Essays in African American History and Culture

Black Vignettes:

Rosalynn Shropshire West

Shropshire West Publishing

Black Vignettes:
Essays in African American History and Culture
All Rights Reserved.
Copyright © 2010 Rosalynn Shropshire West
V7.0

Shropshire West Publishing

ISBN: 978-0-615-24436-5

Library of Congress Control Number: 2009922196

PRINTED IN THE UNITED STATES OF AMERICA

To Kim
My first Publisher

To Stephanie
My first Editor

To Mt. Olive
My first Readers

To the West Family
My first Love

To all of our Sons and Daughters
My hope for them is that they realize their future and appreciate their past

To the Memory of Rita
My Friend

Roz Song

I sense it, I feel it, I need to know,
About my black roots and how far they go
School is a drag and a mystery
When it teaches a history that doesn't include me.
Sure, it was mean, and cruel, and not too hip,
To cross an ocean in a big slave ship.
Well that wasn't my beginning and it wasn't my end.
Still, I need to know just where I've been.
Was I a prince, a pasha, or an African queen?
Was I a great cleric like St. Augustine?
Did I wear a headdress with more than one bauble?
Did I found a city like Jean DuSable?
Did I cross the Alps with elephants in tow?
Did I reach the *top* through the artic snow?
On a Pharaoh's barge, did I sail the Nile?
Did I plan *D.C.,* mile after mile?
It seems a shame and a very great pity
That the *Dreamer* had to march on such a fine city!
With eloquent oration King did vex.
But not with the militancy of a man named *X.*
Let's learn black history as a matter of pride.
To deny our roots is genocide!
Africa is our mother – she gave us our start
To see her disregarded just breaks my heart.
We've been too important on that shore and this,
When I see us excluded, I feel amiss.
Maybe some others can't understand,
Why we're so true to our native land.
Don't they know that humanity is
The acceptance and tolerance of our differences?
Let's learn all cultures, for we're a brotherhood!
Accept every heritage for our nation's good.
And dig into history, every crevice and crack,
It just might surprise you how much is black!

Rosalynn Shropshire West

A great many of the essays in *Black Vignettes* are not found in the garden-variety black history script. United States history books, when describing the American Revolution, do not include information on people like Colonel Tye, a Revolutionary War era runaway slave named Titus who fought for his personal independence. Americans will not speak of him because he fought for the British. And the British will not speak of him because they are possibly still smarting over the loss of those Thirteen North American Colonies. But the reader will meet him in the essay, *Colonel Tye*. And they will certainly meet other black revolutionaries like him.

And what, if anything will you read of Cathay Williams, the only documented female Buffalo Soldier? Is her story included in *Black Vignettes*? You bet it is! History is not just "his story" but it is "her story," too. Black women have been excluded from many mainstream history books, not because of race, but because of gender. The broad-culture marginalization of women is hereby corrected in this book. It includes many essays that feature the contributions of black women. Excluding women would be a disservice to the all-inclusive spirit of this book. The excitement and energy of the accomplishments and achievements of black women are well chronicled within these pages.

Black Vignettes has many essays of historical accounts of events not directly relating to African American history. But their addition is a necessary feature for any history book and their inclusion will be shown to have an impact on African Americans and their history. By no means should these inclusions be considered space fillers. For instance, blacks did not have any part in the creation of the Confederate States of America. But in reading the essay *The Confederacy*, the reader will come to understand the black influence on its formation, and its impact on blacks.

The biographical essays pertaining to African Americans in *Black Vignettes* are methodically filled with events and incidents in the lives of scores of black personalities. Many of these characters will be well known to the reader. But by the same token, many more in this book will be introduced to reader for the first time. It is guaranteed that the readership will never be bored or disinterested like they were in school. The succinctness of the essays will leave the readers wanting more, and may even invite their interest to a more intense self-motivated and independent study.

The charm of *Black Vignettes* can be particularly found in its cultural aspect. Many of its essays are more appropriate for *black culture* than for *black history*. But sometimes the lines between culture and social history are just a bit blurred. They are entwined enough to even be interchangeable. In the historical essay, *Double Dutch*, there are reminisces of my early childhood in Haughville, a black neighborhood in Indianapolis, Indiana. In that poor social setting, a favorite summer pastime for girls was jumping rope. Double Dutch was a favorite for groups of girls. The boys, on the other hand, would engage in the comical and verbal adroit game of *Playing the Dozens*, which has antecedents in African joke-telling tradition. Both essays are a part of the cultural appeal of the book.

All of the essays in *Black Vignettes* were compiled over a period of seven years. They appeared routinely in the weekly church bulletin, the *Olive Branch*, at Mt. Olive Missionary Baptist Church in Indianapolis. I began it as a black history project for myself in January 2000. There was no fanfare to herald the commencement of these black history articles to the congregation because, honestly, not even I knew where or how far I could take my project. But by the time the 100th article was issued, I knew clearly that my black history project was really my practice run for this book. And my church had become my first readership.

One thing has remained abundantly clear for many years; black people are hungry for black history. That fact has been apparent to me from the first time I was asked to speak for a Black History Program. I have long thought that if the historiographers, those who record history, would be inclusive of all those who actually make history, there would be no need for February as National Black History Month, or March as National Women's History Month. Being a member of both groups, it is evident that both groups have been severely marginalized. American History has never been entirely objective. That's because those who write it are subjective and biased in viewpoint. And very often, historiographers tend to overlook that which they deem to be "the other." Since black is not white, and woman is not man, both have been *otherized*.

History does not happen in a vacuum. It is not a set of isolated events. History is interwoven stories, imposed upon by intertwining events. It is rich in content and its layers are diverse and have texture. Just as United States history cannot exclude black achievement and accomplishment, black history cannot be extracted from the full context of United States History and examined separately. In every black history essay in *Black Vignettes,* there are references and obvious connections to the examination of U.S. History in its entirety. Within contextual timeframes, as it is relevant to a particular essay, there is reference to the timeline continuum of which it is a part. One cannot speak of the United States in the 1850s without speaking to the sectional strife occurring at the same time, or slavery as the reason for so much of it. And if one dialogues about the Great Depression of the 1920s and 1930s, then the Great Migration of African Americans to the industrialized North fits within that context and must be included in the discussion.

Finally, no one man owns history. But every man owns his own story. Every man, or woman, has the right to have that story told from his or her own perspective. For that reason, everyone is his own historian. Whatever *Black Vignettes* comes to symbolize to the reader, I hope you will see in it my love of history as whole and complete. It is neither black nor white. Neither is it right or wrong. It is neither good nor bad. It is uniquely objective. To those who read this history book, I hope it will come to signify pride of African heritage. I hope it will bring you to the bold realization that you have value and worth as human beings. I hope you will know who you are and what you represent. Mostly, I hope you will come to the awareness that history is never about the past. It is always about the present. For it is only here and now that history can answer the questions that we pose to it:

What was…?
　　　　When was…?
　　　　　　　　Who was…?
　　　　　　　　　　　　Why was…?
　　　　　　　　　　　　　　　　How did…?
　　　　　　　　　　　　　　　　　　　　When did…?
　　　　　　　　　　　　　　　　　　　　　　　　Why did…?

Happy Reading,
Rosalynn Shropshire West

RALPH ABERNATHY (1926-1990)

R alph Abernathy was an African American civil rights leader and an advocate of nonviolence as a means of social change. He is best known as the chief aide and closest associate of Dr. Martin Luther King, Jr., and helped King to organize the Montgomery Bus Boycott to protest transportation segregation in 1955. Abernathy also co-founded the Southern Christian Leadership Conference (SCLC) in 1957.

He was born Ralph David Abernathy on March 11, 1926 in Linden, Alabama. He was the tenth of twelve children born to successful middle-class farmers, William and Louivery Bell Abernathy. But his grandfather had been a slave. His early education came from local schools. Abernathy served overseas during World War II and took advantage of the G.I. Bill to further his education. He was ordained as a Baptist minister in 1948 and earned a B.S. degree in Mathematics from Alabama State University in 1950. When his interested shifted to social issues, he earned an M.A. degree in Sociology from Atlanta University in 1951. In that same year he married Juanita Jones, a schoolteacher and became the pastor of the First Baptist Church in Montgomery.

A few years later in Montgomery, Abernathy became acquainted with Dr. King, who was the new pastor of the Dexter Avenue Baptist Church. They, along with other clergymen, formed the Montgomery Improvement Association (MIA) in 1955 to force the bus company's racial desegregation in 1956. With the fresh success of the boycott behind them, the two men then formed SCLC in 1957 to give organizational structure to protests against segregation. As King became the first president, Abernathy served as secretary-treasurer, serving as vice president later. After King's death, he assumed the presidency and served until 1977.

In 1961 Abernathy became pastor of the West Hunter Street Baptist Church in Atlanta. But he remained socially active and was frequently jailed with King for acts of civil disobedience. And as a high-ranking officer of SCLC, he spent much of his time on the road traveling with King. In fact, since their first meeting, their lives seemed to run parallel to each other. They both had their homes bombed by segregationists. They both helped to plan the 1963 March on Washington. They both attended the funerals of the four young bombing victims in Birmingham, Alabama.

Abernathy never wavered in his support for nonviolent protest. From 1957 to 1965, one protest followed another, and he helped to lead most of them. His and King's efforts, along with many other dedicated activists led to the Civil rights Act of 1964, the Voting Rights Act of 1965, and many other vital legislation. Upon Dr King's assassination in 1968, Abernathy was propelled into a new and more vital leadership role within the SCLC. But it proved too difficult to fill King's charismatic shoes.

As president of SCLC, Abernathy presided over the 1968 Poor People's Campaign in Washington, D.C., a march that failed miserably. He watched powerlessly as the Civil Rights Movement became fragmented, no longer held together by King's vision and dynamic leadership. He resigned the presidency and ran unsuccessfully for Andrew Young's Atlanta Congressional seat. He returned to the pastorate to lead the West Hunter Street Baptist Church in Atlanta. His biography, "And the Walls Came Tumbling Down," was published in 1989. In it, he confirmed long existing rumors of King's adulterous affairs. It also drew criticism for Abernathy's conservative political stance and the book's overall bitter tone.

For all the criticism heaped upon him in his last years, Ralph Abernathy started as part of the new breed of Baptist ministers. Not just socially active, but educated, articulate, and sophisticated. And they dominated the Civil Rights Movement and made us proud. The 1960s confirmed them as determined but peaceful warriors, confronting social injustice and resisting it in a nonviolent way. Let us all remember them, for they were often beaten back, but never beaten down, and they will never come this way again.

I n the American South, the Christmas holiday for slaves was a welcome break from all the usual toil of their lives. As Christmas approached, many slaves felt the lightness of the holiday atmosphere. For some, Christmas only signified a break from the daily hard work they had endured throughout the year. While each slave-owning household was different, most slaves received at least a few days off to celebrate with their families and visit nearby plantations. Christmas was the only time of the year slaves were allowed to move about the countryside with any freedom.

In Virginia, slaves began getting ready for Christmas weeks in advance. The season began with a number of festivities. Corn shucking was one of the more memorable events. During the end of November and the beginning of December, large plantation owners sent invitations to the slaves of neighboring planters to come and shuck corn on a particular night. At the event, one to two hundred slaves sang and shucked corn throughout the night. A break was given and supper was served. After an hour of eating and drinking, the slaves continued working into the early morning hours. Thomas Jefferson's slaves at Monticello were given a break for several days, and special food rations including turkeys and pigs were distributed.

When Christmas day arrived, slaves would also receive presents from their masters. Within the slaveholding aristocracy, any master who did not give his slave a gift was looked down upon by other slave owners and considered unworthy to be counted among the slaveholding elite. As recorded by Harriet Jacobs in her narrative, Incidents in the Life of a Slave Girl, even slave mothers who had little to give, "tried to gladden the hearts of their little ones on the occasion of Christmas by making new garments and playthings for them."

As Frederick Douglass recounts, the holiday was a time in which slaves could do as they wished. While he recalled that many slaves did have the freedom to see their families, participate in sports activities, such as wrestling, boxing, running, and hunting; getting drunk was the most encouraged activity by slave owners. By Douglass' account in his slave narrative, "those holidays were among the most effective means in the hands of slaveholders of keeping down the spirit of insurrection among slaves." Douglass believed that by keeping slaves drunk, slave owners tried to prevent plans for insurrection, since a sober and thoughtful slave was more dangerous. Christmas leisure was nothing more than a means for slave owners to pacify their slaves.

While Douglass remembered the negative aspects of the holiday, Booker T. Washington recalled the fond childhood memories he had of Christmas in his powerful autobiography, *Up From Slavery*. Scores of black children would scurry to the plantation homes of the masters and ask for "Christ'mus Gifts!" During slavery he wrote, "it was a custom generally observed throughout all the southern states to give the colored people a week of holiday at Christmas, or to allow the holiday to continue as long as the 'Yule Log' lasted." But Washington, like Douglass, added: "the male members of the race, and often the female members too, were expected to get drunk." With the encouragement toward drunkenness, and with little to remind them of the coming of Christ, the sacredness of the season was not completely lost.

For a people who had no reason otherwise to celebrate a slave's life found reason to hope in the life of Christ. The Christmas holiday evoked many different feelings. Some slaves were excited about the holiday, especially the children, while others looked forward to the break from work. Some sought the opportunity to reunite with family members who had been sold to other plantations. Still others found time to engage in industrious activities such as quilting and carpentry. With so much expected holiday movement, Christmas surely must have presented an excellent opportunity for some to escape from slavery altogether. But one thing was certain; after the holiday was concluded the slaves that remained enslaved had to go back to their ceaseless toil until the next Christmas.

ALVIN AILEY (1931-1989)

Alvin Ailey was a dancer and choreographer who founded the Alvin Ailey American Dance Theatre (AAADT) and incorporated African American styles and themes into dance performance. Two of the most significant awards Ailey received for his achievements in dance were NAACP's Springarn Medal (1976) and the Samuel H. Scripps American Dance Festival Award (1987).

Ailey was born in Rogers, Texas on January 5, 1931. He grew up in a single parent home headed by his mother, Lula Cooper. As a boy he helped her pick cotton. In 1942 they moved to Los Angeles, where his mother found employment in World War II aircraft industry. Ailey attended George Washington Carver Junior High School and Jefferson High School in Los Angeles. At the University of California at Los Angeles (UCLA) Ailey studied literature.

It was on a Carver field trip to the Ballet Russe de Monte Carlo that Ailey first became enamored with concert dance. He was further inspired by performances of the Katherine Dunham Dance Company. But his formal dance training did not begin until 1949, when a high school friend, Carmen de La Vallade, introduced him to Lester Horton, his first dance instructor. Horton was the founder of the first integrated dance company in this country.

After Horton's death in 1953, Ailey became director of the company and began to choreograph his own works. In 1954, he and his friend, Carmen were invited to New York to dance in the Broadway show, House of Flowers, by Truman Compote. In New York, Ailey studied with many outstanding dance artists, including Martha Graham, Doris Humphrey, and Charles Weidman. He also took acting lessons from Stella Adler. The versatile Ailey won a number of acting roles, continued to choreograph, and performed as a dancer.

It was in 1958 that Ailey assembled his own modern dance company. He dedicated AAADT to his vision of the preservation and enrichment of American modern dance heritage and the uniqueness of black cultural expression. Also in 1958, he created *Blues Suite*, inspired by a bar in Texas called the Dewdrop Inn. In 1960 he choreographed *Revelations*, the classic masterpiece of American modern danced based on his religious heritage at the Mount Olive Baptist Church he attended as a boy. His 1971 ballet, *Cry*, a tribute to black women, is dedicated to his mother. Ailey stopped dancing in 1965 and reduced his choreographic assignments during the 1970s in order to seek more funding for his growing dance enterprise.

In addition to the AAADT, the Alvin Ailey Dance Center School, founded in 1969, is dedicated to educating dance students in the history and art of both modern dance and ballet. The school's curriculum includes courses in choreography, dance technique, music for dancers, and theatrical design. Pursuing Ailey's goal of preserving and building upon great ballets, both classic and contemporary, his dance company had performed 150 ballets by 50 choreographers.

Throughout his lifetime, Ailey created over 50 dances for AAADT and some 79 ballets, many of which have appeared in the repertoire of major dance companies, including American Ballet Theatre, Joffrey Ballet, Dance Theatre of Harlem, Paris Opera Ballet and La Scala Ballet. His dance troop toured the world so extensively that by 1989 they had performed for an estimated 15 million people in 48 states and 45 countries on six continents.

Alvin Ailey was a world-class choreographer who combined the African American experience with modern dance, giving modern dance mass appeal. But more importantly, he used his art to celebrate the brotherhood of humanity, and to bring exuberant joy through dance.

IRA ALDRIDGE (c. 1807-1867)

Ira Frederick Aldridge was one of the finest Shakespearean actors of all time. His most famous role was Othello, but he played many other roles such as *Macbeth, King Lear*, and Shylock in the *Merchant of Venice*. He was such a great actor that he was commanded to perform before the Crowned Heads of Europe. He was the first African American to be knighted.

The date and place of his birth are variously listed as July 24, 1803, 1805, and 1807, in Senegal, Africa, Baltimore, Maryland, and New York City. His parents were known to be Rev. Daniel and Luranah Aldridge, poor citizens of the class known as "Free Negroes." Rev. Aldridge was a straw vendor by trade, but had high standing in the Old Zion Church. Ira was educated in New York City's African Free School established in 1787 by the Manumission Society. The main purpose of the school was to create a Negro intelligentsia that later participated actively in the leadership of the Abolitionist Movement. Aldridge also attended Schenectady College, and later, the University of Glasgow in Scotland where he received several medals for Latin composition.

At one time Aldridge was apprenticed as a carpenter under a German immigrant and learned German as well as carpentry. He left Maryland to further his education in New York. It was at Schenectady College that he became interested in acting. Before going abroad, he was very active in New York amateur theatre. Aldridge made his professional stage debut as the first black actor at Royal Coburg Theatre, London on October 10, 1825. He played the role of Prince Oroonoko of Africa, sold into slavery in the melodrama The Revolt of Surinam: A Slave's Revenge.

Aldridge toured the established theatre circuits in Great Britain for twenty-seven years as the star of about sixty roles in melodramas, romantic dramas, operettas, comedies, and Shakespearean plays. He first played Othello at Royal Covent Garden in 1833. His first white role was that of Dirk Hatteraick in Guy Mannering. Aldridge completed his first tour of the European Continent in 1852. He became acquainted with Leo Tolstoy and fluent in the language while touring Russia. And he was presented to Duchess Saxe-Coburg-Gotha, which is the original family name of the Windsor sovereigns of Great Britain.

During the last fifteen years of his life, Aldridge performed in Belgium, Germany, Austria, Hungary, Switzerland, France, Sweden, Russia, and the

Ukraine. He appeared by royal command of archdukes and kings. Crowded theatres greeted him everywhere. Princes and people were eager to see him and honors of every kind were showered upon him. Aldridge became the first actor to be knighted when Duke Bernhard of Saxe-Meiningen bestowed on him the Royal Ernestinischen House Order in 1858.

Honored as an African prince and German baron, he remained a man of the people. Aldridge expressed his discontent over some of his people being held in chains. Following performances he appealed to audiences for respect for his African race. England's Anti-Slavery Society referred to Aldridge's majestic presence on stage as a significant contribution in the struggle for the abolition of slavery. With his personal wealth, he contributed to the fund-raising campaigns of black conventions prior to emancipation in the United States.

Aldridge was married to an English woman, Margaret Gill in 1825. And in 1865, he married Countess Amanda von Brandt, his former mistress with whom he already had a child, Ira Daniel. He fathered five children. All were accomplished in areas of music and languages. Ira Aldridge died while on theatrical tour of Poland and was buried with State Honors. His gravesite is a national shrine cared for by the Society of Polish Artists of Film and Theatre in Lodz, Poland. Naturalized as a British subject in 1863, his name is inscribed at the Shakespearean Memorial Theatre in Stratford-on-Avon and a chair is dedicated there to the memory of Ira Aldridge.

AFFIRMATIVE ACTION: THE 1964 CIVIL RIGHTS ACT

I n the 1960s, the most important domestic initiative in the United States was the effort to provide justice and equality for African Americans. It was singularly the most difficult commitment, and the one that produced the severest strains on American society. But it was also the one that could not be avoided. African Americans took bold steps to ensure that the nation would have to deal with the problem of race.

Until the mid 1960s, legal barriers prevented African Americans and other racial minorities in the U.S. from entering many jobs and educational institutions. While women were rarely legally barred from jobs or education, many employers would not hire them and many universities would not admit them. The 1964 Civil Rights Act prohibited discrimination in public accommodations and employment. A section of the Act known as *Title VII*, which specifically banned discrimination in employment, laid the groundwork for the subsequent development of Affirmative Action. The Equal Employment Opportunity Commission (EEOC), created by the 1964 Civil Rights Act, and the Office of Federal Contract Compliance, became important enforcement agencies for Affirmative Action.

"Affirmative Action" is the name given to policies used in the U.S. to increase opportunities for minorities by favoring them in hiring and promotion, college admissions, and the awarding of government contracts. Depending on the interpretation, minorities might include any underrepresented group, especially one defined by race, ethnicity, or gender. Generally, Affirmative Action has been undertaken by government, business, and educational institutions to remedy the effects of past discrimination against any group, whether by specific corporate entities, or by society as a whole.

President Lyndon B. Johnson first used the term "affirmative action" in a 1965 executive order. This order declared that federal contractors should "take affirmative action to ensure that job applicants and employees are treated without regard to their race, color, religion, gender, or national origin." While the original goal of the Civil Rights Movement had been equal justice, simply ending a long-standing policy of discrimination did not go far enough for many people. Responding to continuing racial inequalities in the work force, in 1969, President Richard M. Nixon was the first to implement federal policies designed to guarantee minority hiring.

9

President John F. Kennedy had long been sympathetic to the cause of racial justice, but he was hardly a committed crusader. Like many presidents before him, he feared alienating Southern Democratic voters and the powerful southern Democrats in Congress that represented them. His administration worked to contain the racial problem by expanding enforcement of existing laws against segregation statutes.

The assassination of President Kennedy in November 1963 gave new impetus to the battle for civil rights legislation. Within days of assuming the office of the presidency, Johnson, in an address to a joint session of Congress, promised that Kennedy's commitment to civil rights would be carried forward and translated into action. The ambitious measure that Kennedy had proposed in June 1963 was hopelessly stalled in the Senate after having passed through the House of Representatives with relative ease. Early in 1964, Johnson, a Southerner, was applying both public and private pressure to make sure that the legislation would be passed on his presidential watch.

President Johnson orchestrated a campaign for a civil rights bill untainted by compromise. As a once Senate Majority Leader, he knew what it would take to pass the legislation and end the filibuster surrounding the bill. Johnson brought the full weight of his power and persuasive abilities to secure the votes of doubtful Senators. And, after much effort, the bill won Senate approval in June 1964. On July 2, 1964, with much pomp and circumstance, Johnson signed the wide-sweeping bill into law.

The significance of the 1964 Civil Rights Act lies more in what it did rather than what it was. It effectively outlawed racial discrimination in public facilities and employment, authorized the attorney general to initiate suits to enforce school integration, and allowed for the withholding of federal funds in all cases of non-compliance. While the legislation was directed specifically at removing the barriers to equal access and opportunity that affected African Americans, it vastly expanded the scope of federal protection for the rights of women and other minority groups who experience discrimination.

Civil Rights legislation was nothing new in the United States. At the end of the American Civil War, a frenzy of laws was enacted in support of the freed slaves. From 1865–1869 this reunified nation enacted the Thirteenth, Fourteenth, and Fifteenth Amendments to the U.S. Constitution. Those amendments respectively freed the slaves, granted black male suffrage, and bestowed citizenship. But it would take nearly a century before federal protections were guaranteed with enforcement provided by the 1964 Civil Rights Act.

In recent history there have been some landmark assaults on the idea of Affirmative Action, but not on the 1964 Civil Rights Act per se. And the assaults have come from every quarter. Justice Sandra Day O'Connor, the first woman to sit on the U.S. Supreme Court has written: "All governmental action based on race should...ensure that the personal right to equal protection of the laws has not been infringed." In the same ruling, Justice Clarence Thomas, only the second African American to sit on the Supreme Court wrote in agreement with O'Connor: "Government cannot make us equal; it can only recognize, respect, and protect us as equal before the law."

Some detractors are of the opinion that Affirmative Action has not uplifted poorer blacks, only the black middleclass. Furthermore, others have commented that Affirmative Action has stigmatized African American achievement. And it has caused dependencies to develop. But on the whole, conservatives have mounted more attacks on Affirmative Action than liberals have mounted defenses. It is an indication that today even many liberals are less confident about the program's effectiveness. In some circles, Affirmative Action is often referred to as "reverse discrimination." But defenders of Affirmative Action do make a strong case for its continuance.

The 1964 Civil Rights Act was a landmark piece of legislation. It became the *Magna Charta* for racial minorities, women, and other deprived groups. Not only did *Title VII* of the Act outlaw discrimination in a variety of employment practices on the basis of race, religion, and gender, it also established the Equal Employment Opportunity Commission (EEOC) to enforce that law. Since 1964, Congress has amended the Act to include the passage of the 1972 Civil Rights Act to extend protection to private and public sectors; and passage of the 1978 Civil Rights Act to extend protection for pregnant employees so that they are entitled to receive medical benefits.

The 1964 Civil Rights Act, though originating from injustices against African Americans, raised the consciousness of America so that equal justice is now more far reaching. But as it continues to expand into a broader and more sweeping law its continued effectiveness could be undermined by ever increasing tax cuts. Affirmative Action policies have prodded business and industry to integrate. It has opened the door and has helped to create a level playing field for groups victimized by exclusionary practices. Corporate Boardrooms and university campuses alike have benefited from a diverse population. But the question yet remains: Can Affirmative Action, or any government mandate, compensate African Americans for a century of past injustices?

THE AFRICAN METHODIST EPISCOPAL CHURCH

The African Methodist Episcopal (AME) Church is a Protestant denomination organized by and specifically for African Americans. Officially, it was formed in 1816, but it was clearly a concept in practice long before then. The first congregation of what later became the AME Church began in 1787 by a group of black parishioners of Saint George's Church in Philadelphia. Led by the itinerant preacher and former slave, Richard Allen, blacks withdrew from the church in protest against racial prejudice.

In November 1787 Richard Allen, Absalom Jones, and other black Methodists arrived at Saint George's to attend Sunday services. They were directed toward a newly built seating gallery and mistakenly sat in its "white" section. During prayers, white ushers pulled the black worshipers to their feet and demanded that they sit in the "proper" section. Humiliated, the group left the church and thus began the idea of separate church meetings. There were other incidents of persistent racism as well. White pastor would refuse to take black infants into their arms to christen them. Blacks were required to wait until all whites were served the Lord's Supper before being admitted to the table. And there were also unspoken conflicts over black access to burial grounds.

In response to such discrimination, African American Methodists in Baltimore and Philadelphia began holding separate prayer meetings as early as 1786, a mere two years after the founding of American Methodism. Allen tried to buy a separate building for such meetings, but abandoned the idea in the face of white hostility. But Allen and Jones instead formed the Free African Society, a benevolent organization whose commitment to abolition and the aiding of blacks in times of need became a model for other societies nationwide.

By 1794 Philadelphia's black Methodists had raised enough money to build their own church but a majority of the congregation voted to align with the Episcopalians rather than the Methodists. They named it St. Thomas African Episcopal Church. Allen, however, continued to believe that no other religious sect suited blacks as well as the Methodists. He purchased a blacksmith shop with his own money and converted it into a storefront church. The Methodist bishopric named it Bethel African Methodist Episcopal Church.

By 1816 some black Methodists, still facing persistent discrimination, had come to believe that separate churches were not enough. On April 16, representatives from five congregations met at Bethel to discuss their legal independence from the main body of the Methodist Church. Voting to organize under the name of the African Methodist Episcopal Church, they then successfully sued for independence before the Pennsylvania Supreme Court. Richard Allen, the founder of Bethel AME Church, became the first bishop of the AME denomination.

The new AME Church was not greatly different from the original Methodist Church. Baptism and communion practices were much the same, and hymn singing during worship remained a prominent feature of service. But cultural differences distinct to African Americans assumed a greater importance. AME services became more fervent and were distinguished by spirituals and spontaneous shouting. The church was also distinguished by its commitment to political agitation.

At 220 years old in concept if not in practice, the AME Church remains dedicated to Methodist theology and the black experience. However colorful its historic beginnings, the AME Church has led that long list of denominations making up the "Black Church," the institution which has provided stability, leadership, and moral guidance to predominantly African American congregations within the United States and throughout the African Diaspora.

NOBLE DREW ALI (1886-1929)

Noble Drew Ali was an African American cult leader who founded the Moorish Science Movement in 1913. His teachings were a hodgepodge mishmash of confused Bible teachings adulterated by Islamic doctrine. Thrown into this terrible soup were mixes of Buddhism and Taoism. Ali's teachings were collected into a "Holy Koran," but it is not to be confused with orthodox Islam's holy book.

He was born Timothy Drew on January 8, 1886, in Simpsonbuck County, North Carolina. Nothing is known of his early family life except that he was raised by the Cherokee and adopted into the tribe. He received very little formal education. And at age sixteen he began working as a circus magician. During this time, and in the years prior to World War I, he traveled extensively abroad and encountered cultures of the Middle and Far East. Middle Eastern religions, especially Islam, with its lack of racial consciousness, particularly intrigued him.

He claimed to have gotten the title "Ali" from Sultan Abdul Asis Abn Saud during a visit to Mecca, and thereafter began referring to himself as Noble Drew Ali. While traveling in North Africa, Ali studied under an Egyptian cultist named Suliaman, a magus who is said to have recognized Ali as the reincarnation of a former cult leader. Suliaman also claimed to be the last member of a cult of high magic practiced for centuries in the pyramid of the ancient Egyptian Pharaoh, Cheops. Ali invited Suliaman back to the United States with him to set up a temple where he could preach his newfound doctrine.

Based all the instruction that he had received, Ali contended that African Americans in fact were Asiatic Moors or Moabites; that their homeland was Morocco, not Ethiopia; that religiously they were Islamic; and that Ali himself had been sent by Allah to tell them that their collective identity had been stolen by Christian Europeans. Ali held that once their true identity was reestablished and their true religion codified, Moorish Americans would experience empowerment, thereby prevailing over the racial and economic oppression they had suffered in times past in the U.S.

To affirm this new identity, Ali issued "Nationality and Identification Cards" to his followers. He also created a sixty-page catechism comprising Christian

Bible passages, the words of Marcus Garvey, anecdotes of the life of Jesus from the Levi Dowling book *The Aquarian Gospel of Jesus Christ*, and Ali's own strict codes of dress, diet, and morality. He started his first temple, the Canaanite Temple, with Dr. Suliaman, in Newark, New Jersey. His second temple, and the most well known, the Moorish Science Temple of America, was established in Chicago.

At its peak, the Moorish Science Movement had a membership of between 20,000 and 30,000, with temples in Detroit, Harlem, Pittsburgh, Newark, Chicago and numerous other cities across the South. In 1929, Ali's leadership was challenged by his business manager, Sheik Claude Green, who was later found murdered in Chicago. Adherents of Moorish Science often assigned themselves titles like sheik, and even added "Bey" or "El" to their surnames. Although Ali was not in town at the time of Green's murder, he was arrested and held for questioning upon his return. He was released on bond, but died before his trial. The cause of death, possibly police brutality, was never determined. The date of his death is also disputed.

Like Marcus Garvey, Noble Drew Ali preached the importance of racial pride and unity of all black people. But unlike Garvey, Ali was not predominantly Christian in his worldview. Nor did he adopt any Christian rituals of worship. Had he done so, it is quite possible that he would have had a much larger following. Even though Islam was the biggest threat to Black Christianity in the 1960s, Christian theology is still much too deeply entrenched in the African American psyche to be usurped by any ideological substitute.

ALLEN ALLENSWORTH (1842-1914)

Allen Allensworth was one of the most remarkable people of post-Civil War America. He was a strong proponent and tireless advocate for black self-help to elevate the whole race. He was a businessman, minister, Army Chaplain, twice a delegate to the Republican National Convention in 1880 and 1884. And he was the founder, lent his name to, and was the leading citizen of California's only black community.

Allensworth was born into slavery in Louisville, Kentucky on April 7, 1842. At a young age he displayed evidence of resistance to any system that would deny him the opportunity for an education. He was sold at the age of twelve because it was discovered that he could read and write. By the time he turned twenty-one, the Emancipation Proclamation had effectively given blacks the right to enter the United States armed forces. Allensworth ran away and served in the 44th Illinois Infantry Hospital Corps as a civilian nurse. He then worked on a hospital ship and finally enlisted in the Navy in 1863, serving on gunboats Queen City, Tawah, and the Pittsburgh. Allensworth rose to the rank of Chief Petty Officer in the Navy and returned to civilian life after the war.

Allensworth worked in the commissary of the St. Louis Navy Yard until he could save enough money for his first business venture with his brother. They went into the catering business in 1867 and began operating two restaurants in St. Louis. Still eager for a formal education, he enrolled in the Eli Normal School in Louisville. He also taught in a Freedmen's Bureau school in Christmasville, Kentucky in 1868. By 1871, Allensworth was ordained into the ministry in Louisville and preaching for the Fifth Street Baptist Church. He also functioned as the financial agent of the General Association of the Colored Baptists in Kentucky, superintendent of Sunday schools of the state Baptist convention, and missionary for the American Baptist Publication Society in Philadelphia.

In 1877, Allensworth married Josephine Leavell who was also a school teacher and talented pianist. The couple had two daughters. But family life did not deter Allensworth from extensive travel for various civic and work related reasons. In 1884 he lectured in New England and became the pastor of the Joy Street Baptist Church in Boston. He also served as pastor of the Union Baptist Church in Cincinnati. And in every sermon and lecture, his philosophy of black economic empowerment was evident.

Allensworth petitioned President Grover Cleveland to become a chaplain to one of the four regiments of black soldiers. And in 1886, he became the chaplain of the 24th Infantry with the rank of Captain. While stationed in the Indian Territories of New Mexico, Utah, and Montana, he established separate school programs for enlisted men and children, which were implemented by other chaplains throughout the Army. He addressed the National Education Association Convention in Toronto in 1891 with the topic: "The History and Progress of Education in the U.S. Army." He served as a recruiter in Louisville during the Spanish-American War and later rejoined the 24th Infantry during the Philippine Insurrection. Allensworth retired as a senior chaplain in 1906 and was promoted to the rank of Lieutenant Colonel.

In 1908 Allensworth moved to Los Angles and began advertising for residents to establish an all black township north of Bakersfield. He established a business to aid African Americans wishing to migrate west. He sold lots in Tulare County, for a town that would become "Allensworth." With residents numbering over one hundred, it became a market center that included all the modern amenities of a thriving town: churches, hotel, retail shops, post office, drugstore, stable, school, and railroad station.

But early on the town showed signs of strain by a series of crises that beset it. The Santa Fe Railroad was rerouted, slowing the town's economic progress. It lost its water supply after the water company reneged on the contract. It is sad that Allen Allensworth's advocacy for black self-reliance and mutual assistance could not produce the necessary resources to keep the area from becoming a ghost town by the 1940s.

"And if a house be divided against itself, that house cannot stand."
– Mark 3:25

T he Civil War was a defining moment in Africa American history. Although many factors can be cited as causes of the war, the question of slavery and by extension the question of the future of Africans in America stand at the core of its causes. President Lincoln and most of the white population of the North clearly stated, and sincerely wanted to believe, that the single purpose of the war was to preserve the Federal Union. But black people, slave and free, knew that the South's unyielding commitment to chattel slavery was the real reason underlying its claims to states' rights and independence from the North.

Historians have long debated the causes of the Civil War, whether it was necessary and inevitable or whether it was an irrepressible conflict. They proposed many and assorted reasons for the war: the competition to control the West and thus the future of the country; the North's small farmer vs. the South's large plantations; the North's growing industrial capitalism vs. the South's unchanging agriculture economy; the democratic culture of Northern Puritanism vs. the aristocratic culture of Southern Cavaliers – all unresolved contradictions which sprang not only from America's own origins, but from the two sides in the English Civil War from which North and South was descended.

All the theoretical discussions became academic on April 12, 1861, however, when South Carolina, the first state to secede from the Union, opened fire on Fort Sumter, the United States installation in Charleston Harbor. Firing on the American flag, troops, and fortifications, was an open act of treason. President Abraham Lincoln could only respond accordingly. To the South, it was an open declaration of war, for it had already organized itself into a new and sovereign nation – the Confederate States of America (CSA). The CSA had elected its own President, Jefferson Davis, and formed its own bicameral Congress. It had even ratified its own Constitution, albeit eerily similar to the USA.

Alexander Stephens, the Confederacy's Vice President, spelled out what the dissolution of the Union, the creation of the Confederacy, and the Civil War were fundamentally about. In his speech in March 1861, a month before the beginning of the war, he voiced the South's true and lasting mind-set about blacks:

> *"The Confederacy's foundation is laid, its cornerstone rests on the great truth, that the Negro is not equal to the white man; that slavery subordination to a superior race is his natural and moral condition. This, our new government is the first, in the history of the world, based upon this great physical, philosophical, and moral truth."*

Stephens' statement makes it clear that while the North may have believed it was fighting to preserve the Union, the South, like African Americans both slave and free, knew better than Lincoln himself that the nation could not exist "half slave and half free." So great were the emotions over slavery that when the Civil War ended, there were 625,000 men, black and white, and on both sides, left dead because of it. The total number of casualties from that war alone was greater than the combined total casualties of any war in which the U.S. has since been engaged. That includes the carnage of the current War in Iraq.

Southern partisans called it "The War of Northern Aggression." Abolitionists called it "The War of the Slaveholders' Rebellion." Those who pretended the conflict was value-free simply called it "The War Between the States." But what shall we, as a people, call the Civil War today – a mere 143 years after it ended? We should call it what it was: the emancipation of over four million people and an end to their brutal enslavement that had lasted 231 years. For African Americans, the Civil War is value-laden. And eleven generations are looking back at us to assess what value we place on their freedom and ours.

C inque was a Mende rice farmer from Sierra Leone, West Africa. He was seized and carried away into slavery in 1839. A Portuguese slave ship took him and many others through the brutal Middle Passage to Cuba where they were purchased to work on sugar plantations. In Havana, two Spaniards placed him and fifty-two other Africans aboard the slave ship *Amistad* bound for Puerto Principe, Cuba. With the Africans were their purchasers, the captain and his two slaves, two crewmen, and the cook.

Late one night, Cinque picked his iron locks with a nail. Releasing the other captives, they surprised the captain and the cook, killing them both. They tied the owners of the "cargo" to the bridge and instructed them to steer the ship east, into the rising sun and back to Africa. However, unable to navigate by the stars, the Africans were tricked at night as the owners sailed west and north toward the United States. For nearly two months the *Amistad* zigzagged in the Atlantic Ocean until finally boarded by crewmembers of an American naval vessel.

The Americans were shocked to find only Africans in charge of the ship. They ordered them below deck at gunpoint and steered the ship to New London, Connecticut. Upon arrival there, the Africans, with the exception of three small girls, were arrested and charged before the U.S. Circuit Court in New Haven for murder and mutiny. Despite language barriers and cultural differences, the Africans found many supporters in the New Haven and New York City areas. An *Amistad* Committee was formed to raise money for their defense. The American Missionary Association, whose goal it was to abolish slavery, was formed out of the *Amistad* Committee.

The language problem presented the court with serious difficulties until James Covey, a Mende sailor working aboard a British frigate, was located and used as the official interpreter. Once Covey began interpreting, more details of the heroic story began to unfold. He explained that Cinque told him that they had been kidnapped from their homes in Sierra Leone and taken to Cuba against their will. Public sentiment, already anti-slavery, grew more in favor of the Africans. Northern Abolitionists rallied in their support claiming that since the Africans had been taken from their own lands without their consent they had a right to use any means necessary to obtain their freedom, just as any other free men would do.

21

The *Amistad* case attracted national and international attention and was called the "trial of the century." There were many legal details and fine points of the law to be decided in this case. The Africans had killed men in international waters and stolen a vessel. But the international slave trade had been banned by international treaty and the Spanish and Portuguese were in violation of the law by kidnapping Africans.

The *Amistad* affair aroused much controversy and interest in the United States because of the intensifying antislavery struggle between the North and the South. The case was appealed all the way to the Supreme Court. It was argued for eight hours to a favorable conclusion on March 9, 1841 by then former President John Quincy Adams. Later Adams would express his prophetic feelings that the practice of slavery had to be ended in the United States. He is quoted as saying: *"The practice of judging some people to be slave because of their color and some to be free because of theirs is intolerable and not within the bounds of human decency."*

Before they were freed, Cinque and the other mutineers learned much in the United States. They learned to speak English, studied the laws and political systems, and were regularly taken to the Christian churches in the New England area. When the group left for Africa, several missionaries accompanied them. They believed that Sierra Leone would be a good place to establish a Christian mission against the slave trade. Cinque and the others arrived home in January 1842, three years from the start of their voyage, their number greatly reduced by disease and death, never again to find the families from whence they were taken.

MARIAN ANDERSON (1897-1993)

M arian Anderson was a classical music pioneer known for her wide-ranging repertory of art songs, operatic arias, and spirituals. In 1955 she became the first African American soloist to perform at the Metropolitan Opera. It was with talent alone that she convinced the American musical establishment that blacks should be given a fair chance to succeed at the highest levels of classical music. And in so doing, became one of the most celebrated singers of the 20th century.

She was born in Philadelphia on February 27, the eldest of three daughters. Her father, John, was an ice and coal dealer; and her mother, Anna, although trained as a teacher, took in laundry and worked as a cleaning woman. Throughout her childhood, Anderson's family was poor. Her father died from injuries received at work, and the family's financial situation worsened from there. From an early age, Anderson was clearly talented. She joined the junior choir at the Union Baptist Church when she was only six and became known as the "baby contralto." In addition, she taught herself to play the piano, eventually learning to self-accompany during recitals.

Anderson joined the church's senior choir at age thirteen and began singing professionally and touring during high school to earn money for the family. By graduation from South Philadelphia School for Girls, she had earned enough to help her family purchase a home. In 1924 she gave a Town Hall concert in New York that was so poorly received by critics that she refused to perform for a year. But in 1925 she won the opportunity to appear at Lewisohn Stadium with the New York Philharmonic Orchestra, winning first place over several hundred other contestants.

Despite scoring a triumph at the concert, Anderson made little immediate progress in her career. Other than an engagement with the Philadelphia Orchestra, she found major opportunities for concert or opera performances difficult to obtain because of race prejudice in the United States. Between 1925 and 1935 she studied and toured in Europe, and her career began to develop. In 1939 the Daughters of the American Revolution (DAR) denied her request to perform at Constitution Hall in Washington, D.C. because she was black. First Lady Eleanor Roosevelt resigned from the DAR in protest. Also reacting to the outrage was Secretary of the Interior, Harold Icles, who arranged for her an open-air concert at the Lincoln Memorial on Easter

Sunday at which 75,000 people attended.

During the 1940s, Anderson engaged in a very heavy concert schedule. Having mastered music in German and French, she learned songs in Swedish, Norwegian, and Finnish. And in just one twelve-month period, gave over one hundred concerts in Scandinavian countries. A new accompanist, Kosti Vehanen, helped her to extend her personal repertory, until she commanded a body of several hundred songs, including opera arias, patriotic anthems, and hymns. Eventually Anderson mastered the masters. Works by Bach, Brahms, Handel, Rachmaninoff, Saint-Saen, Schubert, Strauss, and other composers filled her repertoire. During World War II Anderson gave many concerts to support the war effort, one of which was held in Constitution Hall, where the DAR finally allowed her to perform.

Anderson was especially fond of Spirituals. In her own words: "I love them because they are truly spiritual in quality, they give forth the aura of faith, simplicity, humility, and hope." Among the spirituals with which she became especially associated were "Crucifixion" and "My Lord, What a Morning." She used the latter to entitle her autobiography in 1956. Marian Anderson won many awards and accolades for her striking voice and exceptional vocal range. Her career spanned four decades. She was a Diva in the true sense of the word. History esteems Marian Anderson not only for her gift, but also for her poise, her indomitable spirit, and her quiet human dignity.

A *mos 'n' Andy* was a popular American radio and later television series based on racist and exaggerated stereotypes of black life. On the radio, the show ran for nearly thirty years with the voices of its two white creators, Freeman Gosden and Charles Correl, using Black Vernacular English. But the television program lasted only two years before it was canceled amid growing protests from the black community.

It began as the *Sam 'n' Henry* radio show, as it was first called, in 1926 in Chicago. The show portrayed its two black characters in full racial stereotype, complete with broken English. The characters were renamed, *Amos 'n' Andy* in 1928 and were crafted to reflect white stereotypes of African American life and culture in Harlem in the years following the Great Migration of the 1920s. Amos was portrayed as the weak and submissive "Uncle Tom," while Andy was lazy and pretentious. The prototypes for the *Amos 'n' Andy* characters came from a 1921 all-black musical revue, *Shuffle Along*. This famous musical had lyrics and music by Eubie Blake and Hoosier native, Noble Sissle. Langston Hughes credited *Shuffle Along* with sparking the Harlem Renaissance.

The adventures of *Amos 'n' Andy* presented other characters like, George "Kingfish" Stevens, an inept schemer; the Lawyer Calhoun, an underhanded crook that no one trusted; "Lightin'," the slow-talking, slow-moving, slow-witted janitor; Sapphire Stevens, George's shrew of a wife; Sapphire's Mama, the aggressive domineering mother-in-law; and Andy's girlfriend, the infamous Madame Queen. The basis for these characters was derived largely from stereotypical caricatures of blacks that had been communicated through several decades of popular American culture and, most notably, motion pictures.

But by the time *Amos 'n' Andy* debuted on the CBS Television Network in 1951, there was within black America the emergence of a new political consciousness and a new awareness of the importance of image. Post World War II African Americans looked to the new medium of television to nullify decades of racist and offensive caricatures and ethnic stereotypes. Hollywood was now presenting it first glimpses of black soldiers fighting alongside white soldiers and black entertainers appeared in sequined gowns and tuxedos instead of bandanas and overalls. Black characters were finally being presented as lawyers, doctors, teachers, and other contributing members of society.

Especially abhorrent in the *Amos 'n' Andy Show* was the portrayal of the black professional class. Every character was either a clown or a crook. Black doctors were shown as quacks and black lawyers were inept. This insult to the black middleclass, however, would not go unchallenged. The NAACP launched an official protest of the show, outlining a specific list of items it found objectionable. They sued CBS and sought, but failed, to get an injunction against the show's premier episode.

The significance of *Amos 'n' Andy*, with its almost thirty year history as a highly successful radio show, its brief and contentious years on network television, it banishment from prime-time and subsequent years in syndication, and its reappearance in videocassette format, is not difficult to explain. Whites loved it. It reaffirmed their already racist notions of black society. The black community, on the other hand, was acutely divided on the issue. While black denunciation of the show was not universal, all African Americans resented the negative stereotype of their culture and the demeaning use of their dialect.

Many blacks saw the television version of *Amos 'n' Andy* as a means to showcase black talent. With its good writing and talented cast, the show was great comedy and commercially successful. But some blacks deemed the show an insulting return to the days of "blackface" Minstrelsy. They caused a controversy to surround the television version that would almost equal the popularity of the radio version. Still, even with so much contention looming, the network reluctantly canceled the *Amos 'n' Andy Show* in 1953. But it remained in syndication until 1966, and is now available in videocassette and DVD formats.

M aya Angelou is a writer, poet, playwright, educator, singer, dancer, actress, producer, director, and civil rights activist. She has been a success on many creative paths on her journey to self-realization. She is especially celebrated for her writings, which attest to her gift for survival in the face of hardship, personal trauma, and injustice. Many of her poems like *And Still I Rise* and *On the Pulse of Morning* offer hope in the face of any adversity. And some of her poems like *These Yet to Be United States* illuminate adversity.

She was born Marguerite Annie Johnson in St. Louis, Missouri, on April 4, 1928. She was the second child of Bailey Johnson, Sr., a doorman and naval dietitian and Vivian Baxter Johnson, a boardinghouse proprietor and registered nurse. She was quickly called "Maya" because her young brother, Bailey, Jr., could not pronounce her name. Soon after her birth the family moved to Long Beach, California where her parents' marriage broke up soon after. At age seven Maya was traumatized to the point of not speaking for five years after being assaulted by her mother's boyfriend.

While attending George Washington High School and studying dance and drama at the California Labor School, Maya, at age sixteen, became the first black and the first female streetcar conductor in San Francisco. In August 1945 she graduated high school, and a few months later, gave birth to her son, Guy Johnson. During the next several years she held a number of low-level jobs to make ends meet. She was married briefly in the early 1950s to a sailor, Tosh Angelos. When the marriage ended, she took a job as a cabaret singer and dancer using the stage name Maya Angelou.

Maya toured Europe and Africa in a production of Gershwin's opera *Porgy and Bess*. When she returned to the U.S. in 1955, she appeared in a film and recorded an album. In the late 1950s she moved to New York City where she sang at the Apollo Theater in Harlem, performed at other venues, and attended meetings of the Harlem Writers Guild. From 1960 to 1961 Maya was active in the civil rights movement, serving as the Northern coordinator for the SCLC. In 1961 she moved to Africa with her second husband, South African freedom fighter and lawyer, Vusumzi Maké. She spent the next five years living in Egypt and Ghana, working as a journalist and a university professor. After divorcing, she returned to the U.S., resumed work with the Harlem Writers

Guild and published her autobiography, *I Know Why the Caged Bird Sings* (1970).

For the past five decades Maya has been a prolific writer of plays, essays, fiction, film scripts, documentaries, and poetry, but only a few can be listed here: *Freedom Cabaret* (1960); *The Least of These* (1966); *Black, Blues, Black* (1968); *Just Give Me a Cool Drink of Water 'fore I Die* (1971); *Georgia, Georgia* (1972); *All Day Long* (1974); *Gather Together in My Name* (1974); *Oh Pray My Wings Are Gonna Fit Me Well* (1975); *Singin' and Swingin' and Getting' Merry like Christmas* (1976); *And Still I Rise* (1978); *The Heart of a Woman* (1981); *Sister, Sister* (1982); *All God's Children Need Traveling Shoes* (1986); *I Shall Not Be Moved* (1990); *Poetic Justice* (1993); *The Complete Collected Poems of Maya Angelou* (1994).

Maya has kept her personal life very private, but her artistic achievement speaks volumes. She says her work shows her survival: "You may encounter many defeats, but you must not be defeated." She has received accolades, honors, and awards too numerous to mention. But in 1993 she was invited to recite her poem, *"On the Pulse of Morning,"* at President Bill Clinton's inauguration. It was only the second time a poet had been asked to share in that way. As if from the title of her 1993 collection of essays, Maya Angelou clearly says: *"Wouldn't Take Nothing for My Journey Now."* She is a phenomenally gifted artist. She is a phenomenally prolific writer. She is a phenomenally multi-talented individual. Maya Angelou is quite simply, a *phenomenal woman.*

J ames Armistead was born into slavery in Virginia. He became one of the most important counter espionage agents in the American Revolutionary War. He offered himself for duty in the war without even the promise of freedom in return. Armistead was hired by the British to be their spy but instead spied on them.

With his owner's permission, Armistead was only twenty-one when he volunteered to fight in the Continental Army. He was initially placed in the service of Marie Joseph Marquis de Lafayette. When it was quickly discovered that Armistead could read and write clearly and concisely, another task was designed for him. A task more suited to the needs of the Continental forces at that time. Lafayette dispatched Armistead to the headquarters of British General, Lord Charles Cornwallis. Armistead pretended to be a runaway slave seeking work and offering a promise of useful espionage capabilities. He was a good actor. He also acted as Cornwallis' personal valet. Armistead was then in good position to hear and overhear sensitive information.

Armistead took to the role and began providing Lafayette with information that enabled Lafayette and George Washington to trap Cornwallis' forces at Yorktown. His reports had enabled American ground forces and a menacing French fleet to thwart Cornwallis decisively. So effective was Armistead's intelligence reports and counter espionage activities that General Lafayette later wrote:

> *This is to certify that...James had done essential services to me while I had the honour to command in this state. His intelligences from the enemy's camp were industriously collected and more faithfully delivered. He properly acquitted himself with some important communication I gave him and appears to be entitled to every reward his situation can admit of.*

The brevity of Lafayette's testimonial understated this intelligence agent's resourcefulness. And it made no mention at all of the courage it took for Armistead to knowingly risk his own life in order to help the American cause. He took full advantage of the British eagerness to enlist slaves to disrupt American production. Armistead further jeopardized himself by pretending to supply the British with information and feigning loyalty to them. He secreted communications out of the British camp daily to relay to Lafayette. These messages were taken directly to Lafayette who promptly acted upon them. Every moment spent in the British camp increased Armistead's risk of exposure.

Cornwallis feigned illness at the surrender of his troops and sent a subordinate to deliver his sword to Washington. But before returning to England, the defeated Cornwallis did pay a courtesy call to General Lafayette. To his surprise, at Lafayette's headquarters, he found Armistead who had been in the employ of the British to spy on the Americans, but who had in actuality been a counter spy.

A few years after the war ended, Armistead expressed his continuing admiration for the Marquis de Lafayette by calling himself "James Armistead Lafayette." The Virginia General Assembly rewarded him for his service to the revolution with emancipation. In 1818, he petitioned the state for relief, and acquired after thirty years, a veteran's pension for his part in the war.

James Armistead's vital contributions to the astonishing defeat of British forces in America when joined with those of so many other African Americans, made the achievement of American Independence a prize shared jointly by blacks and whites. The American Revolution formed a major turning point in the history of Africans in America. Slavery in the North became almost nonexistent. But in the South, where agrarian economies depended heavily on it, the institution of slavery continued for nearly ninety more years.

LOUIS ARMSTRONG (1901-1971)

L ouis Armstrong was an African American vocalist, trumpet and cornet virtuoso, and one of the most innovative and influential jazz musicians in the world. Jazz is the African American art form that evolved from the Blues in the early 20th century. Armstrong laid the groundwork and set the standard for all other jazz performers. More than anyone else, he was responsible for popularizing jazz for a broad audience.

He was born Louis Daniel Armstrong in New Orleans on July 4, 1901. He grew up in abject poverty and could not attend school beyond the fifth grade. His father abandoned the family about the time of Armstrong's birth and his mother raised him in the slums of the city. As a youth, he joined a vocal quartet and sharpened his musical ear for harmony by singing with the group on city streets. From 1912 to 1914 he was incarcerated for delinquency at the Colored Waif's Home in New Orleans. While there, Armstrong learned to play brass instruments and dedicated himself to becoming a professional musician.

When he was only sixteen Armstrong attracted the attention of King Oliver, who played the jazz cornet in the New Orleans style. Armstrong's apprenticeship with the respected musician lasted for two years until Oliver left for Chicago. Armstrong played in the New Orleans jazz band of trombonist Kid Ory, and later with pianist Fate Marable, who performed on the riverboats of the Mississippi. In 1922 he re-joined Oliver's Creole Jazz Band in Chicago and made his first record.

Armstrong moved to New York City in 1924 where he joined the band of pianist Fletcher Henderson and expanded his reputation as a leading soloist in the style of music known as "hot jazz." After 1925 he began leading his own band and also recorded with some of the most renowned singers of the time. In these recordings, considered the most enduring pieces in jazz history, Armstrong abandoned the traditional collective improvisation of New Orleans-style jazz and transformed the music from a group art into an art form of the individual soloist. He was one of the first artists to record "scat singing," which is the singing of improvised wordless sounds rather than formal lyrics.

In the 1930s and 1940s Armstrong led the Big-Band Era and actively pursued a career as a popular entertainer in motion pictures. He was the first African American to appear regularly in feature films, eventually appearing in over fifty motion pictures and several musical short films. When big band music went into commercial decline, Armstrong formed a septet call the All Stars, which featured, at various times, some of the great jazz artists. This band, which he led until 1968, was largely a vehicle for his own playing and singing. Because of his vocals, a number of his records became hits, including *Blueberry Hill* (1956), *Mack the Knife* (1956), the Grammy Award winning *Hello Dolly* (1964), and *What a Wonderful World* (1967).

In 1956 Armstrong penned his autobiography *Satchmo*. He accumulated many affectionate nicknames over the course of his career, including "Dippermouth," "Satch" and "Pops." But the most enduring and the most endearing was "Satchmo," which essentially means satchel mouth. He became the unofficial musical ambassador from the United States, performing all over the world, touring Europe several times and performing before a crowd of 100,000 in Ghana. His gravel-voice song styling became his musical signature toward the end of his career. His voice became just as well known as his trumpet playing.

Louis Armstrong received many posthumous awards. In 1972 he was selected for a Grammy Lifetime Achievement Award. He received two Grammy Hall of Fame Awards in 1974 and 1993. In 1976 a statue dedicated to him was erected in New Orleans and a park was named in his honor. In 1996 Queens College, which preserves all his archives, announced plans to turn his longtime Queens Borough home into a museum in his honor. Louis Armstrong was a musical giant. Even in death Satchmo remains larger than life. Even in this millennium, his vocals and trumpet-playing style are easily the most recognizable.

CRISPUS ATTUCKS (c. 1723-1770)

On March 5, 1770, Crispus Attucks became the first casualty of the American Revolution when he was shot in the right chest and killed in what became known as the Boston Massacre. Samuel Adams, a prominent leader of the struggle against the British domination of its thirteen North American Colonies, called upon dock workers and seamen in the port of Boston to demonstrate against British military presence. Crispus Attucks responded to that plea. Possibly a runaway slave, Attucks was a proper rebel, a man who loved freedom and knew well its worth, a sailor fond of the freedom that being at sea brought, and a whaler full of adventure.

Crispus Attucks and forty to fifty others armed themselves with clubs, sticks and snowballs, taunted and pelted British regulars until they were fired upon. Five Americans were killed, including Attucks. Several more were wounded as eight soldiers fearfully sent a barrage of musket fire into the crowd. The victims were immediately hailed as martyrs for liberty. All eight soldiers were jailed and tried for murder in American civil court. John Adams, who became the second President of the United States, defended them. The British soldiers were acquitted on grounds of self-defense.

John Adams reviled the mad behavior of the crowd. He called the American patriots *"a motley rabble of saucy boys, Negroes and mulattos, Irish teagues and outlandish Jack Tars."* Building on eyewitness testimony that Attucks shaped and dominated the fray, Adams decried Crispus Attucks as the self-appointed leader of the dreadful carnage. Because of Attucks' imposing height and his brawny physique, Adams was prompted to describe him as "a man of terrifying looks."

Attucks' death is well documented, but little is known about his life. Historians only surmise that he was a runaway slave of mixed heritage. His father was said to be African and his mother was a Natick Indian. The word "attuck" is Natick for "dear." In colonial America, the offspring of black and Indian parents were considered to be mulatto. History does know that Attucks believed in or at the very least, was in sympathy with the cause of American liberty. If indeed he was a runaway slave, he also believed in his own right to exist as a free person. In 1750, the Boston Gazette published an ad for the return of a runaway slave named "Crispus" which included an accompanying reward in the amount of £10 (ten pounds sterling):

"Ran away from his master, William Brown of Framingham, on the 30th of September last, a mulatto fellow, about 27 years of age, named Crispus 6 feet 2 inches high, short curled hair, his knees nearer together than common, had on a light colored bearskin coat. All manner of vessel and others are hereby cautioned against concealing or carrying off said servant on penalty of law."

As a slave in Framingham, Attucks had been known for his skill in buying and selling cattle. As a twenty-year runaway he was mostly a sailor. He worked with a whaling crew that sailed out of Boston harbor. He also worked cargo ships out of the Bahamas. At other times he worked as a rope maker in Boston. Despite laws and customs regulating the burial of African Americans, Crispus Attucks was buried in the Park Street Cemetery in Boston along with other honored dead.

Although Crispus Attucks was credited as the leader and instigator of the event known since as the Boston Massacre, debate continues to rage as to whether he was a hero and a patriot, or a rabble-rousing villain. That debate notwithstanding, Attucks has been immortalized in poetry as *"the first to defy, the first to die,"* and has been lauded as a true martyr in the cause of American liberty. He stepped off the Boston docks onto the pages of American history as a man who loved freedom enough to run away from slavery and enter into the battle for American Independence.

CRISPUS ATTUCKS HIGH SCHOOL (1927-1986)

C rispus Attucks High School, named for a black Revolutionary War period hero, opened in 1927 in Indianapolis, Indiana amid a storm of racial protest. The school was founded on the separation of the races. It was this kind of racism – a segregated high school designed to keep black students separate from white students – which brought the school into being. But despite the original intention, Attucks High School became a great source of black pride, a beacon of cultural unity, and a galvanizing force in the Indianapolis African American community.

The supporters of the creation of an all black high school included the Capitol Avenue Protective Association, which had sought to prevent blacks from moving to the city's north side. Black leaders balked at the notion of a separate high school. They felt that no one section of the population could be segregated without taking from it the advantage of the common culture. But black resistance failed in the face of a grass-roots drive for a segregated high school. White civic leaders appeared before the school board, arguing that black education would thrive in a racially segregated environment. The board then approved construction of a building in the northwestern part of the city, near the heart of Indianapolis' largest black section. All Indianapolis black high school students were thereafter required to attend the new school, even seniors who had attended other Indianapolis high schools for three years.

Although the Ku Klux Klan (KKK) did not directly establish Attucks High School, its pervasive influence in 1920s Indiana politics helps to explain the forces that created such a dramatic example of racial separation. With the Klan promoting white ethnic consciousness, Indiana became the largest and most powerful Klan state in the north. Grand Dragon, D.C. Stephenson, informed on Governor Ed Jackson as having received Klan bribes. When Attucks opened its doors in 1927, the KKK, in full Klan regalia, led a parade past the school in a procession that took an hour to pass.

Yet African Americans transformed the school that had been forced upon them into a unifying symbol. Black opposition to the school's opening ebbed as the first principal, Matthias Nolcox, combed the east coast and as far west as Kansas in search of the finest black faculty available. Attucks had a higher percentage of teachers with advanced degrees than any other area high school. Some like Joseph C. Carroll and John Morton-Finney had earned doctorates and would have taught at the university level had they been white. An active club life, led by the student council, also flourished. And its sports program excited everyone.

The Crispus Attucks athletic program was a popular diversion in Indianapolis black community throughout the school's existence. Not just athletic success, but also the athletes' discipline and status as "Attucks Tigers" fed the students' prestige in the community. The Tigers aggressively played with skill and dignity. African Americans were proud of their winning and also how they won. After the Indiana High School Athletic Association (IHSAA) opened its tournaments to all high schools in 1942, Attucks gained widespread exposure. Winning city, regional, and state championships promoted it as a powerful agent of black achievement and equality.

During Principal Russell A. Lane's tenure (1930-1957), the school achieved it highest educational stature. Lane held three advanced degrees and was an able administrator. Through a series of initiatives, he prompted the expansion of the school building. He also enhanced the curriculum to include college algebra, economics, sociology, current events, and five foreign languages. He promoted an extension of educational programs to include vocational subjects and a popular evening school that served both adults and teens. Lane further encouraged a sense of black self-awareness, establishing clubs for black literature, music, and history. Over the course of his tenure, Attucks established itself as the central institution in black Indianapolis. It was a source of pride, the base for community organization, and a training ground for future success.

H istorically, Indiana Avenue has been the very center of the social, political, and cultural life of black Indianapolis, Indiana. It is located within the Mile Square of Downtown Indianapolis. It cuts a diagonal swath from Capitol Avenue to the edge of the White River, on the near Northwest side. During its prime in the 1930s and 1940s, Indiana Avenue was the "Broadway" of black Indianapolis. What Harlem was to black New Yorker's, the Avenue was to black Hoosiers. And like Harlem, the Avenue was the bi-product of racial segregation. By the turn of the twentieth century, the African American community was well established in Indianapolis. The largest number lived along Indiana Avenue in feeder areas from New York Street to Tenth Street near City Hospital (now Wishard Hospital). Waves of black immigrants from the South before World War I and during the Great Migration increased the black urban population.

Black businesses in Indianapolis clustered around the Avenue and adjacent streets to serve the physical needs of the black population. Everything that a person might want could be purchased in an eight-block segment along the Avenue. By 1916 there were 33 saloons; 33 restaurants; 26 grocery stores; including meat and poultry markets; 17 barbershops and hair salons; 16 tailors and clothing retailers; 14 shoe repair and shine parlors; 13 dry goods stores and drugstores; pool halls, funeral parlors; and the offices of lawyers, doctors, dentists, and real estate agents. Catering businesses and bakeries, often owned by black women, also had white clientele.

The Walker Manufacturing Company, established in 1910 by Madame C.J. Walker, the nation's first black millionaire, commissioned the building that would become the cornerstone of the Avenue, the Walker Building. It housed the manufacturing company, the beauty school, the theatre, a restaurant, and office space for black professionals. Black doctors, dentist, and lawyers were barred from renting space in downtown buildings. Mme. Walker had profits grossing over $100,000 a year. And she was a heavy investor in real estate on and around the Avenue. She also supported the local NAACP, Senate Avenue YMCA, Flanner House, and local black churches.

The Avenue was also home to a vibrant club scene. It thrived during the Prohibition era, the Great Depression, and the war years. At the Sunset Terrace one could hear Count Basie, Lionel Hampton, Eddie Vinson, B.B. King, and other big band and blues acts. Some of the era's great jazz musicians and singers got their start on the Avenue, including the Hamptons, Wes Montgomery, Leroy Vinegar, Freddie Hubbard, Jimmy Lunsford, Jimmy Coe, J.J. Johnson, Earl Walker and the original Inkspots. The lively Jazz and Blues scene became a frequent stop on the "Chittlin' Circuit" attracting artists like Ella Fitzgerald, Dinah Washington, and Duke Ellington.

Unlike other historic black districts, the Avenue was not destroyed by the rioting of the late 1960s, freeway construction, or misguided redevelopment. Instead the area suffered gradual abandonment by the black middleclass. A second wave of black migration occurred during and after World War II. By the late 1950s, the black middleclass fled the area leaving it to the black underclass. The integration thrust of the 1960s allowed the decline of the Avenue to accelerate. By the 1970s, the Avenue and its feeder neighborhoods were in the throes of urban blight. These things, coupled with the massive building expansion of Indiana University-Purdue University Indianapolis, caused the decline of the Avenue.

In the 1980s Indiana Avenue and its feeder areas underwent the process of urban renewal. The project was completed by 1996, but spin-off effects are ongoing as revitalization continues on the streets surrounding Indiana Avenue. But some things never change. African Americans, ever conscious of the street's cultural significance, never call it by its correct name, "Indiana Avenue." It is simply referred to as "The Avenue." And by that, everyone in Indianapolis understands what is meant.

PEARL BAILEY (1918-1990)

P earl Bailey was an actress, singer, dancer, comedienne, and author. She was known for her comedic timing and charm; honored for her service to American troops; and named by President Richard M. Nixon as a special delegate to the United Nations.

She was born Pearlie Mae Bailey in Newport News, Virginia on March 29, 1918, but soon the family moved to Washington, D.C. She was the youngest of four children and the only daughter born to James Bailey, a revivalist minister, and Ella Mae Bailey. By the age of three, Pearl was already singing in her father's church choir. After her parents' divorce, she moved with her mother and stepfather to Philadelphia, attending elementary and high school there.

Bailey's stage singing debut came when she was 15 years old. One of her brothers entered her in an amateur contest at Philadelphia's Pearl Theater, where she won first prize. A few months later she won a similar contest at Harlem's famed Apollo Theater. She decided to pursue a career in entertainment and dropped out of high school. She danced briefly for the band of Hoosier-born Noble Sissle. Soon after, she was singing and dancing in Philadelphia's black nightclubs in the late 1930s and performing in other parts of the East Coast. In 1941, during World War II, she toured the country with the United Service Organization (USO), entertaining American troops.

After her tour with the USO, Bailey settled in New York City. As a talented and successful nightclub performer, she was led to other talented acts such as Cab Calloway and Count Basie. In 1946, she made her Broadway debut in *St. Louis Woman* and won the Donaldson Award for most promising newcomer of the year. She went on to appear onstage in *Arms and the Girl* (1950), *House of Flowers* (1954), and *Bless You All* (1954). In 1967 she won a Tony Award for her role of Dolly Levi in the all-black version of *Hello Dolly*. Bailey also had a thriving movie career, making her debut in *The Variety Girl* in 1947. She had larger roles in *Isn't It Romantic?* (1948), *Carmen Jones* (1955), *That Certain Feeling* (1956), *St. Louis Blues* (1958), *Porgy and Bess* (1959), *All the Fine Young Cannibals* (1960), *The Landlord* (1970), *The Last Generation* (1971), and *Norman, Is That You?* (1976).

Between concert touring and stage and screen performances, Bailey also recorded many record albums. She made regular television appearances on the variety shows of Ed Sullivan, Perry Como, and Dean Martin. She even made an appearance on the short-lived Nat King Cole Show, and hosted her own variety series, *The Pearl Bailey Show* (1971). She appeared in television movies, *Member of the Wedding* (1982), and *Peter Gunn* (1989). Bailey also found the time to author several books: *The Raw Pearl* (1968), *Talking to Myself* (1971), *Pearl's Kitchen: An Extraordinary Cookbook* (1973), *Duey's Tale* (1975), *Hurry Up, America, and Spit* (1976), *Between You and Me: A Heartfelt Memoir on Learning, Loving, and Living* (1989).

Bailey became known at home and abroad for being an ambassador of goodwill. The March of Dimes in 1968 and the USO in 1969 named her Woman of the Year. She announced her show business retirement in 1975 and yet continued to appear on TV and in films. Also in 1975, she accepted a presidential appointment as a member of the American delegation to the United Nations, and served in that capacity for life. Her last years were marked by two extraordinary events. In 1985, at the age of 67, she graduated from Georgetown University in Washington, D.C. with a B.A. in Theology. And, in 1988, President Ronald Regan presented her with the Presidential Medal of Freedom, the nation's highest civilian honor.

Bailey's life transcended show business. And it transcended race. She was a woman of remarkable intelligence with a wide-range of interests. It is always a privilege to showcase talented, artistic, and highly honored African American women such as the indomitable Pearl Bailey.

JAMES BALDWIN (1924-1987)

James Baldwin was an African American and an important writer of essays, poetry, plays, short stories, and novels. As a period writer, he was greatly influenced by the Civil Rights Movement. In fact, he lent the most vital and critical voice to the movement. He later became an outspoken proponent for gay rights.

He was born James Arthur Baldwin was born August 6, 1924, in Harlem, New York City. He was the eldest of his mother's nine children. His real father was unknown. His stepfather was a preacher who was very strict. His mother cleaned houses while James baby-sat his younger siblings. The family was very poor. As a youth, Baldwin found pathways leading out of poverty and at the same time enriched his understanding of where he came from. He had two great passions – books and school. He loved to read and found much to occupy his time in the Harlem branches of the New York Public Library. His teachers soon began to recognize his genius.

Baldwin was a child preacher in the Mt. Calvary Church under the charismatic Pentecostal ministry of Mother Rosa Horn. He grew out of "sanctified shouting," but not beyond the spiritual gift to witness. In public school he studied under Harlem Renaissance poet Countee Cullen, and he began to write. He graduated from DeWitt Clinton High School in 1942. He left home and stopped preaching immediately afterwards. He moved to Greenwich Village and followed the bohemian life-style and lived openly gay, like so many of the many other artists living there.

Baldwin was soon able to have his writings published. But most Americans thought of him only as a "Negro writer." He wanted to be known for his talent, not his race. In 1948 Baldwin won the Rosenwald Fellowship for writing. He decided to use this money to move to Paris, France, the home of other African American expatriates like Josephine Baker and Richard Wright. In Paris he lived modestly and continued to write. Despite his discovery of French racism, he knew that blacks in France were much better treated than those in the U.S. France would remain his home until he died. Baldwin came to share many European friendships. He even discovered a father figure in Beauford Delaney, a troubled expatriate African American painter.

Baldwin's first novel, *Go Tell It on the Mountain*, was largely autobiographical and published in 1953. The book was a huge success and made him famous. In 1955, he published *Notes of a Native Son*, a book about his own life and ideas. More novels followed: *Giovanni's Room*, 1956; Nobody Knows My Name, 1961; *Another Country*, 1962. In 1963, he published a book of essays about race relations in America, *The Fire Next Time*. It was a shocking expose, highlighting racism as a deadly disease for blacks and whites alike.

Other important Baldwin works included many plays: *Blues for Mr. Charlie*, 1964; *Going to Meet the Man*, 1965, *Tell Me How Long the Train's Been Gone*, 1968; *No Name in the Street*, 1972; *If Beale Street Could Talk*, 1974; and *Just Above My Head*, 1979. Baldwin concluded his writing career just as his life was coming to an end. His later works explored the family dynamic. *Jimmy's Blues,* a book of poems; *The Price of the Ticket,* a book of essays; and *The Evidence of Things Not Seen,* another book of essays, were all published in 1985, his most prolific year.

It was during the Civil Rights Movement that Baldwin returned to the United States and made his first visit to the American South. There he met Dr. Martin Luther King, Jr. and heard him speak for the first time in person. From then on, Baldwin gave much of his time and money to civil rights causes. He saw Southern whites trapped in their own racist mythology, and blacks made heroic in their struggle against it. Among his many honors, James Baldwin has earned a place in history as a great intellectual writer and a strong eloquent voice in the African American struggle.

BENJAMIN BANNEKER (1731-1806)

Benjamin Banneker was born to free blacks in rural Maryland in 1731. His mother was a mulatto named Mary and his father was an African named Robert. Robert had no surname so he acquired his wife's name after they were married. Mary was the daughter of a freed African prince, Bannka, and an indentured Englishwoman named Molly Welsh. It was Banneker's grandmother who first taught him to read and write. He attended integrated private schools, and obtained an eighth grade education. By all accounts, he excelled in mathematics, but was largely self-taught. He was an astronomer, author of almanacs, surveyor, humanitarian and inventor.

Banneker spent all his life on his family's 100 acre farm on the Patapsco River in Baltimore County and never married. His time was spent in study and invention. In 1753, he began to tinker with a pocket watch taking it apart and putting it back together several times. Using that watch as an example, Banneker produced the first wooden clock ever built in the United States. It was made entirely of wood and each gear was carved by hand. His clock kept perfect time, striking every hour for more than forty years. News of his clock caused such a sensation that people came from everywhere to see it, and to see the genius who assembled it.

In the years following his parents' death, Banneker became a modest gentleman tobacco farmer, who divided his time between managing an efficient farm and working on mathematical calculations. During the Revolutionary War period, a neighbor introduced Banneker to the science of astronomy that he quickly mastered. His aptitude in mathematics and knowledge of astronomy enabled him to predict the solar eclipse that took place on April 14, 1789. In 1792, Banneker began publishing an almanac that was widely read and became the main reference for farmers in the Middle-Atlantic states. It offered weather information, recipes, medical remedies, poems world peace and anti-slavery essays. His was the first scientific book written by a black man in America, and it was published annually for more than a decade.

Banneker's primary reputation stems from his service as a surveyor on the six-man land survey team which helped design the plans for the new federal capitol in Washington, D.C. President Washington had appointed Banneker to the team, making him the first black presidential appointee in the United

States. Banneker helped in selecting the sites for the U.S. Capitol building, the U.S. Treasury building, the White House and other Federal buildings. Banneker later related that his participation in the survey became the greatest adventure of his life.

When the chairman of the civil engineering team, Major Pierre L'Enfant, abruptly reigned from the project and returned to France with the plans, Banneker redrew the plans from memory. His recall of the project was so keen he was able to reproduce it in its entirety. Washington, D.C., with its grand avenues and buildings, was completed and stands today as a monument to the genius of Benjamin Banneker.

Banneker's preoccupation with science and mathematics in no way diminished his concern for the plight of Africans in America. In a twelve-page letter to then Secretary of State, Thomas Jefferson, he refuted Jefferson's statements that blacks were inferior to whites. He even said that whites "counteract [God's] mercies, in detaining by fraud and violence, so numerous a part of my brethren under groaning captivity and cruel oppression." Banneker further recommended to Jefferson that "you and all others...wean yourselves from those narrow prejudices which you have imbibed with respect to [blacks]."

Benjamin Banneker was an early abolitionist, astronomer, mathematician, inventor, writer and compiler of almanacs. Under circumstances less than ideal, his career demonstrated the intellectual and practical accomplishments African Americans could make when given the same opportunities as whites. Banneker's exemplary life and extraordinary career dispelled the myth of the inferiority of blacks.

IDA B. WELLS BARNETT (1862-1931)

I da B. Wells Barnett was an African American educator, zealous social and political activist, and the most well known anti-lynching crusader even before the turn of the twentieth century. She was an ardent supporter of the United States Constitution and felt it applied to all citizens. And when she saw it violated or denied to anyone based on the common color and gender biases of the day, she taught against, wrote in protest of, and marched to raise awareness of, anything that was an infringement of civil rights.

Ida B. Well was born to slave parents in Holly Springs, Mississippi. She was educated at Rust University, a high school and industrial school for former slaves established in 1866. Her earliest jobs were in the teaching profession. She actually began teaching at a country school at the age of fourteen. Moving to Memphis in 1884, she continued to teach while attending Fisk University in Nashville during the summer.

Due to a lawsuit involving her refusal to give up her seat in a Jim Crow railroad car designated for "whites only," Wells lost her teaching job and subsequently turned to journalism. For some time she wrote a local African American weekly, *Living Word,* and in 1891 she became co-owner and editor of the Memphis weekly, *Free Speech.* On March 9 of the following year she printed an article that denounced the lynching of three of her friends, Thomas Moss, Calvin McDowell, and Henry Stewart, accused of raping three white women. She revealed in print the names of those responsible for the lynching. Her article angered so many Memphis whites that a mob of them demolished her printing press, destroyed her office, and forced her to leave town.

Although the offices of the Memphis *Free Speech* were destroyed by an angry mob, the event launched Wells' lifelong career as an anti-lynching crusader. After being forced out of Memphis, Wells fled to New York City where she was hired by another African American Weekly. Her anti-lynching campaign took her on lecture tours across the country and twice to England. Wells eventually settled in Chicago, and in 1895, she married Ferdinand L. Barnett. In Chicago she resumed her moral advocacy, contributing to newspapers and periodicals. Her hard-hitting articles led the fight not only against lynching, but also chain gang and sharecropping injustices. Wells also founded and headed the *Ida B. Wells Club* that opposed all racial injustice.

In 1898, Wells led a delegation to President William McKinley to protest lynching, and that same year she became secretary of the National Afro-American Council. Some ten years later Wells founded the Negro Fellowship League. In 1910 Wells helped to found the National Association for the Advancement of Colored People (NAACP). In founding the NAACP, she worked closely with other notable co-founders, such as W.E.B. Dubois. In 1913, she was appointed adult probation officer in Chicago, and two years later she was elected vice-president of Chicago's Equal Rights League.

Ida B. Wells Barnett served at some of the leading papers of her era including *The New York Age, The Chicago Defender,* and *The Chicago Conservator,* a paper jointly owned by her husband, Ferdinand Barnett. The State of Tennessee has recognized Wells as one of its leading historical figures in communication. Few communities can boast of anyone as bold and brave as Ida B. Wells Barnett. Never fearful of her own life, although she was placed in some difficult situations, Wells never wavered from her cause.

Blacks have been tremendously tested by the circumstances of being African in America. Yet in every generation there have been men *and* women who have taken up the task of fighting against social and political injustices. Ida B. Wells Barnett's career as a determined teacher, pioneer journalist, passionate speaker, fearless anti-lynching crusader, suffragist and women's rights advocate, co-founder of the NAACP, and tireless political activist, has left us with one such legacy.

COUNT BASIE (1904-1984)

C ount Basie was an African American jazz pianist and bandleader. He was one of the leading musicians of the swing era of the 1930s and 1940s. The Count Basie Band was famous for its outstanding rhythm section. He led one of the foremost jazz big bands. He featured numerous outstanding instrumental and vocal soloists, and talented music arrangers. His career spanned fifty years as he continuously produced light, but relentlessly forward-moving rhythmic propulsion that was the epitome of the swing sound.

He was born William James Basie in Red Bank, New Jersey on August 21, 1904. He played drums as a child before learning the piano. His mother was his first piano teacher, but he was greatly influenced by the stride piano styling of the musicians of the 1920s. In his late teens, he toured extensively on the vaudeville circuits as a solo pianist, an accompanist for other artists, and music director for blues singers, dancers, and comedians. This provided an early training that would prove significant in his later career.

In 1924, barely out of his teens, Basie moved to New York City. There the ragtime-derived styling of Harlem jazz pianists Fats Waller and James P. Johnson influenced him. While based in Harlem, he toured the Midwest and South extensively. When a tour collapsed in 1927, leaving him stranded in Kansas City, Missouri, Basie secured work there playing theater organ for silent movies. He also joined the Blue Devils, a band led by bassist, Walter Page. But in 1929, Basie was invited to join the Kansas City Orchestra of pianist Bennie Moten. It was the leading jazz band in the region at that time. Basie remained with the group until Moten's death in 1935.

After death of friend and mentor, Bennie Moten, Basie formed a new band called "Count Basie and His Barons of Rhythm." There were several members of Moten's band in the new Basie endeavor. In 1936, the group moved to New York City, and a year later began recording as Count Basie and his Orchestra for the Decca recording label. By 1939 the band was made up of fifteen instrumentalists and two singers, Jimmy Rushing and jazz great, Billie Holiday, who was later replaced by Helen Humes.

At first, Basie performed in a two-handed ragtime style. But in the mid 1930s, he switched to a relaxed, spare style. His musical styling was imbued with subtlety and wit. It led beautifully into the solos of his instrumentalists. The

Basie Band was dominated by great soloists like; Lester Young and Herschel Evans, tenor saxophonists; Buck Clayton and Harry "Sweets" Edison, trumpeters; and Dicky Wells, trombonist. And there was, of course, Basie himself who had embraced a new mellow style, different from his youth.

Musical arrangements of the Count Basie Band were written in a relatively straightforward manner when compared to the more intricate scores of Duke Ellington. Some of the Basie band pieces, such as "One O'Clock Jump" (1937) were made up in rehearsal and memorized, rather than written out. The band often made up short, repeated phrases that were usually played as a background for its instrumental soloists. Another musical hallmark of the Basie style was the reliance on the blues, both blues chord progressions, and blue notes, which are certain flatted notes in a musical scale. After World War II ended in 1945, changes in the economy and in American musical tastes sent the big bands into commercial decline. Eventually, the changed economic realities of touring with a band affected the Basie Orchestra, too.

In 1950 Basie dissolved his large ensemble and began touring with a small group of six to nine instrumentalists. But by 1952, he had reassembled his big band. This time, written arrangements were standard operating procedure. By then, the band had a different sound and style than it had in the 1930s and 1940s. Basie's arrangers now included Neil Hefti, Ernie Wilkins, Benny Carter, Thad Jones, and the great Quincy Jones. *April in Paris*, *Shiny Stockings*, and *Lil' Darlin'* became perennial favorites among the enthusiastic Basie audiences. Count Basie became an enduring music institution for fifty years, translating the Count Basie 1930s sound into the 1980s.

D aisy Bates was one of the twentieth century's most prominent civil rights activists. With her husband, she ran a newspaper and used it to feature exposés on racial injustices and educational disparities in Little Rock, Arkansas. Bates distinguished herself as the key figure in the now historic 1957 integration of Central High School in Little Rock. Her memoir of the episode, "The Long Shadow of Little Rock," is viewed as a primary text of the history of American race relations.

She was born Daisy Lee Gatson in 1920, in Huttig, Arkansas. She barely knew her parents. Three white men had abducted her mother, and her body was later found in a local pond. Mentally and emotionally overburdened by this overt act of mob violence, her father left town. He placed Daisy in the care of family friends, Orlee and Susie Smith, who raised her as their own.

In 1941 Daisy Gatson married L.C. Bates, a journalist, and together they started a newspaper, the Arkansas State Press, in Little Rock. In the early months of the newspaper, circulation reached ten thousand. It became the leading African American newspaper in the state and a powerful voice in the Civil Rights Movement. The couple launched a crusade against all forms of injustices perpetrated against blacks. They became a strong force in championing the cause of civil rights.

In 1942, Daisy covered a story involving the murder of a black soldier by city police. She reported that the killing was "one of the most bestial murders in the annals of Little Rock." She went on to say that after the officer had thrown the soldier to the ground, he fired five shots into his prostrate body. A few days after her report, the paper lost substantial amounts of advertising from white patrons. The future of the newspaper looked grim, but with the continued hard work and determination of the Bates' circulation rose to over twenty thousand. And they expanded their crusade to include better housing conditions, jobs and courtroom representation for blacks.

It was as president of the Arkansas state conference of the NAACP that Daisy Bates came to national prominence. When the 1954 Supreme Court decision of Brown v. Board of Education declared that segregation in public schools was unconstitutional, she took the national spotlight as a promoter in desegregating Central High School in Little Rock. Mrs. Bates coordinated the efforts of placing nine black students in the all-white school. Of the seventeen black students selected for enrollment by the NAACP, eight withdrew out of fear. The remaining students came to be known as the "Little Rock Nine."

When the nine black students attempted to enter Central High, National Guardsmen barred the entrance by order of Arkansas Governor Orval Faubus. Violent, rioting crowds of whites surrounded the school and harassed the blacks students as they walked away. The students were exposed to name calling, curses, shoving, thrown bottles and rocks, and spitting. White reaction to integration was so violent, it forced President Eisenhower to order 1,000 troops of the 101st Airborne Division of the United States Army to protect the Little Rock Nine so that they could enter the school. As commander-in-chief of the nation's armed forces, the president usurped the power of the governor by mobilizing the Arkansas National Guard. The guardsmen were then ordered to keep the peace, which meant they had to fight back the white mobs.

Daisy Bates was the students' leading advocate, escorting them safely to school until the crisis was resolved, and continuing the fight for equal rights long after the incident. She spoke at the March on Washington in 1963, pledging to stop fighting only when African Americans could sit, walk, kneel and study in any public place in this country. In recognition of her outstanding efforts, she received citations and honorary degrees from more than forty organizations. Daisy Bates was just one spark…that ignited the flame…that burned down the house…that "Jim Crow" built.

PATRICIA E. BATH (1949-)

D r. Patricia Bath is an eye surgeon, professor of ophthalmology, inventor of the Laserphaco Probe for the treatment of cataracts, and co-founder of the American Institute for the Prevention of Blindness (AIPB). She has been a trailblazer for women and African Americans in the medical profession, being the first African American woman to receive a patent for a medical invention.

She was born Patricia Era Bath in Harlem, New York City in 1949. She attributes her determination and love for learning to her parents. Her father, Rupert Bath, was an immigrant from Trinidad. Her mother, Gladys, was a housewife for the early years of her children's lives. She encouraged Patricia's interest in science by giving her a chemistry set. And her mother did not go to work until the children were in middle school. Bath recalls that her mother scrubbed floors so that she could attend medical school.

Growing up in Harlem, an area some regard as impoverished and dangerous, is full of happy memories for Dr. Bath. Her parents gave her a strong set of values that included a love of family above material things, self-reliance, and a thirst for knowledge. After attending public school in Harlem, Bath entered Charles Evans Hughes High School, graduating in only two and a half years. Her first biology course opened a new world for her. She spent extra hours helping in the lab, was the editor of the school's science paper, and won several science awards. At age sixteen, she was selected to attend a National Science Foundation summer program for high school students at Yeshiva University. Mentored by Rabbi Moses Tendler and Dr. Robert Bernard in the program, she did innovative work in cancer research that made national headlines.

Bath studied chemistry and physics at Hunter College in New York and received a B.A. in 1964. She received her medical degree in 1968 from Howard University in Washington, D.C. She was an intern at Harlem Hospital (1968-69) and completed a fellowship in ophthalmology at Columbia University (1969-70). She completed a three-year residency at New York University (1970-73). In 1974, after completing a fellowship in Corneal and Keratoprosthesis Surgery, Bath moved to Los Angeles and joined the faculty of UCLA as an assistant professor of surgery and ophthalmology.

At UCLA in 1976, Bath and three colleagues founded the AIPB, an organization whose mission is to protect, preserve, and restore the gift of sight. The AIPB also supports global initiatives to provide infants with protective anti-infection eye drops, to ensure that children who are malnourished receive vitamin A supplements essential to vision, and to vaccinate children against disease that lead to blindness. As director of the AIPB, Bath travels widely performing surgery, teaching new medical techniques, lecturing, and donating equipment.

It was in 1981 that Bath conceived of an invention that would use a laser to remove cataracts, a cloudiness that forms in the lens of the eye causing blurry, distorted vision and the leading cause of blindness. Her Laserphaco Probe consists of an optical laser fiber surrounded by irrigation and aspiration tubes. The probe is inserted into a tiny incision in the eye and laser energy vaporizes the cataract and extracts the resulting debris in seconds. She has held the patents on the apparatus, concept, and modifications to the device since 1988 and her invention is used in many countries. The proceeds from the licensing of the probe support the work and programs of AIPB.

Bath is a groundbreaking physician and an historic inventor who has given of herself and her genius to make the world a brighter place for those facing blindness from cataracts and glaucoma. She is quoted as saying that the *"limits of science are not the limits of imagination."* Let us keep sight of Dr. Patricia Bath and all black inventors who continue to make a difference in the world.

JAMES PIERSON BECKWOURTH (1798-1866)

J im Beckwourth was an African American who played a major role in the early exploration and settlement of the American West. He is perhaps most famous for his 1850 discovery of a passage through the Sierra Nevada Mountains, the Beckwourth Trail, which helped many pioneers reach California faster and easier. Although there were people of various races and nationalities on the great American frontier, Beckwourth was the only African American who in 1856 recorded his remarkable life story entitled, The Life and Adventures of James P. Beckwourth, Mountaineer, Scout, and Pioneer, and Chief of the Crow Nation of Indians. The title is a bit long, but it encompassed most of who he was, and all of what he did.

Beckwourth was born on a plantation near Fredericksburg, Virginia in April 1798. He was the second oldest of thirteen children born to a slave woman by her master. History records nothing else about his mother, but his father is reported to have been a Major in the Revolutionary War. In 1806, the family moved, slaves and all, to a property outside St. Louis, Missouri, between the fork of the Mississippi and the Missouri Rivers. It was all wilderness at that time, inhabited by many Native American groups, and French and Spanish fur trappers. Beckwourth completed four years of school and then completed a five-year apprenticeship as a blacksmith in St. Louis.

After a bad ending to his apprenticeship, Beckwourth returned briefly to his father's settlement. While in St. Charles, Missouri, on his way to New Orleans, Beckwourth met Jean-Batiste Pointe DuSable, the black trapper and fur trader who founded Chicago. DuSable told fascinating stories about trapping wild animals, hunting buffalo, and tracking through the newly acquired Louisiana Territory. That was all that Beckwourth needed to hear. He returned to St. Louis and in 1823 he signed on with the Rocky Mountain Fur Trading Company. Living in the wilderness, he soon became an expert hunter and trapper. He also learned the ways of the Indians and the languages of the Crow and Blackfoot.

In 1825 Beckwourth left the trading company and went to live among the Indians for six years. He married Indian women, including the daughter of a Crow Chief. He was given the name Morning Star, but after leading the Crow into battle against their fierce Blackfoot enemies, he was renamed Bloody Arm. Traveling between the western and southern frontiers, he engaged in a myriad of occupations. In the 1830s Beckwourth served as a U.S. Army scout. He fought in the Third Seminole war against the Black and Seminole alliance in Florida in 1842. He even participated in the California Bear Flag Rebellion in 1846. While traveling with his wife in 1848, Beckwourth acted as a guide for General John C. Fremont.

Beckwourth was also a gold prospector in the California gold fields after he discovered the passage to California that still bears his name. He opened two trading posts and also became a rancher. The love of the mountains never left him so he continued to hunt and trap. There have also been tall tales spun around the persona of Jim Beckwourth that may be patently untrue. It is reported that he was once a Pony Express Rider. Although some riders were black, this seems unlikely since the Pony Express was in operation from April 1860 to November 1861. Jim would have been over sixty years old by then and the average age of Pony Express riders was twenty. But he may have worked in another capacity at a station along the express route. He died suddenly and mysteriously in 1866, possibly of food poisoning, after trying to negotiate a peace treaty toward the end of the Cheyenne War.

James Pierson Beckwourth was an unusual man, even for his times. Legally, he was born a slave, but was never treated as such because his father recognized him as a son. He was part of that daring, brutal frontier tradition that opened the wilderness to exploration and settlement. And he was clearly suited for that life. His adventurous and dangerous exploits, mostly documented in his autobiography, have long been forgotten. But his discovery of the Beckwourth Pass, which is still used by the Pacific Railroad and the U.S. Interstate Highway system, will forever stand as a testament to his pioneering spirit.

MARY MCLEOD BETHUNE (1875-1955)

Mary McLeod Bethune was an African American educator, early participant in the Black Club Women's Movement, university founder, and advisor to four United States Presidents. She was the founder of the Daytona Normal School for Colored Girls and oversaw its merger with the Cookman Institute to form Bethune-Cookman College. She was the founder and first president of the National Council of Negro Women. She was the best-known and only female New Deal advisor to President Franklin D. Roosevelt.

She was born Mary Jane McLeod on July 10, 1875, near Mayesville, South Carolina. She was the fifteenth of seventeen children born to former slaves Samuel and Patsy McIntosh McLeod. Her mother continued to work for her former owner and her father was finally able to buy five acres of land that he named "Homestead," and built a home for his family. Sam McLeod was able to find all of his "sold off" children after slavery ended and brought them back to his land. Mary spent her early years in the family's cotton field and could throw 250 pounds by age eight. This time spent in the fields helped shape her work ethic and values regarding the importance of labor. But it could not suppress her yearning for education.

Mary had a burning desire to learn how to read and write and was not happy until she was allowed to attend Mayesville's one room schoolhouse. She became the prize student of Emma Jane Wilson, the school's only teacher. Early on she expressed a wish to be a teacher, received a scholarship, and spent seven years at the Scotia Seminary in North Carolina. Religion was central in her vision of progress for the African American community. Upon graduation from Scotia in 1894, Mary was awarded another scholarship to attend the Moody Institute for Home and Foreign Missions in Chicago. She also studied at the Moody Bible Institute and worked in a Settlement House while living in Chicago. Mary's goal was to become a missionary to minister to the spiritual and educational needs of the youth of Africa. When her application to the Presbyterian Board of Missions in New York was turned down for an appointment to Africa, she began teaching in the United States. She returned home and became Miss Wilson's assistant. Later she accepted an appointment at the Haines Institute in Augusta, Georgia. It was here that she gained experience in primary, grammar, elementary, normal and industrial courses. She met and married Albertus Bethune in 1898. They had one son, Albert born in

1899. For reasons not found in their public personas, Mary and Albertus lived "uncoupled" lives for the vast majority of their marriage.

Bethune established the Daytona Normal and Industrial School for Negro Girls in 1904. She labored for the next twenty years dividing her time and energy between making the school a success and building a national reputation for herself. She was a civic leader and a zealous political activist. Her black voter registration drive earned her a visit from the local Ku Klux Klan. She was elected president of the Federated Colored Women's Clubs. She organized to combat school segregation and the lack of health facilities for black children. In 1924 she became the president of the prestigious National Association of Colored Women's Clubs. In 1935 she founded the more politically cognizant National Council of Negro Women.

Presidents Calvin Coolidge and Herbert Hoover both requested Bethune's services on advisory boards. In 1932, President Franklin D. Roosevelt asked her to serve on the advisory board of the National Youth Administration (NYA). She was so successful in establishing the foundation of the NYA that President Roosevelt called upon her to set up an Office of Minority Affairs. Her title was changed to Director of the Division of Negro Affairs. She was also an advisor for Roosevelt's unofficial "Black Cabinet." President Harry D. Truman sent her as a diplomatic emissary to Haiti and Liberia, and to the charter meeting of the United Nations.

Mary McLeod Bethune lived an amazing life that spanned the generations from the Reconstruction to the onset of the Civil Rights Movement. She saw Jim Crow Laws become deeply entrenched in the South. But then she saw black people working together to provide monumental services to their downtrodden communities. She saw women disenfranchised as citizens, but then she saw them as they cast their first votes toward full citizenship. As a young girl, she heard the Supreme Court ruling: "Separate but Equal is OKAY." But as a seasoned, mature, woman, wizened by years in the struggle for equality and social justice, she heard the Court rule: "Separate but Equal is NOT OKAY, and what were we thinking?"

Mary McLeod Bethune died at the age of 79. She was the most famous woman of her era and the only black woman to have a national monument erected in her honor in Washington, D.C. In her living and in her dying, she left a legacy of love, hope, faith, service, advocacy, and racial dignity. It has been said of Mary McLeod Bethune that her achievements were so great, and her contributions so monumental, that to write, speak, or even present American history without including her, would be to leave out a great chapter.

T raditionally in the United States, separate churches allowed blacks to assume leadership roles denied to them in racially integrated assemblies, and to worship in culturally distinctive ways. African slaves in the American South achieved two extraordinary cultural and social accomplishments. First, despite the variety of ethnic groups, linguistic groups, cultures, and religions the slaves came from in Africa, they welded themselves into a single people. Secondly, the slaves transformed the evangelical Protestantism of the American South into an isolated phenomenon that, despite its important internal differences and divisions, was unified by shared suffering and the shared hope of deliverance. The Black Church is the coalescing factor that fuses black people together even today. It has planted the seeds of our educational endeavors, social welfare initiatives, and political protests.

The slaves brought their own religious sensibilities and culture into the world that they found. And emphasized within biblical Protestantism the themes and components most relevant to them and their situation. The result was, and still remains, a distinct and unique entity. In artistic African style, the slaves told and retold the stories of the Bible by turning them into the Negro Spirituals. Slaves were largely illiterate, but when the spirituals are strung together, they in fact constitute the entire biblical narrative text. The songs were not penned by any one author, but composed in community, by a shared experience.

One of the most remarkable features of the early Black Church was its creative appropriation and adaptation of the Bible, the basis of Protestant authority. Africans identified with the enslavement of the children of Israel in Egypt, and Israel's eventual deliverance under Moses. In the New Testament the slaves also identified with the birth of Jesus as an innocent child and His unjust humiliation, suffering, and death. W.E.B. Dubois was one of the first to write about the slaves' religion. He argued that the spirituals spelled out the slaves' deep religious faith, and at the same time, the unique way that their faith was interwoven both with protest against oppression, and demonstration on behalf of freedom.

For good reason, slaveholders in the American South feared the Black Church as a potential base for insurrection, and tried to control it. By law, for instance, slaves could not gather for worship unless a white person was present. On lax plantations, a white child occasionally fulfilled that technical requirement.

Even with restrictions, the Black Church developed as the African American institution least under white control. It was the institution with the most African survivals, the one in which indigenous leadership could develop, the one most reflective of African American people and their experience, and the one that became the heart and soul of the black community, slave and free.

The North was the first to see the formation of the Independent Black Church Movement. Many black churches had their origins in white churches, but for various reasons, especially those actively involved in discrimination, began to splinter into separate all-black churches. With the Baptist Movement in particular, autonomy happened partly as a result of heightened black consciousness, partly in reaction to discrimination from southerners, and partly in response to paternalistic condescension of northerners. The formation of separate black churches, which moved at a fever pace in the early nineteenth century, only intensified during the Reconstruction era in the late nineteenth century.

Even in this new millennium, the black family remains the primary unit of the Black Church. The historic Black Church was a gathering of families and extended families, worshiping in a sanctuary that they erected themselves, on land hallowed by their dead buried there. Even with the urban migration of African Americans in the twentieth century, there is still a country-like feel to black worship. It is pure, personal, and passionate. And even if fewer of us are related by blood in today's Black Church, African Americans will always be related by the shared experience of being black in a nation that has yet to value the black in us.

W E.B. Dubois, in 1918, made a statement about black churchwomen that remains true even today: *"Black women are the main pillars of those social settlements which we call churches; and they have with small doubt raised three-fourths of our church property."* Even now if we query the top leadership of secular black women's organizations, we would find that they have received their impulse, organizational skills, and values from working within the Black Church.

Historical and contemporary evidence has underscored the fact that the Black Church could scarcely have survived without the support and the active participation of black women. Through various church auxiliaries and missionary societies, black women have performed numerous and vital services for their churches. In the Baptist tradition especially, they have conducted a myriad of services while being excluded from official leadership positions. But within Methodist denominations, especial the African Methodist Episcopal (AME) Church, women have already reached the upper echelon of leadership.

When disasters of economic depression, bankruptcy, and disease struck the black communities in each decade from the collapse of Reconstruction in the 1870s to the Great Depression of the 1930s, churchwomen were there to keep communities functioning. They created orphanages and launched charities to support widows and the aged. They created and taught Sunday Schools. They did, and continue to do, missionary work and participate in endless fundraisers to furnish churches and to pay church mortgages. Despite the importance of women in the life of the Black Church, the offices of preacher and pastor remain a male preserve and are not generally obtainable for women. Even Baptist Deacon Boards of most black churches have remained sacrosanct for males. But in recent years, however, Church Trustee Boards have become an alternative haven for women seeking leadership roles.

Prior to the late 19th and mid 20th centuries, black churchwomen were never officially recognized or ordained as preachers and pastors by any black church. Instead, women were required to transfer their ministerial energies into activities more socially acceptable. In the antebellum south, they became exhorters, making persuasive speeches to slaves to encourage them toward moral rectitude. In the antebellum north, they founded benevolent organizations. Even in this 21st century, most men feel that a woman preacher is a direct contradiction of God's divine authority. For this reason alone, most black women preachers are taking for themselves the title of "Minister." If they find the occasion to preach, they do it happily. If not, they simply minister to the needs of the congregation. Many of them are finding the opportunity to minister for the churches' outreach programs.

Since women could not become preachers, large numbers of religiously motivated black women felt that they were called to teach and to evangelize. The vocation of education attracted numerous black women because the educational needs of the black community were great, especially after the Civil War when thousands of former slaves crammed the churches that often doubled as schoolhouses. Teaching was also attractive because it was considered a proper female vocation by the larger society. In the black community teachers are still highly respected. And women continue to compose the vast majority of the teaching staff in the Black Church. In the 20th century, black women evangelists became commonplace. They are in great demand and invited to speak whenever women are in charge of any church fundraiser.

By the late 19th and mid 20th centuries, black women had become religious missionaries to as far away as Africa, and as close by their immediate communities. In sprawling urban cities and in isolated rural areas, black women minister to the social ills that plague society and fulfill the spiritual purpose set forth by the Church. In the absence of an egalitarian process in the Black Church, and in the presence of an unspoken gender bias, black women have always, and still continue, to speak to the particular condition and the peculiar struggle of black people.

African religious leadership predominated during slavery. And even in that oppressive environment, a slave preacher, or exhorter, could use the Black Church to transform blacks into a single and culturally unique people. It was through the black preacher that people of diverse languages and customs, different cultural and religious traditions, brought here from different parts of Africa, and thrown into slavery, were given their first sense of unity and solidarity.

Strong independent and semi-independent black churches reflected an eagerness for self-direction and leadership. These churches, mainly Baptist and Methodist, became the leadership training institutions for slave and free communities. One qualification that the black preacher among the slaves needed to possess was some knowledge of the Bible. However imperfect or distorted his knowledge of the Bible might be, the fact the he was acquainted with the source of sacred knowledge, which was in a sense the exclusive possession of their white masters, game him prestige in matters concerning the supernatural and the religious among his fellow slaves.

The black preacher's knowledge of scripture had to be combined with an ability to speak and communicate his special knowledge to slaves. Since any part of his congregation might contain non-English speaking new arrivals, the black preacher dramatized the stories of the Bible. The slave preachers were noted for the imagery of their sermons. In the true African style of strong oral tradition, the black preacher, slave or free, told the slaves the story that led to know God.

The black preacher also needed to possess the ability to sing. So much of his preaching consisted of singing sacred songs that have come down to us as the "Negro Spirituals." Those songs represent what the slaves understood from the sacred scripture. When all of them are strung together they complete the biblical narrative. But those songs also represented the hopes and sorrows as well the shared experience of a united people. In the North black preachers preached against the institution of slavery, in the South, black preachers could only sing out against it.

Early black preachers slave and free, also became the interpreters of the African American social and political agendas, placing themselves between the white man and the membership of their congregations. Forced by this position to assume a leadership role, the black preacher often became the lead off witness against slavery. This assumed leadership role was well continued into the twentieth century as they fought against racism and social injustice. It was this role, stemming from the black protest tradition, which fomented the Civil Rights Movement. And it was black clerical leadership that propagated the movement.

By their tone and behavior, black preachers taught their congregants what to think and how to regard the leading social and political issues of the day. Determined to throw off the shackles of inferior treatment in the North and slavery in the South, the early Africans in America found religion to be a strong and resolute ally in their struggle. Black preachers were the first line of offense in the struggle for decency and respect. They took to the pulpit as a justifiable avenue of protest, admonition, exhortation, and indeed, if need be, insurrection.

Many of the notable slave revolts in the South were the work of black preachers who had seen certain "visions." Denmark Vesey used the deacons of a local black church to combine the rich imagery of the Israelite enslavement with African religious customs in his rebellion in 1822. Nat Turner was quite a gifted preacher before he skillfully organized his own insurrection in 1831. But Vesey and Turner were not unique. They are just two examples of the many black preachers who struggled under the oppression of being African in America.

CLEO BLACKBURN (1909-1978)

Cleo Blackburn was an African America businessman, civic leader, educator, ordained minister, social worker, and the Executive Director of Flanner House, a human and social services agency, for nearly forty years. Blackburn received numerous honors and accolades from academia, and the business and social services communities for his many and varied contributions to the Indianapolis community and for his accomplishments across Indiana.

He was born Cleo Walter Blackburn in Jackson, Mississippi on September 27, 1909. He was the youngest of twelve children born to David and Sarah Sneed Blackburn. Blackburn was a product of the Jim Crow South with all the segregation, discrimination, and social injustice attendant to it. He attended Southern Christian Boarding School. It was one of the eighty-three black boarding schools scattered throughout the south for elementary and secondary education. Historically, black boarding schools were the result of segregation that prevented blacks and whites from attending the same schools. But they provided a quality education for black youths in a residential campus setting.

Blackburn's post-secondary education began in Indiana with a B.S. in Theology from Butler University and an M.S. in Sociology from Indiana University. While in the graduate program at I.U., it was intimated that he participated as a research assistant for the Kenzie Report as part of the now famous behavioral science project. Blackburn also earned an M.S. from Fisk University in Tennessee and a Ph.D. from DePauw University. His honorary degrees included: D. Div. Degrees from Northwest Christian College in Eugene, Oregon, and Drake University in Des Moines, Iowa.

Blackburn was appointed Executive Director of Flanner House in 1936. It was a settlement house for African Americans, founded in a cottage donated by Indianapolis mortician, Frank Flanner in 1898. Settlement Houses flourished at the end of the 19th, and turn of the 20th century. They were established to provide social and health services for the urban poor. Under Blackburn's direction, Flanner House expanded its programs and services. He was instrumental in making it a model with national recognition. Flanner House became the first of its kind in aiding people to build and own their homes at a lower cost. The program made it possible for mortgages to be more easily negotiated by families with limited incomes. Blackburn was responsible for

63

nearly 400 new homes built using the Flanner House model. He was the originator of the concept of "sweat equity," a plan that allows people to obtain affordable housing by participating in the building process.

In 1948, Blackburn founded the Board of Fundamental Education. It was designed purely for the purpose of developing and implementing innovative programs to address comprehensive social problems of the poor and underserved in areas of health, education, housing, and employment. In tackling these issues Blackburn sought to effect positive change in the African American community, located north and west of the "Mile Square." National attention to his work came from continuous local and syndicated print media. But in 1961 Dr. Blackburn was recognized through a national television broadcast.

Blackburn's value system was heavily steeped in the Disciples of Christ and Quaker traditions. He served as president of Jarvis Christian College, DC, a historically black college in Hawkins, Texas. The many service programs on which he worked proved that he willingly crossed any boundaries and all color lines to help make America a better place. He was on the Board of Trustees of Earlham College. And worked with the American Friends Service Committee, which is the service arm of the Quaker Church. He spent summers working on service projects for Native Americans in Ashland, Wisconsin.

Dr. Cleo Blackburn had many honors conferred on him reflective of his unending servant hood that are too numerous to list here. Let it suffice to say that Dr. Blackburn was a dedicated community services innovator, a sincere churchman, and loving husband and father. He was truly "a man for all seasons."

EUBIE BLAKE (1883-1983)

Eubie Blake was a pianist, composer, and bandleader. He wrote over three hundred songs. History will always remember him for the music from notable all-black Broadway revues such as *Shuffle Along, Swing It, Blackbirds, and Chocolate Dandies*. With a long musical collaboration with Hoosier native Noble Sissle, Blake legitimized the black musical as a genre and set a standard for numerous imitators that followed. His life was the basis for the 1978 hit Broadway show, *Eubie.*

He was born James Hubert Blake on February 7, 1883, in Baltimore, Maryland. His parents were former slaves and he was the only one of eleven children to survive to adulthood. Young Blake taught himself the organ after his parents put a $75 organ in their home for 25 cents per week. It took nearly six years to pay it off. By age fifteen, he was playing piano in Baltimore's nightclubs, and was active on the vaudeville circuit.

By the early 1900s, Blake was already an exceptional pianist who was giftedly inclined toward the stride piano stylings of Ragtime music. His first recordings and piano rolls were made in 1917. As an early pioneer of Ragtime, he was often far ahead of his time. He had to drastically simplify his music just to get it published. People found it hard to digest the progressive nature of his music, especially publishers. In his compositions were shown evidence of Jazz harmony, even though Jazz had not yet evolved as a musical art form. His piano playing directly influenced the great Fats Waller. But as was often the case, Blake was the only one who could play his own music.

Blake's career took off when he began a long and productive partnership with bandleader and songwriter Noble Sissle in 1915. In 1921, their show, Shuffle Along was a hit musical on Broadway, continuing until 1928. It was that show that made it possible for people of color to present real African American song, dance, humor, and style to a broad American audience. Black artists were changed as a result of "Shuffle Along," able to make money and be recognized by performing elements of their own cultural tradition. Being exposed to unique cultural performances also enriched whites.

Blake was a prolific songwriter. Most of his songs depended upon the highly syncopated rhythms of Ragtime. Some of the most famous Blake compositions include: "Eubie's Slow Drag" (1910), "I'm Just Wild About Harry" (1921),

"You Were Meant for Me" (1922), "Memories of You" (1930), "Roll Jordan Roll" (1930), and "Eubie's Boogie" (1969). Some of the Blake compositions sparked dance crazes like "That Charleston Dance" (1924), "Baltimore Buzz" (1930) and "Trucking On Down" (1935). Toward the end of his life, Blake received many honorary degrees for his music, and in 1981, he received the prestigious Presidential Medal of Honor.

During World War I, Blake toured with bandleader, James Reese Europe. He took over as leader of the famous 369th Infantry Band after Europe's death in 1919. During World War II, Blake was a featured USO performer. He went into semiretirement after the war to study composition formally. He earned a degree in music from New York University. Evidently Blake was an excellent music student because he earned a four-year degree in only two years. He came out of retirement and reappeared in a number of Ragtime revival shows in the 1950s, and talk shows in the 1960s and 1970s.

Eubie Blake was a vibrant personality who composed vibrant music. And that vibrancy did not diminish with age. He remained a music icon for the greater part of the twentieth century. He lived for exactly one hundred years and five days, a life completely surrounded by music. He was the last survivor from the golden age of Ragtime. He was the first to pioneer Jazz in an age that had yet to name it. He was a genius on so many musical levels that it is hard to place him in any single category. Let it suffice to say that James Hubert "Eubie" Blake was the finest at any and everything he did.

THE BLACK CLUBWOMEN'S MOVEMENT

The Black Women's Club Movement in the United States was another manifestation of the struggle of African Americans to become socially self-sufficient. For 200 years clubs, mutual aid societies, sororities, benevolent associations, and organizations established by black women have played beneficial roles in various communities in the United States and throughout the African Diaspora. The Black Women's Club Movement received almost no support from white women who even went so far as to exclude black women's clubs from their national organization, the General Federation of Women's Clubs.

Black women had for generations recognized the advantages of association. Their clubs were moral and benevolent societies, but many had the dual purpose of working to abolish slavery. The Colored Female Religious and Moral Society of Salem, Massachusetts, from its inception in 1818, promised to "charitably watch over each other." By 1830 Philadelphia had at least twenty-seven female mutual aid societies. One of them, the Daughters of Africa, bought groceries and supplies for the needy, lent money, and paid sick benefits to society members in emergency situations. The Ladies Benevolent Society of Detroit was created in 1867 to provide sick and death benefits to its members. Also in Detroit, the Willing Workers made and sold quilts, using proceeds to provide baby clothes and general care for poor children.

There is no doubt that clubwomen were generally from the middle-class and upper-middle class, looking to provide role models and opportunities for the less fortunate. But clearly black women captured the spirit of cooperative work for the collective good and put it to work in their communities. These associations of black women's clubs became even more prominent in the period following the Reconstruction era and on through the turn of the 20th century, and are still providing black women with a forum to speak out for change

By the 1890s organized black women branched out and extended their activities to institution building, or community development. The Woman's League of Kansas City established an industrial home and school to teach cooking, sewing, and other useful employments in 1893. The clearest evidence of institution building among clubwomen came after the creation of the National Association of Colored Women in 1895. It was the first national black organization. The NACW took as its slogan, "Lifting As We Climb." Its membership organized mothers' clubs throughout the country where they taught domestic science, child-care, and health classes. They financed, organized, and maintained kindergartens, homes for the aged, orphanages, hospitals, settlement houses, and other institutions that African Americans needed but, due to racial discrimination, did not receive from their local governments.

In the 20th century the scope of the Black Women's Club Movement changed as women like Mary McLeod Bethune began to explore the potential for influencing political change. In 1935 she founded the National Council of Negro Women (NCNW) to effect positive change for African American women by emphasizing community and political activism. NCNW began an immediate lobby for national and international causes such as the creation of the Federal Employment Practices Commission and the establishment of the United Nations. The NCNW motto, "Leave No One Behind," is currently echoed in familiar federal education legislation, the "No Child Left Behind" Education Act (2002).

The Black Women's Club Movement was instrumental in capturing the spirit of collective work and responsibility long before the introduction of the 1970s Kwanzaa principle of "Ujima" that has the same meaning. Clubwomen advocated an African communitarian value system necessary to build our communities. And black clubwomen are still serving the African American community with the same moral obligation to put into cultural practice all that we know to be right. And as we enter this new century, even this new millennium, we are still inspired to lift as we climb, still committed to leaving no one behind, and still upholding the tradition of black clubwomen.

T hroughout the South in 1865 and early 1866, state legislatures were enacting sets of laws known as "Black Codes." The statutes and laws were modeled after, and bore a remarkable resemblance to, the pre-Civil War Slave Codes. Just as Slave Codes denied African Americans any legal status besides that of property, Black Codes defined the freedmen as legally subordinate to whites. In losing the war and having to ratify the Thirteenth Amendment, Southern states had to concede that slavery, as an institution of Southern life, had come to an end. And yet they still wanted to establish control over the freedmen in ways that secured white dominance.

Starting in 1865, Alabama and Louisiana joined Mississippi and South Carolina in the creation of laws that were attempts to re-enslave African Americans. By 1866 all of the former Confederate States, except North Carolina, had enacted Black Codes that curtailed African American freedom. Legislators in Georgia, South Carolina, Florida, Alabama, Louisiana, and Texas copied the Mississippi Black Codes, sometimes word for word. In those states, the penalty for intermarriage, the South's ultimate taboo, was "confinement in the State penitentiary for life."

At the heart of these codes was the vagrancy law designed to restrict black mobility that was both a precious right and a liberating force for ex-slaves. The Vagrancy Act permitted the imprisonment of or hiring out of vagrants. Vagrancy was defined as "Negroes" who did not possess work contracts with white employers or who were unemployed. The statute read: "all free Negroes and mulattoes over the age of eighteen" must have written proof of a job at the beginning of every year. The companion to the vagrancy statute was the Enticement Act, making it illegal to lure a worker away from his employer by offering him inducements of any kind. The purpose was to restrict the flow and price of labor by stopping landowners' theft of laborers.

Statutes requiring black skilled laborers and artisans to pay exorbitant licensing fees made it rare for them to be anything besides wage laborers. Furthermore, black children who were orphans, or whose parents were impoverished, were turned over to the state and forced into "apprenticeships" with white businessmen. An important aspect of Black Codes was their unequal system of punishment. They sanctioned whippings only for black workers by white employers but not for white workers. The codes listed specific crimes for the

"Negro" alone: "the vending of spirituous or intoxicating liquors," "mischief," "insulting gestures," and "cruel treatment to animals." In addition, African Americans were prohibited from keeping firearms, which was an infringement of their Second Amendment Right.

Black people found "unlawfully assembling themselves together," day or night, were subject to immediate imprisonment. To counter that statute blacks freely used the church as a meeting place for reasons other than religious. Blacks had no legal redress for their mistreatment, so they relied on the institution most unchanged in their lives – the Black Church. Although the Black Church had to, at times, develop a stance seemingly in support of the established order, it does have a history of social activism of which it can be proud. Whites were rarely held accountable for any crime committed against African Americans. This gave rise to white supremacy groups such as the Ku Klux Klan (KKK). Recognizing the worth of black churches, the KKK often burned them down.

Although slavery was ended in the United States in 1865 with the passage of the Thirteenth Amendment to the U.S. Constitution, the presumptive idea upon which slavery was based is seemingly never-ending. White conjecture that they are innately superior to blacks has guided them through more than 250 years of black slavery, and over 140 years of institutional racism. For a fact, the establishment of Black Codes in the nineteenth century served as the indomitable, almost unshakable, foundation for Jim Crow in the twentieth century.

H istory has long overlooked the insurmountable evidence that within the Confederate ranks were black men who willingly took up arms for the Southern cause during the American Civil War. It has been estimated that over 65,000 blacks were in the army and navy of the Confederate States of America. An overwhelming number of them were used as body servants, cooks, teamsters, blacksmiths, and other labor support personnel for Confederate troops. They were also used as spies pretending to be "contraband." However, nearly 15,000 blacks, slave and free, were outfitted as soldiers and saw actual combat.

The concept was first verbalized in early 1864 when Major General Patrick Cleburne, a first-class soldier, saw the "handwriting on the wall." He proposed to Commander General Braxton Bragg that slaves be armed to fight for their freedom with the Confederate army. Cleburne knew that the Confederacy was out-manned, out-gunned, and generally out-classed by Union forces, and that the South would soon loose the war. The troops of General Ulysses S. Grant had a stranglehold on the Confederate capitol at Richmond and the equally important city of Petersburg in Virginia. General Bragg listened to the proposal in stunned silence, but was obligated to forward the proposal on to Confederate President, Jefferson Davis.

Davis was so appalled by the idea of arming blacks, and so worried about the morale crisis that such an idea would cause, that he suppressed any mention of the Cleburne proposal. In the early days of the war, free blacks had tried to enlist in the Confederate army. Black militia units, most notably in Louisiana, rushed to join the war. The Confederacy did not accept the black militia for army duty, but did hire them for combat support services. Often, their rate of pay exceeded that of Confederate privates. Depending on the value of the service, the black pay rate exceeded that of many junior officers. War profiteering has been a phenomenon in America since the Revolution, and is not the exclusive domain of whites.

By late 1864, it was becoming apparent to even the most optimistic Confederate that the North was winning the war. Northern population was 20 million strong. Southern population was only 9 million, and 4 million of them were slaves. Atlanta had fallen before General George Sherman as he marched to the sea. Union armies had achieved terrific victories in Virginia's

Shenandoah Valley. And all southern hope failed as northern voters re-elected Abraham Lincoln as president. In an act of desperation, Davis embraced the idea of allowing blacks to enlist in the Confederate army as soldiers. The Confederate Congress began diligently looking into enacting laws allowing the enlistment of blacks.

Representatives from the Deep South were especially interested in getting blacks to enlist. Their land was receiving the most damage at the hands of Yankees like Sherman. Some in the Confederacy saw the measure as an admission that the South was wrong from the beginning on at least two counts. First, the South was wrong in denying the government the right to interfere with the institution of slavery by emancipating slaves. Secondly, and the most damning, if the South offered slaves their freedom they confessed that they were hypocritical in asserting that slavery was the best state for Negroes after all.

In February 1865, after months of stalling, the Confederate Congress passed an act allowing immediate enlistment of at least 300,000 black men. The Confederacy went a step further and ordered that the blacks were to be treated with all the same courtesy accorded white soldiers. General Robert E. Lee did not wait for congressional enactment. He had already begun recruiting and arming black soldiers throughout Virginia. Black Confederates saw action in the first Battle of Bull Run in 1861. And over 3,000 black Confederates fought against General Stonewall Jackson's occupation of Frederick, Maryland in 1862.

For the Confederacy, the best use of black soldiers never materialized. The enactment came much too late in the war. Had the South achieved its goal, it would have had a larger fighting force than the North which employed 186,000 blacks. For those of us who believe that the Civil War was only about slavery should perhaps reconsider that notion in view of the contradiction provided by the Black Confederate Soldier.

Almost totally missing from the traditional history of the American West is the role of the black cowboy as well as other black pioneers. Even before the nineteenth century, they traveled through and settled in, the vast territory west of the Mississippi River that extended from the Rio Grande along the Mexican border and northward to the Canadian border. Racism is the usual suspect for the deliberate exclusion of blacks by artists, writers, photographers, and even historians. Hollywood producers who not only excluded them, but also slanted and twisted the facts regarding the overall western scene and extended that exclusion into the twentieth century.

The true history of the West has become a myth based on folk heroism. History has been replaced by fiction, and this fiction is perceived by millions of people to be fact. With the exception of the occasional subservient characters, blacks were "fenced out" of the story of the settling of the American West. The real cowboys were black, white, red, and brown. Practically all people of color including Mexicans, Native Americans, and African Americans, were negatively stereotyped. However, they were portrayed as "bad guys," hoodlums, renegades, or just plain lazy and irresponsible. But nothing was further from the truth.

The black cowboy's life was hard, tedious, and lonely with very few luxuries. However, they lived a more dignified life and were not burdened with the constraints place upon many African Americans throughout the country. Those living in the South, barely surviving as sharecroppers, while being subjected to harsh treatment during the emergence of Jim Crow, did not live nearly as well as the black cowboy in the Old West. The cowboy herded and branded cattle. During the zenith of the cattle drives, they rode the trails from Texas northward to grasslands or railheads on the plains. The real cowboys were black, white, brown, and red. They ate the same food; slept on the same ground; performed the same jobs; and were subjected to the same dangers.

A typical cowboy crew consisted of one trail boss, eight cowboys, a wrangler to take care of the horses, and a cook. It is estimated that an average crew would have included two or three black cowboys. It is possible that 15% to 25% of all cowboys were black. While black cowboys seldom if ever became trail bosses, many of them owned their own cattle and land on which to raise them. After the emancipation of the slaves at the end of the Civil War, thousands of blacks went to work on ranches throughout south and west Texas, and subsequently rode the cattle trails northward. Although all western states and territories had their share of black cowboys, the largest contingent of them prior to and immediately after the Civil War could be found in the wide coastal prairies and bayous along the Gulf of Mexico below Houston, Texas, and from the Guadalupe River eastward to Louisiana.

Another center of black cowboys prior to the movements westward to Texas was in the Savannahs of southern Florida. This group was made up of mostly black runaways from the plantations in Georgia and South Carolina in the Seminole Indian Nation inside Florida. They became herdsmen on foot and on horseback. Many left Florida with the Indians as they were hassled into Oklahoma and other western territories. Most black Seminoles feared re-enslavement and did not assemble themselves to go west with other Seminoles. Although not willing to go west, some black Seminoles went south into Mexico and joined the Mexican army.

The history of the black cowboys began long before nineteenth century America. Gambia and other African countries were known to be the lands of large cattle herds and the populace possessed innate skills in controlling and managing the movement of these animals. They were called herdsmen in Africa. And they conducted the animals while on foot. But those African Americans who possessed such cattle herding skills in America, mounted horses to move, drive and conduct vast herds were called cowboys.

THE BLACK VERNACULAR ENGLISH

Black Vernacular English is the colloquial speech idioms characteristically spoken by some segments of the African American population. However, all African Americans easily understand Black English. It is several distinctive, oral-based languages, encompassing dialect speech patterns, with roots in African, Caribbean, and African American history and culture. Each of these black vernacular languages emerged within a particular racial and cultural context. Most significantly, the roots of Black English lie in the experience of American slavery and in the cultural collisions between the many and varied West African linguistic groups and the English speaking dominate culture.

Although Black English is not to be considered substandard or nonstandard, it can certainly be thought of as informal. It is grounded in an oral tradition that is subject to continuous change and innovation. What developed in slavery as a language to circumvent or subvert the white power structure, developed into a highly elaborate speech pattern. Those who feel that Black English has been maintained because whites cannot understand it are incorrect. Whites do come to understand Black English and are constantly using it within their own culture. This borrowing and appropriating of the black vernacular for white use accounts for the rapid turnover in the black vocabulary. Once a word or phrase crosses over to the dominant culture, it is hardly used again, and a new word or phrase is then coined to replace it.

Slaves used linguistic codes, dialects, and gestures that were opaque to slave owners. A black lexicon usually developed by giving special meanings to Standard English words. It is a practice that predates Emancipation. Slaves needed a system of communication that only those in the slave community could understand. A "cracker" is a white person in authority. He was so called because of the cracking sound made by the whips used against blacks. Many West African linguistic groups still do not have the English "th" sounds. The "th" sound was rendered as a "d," a "t," or an "f." For the slaves, to pronounce the word "with," would sound like "wid," "wit," or "wif." Even today, the word "death" is pronounced "def." In today's black vernacular, "def" means great, superb, or excellent, as in Def Comedy Jam. It is derived from an older black expression, "doin' it to def."

Developing a linguistic code was the slaves' way of resisting enslavement.

They were denied their own languages and culture, and then forced to adapt to another. So they pretended not to know correct ways to speak English. In a sense, they refused to spit it back (repeat it) the way it was spit out (originally stated). Black Vernacular English has been a way to Africanized English. Saying uh-huh and uh-uh for yes and no comes directly from the Mandingo language. In the mid 20th century, blacks used Pig Latin to say "foe," which is expressed as "ofay." An "ofay" is a white person and traditionally thought of as the enemy.

In the 1940s, a term for a black person in tune with the latest developments in Jazz was "hipster," and the derogatory term for white hangers-on to the black jazz life-style was "hippies." Decades later, whites appropriated the term "hippie" and use it to denote the drug-laden counter-culture of the 1960s and 1970s. Even that heinous expression, "nigger," in all its negative variant misspelled forms, has become a crossover term applied to everyone. This brings us to the equally distasteful hip-hop idiom, "wigger." This word refers to a white person who has appropriated the black culture but not the black struggle.

Besides having an ever-changing vocabulary, Black Vernacular English has a characteristic grammar. Its most obvious feature being the treatment of the verb phrase "to be." The conjugation of to be, or the lack thereof, in the present tense is stated: "I be / you be / he, she, it be / we be / they be." This Africanized style of speaking English is made even more complex by the existence of Euro-American patterns of English within the black vernacular. If a Standard English word can be misspelled in any way and still be recognizable, then it will be. And yet, there is something abundantly clear to anyone with ears to hear:

"My peeps sho' 'nuff be speakin' some English. We ain't perpetratin'. It's just a Black Thang."

THE BLACK "FORTY-NINERS"

The Gold Rush of 1849 produced a massive movement of people to California following the discovery of gold there in January 1848. Many of these miners were black. Workers at Sutter's Mill in Sacramento Valley discovered gold and tried to keep the discovery secret. But within days word was spread throughout the valley and by the summer, the news had spread up and down the West Coast, across the border into Mexico, and even to the Hawaiian Islands. The following year gold seekers came to California from as far away as Europe, Australia, South America, and China. Free blacks came from as far away as Jamaica and other Caribbean Islands via the Panamanian Isthmus.

By far the greatest number of "Forty-niners," as they were called walked or rode across the North American continent. Some used the Oregon and Mormon Trails over the Great Plains. Others took the Santa Fe and Sonora Trails, and other southern routes. In the two years following the discovery of gold, 100,000 miners had made that trek and 1,000 of them were black. By 1860 more than 200,000 miners had begun prospecting for gold with the number of blacks increasing to 5,000. Most black forty-niners went to California more to seek and make their fortune than to escape a hard life.

Among the earliest black miners were sailors who jumped ship from whaling and other vessels anchored in Sacramento Bay. Being use to foreign places and hard work, and having a degree of independence from long voyages, they did well as miners. When reports of their success began to appear in Eastern antislavery journals, other blacks were probably encouraged to join the Gold Rush. Claims yielding $300-$400 was not uncommon in the earliest days of the Gold Rush. In 1849 alone about $10 million worth of gold was mined. As competition increased, fewer claims would yield such profits. Miners who found practically nothing far outnumbered those who struck it rich. But during the years following 1849, blacks managed to send upwards of $750,000 to the South to buy freedom for family members.

White slaveholding miners who tried to use their slaves to mine gold for them often had problems. One of the unwritten laws in prospecting was that the gold belonged to the man who discovered it. The miners felt that having your slaves find gold for you violated this tradition and often forced slave owners out of the area. Many slave owners prospected in isolated areas or put ads in newspapers trying to sell their slaves. Some would hire their slaves out for tasks other than mining. Still others allowed their slaves to buy their freedom with their profits. Also slaves' attitudes changed, making them less manageable there.

Oftentimes those who fared the best during the Gold Rush era were not the miners, but those who worked at other trades. Someone had to provide goods and services to the miners, such as tools, haircuts and shaves, food items, food services, rooms, laundry and bath services, and entertainment. African American entrepreneurs, especially the barbers and cooks, provided most of these services. Unbelievable prices for supplies were charged. Eggs were $1 each, potatoes $.50 each, bread $1 per slice, shovels $10-$20 each, a blanket $100, a butcher knife $30, and a tin pan for washing gold was $30.

Some historians believe, and offer photographic proof, that black miners preferred integrated settings, and prospected most often with Chinese, Latin American, European, or miners who had come from New England. However there exist on old California maps at least 30 mining camps that prove that black miners worked their own mining settlements. "Negro Bar" settled on the American River in 1849 (later called Mormon Bar) is now part of the city of Folsom. "Negro Slide" was situated in Plumas County on a mountainside between Goodyear Bar and St. Joe's Bar. "Negro Tent" was originally a tent where food, tools, and other supplies could be purchased from blacks. "Negro Hill" situated near Sacramento where one black miner is said to have made over $80,000 before leaving. There were few class, race, and economic distinctions among miners, although whites instinctively sought to keep gold from black and all other non-white miners.

THE BLACK LOYALISTS

During the Revolutionary War, and even before the outbreak of hostilities between the American Colonies and Great Britain, several groups of slaves were petitioning colonial assemblies for their freedom on the Enlightenment Age principle of the "natural rights of man." When the Revolutionary War was well underway, slaves were willing to secure the liberty that they believed to be their birthright. Although many slave and free blacks joined the ranks of the American patriots as early as 1775, they were not welcomed into the Continental Army until 1777.

Early on, the British Colonial officers would offer slaves their freedom if they would fight alongside white Loyalists for the British cause. A large number of slaves became black Loyalists and fought vigorously for the British. Lord Dunsmore, the last Royal Governor of Virginia and Sir Henry Clinton, British Commander in Chief, both issued proclamations in 1775 and 1779 respectively, offering liberty to slaves who would enlist for the Loyalist cause.

Although there were 5,000 black patriots, the number of black Loyalists far exceeded that number. The British wanted to disrupt American production by enticing slaves to leave their masters. But the British offer had even more side benefits for the British. Slaves becoming Loyalists not only increased British manpower in the colonies, it also put American patriot farmers at the disadvantage of having to plant and harvest their own crops without the help of slaves, while they fought for the patriot cause. And then there was the grim dread that every slaveholder held – a full-scale slave insurrection.

It is argued, but history cannot prove, that 50,000 blacks, mostly slaves, were British Loyalists. The Americans also made the offer of freedom for slaves to fight on their side. But their offer came only after the Patriots were desperate for soldiers. There were nearly a million able bodied white men who could have fought for American freedom. But General George Washington could not recruit more than 50,000 whites at any given time. Blacks just as eagerly took up arms to fight for the Patriot cause because of their equally good promise of freedom in exchange for service.

The fact that blacks fought on both sides of the war only speaks to their desire for freedom. In all honesty, they did not favor either cause so much as they favored their own liberty. Some slaves created their own opportunity for freedom by running away from their owners. When British forces occupied southern colonies, thousands of slaves would flock to the British invasion forces. Whether it was Loyalist fervor or just practical circumstances, most runaways offered their services to the British. In all historical truth, very few Loyalist activities lacked the presence of blacks.

While black Loyalists and black Patriots, during the course of the American Revolution, were forced to take separate sides, they were united in their belief of freedom, equality, and all other human rights espoused in the Age of Enlightenment. In some respects the war could be viewed equally as a war of black independence because black Loyalists were just as much moved by ideology as self-interest. Many slaves were convinced, and rightly so, that a British America secure black independence, whereas an independent America would perpetuate their enslavement.

British Royal forces protected black Loyalists as long as the war continued. But when the British were forced to concede defeat to the Americans, the largest single contingency of black loyalists was evacuated to Nova Scotia. Many were shipped to Jamaica, Barbados, and other British territories in the Caribbean. Some even went to London. A small number accompanied the Hessians to Germany. Furthermore, many thousands of black Loyalists were left behind, some to be reclaimed by their owners, and some to continue guerrilla warfare against white America until they were finally defeated in 1786, just one year before the United States Constitution was drafted.

Although history acknowledges that there were African American slaveholders, their existence is not common knowledge. There were black slaveholders in every state that hosted slavery, and yet, their story has not been told. Most Americans, black and white, believe that slavery was a system exclusively maintained by whites to exploit blacks. But in fact, African Americans played a small yet significant role in the annals of that peculiar institution as slave owners. Many free blacks in the Antebellum South believed that slavery was a viable economic system and exploited the labor of black slaves for profit.

Many black slaveholders were former slaves who were manumitted because of their kinship ties to whites, while others were emancipated for meritorious military duty, faithful service, saving lives, and other such reasons. The majority of them never knew the dehumanization of slavery because they had been born to free black or mixed parents. The ranks of the slaveholders included not only free blacks but also "nominal" slaves. The nominal slaves may not have been legally free but often assimilated into the free black community and later became slave owners. The community of black slaveholders had a diverse background that included persons of free and slave status. Once free, blacks could acquire other slaves by various means. The most common was the direct purchase at fair market value.

Black slaveholders inherited slaves from black relatives as well as from white ones. A few owned slaves in West Africa and transported their slaves to the Americas. Not all black slaveholders were from the elite class of black society. The vast majority of black slaveholders used their own industry and worked as artisans, entrepreneurs, and even as unskilled laborers to obtain capital to buy slaves. Quite often, when marriages occurred between free blacks and slaves, the free spouse attempted to buy the freedom of the enslaved spouse. Some slave purchases were brought about not by the bonds of kinship, but by humanitarianism. Free blacks of benevolent disposition or out of the spirit of abolitionism, sometimes used their own money to purchase slaves with the sole intent of emancipating or manumitting them.

In the rare instances when black ownership of slaves is acknowledged in history, the only justification centers on the claim that black slaveholders were simply individuals who purchased the freedom of a spouse, child, or any family member from a white slaveholder only to free them. Although this did indeed happen at times, it is a misrepresentation of the majority of cases of black ownership backed by records of the period. In states like Virginia, Maryland, and South Carolina, many black slaveholders owned family members who could not be emancipated because the state legislatures prohibited freeing slaves who remained in the state. But on record are scores of slaves and large tracts of land owned by blacks in South Carolina.

The majority of the large black planters lived in Louisiana, growing the labor-intensive crop of sugar cane. In New Orleans also there were as many as 3,000 free blacks who owned slaves. The 1860 Census of Louisiana records that wealthy free mulatto planters, Mme. Ciprien Ricard and her son Pierre, owned 168 slaves. Most black slaveholders did not intend to emancipate their slaves and viewed the institution of slavery as a source of labor to be exploited for their own benefit. They not only used slave labor to till the soil of their farms and plantations but also purchased slaves to work in their businesses as skilled and unskilled laborers. Black-owned tailoring and laundry services were expanded by the use of slave labor. Free blacks bought slaves to hire-out and appropriated the proceeds from the labor of the slaves to help support themselves.

Most black slaveholders viewed the institution as a commercial venture, and their attitudes and actions appeared to be similar to those of white slaveholders. In essence, it was the fundamental nature of black slave owners to embrace many of the same attitudes and predilections of the white community. And all the while they had to remain on the fringe of slaveholding society because of their color.

B   lacks began arriving in Indiana as early as the 1740s. Indiana was one
         of the agriculturally sound, heavily forested, river, stream and lake-
         laden territories of the upper northwest ceded by Great Britain to the
newly independent United States of America in 1783. Blacks had come as
slaves and served both French and Indian masters until the French ceded the
Northwest Territory to the British at the end of the French and Indian War in
1763. The white migration into the territory began then. Whites brought with
them contradictory anti-black and anti-slavery sentiments.

On March 1, 1784, Thomas Jefferson, then a member of the Continental
Congress, reported to the congress a temporary plan of government for the
Northwest Territory. But no plan was accepted until the Northwest Ordinance
of 1787. The ordinance provided for the formation of not less than three, or
more than five, states. It defined the boundaries of these states, forbade slavery
and involuntary servitude, and set at 60,000 "free inhabitants," as the
population requirement for statehood there. The region constitutes the present
states of Ohio, Indiana, Michigan, Illinois, and Wisconsin. The Indiana district
was organized in July 1800, but not admitted as a state until 1816. Four years
after achieving statehood, blacks numbered only 1,420 in a population of
147,178.

The prohibition of slavery in the Northwest Ordinance did not alter the status
of blacks in the Indiana Territory. White settlers circumvented the law in
several ways. The most insidious and, sadly, the most successful subterfuge
was the development of "contract servitude" that allowed whites to hold blacks
in apprenticeships or indentured service for periods ranging from ten to ninety
years. Obviously, a form of African slavery did exist in Indiana under the guise
of apprenticeships. The definitive prohibition of slavery would come in the
form of the American Civil War (1861-1865). In the thirty years before the
onset of the war, Abolitionists were demanding the immediate end to slavery in
the U.S.

In Indiana, Quakers were the most active participants in the abolition of
slavery. Levi Coffin, a Quaker in Southern Indiana, consistently violated the
fugitive slave laws by organizing an Underground Railroad that operated from
the southern counties of Indiana to Detroit and into Canada. Because Indiana
was ostensibly a "free" state, many escaped slaves sought refuge here. Quakers

and the few free blacks in the state that had been voluntarily manumitted by their former masters generally aided them. This assistance and the cordial reception of Quakers residing in the south, east, and central areas of the state, and the proximity of river counties bordering the slave states of the Upper South, led to the establishment of free black concentrations and communities in those three sections of the State.

Between 1820 and 1860, the population of blacks in Indiana increased to over 11,000. At the onset of the Civil War, blacks resided in all but six of Indiana's 92 counties. But not everyone was receptive to blacks coming into the state. Many white Hoosiers resented the new black arrivals and feared their competition for land and resources. The Indiana legislature enacted the Black Law of 1831 to discourage black settlement. The law required that all blacks in the state register with county authorities and post a $500 bond as a guarantee of good conduct and as an added protection against their becoming public charges. In 1851 white Hoosier voters approved Article XIII of the State Constitution that explicitly prohibited blacks from coming into the state to settle.

Whites further evidenced their hostility toward blacks with laws denying the right to vote, serve in the state militia, testify against a white man in court, and attend public schools. But the legal status of blacks did improve slightly after the Civil War. However, continuing past the turn of the 20th century were despicable practices that underscored the extent to which whites in Indiana desired to be rid of the black presence. Unprovoked mob violence, murder, lynching, and other forms of terrorism against African American Hoosiers decreased only in the last half of the 20th century.

THE BLUES

The Blues is an African American musical art form that emerged from the southern part of the United States, before the turn of the 20th century. Blues can be vocal or instrumental following a twelve-bar structure. Prominent in the Blues is the use of the "call and response" technique indicative of its West African roots. The Blues has been the influence on such later American and African American musical genres as Ragtime, Jazz, Bluegrass, Rhythm and Blues, Rock and Roll, Popular, and Hip-Hop.

It is first important to stress how the two forms of black music, both religious and secular, reaffirms and reinforces the functional, collective, and committing character of black art forms. All African art is rooted in, and reflective of, life-situations and aspirations. Thus, black music, in its variant forms, expresses these characteristics. This is clear in the Blues that began to take shape in the late nineteenth century. By the twentieth century, it had become a most important type of black expression.

The origin of the term *the Blues* is a reference to being unhappy. There is an equivalent phrase denoting a struggle as having *a fit of blue devils*. The lyrics of all Blues tunes describe a dejected, downhearted, and down in the dumps state of mind. Early Blues lyrics were most likely a single line, repeated two or three times. The current structure is that of a single line, repeated once and followed by a conclusion. More often than not, these lines are delivered in a rhythmic talk instead of being sung. The present day talking to the beat of music would be *rap*. Blues melodies have likewise the same melancholy style.

The origin of the Blues is lost somewhere in the unaccompanied work songs, ring shouts, field hollers, and religious call-and-response rituals of the slave dominated south. It was born in the Mississippi Delta, the Georgia coast, and rural Texas areas where the large black population was often poorest and most isolated. However these songs may have evolved, the Blues express the timeless sadness and melancholy of people struggling with the blue devils of despair. Beneath the sorrow, however, is often another theme: the wisdom of survivors who have perceived that the situation is oddly strange, inconsistent with acceptable behavior, or otherwise inappropriate.

Blues songs are close to tragic but contain close to comic lyricism. So they transcend their victimization to endure with strength, dignity, and even hope. It is likely that wandering singers first performed the Blues. Traditionally the musical prose of the Blues has been simple, earthy, ironic, and often humorous. The Blues were improvised because people who did not read music created them. With great personal intensity, the Blues deal with such themes as mistreatment and abandonment by lovers, disaster, bad luck, loneliness, poverty, the penitentiary, drinking, and escape.

Some historians argue that the blues are secular spirituals. They are secular in their focus on this world, and spiritual in that they are impelled by the same search for the truth of the black experience. The songs are often raucous, coarse, and crass. And the lyrics employ euphemisms that barely disguise their meaning. Often times the lyrics are deficient in refinement of manner and delicacy of feeling. So the connection to the Spirituals is a hard one to make. Other historians feel that the immediate predecessors of the blues were African American work songs that had their origins in West Africa. Still others contend that the Blues is rooted in both secular and religious musical traditions. They cite the training Blues singers had in church, their singing of both hymns and blues, and the tendency to call on the Lord while expressing the deep sorrow consistent to both genres.

It should suffice to say that the Blues is deeply rooted in the totality of the black experience in America. It is curiously connected to the historical and social burden of being black in a racist society. It can be summed up by direct quotes from familiar Blues lyrics: there have been *"hard rows to hoe"* and *"bad news and worse dreams"* for African Americans.

GUY BLUFORD (1942-)

Guy Bluford made history on August 30, 1983 by becoming the first African American in space. To commemorate the event, the National Aeronautics and Space Administration (NASA) brought more than 250 prominent black educators and professionals to Houston, Texas to witness the eighth launching of the space shuttle Challenger.

He was born Guion Steward Bluford, Jr., to educated middle-class parents in Philadelphia. His mother was a teacher and his father was a mechanical engineer. The Bluford's encouraged all four of their sons to set lofty goals. And Guy would set goals that took him out of this world. Bluford graduated from Overbrook High School in Philadelphia in 1960. He received a B.S. in aerospace engineering from Pennsylvania State University in 1964; an M.S. degree with distinction in aerospace engineering in 1974; and a Ph.D. in aerospace engineering with a minor in laser physics from the Air Force Institute of Technology at Wright-Patterson Air Force Base in Ohio in 1978.

Interspersed through his academic achievements was an illustrious career in the military. Bluford enrolled in the Air Force Reserve Officer's Training Corps (ROTC) during college, he then trained to be a pilot at Williams Air Force Base in Arizona. After receiving his pilot wings in 1965 he went through F-4C combat crew training in Arizona and Florida. He was then assigned to the 557th Tactical Fighter Squadron in Cam Ranh Bay, Vietnam, flying 144 combat missions, 65 of which were flown over North Vietnam. Before commencing graduate studies, he was a flight instructor with the rank of Colonel at Sheppard Air Force Base in Arizona for five years.

Bluford assembled an impressive resume before entering the NASA astronaut program. In 1978 he was one of only 35 applicants accepted into NASA out of a field of 10,000. He spent 15 months preparing for his first space flight. Once in space, he helped to launch a $45 million communications and weather information satellite and conducted experiments on the electrical separation of biological fluids in space. While at NASA he also found the time for further study and received an M.B.A. in 1987.

Besides the historic mission in 1983, Bluford completed three other space missions as an astronaut. He flew once more aboard the Challenger in 1985 and twice aboard the orbiter Discovery in 1991 and 1992. The Air Force,

NASA, and numerous African American organizations have recognized Bluford's accomplishments with various awards. About crossing the color line in space exploration, he has commented: "From a black perspective, my flight aboard the shuttle represented another step forward. Opportunities do exist for black youngsters if they work hard and strive to take advantage of those opportunities."

When President Regan called the Challenger crew while they orbited the earth in 1983, he commended Bluford on his groundbreaking achievement. Bluford simply replied that he was *"pleased to be a part of the team."* He has since served that team and this country very well. He spent 29 years in the United States Air Force; and for NASA, flew as a mission specialist and payload commander on four space shuttle missions, logging more than 688 hours in space. In addition, he has written and presented several scientific papers in the area of computational fluid dynamics. In his current position he is responsible for the design, development, integration and operational support of the NASA Fluids and Combustion Facility and associated space flight experiment hardware for the International Space Station.

Retired Air Force Colonel, Dr. Guy Bluford was the little boy who grew up designing and building model airplanes. And he moved through time and space to become the man who turned a new page in the history of aeronautics and space exploration by becoming the first African American to travel in space. Since that historic launch in 1983, NASA has since trained other black astronauts. But Guion Bluford's place is secure in history as the first.

EDWARD ALEXANDER BOUCHÉT (1852-1918)

E dward A. Bouchet was an African American physicist and educator who experienced many firsts in his life. He is most notable for being the first black to graduate from Yale College. He was the first black to be nominated to Phi Beta Kappa. And in 1876 Bouchet received a Ph.D. in Physics from Yale, becoming the first black to earn a doctorate from an American university. In this present time, his name is not well known because he had the misfortune being a highly educated man in a segregated society that imposed numerous racial barriers, thus hindering him from achieving professional recognition.

Edward was born to William and Susan Cooley Bouchet, the youngest and only son of four children, on September 15, 1852 in New Haven, Connecticut. His father was a freed slave and business owner who was prominent in local black affairs. Mr. Bouchet also served as a Deacon of the Temple Street Church. It was the oldest black church in the city and a station for fugitive slaves on the Underground Railroad. Edward attended Artisan Street Colored School, an un-graded, one-room school with one teacher. He also attended New Haven High School from 1866 to 1868.

In 1868, Bouchet was accepted into Hopkins Grammar School, a private institution that prepared young men for the classical and scientific departments at Yale College. He graduated first in his class at Hopkins and prepared to enter Yale in 1870. When Bouchet graduated from Yale in 1874, he was ranked sixth in a class of 124 students. He was nominated to Phi Beta Kappa at that time, but because of his race, was not elected until 1884. Unable to find work as a physicist, he returned to Yale and successfully completed his dissertation on the new subject of geometrical optics. It is the physics of light wave refraction.

Dr. Bouchet then moved to Philadelphia to teach at the Institute for Colored Youth (ICY). It was founded by Quakers and was the city's only black high school. In 1874 a philanthropist named Alfred Cope, who was Bouchet's financial backer for his Yale doctoral studies, also recruited him to establish a new science program at ICY. Bouchet created the chemistry and physics departments at the school. He taught both subjects for 26 years. He resigned in 1902 when ICY dismantled its college preparatory program in the wake of the W.E.B. Dubois–Booker T. Washington controversy over "industrial vs.

collegiate" education for black students. A new set of ICY managers emerged, more amenable to the industrial education philosophy of Washington. When ICY discontinued its classical and scientific programs, it spoke volumes about the immense influence of Booker T. Washington and the "Tuskegee Machine."

Over the next fourteen years, Bouchet held various positions in different parts of the country. He taught math and physics in St. Louis at Sumner High School. It was the first high school for blacks west of the Mississippi River. He was the business manager for Provident Hospital in St. Louis and following that, he was a U.S. customs inspector. Returning to his first love, Bouchet secured a teaching and administrative position at St. Paul's Normal and Industrial School in Virginia. It was later renamed St. Paul's College. In 1908 he became principal of Lincoln High School in Gallipolis, Ohio. He remained there until 1913. An unconfirmed record has Bouchet teaching at Bishop College in Marshall, Texas sometime between 1913 and 1916. In his later years, he retired twice due to illness, the last time in 1916.

Dr. Edward Alexander Bouchet died in his boyhood home at 94 Bradley Street in New Haven and was buried in his family's plot. He never married nor had any children. But he left a great legacy of excellence in teaching and a lifetime of learning. History cannot assess Dr. Bouchet's impact on African American education at the turn of the 20th century. He had spent twenty-six years at ICY in Philadelphia. Although it was a segregated city, it offered a supportive environment for a man of Bouchet's abilities. Philadelphia's black population was the largest in the North, and had made considerable progress in education even before his arrival. Also, Philadelphia had an enriched cultural life that Bouchet so aptly used as the backdrop for the classical education that he so easily provided.

MARY ELIZABETH BOWSER

Mary Elizabeth Bowser served as a Union spy during the American Civil War from 1861-1865. The accounts of her war efforts as an espionage agent were carefully hidden by the Van Lew family, for whom she worked, and by the United States government who benefited the most by her courageous exploits. Her work on behalf of the North continued throughout the duration of the war and she was never discovered.

Many accounts of Mary Elizabeth's life are veiled in mystery. Even exact details of her birth and death are unknown. It is known is that she was born a slave on John and Elizabeth Van Lew's plantation just outside of Richmond, Virginia, possibly in the late 1830s, or early 1840s. As was often the case with slavery, nothing is documented about her birth. There was never a celebration or commemoration for the birth of a slave. Neither is there adequate information as to date of her death that is assumed to be long after the end of Civil War.

Mrs. Van Lew, who long held anti-slavery sympathies, freed all of Van Lew slaves, after her husband's death. As the favorite slave, Mary Elizabeth was sent to Philadelphia to be educated and returned to work for Mrs. Van Lew as a paid servant. It was during this time that she married a free man named William or Wilson Bowser. After the start of the war, Mrs. Van Lew learned of an opening for a domestic servant in the home of the Confederate President, Jefferson Davis. Richmond was the capital of the Confederacy and a hotbed of espionage. She made arrangements for Mary Elizabeth to join the Davis mansion as a servant. At that time, Mary Elizabeth became a part of the Van Lew spy network.

Mary Elizabeth was in frequent contact with the Confederate President and with many important visitors. It was never divulged to Davis, and he never suspected that Mary Elizabeth had received a formal education. Her duties allowed her to move freely about the mansion, including Davis' private study. As she dusted, she would read war dispatches and other important papers left out. Although having to feign stupidity, dull wits, illiteracy, and unconcern, Mary Elizabeth was a woman of uncommon intelligence. She had a photographic memory, a talent that enabled her to recite verbatim the contents of Davis' letters. She had total recall of the conversations she overheard as she served dinners.

Much of the intelligence gleaned by Mary Elizabeth would be passed to Mrs. Van Lew, who would then encode it in cryptic form. However, Thomas McNiven, a local baker, became central in her exchange of information. McNiven sold fresh bread to the Davis mansion every morning. His frequent delivery visits to the Confederate presidential mansion enabled Mary Elizabeth to pass information to him. McNiven, Van Lew, or other Union informers would pass her intelligence to military leaders like Generals Ulysses S. Grant and Benjamin F. Butler.

The contributions Mary Elizabeth made to the nation, at great personal risk to herself, were finally recognized in 1995 when the U.S. Army honored her with induction into the United States Army Intelligence Corps Hall of Fame at Fort Huachuca, Arizona. According to an account assembled by the hall of fame, Jefferson Davis never discovered the leak in his household staff, although he knew the Union Army somehow always kept abreast of Confederate plans.

Rumors persist that Mary Elizabeth kept a personal journal about her exploits during the Civil War, and that her diary still exists today. But this is highly unlikely, since the danger of such a discovery would have caused her reprisals even after the war's end. Celebrations commemorating the end to the American Civil War have past the 140th mark. As we reflect back on our history, let us marvel in knowing that this noteworthy, nontraditional freedom fighter passed this way. And let us esteem the daring and courage of Mary Elizabeth Bowser and the valor of all those who fought to end slavery in America.

BROWN VS. THE BOARD OF EDUCATION

B rown vs. the Board of Education of Topeka, Kansas was the landmark Court case of 1954 in which the United States Supreme Court unanimously declared that to create separate schools for children on the basis of race was unconstitutional. The Brown ruling ranks as one of the most important Supreme Court decisions of the twentieth century, and it effectively set the stage for the 1960s Civil Rights Movement.

At the time of the Brown decision, seventeen southern states and Washington, D.C. required that any and all public schools be racially segregated. A few northern and western states, including Kansas, left the issue of segregation up to the individual school districts. While most schools in Kansas were integrated by 1954, those in Topeka were not. Racial segregation had existed in the United States in the Antebellum (pre Civil War) and the Post-bellum (post Civil War) periods. A number of northern states enforced segregation just as stringently as the South. But before and after the Civil War more than 95% of all blacks lived in the South. So segregation there affected an overwhelming majority of the African American population. After the Civil War ended in 1865, and even after the end of Reconstruction in 1877, the South continued to segregate its schools and other facilities.

The uniqueness of the Brown decision is historically linked to another Supreme Court decision, *Plessy vs. Ferguson.* In 1896 the Court upheld the legality of racial segregation. At the time of that ruling, segregation of blacks and whites already existed in most schools, restaurants, and other public facilities in the American South. In the Plessy decision, the Court ruled that such segregation did not violate the Fourteenth Amendment to the U.S. Constitution. The Court further ruled in Plessy that racial segregation was legal as long as the separate facilities for blacks and whites were equal. This "separate but equal" doctrine, as it became known, was instituted in every aspect of southern society. Railroad cars, schools, and other public facilities in the South were made separate, but they were rarely, if ever, made equal.

The Brown case developed from several court cases involving school segregation from Kansas, South Carolina, Virginia, Delaware, and a related case from Washington, D.C. Other cases also emerged in the 1950s that challenged the legality of segregated schools. Many of them, in various ways, illustrated the unfairness of segregation. In one South Carolina County the average annual expenditure for a white student totaled $179, but for a black student it was only $43. Even in cities, towns, and counties where blacks were in the clear majority, the black schools were much inferior to the white ones. Black teachers earned one-third less than white teachers. Also buses were provided for white students, but not for blacks.

Specifically in the Brown case, Oliver Brown filed suit on behalf of his daughter, Linda, who had to walk six blocks past a white school in her neighborhood to a bus stop, in order to ride the bus to a black school that was two miles from her home. The Brown desegregation case was argued before the Supreme Count by lead NAACP counsel, Thurgood Marshall. Flanked by an impressive legal staff of civil rights attorneys, Marshall argued that segregation was itself inherently unequal and that it denied African Americans their rights to equal protection under the Fourteenth Amendment. Most of the Justices truly favored desegregation. Chief Justice Earl Warren used his political acumen to negotiate a unanimous verdict for desegregation and wrote the opinion for it. But Warren failed to set deadlines for dismantling segregation by simply stating that desegregation should proceed with "all deliberate speed."

The decision of the Supreme Court in *Brown vs. Board of Education of Topeka, Kansas*, on May 17, 1954, was unequivocal in outlawing segregation in public schools. The reaction to the decision was mixed, with the anticipated defiance from the South. But the speed in which desegregation was accomplished was never deliberate enough. It was years before Linda Brown and the twenty plus other plaintiffs in the class action suit attended integrated schools. Nevertheless, the Brown decision was just one step before those giant leaps that eventually struck down all forms of legalized racial segregation.

GWENDOLYN BROOKS (1917-2000)

Gwendolyn Brooks was the first African American woman to receive a Pulitzer Prize. She was a novelist, a leading poet of the post-World War II era, and an important literary figure in the Black Arts Movement of the 1960s and 1970s. Brooks is noted for her adaptation of traditional forms of poetry and for her use of short verse lines and casual rhymes. She was named poet laureate for the state of Illinois in 1968, succeeding Carl Sandburg to that title. She was also appointed to the prestigious National Institute of Arts and Letters in 1976.

She was born Gwendolyn Elizabeth Brooks, the elder of two children of David and Keziah Brooks in Topeka, Kansas. Early in her life, the family moved to Chicago where she received her education and would reside for the rest of her life. Her father was a janitor who had studied at Fisk University in Nashville, Tennessee. Her mother was a former schoolteacher who was the early major influence on her literary career. Mrs. Brooks arranged recitals for Gwen as early as age four. Largely through her mother's urging, Gwen met leading black writers James Weldon Johnson and Langston Hughes, who encouraged her to write poetry.

By age sixteen, Brooks had already published poetry in the Chicago Defender, the leading African American newspaper of the time. Her writing further developed as she participated in the vibrant literary scene of Chicago's South Side during the late 1930s and early 1940s, which included such important writers as Richard Wright and Arna Bontemps. Particularly important in the development of Brooks' writing skills was the poetry workshop at the South Side Community Arts Center. Her poems began to appear in such leading journals and anthologies as *Negro Story* and *Cross Section*. During this time she won many literary prizes including Guggenheim Fellowships.

Critics praised her first poetry collection, *A Street In Bronzeville* (1945), as a clear and moving evocation of life in an urban black neighborhood. The fact that she won the 1950 Pulitzer Prize for her second collection of poems, *Annie Allen* (1949), speaks for itself. Her other works include the autobiographical novel, *Maude Martha* (1953); the children's book, *Bronzeville Boys and Girls* (1956); *The Bean Eaters* (1960); and a volume of poetry, *Selected Poems* (1963). In these works she further developed her art, not just honing her stylistic craft but also enriching her narrative gift through the use of a wide range of situations and characters, both black and white.

In 1967, as the result of attending the Second Black Writers' Conference at Fisk University, Brooks made a distinct change in her writing style. At Fisk she encountered leading Black Arts Movement writers such as Amiri Baraka, who infused her with a new, more militant spirit. She became the black writer of the earlier generation most prominently identified with the movement. This affiliation was seen immediately with a succession of poetry books: *In the Mecca* (1968), *Riot* (1969), *Family Pictures* (1970), *Aloneness* (1971), *Aurora* (1972), *Beckonings* (1975), *Primer For Blacks* (1980), *To Disembark* (1981), *Black Love* (1982), *The Near-Johannesburg Boy and Other Poems* (1987), *Gottschalk and the Grande Tarantelle* (1988), *Winnie* (1988), and *Children Coming Home* (1991).

Gwendolyn Brooks was a prolific writer who used poetry, fiction, non-fiction, and children's books to depict the black struggle. In her lifetime, she received awards and honors too numerous to list here. She had over fifty honorary degrees from various colleges and universities conferred upon her. She reached extraordinary heights as "poet of the ordinary." Her style and language appealed directly to ordinary black readers, and yet she did not sacrifice her characteristic use of words to convey a complex pattern of meanings. Brooks kept her subject matter and her artistic expression firmly rooted in the black experience making her the heir apparent of great poets like Langston Hughes. And yet, she was malleable enough to be influenced by a younger generation that included the militancy of Amiri Baraka.

"Aunt" Clara Brown, as she came to be called, was a woman who faced enormous challenges in her life. As a slave, owned by several men, and a mother who saw her children auctioned off and scattered across the country, she became one of the first African American women settlers of Colorado. Aunt Clara developed into a skillful businesswoman and gained a reputation for community service and philanthropy. She recognized the power of community and built relationships that sustained her throughout her life.

There is much confusion about the early events of Clara's life. Her birthplace was either Virginia or Tennessee, but she grew up in Kentucky from age three, or possibly nine. Her birth date is variously recorded as 1800 or 1803. But historians are certain that she was born a slave in the American South. Some sources report that Clara married at age eighteen and subsequently had four children. Two daughters and a son survived, and one child died at birth. Clara's own account admits to giving birth to four children, but claims they were all sold on the auction block. By age thirty-five her whole family, including her husband, had been separated by the auctioneer's hammer.

Clara was fifty-five when her third owner died and she was able to buy her freedom. Kentucky law demanded that freed slaves leave the state immediately or risk losing their freedom. By 1859 she was living in St. Louis, Missouri. She moved even further west when the Colorado Gold Rush erupted. Joining a wagon train going to Denver, she paid for the trip by bartering her services as a cook, laundress, and nurse. While in Denver, Clara helped two ministers establish a Sunday School.

Clara joined the stream of fortune seekers headed up Clear Creek to Central City, where the first great gold strike had been made on May 6, 1859. In June 1859 she became the first African American woman to reach the Colorado gold fields. In Central City she opened a laundry and worked hard to save money. The town was made up of gold mines, small stores, saloons, and shacks for miners and their families. She organized another Sunday School and help to found a church. She engaged in efforts to help the poor by housing and nursing the needy. Sick and injured miners, of all races, knew they could turn to "Aunt" Clara for help.

Most of Clara's money came from investments in mining claims and real estate. By 1866 she had accumulated a savings in excess of $10,000 and began to actively search for her family. With two of her children known to be dead, and having lost track of her son, Clara returned to Kentucky in an attempt to locate her surviving daughter, Liza Jane. Her daughter was not found then, but Clara was able to help sixteen newly freed slave families relocate to Colorado. In 1879 Clara traveled to Kansas at the request of Frederick W. Pitkin, Governor of the new state of Colorado, as his official liaison to persuade the black "Exodusters" to move to Colorado. Clara delivered Pitkin's invitation and donated some of her own money to support the newly formed black communities.

In 1882, as she was nearing eighty years old, Clara found Liza Jane and a granddaughter, Cindy. She made the trip to Council Bluffs, Iowa to be reunited with what was left of her family. The story of their reunion was widely published in newspapers in Colorado and throughout the Midwest. After more than forty years of separation and searching, Clara's dream had finally come true. She returned her family in Colorado where they lived until her death three years later.

Clara Brown was not just a woman who faced adversity. She was a woman who faced it down with faith in God, determination and purpose, and a love of humanity. Her value system was certainly based on the Christian principles, but they were deeply steeped in the African communitarian tradition. She kept three goals alive as she persevered through her life: family, independence, and community. Her much deserved reputation as the "Angel of the Rockies" lives on in those Colorado communities she called home.

H Rap Brown is the African American activist most famous for his rallying call, "Burn Baby Burn." He came to prominence in the 1960s as a civil rights worker, black activist, and later, Justice Minister of the Black Panther Party. He became a symbol of black radicalism during the Black Nationalist Movement that eclipsed the Civil Rights Movement in the late 1960s.

He was born Hubert Gerold Brown on October 4, 1943, in Baton Rouge, Louisiana. In 1962 he dropped out of Southern University to join the Nonviolent Action Group (NAG) at Howard University. He joined the Student Nonviolent Coordinating Committee (SNICK) in 1964 and was at the center of efforts to register black voters in the South. In 1965 he became the chairman of NAG. But he later became disenchanted with civil disobedience and the mainstream Civil Rights Movement and began advocating violence as a means of bettering the situation for blacks.

Brown was labeled an extremist by the media for his nationalistic views and for his outspoken advocacy of Black Power. In May 1967, when Stokley Carmichael stepped down, Brown was elected National Chairman of Snick. Immediately, he began evicting white members from the organization. He famously declared at a Washington, D.C. rally, "I say violence is necessary. It is as American as cherry pie." He stepped down as SNICK Chairman in 1968 and was made Justice Minister of the Black Panther Party (BPP), a revolutionary black organization. He was arrested several times between 1967 and 1969 for arson and inciting riots.

Brown was harassed by the police and targeted by the counterintelligence program of the FBI. He was charged by the states of Maryland and Ohio with inciting a riot and carrying guns across state lines. Rather than stand trial, Brown went underground, and for two years was a fixture on the FBI's Ten Most Wanted List. He was captured in 1971 after a gun battle with police in a New York robbery. He was tried, convicted, and sentenced to five to fifteen years in Attica Prison. Brown converted to Islam while in prison and changed his name to Jamil Abdullah al-Amin.

After his 1976 prison release, Brown settled in a predominately black neighborhood in Atlanta, Georgia. He became a soft-spoken Muslim leader who preached against drugs and gambling. Seemingly, he no longer advocated violence. He became a leader in the National Ummah, one of America's largest Black Muslim groups. He served as the imam or spiritual leader to Muslim families in and around Atlanta. He was also in charge of the Community Grocery Store. And so it was until the night of March 16, 2000, when two African American Sheriff's Deputies went to his store to serve him for failing to appear on charges of driving without proof of insurance, driving a stolen vehicle, and impersonating a police officer.

Brown exchanged gunfire with the two Deputies, wounding one and fatally wounding the other. According to the surviving Deputy, Brown was the man who fired on them. He left the scene to escape capture. An intensive manhunt ended three days later when Federal Law Enforcement Marshals arrested him as he hid in a field in Alabama. Nearby, police found the car and the gun they said was used in the Atlanta shooting. Brown went on trial in January 2002. He pleaded innocent, claiming he was the victim of a government conspiracy to put him behind bars. His defense relied on factual discrepancies in the account of the shooting by the surviving Deputy.

Brown was found guilty of killing one Sheriff's Deputy and wounding the other in the gun battle at his store. He was sentenced to life in prison. The sad irony of Hubert Gerold Brown, a.k.a. H. Rap Brown, a.k.a. Jamil Abdullah al-Amin, is that he did not practice the nonviolence he later preached. He fell victim to the power structure he tried to change. And that very system he wanted to burn eventually burned him.

HENRY "BOX" BROWN (1815-??)

Perhaps the most ingenious self-emancipated slave was Henry Brown, who was nicknamed "Box" after he had himself crated up and shipped from Virginia to Pennsylvania. It was a 27-hour overland journey by wagon and rail. Even though his friends wrote shipping and handling instructions on the box, Brown still spent a few of those hours on his head and shoulders, or face down, nearly loosing consciousness.

Henry Brown was born a slave in Richmond, Virginia on a plantation in Louisa County in 1815. He was one of eight children. In his autobiography, *Narrative of the Life of Henry "Box" Brown*, he recounted the kind oversight and moral instruction of his mother before the family was separated. Even though a slave, she taught them not to steal, not to tell lies, and to behave in a becoming manner towards everyone. When their first master died, all property, real and slaves, was divided between his four sons. Brown recounts that the separation of families was more barbarous than the use of the whip upon their backs.

Brown and one sister were taken to Richmond, while the other siblings went elsewhere, and their parents remained on the plantation. Brown was fifteen when his family was split up. He was then hired out to a tobacco factory in Richmond where slaves and free blacks worked together. Just as before, his new master was relatively benevolent. Brown was furnished with a new suit of clothes and given money to buy gifts to send to his mother. His master gave orders to current and subsequent overseers that Brown was never to be whipped. Although Brown described his life in slavery as tolerable, he did reach a point when he desired freedom above everything else.

In the 1830s Brown married a slave woman named Nancy, and the couple had three children. He had to use his own money to pay for the privilege of marriage. He was required to rent quarters, pay for clothing and food, and pay Nancy's owner a stipend for the time she spent taking care of her family. In the meantime, he was also paying his owner a portion of his earning from his tobacco factory job. One day Nancy's owner demanded more that his usual share of the Brown family money and threatened to sell Nancy and the children to get it. Brown tried to raise the money, but was unable to do so.

In 1848, Nancy's owner made good on his threat and sold her and the children to another slaveholder, who in turn sent them to the auction house, and then they were sold away to North Carolina. As Nancy began the customary walk south, shackled to other adult slaves and with her children loaded in a wagon, Brown walked with her holding her hand for over four miles. Then he stopped, powerlessly, as his wife and children, and more than three hundred other slaves continued their long trek to the Deep South.

After recovering from the devastation of loosing his wife and children, Brown began to plot an escape to the North. He prayed an earnest prayer to God to lead him to freedom or to give him a sign that he should remain a slave. Almost immediately the idea suddenly flashed through his mind of shutting himself up in a box, and getting it conveyed as dry goods to a free state. With feelings of the divine inspiration of this plan, he engaged the help a sympathetic storeowner and a white member of his Methodist Church, Dr. Samuel Smith, who Brown described in his book as a "conductor of the underground railway." Before dawn of March 23, 1849, Brown, who was 5'8" tall and weighed 200 pounds, squeezed into the wooden crate. The box was lined with canvas, but it was only 37 x 30 x 24 inches. He bored three holes in the box to be able to breathe, and he carried a canteen of water and some crackers to stave-off hunger.

Brown's box reached Anti-slavery Headquarters in Philadelphia where four abolitionists unpacked him. He also became an Abolitionist, lecturing and traveling extensively in the northern United States and Europe as an advocate for the emancipation of slaves. There is no documentation of Brown's life after 1864 when he was living in Wales and working as a performer. History does not record the date or place his death, but I am certain that Box Brown died a free man, having already taken the journey of a lifetime.

STERLING A. BROWN (1901-1989)

S terling A. Brown was an African American educator, author, folklorist, and one of the later poets of the Harlem Renaissance. He took a unique approach to the style of writing poetry by choosing to write in the dialect of country black folk. His extraordinary talent and ability to reveal the humanity of the characters in his poetry won over the most ardent critics of his literary style.

He was born Sterling Allen Brown on May 1, 1901 in Washington, D.C. He was the youngest of six children, and the only son of former slave, Sterling Nelson Brown, and Adelaide Allen. His father was the pastor of Lincoln Temple Congregational Church and professor of Religion at Howard University. His mother was a graduate of Fisk University in Nashville, Tennessee.

Born into the smug and affected black middle-class, Brown attended Washington's segregated schools. He graduated with honors from Paul Lawrence Dunbar High School in 1918. He entered Williams College on a scholarship set aside for minority students. At Williams he was introduced to the radical works of Fyodor Dostoyevsky and Leo Tolstoy. By graduation in 1922, he had performed spectacularly. He was elected to Phi Beta Kappa in his junior year. Earning a BA degree, he won awards for his essays, was awarded Final Honors in English, and graduated cum laude. He went on to earn a MA degree in English from Harvard University in 1923.

Brown was greatly influenced by Jazz and the Blues. They had not been legitimized as African American arts forms yet, but they were having a profound effect on African American writers and poets of that era. He began teaching English at Virginia College in Lynchburg. It was his first exposure to the rural population of the South where he met many colorful characters that would inform his poetry. Brown was popular with his students and invited them to his home to listen to Jazz and read the poetry that was not part of the college's English curriculum.

In 1927 Brown married Daisy Turnbull and began teaching at Fisk University in 1928. He even taught at Lincoln University in Jefferson City, Missouri before accepting a position at Howard University in 1929. He remained at Howard for forty years, only briefly returning to Harvard to do doctoral work and publish his first collection of poetry, "Southern Road" in 1931 and 1932. Brown also spent semesters teaching at Vassar College, Atlanta University, and New York University while still at Howard. Some of the students he taught and mentored at Howard include: actor, Ossie Davis; civil rights activist, Stokley Carmichael; black arts era writer, Amiri Baraka; and Nobel Prize winner, Toni Morrison.

In 1937 he published "The Negro in American Fiction" and "Negro Poetry and Drama." He also co-edited an anthology, "The Negro Caravan." He was the national editor of Negro Affairs for the Federal Writers' Project 1936-1940. It was a federally funded program that hired writers to collect American folklore. Brown treated the subjects of his poetry as black folk heroes. And he was an early champion of Blues and Jazz as legitimate art forms. He received honorary doctorates from Williams and Vassar Colleges, and Howard, Harvard, and Brown Universities. He was elected to the Academy of American Poets and named Poet Laureate of the District of Columbia. Brown continued to publish as late as 1984.

Sterling Brown defied popular Renaissance era black poetry by capturing the vernacular of rural black people. He worked diligently to legitimatize this genre by flavoring and coloring his writings with the pungency of their speech. Although the minstrel and plantation traditions had heavily burdened African American speech with the yoke of racial stereotypes, Brown's poetry was an artistic expression that revealed the humanity that lies just below the surface skimmed by those stereotypes. Brown was one of a few artists that admirably demonstrated the aesthetic potential of black speech when it is centered in a very careful study of African Americans themselves. It is still a vibrant and commanding storytelling tool.

U nited States domestic policy After the American Civil War was focused forcefully on Native American populations. United States infantry and cavalry regiments were assigned to the frontier for the containment of the Indian nations. For the first time on record, this included African Americans of the 9th and 10th Cavalries, and the 24th, 25th, 38th, 39th, and 41st Regiments. They were collectively called the "U.S. Colored Troops." But they became widely known as "Buffalo Soldiers."

At the end of the Civil War, the U.S. faced a dilemma as what to do about the black troops. Southern states did not want armed black men within their borders. And Northern cities did not want black men swelling the number of people competing with whites for jobs. So when Congress established peacetime army, it recognized the value and valor of black troops by sending them westward into Indian Territories. But as soldiers, they were not always fully apprised of the objective of the U.S. government. They marched forth to carry out the orders of their white officers and their white government in Washington, D.C. whose policies were becoming increasingly genocidal toward the native peoples.

It is no painful irony that these intrepid black soldiers took part in the final defeat of the Native American, the first victims of racism in the Americas. But there is an ironic twist in the fact that a number of Native Americans had been slaveholders before they were forced to move westward onto Reservations. Buffalo Soldiers played a tremendous part in the Indian Wars and in the westward expansion of settlers into the U.S. territories. They also protected national parks from fires, illegal poachers, and timber thieves.

Because of their crisp curly hair was similar to the tuft of hair on the buffalo's neck, the Indians called the black soldiers "Buffalo Soldiers." And the name stuck. It became a badge of honor because the blacks knew that the buffalo was a sacred animal to the Indian. From the buffalo came food, shelter, and clothing. In the Native American worldview, the buffalo was sent from the gods who watched over the native peoples. The Indian would not use the term "buffalo" with the intent to slur a class of people.

As the buffalo soldiers dutifully brought a white version of law and order to the frontier, they earned the respect of every military friend or foe that they encountered. They also guarded railroad and telegraph lines, stagecoaches and arms shipments, homesteads and towns. They carried out all orders with no evidence that any were ever questioned. They moved Indian families and nations from one location to another and rode after those who left reservations to seek some freedom or merely to forage for food for starving people. From the Canadian border to the Rio Grande, from St. Louis to the Rockies and into California, the Buffalo Soldiers rolled up an impressive record.

The desertion rate of Buffalo Soldiers was the lowest in the frontier army though their posts were often in the most remote, desolate places. This was at a time when more than one-third of the white enlisted men went absent without leave each year. In 1876, for example, the white Seventh Cavalry had 72 deserters, the Third had 170, and the Fifth had 224, but the black Ninth had only 6 deserters and the Tenth had 18. In an age that offered African Americans few decent jobs, military life appealed to these recruits.

As black men in a white man's army, the Buffalo Soldiers were subject to unusually harsh discipline, bigoted officers, and poor food and recreational facilities. The regimental flag of the Tenth Calvary was homemade, tattered, and worn – unlike the banners of white units that were silk-embroidered and supplied by Army headquarters. Yet their morale was high and some white officers were proud to lead so brave a military force. Eleven Buffalo Soldiers earned the Congressional Medal of Honor in battle against the Ute, Apache, and Comanche. Blacks looked at army life as opportunities for housing, education, pension, and medical benefits. To the Buffalo Soldier, army life was not the storm from which they needed protection. It was the shelter against the storms of life affixed to being African in America.

RALPH J. BUNCHE (1904-1971)

Ralph Bunche was an American scholar and diplomat, known for his work in the United Nations (UN) as the Undersecretary General, responsible for peacekeeping operations and peaceful uses of Atomic energy. He had the distinction of being the first African American to be awarded the Nobel Peace Prize.

He was born Ralph Johnson Bunche in Detroit, Michigan on August 7, 1904. His father, Fred was a barber catering only to a white clientele. His mother, Olive Johnson Bunche was an amateur musician. He spent his early years with his parents, living in Detroit and Albuquerque, New Mexico. But he attributed his achievements to the influence of his maternal grandmother, Lucy Johnson, with whom he lived in Los Angles after he was orphaned at age thirteen. He became the valedictorian of his high school class and went on to graduate summa cum laude in 1927 from U.C.L.A.

The crowning achievement of his academic career came in 1934, when he earned a doctorate in government and international relations from Harvard University. While still a graduate student, Bunche established himself as a professor and an activist for civil rights. In 1928, while completing his doctorate work at Harvard, he joined the faculty of Howard University in Washington, D.C., where he founded and chaired the political science department. In 1936, he published *A World View of Race* based on his research and previous experience as co-director of the Institute on Race Relations at Swarthmore College.

From 1938 to 1940 Dr. Bunche collaborated with Swedish sociologist Gunnar Myral, on the research for Mydral's massive study of American race relations, *The Negro Problem and Modern Democracy* (1944). After years as a scholar of international politics, Dr. Bunche assumed a more active role during World War II. In 1941 he joined the Office of Strategic Services, the predecessor of the Central Intelligence Agency (CIA), where he specialized in African affairs. He moved to the State Department in 1944, and, as the first African American to run a departmental division of the federal government, he continued to work on African and colonial issues. He was a part of the unofficial "Black Cabinet" formed by President Franklin D. Roosevelt to keep him apprised of issues with reference to African Americans. But he would later decline an appointment from President Harry S. Truman.

Dr. Bunche's association with the UN also began in 1944, when he participated in the Dumbarton Oaks Conference, which laid the foundation for the UN Charter signed in San Francisco in 1945. An expert on trusteeship matters, he participated in the writing of the UN Charter. In 1946 Dr. Bunche went to work full-time at the request of the UN's first secretary-general, Trygve Lie. From 1947 to 1954 he served as the principle director of the *Department of Trusteeship and Information from Non-Self-Governing Territories*, which allowed him to assist with the process of de-colonization.

As a senior member of the staff of the UN commission on Palestine, Dr. Bunche participated in the mediation efforts that resulted in the recognition of the State of Israel. He first became known as a peacemaker in 1949, when he defied all expectations and negotiated the armistice that ended the first Arab-Israeli War (1948-1949). In 1950 he won international acclaim for his skill in these negotiations by becoming the first African American to be awarded the Nobel Peace Prize. In 1955 Dr. Bunche was appointed UN undersecretary-general for special political affairs. He held that position until he retired in 1970. In that capacity he oversaw UN peacekeeping operations in the most heated conflicts around the world. He broadened the UN's peacekeeping role by creating the *United Nations Emergency Force*.

Despite the demands of an international career that lasted until just before his death, Dr. Bunche fulfilled extensive academic and civil rights commitments at home. In the twentieth century, when statesmanship was often blurred by politics, and when human existence lay threatened by weapons of mass destruction, Dr. Ralph J. Bunche remained committed to the cause of peace.

THE CAKEWALK

The Cakewalk is a dance form created by slaves in the American South. The Cakewalk dance was always accompanied by the syncopated beat of music that lent itself to the dance form. So in a sense, the Cakewalk is a dance form as well as a music form and can be considered a dual type of entertainment. After the turn of the 20th century, the music evolved into Ragtime with a more sophisticated complexity.

The Cakewalk was the one dance that the slaves created just for their own amusement. It originated on Southern plantations where the slaves had great fun imitating the fancy ball dances of white people. The cakewalk's movements were highly exaggerated, and the whites that watched with amusement never knew that their own formal cotillions and fancy dress balls were being mimicked and mocked more than they were being admired and imitated.

The white power structure that allowed slave celebrations to take place seemingly regarded them as innocent pleasures. But more importantly, slave celebrations were mechanisms of control. A singing and dancing slave was thought to be a happy slave that would not cause much trouble. That may not have been the case though, as slaves sang and danced mainly because it had been a part of their customs in Africa. According to Sterling Stuckey, author of *Slave Culture,* dance had clear antecedents in African tribal celebrations. And like dance in African celebrations, dance at festival time on plantations usually represented some vital aspects of religious expression.

In this context, festivities and dance were combined to show specific kinds of work inspiring the dance movements. While some slaves formed a circle, others in the center danced the motion of labor like swinging a scythe, tossing a pitchfork of hay, hoeing corn, and sawing wood. In true African style, it was the creative and artistic way that slaves used to assess a great deal of the labor they performed on the plantations. This kind of festival dance was the means the slaves had of distancing themselves from the purely exploitative reality of work. They extracted from the experience spiritual and artistic rewards, which helped them to affirm their dignity through labor. And it was, after all, their labor that enabled the planters to grow rich.

The cakewalk was essentially an improvised promenade. Wearing fancy dress, the dancers folded their arms across their chests, threw back their heads, arched their bodies backwards and strutted around. To enhance the excitement, dancers carried a pitcher of water on their heads, which they tried not to spill. The original name of the Cakewalk dance was the "Chalk line dance." But as slices of hoecakes were given as rewards for the best Cakewalker, the name evolved. Later, the Cakewalk prize became vastly decorated dessert cakes being awarded to couples showing the best style and receiving the most applause from the audience.

In modern times, a cakewalk has become a type of raffle-game played at carnivals, funfairs, and fundraisers. Numbered squares are laid out in a path. Tickets are sold to participants, with the number of squares in the path being the maximum number of tickets sold at a time. Similar to a game of musical chairs, the participants walk around a path in time to music, which plays for a duration and then stops. A number is then called out, and the person standing on the square with that number wins a cake. At church socials, the cakes are often donated by members, and multiple cakes are given out, one for each round.

The most modern meaning of "cakewalk" is that of anything that seems to be made easy or effortless. Phrases like "it takes the cake" and "a piece of cake" are the variant forms of the word that have come also to mean something very easy to do, or something of little or no consequence. But the actual dance itself was anything but easy. However fun the slaves made it seem, the dance was still physically demanding and required a bit of acrobatics. So many stylized versions of the Cakewalk evolved by adding steps, stunts, movements, and anything else that might sway the judges.

In the 1890s, a new black musical art form called Ragtime, added a syncopated beat that made the Cakewalk even more sophisticated and stylized. With the addition of sophisticated music, the Cakewalk became the first African American crossover dance. In any event, the new black music and the old black dance re-emerged in the 1890s and everyone, black and white, joined in the fun. The ironic twist to the Cakewalk was that this dance was suddenly being performed by blacks and whites. But if one can follow the circular logic from the beginning, the Cakewalk was a dance created by blacks who were imitating whites who were imitating blacks who were imitating whites.

"CAB" CALLOWAY (1907-1994)

C ab Calloway was an energetic entertainer, gifted singer, excellent
musician and talented actor. He led one of the greatest bands of the
Swing Era of Jazz. He is remembered for his creation of the legendary
"Hi De Ho" shout, and no one will ever forget his signature musical piece,
Minnie The Moocher.

He was born Cabell Calloway III to Cabell Calloway Jr. and Martha Eulalia
Reed Calloway in Rochester, New York. He was the second of six children.
His father was an attorney who dabbled in real estate. His mother was a teacher
and church organist. By the standards of the day, they were a middle-class
family. When Cab was six, the family moved to Baltimore, Maryland. At age
eight, his father died. It took his mother, all his siblings, and the entire church
family to help him recover from that devastating loss.

In his youth, Calloway sold newspapers to earn money. He was very active
with the Bethlehem Methodist Episcopal Church, where he performed in the
choir and eventually sang solo. After graduation from Frederick Douglass High
School, Calloway did not attend college to become an attorney as his father
had wished. He became an entertainer like his older sister, Blanche. Cab joined
her in Chicago where she had gotten him a job as a singer in a quartet. The
group began the circuit of singing in the clubs of Chicago.

In 1925, his career took off. He had landed a job as a drummer for the house
orchestra at the Sunset Café. He soon organized his own orchestra, becoming
its leader and vocalist. Calloway possessed great star power and audiences
loved his performances. He learned to "scat" from the great Louis Armstrong
and then developed his own unique style. Also in 1925, he received his first
recording contract. By 1929 he was booked at the Savoy Ballroom in Harlem.
But he was not the success he hoped to be at the Savoy so the resilient
Calloway dissolved that band and landed a role in an all-black musical revue
on Broadway.

Calloway later began leading a band called the Missourians. Almost
immediately, he changed their name to "Cab Calloway and His Orchestra." He
was noticed by Duke Ellington and invited to play alternating engagements at
the Cotton Club while each toured Europe. Changing his signature song from
St. James Infirmary to *Minnie the Moocher* was also a marker of his success.

111

Even improvising his hi-de-ho shout after forgetting words to a new song was fortuitous. Also enabling Calloway to develop a reputation as a musical class act were band members like Benny Carter and the great Dizzy Gillespie.

Calloway became success in other media. He published a *Hipster Dictionary* in 1938, selling more than two million copies. In it he explained the "jive" language used by jazz musicians. NYU gave him the honorary title of "Dean of American Jive." Callaway attained such stature that many of his performances were carried live on radio. He also had his own program call the "Cab Calloway Quizzical," a satire on the quiz shows popular at that time on radio. He was a fixture in musical films, debuting in *The Big Broadcast* in 1932, and appearing with Lena Horne in *Stormy Weather* in 1943. He appeared on Broadway and toured with *Porgy and Bess* in the role of "Sportin' Life," the well-dressed cad that many say was a part written just for him. During World War II Calloway was one of the first to serve with the USO shows to entertain American military troops overseas.

As the popularity of big band music was waning, Calloway disbanded his orchestra in the 1950s, but frequently regrouped it to play special engagements. He continued in films until the 1980s, appearing in *St. Louis Blues*, *The Cincinnati Kid*, and *The Blues Brothers*. In the 1960s Calloway returned to Broadway in the all-black version of *Hello Dolly*, starring Pearl Bailey. Most entertainers can define a seminal moment when their careers simply took off. But Cab Calloway's career skyrocketed. He was the consummate entertainer, competently performing live, leading an orchestra or at the piano or on drums, on radio, in movies, and on Broadway. And he will certainly be remembered where and whenever "scat" is heard, where and whenever "hi-de-ho" is shouted, where and whenever *Minnie the Moocher* is sung.

STOKLEY CARMICHAEL (1941-1998)

I f there is one person most closely associated with the Black Power Movement of the late 1960s and early1970s, it is Stokley Carmichael. He was the quintessential Black Nationalist. He coined the phrase "Black is Beautiful" and encouraged African Americans to stop processing their hair and grow those huge Afros that defined us. And he made liberal use the word "Black" instead of the traditional, more accepted word "Negro" when referring to African Americans.

Stokley Carmichael was born in Port of Spain, Trinidad, on June 29, 1941. His family moved to the United States in 1952 and encouraged him to excel in school. In 1956 he won admission to the selective Bronx High School of Science. He entered prestigious Howard University in 1960 and soon afterwards joined the Student Nonviolent Coordinating Committee (Snick) that was the student arm of Martin Luther King's organization, the Southern Christian Leadership Conference (SCLC). In 1961 Carmichael became a "Freedom Rider," one of black and white college students who trained in nonviolent techniques as they rode through the Deep South to challenge the region's deeply entrenched segregation laws.

In several places on the journey during those Freedom Summers, the students were beaten by white mobs. Carmichael was even arrested and jailed for 49 days in the notorious Parchman Penitentiary in Jackson, Mississippi. After obtaining a philosophy degree from Howard in 1964, Carmichael continued his Civil Rights work. In 1965 he moved to Alabama to work with the voting rights campaign and helped to organize Lowndes County Freedom Organization (LCFO). His success in attracting black support for LCFO led to his election as chairman of Snick in 1966. Under Carmichael though, the group was no longer what Dr. King had envisioned.

After release from his 27th arrest in 1966, Carmichael made his now famous "Black Power" speech. He called for black people in this country to unite to recognize their heritage, and to build a sense of community. He also advocated that African Americans form and lead their own organizations and urged a complete rejection of the values of white society. The following year Carmichael joined with Charles Hamilton to write Black Power (1967). It was a authoritative manifesto of politics and economics. Many established Civil Rights groups and their leaders accused him of "reverse racism" and rejected his militant point of view. Carmichael began to criticize Dr. King and his ideology of nonviolence and led Snick away from the goals of SCLC.

Carmichael eventually joined the "Black Panther Party" when he became the honorary prime minister. He changed his short haircut, white shirt and tie appearance and grew a large Afro and wore African Dashikis. Young people everywhere followed his ideological and stylistic lead. When Carmichael denounced the U.S. involvement in the Vietnam War, his passport was confiscated and held for almost a year. When it was returned, he moved with his wife, South African Singer and Songwriter, Miriam Makeba, to Guinea, West Africa. He wrote another defining book, Stokley Speaks: Black Power Back to Pan-Africanism (1971).

Carmichael established the All-African People's Revolutionary Party and worked as an aide to Guinea's Prime Minister, Sekou Toure. He adopted the name Kwame Toure and continued in his belief that African people throughout the Diaspora should unite. After the death of Toure in 1984, Carmichael was arrested by the new military regime, charged with sedition, but was released after three days. Guinea remained his permanent home, although he returned to the U.S. occasionally to lecture. Stokley Carmichael, a.k.a. Kwame Toure, died in 1998, still the revolutionary. He had gone from a nonviolent integrationist, seeking equal rights, to a clinched-fist militant Black Nationalist demonstrating and calling for "Black Power." And a whole generation of African Americans raised up to heed his call.

WILLIAM H. CARNEY (1840-1908)

William Harvey Carney was the first, and one of only twenty-two courageous African American to receive the Medal of honor for heroism during the American Civil War. Carney was a Sergeant of Company C in the 54th Massachusetts Infantry. He was part of the contingent that led the assault on Fort Wagner in Charleston, South Carolina. In that one deadly battle on July 18, 1863, 1,500 black soldiers lost their lives in a battle that did not even last the whole day.

He was born to a freeman and a slave woman on the Carney plantation just outside of Norfolk, Virginia in 1840. In his early childhood, William attended a private school that was conducted secretly by a minister. Upon the death of their owner, Major Carney, William and his mother were manumitted and relocated to New Bedford, Massachusetts in 1856. Carney assisted his father who had joined many other free or freed blacks who worked at sea or on the harbor docks.

Carney continued his education as he worked the docks of New Bedford. In fact, he was studying for the ministry when he learned that the first regiment of black soldiers, the 54th Massachusetts Infantry, was being formed. He was twenty-three years old when he enlisted in the Morgan Guards, which was later integrated into the 54th. Carney was quoted as saying: "I can best serve my God by serving my country and my oppressed brothers."

Carney's Company C was completely engaged in the disastrous battle at Fort Wagner. Upon reaching the top of the slope of Wagner's wall, Carney saw that the color guard, the soldier who carried the national flag, had been mortally wounded. He ran to pick up the colors, taking a direct shot to his hip as he did it. He was pinned against the Fort for more than an hour under a barrage of enemy fire before carrying the flag back to his company. Carney held his position on the slope of Wagner's wall and kept the "Stars and Stripes" up and waving.

Sergeant Carney was wounded again in the chest, arm, and leg by Confederate fire while carrying the flag back to his unit. He passed through a makeshift enemy line, encountering small squads of or single enemy gunfire. He would later say to his regiment, "Boys, the old flag never touched the ground." Sadly, Carney also witnessed the death of Col. Robert Gould Shaw, commander of the 54th Infantry. Carney recalled that as he reached his comrades, he "tried to hurrah; in fact, I did hurrah, and the boys hurrahed for the flag that had been brought back to them and the man that brought it." Even before being medically treated for multiple gunshot wounds, Carney was reluctant to release his hold on the flag. He finally turned it over to another member of Company C.

In 1864, Carney was released from active duty for disabilities related to his battle injuries. He went back to New Bedford, before leaving for California. In 1870, he resettled in New Bedford and became one of their four federal letter carriers. It was in 1900 that he received the Medal of Honor commendation. Carney worked for the postal service for thirty-one years, retiring in 1901. He was in great demand as a leader of Memorial Day parades and speaker at other patriotic events. In 1904, he was the Memorial Day orator at the Shaw Monument on the Boston Common.

The courage and valor of the brave 54th and 55th Regiments of Massachusetts, as well as other all-black units are well preserved in the annals of American military history. William H. Carney was just one of countless brave soldiers who risked their lives to put an end to the institution of slavery in America. He was honored with the Congressional Medal of Honor for his exploits, but had to wait thirty-seven years to receive it. Another quote from this modest American hero was: "I only did my duty." As we approach another anniversary of the end of the American Civil War, it is our duty as African Americans to venerate William Carney by giving him one more "HURRAH!"

GEORGE WASHINGTON CARVER (1860-1943)

George Washington Carver was an African American botanist and agricultural chemist. And he was undoubtedly one of the greatest scientists of all times. He revolutionized and revitalized the sagging agricultural industry of the South between 1900 and 1930. The products he developed from peanuts, soy beans, and sweet potatoes, eliminated the South's dependency on cotton as its primary cash crop. He held only three patents on his discoveries while giving hundreds away to benefit people.

Carver was born of slave parents on the Moses Carver plantation, near Diamond Grove, Missouri, in 1860. Although Carver's early education was sketchy, he left the place of his birth at age ten. He eventually settled in Kansas, where he worked his way through high school. When the Headmaster of the first high school saw that he was black, Carver was promptly told to leave. Disillusioned, yet determined, he remained in Kansas working odd jobs as a farm hand, a cook and a laundry helper while obtaining his high school education.

Carver was twenty-five years old when he started his freshman year at Simpson College in Iowa. After two years, he entered what is now Iowa State University at Ames, Iowa. While there, Carver did outstanding work in botany and agricultural chemistry. After graduation, he remained at Iowa State to pursue another degree. Because of his outstanding work with plants and soil, Carver was made an assistant instructor in botany and was appointed greenhouse director.

While on the faculty of Iowa State, Carver continued his studies, specializing in bacteriological systematic botany. However in 1896, he received a letter from Booker T. Washington, president of Tuskegee Institute, asking for Carver's instructional help. Dr. Carver became the director of the Department of Agricultural Research at Tuskegee where he remained for the next forty-seven years. He spent the remainder of his life there as an agricultural scientist.

While at Tuskegee, Dr. Carver readily won the acceptance of former slave as he taught them agricultural techniques that increased their self-sufficiency. He gradually won the acceptance of the white southern farmers, promoting his idea of "plant rotation" to keep the soil enriched with vital nutrients. The cotton plant had been grown in the south for two hundred years, depleting the soil's mineral. Carver taught them to plant peanuts, clover, and peas, since these crops would replenish the minerals as they grew. The roots of these plants brought nitrogen to the soil.

In his exhaustive experiments with peanuts, Carver developed several hundred industrial uses for peanuts, sweet potatoes, and soybeans and developed a new type of cotton know as the Carver Hybrid. He synthesized over two-dozen products, such as milk and cheese, from the peanut. He eventually developed over three-hundred different products: including instant coffee, face cream, ink, shampoo and soaps made from the oils, proteins and chemicals of peanuts. New industries appeared which made use of these peanut products, and the South began to prosper economically. He produced similar results with sweet potatoes, pecans and southern clay.

In 1916, Dr. Carver received an honor given to few Americans when elected a Fellow of the Royal Society of Arts, Manufactures, and Commerce of Great Britain. In recognition of his many other accomplishments, he was awarded the NAACP's Springarn Medal in 1923. In 1935 he was appointed collaborator in the Division of Plant Mycology and Disease Survey of the Bureau of Plant Industry of the U.S. Department of Agriculture. In 1940 he donated his life savings of $33,000 to establish the George Washington Carver Foundation, which helped to provide research opportunities for scientists. This foundation still thrives today. Dr. Carver died at Tuskegee, on January 5, 1943. His birthplace in Missouri was established as a National Monument in 1943.

CHEROKEE BILL (1876-1896)

T he history of the American West is filled with drama and lawlessness. Many of the stories of daring deeds and wild living have come down to us through movies, television, and books written about the old West. But hardly any story, written or otherwise, ever related that there were black lawmen and black outlaws. There were even black cowboys, cowpunchers, and rodeo stars. Cherokee Bill comes out of that tradition of the old West and was probably one of the most infamous leaders of any outlaw gang.

He was born Crawford Goldsby on February 8, 1876 on the military reservation of Fort Concho, Texas. He was the second of four children born to Ellen Beck and George Goldsby. His mother a mixture of Cherokee and black, and her grandparents had been enslaved to the Cherokee Nation when they were still cotton and tobacco planters in Georgia. His father was also biracial and a Buffalo Soldier with the famed Tenth Cavalry. Cherokee Bill's ancestry was a very telling mixture of black, white, and red. His father abandoned his family when Bill was only three. His mother moved the family to Fort Gibson in the Indian Territory, but left Bill in the care of a family friend, Amanda Foster.

"Aunt" Amanda was an elderly black woman who raised Bill until he was seven years old. She enrolled him in the Indian School at Cherokee, Kansas. He remained there until he was ten years old. From there bill was sent to the Catholic Indian School at Carlisle, Pennsylvania. After two years, he returned to his mother at Fort Gibson. But by then his mother was remarried to William Lynch, another Buffalo Soldier with the Ninth Cavalry. Bill and Lynch could not get along and Bill began to associate with unsavory characters, drink liquor, and rebel against authority.

In his early teens, Bill's brushes with the law were mostly for minor offenses. He was considered to be very good with a gun at this time, but not of his offenses were gun related. When he was fifteen he went to live with his older sister, Georgia, and her husband, Moses Brown. They lived near Nowata, Oklahoma Territory on land distributed to them based on Ellen's status as a free person of Cherokee descent. But Bill did not live there very long due to the intense dislike he had for his brother-in-law. Eventually, Moses Brown became one of the men Bill would kill. He returned to Fort Gibson and lived for a while with his mother's relatives.

At seventeen, Bill began to work odd jobs cleaning and sweeping stores and working on a cattle ranch. He began by working for room and board and was later paid wages. His first serious trouble started when he was eighteen. He was severely beaten by a black man named Jake Lewis. The reason for the fight is unclear. Either it was about Bill's younger brother, or it was over a woman. Two days later Bill shot the man twice with a six-shooter, leaving him for dead. Lewis recovered and Bill became a wanted man for attempted murder.

Bill fled to the Cherokee Nation where authorities there attempted to arrest him. He then escaped to the Creek and Seminole Nations and joined up with other outlaws like Jim and Bill Cook, also mixed blood Cherokees. It was during this time that Crawford Goldsby gained the alias of "Cherokee Bill." It was also at this time that the Cook gang was formed. Many of the members were black men or a mixture of Cherokee and black. The gang's crimes included gun fights with lawmen, killing many. They robbed stores, banks, trains, people and stage coaches. Bill, more than the others, was known to have killed many innocent bystanders. It is reported that he murdered at least fourteen men.

For more than two years during the last decade of the nineteenth century, Cherokee Bill led a reign of terror throughout Indian Territory. But in the end, he paid the price of an ignoble life by being hung on a gallows built just for him. He was chased down by all that he was – black, white, and red men – U.S. Marshals and Indian Scouts. He was made to pay with his life for all lives he had taken.

SHIRLEY CHISHOLM (1924-2005)

S hirley Chisholm was the first African American woman ever elected to the United States Congress and was re-elected to serve a total of six terms. She was also the first black and the first woman to seek the nomination of a major political party for President of the United States. To this day, she is the only African American woman to come close to winning the nomination with 162 delegates.

She was born Shirley Anita St. Hill in Brooklyn, New York, on November 20, 1924, to Charles and Ruby St. Hill. She was the oldest of four daughters born to these struggling Caribbean immigrants. When she was three, Shirley and her two sisters were sent to live with their maternal grandmother where they received an early childhood education in the strict, traditional style of British Barbados. After seven years the girls rejoined their parents in the U.S.

In 1946 Shirley graduated cum laude from Brooklyn College with a degree in sociology. During graduate studies at Columbia University, she met and married Conrad Chisholm in 1949. While she earned a master's degree in child education, Chisholm taught at a Harlem nursery school and was supervisor of the largest nursery network in New York. It was through administering to hundreds of children, most of them African American and Puerto Rican, that Chisholm learned the executive skills that would serve her well in the political arena.

In 1953, as a key member of the Seventeenth Assembly District Democratic Club, Chisholm waged a successful political campaign to elect an eminent attorney to the municipal court. Her own political career took off in 1964, when she won by a landslide her campaign for the New York State Assembly. As an assemblyman (1965-1968), she authored legislation that instituted a program that provided college funding to disadvantaged youths, and successfully introduced a bill that secured unemployment insurance for domestics and day-care providers. Throughout her political career, Chisholm was a strong supporter of increased spending for education, healthcare, and other social services.

In 1968 Chisholm won a seat in the U.S. House of Representatives, where she served on a number of committees, including Agriculture, Veteran's Affairs, Education and Labor. She campaigned for a higher minimum wage and federal funding for day-care facilities. She was true to her campaign promise, *"to vote against every money bill that comes to the floor of this House that provides funding for the Department of Defense."* She also delivered important speeches on the economic and political rights of women and fearlessly criticized the Nixon administration during the Vietnam War. While she advocated black civil rights, she regularly took up issues that concerned other people of color, such as Spanish-speaking migrants and Native Americans.

As the first black Congresswoman, Chisholm battled racism from white members of Congress and fought the gender bias she encountered from the male-dominated Congressional Black Caucus. But nothing deterred her from her goals. In 1972 Chisholm put together a coalition of black, feminists, and other minority groups and sought the Democratic nomination for President of the United States. She was unsuccessful in her attempt, but compared herself to Al Smith, the unsuccessful 1928 Catholic presidential hopeful who paved the way for John F. Kennedy, the first U.S. Catholic President.

As Chisholm's seniority increased so did her stature in Congress. In 1977 she joined the powerful House Rules Committee. She recognized the value of party loyalty, but did not support the Democrats if it compromised her principles. Chisholm retired from Congress in 1983 but remained politically active and supported various causes. She left a lasting record of her political and social career in two remarkable autobiographical books: *Unbought And Unbossed* (1970), and *The Good Fight* (1973). Shirley Chisholm championed the causes of the populace earning her the title: "Candidate of the People."

The slaves in the American South were not Christian when they were brought here from various parts of West Africa. And most planters in the American South were indifferent to the religious upbringing of their slaves, rejecting the notion that their property was entitled to seek religious salvation. They reasoned that slaves lacked the common sense and reasoning abilities needed to grasp the tenets of Christianity. And of course, they secretly feared that an unwavering focus on the rewards of Christian faith was the first step on the road to setting the slaves free.

White Southern churches helped to reinforce the slave system by providing ethical, religious, and biblical rationales for human bondage and by behaving in paternalistic ways. When they did provide religious instruction and worship for their slaves, it had nothing to do with the Bible. Slaves were, however, taught the biblical commandment against stealing. The planter's purpose for this and for any other religious education was simply to prevent loss and to reinforce the whole institution of slavery.

Slaves were taught ethics and morals from a slave catechism. The following is an excerpt from a religious catechism written for slaves. It was published in the "Southern Episcopalian" in April 1854:

> Question: Who gave you a master and a mistress?
> Answer: God gave them to me.
>
> Question: Who says that you must obey them?
> Answer: God says that I must.
>
> Question: What book tells you these things?
> Answer: The Bible.

Of course, not all slaves subscribed to the docile, whitewashed version of Christianity preached by their masters. Instead slaves reached deep into themselves, reestablished a dim and distant link with a long-ago homeland many of them had never seer. The spirit with which they worshiped was vitally expressive, physically unleashed, musical, and mystical. It was an earthly combination of what they inherently knew and what they had come to know about true Christianity. As slaves accepted Protestant Christianity, they discarded the interpretation represented by slave catechisms, and emphasized the Bible and Christian theology's image of liberation. They accepted too, the water baptism as a symbol of their faith. But they also knew they had also been baptized by the trials and hardships of their enslavement.

The slaves had no doubt that their masters had misrepresented Christian principles. Slavery was not "God's plan" for them. To the slave, slavery was a glaring sin that only emancipation could correct. And even today, there are seminal moments when it is crystal clear that this nation has not yet found peace from that sin. But as the slaves accepted Christianity, they shaped it to fit the particulars of their oppression, drawing the strength and perseverance needed to believe in something beyond their bleak and dismal reality. This holds true even today as we, the descendents of slaves, incorporate our faith into the social, economic, and political situation we have inherited in America.

The slaves identified with the Supreme Being in a deeply personal way. God the Father was the creator and the maker of all things. The slaves were in awe of the elements and the forces of nature that God alone commanded. They also identified with the suffering of Jesus Christ, especially in His innocence. The indwelling Holy Spirit was a snug fit into many existing African cosmologies. And finally they identified with God's people, the children of Israel. For they too were forced into bondage in a strange land. Although God had given them an extraordinary burden to bear, He was still on their side. And like His deliverance of the Israelites, the slaves felt that their God would surely deliver them as well.

THE 1964 CIVIL RIGHTS ACT

I n the 1960s, the most important domestic initiative in the United States was the effort to provide justice and equality for African Americans. It was singularly the most difficult commitment, and the one that produced the severest strains on American society. But it was also the one that could not be avoided. African Americans took bold steps to ensure that the nation would have to deal with the problem of race.

President John F. Kennedy had long been sympathetic to the cause of racial justice, but he was hardly a committed crusader. Like many presidents before him, he feared alienating Southern Democratic voters and the powerful Southern Democrats in Congress that represented them. His administration worked to contain the racial problem by expanding enforcement of existing laws against segregation statutes.

The assassination of President Kennedy in November 1963 gave new impetus to the battle for civil rights legislation. Within days of assuming the office of the presidency, Lyndon B. Johnson, in an address to a joint session of Congress, promised that Kennedy's commitment to civil rights would be carried forward and translated into action. The ambitious measure that Kennedy had proposed in June 1963 was hopelessly stalled in the Senate after having passed through the House of Representatives with relative ease. Early in 1964, Johnson, a Southerner, was applying both public and private pressure to make sure that the legislation would be passed on his presidential watch.

Johnson orchestrated a campaign for a civil rights bill untainted by compromise. As a once Senate Majority Leader, he knew what it would take to pass the legislation and end the filibuster surrounding the bill. Johnson brought the full weight of his power and persuasive abilities to secure the votes of doubtful Senators. And, after much effort, it won Senate approval in June 1964. On July 2, 1964, with much "pomp and circumstance," Johnson signed the wide-sweeping bill into law.

The significance of the 1964 Civil Rights Act (CRA) lies more in what it did rather than what it was. It effectively outlawed racial discrimination in public facilities and employment, authorized the attorney general to initiate suits to enforce school integration, and allowed for the withholding of federal funds in any case of non-compliance. While the legislation was directed specifically at removing the barriers to equal access and opportunity that affected African Americans, it vastly expanded the scope of federal protection for the rights of women and other minority groups who experience discrimination.

Civil Rights legislation was nothing new in the United States. At the end of the American Civil War, a frenzy of laws was enacted in support of the freed slaves. From 1865–1869 this reunified nation enacted the Thirteenth, Fourteenth, and Fifteenth Amendments to the U.S. Constitution. They respectively freed the slaves, granted black male suffrage, and bestowed citizenship. But it would take nearly a century before federal protections were guaranteed with enforcements provided by the 1964 Civil Rights Act.

The 1964 Civil Rights Act was a landmark piece of legislation. It became the "Magna Charta" for racial minorities, women, and other deprived groups. Not only did Title VII of the act outlaw discrimination in a variety of employment practices on the basis of race, religion, and gender, it also established the Equal Employment Opportunity Commission (EEOC) to enforce that law. Since 1964, Congress has amended the Civil Rights Act to include the passage of the 1972 Civil Rights Act to extend protection to private and public sectors; and passage of the 1978 Civil Rights Act to include protection for pregnant employees so that they are entitled to receive medical benefits.

The 1964 Civil Rights Act, though originating from injustices against African Americans, raised the consciousness of America so that equal justice is now more far-reaching. But as it continues to expand into broader and more sweeping law, its effectiveness is being undermined by ever increasing tax cuts.

HENRI CHRISTOPHE (1767-1820)

Henri Christophe was born a slave on the Caribbean island of Grenada. He became the president of Haiti in 1807, and its king in 1811. He was one of the revolutionary leaders of Haiti whose slave uprising became a struggle for independence. Many of the details about Christophe's early life are unclear. At a young age he was a runaway slave, eventually becoming the property of a French naval officer and then a planter on the French colony of Saint-Domingue (Haiti). He took his own life after suffering a stroke that left him partially paralyzed. Despondent, deserted by his soldiers and nobles, and with rebellion fomenting, Henri Christophé, the first black king in the Americas, shot himself in his Sans Souci palace.

Christophe was present among the 800 Haitian soldiers in a contingency of 3000 French troops sent by the Marquis de Lafayette to buttress the American fight against the British. Since France supported the American patriots against their historical enemy, England, troops were gathered from all over the French empire. Christophé was only twelve years old when he was purchased by a French commander and taken as an aid and servant to Savannah, Georgia. He fondly recalled his discovery at Savannah of the concepts of liberty. He had never before heard the term, but even as a youth, Christophé felt the American inspired concepts of liberty, freedom, and equality should find a home in Haiti as in the United Sates.

The battle of Savanna in 1779 was a turning point in the American Revolution. What British troops came to face for the first time in their history was a formidable army of black soldiers. These strangely recruited black forces from Haiti had been held in reserve to dig trenches, to drive horses, and to serve officers. But when the Haitians were finally engaged in the battle, their role was decisive. The French and American forces were so terribly decimated that the survivors could have been slaughtered. But the war-ready Haitians stopped the carnage and saved the day.

Sometime after his North American adventure, Christophe obtained his freedom. In 1794, with the Haitian Revolution already in progress, Christophé joined the forces led by the black rebel General François Dominique Toussaint-L'Ouverture. Toussaint quickly made Christophé a brigadier general. In fact, Toussaint made many alliances with all those inspired veterans of the Savannah campaign, but he depended most on Christophé to vanquish foes, deliver secret messages, or to destroy entire villages. Across the ten years of endless fighting in Haiti, Christophé and Toussaint-L'Ouverture formed the most formidable army on the island.

In 1806 Chistrophe and Alexander Sabes Petion secured the overthrow of Jean-Jacques Dessalines, who had proclaimed himself emperor after the capture of Toussaint. In 1807 Christophe was appointed president of northern Haiti. However, civil war erupted between Christophé and Petion, and in 1811 Christophé was proclaimed King Henri I of a united Haiti. Christophé had wanted Haiti to be an example of what black leadership and black people could accomplish and he desperately wanted to emulate what he had observed in the North American struggle for liberty.

Sadly though, Christophe's reign was cruel and bloody. He used forced labor to improve the economy. He implemented agricultural programs similar to those accomplished under Toussaint, which largely maintained the plantation system though without slavery. This system proved to be financially successful but created a highly divided society with a small black elite controlling most of the land and wealth. To his credit, Christophe also pursued many educational reforms and attempted widespread social reforms. But he used coercion and paternalism to instill these values.

The whole world had watched the United States in its quest for liberty. The leaders of the small French colony of Haiti tried to emulate the North American experiment in liberty but failed to fully recreate a true republican form of government. And yet, Haiti did abolish slavery. Something the United States did not do until 1865. In 1801 Haiti emerged as the second independent republic in the Americas, but the first to free its slaves.

T he first penal systems in the United States were established to furnish a structure combining separated confinement with collective work. In these initial penitentiaries, the states' private citizens were given contracts to operate factories within the prisons. The prisoners were also leased out to private bidders to be housed, fed, and worked as slaves. This came to be known as the Convict Lease System. Through this system, bidders paid an average of $25,000 a year to the state, in exchange for control over the lives and labor of all convicts. The system provided revenue for the state and an immense profit of unwaged and unprotected workers for plantation owners and the captains of private industry.

The convict lease system became the closest thing to slavery to survive the Civil War. Reported stories about it cover the bleak panorama of race and punishment in the darkest corners of the American South. Convict lease camps became almost the exclusive domains of African Americans in the years following the Reconstruction era. As slaves, blacks were the traditional victims of violence and exploitation in the South. The ex-slave then became a scapegoat for the South's humiliating defeat. And the mechanism of control for the freedmen became the convict lease system.

The most brutal form of convict leasing arose in the penal systems of southern states. Convict leasing functioned with the Black Codes to re-establish and maintain the race relationship of slavery by returning control over the lives of African Americans to white plantation owners. When slavery was legally abolished, Slave Codes were rewritten as Black Codes to criminalize the freedoms of African Americans. The Mississippi Black Codes were copied, sometimes word for word, by legislators in Alabama, Florida, Georgia, Louisiana, South Carolina, and Texas. Black Codes listed specific crimes for the freedmen alone, including vagrancy, mischief, insulting gestures, cruel treatment to animals, and the selling of intoxicating beverages. Free blacks were also prohibited from keeping firearms and from cohabiting with whites. The penalty for intermarriage, the South's ultimate taboo, was life imprisonment.

Most black prisoners were sent to convict lease camps, which were organized on a deadly combination of racism and profit. Racial and economic motivations were far more central to convict leasing than public safety or rehabilitation. Owners of mines, plantations, railroads, and other industries would contract with states to lease the labor of men sentenced to jail. The prisoners would then be sent to work camps where they would work six or seven days a week, from before dawn to after dark. They cleared snake and alligator swamps, dug coal in gas-filled mines, built railroads, and gathered turpentine in hundred degree heat. They worked in the most appalling conditions. They ate and slept on bare ground, without blankets and mattresses, and often, without adequate clothing.

From its inception, the convict lease system was criticized as cruel and brutal by social reformers. Prisoners were treated inhumanely, beaten, denied medical treatment, and poorly fed and clothed. Black prisoners routinely died of shackle poisoning, malaria, scurvy, frostbite, sunstroke, dysentery, snakebite, and murder by violent sadistic guards. It was not uncommon for them to be beaten or tortured to death. If they did survive the beating, the wounds did not heal, causing a later death from infection. The death rate was as high as 45% in many camps, and no less than 15% in other camps. By comparison, in the North, the death rate for prisoners was only 1%. At a time in history when blacks were lynched on an average of one hundred per year, the convict lease system brutally claimed many thousands annually.

By the turn of the twentieth century, an estimated thirty thousand African Americans, one quarter of them children, were condemned to hard labor in convict lease camps for minor infractions of the law. And to supply this great demand for convict labor, sheriffs, judges, and entire legal systems were duplicitous in continued institutional racism against African American men, women, and children in the United States.

THE CIVIL RIGHTS MOVEMENT

C *ivil Rights* – the very words are synonymous with the 1960s. During much of the decade, the Civil Rights Movement dominated the national consciousness. Twentieth century America had never witnessed anything quite like it. The movement was an effort to break down the barriers that kept African Americans from enjoying full citizenship participation in American society. In essence, it was about obtaining for African Americans their basic legal rights as citizens. These same rights had been established nearly a hundred years earlier during Reconstruction, but were denied by unjust laws and customs of racial segregation.

Segregation kept black people from public schools; public transportation was limited to them, and access to public facilities was denied to them altogether. It also kept them from privately owned places like stores and restaurants supposedly open to the public. When African Americans began to challenge the established systems of segregation and long held patterns of racial injustice that had remained in place a century after the demise of slavery, the Black Church came to play a central role in the emerging Civil Rights Movement. It would prove to be yet another example of how religion could be used in support of a political cause. The Church provided the leadership, physical space, financial support, and ideological component upon which the whole movement rested.

The philosophy of the Civil Rights Movement was moralistic and expressed Christian principles of brotherhood and love familiar to the Black Church. Denominational lines were transcended as individual churches expressed solidarity with each other and with the movement. The Black Church was convinced within its own mind and it convinced the world that its cause was a righteous one. Because of the Church's heavy involvement in the Civil Rights Movement, some scholars have called the movement a Black Church "revival." The Black Church had certainly had revivals before. But what was different about this revival that caused it to manifest itself with marches, rallies, and picket lines? The answer can perhaps be found in the broader American culture, changes within the black community, and a focus on the international scene.

Even though the Civil Rights Movement was born in the culture of the Black Church, it was not completely unaffected by, nor isolated from events outside its doors. One such event was *Brown v. the Board of Education,* in 1954. That Supreme Court case was a landmark decision that struck down the "separate but equal" doctrine that kept black children segregated in public schools that were inherently unequal. The *Brown* decision literally opened the door for other assaults on segregation in America. Subsequent decisions outlawed discrimination in all government facilities or facilities involved in interstate commerce, such as parks, libraries, hospitals, and public transportation. Existing state laws against racial intermarriage were also ruled invalid.

Also on the international scene in the 1960s were African nations throwing off the yoke of Western European Colonization. The post-war United Nations mandate of "self-determination" for all peoples finally found its expression in Africa. It remains the most exploited continent on earth by virtue of colonization within in and the various slave trades out of it. American capitalism would carry on ideological warfare with Russian communism in most unique ways. But first, in *cold war* America, the leader of the *free world* needed to substantially improve its image by making a serious attempt to extend freedom to all within its own borders.

Of course the origins of the Civil Rights Movement can be linked to the political culture of the 1950s and 1960s. But it was the Black Church that seized upon the politics of the day and became the strongest advocate of what it deemed to be a moral crusade. The Civil Rights Movement was religious in scope and it paradoxically defined itself in religious terms to achieve a political end.

E ldridge Cleaver was an author of books and pamphlets and a social activist in the volatile 1960s. He was also a charter member of the Black Panther Party (BPP), serving as its first Minister of Information. But he was more than the spokesman for the party he was the spokesman for an entire militant generation.

He was born Eldridge Leroy Cleaver in Wabbaseka, Arkansas in on August 31, 1935. His parents were of the class known as the working poor. His father was a dining car waiter who played piano and his mother was a maid. They moved to Phoenix, Arizona before settling in California where Eldridge grew up in the Watts section of Los Angles. He ran into trouble with the police early and often. It started with petty larceny and moved to marijuana convictions. He spent much of his youth in reform schools.

As a young adult, Cleaver's crime sprees escalated to sexual assault and attempted murder. He was convicted and sent to the tough prison systems at San Quentin and Folsom and served a total of nine years. While in prison, he took the opportunity to self-educate. He fell under the political influence of Malcolm X and the Nation of Islam theology. He immersed himself in the leftist writings of Karl Marx and Vladimir Lenin. He devoured the work of African American writers like Richard Wright, James Baldwin, and W.E.B. Dubois. He loved counter-culture writings of Norman Mailer and Allen Ginsberg.

Against the backdrop of the California penal system and a steady diet of leftist politics, Cleaver began to write for himself. With the help of his attorney, he came to the attention of various literary figures, including Mailer, who petitioned the parole board for his release. His release in 1966 coincided with the founding of the BPP by Huey Newton and Bobby Seale. Upon hearing Cleaver's political rhetoric, Newton instantly appointed him the spokesman for the BPP. Cleaver was by now a fully committed revolutionary and called for armed insurrection and the establishment of a black socialist government.

In 1968, Cleaver published *Soul On Ice*, a series of essays written while he was in prison. The book was a gifted cultural criticism and established him as one of African America's most important political figures. It also invited the scrutiny of federal authorities. Throughout the 1960s the FBI employed hard-hitting counter intelligence measures to cripple the most important black activist groups. On April 6, 1968 BPP members, including Cleaver, while traveling in two cars, exchanged gunfire with Oakland police. The panthers fled to a building basement and were tear gassed into surrender. Cleaver was wounded in the leg and another Panther was killed.

Rather than stand trial on "trumped up charges," Cleaver fled to Mexico. He later moved to Cuba, France, and then to Algeria. During his self-imposed exile, Cleaver had disagreements with Newton and in 1971 was expelled from the BPP. Soon after, Cleaver formed the Revolutionary People's Communication Network, with his wife, Kathleen, returning to the U.S. to establish it. In 1975, he returned home and was tried for the 1968 shoot-out. But by then Cleaver was a professed born-again Christian and the court was very lenient. Given five years probation, he was ordered to perform 2,000 hours of community service.

After his 1975 trial he started the "Cleaver Crusade for Christ." But his Christian witness was perverted when he tried to combine Christianity with Islam, even calling it "Christlam." For a while he advocated the religious ideas of Sun Myung Moon and flirted with Mormonism. He published *Soul On Fire* in 1978 to try to explain his religious convictions. His expanded drug use caused him to do many other irrational things. Most notably, he supported Ronald Reagan in 1980 and divorced his wife in 1985.

Eldridge Cleaver died in 1998 with his family refusing to allow the hospital to disclose the cause of death. His last final years were consumed with escalating drug addiction battles. It is sad to think that after winning the war for social change, he lost this important battle with himself.

JOHNETTA B. COLE (1936-)

J ohnnetta Cole is an African American anthropologist, administrator, educator, and social activist. In addition to being an expert in cross-cultural studies on race, sex, and class, in 1987, she became the first black woman to become president of Spelman College in Atlanta, Georgia. Spelman is the oldest, largest, and most respected historically black college (HBCU) for women in the United States.

She was born Johnnetta Betsch in Jacksonville, Florida, on October 19, 1936. She was the middle child of John Thomas Betsch, Sr. and Mary Frances (Lewis) Betsch. Her mother was a professor of English at a college in Jacksonville and later the Treasurer and Vice President an insurance company that her maternal grandfather helped to found. Her father was an executive in his wife's family business, a civic volunteer, and a social activist.

Johnnetta was a good student early on, due in part to an early love of reading. She spent a great deal of time at Jacksonville's black public library, which had been named for her mother's grandfather. She excelled at the segregated high school she attended and entered the early admissions program at predominately black Fisk University in Nashville. She transferred to Oberlin College in Ohio and received her B.A. in sociology in 1957. She did graduated work at Northwestern University in Evanston, Illinois and earned an M.A. in anthropology in 1959.

In 1960, Johnnetta married Robert Cole, the son of an Iowa dairy farmer. The couple moved to Liberia, where she spent two years engaged in anthropological fieldwork. She also did field research in the Caribbean island nations of Cuba, Haiti, and Grenada. In 1967 Cole received her Ph.D. in anthropology from Northwestern. By 1969 she had become assistant professor of anthropology at Washington State University in Pullman. She also served as the director of the school's black studies program. In 1970 she accepted a position in the Afro-American studies program at the University of Massachusetts at Amherst. She taught there for thirteen years, becoming a full professor and serving for two years as the school's associate provost for undergraduate education.

Also in the 1980s Cole was a visiting professor at Oberlin College, UCLA, Williams College, Hunter College, and NYU. Her defining moment came in

1986 when she applied for, and received the appointment as president of the prestigious Spelman College. Taking office in 1987, she immediately established the school's office of community service. By 1993 40% of students had volunteered for service. She also instituted a mentoring program that paired her students with the Chief Executive Officers (CEOs) of Atlanta-based businesses.

During her tenure as president of Spelman, Cole maintained a close relationship with the students by teaching an anthropology or women's studies class each semester. She was also accessible to students through office visits. She infused new life into the school by engaging in fund-raising activities. By 1992, Spelman had completed a campaign that garnered $113.8 million. It was the largest sum ever raised by an HBCU. Bill and Camille Cosby were the largest individual donors.

During Cole's presidency, Spelman College became the first HBCU to receive a number one rating in *U.S. News and World Report's* annual college issue. Money Magazine ranked Spelman as the number one HBCU, the number one women's college, and number seven in the nation, overall. With academic awards and honorary degrees too numerous too mention, Johnnetta Betsch Cole, still finds time to promote self-enrichment through education, equality through advocacy, and service through volunteerism. She has a record of distinguished achievement in all her endeavors. Even her 1986 landmark book, *All American Women,* broke new ground in Women's Studies programs.

NAT "KING" COLE (1919-1965)

Nat King Cole was an African American pianist and singer. He was one of the most stylistically advanced jazz pianists of the 1940s. And he was also one of the most talented vocal artists of the 1950s and 1960s. His voice had enormous appeal and was quite popular for radio, television, and movies.

He was born Nathaniel Adams Coles in Montgomery, Alabama. His birth date has been variously reported between 1915 and 1919. He was one of six children born to Edward, a Baptist minister and Perlina Coles. When Nat was very young, the family moved to Chicago where his father was offered the pastorate of a Chicago area church. His mother became the choir director at her husband's church and the children were introduced to music early on. All four of the boys would become professional musicians.

Cole's mother was his first music teacher. As a small child, Nat could play jazz, gospel, and classical tunes on the piano. He would also stand in front of the radio with a ruler in his hand and "conduct" the orchestra being broadcast. At age twelve, he began taking formal lessons in piano and also began playing the organ at his father's church. If his keyboard skills were not needed, he was put into the choir stand.

While attending Wendell Phillips High School, Cole became enamored of jazz music. He also participated in the music program of Walter Dyett at DuSable High School. The African American neighborhood of Bronzeville, on Chicago's Southside, was the center of jazz in the 1930s. Nat and his brother Eddie went as often as possible to hear jazz and to be with the jazz musicians. When they could not afford the price of admission to a performance, the brothers would stand in the alleys listening at the stage door. Nat was most influenced by the piano style of Earl "Fatha" Hines.

Cole began his performing career while he was still a teenager. He dropped the "s" from his last name and organized two musical groups, a fourteen-piece band called the Rogues of Rhythm, and a quintet called Nat Cole and his Royal Dukes. He would play with whichever group could get a booking. In addition to music, sports played a big role in his adolescence and his talent on the baseball diamond drew some interest from the scouts of the Negro Leagues.

Cole's brother Eddie, a bassist, soon joined his band and they recorded for the first time in 1936. Nat had some success as a local band in and around Chicago and recorded for some black music labels. He was also a regular performer at clubs. In fact, he picked up the nickname "King" performing at one Chicago club. He toured with a revival of Eubie Blake's *Shuffle Along*. When it suddenly failed in Long Beach, California, Cole decided to remain on the West Coast. He was married twice and had five children.

He formed the Nat King Cole Trio while in Long Beach but the group became a greater success once it relocated to Los Angles. The Trio played in L. A. throughout the late 1930s and recorded many radio broadcasts. He also enjoyed a few small movie roles, playing himself. He did not achieve widespread popularity until he recorded "Sweet Lorraine" in 1940. Cole signed with the fledgling Capitol Records in the early 1940s and remained with the company for the rest of his career. He released such hits as: *Straighten Up and Fly Right; Get Your Kicks On Route 66; The Christmas Song; Walkin' My Baby Back Home; Mona Lisa; Pretend; Darling Je Vous Amie Beaucoup, Smile, Nature Boy*, and *Unforgettable*.

Cole also had a half-hour variety show that showcased much of the black talent of the late 1950s. After a year on the air, he canceled the show because he could never get national sponsorship. He later quipped that, "Madison Avenue is afraid of the Dark." If Nat King Cole had lived, I'm sure he would be taken aback by the overabundance of marketing for today's African American music. He would surely be surprised by the acceptance of black programming on stations like BET, UPN, and WB. Madison Avenue is no longer afraid of the dark. In fact, it seems that they have finally seen the light.

BESSIE COLEMAN (1892-1926)

B essie Coleman was the first African American woman to become an airplane pilot and the very first American woman to obtain an international pilots license. Known to an admiring public as "Queen Bess," she earned wide recognition for her aerial skills that were breathtaking to watch.

Bessie was born in Atlanta, Texas. She was the tenth of thirteen children born to George and Susan Coleman. Her early education was interrupted by long cotton-picking seasons that caused local schools to shut down so that the children could help with the harvest. When Bessie was nine, her father, who was of Native American descent, left the family to return to Oklahoma. Bessie's mother remained in Texas, taking in laundry and picking cotton to support herself and her children. Bessie was herself a laundress, earning money from washing and ironing to pay for her secondary and college education.

In 1910 Bessie enrolled in the preparatory school of the Agricultural and Normal University in Langston, Oklahoma, but her money ran out after only one semester. She was forced to return to Texas and resume her job as a laundress. By 1915 she had grown weary of domestic work and left to join her brother in Chicago. From that time on, Chicago was Bessie's adopted home. She enrolled in an area beauty school and completed a course in manicuring.

Bessie's charm and good looks earned her a good living in salary and tips. Those same attributes also earned her many admirers, one to whom she was briefly married in 1917. After mingling with many of Chicago's wealthiest and most powerful black citizens, Bessie pursued what initially seemed an impossible dream. In the early 1920s, women pilots were rare and black women pilots were non-existent. Having listened to her brother's wartime tales of French aviatrixes, a career in flying offered an irresistible challenge to her.

Bessie ignored all the obstacles presented by her gender, race, and limited education, and accomplished her goal. After receiving a string of rejections from American aviation schools, Bessie completed a basic French course and set sail for France to enroll in an aviation school there. The money she had saved from working, together with gifts from a number of wealthy sponsors, enabled Bessie to pay for her passage to Europe and flying lessons. In June of 1921, after completing seven months of instruction and a rigorous qualifying examination, she received her pilot's license and earned a permanent place in history.

In August of 1921, Bessie returned to the U.S. with confidence, enthusiasm and impeccable credentials. She added to that her mix of talent and daring she already possessed and began a career as a barnstorming stunt pilot. Throughout her flying career, Bessie Coleman delivered stunning demonstrations of daredevil maneuvers, including figure eights, loops, and near-ground dips, to large and very enthusiastic crowds. She performed in air shows in cities around the country, gaining wide acclaim. The Firestone Rubber Corporation hired her to do aerial advertising in California.

Although she continued to perform aerial exhibitions, Bessie was increasingly aware of the potential power lecture platforms held as a means of inspiring other young African Americans to pursue careers in aviation. She spent the last year of her life speaking at schools, theaters, and churches around the country, accompanying each lecture with stimulating film clips of her aerial displays. Bessie's last dream was to establish a flying school. But that vision ended with her untimely demise.

On April 30, 1926, Bessie and her aircraft mechanic took her new plane out for a practice run. A mechanical failure occurred and Bessie was hurled out of the plane and plunged move than 500 feet to her death. During her distinguished, albeit brief career as a performance aircraft flier, she appeared at air shows and exhibitions across the United States. Some of the approbation she received is still evident today as "Bessie Coleman Drive" at O'Hare International Airport in Chicago is named in her honor.

FANNIE JACKSON COPPIN (1837-1913)

F anny Jackson Coppin was one of the first African American school principals in the United States. She was a church and civic leader, writer on women's issues, and one of the leading black educators of the nineteenth century. Coppin worked tirelessly to make education available to all African Americans. Coppin State University in Baltimore, Maryland is named in her honor.

She was born Frances Marion Jackson, a slave in Washington D.C. in 1837. She was the daughter of a slave mother and a white father. An aunt purchased her freedom when she was twelve years old and sent her to live with another aunt in New Bedford, Massachusetts. Later, the aunt moved to Newport, Rhode Island where Fanny became a domestic servant at age fourteen and used her earnings to hire a private tutor for three hours a week. Her employer, George Henry Calvert, whose cultured lifestyle made an indelible impression on her, allowed her to pursue her studies for one hour every afternoon.

By then, Fanny had purposed in her heart to get an education and become a teacher to her people. She later attended the segregated Newport public schools and briefly attended Rhode Island Normal School before moving to Ohio to attend Oberlin College in 1860. While still a student in 1863, Fanny established an evening school for freed slaves migrating to Ohio during the Civil War. She was elected class poet and became a member of the prestigious Young Ladies Literary Society. Even as a student, Fanny established a reputation as an effective educator.

When Fanny graduated Oberlin in 1865, she became one of the first black women to earn a bachelor's degree from a major U.S. college. She was offered a teaching position with an historically black college, the Institute for Colored Youth (ICY) in Philadelphia. It later became Cheney State University. Afterward, she became the principal of ICY making her the first African American woman director of a coeducational institution, and overseeing male and female teachers. It was the highest educational appointment held by a black woman at that time. In her thirty-seven year association with ICY, Fanny trained many notable black leaders and helped to shape the patterns of black education in the late 19th century.

The industrial department of ICY established under Fanny's leadership was the first trade school for blacks in Philadelphia. It was an immediate success and had a waiting list for admission throughout its existence. She had anticipated Booker T. Washington's call for vocational training for blacks by establishing an industrial department in the 1880s. In fact, she was often compared to Washington for her efforts to help promote self-reliance among blacks.

Fanny also found time to write articles on women's issues for the "Christian Recorder," the national newspaper for the African Methodist Episcopal Church. She was president of the local "Women's Mite Missionary Society." She was also the national president of the Women's Home and Foreign Missionary Society of the AME Church. Her civic responsibilities also involved the causes of women. She was the Vice President of the "National Association of Colored Women." Politically, she was a strong proponent of women's rights, including the right to vote. Her speeches encouraged women to strive for the same educational and employment rights that men had.

In the fall of 1881, Fanny married Rev. Levi Jenkins Coppin, a minister of the AME Church. He became pastor of Philadelphia's historic Mother Bethel AME Church in 1896. Their marriage opened a wealth of missionary opportunities for Fanny. When Coppin was made Bishop of Cape Town, South Africa in 1902, Fanny accompanied him and traveled thousands of miles organizing mission societies as well as mission schools. Upon returning home in 1904, Fanny continued to teach and enlighten her students by opening their minds and understanding to the endless possibilities that education could offer.

*"Weel about and turn about do jes so /
Ev'by time I weel about I jump Jim Crow"*

T he name "Jim Crow" has been haunting the American consciousness since the early-middle nineteenth century. Thomas "Daddy" Rice, a white minstrel performer heard an elderly black stable worker dancing and singing the above limerick. Rice incorporated the song, dance, and shabby clothes into his minstrel act and the black character of Jim Crow became a featured staple of Minstrelsy by the mid-nineteenth century. "Jim Crow," then, effectively became a phrase to slur an entire class of people, on the same reprehensible level with the word "nigger."

Jim Crow laws were southern statutes that effectively segregated people by race. In 1883, in a group of decisions known as the *Civil Rights Cases*, the United States Supreme Court struck down the Civil Rights Act of 1875 that had forbidden racial segregation in public accommodations such as hotel and trains. Under Jim Crow laws, separate facilities for black and white train and streetcar passengers, separate schools, and separate entrances and reception areas in public buildings were built in the South. Separate restrooms and drinking fountains as well as special visiting hours for blacks at museums became fixtures of southern life.

Eventually, the Court validated state legislation that discriminated against blacks. The Court held that separated accommodations did not deprive blacks of equal rights if the accommodations were equal. The Court also came to conclude that it could prohibit state governments from discriminating against people because of race, but could not restrict private organizations or individuals from doing so. Thus railroads, hotels, theaters, and the like could legally practice segregation. Even before these decisions, white Southerners were working to strengthen white supremacy and separate the races to the greatest extent possible.

Jim Crow laws were nothing more than thinly disguised Black Codes, which had previously been the states' Slave Codes. Another illustration of the movement from subordination to segregation of African Americans came in the form of voting rights. In some states, disenfranchisement had begun almost as soon as Reconstruction ended. But in other areas, black voting continued for some time after Reconstruction, largely because conservative whites believed they could control the black electorate and use it to beat back the attempts of poor white farmers to take control of the Democratic Party.

But Jim Crow laws also stripped blacks of many of the modest social, economic, and political gains they had made in the more fluid atmosphere of the late nineteenth century. They served, too, as a means for whites to retain control of social relations between the races in the newly growing cities and towns of the South, where traditional patterns of deference and subjugation were more difficult to preserve than in the countryside. What had been maintained by custom in the rural South was to be maintained by law in the urban South.

Laws restricting franchise and segregating schools were only part of the network of state statutes known as Jim Crow laws. By the first years of the twentieth century blacks and whites could not ride together in the same railroad cars, sit in the same waiting rooms, use the same washrooms, eat in the same restaurants, or sit in the same theaters. Blacks were denied access to parks, beaches, and picnic areas; and they were barred from many hospitals. Oftentimes terrorizing brutalities such as lynching in rural areas and firebombs in urban areas were used to reinforce Jim Crow statues.

Jim Crow was originally the name of a popular cartoon and minstrel character in the late nineteenth century. But the name has since come to personify racial hatred, bigotry, and the institutionalized oppression of African Americans. It was considered to be the legally based, state supported, American version of the South African Apartheid System.

P aul Cuffe was a philanthropist, merchant, ship builder, and sea captain who advocated the mass emigration of free blacks to Africa. One of ten children, he was born free on Chuttyhunk Island, Massachusetts. "Cuffe" is the Anglicized version of his father's African name which was Saiz Kofu. Paul's father was of the Akan ethnic group, but was enslaved to the subjugating and hegemonic Ashanti people of West Africa. Kofu was sold and brought to America at age ten. He became a skilled carpenter, bought his freedom, and educated himself. Paul's mother, Ruth Moses, was Native American.

Paul began working on whaling ships when he was just fourteen. When his father died he brought a ship with his inheritance. Convinced that commerce would make him more of a fortune than agriculture, he taught himself math and navigation and in 1776 began sailing his own vessels. During the American Revolutionary War he made his living as a blockade runner, smuggling goods in and out of American harbors past British patrol ships. This proved to be lucrative for Cuffe, but after the war he returned to whaling domestically and internationally, which provided the bulk of his great wealth.

Cuffe's ships were staffed exclusively by blacks, which he hoped would demonstrate their equality to all observers. Members of his extended family served as his crew or operated his businesses. He owned all or part of at least ten ships during his lifetime, building or supervising in the construction of them at his shipyard. In addition to his shipping interest, he had investments in farming and fishing businesses. He was also invested in other business concerns with wealthy Quakers. In 1808 he joined the Society of Friends (Quaker) religion.

Even when working to pursue his fortune, Cuffe worked to benefit others, especially as it pertained to fighting discrimination. In 1780 he and his brother refused to pay taxes in protest against the Massachusetts state constitution that excluded blacks and Indians from voting. In their complaint the two brothers alluded to "taxation without representation," the main argument that the North American Colonists used against the British. Although their complaint did not gain them the vote, it did reduce the family's taxes.

Angered by the incident and believing that Africans were exploited, Cuffe sent a petition to the Massachusetts legislature, appealing his case. He wrote that blacks should be granted immunity from taxation since they *"had no voice or influence in the election of those who tax us."* His case was argued in the legislature. When the appeal was decided, a law was passed granting Africans the same rights as whites in the state. Cuffe's stature rose among blacks and he was recognized by blacks and whites as a leader in the black community.

Cuffe donated large sums for a Quaker meetinghouse and built an interracial Quaker school. He felt that education was valuable to all people and that no one should be denied the opportunity to learn. The Cuffe School was an example of what education ought to have been for all citizens. His religious ties brought him into close contact with British and American abolitionists. Near the end of his life, Cuffe supported the American Colonization Society that sought to repatriate free blacks to Africa. He was personally responsible for repatriating thirty-eight people to Sierra Leone, West Africa, aboard his ships, and supplied with all necessities for their new environment.

Paul Cuffe was completely unaffected by his great riches. He was the wealthiest person of African descent during the 1790s. And at his death his estate was valued in excess of $300,000. But his legacy was not just the wealth of money, but wealth of integrity, purpose, and resolve. Throughout his life he remained committed to the ideals and principles espoused during the American Revolution and wanted only to have those same rights of citizenship conferred on the Africans in America.

COUNTEE CULLEN (1903-1946)

Countee Cullen was a poet, anthologist, novelist, translator, children's writer, playwright, and the best-known literary figure of the Harlem Renaissance. Recent scholarship reveals that he was born Countee Porter on March 30, 1903, in Louisville, Kentucky. His mother was Elizabeth Thomas Lucas, who died in 1940; nothing is known of his father. He lived with Amanda Porter, assumed to be his grandmother, in the Bronx until her death in 1917. Shortly afterwards he went to live with Rev. and Mrs. Frederick Cullen, pastor of Salem Methodist Episcopal Church in Harlem. Although never formally adopted by the Cullen family, he assumed their name in 1918.

Cullen enrolled in the respected, almost exclusively white, Dewitt Clinton High School for boys in Manhattan in 1918. Among other things he became a member of the honor society, served as vice president of the senior class, associate editor of the school's literary magazine, editor of the school's newspaper, an officer of the Inter-High School Poetry Society. In addition, his poetry appeared regularly in school publications, and he won a citywide poetry contest.

His college career was even more distinguished. Cullen attended New York University on a New York State Regents Scholarship, elected to Phi Beta Kappa National Honor Society in his junior year, before receiving a bachelor's degree in 1925. His poems were published frequently in the college magazine, of which he eventually became poetry editor. He was also published in other notable magazines such as *Harper's, Century,* and *Nation.* His first collection of poetry, *Color,* was published in his senior year at NYU. In 1926 he received a master's degree in English and French from Harvard University and won the *Crisis* magazine award in poetry. From 1926 to 1928 he was assistant editor of *Opportunity: A Journal of Negro Life* for which he wrote a feature column, "The Dark Tower." In 1927 he published his second volume of poetry, *Copper Sun.*

By the late 1920s, Cullen had become the most popular black poet in the United States, and had won more literary prizes, from black and white sources, than any other black writer. 1928 was a watershed year for him. He received a Guggenheim Fellowship to study in Paris, published his third volume of poetry, *The Ballad of a Brown Girl,* and, after a long courtship, married Nina Yolande Dubois. Marrying the only daughter of W.E.B. Dubois reinforced

Cullen's celebrity. Their lavish wedding, performed by Rev. Cullen, was attended by over 1000 guests and was one of the major social events of the Harlem Renaissance. It appeared literally to place Cullen, and his generation of black intellectuals, in the position of being heir to Dubois.

The marriage was disastrous and ended quickly. They were divorced by 1930. It had an adverse effect on Cullen for the rest of his life. He did not attempt marriage again until 1940. His career changed after his divorce. In 1929 he published *The Black Christ and Other Poems*, on which he had worked for two years. He considered it to be his masterpiece, but was bitterly disappointed when the book was not well received. From the 1930s onward, his work was no longer universally acclaimed but he remained popular. He was offered teaching positions at various universities but preferred to teach French at Frederick Douglass Junior High School, where his most distinguished pupil was the future writer, James Baldwin.

Countee Cullen called upon black writers to create a representative and respectable race literature while insisting that the artist not be bound by race or restricted to racial themes. With his considerable academic training, higher than other writers and poets of the Harlem Renaissance, it was an easy call to make. He wrote in the tradition of Keats and Shelley, with genuine skill and compelling power. And he understood himself as a poet, never employing jazz or free-style techniques, but always true to his own form of poetic expression.

DOROTHY DANDRIDGE (1922-1965)

D orothy Dandridge was one of the most beautiful women of the twentieth century and one of the most accomplished actresses of her time. She set a new standard for African American film stars and forever changed the way Americans viewed women of color on the silver screen. Although often forced into playing stereotypes, she rose above the material and forced critics and audiences to take black actresses seriously.

She was the younger of two daughters born to Cyril Dandridge, a cabinetmaker and minister; and Ruby Jean Butler Dandridge, an aspiring entertainer. Her parents separated near Dorothy's birth on November 9, 1922. As Dorothy and her older sister, Vivian, grew up, their mother helped them into the field that she knew best – entertainment. Ruby Jean wrote material for the act she called the "Wonder Kids." The act consisted of Dorothy and Vivian touring the country, singing, dancing, and performing comedy skits at schools, churches, and social gatherings.

In the early 1930s Ruby Jean had settled in Los Angeles and found work in radio, television, and films. Her daughters, while enrolled in school, also continued their careers as the three Dandridge Sisters, singing with Etta Jones. The girls had brief appearances in several films. By age sixteen, Dorothy and her "sisters" were appearing at the Cotton Club in Harlem. The trio split up in 1940.

Early in her solo career, Dorothy appeared in more than a dozen short musical films, notably as the "dream girl" of the Mills Brother singing group in *Paper Doll* (1942). She played bit parts in feature movies, such as *Sun Valley Serenade* (1941); *Drums of the Congo* (1942); *Lucky Jordan* (1942), and *Hit Parade of 1943* (1943). In 1942 Dorothy married Harold Nicholas of the famed Nicholas Brothers tap dance team. The marriage ended in divorce. And the couple's severely brain-damaged daughter was eventually put into a private institution.

Dorothy had always aspired to be a film actress and she began to devote herself to that aspiration on a full-time basis. To support herself and to make contacts, she first established a nightclub singing act, appearing in important clubs across the country. In 1951 she performed with the Desi Arnaz Band, and in 1952 her performances at one New York City nightclub saved it from bankruptcy. At the same time she was appearing in low-budget films including *Tarzan's Peril* (1951), *The Harlem Globetrotters* (1951); and *Jungle Queen* (1951).

Dandridge gave a wonderfully strong performance as a southern schoolteacher when she was cast opposite Harry Belafonte in their first film, *Bright Road* (1953). But her breakthrough role was in the lead in *Carmen Jones* (1954), and she became the first black actress to be nominated for an Academy Award in the category of Best Actress. Her next film, *Island in the Sun* (1957), the first mainstream film to portray an interracial romance, was not critically received. And again in 1959, she received high praises for her film role of "Bess" in *Porgy and Bess*. Despite film successes and being featured on the cover of magazines, she still had difficulty finding suitable leading roles.

Hollywood did not know what to do with Dorothy Dandridge. There were few opportunities for a black woman who would not pander to playing the role of comedic or docile maids. In words from her autobiography "Everything and Nothing: The Dorothy Dandridge Tragedy," she would say: *"I was to reach a high and also the beginnings of a decline inevitable for a Negro actress for whom there was no place else to go."* She was a major star and a leading lady with immense range and talent. But since there were very few black leading men, she was cast opposite white actors. But in the casting, another kind of film stereotype was created – that of a black coquette, living a self-destructive life. Tragically, she died of an overdose of antidepressants in 1965. In a number of ways Dorothy Dandridge's life imitated her art.

ISOM DART (1849-1900)

When daring stories are told of the American Old West, few if any speak of the African American experience. When ballads are sung of heroic good guys and infamous bad guys, none are ever black. These fabled versions of the Old West are inaccurate. Since they do not depict people of color, they are slanted at best. For well over a century, a biased version of the Old West went unchallenged. But when the all-inclusive truth was told, there was a long list of black adventurers, cowboys, miners, and trailblazers who gave added dimension to the American West. One such daring story is that of Ned Huddleston, a.k.a. Isom Dart.

Huddleston was born to slave parents on a plantation in Arkansas in 1849. When the Civil War began in 1861, as it was with other slaves in the South, he was forced into the service of the Confederacy. At age twelve he was used as an officer's orderly. As the war continued, and as things went badly for the South, he developed his talents as a thief by foraging for the Confederate Army. At age sixteen, as the war was nearing its end, he ran away. Like so many runaway slaves he found refuge in Mexico where he worked as a rodeo clown.

After the end of the war Huddleston returned the United States, but stayed in the West, never returning home again. With skills he learned foraging during the war, he joined the Tip Gault gang of horse thieves. He stole horses and swam them across the Rio Grande to sell. Once while he was away from the camp, white ranchers and their private posse, killed all of the gang members in an ambush. Dart was out burying a friend who had been kicked to death by a horse. He survived by spending the night in the grave alongside his dead friend. After that harrowing experience, he began using the alias, Isom Dart, and went to live in the Oklahoma territory.

Dart gave up stealing for a while and became a prospector and then a broncobuster. His skill as a rider was unequaled, but he never entered any of the cowboy contests. It is reported that he repeatedly tried to give up his criminal ways and each time he returned to them. Eventually he returned to his horse stealing habits and also began to rustle cattle with a Mexican friend. Once he was captured by a county sheriff and during the trip to jail, he saved the sheriff's life. Out of gratitude, the sheriff testified on Dart's behalf so passionately that he was acquitted.

Dart was arrested on a number of occasions for stealing cattle but never received any jail time. Some of his other activities also caused him to have brushes with the law. In northwest Colorado he was involved in gambling and fighting. No matter how hard he tried he could not keep to the "straight and narrow." He was even involved in range wars in Colorado. During one of the times that he "went straight," Dart earned enough money breaking horsed that he was soon able to buy a small horse ranch. But sadly, he always remained a wanted man with outstanding warrants.

Even as Dart involved himself in outlaw activities, he was variously described as a "good man." In addition to his skill as a horseman, he was known for his ability to hunt and track, as well as his ability with guns. In authentic sepia photographs, Dart is pictured as a tall husky, black man with two pistols tucked in his belt, wearing a large hat, light shirt with a bandana around his neck, jeans, chaps, spurs, and a jacket. He is also pictured on horseback with other companions.

One morning, while standing outside his cabin in Brown's Park, Colorado, he was ambushed from the surrounding rocks by Tom Horn, a white bounty hunter who later claimed the reward. Dart was only fifty-one when he was shot in the back and killed. African Americans carried a heavier burden and paid a higher price for pioneering the Old West. But what they expected, and largely received, was equal protection under the law – to be judged by deeds and not by color.

MILES DAVIS (1926-1991)

M iles Davis was the quintessential jazz musician. He was a trumpeter, composer, bandleader, and one of the most influential and respected figures in the history of jazz. He was a leading figure in the bebop style of jazz and in combining styles of jazz and rock music. As a trumpeter, he was a master of improvisation and played complicated melodies with great subtlety and expressiveness. As a bandleader, he assembled classic groups and allowed them the freedom to experiment and develop. Musicians around the world have imitated the recordings of Davis and his groups.

He was born Miles Dewey Davis III in Alton, Illinois, but he grew up in East St. Louis. His father was a prominent dentist and his mother was a classically trained pianist. He received his first trumpet at age thirteen and two years later was a member of the Musicians' Union. By his mid-teens, Davis was playing in the St. Louis area with a local band on weekends. In 1944, after graduating from high school, he went to New York City to study classical music at the Juilliard School of Music but he never graduated. He gained his musical education and an early reputation playing the jazz clubs on 52nd Street

In New York, Davis began playing with saxophonist Charlie "Bird" Parker, trumpeter Dizzy Gillespie, and other pioneers of the new jazz style known as "bebop." It was playing with Parker that led to the development, improvement, and refinement of that Davis improvisational style. In 1950, he released an album, *The Birth of Cool*, which gave rise to a slower, smoother and more subdued style of bebop. And by the mid-1950s, Davis had developed one of the most distinctive styles in all of jazz, preferring simple, lyrical melodies to the speedier, flashier ones. He often used a Harmon mute to get a pinched, quiet sound. Some of those classic albums include: *Round about Midnight* (1956), *Miles Ahead* (1957), *Milestones* (1958), and *Kind of Blue* (1959).

Also by the mid 1950s, Davis was leading the finest jazz combos that included jazz greats like John Coltrane, Cannonball Adderly, Wayne Shorter, and Herbie Hancock. The albums recorded by these groups, represented major landmarks in the evolution of jazz. *Kind of Blue* was the best-selling jazz album ever and is considered by jazz aficionados to be one of the finest jazz albums ever made. It was the first significant example of modal jazz and continues to exert a profound influence on young jazz musicians everywhere.

In the early 1960s Davis began playing louder and using high notes and quick phrases more frequently. Some of his more notable albums of the 1960s include: *ESP* (1965), *Miles Smiles* (1966), and *Nefertiti* (1967). By the end of the 1960s he began to make use of the electronic instruments, rhythms, and song structures of rock music. His manner of playing the trumpet did not change much, but his musical surroundings were dramatically different. Although many Davis fans disliked his fusion of jazz and rock music styles, bebop musicians followed his lead and imitated his new style in the 1970s.

From 1975 to 1980, Davis experienced a period of reclusive inactivity, supposedly because of injuries in an automobile accident and the subsequent onset of several illnesses. He was known to use heroin and cocaine at various times in his life. If the addiction was strong, as in the case of so many artists, he could have also been battling those demons as well. In 1981 Davis married long-time love-interest, actress Cicely Tyson, but the couple later divorced. Throughout the 1980s Davis released several jazz and rock fusion albums such as: *The Man with The Horn* (1981), *Decoy* (1983), and *You're Under Arrest* (1985).

Davis was a major musical force of the last half of the 20th century, winning nine Grammy Awards and being inducted into the Grammy Hall of Fame three times. Indicative of his genius was his cool aloofness on stage, and his brooding, reclusiveness off stage. And yet, even with all that, Miles Davis remained a milestone in the field of jazz, and miles ahead of any other jazz artist of his time.

D ouble Dutch is a game of jump rope played by African American girls in which players have to jump over two ropes instead of one. The ropes are turned around and over each other in "eggbeater" fashion. Speeds alternate between fast and slow, depending on the inclination of the players turning the ropes for the jumper. In terms of speed, some jumpers can approach 200 beats per minute. Some can twirl batons, do handstands, or even jump a regular rope, all while they are jumping the "eggbeater" ropes of the Double Dutch game

Many believe that the Dutch, who were the original settlers of the Dutch Colony of New Amsterdam, brought the double rope style to America. In various European wars though, the Dutch lost their overseas colonies to the British. New Amsterdam became the British Colony of New York. But Dutch words like "Harlem" and "Amsterdam" Avenue continue to this day in New York City. No one knows with any certainty where the name "Double Dutch" originated. It is speculated that the history of the term is tied to the rope making techniques of those early Dutch settlers. They twisted hemp fibers into twine, turning their arms like eggbeaters, similar to the way Double Dutch game ropes have been turned for generations by African American girls.

There are many variations on the basic pattern of Double Dutch. Usually two turners face each other, holding two strands of rope 12 to 15 feet long. They turn each rope inward in an alternating pattern. The jumper synchronizes with the turning ropes, and enters them in a jumping motion. Double Dutch reflects the Africanized character of other black children's games because of the rhymed chants accompanying the game. The turners establish the beat with a rhyming children's song like:

"Oh Mary Mack, Mack, Mack, All dressed in Black, Black, Black.
With Silver Buttons, Buttons, Buttons. All Down Her Back, Back, Back..."

Double Dutch, like many games among black youth, became popular in urban areas because it could be played anywhere and did not require expensive toys or equipment. My grandmother's clothesline was an ever-ready jumping rope in our Haughville neighborhood. That withstanding, 25-feet of clothesline rope could be purchased at local area Hardware Stores for 25-cents. Also, clothesline had a better weight and was more substantial than the toy ropes found in dime stores.

The Double Dutch tradition originally began as a boys' game, but girls took it over in the twentieth century and it has become a training ground for developing rhythm, coordination, and style. It was a highly competitive game testing dexterity, concentration, and the ability to look "cool" while displaying great stamina. Double Dutch became to African American girls, what basketball has become to African American boys.

Traditionally Double Dutch is played on the street by girls of grammar and junior high school age. For generations, the pulse of rope against concrete punctuated by syncopated jumping has drawn African American girls to play outside. The age-old children's game is still played by loose gatherings of girls on school playgrounds and on neighborhood sidewalks. As girls show off their fancy footwork while trying to out jump each other, they are also having wholesome and healthy fun. More recently, Double Dutch can be seen as a backdrop in the "One Less" T.V. commercials raising awareness about cervical cancer.

While most often played by urban black girls, Double Dutch is no longer exclusive to one ethnic group. And this heart-healthy aerobic exercise shows no signs of slowing down. Organized Double Dutch League Competitions founded in New York City in 1974, have swept the country. The game has expanded to include thousands of participants. Each year teams come up with new and innovative routines, which have become more elaborate as players' skill levels increase.

MARTIN R. DELANY (1812-1885)

M artin Robison Delany was a man of rare intellect. During the course of his life he was an author, columnist, physician, Abolitionist, colonizationist, and the highest-ranking army officer during the Civil War. His militant, Black Nationalist views on the treatment of African Americans established a unique place for him in American History.

He was born on May 6, 1812 in Charles Town in western Virginia. His mother, Pattie Peace Delany was freeborn, but his father, Samuel Delany was a slave. Martin grew up listening to proud stories of his African ancestry from his grandmother Gracie Peace. His mother's people were from the royal lines of the Gola and Mandingo ethnic groups of West Africa. In 1822 Pattie Delany took her five children and fled to avoid imprisonment for knowing how to read. They traveled to Chambersburg, Pennsylvania, and a year later, Samuel bought his freedom and rejoined his family. Meanwhile Martin and the other Delany children continued their education. Delany left home in 1831, traveling on foot across the Allegheny Mountains into Pittsburgh, where he remained until 1856.

Delany continued his studies at an African Methodist Episcopal (AME) night school. He also studied medicine, and under the tutelage of a white physician, became qualified to practice a variety of medical procedures that were common at that time. In addition, Delany became an officer of the Pittsburgh Anti-Slavery Society, Underground Railroad activists, and the organizer of various literary and moral reform groups among the growing number of fugitive slaves then settling in the area. In 1836 he served as a delegate to a colored convention, traveling both to Philadelphia and New York in this capacity. It was during this time that he met and married Catherine Richards. The couple had six sons and one daughter. He named his children in honor of great blacks in history. For example, two of his sons were named Toussaint L'Ouverture Delany and Alexander Dumas Delany; his daughter was named Ethiopia Halle Delany.

Delany had a varied career. In 1843 he began practicing medicine, even attending Harvard for a brief time (1850-51). He published *The Mystery* from 1843-47, the first black owned newspaper west of the Allegheny Mountains. It went out of business due to lack of funds. He also co-edited *The North Star* with Frederick Douglass (1847-49). In addition to writing for Douglass' paper,

Delany wrote numerous anti-slavery pamphlets and was extremely active in speaking to Anti-Slavery gatherings throughout the East and Midwest. He made as many as three speeches a day, and at great danger to himself. On one occasion in Ohio, he barely escaped being lynched for his black nationalist, anti-slavery remarks. Even Douglass felt that Delany was too militant in his writings and in his speeches. In 1852 Delany published his first Black Nationalist treatise that drew harsh criticism from white Abolitionists and the liberal white press.

Also in the tumultuous 1850s, Delany embraced colonization to Africa for African Americans, and traveled there several times. In 1858 he sailed to Nigeria to sign a treaty with a chief for black workers to emigrate and grow cotton for export. But with the advent of the Civil War, that dream died. He served as a recruiting officer, raising black troops for the Union army. In 1865, he was commissioned a major and transferred to South Carolina, making him the first African American to be given a field command. Following the war, his work for the Freedmen's Bureau led to political office during Reconstruction.

Delany was a man ahead of his time. He was committed to black equality and social justice. He spoke and wrote of a proud black heritage at a time when leading theorists debated whether or not there was such a thing. He was the forerunner of such forward thinking Black Nationalists like Marcus Garvey and Malcolm X. Martin Delany was not a man who simply marched to a different drummer, he was the drum major who led the drum line.

OSCAR DE PRIEST (1871-1951)

Oscar De Priest was the first African American elected to the United States Congress since Reconstruction and the first-ever African American congressman from the North. Oscar Stanton De Priest was born to former slaves. His father was a part time farmer and hauler, and his mother was a laundress. They fled Alabama when Oscar was only seven years old to escape post Civil War racism and poverty. The family settled in Kansas as part of the *Exoduster* Migration.

De Priest left home at age seventeen, living first in Ohio and then in Chicago. He worked as a painter and decorator. By 1905 he owned his own painting and decorating business. By 1915 he was capitalizing on the Great Migration that brought tens of thousands of blacks to South Chicago by opening a lucrative real estate practice. De Priest became active in politics, delivering black votes to Chicago's powerful Republican Party. He was rewarded in 1904 when he was elected as a Cook County commissioner. He remained in that post for four years.

In subsequent years, De Priest threw his support to both black and white candidates, Republicans and Democrats, and in 1915 became Chicago's first black alderman on the Republican ticket. Two years later, He was indicted for ties to organized crime. Although acquitted in 1918, with the help of Attorney Clarence Darrow, he stepped down from the city council pending elections. But through it all, he continued selling real estate and practicing politics, eventually becoming the leading black broker of power for Republican mayor William "Big Bill" Thompson.

When one of Chicago's incumbent congressmen died during the 1928 election campaign, a Republican committee selected De Priest to replace him. Again indicted for underworld activities, De Priest nonetheless defeated his white Democratic opponent, largely on the strength of the black vote. In 1929 he became the first African American in Congress in 28 years, the first elected since Reconstruction, and the first elected from the North. After the election, the indictment was dropped for lack of evidence.

While in Congress De Priest launched several unsuccessful measures related to race. One bill would have had counties paying lynching victim's families $10,000. He opened a rancorous debate by proposing that blacks be allowed to eat in the House restaurant. As a member of the House of Congress, the

159

prohibition did not apply to him.

Among De Priest's successes was a bill that prohibited the Civilian Conservation Corps (CCC), a New Deal work program, from discriminating against blacks in the hiring process. De Priest also increased Congress' appropriation to Howard University and sent black appointments to the U.S. Military Academy at West Point and the U.S. Naval Academy at Annapolis.

De Priest ignored threats to his life and spoke widely in the South where he urged blacks to organize and vote. His years in Congress saw the abandonment of the Republican Party by African Americans in favor of the Democratic Party. Although De Priest survived the sweeping Democratic elections of 1930 and 1932, he was vulnerable for his refusal to support aid to the poor and place taxes on the rich. In 1934 a black Democrat defeated him. He did serve again as a Chicago alderman from 1943-1947, but never again in the U.S. House of Representatives.

Blacks in the North did not face legal barriers to voting, and actively participated in the political process. But blacks in the South had to organize to fight against the barriers to their civil rights. Unfortunately, Oscar De Priest died before he could see the full effect of the Civil Rights Movement of which he is noted to be an historic pioneer.

"FATHER DIVINE" (1879-1965)

Father Divine was an African American cult leader and founder of the Peace Mission Movement. His movement grew to include tens of thousands of people in several cities along the east coast. He amassed millions of dollars in assets and lived lavishly. And he surrounded himself with lovely young women, while encouraging his followers to lead austere and celibate lives. Divine did not discuss his early life, so history has had to struggle to fill in the gaps before 1915. Particularly reprehensible about Divine was his penchant for encouraging his followers to call him "God."

He was born George Baker, Jr., the son of George Baker, Sr., a day laborer, and Nancy Smith, a domestic worker. He was born in either Rockville, Maryland or near Savannah, Georgia. The date of his birth is variously reported as 1879, 1880, and 1882. It is known that he moved to Baltimore at age twenty, where he was active with the Baptist denomination and soon began an itinerant ministry throughout the South. Southern whites regarded his preaching as dangerous, which means he preached racial equality, and he was jailed for it. History records that he was present in Los Angles at the revival that gave birth to the modern Pentecostal Movement in 1906. His rise to prominence began in 1915 when he began calling himself "Major J. Divine."

Divine took a small group of followers to Harlem, New York City and began preaching. The movement, in which he became known as Father Divine, evolved gradually. And in 1919, he established his first communal dwellings at his estate in all-white Sayville on Long Island. His followers called it the "Heavens." He was soon welcoming visitors to free Sunday banquets and prayer services. By 1926 the Peace Mission Movement had became interracial in scope. But the continued presence of African Americans was a threatening sight for his white neighbors. Divine's worship services attracted thousands of people and generated much too much noise to suit them.

Things collimated in 1930 when, Divine was arrested and found guilty on charges of disturbing the peace and running a public nuisance. He received the maximum fine and sentence of one year in jail by the biased Judge, Lewis J. Smith. One of the most renowned anecdotes about Father Divine came three days after his sentencing when the fifty-five year old judge dropped dead of a heart attack. In response to the judge's death, Divine responded: *"I hated to do it."* The timing of Smith's death and Divine's comment were not lost on the growing legions of his followers. At that point the Peace Mission moved to Harlem, which was then caught up in the throes of the Great Depression. From the beginning Father Divine had ministered to the whole person, body and soul, and that approach found an eager reception among the thousands of impoverished African Americans in Harlem.

Divine's movement rapidly built up a network of businesses, including restaurants, grocery and clothing stores, gas stations, hotels, farms, and many other enterprises. All his businesses provided high quality goods and services inexpensively, and not coincidentally, created jobs for his faithful followers. Father Divine's first wife was a black woman named Peninniah, a longtime follower and stalwart worker for the Divine cause. Divine taught that his followers would not die, but Peninniah did die in 1943. And in 1946, he married one of his young secretaries, a white Canadian named Edna Rose Ritchings. She took the movement name of "Sweet Angel" and became a strong leader in her own right. When Divine died in 1965, she was able to sustain the organization that would have perished without its charismatic leader.

Divine amused many who observed him. Others were simply perplexed to witness the duping of Christians seeking heaven on earth. Although he built up a following that deserted their traditional churches, and had the colossal effrontery to be called God, his movement was as much social as it was religious. That Father Divine could flourish was a testament to the extent of the social problems under which the United States suffered at that time. And it was one more indication of the tremendous social and political frustrations that characterized most blacks and some whites in the early 20th century.

ISAIAH DORMAN (c. 1821-1876)

Isaiah Dorman was an African American frontiersman, interpreter, and, in the end, a soldier. He was the only black man known to have been present during the Battle of the Little Bighorn, which began on June 25, 1876. In every biography ever written about George Armstrong Custer, this black interpreter and guide is always mentioned. While the countless films made about "Custer's Last Stand" never even include Dorman's character. History records him as the only black man to die at the Little Bighorn River.

No one really knows how or why Dorman went west. But it is believed that he was a runaway slave from the D'Orman family of Louisiana in the late 1840s. Wanted Posters of that period shows that a Negro slave named Isaiah was a fugitive. At some point after his escape, he settled among the Lakota Sioux Indians in the Dakota Territory around 1850. There are stories from Sioux history depicting him as living peaceably among them, describing him as "Wasichu Sapa," which means "black white man." He learned their language, adopted their customs, and married a Santee Sioux woman. Dorman worked as a trapper and trader, and was known to travel with a horse and a mule. Since he was a runaway slave, he had to avoid all contact with white settlers.

There is not enough historical documentation to complete Dorman's life story. He first appeared in army records on November 11, 1865, when he was hired as a mail courier to make the 300 mile round trip between Fort Wadsworth and Fort Rice, Dakota Territory. He earned the substantial sum of $100 per month. The work, while paying well, was not regular and he also worked intermittently chopping wood. By 1867, army work had dwindled. Dorman took a job with the firm of Durfee and Peck as a "woodhawk." They were woodcutters that cut and stacked wood along the Missouri River for the use of Riverboats at the rate of $1.50 per cord. He relocated in 1869 to the Standing Rock Indian Agency. In September 1871, he was hired as a guide and interpreter by the army to escort the Northern Pacific Railroad survey team for $100 for one month. His last job for the army was that of interpreter at Ft. Rice for $75 per month.

The Sioux considered the Black Hills of Dakota holy ground. The Federal government had pledged that white people would not be allowed to settle there nor desecrate their sacred space. But when gold was discovered in the Black Hills, white settlers steamed in and the government violated its own treaty.

When the government did nothing to stop the influx of whites, the Sioux rose up to defend their ancient land. To counter the Sioux uprising, the army sent Colonel Custer, commander of the U.S. Seventh Cavalry, against them.

Dorman's expertise with the Sioux language came to Custer's attention. At his specific request, Dorman became a guide and interpreter accompanying his Little Bighorn expedition. When Custer's column found the Sioux camp on the Little Bighorn River in the afternoon, he ordered his command split into separate groups. He ordered Major Marcus A. Reno down into the valley to attack the south end of the camp. Custer himself took another group of troops and attacked from the heights across the river from the camp. Most of Custer's men were killed with him.

Dorman was assigned to Major Reno's troops as he headed south across the river. Reno's raid was short-lived as Sioux warriors successfully confronted them. The contingent dismounted and spread out to fight on foot. By then, Dorman had been wounded and had become partially pinned under his dead horse. Eyewitness accounts describe the Sioux as pointedly angry at Dorman's betrayal of them by riding with the white cavalry. And they give gruesome details of his post-mortem mutilation at Sioux hands. For Isaiah Dorman, the battle of the Little Bighorn lasted almost two days and ended in his agonizing death. His legs riddled with bullets, arrows filling his chest, neck, and head, and all from Native Americans with whom he had formed close kinship ties.

FREDERICK DOUGLASS (c. 1817-1895)

Historically, the best known of all Abolitionists, black or white was Frederick Douglass. He was born in slavery, in 1817 in Tuckahoe, Maryland. The actual day is unknown because records of slave births were not that stringent. The year and mother's name was all that was required. Frederick would later adopt the date of February 14th as his birthday because his mother, Harriet Bailey, had always called him her "little valentine." He knew little of his mother other than she was a slave field hand on a plantation twelve miles away. She died when Frederick was about nine years old. He knew even less about his father. But it was rumored that he was the son of his white slave master, Aaron Anthony.

As a slave, Frederick suffered gross maltreatment. To keep from starving, on many occasion, he competed with his master's dogs for table scraps and bones. In 1825, he was sent to serve as a houseboy in the home of Hugh and Sophia Auld in Baltimore. Mrs. Auld grew fond of him and sought to teach him to read and write. By the time her irate husband discovered it and put a stop to it, Frederick had acquired enough of the rudiments to carry on by himself.

His life in Baltimore was interrupted in 1832, when he was sold to another master and sent back to Tuckahoe's brutal plantation environment. After four years, Frederick and several other slaves attempted to escape. However, their effort proved unsuccessful when one of the slaves revealed their plan. Viewed as a "bad slave", Frederick was sent to a slave breaker, who whipped him mercilessly. He endured the mistreatment until he fought back. Soon thereafter he was again returned to Baltimore.

Douglass met Anna Murray, a free black woman, whose love and encouragement heightened his quest for freedom. On September 3, 1838, Frederick, dressed in a sailor's uniform and carrying false identification papers provided by a free black seaman, managed to reach New York City. There he met David Ruggles, an Abolitionist, who sheltered Frederick until his marriage to Anna. Before the ceremony, Frederick changed his surname from Bailey to Douglass. The couple then moved to New Bedford, Massachusetts.

Douglass began reading the *Liberator,* an Abolitionist newspaper, and frequenting Anti-Slavery meetings, and on one occasion was unexpectedly called upon to describe his former enslavement. The audience included some of the most prominent Abolitionists: William Lloyd Garrison, Wendell Phillips, and William Collins. After hearing Douglass' story in such a rich and powerful voice, and seeing his towering, erect, posture, which illustrated dignity and strength, the other Abolitionists urged him to become and anti-slavery lecturer.

Frederick Douglass became the most influential voice against slavery in the United States. His enunciation and command of the English language armed him with profound and persuasive arguments that he reinforced with a quick wit and vivid imagery to describe the horror of slavery. So eloquent were his speeches that the public began to question if this well-versed man was ever really a slave. At the risk of capture, and to remove all doubts about him, he published an account of his experience; *Narrative of the Life of Frederick Douglass* was published in 1845.

Because this detailed account jeopardized his freedom, Douglass was forced to go abroad and remain there for two years. He lived and lectured in England, thus gaining international recognition for the American Abolition cause. Upon his return, he legally secured his freedom and launched his own newspaper, the *North Star* with Martin R. Delany. The two reformers used the publication to speak out against slavery and advocate for women's rights. The paper's name was later changed to *Frederick Douglass' Paper*. He moved to Washington, D.C. and entered public service and the diplomatic corps through various high-level federal appointments. With all that Frederick Douglass was, on every avenue he traveled, he continued to speak out against injustices of every kind when and wherever he found them.

The "Dozens" is a verbal ritual played by African American youths, which includes, but is not limited to, speaking negatively about someone's family members, coming up with outlandish, highly exaggerated, and humorous "insults." It has also been called "playing the dozens," "sounding," "jonsing," and "wolfing." The dozens is most popular among adolescent boys who usually perform in front of a neutral audience of friends, associates, classmates, or anyone else who understands the goals and rules of the insult ritual. The group openly comments on the performance of each player, judging their relative abilities and urging them on:

"He's talking about YOUR mama so bad, he's making ME mad!"

The objective of the dozens is twofold. First, one must outtalk one's competitor, thereby getting the most laughs from the audience participants. And secondly, one must not loose emotional control. No respect is given to emotionalism that escalates into a fight. The fundamental rule is that the insult must not be literally true because truth takes the group out of the realm of "performance art" into reality. Since the insults are too outlandish to be true, no offence can be taken and no fight can be started. Although the dozens could end in violence, it is not the planned or even the preferred end to which the ritual wants to avail itself.

The players must develop the ability to remain poised and master the verbal dexterity to respond quickly and creatively to their opponent's insults without becoming angry. To be sure, violence is always a possibility, but it hardly ever happens. Resorting to violence would be a sharp break with the rules governing the ritual, and whoever breaks with the rules in that manner is the automatic looser. When players lost the game, it showed that they had exhausted all verbal skills.

The exact origin of "the dozens" is uncertain. In many ways it seems to resemble traditional African "joking relationships" and draws heavily on African oral tradition. Since the dozens incorporates an element of joke telling, like "signifying," "rapping," and "toasting," playing the dozens reinforces the high value black Americans place on verbal skills. Like the joke, the insult is never based in truth. Once truth enters the performance or the joke telling, its life is ended.

167

The history of the term "the dozens" may have originated during slavery, wherein slave auctioneers sold old or infirmed slaves in lots of twelve. Thus slaves sold in lots of a dozen were "defective merchandize" or were inferior in some way. The ritual itself is in no way connected to slavery. However, because of the entertainment factor, it could conceivably resemble a minstrel show in that jokes are performed by a few for the entertainment benefit of an audience.

What usually happens in playing the dozens is that it evolves into a higher form of "stand-up" comedy, which might not include the ritual insult. It can become a battle of wits in which the youths will make self-deprecating remarks. They try to make the most humorously, derogatory comments about themselves, while trying to top their competitor. It becomes a hilarious game of one-up-man-ship and the rules are nearly the same. Whoever is judged to be the most humorously self-deprecating, will win:

1st Person: **"We are so poor, we have to sleep six to a bed!"**
2nd Person: **"You have a bed!?"**

With the high level of comedic sophistication shown by stand-up comedians like Bill Cosby and Sinbad, and the quick wit shown by D.L. Hughley and Chris Rock, we are not left to imagine that they must have been very good at "Playing the Dozens."

CHARLES DREW (1904-1950)

C harles Richard Drew was a world-renowned surgeon, medical scientist, educator and authority on the preservation of blood. His research led to significant discovery in the techniques for separating and preserving blood and advancing work with blood plasma. This discovery revolutionized blood storage and blood transfusions. His pioneering endeavors in the field of blood plasma preservation left mankind an important legacy – the Blood Bank.

Born on June 3, 1904, in Washington, D.C., he was the eldest of five children born to Charles and Nora Drew. He was an outstanding athlete and scholar. In 1922 Drew graduated from Dunbar High School lettering in four sports (football, basketball, swimming, and track). Aided by an athletic scholarship and part-time work as a waiter, he graduated with high academic honors from Amherst College in 1926. Drew went on to become an instructor of biology, chemistry, and Athletic Director at Morgan State College in Baltimore, Maryland.

Drew applied to attend Howard Medical School but was denied entrance because he lacked credits in English. Now wanting to wait to acquire the credits, he enrolled in McGill University Medical School in Montreal, Ontario, Canada in 1928. Because of his brilliant scholarship, he was inducted into a Medical Honorary Society. It was at McGill that he became interested in blood research. Because of his discipline and enthusiasm for science, Drew was invited to work as an assistant on a blood research project. He received his Doctor of Medicine degree in 1933.

After internships at the Royal Victoria Hospital and the Montreal General Hospital, he taught at Howard University's Medical School. Later, he researched a process for blood preservation at Columbia Presbyterian Hospital in New York City. During his two years at Columbia, Dr. Drew developed a technique for the long-term preservation of blood plasma. His technique involved dehydrating blood and reconstituting it with water before it was to be transfused. He also earned his Doctor of Science in Medicine degree in 1940 with a brilliant dissertation entitled "Banked Blood."

The importance of Drew's research was underscored by the fact that Europe was at war and thousands of soldiers who would have been mortally wounded prior to his discoveries were saved. During World War II, England suffered heavy casualties and called upon Drew to initiate its military blood bank system. He introduced preserved blood plasma on the battlefield. His process for preserving blood and shipping it over great distances greatly helped the British who were being heavily bombarded by the Germans. This system worked so well that the British asked Drew to organize the world's first mass blood bank project.

In 1941, the American Red Cross (ARC) appointed Drew director of its first Blood Bank. However, the ARC's decision to follow the War Department's directive to separate blood by race caused Drew to resign his position. He called the order a "stupid blunder." This issue caused widespread controversy. He further stated that "the blood of individual human beings may differ by blood groupings, but there is absolutely no scientific basis to indicate any difference according to race." Following that incident Dr. Drew returned to Howard University to teach surgery at its medical school, where he was named Chief Surgeon.

Dr. Drew died as a result of an automobile accident while on a trip to a medical meeting at the Tuskegee Institute in 1950. The irony of his death was that he could have been saved if he had received immediate medical attention following the accident. Discrimination by the nearby white hospital did not allow Drew the blood transfusion needed to save his life. He had devoted his life to research that could have prevented his death, but was denied access to the practical application of his own methods and procedures. But Dr. Charles Drew yet lives in the annals of medical history; and today, every blood bank in the world is a living memorial to his genius.

W.E.B. DUBOIS (1868-1963)

W E.B. Dubois was one of America's most brilliant scholars. His talents allowed him to carry many labels: educator, historian, sociologist, philosopher, and civil rights activist. Dubois was a professor of Greek, Latin, German, English, Economics, and History. He authored over one hundred books, articles, and poems; he edited publications on virtually every aspect of African American history, life, and culture. But his place in history was earned when he became the first African American to receive a PhD from the premier institution of higher learning in the United States, Harvard University.

He was born William Edward Burghardt Dubois on February 23, 1868, the only child of Alfred and Mary Silvina Dubois, in Great Barrington, Massachusetts. From early childhood, Dubois exhibited a remarkable intellect. He was the only black graduate from Great Barrington High School in 1884. In 1888 he received a B.A. from the prestigious Fisk University. In 1890, he earned another B.A., cum laude, in 1891 a Masters Degree, and finally a Ph.D. in 1895, all from Harvard University. In 1896, he married Nina Gomer, a former student, and later had two children. His daughter, Yolande, was briefly married to the talented African American poet and Harlem Renaissance celebrity, Countee Cullen.

With truth, intellect, and the vigor of his pen, Dubois' entire life was spent trying to unbind the enslaving shackles of racism and prejudice. He introduced his first work of importance, "The Suppression of the African Slave Trade" in 1896. It was 335 pages long and required voluminous research that he supported with abundant footnotes, lengthy appendices, and a fifteen-page bibliography. It became an indispensable source for the study of the Transatlantic Slave Trade. His was the first study of scientific importance by an African American on the social conditions affecting blacks.

Dubois received even greater acclaim as a great American essayist when he authored "The Souls of Black Folk" in 1903. It became the classic of the times and was widely quoted. In it, he identified "the color line" as the twentieth century's central problem, and dismissed the philosophy of accommodation advocated by Booker T. Washington. All of Dubois' scholarly works would adhere to his profound idea of "seeking the truth on the pure assumption that it is worth seeking." He was such a fierce antagonist of racial injustice and a great leader of protest that he can truly be called an authentic American radical. Dr. Dubois founded the Niagara Movement in 1905 that later became the National Association for the Advancement of Colored People (NAACP). For many years he edited its journal, "Crisis." He always espoused and associated with movements that advocated immediate and full citizenship rights for blacks.

Increasingly, Dr. Dubois looked beyond American race relations to international economics and politics. In 1915 he wrote "The Negro," a sociological examination of the African Diaspora. In 1919, he led the Pan-Africa Congress in Paris to focus world opinion on the problems of black people everywhere. He urged Great Britain to give governmental rights to its colonies in Africa and the West Indies. Throughout the 1930s and 1940s he became one of most controversial black leaders in the United States. During the 1950s he was the leader of the World Peace Information Center that held close ties to the Communist Party. His association with it led to his indictment as an unregistered foreign agent. He was acquitted but his open sympathies toward the Soviet Union caused the U.S. State Department to bar him from foreign travel until 1958.

In 1960 Dr. Dubois accepted an invitation to long-time friend, Kwame Nkrumah's inauguration as the first president of Ghana in West Africa. He remained there to live out his life. In 1963 Dubois wired Dr. Martin Luther King, Jr. a message that was read at the historic March on Washington. Sadly, just days later, he succumbed to his ninety-five years of life and died as a citizen of Ghana. W.E.B. Dubois was an intellectual giant. The scope of his interest, the depth of his insight, and the sheer majesty of his prolific writings bespeak a level of genius unequaled even among scholars in these modern times.

PAUL LAURENCE DUNBAR (1872-1906)

P aul Laurence Dunbar was the first African American literary figure to achieve national and international recognition, appealing to both black and white audiences. His writing contains powerful nuances that still move readers. His popularity was based in part on his ability to write in dialect, through which he captured black folk speech.

> *Gloom tu'ns into gladness...joy drives out de doubt*
> *when the oven do' is opened, An' de smell comes po'in out*

He was born the son of two former slaves in Dayton, Ohio on June 27, 1872. He was taught to read by his mother, Matilda Murphy Dunbar, and he absorbed her homespun wisdom. His father, Joshua Dunbar, who had escaped from slavery in Kentucky, and served in the famous Massachusetts 55th Regiment during the Civil War, also lavished stories on him. While Paul himself was never enslaved, he was one of the last generations to have ongoing contact with those who had been. Thus he was steeped in the oral tradition during his formative years and he would go on to become a powerful interpreter of the African American folk experience in literature and song. He would also champion the cause of civil rights and higher education for blacks in essays and poetry that were militant by the standards of his day.

> *So you see de Lawd's intention, Evah sence the worl' began*
> *Was dat His almighty freedom should belong to evah man.*

Dunbar attended the public schools of Dayton. During his years at Central High School, he was the only student of color. But he distinguished himself in many other ways. He was class president, editor-in-chief of the school paper, president of the literary society, and class poet. His poetry grew more sophisticated with his repeated readings of John Keats and William Wordsworth. Later he added American poets John Greenleaf Whittier, Henry Wadsworth Longfellow, and James Whitcomb Riley to his list of favorites as he searched for his own poetic voice that would lead him to incorporate the voices of his parents and the stories they told him. After high school graduation in 1891 Dunbar could not find work in journalism. He took a job as an elevator operator in a Dayton hotel but continued to write poetry.

Dunbar became well known as the "elevator boy poet" after a reading at the

Western Association of Writers, held in Dayton in 1892.In 1893 he self-published his first volume of poetry, *Oak and Ivy*. Later that year he obtained the patronage of Frederick Douglass after their meeting at the World's Columbian Exposition in Chicago. He became a crossover literary sensation with the publication of *Majors and Minors* (1895) and *Lyrics of Lowly Life* (1896). During his lifetime, he published eleven volumes of poetry, and many other fictional works and short stories. In 1898 Dunbar married Alice Ruth Moore and they became a celebrated literary couple during their brief marriage. But the effects of tuberculosis and alcoholism caused the couple to separate permanently in 1902. They had no children but remained close friends even until Dunbar's early demise at age thirty-four.

While Dunbar sought an appropriate literary form for the representation of the African American vernacular expression, he was deeply ambivalent about the critical acclaim this area of his work received. His poetry in Standard English verse was never able to transcend the genius of his dialect poetry. Lines from *The Poet*, one of his last poems bespeak his profound melancholia:

> *He sang of life serenely sweet,*
> *With, now and then, a deeper note,*
> *From some high peak, nigh yet remote,*
> *He voiced the world's absorbing beat,*
> *He sang of love when earth was young,*
> *And love itself was in his lays,*
> *But, ah, the world it turned to praise*
> *A jingle in a broken tongue.*

KATHERINE DUNHAM (1909-2006)

Katherine Dunham was one of the most popular and historically important dancer-choreographers of the 20th century. She led a dance troupe that performed African, African American, and Caribbean dance movements to diverse audiences throughout the world from the 1930s through the 1960s. Dunham helped to lay the foundation and provided innovations during the formative years of modern dance.

There are conflicting dates as to when Dunham was born. But she was born in Glyn Ellen, Illinois, a suburb of Chicago, in 1909 or 1910. She was the second of two children born to her parents, Albert Dunham who was of Malagasy and West African descent; and Fanny Taylor Dunham of French-Canadian and Indian ancestry. Her mother died when Katherine was very young, leaving her and a brother, as well as two older children from a previous marriage. Left with relatives while her father traveled as a salesman, Katherine developed an interest in the performing arts.

Dunham grew up in Joliet and attended local schools. She graduated from Joliet High School and Joliet Junior College. She later became one of the first African Americans to attend the University of Chicago where she earned bachelor, master, and doctoral degrees in anthropology, specializing in dance. She paid her way through school by giving dance lessons and working as an assistant librarian. A Rosenwald Fellowship supported her in graduate school. Aided by a Guggenheim Fellowship, Dunham completed groundbreaking work in Caribbean and Brazilian dance anthropology, launching a new academic discipline. She did more than study Afro-Caribbean cultures she literally absorbed them. She was one of the first Americans to appreciate the aesthetic beauty of voodoo ritual and its implication for dance anthropology. And she became an avowed mystic and devotee in the process.

In 1931 Dunham established her first dance school in Chicago. She made her dancing debut in 1933 in the ballet, *La Guiablese*. And in 1934, she began one of the most successful dance careers in the history of American and European theater. It led her to leading roles in musicals, operas, cabarets, and films. Her own ballet, *L'Ag 'Ya,* based on a fight dance from Martinique, was accepted by the Federal Works Progress Administration and performed in 1936 in Chicago. In 1937, she established her first ensemble company with fifteen dancers while serving as director of the New York Labor Stage.

Dunham set out for the Caribbean in 1936. While traveling in Martinique, Jamaica, Trinidad, and Haiti, she observed firsthand some of the dances that African slaves brought to the New World. Based on her fieldwork in the Caribbean, Dunham published: Katherine Dunham's *Journey to Accompong* (1946), about a maroon society that had escaped to the Blue Mountains of Jamaica. She followed with a second book in 1947 based on subsequent research in Haiti on the influence of Haitian culture and history on dance. She also ran a dance studio in New York City from 1945 to 1955.

Dunham also created dance innovations based on her research in both Afro-Caribbean dance and cultural anthropology. She perfected a new dance technique called "dance-isolation." It involved the movement of one part of the body while other parts were kept stationary. Her work has also included a considerable element of theatricality, which has been both praised and criticized, and has been mislabeled as primitive. But her dance philosophy has always suggested the primal in the sense she believes that everyone needs movement, as in dance, to live. In short, she believed then, as she believes now, that dance is liberating.

With a PhD in anthropology, Katherine Dunham took a scholarly approach to ethnic dance. Her dance concerts were fluid, kinetic, and esthetically exciting. They were based on a profound understanding of the peoples and cultures represented in the dance, and her keen knowledge of social values and human psychology. Katherine Dunham was truly the most competent modern dance innovator of all time.

JEAN-BAPTISTE POINTE DUSABLE (c. 1745-1818)

Jean-Baptiste Pointe DuSable established a fur trading post in the 1770s on Lake Michigan in Illinois. It was the area that would come to be known as the city of Chicago. The site where he constructed his log house, on the southwest shore of Lake Michigan, is accepted as the original settlement of Chicago. DuSable conducted a thriving business throughout his career as an explorer, trapper, and trader in the Northwest Territory.

DuSable was born in St. Marc on the French colonial island of Saint-Domingue, which is present day Haiti. His mother was an enslaved African and his father was French sailor. After his mother's death, his father sent him to Paris to be educated. He received an excellent Catholic education in France and came to greatly esteem European art. In his later years, he was a collector of fine French art. As a young adult, he worked aboard his father's ships as a seaman for a few years. At age twenty he was shipwrecked in the Gulf of Mexico. It was at that point that DuSable entered North America through the Spanish-controlled port city of New Orleans.

DuSable had to be hidden by Jesuit priests on the outskirts of New Orleans until he recuperated from the ordeal of being shipwrecked. As a black man, he was fearful of being enslaved. So he sailed up the Mississippi River to get out of Southern slave territory and to explore the Northwest Territory that was controlled by France. It was on the unsettled North American frontier that the DuSable adventure began. By the 1760s he had become a trailblazing figure of heroic proportions. He was tall, dark, and possessed striking features. From his Paris education, he became quite polished. For ten years he traveled by horse and small caravan through the forests and immense prairies as far north as the Great Lakes. He was able to journey so far and endure such difficult conditions because of the great friendships he made with various Native American indigenous peoples.

DuSable married into and remained a good friend of the Illinois Indians. He lived with and later married a Pottawatomie Indian woman named Kittihawa. The couple had two children, a son and a daughter. But they were not married before a priest until 1788. It was then that Kittihawa was given the Christian name of Catherine. The couple also had a host of notable friends. Included among them were Chief Pontiac of Michigan, and Kentucky woodsman, Daniel Boone. DuSable was more than a frontier fur trapper. He was known for his easy relationships with red and white men. But he must have maneuvered with the skill of an experienced diplomat as he witnessed Illinois slip from French to British to United States control within a short span of twenty-one years.

The French lost the Northwest Territory to the British during the French and Indian War (1756-1763). In Europe it was called the "War for Empire." As Great Britain, France, Spain, and the Netherlands warred with each other in Europe it put their overseas colonies in constant jeopardy. Great Britain acquired the Dutch Colony of New Amsterdam, renaming it New York. It also won from France the Northwest Territory, which included Illinois where DuSable had settled. Great Britain had essentially won the war for overseas empire, only to later have its North American Colonies fight them for independence during the American Revolution (1776-1783).

As a Frenchman in a land recently taken by the British, DuSable fell under suspicion. He was arrested by invading British troops and detained for many months as a probable French agent during the French and Indian War. It was local Indians that demanded and obtained his release. At the end of those hostiles, DuSable returned to trapping and trading with the Indians. He was again arrested by the British during the American Revolution for "treasonable intercourse with the enemy." For his commerce with the rebellious North American colonists, British soldiers curtailed his activities and limited his movements to a settlement on the St. Charles River. But this well-educated, urbane, highly capable frontiersman soon impressed even the British.

DuSable stood in awe of the wilderness area on the Southwest shore of Lake Michigan. The Native Americans called it "Eschikagou." It was later translated to "Chicago" by the American traders. In 1774, DuSable built a trading post there and by 1779 it was a thriving business, teeming with Indian and white traders alike. His store and home swelled to include a 40 x 22 foot log cabin, a bake house, a dairy, a smokehouse, a poultry house, a workshop, a barn, and a mill. DuSable made his primary living as a trader, but he was also the local miller and cooper, a farmer, a trapper, and an explorer. He also purchased and developed 800 acres of land in Peoria, but Chicago remained his great love and he lived there until 1800.

DuSable was always closely aligned with the Indians of the region. But in 1800, he lost a bid to be elected tribal chief. Because he was growing older, or because he was defeated in the election for tribal chief, or perhaps because he was now a grandfather, DuSable decided to sell his Chicago home and trading station. He and Kittihawa moved into his daughter's new home in St. Charles, Missouri. For the sale of his property and houses alone, DuSable received

$1200. In separate trades, he also sold thirty head of cattle, thirty-eight pigs, two mules, and hundreds of chickens. He became even wealthier after the sale of all his goods, which included many French works of art. Real Estate records suggest that DuSable lived in St. Charles at least from 1805 until 1814. Sadly though, as old age overtook him, he did have to seek public relief. DuSable died in 1818, and true to his faith, he was buried in the Catholic Borromeo Cemetery in St. Charles, Missouri.

The Jean-Baptiste Pointe DuSable story is just one of the many amazing narratives of eighteenth century Africans in America. He found success first living on the peripheries of Native American societies and then as an entrepreneur, trading with various white and native groups. He was the epitome of the creolization that took place in the Americas. For in DuSable were the three cultures linked. The red, white, and black, and all of them melding into the free enterprise system of capitalism that has since come to represent the American Way.

The "Ethiopian Regiment" was the name given to runaway slaves who fought for the British during the American Revolutionary War. Blacks had frequently participated in wars against the French and the Indians, thus developing a tradition of military service that was still strong at the time of the War for Independence. Hostilities between the British and their thirteen rebellious North American Colonies began as early as 1770 when Crispus Attucks, a black man, became the first American patriot to die for the cause of liberty in the Boston Massacre.

But in the fall of 1775, while General George Washington was moving to officially bar further black enlistment in the Continental Army, his British counterpart, John Murray, the Earl of Dunsmore, was designing another tactic. Lord Dunsmore issued a formal proclamation that granted freedom to all slaves and indentured servants if they were willing to bear arms for His Majesty, King George III. It was a stroke of genius and a savvy plan to make a shambles of the American economy, and to fill out the British ranks with slaves who were essentially fighting for their lives. And without slaves to guard their homes and do all manual labor, patriot farmers would be forced to desert the Continental Army and return to their homes to safeguard their property and protect their families.

In issuing this proclamation to slaves, Lord Dunsmore could disrupt production in the thirteen American colonies by procuring a body of soldiers who were fighting for their own personal liberty and leaving the Americans short-handed in the process. He called his recruits the "Ethiopian Regiment." Many white Americans feared that the Dunsmore proclamation would spark a full-scale slave insurrection. History has recorded far more isolated slave rebellions than slaveholders had ever wanted to admit. The main slave resistance technique was to run away. But instead of a slave insurrection, the Dunsmore proclamation created an elite, fierce, fighting force of black soldiers that defeated the patriots in almost every battle.

Although Washington had 1,000,000 able-bodies patriots that could have been soldiers for the American cause, he was never able to recruit more than 50,000 at any given time. And at least 5,000 of his solders were blacks fighting heroically on the patriot side. But because of the creation of the Ethiopian Regiment, possibly ten times that many blacks fought for the British on the loyalist side. Two thousand came from the Virginia Colony. While Dunsmore's proclamation never sparked a full-scale slave insurrection, it did cause a flood of slaves to file into British camps. Although Lord Dunsmore was the Royal Governor of the Virginia Colony, his offer of freedom for slaves was good in all the other colonies. And blacks from all thirteen donned the British uniform and proudly wore their "redcoat" to mark the change of status.

Because of the idea of slaves taking up arms against their former owners raised such a specter in the minds of southern planters, those who had been uncommitted to either side suddenly began to support the patriot cause. Even irate northern patriots in New York burned Dunsmore in effigy. And as for Washington, a Virginia slaveholder on his very large Mount Vernon estate, the thought of blacks armed against whites was beyond terrifying. The Ethiopian Regiment threatened the very foundation of the entire plantation system. Many of the slaves answering Dunsmore's call were skilled in the jobs that made a plantation run efficiently. As the commander-in-chief of the Continental Army, Washington knew that Dunsmore had a workable plan, and that it made him the most formidable enemy that America had.

For the many free blacks who considered themselves patriots, and for some whites as well, Dunsmore's clever gambit underscored the contradiction of racial enslavement within the patriot cause and made them look to broaden the bounds of the American Revolution. One of the most interesting outcomes of the war, and the most advantageous to blacks, was that slavery was effectively ended in the North. As new state constitutions were drafted, only the southern states clung tenaciously to slavery. It would take another hard-fought war to end the institution of slavery in what would become the United States of America.

DUKE ELLINGTON (1899-1974)

Duke Ellington was the world's foremost composer and arranger. He was also a pianist, orchestra leader, and was one of the founding fathers of Jazz music. In his lifetime, Ellington was recognized as the composer and performer who possessed a level of sophistication unparalleled in the history of Jazz.

He was born Edward Kennedy Ellington in Washington, D.C. on April 29, 1899. His parents, James Edward Ellington and Daisy Kennedy Ellington encouraged his creative expression by providing him with piano lessons at age seven. But he was largely self-taught, and by age twelve he was composing quality music. The black schools in D.C. provided him with an education at elementary, middle, and high school levels. He excelled in sports and fine arts. He was awarded a scholarship to the Pratt Institute of Applied Arts in Brooklyn, but he chose to pursue a music career instead.

Ellington was nicknamed the "Duke" by boyhood friend, Edgar McEntree, who admired his regal air and also encouraged Ellington's piano playing. His earliest influences were the ragtime pianists. He came under the tutelage of prominent Washington musicians at local theaters and cafes. He composed *Soda Fountain Rag* at age fifteen. He made his professional debut at age seventeen. In 1918 he married Edna Thompson. Their son, Mercer, continued the orchestra after his father's death. Fats Waller encouraged Ellington to return to New York in 1923 after not having much success there the year before.

Ellington's ensemble finally began to be recognized in New York, securing a downtown engagement at Club Hollywood. For the *Okeh* and *RCA Victor* recording labels, he composed and recorded such works as *Creole Love Call*, *Black and Tan Fantasy*, *Black Beauty*, and *The Mooch*. Between 1927 and 1928 the core of the Ellington Orchestra was formed. In 1927, after King Oliver unwisely turned down Harlem's Cotton Club, Ellington secured the engagement using the name "Duke Ellington Orchestra." During those formative Cotton Club years, he developed his signature style that would quickly bring him worldwide success. By 1929, the Duke Ellington Orchestra had been heard on nationwide radio and had participated in a film, *Black and Tan,* for which Ellington had composed the music.

During the 1930s, Ellington appeared in such films as *Check and Double Check, A Day at the Races*, and *A Cabin in the Sky*. He composed one of his most celebrated compositions, *Mood Indigo*. He became and international celebrity by twice touring Europe. He composed pieces for the film *Symphony in Black*. And in 1939, Ellington began his musical association with the legendary Billy Strayhorn, who became his principal musical collaborator for more than twenty-five years. The most recognizable of the Ellington-Strayhorn collaboration was his orchestra's signature pieces, *Take the A Train*, and *Satin Doll*. In the 1950s Ellington wrote the complete musical score for the film, *Anatomy of a Murder*.

Ellington brought a level of style and sophistication to Jazz that had not been seen before. Although he was a gifted piano player, he used his orchestra as his principal instrument. He composed and arranged music that gave everyone in the orchestra a chance to express himself. And he was a prolific composer. There are hundreds of compositions to his credit, including suites, concertos, and movie scores. His adaptability and ability to grow with the times kept the Duke Ellington Orchestra a major force in Jazz until his death in 1974. Even today, his memory lingers on and is an inspiration for all Jazz musicians.

Duke Ellington's career spanned more than sixty years. His style was so timeless that it outlived Ragtime, his first musical inspiration. It outlived the Swing music of the Big Band Era, where he earned his first musical success. It crossed boundaries in that it was, and is yet today, disseminated all over the world. His music is still recognized as uniquely his. He had a unique genius for instrumental combinations, Jazz improvisation, and arranging that brought the world that inimitable "Ellington Sound," and it found consummate expression in the music that celebrated the African American experience.

RALPH ELLISON (1914-1994)

alph Ellison was a teacher and modernist author whose novel, *Invisible Man*, gained wide critical success in 1952. On the strength of his first and only, seminal writing, he was catapulted to national and international acclaim. It won the National Book Award in 1953. In 1965 literary critics named it one of the most important works of the 20th century.

He was born Ralph Waldo Ellison in Okalahoma City. His well read father, Lewis Albert Ellison, an ice and coal vendor and construction worker, named him after the famous American poet and philosopher, Ralph Waldo Emerson. His mother, Ida Millsap Ellison, had to support herself and the children by working as a domestic after her husband was killed in an accident. Mrs. Ellison was also a socialist and political activist who was arrested on several occasions for violating state segregation laws.

Even though Ellison attended segregated public schools, he viewed the United States as a land of infinite opportunity and was influenced early on by the myth of the American frontier. He lived in a close-knit black community that supplied him with images of courage for his later writings and inclined him toward music. In high school, he was the first chair trumpet player. With the help of a music scholarship, he studied at the Tuskegee Institute in Alabama from 1933 to 1936. However, he dropped out to pursue a career in art.

Ellison moved to New York City to study sculpture, but again abandoned his plans after a chance meeting with Langston Hughes and Richard Wright. They encouraged him to pursue writing and led him to join the Federal Writers' Project. He collected black folklore stories and oral histories from the elderly. He also began writing essays and short stories for various periodicals. He became an editor for the *Negro Quarterly* before starting his novel. His writing was greatly influenced by Ernest Hemingway, George Bernard Shaw, and T.S. Elliott.

Refusing to enlist in a segregated army, Ellison served in the Merchant Marines as a cook from 1943 to 1945. He did not begin writing *Invisible Man* until after the war. From the 1930s to the 1950s he wrote primarily short stories and essays. *Invisible Man* made him an instant celebrity. The mentoring friendship Ellison had developed with Wright soured as Ellison gradually rejected Wright's aesthetic and communist politics. But he matured into a style that was uniquely his own.

Invisible Man was a milestone in American literature. It remained on the bestseller list for sixteen weeks, establishing Ellison as one of the key writers of the century. And it continues to engage readers today. It tells a story of a nameless African American, who is losing his sense of identity in a world of prejudice and hostility. He feverishly journeys from one experience to another, from the South to the North. It describes the character as growing up in a black community in the South, attending a black college from which he is expelled, moving to New York and becoming the chief spokesman of the Harlem branch of the *Brotherhood*, and retreating, amid violence and confusion, to the basement lair of the invisible man he imagines himself to be.

Ellison combined his writing career with teaching and lecturing on various college campuses. From 1970 to 1980 he was the Albert Schweitzer Professor at New York University (NYU). Honorary doctorates were bestowed upon him from Harvard and Wesleyan, and presidential citations from Richard M. Nixon and Ronald Reagan. Ralph Ellison was controversial, stating that blacks were shaped more by the American experience than the African. He was a modernist writer who could masterfully synthesize the black experience into the black identity. He retired from teaching but continued the work on his second novel, *Juneteenth*, for forty years. It was published posthumously in 1999.

EMANCIPATION PROCLAMATION

The Emancipation Proclamation stands as the most unique document in American History. It is the first official United States document to mention the words "slave" or "slavery." The United States Constitution never explicitly stated those words in print until it abolished slavery with the enactment of the Thirteenth Amendment. When the Constitution spoke of "citizens" it meant white males. When it spoke of "others" it meant black people in general and slaves in particular. The distinctiveness of the Emancipation Proclamation lies in the fact that it never really freed any slaves. And the irony of the document lies in the fact that slavery still existed at the end of the Civil War, but only in the North.

President Abraham Lincoln signed the Emancipation Proclamation into law on January 1, 1863. As it dryly stated, "all slaves within any State, or designated part of a State, then in rebellion, shall be then, thenceforward, and forever free." The states affected were enumerated in the proclamation. Specifically exempted were slaves in parts of the South already held by Union armies. When Lincoln issued the proclamation, two years after the Civil War began; it marked a bold departure from his policy to merely save the Union.

Even before the issuance of the Emancipation Proclamation Lincoln knew that there were many reasons it could not be enforced in the rebel states. The South was no longer part of the United States and Lincoln was no longer their president were the two most obvious reasons. The eleven seceding states were now the Confederate States of America. Immediately after the confirmation of the election of Lincoln as president, South Carolina led the secession and her ten confederate sister-states followed. By March 11, 1861, all eleven states had unanimously ratified a permanent constitution similar to that of the U.S., selected Jefferson Davis of Mississippi as president and Alexander Stephens of Georgia as vice president; and had installed a bicameral legislature.

When Lincoln issued the Emancipation Proclamation, he did so not as the U.S. President, but as the Commander-In-Chief of the U.S. military. As a U.S. President he had no authority over another sovereign nation, which is what the South had become. But as Commander-In-Chief of the military, he could make the proclamation an enforceable war aim. He described the proclamation as a "fit and necessary war measure." In the last paragraph, Lincoln wrote that it was "sincerely believed to be an act of justice warranted by the Constitution upon military necessity." What the proclamation explicitly did was to expand the ranks of northern enlistment to include black soldiers and sailors for the first time during the war. More than 186,000 black men fought under the Union flag. Up to that point the North had not shown itself to be a superior fighting force and was well on the way to loosing the war.

Many historians regard the Emancipation Proclamation as one of the great documents of state. But many more historians discount it as the document that actually freed the slaves. If the document was essentially a war measure, like Lincoln said, it had the desired effect of creating confusion in the South and depriving the Confederacy of much of its valuable labor force. If it was a diplomatic document, it succeeded in rallying to the Northern cause thousands of English and European laborers who were anxious to see all workers gain their freedom throughout the world. But if it was a humanitarian document, it gave hope to millions of blacks that a better day laid ahead. And it renewed the faith of thousands of antislavery crusaders who had fought long and hard to win freedom in America.

So, what was the significance of the Emancipation Proclamation if it did not really free the slaves? Why then do we as African Americans celebrate it every January in our churches? It is simply this: that for the first time in U.S. history, the proclamation openly committed a U.S. president and the federal government to the long-term fight for the eradication of slavery. And that fight came to fruition only with the ratification of the Thirteenth Amendment to the U.S. Constitution on December 4, 1865.

JAMES REESE EUROPE (1881-1919)

J ames Reese Europe was an African American bandleader, arranger, composer, and the most influential musician at the turn of the 20th century. While serving in World War I, he was the bandmaster of the glorious 369th Infantry, an African American regiment. He was also a major figure in the transition era of ragtime to jazz, and the inspiration for the beautiful music of American composer, George Gershwin.

James Reese Europe was born in Mobile, Alabama on February 22, 1881. His parents were both musicians and instilled the love of music into their children. At age ten, Europe moved with his family to Washington, D.C., where he studied violin and piano with the assistant director of the Marine Corps Band, Enrico Hurlei. The family lived just doors from John Phillip Sousa. Sousa and the Marine Band long claimed a tight relationship with Washington's black community. Many if the band members taught other promising black children. Europe and his sister Mary entered a music-writing contest when he was fourteen and he came in second to her.

In 1904, Europe moved to New York City to continue his musical studiers. He became a favorite on the club scene, playing piano in cabarets. He also played and directed on Broadway for shows starring black comedian, Bert Williams. Europe became the band director for the famous dance duo, Vernon and Irene Castle. He was instrumental in helping the couple develop their most famous dance creation, the Fox Trot. In 1910 Europe founded one of the most unusual African American organizations of that time. The Clef Club was unique in that it was part fraternal organization and part union. The Clef Club purchased a building on West 53rd Street that served as both a club and a booking office.

Under Europe's leadership, the Clef Club functioned as a clearinghouse for all types of entertainers. It was also actively involved in improving the working conditions of all entertainers and musicians. The Clef Club proved exceptionally successful, generating over $100,000 a year in bookings at its height. With Europe as conductor, the Clef Club Orchestra appeared at Carnegie Hall annually from 1912 to 1914. The Carnegie Hall concerts gave the orchestra respectability with white audiences. And with those engagements, Europe achieved professional notice as a composer and conductor.

As World War I was progressing, Europe enlisted as a private, but was

189

promoted to Lieutenant after passing the officer's exam. His commander realized the importance of parades, music, and marching bands in establishing morale. He asked Europe to create the finest band in United States Army history. It was to be attached to the newly formed all-black 369th Infantry Division. Upon arriving in France, the band was given orders to entertain troops too infirmed for duty. When American entertainment organizers got word that Europe was in France, the band played in many places. Europe's musical style was really quite simple – jazz up the familiar favorites, and bring down the house.

In the last months of the war, Europe's concerts held Allied audiences spellbound. Once his band played to 50,000 people. But it was nothing compared to he rousing homecoming the marching band of the 369th Infantry received as they paraded up Fifth Avenue and on home to Harlem. Europe then returned to civilian life in the same role that he had left composer and bandleader. He began to prepare a national tour for the 369th Infantry Band. But sadly, a drummer stabbed him to death because Europe had given him a severe reprimand during a strenuous rehearsal.

It is not unfair to speculate that the whole history of jazz might have been different had James Reese Europe not met a premature death. He had achieved so much in his short life that surely he would have gone on to receive even greater accolades, like the ones that awaited his fellow jazz musicians, Eubie Blake and Noble Sissle. But of all his contemporaries, James Reese Europe's story is perhaps the saddest of all. For at the time of his early death, all that he was to be, had yet to be.

190

An "Exoduster" was an African American who migrated from the South to Kansas and other points west during the post-Reconstruction years following the Civil War. Their journey took them as far west as Oklahoma. But it was the political and social climate of prejudice and racial discrimination that led them to establish all-black townships in Kansas and Oklahoma. As the Compromise of 1877 brought Reconstruction to a close with the withdrawal Federal soldiers from the occupied South, blacks began to face almost as much peril as slavery had caused. Their rights of citizenship were essentially denied as terrorist groups like the Ku Klux Klan and White Citizens Councils erected barriers to acquired freedoms.

African Americans understood that land ownership provided the best economic foundation for political and social independence, yet most were unable to secure acreage for their families. This apparent lack of progress, coupled with organized acts of violence against them, initiated a westward migration movement. In May 1879, blacks from throughout the South gathered in Nashville, Tennessee to discuss the continuing violence against their families. The body of that convention adopted a report that set forth its grievances and its proposed remedies.

The convention also encouraged black people to emigrate to the North and West in search of better living conditions. A group of Mississippi freedmen proposed to move en masse to New Mexico or Arizona. North Carolina blacks circulated pamphlets describing land available in Nebraska under the Homestead Act. Others opted to leave the South for Missouri, Indiana, and Colorado. But the greatest interest centered on Kansas, which became the destination of tens of thousands of refugees from oppression and domestic terrorism. Kansas had been the home of legendary Abolitionist, John Brown, and it had a more progressive reputation than many of the other points of destination.

If nineteenth century blacks understood correctly the Thirteenth, Fourteenth, and Fifteenth Amendments to the United States Constitution, and they indeed did, they knew that they were entitled to freedom, citizenship, and the right to vote. But if they could not enjoy that status, they wanted the government to set aside one of the Territories for their settlement. Although Congress evinced no interest in doing any such thing, blacks throughout the South took up the cry of internal emigration in the late 1870s. Just as enslaved blacks had believed that the North was their promise land, the Exodusters now believed that the West would prove to be their new promise land.

The Kansas migration in 1879 was by far the largest southwest movement of people. Over 40,000 African Americans went to Kansas in less than two years. Nationally prominent black leaders, including Frederick Douglass, opposed the Kansas migration, fearing it amounted to a tacit abandonment of the struggle for citizenship rights in the South. But the movement generated immense excitement among ordinary blacks. Even the name they gave it, "the Exodus," suggested that it tapped deep religious convictions. They drew upon biblical illustration, just as they had done all through slavery, to identify with the children of Israel and their flight from Egypt. History was compelled to repeat itself as African Americans were forced to seek new homes beyond the reign and rule of yet another Pharaoh.

To countless African Americans leaving the oppressive South, the West offered the prospect of political equality, access to education, economic opportunity, freedom from violence, and liberation from the presence of the old slave owning class. The Exodus offered the practical independence that Reconstruction had failed to secure. Few Exodusters found life in the West completely idyllic. Lacking the funds or experience to take up plains farming, blacks settled for menial jobs in western towns. But few, if any, succumbed to disappointment sufficiently enough to return to the South. Blacks were convinced that the whites of the defeated South would stop at nothing to vent their frustrations on blacks that had achieved the status of freemen in America.

WALLACE D. FARD (1877?-1934?)

Wallace D. Fard was the founder of the religious cultural community that evolved in 20th century America known as the Nation of Islam (NOI), a.k.a. the Black Muslims. It was a splinter group of another quasi-religious cult, the Moorish Science Movement founded by Noble Drew Ali.

It was obvious to all who knew him that Fard sprang from humble beginnings. But because his origins were obscure, he made claims that were virtually unverifiable. History has had difficulty tracking his early life because of his use of so many aliases with variant spellings. In 1929 he claimed to be the reincarnation of Noble Drew Ali, thereby adopting the name Farrad Mohammad Ali. He used two aliases that were decidedly western, Wallace Delaney Ford and Wallace Dodd Ford, possibly indicating that he was really African American after all.

History disagrees on the year of Fard's birth. It has been variously reported as 1877 and 1891. Fard's birthplace is also in question. It is usually reported to be Mecca, Arabia. But it could have been in India, England, the West Indies, New Zealand, or Oregon in the United States. By the same token, his ethnicity is also in dispute. Was he from the Kuraishi tribe of Arabia, as he claimed, or was he Indian? Was he of Polynesian descent or was he a British subject? If he was really from Oregon, his racial background must have included Native American. Whatever his ethnicity or heritage, Fard was known to have passed for white when he was arrested in the U.S.

After various encounters with the law, Fard was sentenced to three years in San Quentin Prison for dealing narcotics. Upon his release, he settled in Detroit where he became involved with the Moorish Science Temple. Fard was a door-to-door notion's peddler, selling silks, raincoats, and trinkets to residents of Paradise Valley, a Detroit neighborhood. It was an enclave of African Americans with southern roots who had moved to the industrial north during the Great Migration. Fard identified his wares as those made by African peoples, and satisfied his customers with a sense of cultural identity and stories of a common heritage.

In 1930, after his local popularity grew, Fard announced the formation of the Temple of Islam, which later became Temple #1 of the Nation of Islam. Beside his travelogue and anecdotal stories, he proscribed a diet and a moral code for African Americans to follow. He then began to address deeper theological issues. He cited the Bible, but only to debunk it. He called Christianity "the religion of slave masters" and completely rejected its tenets. Fard espoused Islamic religion with Black Nationalism interjected. He advocated an independent republic of African Americans within the United States. His separatist doctrine depicted whites as "blue-eyed devils" that exploited, oppressed, and even murdered black people.

Fard went on to establish the University of Islam, which was the temple's school. He established a school for young women as well. He also formed the Fruit of Islam, an elite corps of male bodyguards. And he instituted the practice of dropping Western European surnames in favor of an "X" to denote a complete break with white America and the odious slave heritage. All of this, and the fact that the police connected a murder to the NOI, brought Fard under police scrutiny. He was arrested and released, ordered to leave Detroit, and thereafter went into hiding

At some point Fard became even more delusional and began thinking of himself as a deity. Elijah Muhammad, who had formed Temple #2 in Chicago in 1933, asked Fard to state his real name. Fard reportedly answered: "My name is Mahdi; I am God, I came to guide you into the right path that you may be successful and see the hereafter." After a June 1934 meeting with Muhammad, Wallace D. Fard was never seen again. He disappeared from the American scene in 1934, just as mysteriously as he had appeared in 1930, without herald, without fanfare, without a trace.

T he Jubilee Singers were, and remain to this day, a choral group from Fisk University that introduced African American Spirituals to a worldwide audience in the 1870s. And they helped to preserve black work songs, anthems, and spirituals. They were the first internationally acclaimed group of black musicians who attained recognition and fame, and along the way, financed the growth of their school. This group of artists introduced the slaves' song to the world by collecting, archiving, performing, and thus preserving this music from extinction.

George L. White, the vocal-music teacher at Fisk University, founded the Jubilee Singers in 1867. The university itself had been established in 1866 to educate newly freed black slaves. Since few students could afford the tuition, the school needed other sources of revenue to sustain itself. Most students engaged in work-study programs to meet their tuition bills. But it was White who came up with the idea of a performing chorale as a way to raise money for the school itself. It is a music tradition that still continues at Fisk and other historically black colleges.

It was also White who gave the Jubilee Singers their name. In Old Testament history, after the lapse of seven Sabbaths of years (forty-nine years), the trumpet was to sound throughout the entire land, and the fiftieth year was to be proclaimed and hallowed as the Jubilee year. The observance of Jubilee was obligatory upon the Israelites after they had taken possession of the Promised Land and had cultivated the soil for forty-nine years. Every Israelite who through poverty had sold himself into slavery, if he was unable to redeem himself or had not been redeemed by a kinsman was to be set free. To White, the term "Jubilee Singers" seemed most appropriate since most of the students at Fisk University at that time were former slaves

After several successful local appearances in and around the Nashville, Tennessee area, and later in the North and throughout South, the reputation of the chorale ensemble began to spread. In 1871 the singers embarked on a tour of the Northeast United States, performing mainly in churches before white audiences. Within their first decade of touring, the singers had performed throughout the U.S. and Europe. Their repertoire included anthems, popular ballads, and operatic excerpts, but their most popular pieces proved to be African American Spirituals and work songs, which many in their audiences were hearing for the first time.

Highlights of their first tour included a performance before 40,000 people at the World's Peace Jubilee in Boston in 1872 and a concert for President Ulysses S. Grant in Washington, D.C. That first tour was a great success and spurred widespread interest in plantation hymns and other Southern black folk music. The singers eventually performed in European countries, including a performance before Queen Victoria in London, England. The painting by British artist Edmund Havel of the original Jubilee Singers, a ceiling to floor mural, was commissioned by Queen Victoria and still hangs with the university collection in Nashville.

During the Reconstruction era of the American South, black institutions of higher education fielded many groups of singers, quartets, and vocal chorales that were always prepared to sing Negro Spirituals. But the earliest and most famous of these groups were the Fisk University Jubilee Singers. At a time when white minstrel musicians in "blackface," using vulgar caricature and racial affectation, performed most black music, this small group of eleven exceptionally well-trained and talented young people preserved history. And they achieved distinction for their accurate and stirring performances of traditional black spirituals. In terms of musical history, the significance of the Jubilee Singers is that they introduced to the world a magnificent body of folk music that celebrated life, survival, and ultimate victory.

THE FIFTY-FOURTH MASSACHUSETTS INFANTRY

T he Fifty-Fourth Massachusetts Volunteer Infantry was an African American regiment made up of free blacks that fought with the Union Army. The story of the "54th Mass" is composed of the kind of excitement from which movies are made. During the American Civil War, black soldiers were able to play a significant role in the fight against slavery. There were several all-black units, but the 54th Mass became the most famous. Their courage and valor quieted those whites that had doubted black ability to fight with enough discipline to be led into battle, and it inspired many other blacks to join their ranks.

Northern whites were opposed to enlisting blacks for military service. But the Emancipation Proclamation of 1863 was explicit in allowing blacks into the military. Even white Union soldiers were hostile to their black counterparts. They questioned whether blacks had the intelligence and discipline to be soldiers. People worried that armed blacks were nothing more that bandits. Then there was the most damaging accusation of all that once under fire, black soldiers would show cowardice and run. In the South, blacks in the Union Army were even more detested. If captured, black soldiers were immediately executed or at the very least, re-enslaved for Confederate use.

The 54th Mass was one of the first African American Civil War Regiments to be formed. It was organized in March 1863 at Camp Meigs in Readville, Massachusetts by Robert Gould Shaw, a member of a prominent Boston abolitionist family. Governor John Andrews appointed Colonel Shaw in February 1863. The enlisted men in the regiment were former slaves and free blacks from the North. Charles and Lewis Douglass, the sons of Frederick Douglass, were the most well known of the all the recruits. All the officers were white and from prominent abolitionist families. After training, the unit was sent to Hilton Head, South Carolina. It was there that their actions proved worthy of historical record.

On July 18, 1863, the 54th Mass was ordered to lead the attack on the heavily armed, impregnable, Fort Wagner. They were bombarded by heavy gunfire from Confederate soldiers as they charged ahead. Casualties were high with 250 soldiers, including Colonel Shaw, killed by the end of the battle. While the attack was unsuccessful, the battle brought the unit it greatest recognition. The 1989 movie *Glory*, while wonderfully dramatized, and very well acted, was a less-than-perfect synthesis of this noble story.

The regiment received high praise for their bravery while William Carney, a twenty-three year old enlisted man, was the first African American to receive the Congressional Medal of Honor. The 54th Mass participated in other battles in Charleston for the duration of 1863. In February 1864, they were assigned to help the forces in Jacksonville, Florida. They went on to the battle of Olustee where they, along with other black troops, fought with white Union regiments on the front lines.

While the 54th Mass participated in the most heated battles of the war, it should be noted that they remained steadfast in their commitment to black freedom even though all the African American soldiers received less pay. Black soldiers received $7 a month while whites received $10. As usual, it took an act of Congress to end the disparity. The soldiers of the 54th, however, had already refused to accept any pay until it was equal to that of white soldiers of the same rank. Following the battle of Fort Wagner, the movement to equalize pay grew in strength, and in the summer of 1864 Congress enacted a law to equalize pay of all soldiers. At that time soldiers of the 54th Mass received their back wages as well.

Thousands of African Americans answered the call to fight in the American Civil War. Over 180,000 blacks enlisted in the Union Army, while another 10,000 served in the Union Navy. They served mostly in all-black units and received high marks for their bravery and performance. While African American soldiers have continued to fight in subsequent wars for the United States overseas, their biggest enemy remains the vilifying racism that they endure at home.

HENRY O. FLIPPER (1856-1940)

Henry O. Flipper had a productive life. He was a Buffalo Soldier, civil engineer, author, newspaper editor, land surveyor, cartographer, special agent for the United States Justice Department, and Assistant to the Secretary of the Interior. But his place in American history is discernible as the first African American graduate of the United States Military Academy at West Point.

He was born Henry Ossian Flipper on February 21, 1856, in Thomasville, Georgia. He was one of five sons born to the slave family of Festus and Isabella Buckhalter Flipper, Sr. Festus Flipper established himself in a successful shoemaking business at the end of the Civil War. Henry's education began when he was eight years old in the wood shop of another slave who taught school at night. In late 1865 he began studying in schools established by the American Missionary Association and in 1869 he entered the newly established Atlanta University.

In 1873, Flipper received an appointment to West Point by Rep. James C. Freeman of Georgia. As a cadet, he excelled in engineering, law, French and Spanish. He survived the hostility from other cadets and the lack of friendship from the instructors to graduate in 1877. He was ranked 50th in a class of 76 and commissioned as a Lieutenant. At age 21 Henry became the first black graduate of West Point. He was later assigned to Fort Sill, Oklahoma in 1878 and became the first black officer assigned to the historic 10th Cavalry of Buffalo Soldiers. His first task as an army engineer was to order a drainage ditch dug to rid the area of standing water to combat malaria fever from mosquitoes. It was assessed to be an engineering marvel, and today stands as an historic landmark.

In 1880 Lt. Flipper was ordered to Fort. Davis, Texas. It was there that he would face his greatest challenge. He was named acting quartermaster but relieved of those duties and court-martialed for embezzlement and "conduct unbecoming and officer and a gentlemen." He was found not guilty of embezzlement but guilty of misconduct and dismissed from the corps.

Flipper maintained his innocence for the rest of his life but the matter was never redressed in his lifetime. Prior to the court-martial, Flipper had distinguished himself as an officer tackling such duties as leading scouting expeditions, post engineer surveyor, post adjutant, post construction supervisor, and commissary officer.

Despite his disgrace, Lt. Flipper continued his life and legacy. He wrote the first personal narrative by a black man on the Western frontier and was one of the first blacks in the U.S. to gain prominence in the engineering profession. He remained in the Southwest until ill health in later life retired him to Georgia. Flipper was an avid student of Southwestern history and published articles in *Old Santa Fe* Magazine, the forerunner of the New Mexico Historical Review. He also wrote *The Colored Cadet at West Point* (1878), an account of his military academy experiences. His second book, *Negro Frontiersman: The Western Memoirs of Henry O. Flipper* (1916), was published by his family after his death. His other works included *Spanish and Mexican Land Laws: New Spain and Mexico* (1895), for the Department of Justice.

The federal and state and local governments took advantage of his skill and training, and repeatedly hired him as a civil engineer. His work, his incorruptibility and the confidence his employers had in him often resulted in the return of large amount of land to public domain. He served as a translator for the United States Senate Committee on Foreign Relations and later helped build a railroad in Alaska.

In 1978, the Army, in an effort to erase its own prejudice history, expunged Flipper's record and granted him an honorable discharge. The body of Lt. Henry O. Flipper was exhumed and re-interred with full military honors. In 1999, President Clinton not only gave him a full pardon but also acknowledged the lifetime accomplishments of this embattled army officer and consummate civilian gentleman.

BARNEY LANCELOT FORD (1824-1902)

Barney Lancelot Ford was born a slave but made, lost, and remade several fortunes before he died at the age of seventy-eight. At his death he was listed as one of Denver's most prominent citizens. He had used his accumulated wealth to help black people by giving money, food, and jobs to newly freed slaves. With longtime friend, Henry Wagoner, Ford started schools for blacks that taught basic elementary education, and the rules of government as the foundation for good citizenship.

Ford was born into slavery on January 22, 1824 at Stafford Courthouse, Virginia, but lived in North Carolina until age seventeen. His mother, Phoebe, instilled in him many aspirations that did not include slavery. In fact, she raised him to look for any opportunity to escape slavery. Phoebe drowned during her own escape attempt. After his mother's death, his owner sold him to a slaveholder in Georgia where Barney drove hogs and mules from Kentucky to Georgia. He also worked on the cotton barges and was a cook. His owner later moved to St. Louis and hired Ford out as a steward on a Mississippi Steamboat. In Quincy, Illinois, Ford seized the opportunity to escape and made his way to Chicago with the aid of the Underground Railroad.

In Chicago, Ford met Wagoner and the two men engaged in several enterprises together. They taught themselves to read and write as they continued the work of the Underground Railroad. They also helped runaway slaves to learn to read and write. Ford married Wagoner's sister, Julia; and the couple had three children. Before they married though, Julia helped Barney pick out a last name. While walking in Chicago, they saw a name on a train engine, the "Lancelot Ford." Barney liked the sound of it and immediately annexed it to his name.

Ford had wanted to join the California Gold Rush in 1849, but was fearful of traveling overland because he was a runaway slave. He and his wife decided to take a steamship by way of Panama to California that was quicker and safer. While in Nicaragua, Ford saw many business opportunities and decided to stay. They opened the United States Hotel and Restaurant in 1851. Many important people stayed there before it was destroyed in a racial and political dispute between the U.S. and Great Britain. The Fords returned to Chicago with their savings and opened a livery stable that also became an Underground Railroad station.

In 1860 Ford headed west again, this time participating in the Colorado Gold Rush that began in 1859. He was not allowed to book passage on a stagecoach so he traveled by wagon train. Once in Colorado he was not allowed to rent a hotel room so he boarded with the famous "Aunt" Clara Brown. Ford staked a mining claim in the Colorado gold fields, but territorial law did not allow him to own land so his claim was stolen away. In 1964, the land he had tried so hard to claim one hundred years earlier was renamed "Barney Ford Hill" by Denver authorities.

Undaunted by this loss, Ford became a prosperous tycoon in the hotel, restaurant, and barbering businesses. His luxury Inter-Ocean Hotels, in Denver and Cheyenne were the best in the west. His impressive guest list included President Ulysses S. Grant, and U.S. Generals Sherman and Sheridan. As early as the 1870s, Ford had amassed a personal fortune estimated at $250,000. He continued to help the newly freed slaves, establishing Colorado's first adult education classes for blacks. Colorado lost its first bid for statehood because of Ford's eloquent argument against its discriminatory practices against blacks. He said those practices were inconsistent with the goals of statehood and a violation of the Constitution.

The story of Barney Lancelot Ford, a poor plantation slave, with no name, who rose to the status of rich entrepreneur, is the kind of story from which movies are made. The pioneering spirit of his story, with its drama, pathos, and intrigue, is indicative of those great western sagas that screenwriters should write if U.S. history would ever allow itself to become inclusive of all those who made our history.

"One of dese mornings, bright and fair, /
gonna take my wings and cleve de air..."

Slavery in the Americas produced an amazing body of people. It is amazing that they could ever smile and laugh, let alone make up riddles, songs and jokes, and tell stories. As slaves, they were forced to live without citizenship or rights. As property, they were counted as chattel. Only their souls belonged to them. But no amount of hard labor and suffering could suppress their great powers of imagination. And in the black folkloric tradition, they imagined that they could fly.

Slaves resisted slavery in so many ways. Running away was at the top of the list. There were many escape routes attempted by slaves to obtain their freedom. But not every escape was meant to be a physical one. To signify a mental escape, slaves used songs and stories relating to the phenomenon of flying. Flying came to represent a way to flee the dehumanization and oppression fostered by enslavement. This folkloric belief is that the legend of the "flying Africans," who rose up from the slave fields and flew back to Africa, arises out of the crucible of slavery itself. The people could fly off or disappear anytime their physical and mental burden was too great for them to carry. This power was the exclusive property of the African-born slave for the express purpose of returning to Africa.

Flying signified the slaves' willingness to accept and trust in their own experience, and to trust in a truth other than that given to them by slavery. The African American folkloric tradition originated with groups of people, most of who, long ago, were taken from Africa against their will. They were torn from their individual cultures as they left their history, their families and social groups, and their languages and customs behind. Flying, as performed by Africans, and as attested to by African Americans, was an affirmation of black humanity. When they could fly, they resisted the negation of their humanity. When they could fly, they identified the truth of their own self-worth.

African Americans had no trouble accepting the notion that only Africans could fly and not themselves. For Africa was for them a mystical place and a source of great wonder. They knew and fully understood that they could not fly back to a place that they had never been. Before their "Christianization,"

Africa was the "heaven" the slaves' souls would fly to when they were dead. The ability to fly was associated exclusively with native-born African slaves, who were believed to be the only ones to possess the supernatural power capable of such a feat. Africans who had actually seen, touched, and smelled Africa were thought to have a mystical connection to that land and were believed to be able to fly back to it at will. But this was never the case for American-born slaves.

The disconnection to Africa felt by American-born slaves was caused by the "African" in them being forcibly suppressed by slave owners. Slaves were not allowed to speak their own languages. They were forced to speak English, but paradoxically forbidden to learn to read or write it. They could see freedom, but not experienced it. They could work the land, but never possess it. They came here with names, but would never be called by them. Sadly, American-born slaves lost their mystical connection to Africa. They lived under conditions more brutal than any group of people have ever had to endure.

Singer, R. Kelly, has written a song he has aptly entitled, *I Believe I Can Fly*. As stated above, that is not a unique concept to people of African descent. It is substantiated in folktales concerning the African experience in America. What gives us pause is whether R. Kelly realizes that he has written a song about a concept that is as old as slavery in the Americas. What is fascinating is that R. Kelly is in a long line of those African Americans descended from enslaved Africans who believed they could fly – not just in the air, but fly above ceaseless back-breaking work, fly above the pain of family separation, and fly above the circumstance of slavery itself. They believed they could *fly...fly...fly...*

JAMES FORMAN (1928-2005)

J ames Forman was a writer, civil rights activist and political philosopher who is perhaps best known as the leader of the Student Nonviolent Coordinating Committee (SNICK) in the 1960s. Under his leadership, SNICK hammered out a role among traditional civil rights organizations that was edgy and aggressive. Forman also published two bestsellers *The Making of Black Revolutionaries: A Personal Account* (1972) and *Self-Determination: An Examination of the Question...* (1984)

Forman was born in Chicago and did not meet his real father until his teens. He spent the first six years of his childhood with his grandmother on a farm in rural Marshall County, Mississippi. After that, he spent every summer with her. His character was formed by the stress she placed on education and by the despicable legacy of well-enforced Jim Crow laws. His experiences in the segregated South also proved important in developing his social consciousness.

Forman graduated from Chicago's Englewood High School in 1947. He went on to attend Wilson Junior College before joining the U.S. Air force. At the end of his tour of duty, he enrolled at the University of Southern California (USC). As his second semester was beginning, he was beaten and arrested by the police where he was beaten again while in custody. The trauma and humiliation was too much for Forman, and it triggered a complete mental and emotional breakdown. When well, Forman transferred to Roosevelt University in Chicago and excelled in the intellectually challenging environment and became a force in student politics. He graduated in 1957 and attended Boston University as a graduate student.

Forman's entrance into the Civil Rights Movement was very gradual. In 1958 he traveled to Little Rock, Arkansas to cover the school desegregation crisis for the Chicago Defender. In 1960, he joined the Congress Of Racial Equality (CORE), providing relief services to sharecroppers in Tennessee who had been evicted for registering to vote. In the same year he began working with the Freedom Riders, who got him involved with SNCC. In 1961 he moved south to join SNCC and began activism full-time. His organizational skills, as well as his maturity and experience, thrust him into leadership roles at SNCC. Having served in the air force during the Korean conflict for four years, he was ten years older than the young people at SNCC.

Forman supervised staff and directed fundraising, serving as the Executive Secretary from 1964 to 1966. In addition, he participated in many of SNICK's direct action protests and helped to organize voter registration drives in Alabama and Mississippi. He was harassed, beaten, and jailed on many occasions. Soon after the Freedom Summer of 1964, disagreements over the direction, tactics, and strategies of SNICK consumed its leadership. Forman was adept at keeping all factions busy with the agenda at hand. But his increasingly militant stance brought growing tension with Martin Luther King and the Southern Christian Leadership Conference (SCLC). SNICK began cooperating on various levels with the Black Panther Party until an even more radical faction, led by Stokely Carmichael, usurped power in 1968.

Forman left SNICK to seek economic development opportunities for black communities in the U.S and in Africa. He became one of the first African Americans to call for reparations to make up for slavery and the social injustices that blacks have had to endure for centuries. Forman received his first graduate degree from Cornell in African American Studies in 1980. He also received a Ph.D. in 1982 from the Union of Experimental Colleges and Universities with the Institute for Policy Studies in Washington.

James Forman became active in the fight to gain statehood for the District of Columbia. In July 2004, with his body ravished by cancer, he was part of a "Boston Tea Party." Delegates from the District threw tea bags into Boston Harbor to protest the disenfranchisement of Washingtonians. The irony of that event was that Forman's last protest against America was the same as America's first protest against England.

CHARLOTTE FORTEN (1837-1914)

C harlotte Forten was a 19th century African American educator, writer, and poet. She descended from the illustrious Forten and Purvis families, renowned for their wealth and abolition sentiments. She was the first northern black educator to go south to teach former slaves. Today we are left to remember her mostly through her personal diaries that record sensitive, intelligent, and cultured reflections, and provide a unique, firsthand narrative account of her life and experiences.

Charlotte was born in Philadelphia to Mary Woods and Robert Bridges Forten on August 17, 1837. Her mother died when she was only four years old. Although born into a life of affluence and privilege, she dedicated her life to the Abolitionist cause and the moral and intellectual improvement of her people. Her grandfather was James Forten, a wealthy New England ship builder. Her uncle was Robert Purvis, another prominent black Abolitionist. Charlotte was no ordinary young woman. She was a part of the free black elite. The Fortens were also strong proponents of black equality. And as a teenager, Charlotte followed all the racial issues of the day. The diary Charlotte began keeping at age sixteen also contains reflections about the concerns affecting Philadelphia blacks.

Charlotte led a protected life. She was not permitted to attend Philadelphia's segregated schools. Instead, the Forten family wealth allowed her to have private tutors. To further her education, she attended Higginson Grammar School in Salem, Massachusetts. She was the only black student at the school but excelled in literature and poetry. She also completed additional studies and earned a teaching certificate from Salem Normal School the next year. While living in Salem, her father placed her under the guardianship of another notable black couple, Charles and Sarah Redmond. Charlotte's admirers and mentors included such celebrated figures as John Greenleaf Whittier, William Lloyd Garrison, and Wendell Phillips.

In 1856, Charlotte received a teaching assignment at the integrated Epes Grammar School, making her the first black teacher of whites in Salem. She became a member of the Salem Female Anti-Slavery Society, where she was involved in networking and fundraising, and proved to be influential as an activist and civil rights leader. One of her greatest joys was attending abolition speeches and rallies. She remained at Epes for two years when illness forced her to resign and return to Philadelphia. While recuperating from tuberculosis, Charlotte began writing poetry with an activist theme and was published in "The Liberator." One of her poems, "Glimpses of England," received critical acclaim. She also served as a correspondent for the "National Anti-Slavery Standard" and the "Atlantic Monthly."

In 1862, Charlotte was the first black teacher to travel south to teach freed slaves. At the height of the Civil War, she wholeheartedly participated in the project at Port Royal, South Carolina, designed to help educate the thousands of destitute and illiterate slaves set free by the Emancipation Proclamation. In addition to teaching, after the attack on Fort Wagner, she tended to the soldiers, mended their clothes, and wrote letters for them. All of this additional activity weakened her already frail health. Near the end of 1863, Charlotte sailed from St. Helena Island to New York, Philadelphia, Boston, and Salem to visit with friends and to recover her health.

In 1864 Charlotte published "Life on the Sea Islands" in the Atlantic Monthly Magazine and drew huge attention from Northern readers. At age forty-one, she married Francis Grimké, a much younger author, law student, and minister. Their only child, Theodora, died in infancy. Charlotte maintained faithful journal entries until she returned to the North. After her return, the entries were less frequent. Her later writings touched on her life with Grimké and Theodora's death, but they are fewer in number compared to the daily entries she made in her youth. The diaries of Charlotte Forten Grimké are some of the rarest extant documents that inform on the life of a free black woman of status in the Antebellum North.

JAMES FORTEN (1766-1842)

James Forten was a wealthy businessman and reformer and one of the most influential black men of post Revolutionary War America. He used his wealth and prominence to influence policy and practice toward African Americans and became one of the country's best-known Abolitionists.

He was born to free African American parents in Philadelphia on September 2, 1766. His father, Thomas, was a worker in the Philadelphia shipyards. In his only year of formal schooling, Forten learned to read and write and do sums in his arithmetic book. His education came to a sudden halt in 1776 when his father accidentally drowned in the Delaware River. To help support his family he worked first in a grocery store and then entered Militia service that took him away from home briefly.

In 1781 Forten was recruited aboard the twenty-two-gun privateer, *Royal Louis,* when he was a 6'2" fourteen year-old. As powder boy he had the extremely hazardous duty of carrying canvas buckets of water, gunpowder, and cannonballs from the powder magazine below decks up a ladder to his gun crew and then race down for a fresh round under heavy enemy fire. During one engagement, the ship was surrounded by three British warships and forced to surrender. Forten and the surviving crew was taken to a British prison ship and remained until the end of the war.

In 1786 Forten was apprenticed to a sail maker named Robert Bridges, the same man who had employed his father years previously. He learned all the skills required to fit out the sails of ships. Within two years, he was promoted to foreman and had the new experience of supervising forty workers, black and white. In the next few years, as Forten learned to manage the business, the elderly Bridges finally offered to sell it to him in 1798. Upon buying the business Forten promptly announced that he would not take orders for sails of ships in any way engaged in the slave trade. Much of his income would come from a new laborsaving device for hoisting sails that he invented, the hand-cranked winch. Its patent and his sail making business helped him amass assets that would make him a millionaire by today's standards.

In 1787, while the U.S. Constitution was being drawn up in Philadelphia, Forten, Rev. Richard Allen and Rev. Absalom Jones were forming the Free African Society, a benevolent organization to help free blacks in times of illness, unemployment, or other emergencies. After the first Fugitive Slave Act was passed in 1793 Forten began to devote his money and his efforts to buying freedom for slaves and asserting himself politically to protect their rights. For forty years he gave free classes in his home and then in St. Thomas Church teaching black children to read and write and do arithmetic. He also helped to launch the Infant School for Colored Children, forerunner of the modern day *Head Start Program*.

During the War of 1812 Forten recruited 2,500 blacks to defend Philadelphia. He was a strong supporter of the radical abolitionist newspaper, *The Liberator*, published by William Lloyd Garrison of Boston. Forten esteemed his long-time friend, Paul Cuffe, but was suspicious of the American Colonization Society of which he was a part. He wrote many letters to Cuffe expressing his fears of it. In 1833 Forten organized the American Anti-Slavery Society at his Philadelphia home on Lombard Street. He was elected president of the American Moral Reform Society in 1835, a reform organization that held both a temperance and women's rights position.

Forten used his own resources to become a noted pamphleteer, which was the 19th century version of social activism. In all his speaking, writing, and doing, he never ceased to espouse the rights of Africans in America. When James Forten died at the age of seventy-five, his funeral was well attended by over five thousand blacks and whites, men and women, rich and poor. The newspapers noted the passing of the city's leading sail maker under the headline *"Death of an Excellent Man."* It was a fitting title for a man who possessed so much integrity, and for the man who in essence was the elder statesman of black America.

The phrase "40 acres and a mule" probably stems from a field order given in 1865 to former slaves in Savannah, Georgia. On January 16, 1865, General William Tecumseh Sherman of the Union Army issued "Special Field Order # 15." This order reserved the Sea Islands and areas of coastal South Carolina, Georgia, and Florida for the freed slaves. Each person or family of persons was to receive a 40-acre plot of agriculturally fit land. And with General Sherman's permission, the army could also loan mules to former slaves. About 40,000 freedmen settled 400,000 acres of land within six months. But they were never given legal titles to the land, and in the end the government broke its implied promise and drove them off.

Nearing the end of the Civil War, black preachers and other leaders of Savannah met with General Sherman and indicated that freedom meant having their own land. Sherman, in his now historic "March to the Sea," had just cut a swath of desolation 250 miles long through Georgia. His aim had been to demoralize the South. The order issuing land to ex-slaves aided the process. Sherman granted the wishes of the black leaders. In 1866, Congress attempted to make Sherman's order official government policy by the passage of a bill strengthening the Freedmen's Bureau and authorizing it to make forty acres of land from confiscated Confederate property available to each household of ex-slaves.

This legislation was designed to make the freedmen self-sufficient and to compensate for 246 years of free labor. When President Abraham Lincoln issued the Emancipation Proclamation in 1863, the four million freedmen had nothing on which to subsist. "Freedom" was all they had. They were bereft of food, goods, clothing, money, and land. They did not have legal names or legal status. They had not yet been granted citizenship or the right to vote. Receiving the confiscated property of their former owners would have greatly eased their situation.

But this opportunity to establish a base of self-sufficiency for themselves and for future generations of African Americans would never be realized. President Andrew Johnson, Lincoln's successor, vetoed the bill. Congress was either unwilling or unable to override his veto. Johnson was a racist and a southerner with sympathies for the vanquished South. He was totally against Reconstruction and had no intention of confiscating southern property. He gave the land back to white planters. Blacks could stay on the land if they signed labor contracts. But those who resisted were forcibly evicted.

The phrase "40 acres and a mule" has come to represent the consummate failed promise to African Americans. It is symbolic of reparations for enslavement, and has been a recurrent theme in African American culture and throughout the black experience since Reconstruction. Black filmmaker Spike Lee used the expression lightheartedly to name his production company. Rapper Nelly used a play-on-words on his Compact Disc, *Welcome to Nellyville*: *"give me 40 acres and a pool."* Ultimately underlying the concept of "40 acres and a mule" was the notion of economic justice. It has to be recognized as the earliest form of Reparations paid to the freed slaves of the American South.

Even though freed slaves did not obtain the desired compensation for that period of enslavement, it did not end their desire for such justice. Black folklore revived the notion of a gift of land several times after the Civil War, but nothing ever happened. The whole episode typified bitter betrayal by the United States, and the African American loss of faith in government help. And yet, African Americans continued to maneuver around obstacles and achieved land ownership. By the 1890s and through the turn of the early 20th century, blacks had accumulated millions of acres of rural property. As members of the African Diaspora, enduring in the Americas, under unique circumstances, we can add this to our description of grace: "A PEOPLE ONCE OWNED AS "PROPERTY" CAME TO OWN <u>REAL</u> PROPERTY"

THE FREEDMEN'S BUREAU

The Bureau of Refugees, Freedmen, and Abandoned Lands was the principal agency by which the newly freed slaves in the American South were acculturated as citizen of the newly reconciled United States of America. It was established as part of the U.S. War Department by an act of Congress in March 1865. It became known as the Freedmen's Bureau because its primary aim was to provide assistance to the newly emancipated slaves of the South after the American Civil War. The Bureau was originally created for one year, but was given extensions and continued its efforts for seven years altogether.

As its rather lengthy title suggests, the bureau's responsibilities went beyond giving aid to blacks. It initially extended aid in the form of food, shelter, and clothing to whites as well. Refugees were the whites living in the Confederacy while loyal to the Union. Those whites and the former slaves needed immediate medical relief as well the already mentioned assistance. The bureau was also given a charge to disperse of Confederate owned land confiscated by Union armies. It was to resettle a portion of the freed population on the 850,000 acres of abandoned and confiscated throughout the south, but the rate at which President Johnson pardoned Confederates and restored their land frustrated the effort. Still that small amount of acreage would not have been enough to resettle 4,000,000 freed slaves.

Even before the establishment of the Freedmen's Bureau, the Union army had already become the chief relief agency. Field commanders dealt with the urgent demands of needy blacks and whites. There was no clear policy directing the effort as significant legal and logistical questions arose. The issue of slavery presented peculiar difficulties to the generals in the field. Before the war's end, the avowed policy of the administration was that of non-interference with slavery in the occupied states and the enforcement of laws, including the Fugitive Slave Act. Many military officers obeyed the pro-slavery orders under protest, or mere simulated obedience while secretly aiding the escape of fugitives.

The Freedmen's Bureau did not accomplish all that it was organized to do, but it was not a total failure. It was a tremendous temporary relief agency. It took responsibility for furnishing food and medical supplies to blacks, most of whom were destitute, and to needy white refugees as well. The Bureau issued millions of food ration packages and established over forty hospitals. $20 million in various types of relief and assistance helped the African Americans in their transition from slavery to freedom. The Bureau was also concerned with the regulation of wages and the working conditions of blacks. Many white planters tried to re-enslave its agriculture work force through illegal contracts that cheated blacks out of their wages and created coercive working conditions that resembled their former enslavement.

In establishing and maintaining schools for the illiterate former slaves, the Freedmen's Bureau also created the first public school system the South had ever known. An additional accomplishment of its educational initiative was the establishment of higher educational institutions. Some of the traditional black colleges like Howard, Fisk, and Atlanta Universities and Hampton Institute were created by the Freedmen's Bureau. Those colleges and universities remain as a great legacy for African Americans who, under slavery, had been denied the opportunity of an education.

It was onto a crowed stage that the Freedmen's Bureau debuted in the first place. It was organized only one month before Robert E. Lee surrendered to Ulysses S. Grant at Appomattox Courthouse. Congress assigned to it all the responsibilities previously shared by military commanders. Perhaps the Bureau's only failure came in the handling of the 850,000 acres of confiscated and abandoned lands. For various reasons the plan was forsaken as the President Andrew Johnson returned confiscated land to former Confederate owners. This caused severe disappointment to African Americans who had hoped thereby to establish themselves as independent farmers. They knew at that time that it was only the concept of land ownership that made all men free and equal in America.

During the Civil Rights Movement, African Americans adapted many Negro Spirituals and black gospels to meet the immediate needs of the black community. Movement songwriters revised many of the spirituals by inserting new political lyrics. The revised lyrics expressed the desire for equal treatment and a better life. God was not excluded from the music, but many spiritual were rewritten for the direct purpose of rallying people to action. God was viewed as the spiritual leader of the movement. Scripture taught that He had sent His Son to die for the world and that every believer had been "set free" by that death. The movement had not forgotten the *"God of our weary years, God of our silent tears,"* it had simply moved Him to the forefront of the battle.

The songs of earlier generations were sung with new lyrics and new meaning. As a result, the repertoire of civil rights songs was extensive. It was expanded by the many variations as these songs were sung by different people and crafted to fit local situations all across the South. The Civil Rights Movement was often called "the singing revolution" because time after time song came to the aid of the civil rights demonstrators. In moments of crises, singing would ease tension. At street rallies, church meetings, in jails and prisons, on dangerous marches, songs helped demonstrators to center themselves on their goals. No other movement in American history has granted a greater role to song and to mass singing.

By 1961 singing was a habit and it was sustained well into 1966. Often these songs were called "freedom songs" or "movement songs." Many civil rights leaders had favorite songs that they adapted specifically for the movement. The favorite spiritual of Dr. Martin Luther King, Jr. was *We Shall Overcome*. It is easily the best-known adaptation of a Negro Spiritual. Since King emerged as the national symbol and spokesman of a vital new civil rights era, his favorite song became the signature piece of the movement. *Ain't Gonna Let Nobody Turn Me Around* was another one of the more powerful songs of the Civil Rights Movement. It provoked an attitude of determination in marchers. Although they were peaceful, they knew their peaceful protest would be met with hatred and violence. That song gave strength and courage to marchers and was a constant reminder that their cause was just. Fannie Lou Hamer was noted for leading a rousing rendition of *This Little Light of Mine* wherever she was – on a program or in the streets.

The movement's mass singing had it roots in the African American music tradition. Since the slave era, black communities had employed songs to communicate messages, to spend leisure time, to elaborate a worldview, to sing praises to God, and to ease their sorrow. Freedom songs drew on this rich heritage, especially that of spiritual and gospel music. While enslaved, many of the messages that blacks communicated made use of *double entendre* (double meaning). When they sang *Wade In The Water* they meant for escaping slaves to walk in shallow riverbeds so that hounds could not pick up their scent. It was not apparent to the enslavers that these religious songs were not about an afterlife, but about immediate, physical freedom.

Freedom songs served the Civil Rights Movement well. But this time, there was no mistaking the lyrics of these songs. There was no "double speaking." The message was easily understood. It was a clear, anguished, and determined protest from those who had been so long denied freedom as citizens and dignity as human beings. And the message was communicated to the world. As a movement song, *Wade in the Water* took on a different significance. It came to mean that God himself would change the existing sociopolitical system *(God's gonna' trouble the water)* if they held on *(wade in the water)*.

All groups of people have nationalistic and cultural songs to aid them in their struggles. But since the 1960s, African American Freedom Songs have helped the world through moments of profound change. South Africans sung them in their fight against apartheid. When the Berlin Wall was torn down in 1989, as the Soviet Union was collapsing, it was the Germans who were singing: *We Shall Overcome.*

THE FREEDMEN AND THE NAMING PROCESS

ompared to the many acute problems facing the newly freed slaves, the question of their names might have seemed the least consequential. But the freedmen felt otherwise. Rather than reveal a degraded past, the names assumed after emancipation reflected a new beginning. It was an indispensable step toward achieving the self-respect, the personal dignity, and the independence which slavery had compromised.

During slavery, many blacks only had a given name. Although most slaves appeared to have named their own children, the master might arbitrarily assign a name, borrowing heavily from classical, biblical, and Anglo-Saxon appellations. The naming process also afforded him a chance to indulge in some humorous whims, and some did so at the expense of the slave's dignity. The slaves were apt to have the same surname as the master. It was a convenient way to identify the plantation to which they belonged. To allow the slave to use his own surname would be sharing an honor due only to his master. And honor was something seldom given to a slave.

More often than many masters realized, slaves adopted their own surnames among themselves. Generally these names were not publicly revealed until after emancipation. But immediately after they were freed these surnames came to light. The freed slaves themselves selected their names. Scarcely ever did a freed slave choose the name of his or her owner, but often took the surname of some other slaveholding family, of which he knew. This would often be done to recognize some compassionate kindness extended that the freedman that he never forgot.

Freedmen, who took the name of an earlier owner, perhaps the first owner he could recall, frequently made the choice out of a sense of historical identity, continuity, and family pride. The idea was not to honor a previous master but to sustain some identification with the freedman's family of origin. Although family pride was reason enough, certain practical considerations also encouraged the selection of names after emancipation. In some instances, the freedmen would have to select a new given name if he had jokingly been given a degrading or belittling name.

Whether it was to enlist in the Union Army, live in the contraband camps, apply for relief at the Freedmen's Bureau office, or, some years later, vote in an election, blacks needed to register both a given name and a surname with Federal authorities. In some instances, Federal officials expedited the naming process by furnishing the names themselves, and invariably the name would be the same as that of the freedman's most recent master. But these appear to have been exceptional cases. The former slaves themselves usually took the initiative in the choosing of a name.

Whatever names the newly freed slaves adopted they were most often making that decision for themselves relevant to their status as African American citizens. Some freedmen did take the name of a previous master, but perhaps not the immediately previous one. If he were to look for a family member, as many did, he would revert to the name they used at the time. The most common names used by freedmen were the names of national leaders. The names of dead presidents like Washington, Jefferson, Adams, Jackson, and Grant were fair game. An insight not lost on former slave, Booker T. Washington.

Sometimes an identifying occupational skill like Smith, Tanner, Shoemaker, or Wainwright would be the moniker they would choose. Even a place of residence or region like Hill, Middleton, Charleston, and Shropshire would suffice. Names denoting colors like Greene, Brown, Black, or Gray were chosen. Often, the name Freeman was selected to signify their new status. In the aftermath of slavery, the freed ex-slaves made the decision to take names suitable for their new status as African American citizens. They achieved much for a people that were bereft of everything, never having had the best of anything. But they knew they were striving toward personal dignity and self-respect and their names would be reflective of that.

ELIZABETH "MUM BETT" FREEMAN (1742-1829)

Elizabeth Freeman was probably born in 1742 to enslaved African parents in Claverack, New York. Her first owner was a Dutchman named Peter Hodgebooma. At the age of six months, John Ashley of Sheffield, Massachusetts, purchased her and her sister, Lizzie. The Ashley family legally owned Freeman until she was nearly forty. By then, she was known as "Mum Bett." Her daughter was known as "Little Bett." Freeman's husband was killed while fighting in the American Revolutionary War.

In 1773, a special committee appointed by voters in the Town of Sheffield and chaired by John Ashley, met in the Ashley home. They discussed concepts of freedom, equality, and the rights of man. The committee wrote their thoughts down in a document that came to be known as the "Sheffield Declaration," a precursor of the Declaration of Independence of 1776. Freeman had listened carefully while the wealthy men she served spoke with the rhetoric of revolution. In that same spirit of revolution, Freeman felt that if "all people were born free and equal," then the laws must surely apply to her as well.

One day, Mrs. Ashley angrily tried to hit Freeman's sister with a heated kitchen shovel. Freeman intervened and received the blow instead. Infuriated by such treatment, she left the house and refused to return. The scar remained a disfigurement on her face for the rest of her life. When Colonel Ashley appealed to the law for her return, Freeman called on Theodore Sedgwick, a lawyer from Stockbridge who had anti-slavery sentiments, and asked for his help to sue for her freedom. Freeman knew Sedgwick as the secretary of the committee that drew up the Sheffield Declaration.

In 1781, near the close of the Revolutionary War, Sedgwick brought suit in the Berkshire County Court of Common Pleas. The Case of *Brom & Bett vs. Ashley* was argued successfully before the court and the jury ruled in favor of Freeman and another slave named Brom. The case was argued based on the fact that Massachusetts had no law that ever established slavery, and if it had, that the new State Constitution would have made that law null and void. The jury agreed with the argument and held that slavery was illegal in Massachusetts and that the plaintiffs were free people. In winning their suit, they became the first African Americans to be freed under the Massachusetts constitution of 1780. In addition, the court ruled that Ashley should pay them thirty shillings in damages and court costs.

After the ruling, despite pleas from Colonel Ashley that she return and work for him for wages, Mum Bett changed her last name to "Freeman" to denote her new status, and went to work for the Sedgwick family. She stayed with them as their paid housekeeper for many years. Eventually, she set up house with her daughter and became a much sought after nurse and midwife. Mum Bett died at the age of eighty-seven. She lived out her life as a free woman in the free state of Massachusetts that her historic case helped to create. One of Mum Bett's great-grandchildren was W.E.B. Dubois, a history maker in his own right.

Elizabeth "Mum Bett" Freeman was buried in the Sedgwick family plot in Stockbridge, Massachusetts. It is believed that she is the only black person buried there. The tombstone of this African American woman, whose suit for freedom helped to bring about the end of slavery in Massachusetts, can still be seen in that old burial ground. It is a fitting epitaph that summed up her life and the way she would have viewed her duty. It read as follows:

> *"She was born a slave and remained a slave for nearly thirty years.*
> *She could neither read nor write*
> *yet in her own sphere she had no superior or equal.*
> *She neither wasted time nor property.*
> *She never violated a trust nor failed to perform a duty.*
> *In every situation of domestic trial, she was the most efficient helper,*
> *and the tenderest friend.*
> *Good Mother, Farewell"*

META WARRICK FULLER (1877-1968)

eta Warrick Fuller was an important African American artist and one of the earliest sculptors to depict black themes and the first to express the suffering and toil of slavery. She was an artist with great talent, and had one of the longest careers in art. She sculpted for museums, churches, libraries, and public works. Her last sculpture, The Crucifixion, honored four black girls killed in a church bombing in Birmingham.

She was born Meta Vaux Warrick to William and Emma Jones Warrick on June 9, 1877 in Philadelphia. Her parents owned beauty and barbering shops, and a catering business. They could afford her a very privileged upbringing with private tutoring, art, dance, and music lessons, and horseback riding lessons. Her father was an art lover who often took Meta to the Philadelphia museums and art galleries. She attended the J. Liberty Tadd Industrial Arts School and had her art project selected as part of Tadd's exhibit at the 1893 World Columbian Exposition in Chicago.

In 1894 Warrick was awarded a three-year scholarship to the Pennsylvania School of Industrial Art, followed by a one-year post-graduate fellowship in 1897. She won many awards for art during her undergraduate and post-graduate tenure. Encouraged toward follow-up studies abroad, Warrick sailed to Paris, France in 1899. She spent the next four years at a prestigious French art school. She became acquainted with the work of famed American artist, Augustus Saint-Gaudens. African American painter, Henry O. Tanner while in Paris, also befriended her. But she received the highest praise and the most encouragement from French artist, Auguste Rodin, one of the most gifted sculptors in history.

By 1900 Warrick was developing a style of her own. Her inspiration came from classic French literature, Greek mythology, and biblical tradition. Some of her sculptures included The Medusa, The Wretched, The Impertinent Thief, and Man Carrying a Dead Comrade. In 1901 her first important sculpture, Secret Sorrow, was of a man eating his own heart, and was exhibited in Paris where she was becoming well known. Upon her return to the United States in 1902, she found a chilly reception for the themes that had received rave reviews in Europe. Warrick then began to construct new images that appealed to a black audience. But in doing so, her work developed an appeal to an even broader American audience.

Warrick created portrait sculptures of Charlotte Hawkins Brown, Frederick Douglass, Richard Harrison, Sojourner Truth, and Harriet Tubman. In 1907 she was the first black woman artist to receive a federal commission from the Jamestown Tercentennial Exposition committee to contribute 150-piece tableaux, illustrating the progress of African Americans since the arrival of the first twenty African slaves in 1619. She won a gold medal for that work. In 1913 Warrick was again commissioned to create a statue for the 50th anniversary celebration of the Emancipation Proclamation for the state of New York.

In 1909 Warrick married Solomon Fuller, M.D., the nation's first black psychiatrist. She moved with him to Framingham, Massachusetts. The couple had three sons. Over the next few decades, Warrick created sculptures that celebrated the African American experience. Warrick is only nominally associated with the 1920s Harlem Renaissance. Her seventy-year career began at the turn of the twentieth century and ended with a focus on the Civil Rights Movement. Warrick's style evolved from Gothic, to African American types, to more realism, to religious subjects. Her sculptures still appear in the San Francisco Museum of Fine Arts, Howard University, and in the New York Public Library Schomburg Collection.

When questioned about her art, she once said: "Tell the world how you feel...take the chance...try, try!" Meta Warrick Fuller lived up to her credo. She told the world by her sculptures how she felt. She took the chance that through her art we would come to know who she was, and possibly, who we are. And in her superb trying, she left for us her signature style of bold and powerful black figures, the likes of which had not been seen on this earth since those created by ancient Africans.

G abriel's Revolt was a slave insurrection that occurred on August 30, 1800, in Richmond, Virginia. It was named for Gabriel Prosser, the instigator and organizer. He was born a slave in 1776 on the Brookfield Tobacco Plantation in Henrico County. Not much is known about Gabriel's background. He was owned by Thomas Henry Prosser, as were his two brothers, Solomon and Martin, and his wife, Nanny. Gabriel could read and write and was an avid Bible student. His slave occupation was that of a blacksmith. It was a skill he would use to gain access to a world beyond the plantation.

Restrictions on slaves had been reduced following the American Revolutionary War. Slaves were allowed to travel and meet evenings and weekends. They could establish regular meetings to socialize and worship. Skilled artisans like Gabriel were often allowed to purchase their freedom. Gabriel, like many slaves in 1800, was inspired of by the ideals of the American Revolution, the first Republic in the Americas; and fully understood the implications of the slave uprising in Haiti that led to the creation of the second independent Republic in the Americas. For some slaves, freedom was more that just a dream; it was a goal that could be realized.

Gabriel wanted to be free, but he also wanted to destroy the institution of slavery for everyone. For months he planned his desperate move, molding bullets, and gathering clubs, swords, and scythes as weapons. He began recruiting men for his plan to overthrow the state of Virginia and to end slavery as early as 1799. He first enlisted his own brothers and then slaves from Caroline, Louisa, Hanover, and Henrico Counties; and from Richmond, Petersburg, Norfolk, and Albemarle. It is believed Gabriel had French conspirators from as far away as South Key, who may have been Haitian. He also had militant abolitionist groups in Richmond. And caught up in the amalgamation were free blacks and a few of the white underclass. It was never confirmed, but Gabriel intended to engage the Catawba Indians as well.

When they were assembled, Gabriel's men would then kill the plantation owners in neighboring areas to insure the secrecy of his plot. His forces would then proceed to Richmond where they expected to meet fellow conspirators from Petersburg. As a combined group, they would separate to carry out missions, including setting fires as diversions, capturing the Richmond Capitol;

and kidnapping Governor James Monroe to persuade him to accept their demands. Gabriel felt that when news of the success of their plan was circulated, other sympathizers would join the plot. When the time came to execute the plan, it failed due to torrential rains that made roads and bridges impassable. Nevertheless, about 1,000-armed slaves stood ready.

Gabriel wanted to reschedule for the next evening but two slaves had already informed on the conspirators and word was quickly sent to the Governor who called up the militia in every county. Cities and towns were alerted and prepared to defend their environs. At this point, not even defensive measures, though attempted, could be executed. The group had to disband. Within days, an alarmed slave state committed all its resources to hunting the conspirators and arresting scores of black people. Gabriel managed to escape for 30 days, but was captured in Norfolk, and tried and executed within two weeks. Some conspirators agreed to testify against the leaders in return for a pardon. In total, 35 men were hanged, but four others escaped from prison, with no record of recapture.

Gabriel Prosser's heroic bid for freedom only served to tighten the grip of slavery in Virginia. In the aftermath of the insurrection, slave codes were also toughened in other southern states. Gabriel's revolt was a subsequent failure, as slave rebellions were apt to be. But Gabriel did herald the cause of independence for himself and for all slaves. It was a cause for which he took extreme measures, and a cause that was universal in scope with his inclusion of Indians and poor whites, and a cause for which he nobly paid the ultimate price.

HENRY HIGHLAND GARNET (1815-1882)

Henry Highland Garnet was a Presbyterian churchman, eloquent Abolitionist, and Counsel General to the West African nation of Liberia. But before that, he was born a slave on a plantation in New Market, Kent County, Maryland on December 23, 1815. His grandfather was a hereditary chieftain from the Congo and became a leader in the slave community. At age nine, Henry's father, George Garnet, escaped from slavery with ten other family members, eventually settling in New York City.

By age eleven Henry was enrolled at African Free School #1, receiving an academic and religious education. As he grew older, he attended Noyes Academy in Canaan, New Hampshire. Before attending the Oneida Theological Institute in Whitesboro, New York, where he graduated with honors in 1840, he spent several years as a sailor and a farmer's apprentice. During this period, Garnet became interested in the activities of the First Colored Presbyterian Church, where he met Rev. Theodore S. Wright, the pastor and one of the state's leading Abolitionists. Wright baptized him into the faith and performed the ceremony when Garnet married Julia Williams in 1842. It was Wright who encouraged Garnet to join the ministry.

After seminary training Garnet attached himself to a black congregation in Troy, New York and transformed the area into an important center for Abolitionism. His church soon became a stop on the Underground Railroad. He became a pamphleteer and published many articles decrying the evils of slavery. On August 21, 1843, at the National Negro Convention in Buffalo, New York, Garnet rose to the prominence of other notable Abolitionists when he delivered a stormy speech to the delegates. At that time, calling for a slave insurrection was so radical that even Frederick Douglass called for its suppression. John Brown, the white radical Abolitionist, was so moved by Garnet's speech that he had copies published and circulated at his own expense.

From 1843 to 1848, Garnet served as the pastor of the Liberty Street Presbyterian Church in New York. In the 1850s Garnet capitalized on his national fame and visited international Abolition Societies in Europe and Great Britain. He raised money in Scotland to minister to blacks in Jamaica. He tried, but failed, to get England to boycott cotton raised in the American South. He served as a delegate to the World Peace Congress in Frankfurt. While abroad, he learned to speak fluent German and French. Illness forced his return to the United States in 1856. When his mentor, Rev. Wright died in 1856, Garnet assumed the pastorate of Shiloh Presbyterian Church.

When the Civil War was eminent, Garnet joined with other black leaders in pushing the reluctant Abraham Lincoln to use the opportunity the war provided to abolish slavery. He also urged the president to allow blacks in the Union Army and helped to organize an African American unit. During the New York City draft riot in 1863, when many blacks lost their lives, Garnet had his life threatened and his church badly damaged by white rioters. In 1864 he moved his ministry to Washington, D.C. where, in 1865, he had the opportunity to be the first African American to sermonize Congress at the ratification of the Thirteenth Amendment.

On November 4, 1881, President James A. Garfield appointed Garnet Minister Resident and Counsel General to Liberia. However, Garnet died a few months later in Monrovia after suffering an asthma attack. But his lifelong dream of traveling to Africa had been fulfilled. He was buried in Africa but the words of his fiery speech yet echoed an eloquent refrain in America:

> *"You cannot be more oppressed than you have been –*
> *You cannot suffer greater cruelties than you have already.*
> *Rather die free men than live to be slaves."*

ALTHEA GIBSON (1927-2003)

Althea Gibson was born in Silver, South Carolina on August 25, 1927, the oldest of the five children of Daniel and Annie Washington Gibson. Her father was a sharecropper until, when Althea was a small child, the family moved to the Harlem section of New York City, where he became a handyman in a garage. Growing up in a tough neighborhood where education was not highly valued, Althea often got into trouble for truancy, and in her early teens she dropped out of school altogether to work a series of odd jobs. Restless and discontent, she kept losing the jobs, and when not working, she loitered in the streets of New York City. It was during this period, however, that her talent for tennis was discovered.

The game of tennis gave Gibson a focus and purpose in life for the first time. Within a year after starting lessons, she won the girls' singles in the New York State Open Championships in 1942. In 1944 and 1945 she won the national girls' singles championship of the predominantly black American Tennis Association (ATA). Gibson's talent attracted the attention of two black surgeons in the ATA. The doctors provided her with advanced tennis instruction, beginning in the fall of 1946, they improved her game so much that in the summer of 1947 she won the first of her ten consecutive ATA women's championships.

In 1949 Gibson graduated tenth in her class from Williston Industrial High School in Wilmington, and that fall she entered Florida State University at Tallahassee on a tennis scholarship. There she kept a full load of classes, played both tennis and basketball, worked as a student assistant in the physical education department, and played saxophone in the marching band. Meanwhile, she also began to make a good showing in predominantly white tennis tournaments, including the 1949 and 1950 eastern and national indoor championships.

In 1950, the United States Lawn Tennis Association (USLTA) relaxed its discriminatory policy and allowed Althea Gibson to become the first African American to play in a major event. In 1951 she became the first African American invited to play Wimbledon, where she reached the quarterfinals. She graduated from college in 1953. And in 1955 she undertook an exhibition tour of Asia sponsored by the State Department. The following year she increased her international reputation by playing in Mexico, Sweden,

Germany, Egypt and elsewhere.

By 1956 she won the French Championship, the first time a black person had won a major tennis singles title. In 1957, with her game perfected, she returned to Wimbledon for the third time and became the first African American to win the singles final. She then teamed up with her defeated opponent and won the doubles championship as well. And in September, Gibson won the U.S. Championship in Forest Hills, New York. The following year Gibson, now the number one female tennis player in the world, successfully defended the same three titles.

In 1959 Gibson, at the top of her game, retired from competition. At that time tennis was not lucrative enough to support her. She wrote the autobiographical book *I Always Wanted to Be Somebody*. In the mid-1960s though, she returned to the world of sports by competing in golf tournaments. In 1964 she once again proved her remarkable athletic skill by becoming the first African American to hold a Ladies Professional Golf Association (LPGA) player's card. By 1968 she had written another autobiography, *So Much to Live For*.

Althea Gibson was one of the greatest athletes of her time, a pioneer who helped open the doors for future generations of sports stars, like Venus and Serena Williams. And she is the benchmark by which all other black women measure their achievement in the sport of tennis. Gibson died in 2003 after having realized the same goals for tennis what Jackie Robinson realized for baseball – crossed boundaries, broken barriers, and smashed stereotypes.

JOSH GIBSON (1911-1947)

J osh Gibson was the great Negro League baseball player who is often called the "black Babe Ruth." His batting feats were mythical and his hitting power was legendary. He spent much of his career as the homerun-hitting catcher with the Homestead Grays and the Pittsburgh Crawfords. Gibson's ability was instrumental in increasing the popularity of the Negro Leagues.

He was born Joshua Gibson to Mark, a steelworker, and Nancy Woodlock Gibson on December 21, 1911 in Buena Vista, Georgia. He attended public schools in Buena Vista before studying electrical circuitry at the Allegheny Pre-Vocational School in Pittsburgh. At seventeen, Gibson married Helen Mason, who died delivering their twins. Distraught, Gibson left the hospital without even naming his children. His parents in Pittsburgh would raise the twins, Joshua, Jr. and Helen, for their son. Gibson never remarried.

Gibson's legendary career began in 1927, with a semi-professional team, the Pittsburgh Crawfords of Compton Hill. His notoriety grew as he won three league home run titles. He played there for two seasons before jumping to the Homestead Grays in 1930. His chance to play professional ball came after the Grays catcher, Buck Ewing, had to leave the game with an injured thumb. Some of the Grays players had seen Gibson play and asked him to take Ewing's place behind the plate. Unpolished as a catcher, but with a powerful 6'2" frame and 210 pounds, Gibson made a lasting impression on the Grays and the host team, the Kansas City Monarchs.

Gibson stayed with the Grays for two seasons, 1930-1931, before going back to the Crawfords who were beginning to rival the Grays as a professional team. He won home run titles in 1932, 1934, and 1936 while wearing the Crawford jersey. Gibson rejoined the Grays in 1937. In that year, the Grays split their home games between Washington, D.C. and Pittsburgh. Before the end of the 1937 season, Gibson, James "Cool Papa" Bell, Satchel Page, and several of the Grays teammates played games in Santo Domingo for dictator, Rafael Trujillo.

Gibson's 1938 and 1939 seasons were just as spectacular as previous seasons. He won home run titles in both seasons, and his first batting title in 1938. He was noted for his long distance drives, supposedly being the only player ever to have hit a homerun out of Yankee Stadium. He played briefly in Mexico and

Puerto Rico in 1941 and 1942. He won the batting title in Puerto Rico with a .480 average and was named the Most Valuable Player. After becoming seriously ill in Mexico, he returned to the Grays in 1942. Despite intermittent health problems, Gibson won homerun titles in 1942, 1943, and 1946. He also won a batting title in 1943 with an incredible average of .521. In that season alone, he hit ten homeruns out of Griffin Stadium, a feat never duplicated by any major leaguer.

Gibson was probably the most powerful hitter in the Negro Leagues. He could destroy pitchers' averages with his powerful swing. And he seldom stroke out. Sports Historians have credited Gibson with 823 homeruns in a career that spanned twenty-two years. Gibson was a slugger without the glitz and glamour of his Negro League counterparts. He was simply known as "Josh" – no nicknames, no monikers, and no labels. His skill at bat was the only showmanship he displayed. In his own right, Gibson could bully pitchers with a smooth, quick swing of authority, making the ball leave the park.

Gibson's biggest dream, his heart's ardent desire was to play Major League Baseball. But that would elude him. He died of a sudden stroke as a result of a brain tumor in 1947, just months before Jackie Robinson became the first African American to enter Major League baseball in the Brooklyn Dodgers lineup. But it would be another twelve years before every Major League team could boast of an integrated lineup. Josh Gibson was inducted into the Baseball Hall of Fame in 1972. It was a fitting compliment to a long and brilliant career, and it added a bit of saccharin to an all too short and bittersweet life.

Nikki Giovanni is an African American poet, essayist, and lecturer, whose work reflects pride in her heritage. She has been called the "speaker of the age" because she gives voice to the African American experience. Her poetic language and rhythms reflect jazz and blues music, and she is considered a leader in the black oral poetry movement. She has become famous for strongly voiced poems that testify both to her evolving self-awareness and the black experience.

She was born Yolande Cornelia Giovanni, Jr. on June 7, 1943, the younger of two children of Jones and Cornelia Watson Giovanni in Knoxville, Tennessee. Almost immediately she was nicknamed "Nikki" by her parents. Her father was a probation officer and her mother was a social worker. Her father's surname came from the Italian owner of his ancestors. As a child Nikki heard stories from her maternal grandfather, John Watson, a teacher and Latin scholar who loved myths. From her mother she heard romantic tales and grew up appreciating the quality and rhythm of the telling of stories.

Giovanni began her writing career as a student involved in the black literary movement of the late 1960s. While attending Fisk University she was a militant civil rights activist. She helped to found the university's chapter of the Student Nonviolent Coordinating Committee (SNICK). After graduating in 1967, Giovanni undertook graduate studies at the University of Pennsylvania School Of Social Work in 1967 and the Columbia University School of Fine Arts in 1968. It was 1968 that Giovanni captured the revolutionary spirit of the militant side of the Civil Rights Movement in her poetry collections: *Black Feelings, Black Talk* and *Black Judgment.*

Giovanni changed the focus of her work from public issues to private ones after the birth of her son in 1969. She explored motherhood, womanhood, and personal relationships. Much of her new body of work, however, extended her earlier interests by speaking directly to black people, celebrating positive features of black life, and suggesting that personal values should be applied toward making the world a better place. Her poetry collections during this period included: *Creation* (1970), *My House* (1972), *Ego Tripping and Other Poems for Young People* (1973), *The Women and the Men* (1975), and *Cotton Candy on a Rainy Day* (1978). Also during this time she wrote the monumental *Gemini: An Extended Autobiographical Statement on My First*

Twenty-Five Years of being a Black Poet (1971).

The focus of Giovanni's work has changed frequently, mirroring her view that life itself is fluid and that change is necessary for growth. Subsequent works have stressed a global outlook and include: *Those Who Ride the Night Winds* (1983) and *Sacred Cows...and Other Edibles* (1988). Giovanni has also written children's books and poems and has made recordings of her poems and of her conversations with prominent African American writers.

Giovanni's writings in the 1990s reflected her maturation as an artist reaching her fifties. While still energetically tackling contemporary issues, she also developed an increasing interest in introspection. In 1994 she published a new edition of *Ego Tripping and Other Poems for Young People* with ten new poems added to her 1973 collection. *Racism 101*, written in 1994, is an extremely important book of essays presented from her perspective as a university faculty member.

Nikki Giovanni has engaged in a wide range of professional activities including: poet, college professor, columnist, lecturer, and writer of children's books. She has been invited to speak on stage, radio, and television. As she speaks the listening audience can bask in her warmth. And though those mediums have aptly called her *the speaker of the age*, her message is timeless. Nikki Giovanni speaks from the heart and touches the soul. She speaks from her intellect and raises our consciousness.

THE "GOLD AND GLORY"

B efore athletes like Jesse Owens, Joe Louis, and Jackie Robinson blazed new trails in their particular sport; a group of African American sportsmen risked their very lives on a barnstorming motor sports tour aptly called the Colored Racing Circuit. It was in an era when black sports heroes were not measured by their athletic ability, but by their ability to withstand intense racial prejudice. These motor sportsmen faced overwhelming challenges to create opportunities for African Americans in the realm of auto racing.

In 1920s Indianapolis, the activities of the Ku Klux Klan cast a pall over the social and political landscape. Parks, clubs, and sports venues like the Indianapolis Motor Speedway were rigidly segregated. It was into this world that the Gold and Glory Sweepstakes was born. In 1924, a group of the city's top black civic leaders and several noted white race promoters came together to form the Colored Speedway Association. It was the concept of successful black contractor and racing enthusiast, William Rucker. The group included Carl Fisher, the Indianapolis 500 Mile Race organizer and promoter; Harry Earl, an official in the Midwestern racing circuit; Harold Dunnington, a writer who promoted black sporting events in the Midwest, and O.E. Schilling, a railway executive who helped finance the organization's initial undertaking.

The Gold and Glory Sweepstakes Race had its inaugural staged on August 2, 1924, at the Indiana State Fairgrounds in Indianapolis. Fifteen African American drivers took their places on the starting line. The vehicles were a menagerie of makes, models, and styles. There were no rules about car or engine size. At the race, one could see Fords and Duesenbergs entered in the sweepstakes. But then one could also see some really wild-looking cars as well. Some drivers, especially the best mechanics, made their own cars. They worked in garages and took old, discarded parts and put them into chassis they molded themselves. Even then, racecars were customized to the drivers needs.

The winning driver of the Gold and Glory Sweepstakes 100-mile inaugural was Malcolm Hannon of Indianapolis. His racecar, the "Barber-Warnock Special" won the race in 1:45:42, with an average speed of 63.5 miles per hour. It was a record time for dirt track racing. It thrilled the crowd of 12,000 race fans who attended and was just as thrilling to the thousands more who read about it newspapers and the many more thousands who witnessed it via

233

newsreels. The success of Indy's Gold and Glory Sweepstakes inspired promoters in other cities to organize their own "Colored Speed Classics," effectively creating an African American Racing Circuit.

In those days, auto racing was a new and burgeoning sport. In fact, the automobile industry was not fully an industry. There were no paved roads and no paved racetracks. One big danger for auto drivers and auto racers was dust. On a racetrack, cars driving around an oval kicked up so much dust for the cars behind them, that it was impossible to see anything. Another problem was ruts or groves in the track caused by continuous car tires. Racetracks and American roads were very bumpy and posed severe risks for drivers.

For twelve years, the Gold and Glory Sweepstakes created a racing spectacle so grand it attracted the attention of national newspaper and newsreel agencies, as well as thousands of spectators from around the country. It was recognized as the greatest single sports event staged annually by black people for the express purpose of showcasing African American racecar drivers. It posted the largest purses and presented the greatest array of black driving talent in the country.

These celebrated drivers and mechanics of the Gold and Glory Sweepstakes embodied the essence and the ardor of the racing event. In relentless pursuit of fame and fortune for themselves, these drivers were also in hot pursuit of the "gold and glory" for their race.

THE "GRANDFATHER CLAUSE"

With the enactment of Jim Crow Laws throughout the post-Reconstruction era South, African Americans were at risk of loosing their lives as well as their liberties. Southern states found many and various ways to render the Thirteenth, Fourteenth, and Fifteenth Amendments completely useless. Eight states led by Mississippi and South Carolina, devised novel responses to abridge African American freedoms, citizenship, and voting rights. But it was Louisiana that actually coined the phrase, "Grandfather Clause."

Grandfather clauses were enacted purely for voting purposes. They were devices added to state constitutions, and passed by some Southern states between the end of Reconstruction and the turn of the twentieth century to deny suffrage to African Americans. It simply meant that those who had enjoyed the right to vote prior to 1867, or their lineal descendants, would be exempt from the educational, property, or tax requirements for voting. Put very simply, a man could have all the voting requirements waived if his grandfather had been a voter of that state prior to 1867.

Because the former slaves were not granted the right to vote until the adoption of the Fifteenth Amendment in 1870, grandfather clauses effectively kept African Americans from voting. By the same token, grandfather clauses virtually assured the right to vote for many impoverished and illiterate southern whites. North Carolina, Virginia, Alabama, Georgia, and Oklahoma fell in line to painstakingly disfranchise African Americans, all the while circumventing the Fifteenth Amendment.

Most Southern states employed three maneuvers to eliminate African American voters from the polls: criminal convictions; poll taxes; and literacy tests. The state of Mississippi changed its constitution in 1890 to bar any person "convicted of bribery, burglary, theft, arson, fraud, perjury, forgery, embezzlement or bigamy" from voting. To deprive African Americans of the right to vote, white officials often arrested blacks and convicted them of offenses to remove them from the voting rolls. However, whites who committed the same such offenses were overlooked.

In addition to the criminal offense maneuver, the states required a poll tax to be paid in February for the election held in November. The voter had to bring the receipt indicating payment to the polling place. Many African Americans were unable to pay the poll tax which was cumulative. That is, if a voter wanted to vote, the poll taxes for previous years had to be paid as well. Many blacks, due to poor living conditions, were unable to keep the receipts for nine months. These receipts were often lost or misplaced between February and November. With another obstruction to voting, blacks would have to demonstrate that they could read and interpret sections of state constitutions. Many educated blacks were denied the right to vote because the sole judge was the registrar.

All whites who would have lost their right to vote if the same rules were applied to them escaped being disenfranchised because of grandfather clauses. Louisiana passed the law in 1898 when it became the third state to change its constitution to keep African Americans from voting. The Louisiana law read in part: "no male person who was on January 1, 1867 or at any date prior thereto, entitled to vote...and no son or grandson of any such person...shall be denied the right to register and vote." Since blacks could not vote until 1870, the law was discriminatory against virtually every African American male.

Although it never made a huge difference to Southern states, the U.S. Supreme Court declared the grandfather clause to be unconstitutional in 1915. It was finally judged to be a violation of the universal male suffrage guaranteed by the Fifteenth Amendment. However, discriminatory voting practices continued in the South until the passage of the 1965 Voting Rights Act. Currently, "grandfather clause" is still in use. But today's definition supposedly has no racial connotation. The term today denotes an "exempt status" and is applicable for various reasons. But still, let us all remain aware of its ugly history.

GRIOT (PRONOUNCED GREE/OH)

G riots are very old men still to be found in the older backcountry villages of Sub-Saharan Africa. They are, in effect, walking archives of oral history. Throughout the whole of black Africa such oral chronicles have been handed down since the time of the ancient forefathers. Certain legendary griots can narrate facets of African history literally for as long as three days without ever repeating themselves. We, as Africans of the Diaspora, have an ancestry that goes back to some time and some place where no writing existed.

Griots were first and foremost historians, the keepers of memories. They did much to keep the knowledge of the past alive. A griot's reputation rose or fell commensurate with his ability to make the story come alive. Africans come from a strong oral tradition, against which there is a western bias. Europe, and by extension, the United States, honors the written word, but not the spoken. Cultures where history is orally transmitted tend to be discounted and devalued.

Griots were trained from childhood. They often came from particular families whose members, for generations, had been griots. Different griot families often used different accompanying instruments to tell or sing their stories. Author Alex Haley, when writing the quintessential "Roots," had to visit the Mandinka griot for his ancestral Kinte clan with three interpreters and four musicians, because the old griot would not talk without music in the background. Since time immemorial, the griot traveled the countryside carrying an instrument, and always prepared to tell either the news of the day, or the story of a lifetime.

During earlier centuries in West Africa, the griot was a bard or minstrel employed at the royal courts of the great Ghana, Mali and Songhay Empires. Griots preserved the memory of the line of descent of all the ruling families and kept the record of battles, victories, and other notable events. In addition, the griot was expected to offer advice on many matters of state. They knew specific monarchs histories and could extract lessons for the rulers from that knowledge.

More importantly, griots represented the common folk. They were the voice of the people beyond the royal courts. They told rulers what the people were saying and thinking. Griots could be outspoken and critical without fear of reprisal. So highly valued were their views that they would not be punished for their criticism. This, more than anything else, aided benevolent rule, and caused democracy to flourish in many African societies. There was also a deeper side to the role of a griot. Interpreting dreams was a griot specialty. Knowing the secrets of healing, spells, charms, and herbal remedies, was another art. Some griots knew how to manipulate sound to produce certain mental effects, such as relaxation and meditation, and could even induce trances.

The griot tradition came to America with slaves from West Africa and continues even today. In the United States, it has found expression in our culture in the many and varied African American art forms. Rappers style themselves after griots with long and tedious monologues set to music. Black choreographer, Garth Fagan, created wonderful dance stories entitled *Griot New York City* with musical accompaniment by trumpeter Wynton Marsalis. Today, all African American storytellers, whether male or female, call themselves "Griot" after the African storytelling tradition.

Black preachers can be considered the spiritual descendants of the griot in that they have seized the opportunity presented by Christianity. They establish reputations based upon their ability to tell and retell "the story" of God's saving grace. Especially in the Baptist tradition, black preachers have developed a unique style of delivery, a kind of singsong sermon that is part speech, part exhortation, part ballad, and part awe-inspiring performance art.

G ullah is the name of an African American people strongly influenced by West Africa. The descendents of slaves who originated in West Africa, Gullah people have occupied the Sea Islands off the South Carolina and Georgia coasts since the seventeenth century. Gullah is the name not only of the people but also of their language and culture. They speak a Creole form of English, a *pidgin* dialect that has become the native language for its speakers, merging elements of several West African languages. The vocabulary is predominantly English but the syntax and grammar are more reflective of African languages.

The Gullah use palm-leaf brooms, fish with traditional cast nets of their own weaving, and retain a diet that is similar to the fare of West Africa. All Gullah handicrafts have a distinctive African flavor. Their sweet grass baskets have a coiled design closely related to those still woven in the Gambia and Senegal. The houses avoid the row-style layout typical of the United States, favoring instead the method of clustering homes around the main home, which belongs to a matriarch. The dead are buried near their mother, as in some West African societies. Although overwhelmingly Christian, the Gullah have incorporated many African cultural traits into their worship.

West African slaves were first brought to the Sea Islands to cultivate indigo, later for rice, and finally for the famous long-staple fine quality cotton. Because of their knowledge of rice growing, they greatly influenced rice growing in South Carolina. Slaves from rice-growing regions in Africa were highly prized in rice-growing regions in the American South. Africans from the Bight of Benin, Nigeria, the Bight of Congo, and Angola were veteran rice growers who needed not to be re-taught the skill. The harsh conditions on the Sea Islands and the backbreaking work of rice planting kept white settlement low. By the end of the eighteenth century, more than 70% of the islands' inhabitants were black.

In November 1861, as the Civil War was commencing, plantation owner on the islands fled to the relative safety of the mainland as Union Naval ships blockaded and patrolled Southern shores. This effectively freed the Sea Island slaves who claimed the abandoned lands as their own. Although the federal government did not allow the freedmen to obtain legal title to the lands, the period did provide the Gullah with experience in independent subsistence farming. After the American Civil War in the mid nineteenth century, the Gullah people remained on the islands with the relative isolation from the mainland preserving their cultural conditions. Like other African Americans, they were often denied their civil rights, but they had their own civil practices, which their remote location allowed them to maintain.

The numbers of Gullah remaining on the islands began to dwindle during the twentieth century. In the 1920s, mainland authorities constructed bridges to many of the islands. The economic opportunities associated with war industries during World War II drew many Gullah away. And in the 1950s and 1960s, developers began to purchase land on the islands, developing the properties for tourism. Most vacationers know Hilton Head, South Carolina as a tourist resort, not as home to a unique African American culture.

Although mainstream American culture has encroached upon them in modern times, Gullah communities still existed during the late twentieth century in small farming and fishing villages, practicing many of the same customs of their African ancestors. In 1979 their numbers were estimated to be a mere 100,000. And if current numbers are smaller yet, there is still a legacy that is too great to be enumerated. The Gullah culture, the people and the language, represent a diffusion of West African cultures that reached these shores by the largest forced migration of people the world has ever witnessed – the Transatlantic Slave Trade.

THE GREAT MIGRATION

From 1915 to the 1930s, 1.8 million Southern African Americans migrated to industrial cities in the North and the Midwest. The influx of blacks into northern cities during this period was called "The Great Migration" because it forever changed the layout of blacks on the American landscape. Black relations with other Americans were fundamentally altered as well. Blacks were no longer stationary agricultural workers, but industrial workers and craftsmen, competing with whites for jobs in the industrialized north.

At its peak, this tremendous population shift saw sixteen thousand blacks per month leaving the South. According to the 1900 Census, there were nine million African Americans, totaling 12% of the nation's population of just over seventy-five million citizens. Over 90% of the nine million blacks lived in the South. The South had been the American homeland of blacks since the earliest days of slavery. By that same 1900 Census, blacks accounted for one-third, or eight million of the South's total population. No one could have predicted that a people so fixed within a region would leave in such great numbers. The causes of that migration were varied but blatant.

At first, blacks crowed into northern cities to get wartime factory jobs. Factory work paid well when compared to farm wages and sharecropping. When World War I began in 1911, it interrupted the flow of European immigrants into the country. Italians, Irish, and Central Europeans had been the primary hirelings for northern factories. Ironically, it was the war itself that caused both an increase boon to manufacturing and a decrease in the labor supply.

The northern labor agents, who offered free transportation to those in search of the factory jobs that the war was rapidly generating, relentlessly recruited southern blacks. Northern manufacturing companies who sent them to the South to solicit African American laborers employed these labor agents. Southern society became apprehensive only when it realized that homes were without housekeepers, farms were without laborers, churches were empty, and sharecropping shacks were deserted. The white citizenry of many Southern towns threatened blacks, while the southern press urged them to remain in the South.

The northern black press did much to persuade blacks to leave the South. One newspaper in particular, the *Chicago Defender* wrote; "To die from the bite of frost is far more glorious than at the hands of a mob." It was an obvious reference to the colder temperatures in the North and the high incidence of the lynching of black people in the South. The National Urban League was essentially created for, and played an active role, in helping African Americans adjust to a totally new, and much different life in the industrial cities of the North.

The Chicago Defender touched on the most alarming reasons blacks sought to leave the South. The Great Migration was due primarily to the African American dissatisfaction with, and their determination to escape oppressive, exploitative race relations in the South. Jim Crow segregation kept blacks in the position of underclass citizens. Fifty years after the end of the Civil War, blacks were virtually prisoners in the rural South. In many places, blacks lived poorly in conditions hardly better than slavery. They were paid the lowest wages, had the least nutritious diets, and suffered generally poor health. And the racial climate had become even more savage and murderous. There was a sudden increase in the number of lynchings by 1919. Even black military veterans were "strung-up" while still in uniform.

Although numerous unfortunate incidents resulted from the wholesale movement of African Americans into the North and Midwest, the migration, coming when it did, gave them an opportunity for industrial employment that they had never before enjoyed. And it relieved the labor shortage during the crucial years of the war. Within a few years, the nation's racial demographics were transformed. Suddenly there were large black communities crowding into Northern cities, some of which in only a very few African Americas had lived in the past. And to this day, blacks remain a big part of the urban experience.

T he decade of the 1960s is known as one of the most volatile times in American social and political history. United States culture was forever changed by it. As a time of tremendous change, society became unstable, unpredictable, and explosive. But on February 1, 1960, four black students from North Carolina Agricultural & Technical State College sat down at the "whites only" lunch counter in an F. W. Woolworth Department Store and quietly and with dignity, asked to be served. This was the opening salvo of a previously unseen student protest movement that shook the South to its very foundation. And it set the stage for student nonviolent demonstrations for the remainder of the decade.

The four young men, Ezell Blair, Jr., Franklin McCain, Joseph McNeil, and David Richmond, were freshmen on academic scholarships at the college. The *Greensboro Four*, as history has labeled them, were seeking much more than the sodas and sandwiches they ordered. They were attacking the social order of the time. "Jim Crow" laws, the Southern formula for racial segregation and discrimination, required black people to stay out of white-owned restaurants, to use only designated drinking fountains and restrooms, to sit in the rear of buses, and in a separate balcony area of movie theaters.

The Greensboro students acted at a time when protests against segregation in schools and on buses were taking place all over the South. But there were few challenges to segregation in privately owned businesses such as Woolworth's. And yet, these four teenagers dared to take on a system so profoundly ingrained in that city, and others in the segregated South. And before the 1960s would end, however, there came nonviolent student protests, in various forms, all over the United States.

The four freshmen in Greensboro selected Woolworth Department store because they especially resented the company's double standard. Everywhere but in the South, black and white patrons sat together at Woolworth counters. Not only was the counter segregated, but also the staff behind it. Waitresses were white, but those who cooked and cleaned up were black. Black patrons could shop Woolworth's general merchandise counters and eat at a stand-up snack bar and bakery counter. But one section of the store remained forbidden territory: the long L-shaped lunch counter, with stainless steel and plastic cushion stools that took up two walls of the first floor.

When Blair, McCain, McNeil, and Richmond were refused service, they remained seated until the store closed for the evening. They returned each morning for the next five days to occupy the lunch counter. They were joined by a group of protesters that grew to hundreds. The students also faced violent white mobs, angered by the possibility of equal treatment for blacks. The sit-ins lasted off and on for five months before Woolworth agreed to full integration.

Within ten days of the Greensboro Four's demonstration, sit-ins were being staged in fifteen southern cities in five states. Within three months, thousands of black students were taking seats at segregated lunch counters and demanding service. If, as generally happened, the students were refused service, they refused to move until arrested. The sit-ins, patterned on the passive resistance techniques of Mohandas K. Gandhi of India, spread across the entire South affecting department stores, libraries, supermarkets, and movie theaters. By the end of 1960, 70,000 black students had participated in or marched in support of the demonstrators, and 36,000 of them had been arrested.

The *Greensboro Four* are recognized heroes of the Civil Rights Movement because their nonviolent demonstration helped to end the strict segregation that defined southern life. Their protest inspired black and white students to do the same at other lunch counters in other cities. The movement they started led to the integration of Woolworth's and other department store chains. The *Greensboro Four* were just four of the sparks...that ignited the flame...that burned down the house...that Jim Crow built.

CHARLES "BUSTER" HALL (1920-1971)

On July 2, 1943, Lt. Charles Hall made history by becoming the first African American pilot to shoot down enemy aircraft in World War II. Hall, a Hoosier native, was one of the 1,000 all-black Tuskegee Airmen who earned their wings as trained fighter pilots; and one of the 450 who flew escort and combat missions over Europe and North Africa during that war. Under the fierce protection of the Tuskegee Airmen, not a single bomber was lost. Their 99th Pursuit Squadron earned over 800 medals for valor.

Charles Blakely Hall was born in 1920, the son of Frank and Anna Hall, in Brazil, Indiana. He had been an outstanding athlete at Brazil High School, lettering in football, basketball, and track, before graduating in 1938. He enrolled at Eastern Illinois University at Charleston in the fall of 1938 and played halfback on the football team during his first two years at the university. In 1941 Hall withdrew from college to enlist in the United States Army Air Corps. His goal was to be accepted in the aviation cadet-training program in Tuskegee, Alabama. After completing basic training, Hall was assigned to Class 42-F, the fourth at Tuskegee Institute.

The 99th Pursuit Squadron was activated in January 1941 to receive the first black pilots to complete flight training. Instruction was accomplished in three phases: primary, basic, and advanced. Hall graduated and was commissioned a second lieutenant in July 1942. He was well liked by his fellow cadets, who often referred to him as "Buster." On June 2, 1943, the 99th flew its first combat mission with Hall and three other Tuskegee Airmen selected to fly that historic mission. The four black pilots flew as wingmen in new P-40s armed with six 50-calibre machine guns manned by four white pilots from the 33rd Fighter Group. No enemy aircraft was encountered, and all planes returned safely without damage. A month later, however, Lt. Hall did engage enemy aircraft and made aviation history in the process.

A flight of U.S. B-25 bombers was being escorted by six escort fighters after completing its bombing runs on the enemy airfield over Sicily, when a pair of German FW-190s dropped in behind the last two bombers for what seemed to be an easy kill. But out of nowhere came Hall's P-40 Warhawk, with the name "Maxine/Knobly II" emblazoned on its nose. Lt. Hall gives an account of his historic mission in his own words: "*It was my eighth mission, but the first time*

I had seen the enemy close enough to shoot at. I saw two FW-190s following the Mitchells just after the bombs were dropped. I headed for the space between the fighters and bombers and managed to turn inside the "jerries" [Germans]. I fired a long bust and saw my tracers penetrate the second aircraft. He was turning to the left, but suddenly fell off and headed straight into the ground. I followed him down and saw the crash. He raised a big cloud of dust."

This modest recount gives the impression that nothing special happened that day. But Lt. Hall received much attention from the press for his feat and was personally congratulated after the mission by General Dwight D. Eisenhower. The black press in the U.S. especially brought the news of Hall's victory to the American public. Buster Hall would fly many more missions with the 99th Squadron during the next several months. In January 1944, Hall became a captain, and members of his patrol group over Italy intercepted seven German fighters that were beginning their strafing run on allied positions at Anzio. The 99th dove into the middle of the German formation, and Hall shot down a ME-109 and another FW-190. For this feat he was awarded the Distinguished Flying Cross by Gen. Eisenhower.

At the time of his honorable discharge in 1946, Hall had achieved the rank of Major. He had been described by his commander as a man totally without fear. In total, he had flown 87 missions before his discharge at the end of his European and North African tour of duty. He relocated to Oklahoma City and worked at Tinker Field. Later he joined the Federal Aviation Agency (FAA), where he was employed until the time of his death in 1971. Charles Blakely Hall is just one historic Hoosier link to the history making Tuskegee Airmen.

LLOYD AUGUSTUS HALL (1894-1971)

L loyd A. Hall was a chemist and a pioneer in the area of food technology, where he developed processes to cure and preserve meat, prevent rancidity in fats, and sterilize spices. His patented chemical processes revolutionized the meatpacking industry and benefited other food products as well. He was born in Elgin, Illinois on June 20, 1894 to Augustus Hall, the first pastor of Quinn Chapel A.M.E. Church, the first African American church in Chicago. His mother, Isabel, fled slavery via the Underground Railroad at the age of sixteen. Hall was an honor student at East Side High School in Aurora, Illinois where he developed an interest in chemistry. He was active in various extracurricular activities including the debate team, track, basketball, and football. By graduation, he had been offered academic scholarships to four Illinois universities.

Hall selected Northwestern University, but chose to work as he obtained a B.S. in Chemistry in 1916. At Northwestern, he met Carroll Griffith, a fellow chemistry major who would later play a significant role in his career. He would eventually earn graduate degrees from the University of Chicago and the University of Illinois. In his first position, he worked as a chemist in the Chicago Department of Health laboratory. Within a year he was promoted to senior chemist. During World War I Hall served as a lieutenant in the Army Ordinance Department as chief inspector of powder and explosives at a plant in Wisconsin. He was subjected to such prejudice and discrimination that he asked to be transferred. That prejudice followed him in civilian life as he attempted to get a job with the Western Electric Company but was denied employment.

During the six years following the war, Hall worked in several industrial laboratories. In 1921, he was made chief chemist at Boyer Chemical Labs in Chicago. By then, he had become interested in the emergent technology of food chemistry. In 1922 he became president and chemical director of the Chemical Products Corporation, a consulting lab in Chicago. In 1924, one of Hall's clients, Griffith Laboratories, offered him space where he could work for them while continuing his consulting practice. By 1925, Hall had become chief chemist and director of research at Griffith Labs. In 1929 he gave up his consulting practice and devoted himself full-time to Griffith Labs until his retirement. In 1939 he and Carroll Griffith co-founded the Institute of Food Technologies, established a new branch of industrial chemistry. During World

War II, Hall was invaluable in solving problems of maintaining edible food for the military.

Before Hall's patented processes, standard meat curing and preservation methods were highly unsatisfactory. It was known that sodium chloride preserved meat, while nitrates and nitrites were used for curing. However, not much was known about how these chemicals worked, and food could not be preserved for any extended period of time. But Hall developed a new salt mixture of sodium nitrate and sodium nitrite. Hall's method of flash-drying the solution formed preserving crystals far superior to any meat-curing salts ever produced.

Hall's next accomplishment was in the area of spices. Although he formulated the process by which meat could now be preserved and cured effectively, the natural spices that were used to enhance and preserve meat often contained contaminants. Spices such as allspice, cloves, cinnamon, and paprika, as well as dried vegetable products like onion powder, contained yeasts, molds, and bacteria. Hall developed a method to sterilize the spices and dried vegetables without destroying their original flavor and appearance. He discovered that ethylene oxide, a gas used to kill insects, would also kill germs in the spices. He used a vacuum chamber to remove the moisture from the spices so that the gas would permeate and sterilize them when introduced into the chamber. This has added great convenience to the food preparation habits of every modern cook. Lloyd A. Hall left a great legacy of innovations in the food preservation industry.

P rince Hall is recognized as the father of Black Masonry in the United States. He made it possible for black men to be recognized and enjoy all privileges of Free and Accepted Masonry. As a result of his dedication, there are nearly 5,000 lodges, forty Grand Lodges, and nearly half a million black Masons in the United States, all under the name of *Prince Hall Masonic Lodges*.

The generally acknowledged facts about the early life of Prince Hall have been in dispute by historians, giving rise to many rumors about his birth. But it is generally accepted that he was born in British Barbados in 1735 of racially mixed parentage. He immigrated to Boston in 1765 by working aboard a ship bound for the British North American Colonies. Hall enlisted in the militia during the Revolutionary War and fought with the Americans.

The record of Hall's Masonic activities is clearly documented. Prince Hall was this country's first black Mason. He was initiated on March 6, 1775, in Lodge # 441, just outside Boston. Shortly afterward, Hall and the fourteen other men initiated with him were given a temporary permit to meet in accordance with established Masonic practices. As Grand Master, Hall later petitioned and received approval for the establishment of Lodge # 459, a regular Lodge of Free and accepted Masons, under the title of "African Lodge # 1." For nine years the black Masons assembled and enjoyed their limited privileges as Masons. They were permitted to bury their dead, but they could not confer degrees nor perform any other Masonic work.

Finally in 1784, Hall petitioned the Grand Lodge of England for a warrant (charter) and received it in 1787. The Warrant to African Lodge # 459 of Boston is the most significant and highly prized document known to the Prince Hall Mason Fraternity. Through it their legitimacy is traced, and on it their case rests. In 1791, His Royal Highness, the Prince of Wales, appointed Hall Provincial Grand Master. Hall then turned his attention to the organization of other black lodges. By 1798, he had established three others, which together constituted the Prince Hall Solidarity.

In addition to his activities as a Mason, Hall also worked diligently to abolish slavery and secure equal rights for blacks in what had become the United States of America. He was very skillful in using legal means to combat slavery and discrimination. He petitioned the Massachusetts state legislature several times. In 1777, when Hall and several other black Masons appealed for the abolition of slavery, the state legislature refused to act. By 1788 he appealed for legislative action to ensure that black citizens be allowed to walk the streets in safety. Within a month the legislature passed the act "to prevent the slave trade, and for granting relief to the families of such unhappy persons as may be kidnapped or destroyed from this Commonwealth."

Hall regularly involved himself in politics. As a taxpayer and property owner, he sued for equal educational facilities for black children. Although this appeal was rejected, in 1798 a group of concerned black parents opened a school in Hall's home. The site for the school was later moved to the African Meeting House, where it operated for twenty-nine years. He was also one of the early proponents of black colonization, encouraging free black immigration to West Africa. Black colonization was a controversial theme that would continue to be so throughout the next two centuries in United States.

Prince Hall was a success at many things in his lifetime: seaman, leather worker, property owner, founder of a school, civil rights advocate, political activist, and African Methodist Episcopal (AME) minister. But history has recorded him first and foremost as a Mason, and the founder of Prince Hall Masonry in the United States.

FANNIE LOU HAMER (1917-1977)

Fannie Lou Hamer was the founder and vice-chairperson of the Mississippi Freedom Democratic Party (MFDP), which successfully unseated the all white Democratic Party at the 1968 Democratic Convention. She earned the title "First Lady of Civil Rights" because of her courage and determination in the face of racial bigotry and hatred. During the Civil Rights Movement, she summed up conditions in Mississippi in her own unique homespun way by saying: *"I am sick and tired of being sick and tired."*

She was born Fannie Lou Townsend on October 6, 1917, to Jim and Lou Ella Townsend, the last of their twenty children. Her parents were sharecroppers in the Mississippi Delta town of Ruleville. Although the family picked between 50 and 60 bales of cotton a year, they lived in extreme poverty with little to eat and no heat or plumbing. Fannie suffered a life-long limp because her leg was broken in infancy and never treated. She learned to pick cotton at age six and only attended school periodically, finally dropping out at age twelve. In the early 1940s, after many of her siblings had moved to the North, she married Perry Hamer, a farm worker and tractor driver. The couple moved into a small house on a cotton plantation in Sunflower County and began sharecropping. They adopted two daughters who eventually provided them with grandchildren.

In 1962 Hamer became involved with the Civil Rights Movement when the Southern Christian Leadership Conference (SCLC) and the Student Nonviolent Coordinating Committee (SNCC) organized a mass meeting in her area. The Delta region was home to poverty-stricken blacks living in the worst conditions in the United States. SCLC and SNCC hoped to register and educate the more than 400,000 African Americans in Mississippi who were being denied their constitutional right to vote by a variety means, including voter registration tests, poll taxes, and violent intimidation.

For Hamer's political involvement, her landlord evicted her from the house her family lived in and they were forced from the land they had sharecropped for eighteen years. A friend quoted her: *"They kicked me off the plantation, they set me free. It's the best thing that could happen. Now I can work for my people."* Afterwards, Hamer joined SNCC as a field worker where she was soon seen by the leadership as a valuable asset because of her brilliant oratory and powerful singing. She also became a living symbol of the dangers faced by civil rights workers after she was unjustly jailed and severely beaten in Winona, Mississippi upon returning from citizenship classes in 1963. When word of her mistreatment reached Dr. Martin Luther King, he demanded her immediate release. King, Andrew Young and James Bevel carried her limp body from jail.

In many of her endeavors for civil rights, Hamer experienced shouts, curses, and even gunfire from angry and abusive crowds of whites. But she came to national prominence in 1964, in the first attempt of the MDFP to unseat the Mississippi delegation at the Democratic National Convention. Hamer was interviewed on national television to question America about its failure to provide equal justice for all Americans. She gave a scathing account of the voting atrocities occurring in the state of Mississippi. In her lifetime Hamer saw the results of her civil rights efforts. The most impressive result of her work with the Council of Federated Organizations, a coalition of SNCC, CORE, and NAACP, was the enactment of the 1965 Voting Rights Act. The U.S. Congress passed the law to ensure the rights of African Americans to register to vote.

By 1968, Mississippi's convention delegation was no longer all white. Also in 1968, Robert Clark was elected to the Mississippi State Legislature, the first black Congressman since Reconstruction. From 1969 to 1974 Hamer ran the "Freedom Farm," a cooperative farm that provided poor blacks with both food and jobs. Fannie Lou Hamer remained an inspiration to many as she continued her civil rights involvement, and as she expanded her work to include issues of poverty and economic empowerment.

JUPITER HAMMON (1711-1806?)

Jupiter Hammon was a slave and the first black poet to be published in the British North American Colonies. He was a devout Christian and all of his poems were written as if they were psalms. They were filled with the spirituality of the Enlightenment Age. He was greatly influenced and inspired by the "Great Awakening," a series of religious revivals taking place in 18th century New England. He was also a preacher for other slaves and free blacks on Long Island, New York.

Hammon was born into slavery on October 17, 1711 on Long Island, New York. He was a slave his entire life and served several generations of the Lloyd family on the Lloyd Manor Estate on Long Island where he died. He lived a privileged enough existence for him to publicly say that he "did not wish to be free." However, he did think that it was advantageous for young people to be free. It was clear in his writings, Hammon thought of himself as "free" by virtue of his salvation. His aspiration was to achieve "perfection" through the study of the Word of God.

Hammon received an unusually extensive education on the Lloyd Manor Estate, from Nehemiah Bull, a Harvard graduate and later noted New England minister. Hammon was basically allowed to engage in any business he wished. This included reading in the extensive Lloyd library, and writing his poetry. Hammon knew how valuable these privileges were and took full advantage of the kindness offered to him. He wrote in the religious tradition of his era. His writings were religious exhortations and dealt with themes of race, slavery, and the alienation of slaves. Since his poems were edited and probably approved by white patrons, his themes of white injustices took on even more important significance as enlightenment philosophy, and later as abolitionist doctrine.

Hammon's first poem, *An Evening Thought* was written on Christmas Day 1760 and published as a broadside in early 1761. It appears to be the first piece of literature published in British North America by a person of African descent. The second existing piece of poetry, published in 1778, honors the young Phyllis Wheatley. Even though Hammon never mentions himself in the poem, it seems that in choosing Wheatley as the subject, he is acknowledging their common bond of slavery. He too adored the wisdom of God that brought them both to these shores and to the beacon of His Son. In 1779 Hammon published *An Essay on the Ten Virgins*. *A Winter Piece* followed it in 1782. It is believed that Hammon composed a set of verses, not yet found and probably still unpublished also in 1782. These verses supposedly celebrate the visit of young British Prince William Henry to the Lloyd Manor House.

The last extant prose to be published by Hammon was *An Evening Improved* in 1783. In his *Address to the Negroes of State of New York* before their African Society on September 24, 1786, Hammon's feelings about slavery are made quite clear. In this speech, he claimed that even though he did not wish to be free himself, slavery was still an unjust system and that he would "be glad if others, especially the young Negroes were free." The fact that Hammon never aspired to be a free man attests to the sheltered and comfortable life he led as a slave of a wealthy and powerful family. His life was one of study and contemplation, not drudge and toil.

Apparently Jupiter Hammon was very content as a slave. But before we judge him as apathetic, we will need to understand how privileged his life was. We already know that very few slaves lived as comfortably or as happily as he did. As African Americans we know what it is to live within this skin. But we cannot, with twenty-first century eyes, look upon an eighteenth century black man and judge his actions. So let us not look askance at Hammon. Only an astute student of history can surmise what it was like to walk in Hammon's shoes before there was a United States. He was comfortable for sure, but I am also sure that his walk as a slave was circumspect. And yet, all Americans, black and white, must acclaim Hammon's poetry in recognition of his role as a founder of the African American literary tradition.

HISTORICALLY BLACK COLLEGES AND UNIVERSITIES

There are more than one hundred Historically Black Colleges and Universities (HBCU) in the United States to date. These institutions of higher learning, whose principal mission is to educate African Americans, have greatly evolved since their humble beginning in 1837, when their primary responsibility was to teach freed slaves to read and write. As we enter the third millennium the HBCU not only offer graduate and post-graduate degrees, they offer African American students a place to earn a sense of identity, heritage, and community.

In the Post-Civil War era of Reconstruction, the origins of the southern HBCU were modest at best. The first black colleges were the result of small donations from church missionary groups and from the Freedman's Bureau. Often, local groups of free blacks and the newly freedmen helped these fledging academies by building and maintaining school buildings, bringing farm produce to feed students, and raising money for them. Many of the former slaves possessed skills such as carpentry and masonry, and were adept at building. Those blacks who were free before the Civil War were entrepreneurs. They sold hams, chickens, and eggs to benefit the new colleges. At Hampton Institute, the very first students were not even taught in classrooms but under an oak tree, later named "Emancipation Oak."

Most students were extremely poor. They came to college shoeless with no possessions other than the clothes on their backs. Frequently they had walked for miles to even get to the colleges. Booker T. Washington walked most of the way from West Virginia to reach Hampton Institute in Virginia. The northern whites who came to teach the eager black pupils found them in need of more than just education. Many of the former slaves did not even have sir-names by which to be called. They found a great supply from many the dead presidents. The names of Washington, Adams, Jefferson, and Jackson were commonly assumed. Some of them assumed a sir-name based on their fathers' occupations: Miller, Tanner, Smith, Carpenter, and Mason. And some continued in the names of their former masters.

At first these colleges were just primary and secondary schools, and taught only basic skills. College classes came much later. For decades, whites administered these colleges, and the schools' educational philosophies often reflected the white concept of black needs in the postwar years. However,

Tuskegee Institute, under the administration of Booker T. Washington, was from the beginning, a school staffed entirely by blacks. It is important to note that the HBCU did not impose age requirements on their students. So classrooms were overcrowded with black people of all ages. In 1865, it was estimated that only 5% of the freedmen could read and write. In 1870, the number had expanded to nearly 20%. And every decade after that showed a marked increase in the literacy rate of southern blacks.

The United Negro College Fund (UNCF) is a Virginia based American philanthropic organization that raises funds for college tuition money for black students and general scholarship funds for thirty-nine historically black colleges and universities. UNCF was incorporated on April 25, 1944. Among the founding organizers was Frederick D. Patterson, then president of Tuskegee Institute and Mary McLeod Bethune, then president of Bethune-Cookman College and the National Council of Negro Women. UNCF was the first consortium to apply the concept of cooperative fund raising to the field of higher education.

The HBCU, with the help of UNCF as its primary funding source, have extended their unique partnership into the new millennium. With an emphasis on education that far surpasses literacy, the HBCU offer business, humanities and technology courses on par with any of the white universities. And assured that African Americans will not abandon their strong tradition of self-help and mutual assistance, UNCF mounts a successful annual marketing campaign to raise many millions of dollars. And they have acquired one of the most widely recognizable marketing slogans in advertising history:

"A MIND IS A TERRIBLE THING TO WASTE."

W C. Handy was a composer, cornetist, bandmaster, publisher and educator. He was considered to be the "Father of the Blues," as was the title of his 1941 autobiography. The Blues, the African American musical genre of great historical and cultural significance, took form in the late nineteenth century and became a major form of black expression. It was in no sense the creation of any one individual, but Handy is credited with making the Blues known to the world.

He was born William Christopher Handy on November 16, 1873, in Florence, Alabama. He was educated in public schools and by his father and paternal grandfather who were both clergymen. He taught school before he was nineteen, but then left home to work in a factory in Bessemer, Alabama because it paid more. In 1893 he organized a quartet that performed at the Chicago World's Fair, an exposition that attracted many musicians. Later he traveled the country, making a career in music with brass bands. For a time, he taught music and was the bandmaster at Alabama A & M in Huntsville.

When teaching music on the college level was no longer satisfying, Handy tried minstrelsy. In 1896 was invited to join Mahara's Minstrel Show as a cornet player for $6.00 per week. They called him "Fess," which was short for Professor, in recognition of his musical abilities. After only one season, he was made bandleader of a 42-piece orchestra. However, his career choice brought criticism from family and friends because minstrelsy was disreputable in the eyes of the black bourgeoisie. But he remained with the troupe until 1903.

Handy spent the next five years as a bandleader in Clarkdale, Mississippi and it was there that he encountered the Blues, as if for the first time. He approached it hesitantly at first, but then, with deepening interest, he seized the loosely constructed folk idiom, performed by unschooled musicians and formalized its 12-bar form. By so doing, he prepared the way for the Blues craze of the 1920s when a more general dissemination of the Blues took place. By his own account, Handy took music "already used by Negro roustabouts, honky-tonk piano players, wanders, and others, from Missouri to the Gulf of Mexico and introduced the Blues form to the general public."

Handy settled in Memphis 1908 and established the Pace & Handy Music Company with partner and lyricist, Harry Pace. The company also served as a booking agent for other dance bands thus controlling the black music industry in Memphis. In 1912, he published *Memphis Blues* which was one of the first Blues to appear in sheet music. According to Noble Sissle, *Memphis Blues* inspired the "Fox Trot," a ballroom dance created by Vernon and Irene Castle. His best-known composition and an American standard, *St. Louis Blues*, followed two years later. It has been one of the most recorded songs in the history of music. Handy was still receiving the royalties of $25,000 per year for it when he died.

In 1918 Handy and Pace moved their company to New York City and it became the leading publisher of music by African American composers. The two dissolved their partnership in 1920, and continued separately in the music industry. Although Handy continued to perform and compose, he became increasingly active as a businessman and impresario. He also published two musical collections: *Blues: An Anthology* (1926) and *Book of Negro Spirituals* (1938).

Throughout his long career, W.C. Handy was a tireless ambassador for African American music. His importance to history lies in his success as a publisher and promoter. Popularizing the Blues was his greatest accomplishment. He took regional black folksongs, little known beyond the southern United States, and ultimately transformed American popular music into a force recognized in the entire world. Though William Christopher Handy was not the only one to play the Blues and Ragtime, he is credited for notating his music for publication thereby preserving it for posterity.

The Harlem Renaissance was that extraordinary flourishing of African American art, music, literature, history and culture in the early 20th century. The first budding may have happened in New York City, but by the 1930s there were garden spots throughout the United States. Although debate brews as to when this rebirth began and when it ended, it is fairly well agreed upon that the best time reference to use would be the era ending World War I until the onset of World War II.

World War I ended with the armistice in November 1919. During the postwar period a distinctly new literary movement emerged in the United States. American writers became interested in numerous social and economic problems. Labor problems received a great amount of attention, as did housing, crime, social planning, and disarmament. Novelists, dramatists, publicists, and other writers also turned to the American race problem. There can be no doubt that the emergence of African American writers in this postwar period stemmed in part from the fact that they were inclined to exploit the opportunity to write about themselves and the black experience.

Strictly speaking, the Harlem Renaissance was not just a literary movement. It was a period of astonishing creativity among African American artists, musicians, actors, as well as writers. And it had many anomalies. First, it was not actually a *renaissance* at all. It was less a *rebirth* of African American culture than it was a sudden *outburst* of it. The age produced race and socially conscious artists who reached back to Africa and into the American black experience to achieve a distinctively blended motif. It was completely Afro-centric in outlook, and completely modern in attitude.

Black artists like Charles Alston, one of the most important muralists during this time, used the *cubist style* to depict contrasts between black and white realities in America. Alston and another artist, Hale Woodruff, were commissioned to do a mural for the Golden State Mutual Life Insurance Company documenting black contributions in the founding of California. The existence of black independent filmmakers like Oscar Micheaux, active during this period, was made possible largely by the great hunger of the African American masses for films that featured members of their race and addressed issues that affected their lives.

A second anomaly of the Harlem Renaissance is that it did not take place exclusively in Harlem. Black culture flourished in many other areas of the country. Jazz, a strictly African American music form, was born in New Orleans, but it was transported to every other major city in America. It was transported to Europe, making it international in scope. The 1920s was defined as the *Jazz Age*. Although New York City was the center of the Harlem Renaissance and the publishing industry was chiefly located there, it still could not claim a complete monopoly on African American literary activity in the decades following the war. Black writers were being published in Boston, Philadelphia, and Chicago literary houses as well.

It was only natural that artists of the Harlem Renaissance in New York City would tend to move in the same social circles. There was a community of spirit and viewpoint that found its expression not only in cooperative ventures of a professional nature, but also in the intimate social relationships that developed in literary saloons and jazz clubs. Perhaps Harlemites felt that form and substance could be given to their efforts through the interchange of ideas in moments of informality. And, if nothing else, if no other commonality could be found, every African American writer, poet, musician, etc., had a kindred spirit and a shared heritage of being black in America.

Harlem Renaissance ideas and influence have long outlived the era. It continues to represent creativity and ingenuity. But it flowered again in the 1960s as the Black Arts Movement. And just as it flooded before as Afro-centric artistic inspiration, it poured out a second time as black social and political unrest.

THE HAT TRADITION IN THE BLACK CHURCH

I f a hat says a lot about a person, then they can speak volumes about a people. Every Sunday morning, black churchwomen attend my church, and worship centers across America, decked out in their finest for worship and praise. And nothing tops off a well-coordinated ensemble like a hat. Following in a strong African American tradition, black women can wear the most extraordinary hats like no one else can.

If the Black Church forged African Americans together as a people, then hats were a part of a cultural and religious tradition that fused congregations of black women together. For us, the descendents of African nobility (and don't think that we're not), dress hats have been the "crowns" of Sunday morning worship. "Sunday-go-to-meeting hats" are more than fashion accessories. They are a tradition that pre-dates the Transatlantic Slave Trade, taking us back to the headdresses worn by women in ancient African cultures.

Slaves entered this country deeply steeped in the African tradition of adorning themselves for worship. In Africa, men often wore masks on the crowns of their heads like hats to venerate dead ancestors. But African women would wear headdresses and even intricate hairstyles that involved delicate beading and expensive cowry shells. The royalty wore diadems. Beaded caps were worn to denote rank and status. Headdresses decorated with feathers and plumes were also highly prized, and remain so.

Adorning the head manifested itself differently during American slavery. Female slaves worked the plantations with their heads wrapped much like their ancestors did in Africa. And as the slaves converted to Christianity, several unique worship customs sprang up. Distinguishing their field clothes from their church clothes was a slave's way of denoting the sacredness worship. Hats became a part of that experience. Slaves and their descendants, who performed backbreaking work during the week, came to know Sunday as a day of religion, rest, and dress. So the head wraps worn during the week were less ornate and far less colorful than the ones worn to Sunday worship.

After the Civil War black women began in earnest to rid themselves of the stigma of having been slaves. They became very concerned with the way they presented themselves. The hat became the way for black women to show others that they were *somebody*. This whole idea of getting dressed up on

Sunday was born of a cultural longing for respectability. Since blacks have historically been held in low esteem, adorning themselves to show pride and to dispel the myth of inferiority has created an African American signature sense of style.

Before the advent of the Civil Rights Movement that eventually ushered in the Black Nationalist Movement, which touted the Afro-style hairdos, black churches were brimming with hats on Sunday mornings. Even the informality that seized the United States after World War II did not diminish the hat tradition with black women. But since the 1960s, hats have undergone a steady decline. However, there are still women who don church hats, showcasing style and grace, and supporting a century's old cultural tradition. In the Black Church today, older members, pastors' wives, and Easter bonneted young girls, keep this tradition alive. And every male in close proximity is expected to politely acknowledge the hat.

The threads of ancestry, religion, and the complexities of African American culture entwine black women and their church hats. The very worship experience often can, and usually does, turn into a celebration of black women in their church hats. They are just as much a part of the Black Church experience as the preaching, the singing, and the shouting. Black women's hats can nod "Amen," shake in disapproval, sway to the music, issue a warning to naughty children, and never fall off a head during a shout. Look around you today, and admire the array of colors and styles of hats. And remember the tradition that it represents. African Americans do very African things, whether it is intricate hair braiding or distinctive hairstyles or the beautiful hats we wear on Sundays. The very next time you are in a Black Church, look around. And you will see that you may be sitting near, or at least glance over at, an amazing hat.

D r. Dorothy I. Height has been a central figure in the Civil Rights and Women's Rights Movements of her lifetime. No African American woman has surpassed her ability as an organizational leader in her roles with the Young Women's Christian Association (YWCA); the Delta Sigma Theta (ΔΣθ) sorority; and especially the National Council of Negro Women (NCNW).

She was born Dorothy Irene Height in Richmond, Virginia, on March 24, 1912. Her parents were James Edward Height and Fannie Burroughs Height. She had one sister and a half brother and sister. In 1916 the Heights moved to Rankin, a small mining town in Pennsylvania. Her father was a building contractor and her mother was a private duty nurse who was active in various civil rights and community service organizations. In addition to being an outstanding student at Rankin High School, Height became active in the YWCA, where she early on developed leadership skills. By the age of fourteen she was elected president of the Pennsylvania State Federation of Girls Clubs. After high school she enrolled at New York University, where she completed her undergraduate work in only three years and earned a master's degree in educational psychology at the end of her fourth year.

Upon graduation and holding two degrees, Height's first job was a teaching position at a Community Center in Brooklyn. Shortly after, in 1935, she became a caseworker for the New York City Department of Welfare, and was soon promoted to an advisory position. It was during this time she became one of the leaders of the United Christian Youth Movement, which gave her the opportunity to travel widely and work closely with first lady, Eleanor Roosevelt. In 1937, Height accepted a post with the Harlem YWCA. She continued to hold leadership positions with the YWCA, first at the local level then at the national level, for the next forty years. Among Height's accomplishments at the YWCA was her help in organizing the historic 1946 conference at which the organization formally committed to integrating its programs.

Soon after joining Delta Sigma Theta sorority, Height took a leadership role in 1939. She was elected vice president in 1944 and became the national president in 1947, a position she held until 1956. During her tenure with the Delta's she expanded the scope of the sorority and drew national and international attention to its work. Under her leadership the sorority created international chapters and was actively involved in world affairs on behalf of women's rights.

In November 1937 as she escorted Eleanor Roosevelt to a function Height caught the attention of legendary activist, Mary McLeod Bethune. Dr. Bethune quickly became Height's friend and mentor. Through her, Height became deeply involved with the National Council of Negro Women (NCNW), the coalition, founded by Bethune, of black women's organizations. In 1957 Height became the fourth national president of NCNW, a position she has held for the past fifty years.

As president of NCNW, Height has traveled the world working to secure equal rights and equal justice for women and people of color. She has organized the council to develop many programs specifically designed to socially enhance and economically stabilize the lives of African American women and their families. And she has lent her leadership services to other organizations. Her distinguished service contributions to the social and political arenas have earned her innumerable awards and honors, including the highest civilian award bestowed by the United States, the Presidential Medal of Freedom in 1993.

Dorothy Height has exerted tremendous influence as an advocate confronting those who would diminish the rights for black women around the world. Her memoir, *Open Wide the Freedom Gates* was a winner of the Centennial Award, and should be view as a primary text of the social history of the first half of the twentieth century in the United States. It is sure to be studied as a first-hand narrative account of this nation's most eventful era.

S ally Hemings is an enigma, a puzzle wrapped in a mystery. For the past 200 years, she has been the most controversial woman in American history. She never held an office, signed a treaty or entered politics, but she stands at the center of the most hotly debated argument in American politics. Sally Hemings was the slave of Thomas Jefferson of whom it is alleged that he fathered seven children with her. Not much is known about Sally Hemings except what is noted in her son's memoirs. She was born in Bermuda Hundred, Virginia, to a slave woman named Elizabeth Hemings. Her given name was probably Sarah. She was one of six children allegedly fathered by John Wayles, Thomas Jefferson's father-in-law. In 1774, upon the death of Wayles, the Hemings clan became part of the inheritance of Martha Jefferson who died in 1782. There are only two known descriptions of Sally. The slave Isaac Jefferson remembered that she was *"mighty near white, very handsome, long straight hair down her back."* A Jefferson biographer quoted his grandson as describing her as *"light colored and decidedly good looking."*

In 1784 Jefferson was appointed to serve as a minister to France. His oldest daughter, Martha, and a slave named James Hemings accompanied him. His two younger daughters, Mary and Lucy, remained in Virginia with other Jefferson family members. Three years later, after the death of Lucy, Mary arrived in Paris accompanied by fourteen year-old Sally Hemings, the sister of James. Some historians have theorized that since Martha Jefferson and Sally were half-sisters, they resembled each other greatly making it understandable that Jefferson could have formed an attachment to her after his wife's death.

Jefferson stayed in Paris for over two years after Sally arrived. The controversy surrounding the two begins in Paris because it was there that it is alleged Jefferson and Hemings began a thirty-eight year relationship, producing four surviving children: Beverley (1798), a daughter named Harriett (1801), Madison (1805), and Eston Hemings (1808). In his 1873 Memoir, Madison Hemings not only states the relationship of his mother to Jefferson as that of "concubine," naming him as their father, but he also provides insight as to why Sally's children were the only slaves ever freed from Monticello:

> *"... and when he was called back home she was enceinte (pregnant) by him. He desired to bring my mother back to Virginia with him but she demurred. She was just beginning to understand the French language*

well, and in France she was free, while if she returned to Virginia, she would be re-enslaved. So she refused to return with him. To induce her to do so he promised her extraordinary privileges, and made a solemn pledge that her children should be freed at the age of twenty-one years. In consequence of his promise, on which she implicitly relied, she returned..."

As early as, 1790 there were rumors among the Virginia gentry that Jefferson and Hemings were romantically involved. But the rumors did not explode on the national scene until 1801. Early in Jefferson's first term as president, James Callender, a muckraking journalist and political enemy of Jefferson accused him of miscegenation, even publishing a timeline that put Jefferson at Monticello for the conception of each of Sally's children. Callender's allegations started one of the most malicious political fights in history. Jefferson's supporters protected him by denying those allegations and others that surrounded him at the time. Jefferson never responded to the allegations or even acknowledged them.

The continued speculation about the paternity of Sally Hemings' children in 1998 prompted scientists to apply newly available DNA testing to the controversy. While it is impossible to claim with absolute certainty that Jefferson fathered her children, the results convinced scientists that it is extremely likely. These results confirmed both longstanding oral histories passed down by Hemings' descendents and the theories advanced by several historians and Jefferson biographers. It also attests to the contradiction that was Jefferson. He authored The Declaration of Independence, and yet he was a slaveholder. He held one family in high esteem and another in bondage. And as for Sally Hemmings, there were contradictions for her as well. She lived her life un-free in a free society, not free to consent to the fathering of her children.

MATTHEW HENSON (1866-1955)

M atthew Henson was the co-discoverer of the North Pole on April 6, 1909 along with Robert Peary and four Inuit men. They were the first people to reach the Pole in the long and treacherous history of Artic exploration, though Henson's victory was diminished by racism in America. He was never mentioned at the time of the discovery, and only in 1948 were his achievements truly recognized. In 1986 he was commemorated on a postage stamp.

He was born Matthew Alexander Henson on August 6, 1866, on a farm that had been used as a slave market in Najemay, Charles County, Maryland. He fled the farm after his parents died, and took to the road again at the age of eleven because of a cruel and abusive foster mother. He went to Washington D.C. and found his uncle. When Henson realized that his uncle could little afford to educate him, he found work as a dishwasher in a Baltimore restaurant.

While working, Henson overheard dinner conversation talk of the sea and of distant lands. At age thirteen he packed up what little he had and signed on the *Katie Hines*, a merchant vessel bound for Hong Kong. He traveled the world for six years. During this time, the captain grew very fond of him and taught him navigation, mathematics, seamanship, and geography. Henson benefited greatly from the mentoring of Captain Childs and found the world a more exciting place than he had ever imagined. He even became fluent in Russian.

Captain Childs died in 1885 and Henson returned to Washington, D.C. and began working in a men's hat store. In 1886, he was introduced to then Lieutenant Robert Peary, a civil engineer with the U.S. Navy and an avid explorer. Henson made such an impression on Peary that he hired him as his personal assistant and took him on a survey expedition to Nicaragua in 1887. This was the beginning of a fourteen-year friendship during which they made seven polar expeditions together.

Until Henson and Peary's expedition of 1909, no one had reached the North Pole or the polar ice cap, one of the bleakest, most enigmatic places on earth. Despite the hundreds of voyages made by the Scandinavians, Dutch, and English explorers, the vast polar sea, covering an expanse of nearly five million square miles was still completely unknown. Henson was indispensable to the Peary expedition. He was the only one fluent in the Inuit language. He lived with them on and off for fourteen years, establishing a family with an Inuit woman, and learning to survive in the Artic climate. He was responsible for much of the material comfort during their missions. He built their headquarters, hunted for food, and drove the dog sled that took them to the Pole.

In 1913 President Taft personally recommended Henson's appointment to the U.S. Customs House in New York in recognition of his exploration of the Artic. In 1944 Henson received a joint medal from Congress honoring the Peary expedition to the North Pole. He was also honored by President Truman in 1950 and admitted to the Explorer's Club. He passed away in relative obscurity in 1955; but in 1988 he was reburied in Arlington National Cemetery with full honors.

In his book, *A Black Explorer at the North Pole* (1912), Henson gave a sagacious account of his artic experience: "*When I reached the ship again and gazed into my little mirror, it was the pinched and wrinkled visage of an old man that peered out at me, but the eyes still twinkled and life was still entrancing. This wizening of our features was due to the strain of travel and lack of sleep; we had enough to eat. I have only mentioned it to help impress the fact that the journey to the Pole and back is not to be regarded as a pleasure outing, and our so-called 'jaunt' was by no means a cake-walk.*" Matthew Henson's astute remark was proof positive that this descendant of slaves possessed the requisite skills and drive to excel even in that most difficult and arduous profession of exploration and discovery.

GEORGE HERRIMAN (1880-1944)

Georﾘe Herriman is considered to be the greatest of American cartoonists. Strong lines, subtle wit, surrealistic desert settings, clever word spellings, and an ironic storyline, that he repeated daily, but managed to keep fresh, characterized his work. He drew the daily and Sunday comic strip "Krazy Kat" for over thirty years and it became the one strip for which he was most famous.

He was born George Joseph Herriman into a Creole family August 22, 1880, at 348 Villere Street in New Orleans, Louisiana. His birth certificate classified him as "colored" And his parents and grandparents were all listed in the 1880 census as mulattos. His father worked as a baker, tailor, and barber in New Orleans, but moved his family to Los Angles to avoid the increasingly restrictive Jim Crow laws in Louisiana. Better opportunities came as George began passing as white. His wife, who died before him, may have been privy to his secret, but his only surviving daughter did not know until after his death.

At age seventeen, Herriman began working as an illustrator and engraver for the Los Angles Herald newspaper. His colleagues began calling him "the Greek," as a way of commenting on his indeterminate ancestry. The fact that he was indeed African American remained a closely guarded secret until his death. His thick curly black hair was attributed to Greek ancestry, a notion he did nothing to dissuade. And he was never photographed without his wearing his Stetson hat to cover his hair. Over the next few years he did many newspaper sports illustrations and political cartoons, and produced several early comic strips, at times producing several daily strips at once. His early strips included "Major Ozone," "Musical Mose," "Acrobatic Archie," "Professor Otto and his Auto," "Two Jolly Jackies," and several others. Most of his early work was only slightly above the average quality of newspaper strips of the time.

Perhaps the first indication of Herriman's unusual creativity and bizarre poetic sense of humor, which would make him famous, surfaced in 1909 with his strip "Goosebury Sprig, the Duck Duke." The next year he began a domestic comedy strip called "The Dingbat Family." After a while Herriman started drawing "The Dingbat Family" as two strips in one. The main action happening with the human family taking up most of each panel, and an unrelated storyline involving a cat and mouse underneath the family's floorboards taking place in the bottom segment of each panel. The strip was then renamed "The Family Upstairs." The cat and mouse strip was then spun off into another strip in 1913, originally titled "Krazy Kat and Ignatz," and finally just "Krazy Kat." It was a phenomenon of illustration and dialogue.

"Krazy Kat" received critical but not popular acclaim. Many readers complained that it made no sense. It was so different. Krazy Kat adores Ignatz Mouse. Ignatz hates Krazy and throws bricks at Krazy's head. Krazy takes this abuse as a sign of affection and always looks for the love notes that should be attached to the missiles. Officer Pupp a police dog that loves Krazy and in attempts to protect Krazy, throws Ignatz in jail. This was the simple premise that sustained "Krazy Kat" for all those years. Herriman played out endless variations on the same theme in a continually evolving comic, using ever-changing formats and layouts, set in surreal and ever-shifting desert landscapes. "Krazy Kat" had an enthusiastic following, including prominent artists and intellectuals like Charlie Chaplin, Ernest Hemmingway, Frank Capra, Walt Disney, F. Scott Fitzgerald, H.L. Mencken and Herriman's publisher, William Randolph Hearst.

The "Krazy Kat" comic strip ended upon Herriman's death in 1944. No one else could reproduce the style, sophistication and laconic wit of his original work. No one else could reproduce the simple plot that was endlessly renewed through constant innovation. Some think that Herriman denied his blackness by passing as white. But I must disagree. I think his body of work spoke for his blackness, but it was so completely over the heads of his audience, that none understood it. The fact that Krazy was drawn as a black cat should have clued us all. And the fact that Krazy's gender could never be firmly established should have alerted us too, that in George Herriman's work, just as in his life, nothing really was as it seemed.

JUSTIN HOLLAND (1819-1887)

The guitar is not original to America, it is considered to be a Spanish instrument. But it may have gone into Spain by way of the invading Moors from North Africa. What entrenched the guitar into American music was the work of Justin Holland, an African American, and perhaps the first master guitar player and teacher in the United States. He created a system for learning the guitar that is still used today. Every modern guitar player owes Justin Holland a debt of gratitude.

Holland was born in Norfolk County, Virginia on July 26, 1819 to free black farmers. He may have been the eldest of the family's eight children. Even as a child, he loved music so much that he would walk ten miles to participate in a songfest every Sunday. His father noticed his talent for music at an early age, but there was little opportunity for cultivating that talent. The family lived near other free blacks in a county that included whites of moderate means who owned slaves, and poor whites who could not afford slaves. Free blacks living in the South dispelled the myths surrounding slavery.

In 1833, when he was only fourteen, Holland left Virginia for Boston. There were two notable reasons for his departure. The first was the death of his parents. Secondly, the South had become an ever increasingly unpleasant place for free blacks to be, especially after the Nat Turner insurrection in 1831. But the black population in Massachusetts enjoyed educational and economic opportunities for advancement unheard of in the South. In Boston, he studied the flute and piano. At a music concert at Boston's Lion Theater, he heard the Spaniard, Mariano Perez, perform on the Spanish guitar. Holland was so deeply moved by the beauty of the sound that he decided to add the guitar to his music studies.

In 1841 Holland entered Oberlin College in Ohio to continue his music education. Oberlin was a hotbed of antislavery thought and activity. The Oberlin staff was peppered with professors who opposed slavery and all its supporting institutions. It was there that Holland entered the fight for greatest cause of his time, the abolition of slavery. He lent his musical talents to abolitionist speeches, rallies, and fund-raisers. After leaving Oberlin, Holland moved to Cleveland and became a hugely successful music teacher. He continued to play the guitar and became one of the world's greatest guitarists. But at that time very little music had been written for the instrument, so he adapted music written for other instruments to the guitar. He single handedly caused an upswing in the use of the guitar in American music.

In 1848 Holland began to publish his guitar arrangements. As more of his written arrangements became available, more people began to learn the guitar. His sheet music sales grew and he soon became a very successful businessman. He taught himself Spanish, French, and Italian to keep up with the music world. Holland seldom performed in public, but instead, concentrated on teaching. Cleveland's 1840s industrialized population included enough individuals of the middle and upper classes to support the fine arts. By the 1830s, the city had formed the Cleveland Musical Society and the Sacred Music Society; and by 1850, it had formally organized musical associations that included several bands, orchestras, choirs, and a music appreciation society.

Not only did Holland compose and arrange guitar music for his students, who they called "The Professor," but he also published his work through a Cleveland based firm. Brainard's published his music and provided for its local distribution through a Cleveland music store and advertised his work throughout the Midwest in a monthly publication. In 1874, he published *Holland's Comprehensive Method of the Guitar*. A newer version, *Holland's Modern Method for the Guitar*, appeared in 1876. His books soon became the standard texts for learning to play the guitar. They were so widely sold, that both texts represent his greatest contribution to music. Sadly, Holland did not live to see African Americans achieve full equality, but the world did see him as a musician without equal.

People have died at all points in the history of civilizations. Those living have always mourned the death of a loved one with some type of ceremony. And African Americans are no different from any other cultural group. Within the African American community, there exists a wide array of burial rituals that are specific to ancestral roots in West Africa. One of the most the distinctive features in African American culture is the name assigned for the funeral service or burial rite. Blacks honor the dead with a *home going celebration*, not a funeral. No other culture has ever designated the term *home going* to mean a funeral service.

To understand the magnitude of the influence that our African-based culture has had on the practice of funeral service, not only in this country but in the entire world, we must go back to the time of ancient African countries like Egypt. Not only did the Egyptians initiate embalming, they also built extravagant monuments as a testament to the life contained therein. This act of preserving the body of a deceased human in order to conduct funeral services over an extended period of time and placing those remains in a container for burial is practiced worldwide as a result of the traditions of ancient Egyptians.

Africans were brought to the Americas by violent force and subjected to inhumane treatment. Laws were enacted and enforced to prohibit slaves from congregating in any form of assembly for fear they would have the opportunity to conspire and plan revolts. This prohibitive policy prevented slaves from having organized gatherings for worship and funeral services. The right to give a loved one the respect and dignity of a proper burial was denied to many slaves. But as they did with worship and other religious practices, the slaves found inventive ways to circumvent the institution of slavery. Slaves were always buried on non-crop producing land and no monument was ever placed over their graves. However, other slaves would always manage to at least place wooden crosses to mark the graves.

When slaves were allowed religious and funeral assembly, it was under the auspices of a white adult male. The slaves' intensity for religious expression was also attendant at each burial service. To the bewilderment of white onlookers, the slaves exhibited behavior contradictory to the nature of the event. They were not somber mourners, but jubilant celebrants of the deceased person. With no hope of ever returning to Africa, slaves felt that death was the ultimate escape. In death the soul could take wings and fly home to be with the God they had come to know as their *strong deliverer.*

To the slaves, death was not viewed as an act of passing away, but as an act of going home. Today that premise continues to dominate the practice of African American funeral customs. Whether blacks continue these customs out of respect for tradition or the belief that social conditions in America have not sufficiently changed is of little consequence. We continue to be surrounded by our traditions. The black funeral tradition and the Black Church are the two institutions most unchanged in black history. And in black churches across America there are announcements being made, not about impending funerals, but about impending home going celebrations. And the funeral procession to the cemetery is a spectacle in and of itself. Even if the deceased was not a well-known individual, the funeral motorcade can be lengthy.

People of color started this method of the commemoration for the deceased who have passed over to the other side. Africans of the Diaspora, whether African American, Afro-Caribbean, or those of African descent in Central and South America, have a history rich in heritage and tradition. And with those traditions, we have achieved what no other cultural group on earth has done. We have transformed a dead body into a living memorial. The deceased live on in our memories. And in so doing, we celebrate the life instead of mourning the loss. It is highly probable that all people of faith are familiar with the Scripture that relates *"it is appointed unto man once to die."* As black Christians commemorate the transition from life unto life-everlasting, we gaze forward and likely think of our own future home going celebrations.

M iss Lena Horne is an African American actress and Grammy Award winning singer. She is one of the most distinguished singers in the history of American popular music. As an actress, she refused to be cast in stereotypical roles, thus helping to transform the popular image of black women on stage and screen.

She was born Lena Mary Calhoun Horne to Ted and Edna Scrottron Horne in Brooklyn on June 30, 1917. Her father was a clerk for the New York State Department of Labor, but he was also heavily involved with the numbers rackets. He deserted the family by the time Lena was three. Her mother was an aspiring actress who eventually left Lena in the care of her paternal Grandmother, civil rights activist and suffragist, Cora Calhoun Horne. In 1924 Lena rejoined her mother, and for the next few years lived a nomadic existence along the East Coast as her mother struggled as an actress.

By the time Horne was eleven, she was again living with her grandparents in Brooklyn, but joined her mother in the Bronx, later moving to Harlem. By the age of sixteen she began working at the famed Cotton Club, first as a dancer, then in the chorus, and later as a solo performer. She was hired for her great beauty but worked diligently to improve her singing voice by taking lessons. Horne developed a sultry, husky, voice that was highly distinctive and capable of considerable depth. She left the Cotton Club and accepted a role on Broadway in "Dance with Your Gods" and then joined the Noble Sissle Society Orchestra in Philadelphia. Under his direction she also began a career that included recordings.

It was in Philadelphia that Horne reunited with her father, who subsequently played an important role in her life and career until his death in 1970. Her father introduced her to Louis Jones, to whom she married and had two children. Horne returned to Broadway in "Blackbirds of 1939" and went on to become the lead singer in the Charlie Barnett Band in 1940. She became a featured performer at the Café Society Downtown, the only non-segregated nightclub in New York. It was there that she became acquainted with entertainer, Paul Robeson, and NAAP Executive Director, Walter White. Both men helped her to develop an appreciation for the need for racial solidarity. She also began playing clubs in Greenwich Village and even performed at Carnegie Hall.

Horne separated from her husband in 1941, later divorcing him in 1944. She moved to Hollywood in 1941 where she was featured at the Little Troc Club. In 1942 Horne began a movie career by signing with Metro-Goldwyn-Mayer (MGM). Her contract stipulated that she would not be asked to play black stereotypical roles. In the following years her screen assignments were as brief appearances as singers in: *Panama Hattie* (1942); *Swing Fever* (1943); *Broadway Rhythm* (1944), and *Ziegfeld Follies* (1946). Her most important film for MGM was the all-black musical, *Cabin in the Sky* (1943), in which she played the temptress, Georgia Brown. MGM lent Horne to 20th Century Fox, where she made another all-black musical, *Stormy Weather* (1943). Performing the title song afterward became her signature song.

During World War II Horne performed on USO Tours and insisted that both black and white soldiers be seated together to in her audiences. She became the pinup girl for thousands of black soldiers. Returning to MGM, she resumed small roles in white musicals, during which she met and secretly married second husband, Leonard Hayton, an Academy Award winning studio music director. Because he was white, the couple endured hate mail from whites and bitter, recriminating remarks from blacks. Horne made many albums that Hayton produced until his death in 1971. Her last film appearance was in *The Wiz* (1978).

Lena Horne more recently made headlines when she refused to allow Janet Jackson to portray her in an upcoming biographical film. For many years Miss Horne has jealously guarded her reputation and image and has steadfastly refused to allow anyone to trash that image. She is a paragon of virtue and good taste. All should esteem this show business legend not for her classic beauty alone, but also for her classic style.

HARRY HOSIER (1750?-1806)

For well over 150 years, people of Indiana have been called, and proudly call themselves, "Hoosiers." Although there are many theories, the origin of the term is not known with any certainty. Most theories present the word as a slur for ignorance. But one theory involves an itinerant preacher of the late 18th and early 19th centuries who was known as "Black Harry" Hosier. He was a heart-stirring evangelist who traveled the eastern seaboard, but never as far west as the Northwest Territory that contained Indiana. Not much more than first-hand accounts from his contemporaries are known about this celebrated African American.

Since most of the bare facts of Harry Hosier's life have eluded historians, they have therefore had to liberally sprinkle probabilities about his life throughout their narratives of him. His birthday is celebrated on July 18, although he was probably born on November 29. His birth year is variously recorded as 1750 or 1758. It is known that he was born into slavery, probably near Bethania, also known as Hoosertown, North Carolina. But his sketchy biography is buttressed with accolades from his acquaintances, and good impressions from those who worked and traveled with him.

Following the American Revolutionary War, it is known that Hosier gained his freedom and was converted to Methodism. His sermon, *The Barren Fig Tree*, preached at Adam's Chapel, Fairfax County, Virginia, in May 1781, was the first documented Methodist sermon by an African American. No recording devices tapped the cadence of Hosier's preaching style. But we must again add to the probabilities of his life. Given his African heritage, his words probably poured out rhythmically, and with a range of volume as resonant as today's black preachers.

Hosier is easily placed in historical context with other figures and events. He and Richard Allen, the founder of the African Methodist Episcopal (AME) Denomination, were the two non-voting African American representatives at the 1784 Christmas Conference that officially organized American Methodism. The Second Great Awakening was the dominant religious development among Protestants in the United States in the first half of the 19th century. Through revivals and camp meetings, sinners were brought to conversion experiences. This style of Christian faith and discipline was very agreeable to Methodists who favored its emphasis on the experiential.

Hosier was a companion on evangelistic trips with Francis Asbury, Thomas Coke, Jesse Lee, and Freeborn Garrettson. Asbury and Coke were the first two Bishops of American Methodism. Coke records that Hosier was one of the best preachers in the world. An amazing power attended Hosier's preaching, although he could not read or write. With his humble spirit he could connect to the enslaved, the poor, and the uneducated. His evangelistic work with Garrettson exemplified a great Christian truth of former slave and former slaveholder, working and ministering together, knowing that in Christ Jesus there is neither *"bond nor free."*

Henry Boehm, an ordained Methodist minister, also adds another eye and ear witness account of Hosier's prowess as a preacher. He describes Hosier as being very black, with a musical voice that could repeat any hymn as if reading it. Hosier could also quote Scripture with great accuracy. He was an immensely popular orator, and many on the Methodist Circuit would rather have listened him than to their educated bishops.

It was the influence of Harry Hosier that can be pointed to as one of the most important factors in the early spread of the Methodist Episcopal Church in America. Even though he was born a slave, and remained illiterate throughout his life, Hosier became one of the most eloquent preachers in American Methodism. And by all historical accounts, *"he died happy in the Lord."*

LANGSTON HUGHES (1902-1967)

L angston Hughes was an African American poet, novelist, newspaper columnist, and playwright. He wrote in many genres, but is best known for his poetry, in which he disregarded classical forms in favor of musical rhythms and the oral and improvisation traditions of black culture. He was recognized as one of the leading stars in the constellation of black writers, artists, and musicians who shaped the Harlem Renaissance. And Langston Hughes was aptly called its *Poet Laureate*.

He was born James Mercer Langston Hughes on February 2, 1902, in Joplin, Missouri. His father, a lawyer frustrated by racism, left the family when Langston was a small child and moved to Mexico. His maternal grandmother raised Langston until he was twelve, when he moved to Lincoln, Illinois, to live with his mother and stepfather. The family later moved to Cleveland, Ohio, where he attended high school. It was during his high school years that Hughes began writing poetry. He contributed to his high school literary magazine and was named class poet in his senior year before graduating in 1920.

Following graduation, Hughes spent a year in Mexico with his father before traveling abroad to Africa and Europe. On the train ride to Mexico, Hughes penned "The Negro Speaks of Rivers," which was published in the June 1921 issue of *Crisis*, the official publication of the NAACP. He moved to New York City in 1924. He enrolled in Columbia University at his father's insistence, but only stayed one year. He finished his college education at Lincoln University in Pennsylvania.

Hughes wrote more than fifty books. His works include the poetry volumes *The Weary Blues* (1926), *The Dream Keeper* (1932), *The Ways of White Folks* (1934), *Shakespeare in Harlem* (1942), *Fields of Wonder* (1947), and the immensely important, *Montage of a Dream Deferred* (1951). He wrote the short-story collection, *The Ways of White Folks* (1934). He also wrote a whole series of short stories based on the fictional character he created for newspaper columns, "Jesse B. Simple," which included *Simple Speaks His Mind* (1950). He wrote two novels, *Not Without Laughter* (1930) and *Tambourines to Glory* (1958). In the autobiographical books, *The Big Sea* (1940) and *I Wonder as I Wander* (1957), Hughes discussed personal topics and inner conflicts, but most readers especially value his insider's portrayal of the Harlem Renaissance.

Hughes also wrote the drama, *Mulatto* (1935), which was the longest running Broadway play by an African American until Lorraine Hansberry's, *A Raisin in the Sun*. But Hansberry used as her title and theme elements referenced from Hughes' poem, *Harlem:*

> *What happens to a dream deferred? /*
> *Does it dry up / like a raisin in the sun? /*
> *Or fester like a sore / and then run? /*
> *...Maybe it just sags / like a heavy load /*
> *Or does it explode? /*

Hughes remained a prolific writer until his death, with many works being published posthumously. When he died on May 22, 1967, he was at work on a new collection of poetry celebrating the Civil Rights Movement and Black Power / Black Nationalist Movements, which was published later that year as *The Panther and the Lash*. In the 1960s, he wrote several successful gospel plays, including *Black Nativity* (1961), which remains a holiday tradition in many cities.

Langston Hughes became the first African American author able to support himself completely by his writings. His work was remarkable for much more than its quantity. Hughes' work captured the essence of "black" America in a way that African Americans felt it had not been captured before. He engaged other African American art forms, namely jazz and black folk rhythms to enhance his poetry. His innovations in form and voice influenced many black writers just as he was himself influenced by the black culture that surrounded him.

A grippa Hull was one of the more than 5,000 black patriots that stood shoulder to shoulder with white patriots in the American Revolutionary War of 1776. In some cases black soldiers were given menial duties, such as digging trenches and becoming the personal valets to white officers. But most blacks who enlisted in the Continental Army were musket-carrying privates who fought alongside white soldiers. Although many questioned the wisdom of arming an oppressed people, both the Americans and the British felt forced to recruit able-bodied men, whether black or white.

Many American regiments were composed entirely of blacks during the war for independence. But many more American regiments, especially in the northern colonies, were racial integrated. Free blacks that enlisted in the armies were promised bounties or land in exchange for military service. In the southern colonies, slaves often fought in place of their owners. Sometime they could win their freedom after the war, but oftentimes they returned to bondage. In the South, especially, slaves found it more advantageous to fight for Great Britain because of the offer of freedom that was guaranteed by the Crown. It is estimated that the number of blacks fighting for the British mother country was ten times greater that the number fighting for her American colonies.

Agrippa Hull was born a free person in Northampton, Massachusetts in1759. At age six his family moved to Stockbridge where he received an education and grew to young manhood working as a farmer. Hull enlisted in the Revolutionary Army in 1777 and served for the duration of the war. He served first as a private in the Third Massachusetts Line Brigade under General John Patterson. Later he was an orderly and friend to Polish patriot, Thaddeus Kosciusko.

In all probability, Hull saw action at the June 28, 1778 Battle of Monmouth in New Jersey. He served under Patterson for his first two years of his enlistment. And Patterson's Third Massachusetts Brigade took part in that battle. Hull was sure to have been one of the more than 800 blacks present at the war's last major engagement in the North. For the remainder of the war Hull was the personal valet of Kosciusko, the celebrated Polish volunteer and master military engineer. Hull was at West Point at the time Kosciusko was engaged in fortifying its strategic high point on the west bank of the Hudson River. Kosciusko, who had taken a great liking to Hull, invited him to return to

Poland with him, but Hull declined. The two did keep in contact through letters after the war.

In 1783, Hull received an honorable discharge from the army signed by General George Washington. He returned to Stockbridge where he was a neighbor to Elizabeth "Mum Bett" Freeman, the first slave to be freed under the new Massachusetts State Constitution. Charles Sedgwick was the attorney of record in the Freeman case. Hull worked as a butler for the Sedgwick family. Hull also obtained the services of Sedgwick to help gain freedom for Jane Darby, a runaway slave who sought refuge in Stockbridge. Hull saved enough money to buy a farm. He married Darby and raised a family. In 1797 Hull was awarded a grant of land in Ohio in acknowledgement of his military service. In a magnanimous gesture, Hull requested that the land be sold to build a school for black children.

The Agrippa Hull story is only one account of the many black soldiers, slave and free, who fought for American liberty. There is no question that African Americans played a significant part during the struggle that would eventually separate the American Colonies from England. Sadly, it would be another century, and another war, before African Americans would obtain the legal definition of "African American." And sadder still, it took two centuries before African Americans would attain full citizenship rights in what became the United States of America.

Zora Neale Hurston was the first African American woman to research, collect, and publish African American and Afro-Caribbean folklore. Her study of folklore dramatically affected her career as an essayist and creative writer. Hurston's interest in anthropology led her to study the folk culture of blacks and to record the wonderful oral culture of stories and songs. As a result she created some of the most vivid images of black life, including manners, traditions, and belief systems, that we have today. Hurston traveled extensively in the southern United States and Caribbean Islands listening to and recording the stories of the African Diaspora.

She was born in Eatonville, Florida on January 7, but the year of her birth is variously listed as 1891 and 1901. She was one of eight children born to Rev. John and Lucy Ann Potts Hurston. Her father was three times elected mayor of Eatonville, the first incorporated black township in the United States. Her mother, a former schoolteacher, taught Sunday School in her husband's church. Hurston's mother died when she was thirteen. Afterwards her father remarried and she had to live with various other relatives.

At the age of fourteen, Hurston left Eatonville to work as a maid and wardrobe assistant with a traveling Gilbert and Sullivan theatrical troupe. In Baltimore she left the troupe to enter Morgan Academy, a predominately black high school from which she graduated in June 1918. She studied occasionally at Howard University in Washington, D.C. until 1924. In 1925 Hurston moved to New York City where she joined the Harlem Renaissance, a literary and cultural movement that celebrated black folk life. During this time she was published in literary magazines and received a bachelor's degree from Barnard College in 1928.

After leaving Barnard College, Hurston pursued graduate studies at Columbia University under the direction of Franz Boas, who encouraged her to return to Eatonville to collect black folklore. From 1929 to 1931 she collected black folk stories in Florida and Alabama. Hurston published the results in the book *Of Mules and Men* (1935). It was the first collection of black folklore published by an African American woman. Her first novel, *Jonah's Gourd Vine* (1934), and all her other novels were strongly influenced by her folklore studies. Hurston used rich characterizations of humanity and not of race, showing how African and European Americans views conflict in the black mind.

Hurston followed her first novel and first folkloric anthropology collection with a string of other novels: *Their Eyes Were Watching God* (1937), *Tell My Horse* (1938), *Moses, Man of the Mountain* (1939), *Dust Tracks on a Road* (1942), and *Seraph on the Suwannee* (1948). During the remainder of the 1940s she wrote articles and essays for several magazines, including the *Journal of American Folklore*, *Saturday Evening Post*, and *Negro Digest*.

In the 1950s, Hurston's income as a writer declined sharply. The royalties from her books dropped, she published no new ones, and she wrote only a few articles and reviews. To earn a living, she took a series of menial jobs while living in southern Florida. She fell into ill health and died in poverty on January 28, 1960. No clarion call was sent out in tribute to her passing, and she was buried in an unmarked grave. It seemed a meager ending to a life that had enriched American culture tremendously through pioneering studies into African American folkloric anthropology.

Zora Neale Hurston was a prolific writer and a fiercely independent thinker. Her studies of black heritage influenced the Harlem Renaissance writers of the 1930s. Her work continues still to impact modern African American authors like Alice Walker and Toni Morrison. It was Walker who discovered Hurston's gravesite and erected a proper monument to salute a writer of such significance. Prophetically, Hurston's life is best summed up by her own words: *"I want a busy life, a just mind, and a timely death."*

THE INDIANAPOLIS CLOWNS (1920-1970)

T he Indianapolis Clowns were an American Negro League team that played variously under the names of the Miami Giants, Ethiopian Clowns, and Cincinnati Clowns. They were the masters of minstrelsy-style baseball playing that many resented, but all knew would draw great crowds, black and white. The Negro Leagues were a segregated baseball league, consisting solely of black teams and players, created out of necessity since blacks had been excluded from existing major and minor baseball leagues since the 1890s.

The Clowns were the most famous black team to play in Indianapolis although technically not the first. The Indianapolis team known as the ABCs was the first black team for Indianapolis. The American Brewing Company owner, Joseph C. Schaf, sponsored them. But because of the national prohibition law, all Indianapolis brewers were out of business by 1918. The heyday of the barnstorming company teams was coming to a close. By 1920 though, the Negro Leagues had been organized and was bringing new vitality to the national pastime and utilizing those barnstorming black players without missing a swing.

The Clowns were as much devoted to showmanship and on field clowning as to serious diamond play. To bolster sagging gate sales, many teams had to add novel attractions to their games. And the Clowns were the ultimate champions of such burlesque baseball as wearing grass skirts and painting their bodies to mimic African cannibals. They even assumed names such as "Selassie," "Mofike," "Wahoo," and "Tarzan." But once admitted to the Negro American League, the Clowns toned down the their pranks and blatant showmanship. They turned their ball club into one of the most popular on the league circuit.

During exhibition games in front of largely white audiences though, the Clowns had to accept the role of burlesque and minstrel funnymen. Predictably, many Negro League players themselves bitterly resented the comic image of the Indianapolis Clowns. But many more had to admit that under their clown image was adroit skill, adept talent, and an intense desire to win. The Clowns willingly accepted any talented player who could increase the gate and win games. On occasion the team spiced up their game by adding the novelty women players to the roster. They had two female second basemen, Toni Stone and Connie Martin. They were skillful players with impressive batting averages. Another time they were graced to have diminutive female right-hand pitcher, Mamie "Peanut" Johnson for their 1953-55 Season.

At the height of the Negro League play during the 1930s, the black leagues remained at best a loosely knit federation of barnstorming teams. And Indianapolis was no different from any other city supporting such teams. But by the beginning of World War II in the early 1940s, National and American Negro Leagues had solidified. And Indianapolis joined with the Clowns team in 1943. The Clowns would eventually call Indianapolis home, remaining here past the duration of the Negro Leagues.

Throughout their tenure in the organized Negro American League, the Clowns had boasted some moderate success. They finished as the league runner-up in both halves of a single division split season during their second league campaign in 1944. The team had to actually divide their time between Cincinnati and Indianapolis during the 1943–1945 seasons. They won the Eastern Division title the final season of 1950. During the early 1950s they had the distinction of signing a young Hank Aaron who would, of course, ultimately become baseball's all-time homerun king.

The integration of organized baseball brought about the demise of all the teams of the Negro Leagues. Following the demise of the Negro League structure in 1950, the Indianapolis Clowns continued their barnstorming show across the nation for another two decades, not disbanding until 1970. They returned to their comedic routines as a measure of financial necessity. The Clowns ended as they had started, as comic geniuses gracing a diamond, skillfully engaged in a game that they loved, and a game that all of America still loves today. The game is so beloved it asserts the title of "America's favorite pass time."

HAROLD JACKMAN (1901-1961)

The Harlem Renaissance was the extraordinary flowering of African American arts and letters that took place in the 1920s and 1930s. And Harold Jackman was its quintessential representative and the personification of the *New Negro* image that accompanied it. He was an educator, male model, editor, theater co-founder, and playwright. He helped to create the history and culture of the Harlem Renaissance through his association with the leading figures of the time and his involvement in the intellectual ferment of the era. Jackman was talented in his own right, but he spent a lifetime promoting the talents of others.

Jackman was thought to be West Indian, but in fact, he was born in London, England. He grew up in Harlem, New York City, where he attended public schools. It was at the Dewitt Clinton High School for boys in Manhattan that he began his lifetime friendship with American poet, novelist, and playwright, Countee Cullen. They were so intellectually compatible that they almost possessed one mind. Their friendship was deep, abiding, and sometimes, inexplicable. Jackman went on to receive a B.A. degree from New York University in 1923, and subsequently, a master's degree from Columbia University.

Jackman possessed distinguished good looks, even in his later years and worked part-time as a model while at NYU and received fan mail from all over the world. He continued to model after college, and as he grew older, he depicted dentists, doctors, lawyers, and business executives. In the March 1925 issue of Survey Graphic, painter Weinold Reiss published his portrait of Jackman on the cover with the title: "Harlem: Mecca of the New Negro." Jackman was a strong advocate of the arts and was a constant source of support for African American artists, encouraging them and promoting their careers.

Jackman was a dedicated teacher and taught social studies for thirty years in the New York Public School system. In his lifetime, he was active in many organizations including the National Urban League (NUL), National Association for the Advancement of Colored People (NAACP), Alpha Phi Alpha Fraternity, the American Society of African Culture, and the Ira Aldridge Society. He was a life member and served on the executive board of the Negro Actors Guild. Jackman was also a skilled journalist and a contributor to two magazines. His journalistic talents were evidenced in his work as

287

associate editor from 1935 to 1937 for the literary magazine *Challenge*. He was contributing editor and later an advisory editor of *Phylon* from 1944 until his death.

Jackman took the story of the Harlem Renaissance to London and Paris where the recounting of the cultural arts of Harlem aroused great interest. He so impressed everyone with the stories of Harlem's arts and letters explosion that he single-handedly caused an influx of Europeans to witness first hand, the great flowering of African American arts. While in America, the concept of the *New Negro* became a cultural phenomenon. Blacks themselves were not "new," but their art, literature, and poetry took on new flavor and a new energy as their artistic and intellectual creativity fused to reflect the black experience.

Jackman could be found at the most elegant of dinner parties in the townhouses and salons of Harlem in the 1920s. He was often the unofficial guide to the night scene showing dignitaries around town. He was frequently the noted guest in the company of other artists like Countee Cullen, Langston Hughes, Arna Bontemps, Claude McKay, and Zora Neale Hurston. Wendell Wilkie, a future Republican presidential candidate, and French royalty and direct descendant of Napoleon Bonaparte, Princess Violette Murat, could be seen as part of the entourage that Jackman squired through Harlem.

Harold Jackman was an authority on the arts and will be forever remembered as a great part of the brilliance that was the Harlem Renaissance. He built collections of the finest African American literature and promoted its preservation. He moved in artistic circles in the United States and Europe. And on either continent, he possessed the sophisticated elegance and the cosmopolitan aura of a true Renaissance man.

MAHALIA JACKSON (1911-1972)

I f any one person could personify the shear majesty of gospel singing it was Mahalia Jackson. It is her tearstained face that we envision and her robust voice we hear when we think of great gospel singing. She did more for mainstream gospel music than any other artist. And throughout her career in music, she refused to sing anything except gospel music, even though the inducement to do otherwise was relentless. From the 1940s through the 1960s, her voice could be heard on radio, television, and even the silver screen. And when she performed live, she would resonate to a packed house.

Mahalia Jackson was born in New Orleans, Louisiana, on October 26, 1911. Her father, Johnny Jackson, a barber, longshoreman, and Baptist preacher, was never a presence in the family home. Her mother, Charity Clark, was a maid and laundress who died when Mahalia was five. The orphaned child grew up in a household with her brother, her father's other children, and six aunts. Some of her relatives played dance music at parties for the rich, and some played blues and ragtime with the blues singer, Ma Rainey.

New Orleans, then and now, was filled with vibrant music of all kinds. Jackson made her singing debut in the children's choir of the Plymouth Rock Baptist Church at age four. Early in her life she absorbed the conservative music tradition of hymn singing at the Mount Moriah Baptist Church, where her family worshipped. She was also attracted to the strong rhythms and emotional abandon evident in the music of a nearby Holiness Church. In addition, she was inspired by the secular music all around her, including a new popular form to which New Orleans was giving birth – Jazz. She had to secretly listen to blues and jazz because most southern church-going blacks at that time associated that music with the Devil.

As a child Jackson dropped out of elementary school to help support the family. In her teens she moved to Chicago, where she sang professionally with the choir of Greater Salem Baptist Church and with the Johnson Gospel Singers, one of the first professional touring gospel groups. In 1929 Jackson met composer Thomas A. Dorsey, known as the Father of Gospel Music. He advised musically, and in the mid-1930s they began a fourteen-year association of touring, with Jackson singing Dorsey's songs in church programs and at conventions. Dorsey's "Precious Lord Take My Hand" became a signature song.

Various people, including then husband Isaac Hockenhull, and jazz great Louis Armstrong, tried to persuade Jackson to abandon gospel singing and perform blues, jazz, and other popular music to increase earnings, but Jackson unwaveringly refused. When she sang, she felt compelled to express her deepest religious convictions. Touring the country singing Dorsey's music proved to be commercially successful and at the same time, spiritually uplifting. And yet, northerners were uncomfortable with Jackson's "holiness emotionalism," and southerners were uncomfortable with her "jazzy worldliness." Her expressive contralto voice infused gospel music with a sensual freedom it had never before known.

By the late 1940s, Jackson had become the official soloist of the National Baptist Convention. In the 1950s she had her own radio and television shows in Chicago, but appeared frequently on other national radio broadcasts and television programs. During this time she also toured as a concert artist, and began appearing less frequently in churches. As a result of this venue change, her arrangements expanded from piano and organ to full orchestral accompaniment. In 1950 she became the first gospel singer to perform at Carnegie Hall, and in 1958 she was the first gospel artist to sing at the Newport Jazz Festival.

Creating a unique style by blending Baptist hymn tradition and blues, she was among the first spiritual performers to introduce elements of the blues into her music. Jackson, more than anyone else, established gospel music as a genre distinct from traditional Negro Spirituals, earning her the title, "Gospel Queen." General critical consensus holds her as the greatest gospel singer ever. She was a major crossover success whose popularity could transverse racial divides. Mahalia Jackson was gospel's first superstar, and even decades after her death, remains for many the major icon of gospel music's transcendent power.

290

*"...music has charms to melt rock...bend the knotted oak...
and soothe the savage breast..."*

– William Congrieve

J azz is an African American musical art form that came into being before the turn of the 20th century in New Orleans. It was a seamless blending of African and European musical influences. Early indication shows the word was spelled J-A-S-S, but it later took on that familiar spelling that we know today. The Blues had a great influence on Jazz, just as it had on Ragtime, and other later forms of African American music. Jazz makes good use of the "blue" or flattened note, improvisation, and polyrhythm. In Jazz, the boundaries of music are challenged to the point that each Jazz musician can achieve a uniquely identifiable sound. With Jazz, African Americans have created an enduring legacy. It has been the crowning achievement of all African American music to date.

Like all black music, it is likely that Jazz roots come from the musical genre that immediately preceded it. That should mean that the Blues gave birth to Jazz. But unlike the Blues, Jazz is highly evolved and has incorporated all other musical forms before it and after it. Since all African American music is born of experience that would mean that not only the Blues, but Ragtime, black work songs, and Negro Spirituals, gave birth to Jazz. And Jazz has that boundless ability to fuse into itself all music that has come after it. And no other musical genre has so many sub-genres: Dixieland, Swing, Bebop, Afro-Cuban, Brazilian, Modal, and Fusion, to name a very few. Jazz is peerless in that it is now the standard by which all other music is critiqued.

No other music has put a stamp on modern literature, the way that Jazz has. The period of American History from 1918-1929 is defined as the "Jazz Age." It was the notable American novelist, F. Scott Fitzgerald (1896-1940), who coined the phrase. His interpretation of the term meant all things modern including attitudes, social mores, values, and of course, the music. Fitzgerald used the phrase to entitle his collection of short stories, "Tales of the Jazz Age." Jazz also influenced writers of the Harlem Renaissance, that extraordinary time of the flowering of African American arts and literature in the early to mid twentieth century. Langston Hughes (1902-1967), the poet laureate of the era, used Jazz to enhance his poetry. His innovation in poetic voice and form, especially in his poem "A Dream Deferred," influenced other black poets.

Although Jazz cannot profess a total self-genesis, it is clearly unlike any other music form before it, and nothing since has measured up to it. Jazz changed the nature of musical culture, not just in the United States, but in the rest of the world as well. If there was ever a truly defining music of a people, Jazz would have to be it for African Americans. And like all black music, Jazz is disseminated and embraced all over the world. And it has not ebbed since its inception over a century ago. But it has continually beaten against the shorelines, each wave swelling differently, but all flooding from the same sea of African American inspiration.

Cross-culturally, Jazz altered social structures. Because there was such a wholesale acceptance of Jazz music in the first half of the twentieth century, black people in the United States and elsewhere began to be treated with much more equality than in all previous decades. Musically, there were many more collaborations between black and white musical artists. Musicians and singers, too, blurred racial lines as their performances featured a confluence of both races.

The history of Jazz is just as hard to pin-point as a definition of Jazz. It is certain that it first flowed out of New Orleans, into Kansas City, into Chicago, and then to Harlem in New York City. But as it flowed northward into the American heartland, it was just as easily flowing southward into Central and South America. It flooded into Cuba and the Caribbean Island nations. It infused itself into the Spanish, Dutch, and French cultures in the islands before it dashed over to Europe. It grew up like a familiar scion in all of Sub-Saharan Africa. It was only there that it was embraced like a "prodigal son," returning home.

Several sources record that Charles Joseph "Buddy" Bolden (1877-1931) was the first Jazz musician. He was a coronet player from New Orleans. He had a keen ear and memory, which augmented his improvisation skills. He is reportedly the first to "rag" the Blues for dancing, thereby creating the new musical genre of Jazz. Ferdinand "Jelly Roll" Morton (1890-1941) was a pioneer of modern Jazz. He was a phenomenal pianist, bandleader, and the first true Jazz composer. In 1915, his "Jelly Roll Blues" became the first Jazz composition to be published. He was known for mixing individual improvisation within rehearsed group arrangements which is now the format for Modern Jazz. If any one artist can be credited with bringing international acclaim to Jazz, it would have to be Duke Ellington (1899-1974). His sophisticated concerto arrangements and compositions are still being copied. Even today, that "Ellington Sound" lives on as a testament to his incredible brilliance.

Because African American music is so universally dispersed, and because Jazz has been the perennial favorite over any other music, and because it is clearly the most imitated of all African American musical art forms, it may be that the origins of Jazz are obscured by now. But our history is quite clear. Jazz was born of a people, whose ancestors were kidnapped from their homelands, stripped of any identity, bereft of any humane treatment; disoriented, devalued, despised, derided, distained and almost destroyed. But from all of that, through all of that, and in all of that, they made music. Their descendents have created what the world had been waiting for. They created Jazz! And the world welcomed it. Now the world knows of that people. It knows of the struggle of that people. It knows of the resourcefulness of that people. It knows of the creativity of that people. And through Jazz music, it knows of the genius of that people. Whatever the situation, whatever the circumstance, whatever the condition, event, incident or accident, African Americans are driven to produce music to express it.

BLIND LEMON JEFFERSON (1893-1929)

lind Lemon Jefferson was the renowned African American singer, songwriter, and musician. He was one of the greatest and most influential blues singers in American history. His reputation rests on a very short recording career in which he recorded nearly one hundred songs from 1926 to 1929. His music reflected a primitive style that could be at once, raw and forceful, and haunting and melancholy. His recordings influenced later generations of folk and blues singers up to present day artists like B.B. King.

He was born Clarence Jefferson on a farm in Couchman, Freestone County, Texas. Most historians put his birth date at 1897, but there are census records to indicate he was born in July 1893. Historians cannot agree on whether he was born blind or was partially sighted throughout his life. The fact that he wore clear glasses instead of dark tinted glasses might suggest that he had very limited vision. His career began close to home, performing gospel music at Shiloh Baptist Church in Kirvin, Texas. By the time he was a teenager, though, he devoted himself entirely to the blues. He earned a living as a singer and guitar player, traveling a circuit through small Texas towns.

In 1917 Blind Lemon moved to Dallas, where he earned money as a wrestler and street musician. For a brief time, he sang with another well-known folksinger, Huddie "Ledbelly" Ledbetter. As his reputation grew, Blind Lemon started traveling further away to sing and play. In the early 1920s, he played in most southern states. The lyrics to some of his songs suggest a familiarity with many different locales. He most certainly penetrated the Mississippi Delta and Memphis, Tennessee regions, where there was lucrative work for an itinerant blues musician. Presumably, he traveled by train, occasionally riding in boxcars.

Blind Lemon was a unique artist, singing solo, self-accompanied, and performing a great deal of original material in addition to the more familiar repertoire of folk standards. He eventually came to the attention of the Paramount Record Company in Chicago. In 1925, he began a recording career that was brief but stellar. He commanded a broad vocal range. And he sang in a loud and passionate, but finely controlled, voice. He was self-taught on the guitar, but the intricacies and often staggered rhythms of his guitar accompaniments also showed superior musical skill.

Blind Lemon created a niche for the male blues artist in an industry previously dominated by back females like Ma Rainey and Bessie Smith. Some of his songs were autobiographical, and others showed sympathy for prison inmates. Many times he recorded different renditions of the same song. His major recordings include: *Long Lonesome Blues, Shuckin' Sugar Blues, Jack O'Diamonds Blues, Black Snake Moan, Match Box Blues, Blind Lemon's Penitentiary Blues, Hangman's Blues*, and *Pneumonia Blues*. His longtime friend and protégé, Ledbelly, recorded the *Blind Lemon Blues* in his honor.

Very little is known of Blind Lemon's adult personal life, but it is known that in 1922 he married a woman named Roberta with whom he had children. He made enough money doing street performances to support his family. Many specifics of his life are not available, leaving room for folklore to spring up in their place. It is said that he could recognize the clink of pennies tossed into his tin cup and reject them as inadequate payment. But pennies could buy bread in those days. It is said that he carried a gun. But he could not see to shoot it. It is said that he was a bootlegger. But he could not have operated a still.

As with his birth, uncertainty still surrounds his death. He was found mysteriously dead on a Chicago street. But Blind Lemon Jefferson will remain indisputably one of the main figures in country blues. He was one of the founders of Texas blues, one of the most influential country blues men of all time, one of the most popular blues men of the 1920s, and certainly the first truly commercially successful male blues performer. Recording only a few short years, he left a legacy of music that has come down to us as the standard of folk and blues, for the enjoyment of the listener and the inspiration of the musician.

M ae Jemison made history as the first African American woman to fly in space. She achieved her trailblazing success in September 1992 as a science mission specialist on the United States space shuttle *Endeavour*. In March 2001, she penned her life story in the autobiography, *Find Where the Wind Goes: Moments from My Life*. About her space journey, Dr. Jemison was quoted: *"I realized I would feel comfortable anywhere in the universe – because I belonged to and was a part of it, as much as any star, planet, asteroid, comet, or nebula."*

She was born Mae Carol Jemison in Decatur, Alabama, on October 17, 1956, the youngest of three children of Charlie and Dorothy Jemison. Her father was a roofer, carpenter, and maintenance supervisor. Her mother was an elementary schoolteacher. Jemison grew up in Chicago, where she became enamored with the idea of traveling to outer space. She read astronomy books and often visited the Museum of Science and Industry. Her interest in space was heightened in 1969 when the *Apollo 11* astronauts landed on the moon.

After graduating from high school in 1973 at age sixteen, Jemison entered Stanford University, from which she graduated in 1977 with a B.S. degree in chemical engineering and A.B. degree in African and African American studies. She also learned to speak Russian and Swahili while in college. She went on to medical and followed those degrees with a medical degree from Cornel University Medical College in New York City. While at Cornell, Jemison served as president of the Medical Student Executive Council and president of the Cornell Chapter of the National Student Medical Association. She also learned to speak Russian and Swahili while in college.

Jemison graduated medical school in 1981 and interned at the Los Angles County – USC Medical Center until July 1982. After that she was in private practice briefly in Los Angles. From 1983 until the summer of 1985 she served in the Peace Corps as a medical officer in the western African countries of Sierra Leone and Liberia, administering health care programs for Peace Corps volunteers and American Embassy personnel.

Returning to the United States in 1985, Dr. Jemison went to work as a general practitioner at CIGNA Health Plans of California, a health maintenance organization. She spent evenings taking further engineering courses at UCLA.

Though he career as a physician was progressing well, she never forgot her early desire to travel into space. Dr. Jemison applied for admission into the National Aeronautics and Space Administration (NASA) space program, and in 1987, after intensive examinations and interviews; she was accepted in NASA's training program. She was one of only fifteen chosen from 2,000 applicants. She trained in Houston, Texas and learned every aspect the space exploration program.

After finishing the training program, Dr. Jemison work at the Kennedy Space Center in Florida for another four years before being chosen for her first mission aboard the space shuttle *Endeavour*. On that historic shuttle mission, her assignment was to conduct experiments on weightlessness, tissue growth, and the development of semiconductor materials. The *Endeavour* successfully completed a mission of 127 orbits of the earth and 190 hours in space. Afterwards Dr. Jemison expressed the hope that her historic flight would help people appreciate the abilities of both women and minorities.

In 1993 Dr. Jemison resigned from the astronaut corps to return to the practice of medicine. She also established the Jemison Group, a company devoted to researching, developing, and marketing advanced technologies, such as a space-based telecommunication system designed to improve health care delivery in developing countries. Dr. Mae Carol Jemison continues to inspire so many with her spirit of adventure and sense of compassion. Her accomplishments are, in a sense, OUT OF THIS WORLD!

JACK JOHNSON (1878-1946)

J ack Johnson was the first African American heavyweight champion of the world. He was also one of many controversial symbols of racial tensions in the United States in the early twentieth century. His athletic ability and flamboyant life-style challenged the codes of white supremacy and racial segregation in the ring and in American society at large. His life and exploits were chronicled in a 20th century movie entitled *The Great White Hope.*

He was born John Arthur Johnson to Henry and Tina Johnson in Galveston, Texas. His father worked two janitorial jobs to support the family. Jack quit school in the fifth grade and went to work at a succession of menial jobs. He painted wagons and trained horses, worked as a baker's assistant, and loaded and unloaded ships on the Galveston docks. But it was while working as a janitor in a gymnasium that he became interested in boxing.

While Johnson trained and fought in Galveston, he established a reputation as the best "colored" boxer in the area. With a string of wins, he turned professional in 1897 and let it be known that he wanted a chance at the title in 1903. There were many qualified black fighters at that time, but none were permitted to contend for the title. Johnson continued to win bouts and agitate for a chance at the crown. Previous white champions, John L Sullivan and Jim Jeffries, had publicly declared that they would not fight blacks. But Johnson eventually fought reigning champion, Tommy Burns, a Canadian in Sydney, Australia in 1908. The fight lasted for fourteen rounds before it was stopped and Johnson was declared the winner.

After Johnson gained the heavyweight crown, the incensed white community angrily declared the need for a "great white hope." They enlisted retired champion, Jim Jeffries to bring Johnson down. The match took place in San Francisco on July 4, 1910. At the time, it was the most lucrative deal in sports history. Both fighters received over $100,000 each. Johnson was in control from the first round. He outscored and generally outclassed Jeffries before the other corner threw in the towel. The racially charged nature of Johnson's win over Jeffries sparked race riots across the nation. Jeffries was to become the first of many white hopes to be defeated by Johnson. Johnson defended his title against five other white fighters over the next two years.

In 113 fights, spanning a 35-year career, Johnson lost only 8 fights. Though physically imposing, well over 6-ft frame, and 220-pound weight class, he was known for his defensive ingenuity and a compact efficient style. He is still considered one of the great counter-punchers of all time. It was his goal to prove himself against the best competition regardless of race. But when he fought whites, he delivered the most strenuous punches, punishing, jeering, and taunting them with that trademark gold-tooth grin.

The one-on-one nature of boxing as well as its use of both physical and mental abilities made the sport a symbolic testing place for whites and blacks. The racial pride of both groups was at issue. But underpinning that pride was the white myth of racial superiority. The boxing ring became a metaphorical arena as well. Whites believed they could demonstrate and maintain their racial superiority, but Johnson believed those stereotypes would fall like his white opponents in the ring.

Jack Johnson's heavyweight crown came at a greater price than just defeating white men in the ring. Blacks were lynched and many more injured in the racial strife that followed. Johnson himself was harassed for the rest of his life, largely because he was a black man who dared to live a flamboyant lifestyle. He flaunted his physical prowess and his success in the face of white America and they hated him for it. He was despised not simply for beating white opponents, but for doing so in a manner that boldly mocked white America's racist notions and crushed their stereotypical opinions of black athletes and black Americans.

JAMES WELDON JOHNSON (1871-1938)

J ames Weldon Johnson was a leading African American novelist, poet, editor, and songwriter, of the Harlem Renaissance. Few could have boasted of such many and varied talents combined with such keen intellect as he did. Not only was he artistically gifted he was an intellectual giant. At various times in his life he worked as, and held degrees in, the areas of anthropology, education, and the law.

He was born James Weldon Johnson on June 17, 1871, in Jacksonville, Florida. He was raised in a middleclass household. His father was a headwaiter in a luxury hotel and his mother was an elementary school teacher. He received exceptional educational opportunities for the time and place. In 1887 he enrolled in Atlanta University, where he emerged as a scholar and athlete and delivered the commencement address in 1894. After a brief stint as principal of his former school in Jacksonville, he formed a legal partnership, becoming, in the process, the first black lawyer admitted to the bar in Duval County, Florida in 1898.

By 1904 Johnson had become involved in Republican Party politics, writing two songs for Teddy Roosevelt's Presidential campaign. He was also treasurer of the Colored Republican Club. In 1906, at the recommendation of Booker T. Washington, Johnson was named United States Consul to Venezuela and served there until 1909. From 1909 to 1912, he was Consul to Nicaragua. At the end of his diplomatic career, Johnson took up residence in New York City and turned his attention to writing, editing, and the social side of politics.

On the domestic side, he became editor of *New York Age* in 1914. He was a field secretary for the National Association for the Advancement of Colored People (NAACP) from 1916 to 1920. And for the next decade, he was the NAACP's first African American Executive Secretary. Johnson became the most effective defender of equal rights for African Americans in the 1920s. Johnson originated the phrase "Red Summer," after the race riots in Washington, Chicago, Knoxville, Omaha, and Charleston. He organized a silent protest march in Harlem against lynching and racial oppression. Johnson was fundamental to the early successes of the NAACP.

Johnson was a prolific writer. In 1900 he penned the lyrics for *Lift Every Voice and Sing*. He also wrote musical comedies and light operas with his brother, J.

Rosamond Johnson. Together, they wrote the score for *Under The Bamboo Tree*. Upon returning from diplomatic service, Johnson anonymously published *The Autobiography of an Ex-Colored Man* in 1912. It was one of the most influential and accomplished novels written by an African American between the Civil War and the Harlem Renaissance. As a poet, Johnson published several collections. *Fifty Years and Other Poems* published in 1917 that documented the African American literary success starting after the Civil War. *God's Trombones*: *Seven Negro Sermons in Verse* published in 1927 celebrated the tradition of the black folk preacher.

Johnson's academic achievements include a charter membership in the American Society of Composers, Authors, and Publishers; visiting professor at New York University; and Chair in Creative Literature and Writing at Fisk University (1930-1938). He is perhaps most widely known as one of the key figures in the African American literary tradition. He stands out as one of the brightest stars in that constellation that was the Harlem Renaissance. His talent and intellect were inexhaustible. But Johnson's place in the annals of African American history is mostly enshrined because of his protest against injustice and his unflinching courage in creating dialogue about the African American experience.

James Weldon Johnson was truly a "renaissance man" in every sense. As a songwriter, poet, novelist, diplomat, playwright, journalist, attorney, and human rights champion, he was truly a man for all seasons. One would be hard-pressed to name anyone who could rival the artistic and intellectual versatility, and commitment to social justice that James Weldon Johnson possessed.

A bsalom Jones was the first African American priest in the Episcopal Church. He was also an eighteenth century abolitionist and a part of the black Masonic movement chartered by Prince Hall. Jones was the epitome of the Revolutionary War era black leadership who knew that the goals of the American Revolution were inconsistent with the institution of slavery in America. But more importantly, he knew that slavery was quite inconsistent with Christianity itself and all the morality ascribed to Christian tenets.

Jones was born a house slave in 1746 in Sussex County, Delaware. He was raised on a plantation known as "Cedar Town." He worked as a handyman and taught himself to read from the New Testament and other books. When he was sixteen years old, he was sold to a storeowner named Wynkoop in Philadelphia. There, he continued his education by attending a Quaker operated night school for blacks. At age twenty-four Jones married Mary, the domestic slave of a man named King. Their marriage was recorded in the register of St. Peter's Anglican Church in 1770. The Wynkoops and the Kings were neighbors in Philadelphia, and both families worshipped at St. Peter's.

Soon after the wedding, Jones composed and circulated an appeal calling for donations and loans to buy his wife's freedom. He reasoned that under Pennsylvania law; any children of their marriage would be freeborn, based on the mother's free status. During the Revolutionary War, Jones made it his business to work until late in the night to assist his wife in obtaining a livelihood and to repay the money borrowed to buy her freedom. Jones had repaid it all by 1778. He also bought a house and lot in South Philadelphia even though he would not be allowed to buy his freedom for another seven years.

In 1787 Absalom Jones and Richard Allen were elected overseers of the first organized African American self-help organization, the Free African Society. The society crystallized the social-communal dimension of African heritage and the Christian faith. Members of the society paid monthly dues for the benefit of those in need. They also established communication with similar black groups in other cities. In 1793 the Free African Society would perform invaluable services of nursing the sick and burying the dead during a deadly epidemic of yellow fever, to which blacks were erroneously thought to be immune.

Both Jones and Allen served as lay ministers for the black membership of St.

George's Methodist Episcopal Church. The active evangelism of both men greatly increased black membership at St. George's which greatly alarmed the vestry. Until 1786, blacks and whites had worshipped together at the church. But the next year the church built a gallery and ordered its black members to sit only there. Jones and Allen were literally dragged from their knelling positions by ushers during prayer and ordered to seats in the gallery. Indignant because black labor and black money had been contributed to the expansion of the church, Jones led the black congregants from St. George's en masse.

For a while, the black congregants of St. George's met at the Free African Society meeting house. But after Jones conferred with William White, Episcopal Bishop of Philadelphia, the diocese agreed to accept the group as an Episcopal parish. But the group advanced three conditions by which they would accept membership in the Episcopal Diocese of Pennsylvania: that they must be received as an organized body, that they have governance over their local affairs, that Absalom Jones be licensed as lay reader, and, after further study, Jones be ordained as minister. In 1794, the group was admitted as St. Thomas African Episcopal Church. Bishop White ordained Jones as a deacon in 1795 and as a priest in 1802.

Absalom Jones led a remarkable life in a seminal period of American history. He was an outspoken proponent of the abolition of slavery before it was fashionable. He also entered into the struggle for blacks to gain control over their religious worship during the independent black church movement. But above all, Absalom Jones demonstrated persistent faith in God, and in the Church as God's instrument.

FREDERICK MCKINLEY JONES (1892-1961)

Frederick Jones was the African American inventor of the first practical refrigeration system for long-haul trucks. It completely revolutionized the food transport industry by eliminating the problem of food spoilage and changed America's eating habits forever. His system was later adapted to a variety of other carriers including ships for international markets and railway cars for home markets. He held over 60 patents in a variety of fields, with 40 in the area of refrigeration alone.

He was born in Cincinnati, Ohio in 1892, orphaned at the age of nine, and never managed to get more than a sixth grade education. He was moved to Covington, Kentucky where a priest raised him until he was sixteen. Upon returning to Cincinnati by hitching rides in automobiles, he developed a fascination for engines. He found work as a garage mechanic where he was later made foreman. By age 19 Jones had built several racing cars that he drove in exhibitions. From the knowledge he gained in his early experience, he developed a self-starting gasoline motor.

After Cincinnati, Jones accepted a job as the chief mechanic on a large farm in Minnesota. He kept expanding his mechanical skills and knowledge through library studies. Jones served as an electrician in the United States Army in France during World War I, achieving the rank of sergeant. After the war, he returned to Minnesota, entered the new area of electronic research, and built a transmitter for a local radio station. In the late 1920s, Jones designed a series of devices for the growing movie industry. When motion pictures incorporated soundtracks, he adapted silent movie projectors to accommodate talking films. He also developed the box-office equipment that delivers tickets and spills out change.

By the late 1930s, Jones was busy designing portable air-cooling units for trucks that would preserve perishable foods transported to markets across the nation. In 1944 he was elected to membership in the American Society of Refrigeration Engineers. At age 50, Jones was one of the outstanding authorities in the field of refrigeration in the U.S. Also in the 1940s he formed a partnership with Joseph Numero to create the U.S. Thermo Control Company. By 1949, the company had grown into a $3,000,000 a year business, manufacturing refrigeration units for trains, ships, and airplanes.

As an inventor, Jones was never satisfied with the improvements he had made in his cooling units. He developed ways that kept the air around the food at a constant temperature. He created other devices that produced special atmospheric conditions to keep fruit from drying out or becoming over-ripe before reaching supermarkets. Still other methods controlled the moisture in the air and air circulation. His inventions made it possible for the first time to transport meat, fruit, eggs, vegetables, butter and other produce that needed refrigeration over long distances at any time during the year.

The crisis of World War II inspired Jones to design and patent a special refrigeration unit that would keep medicines and blood serum fresh for transfusions via air transport. During the 1950s Jones was called to Washington D.C. to advise the government about refrigeration problems. He was a consultant to both the United States Defense Department and the U.S. Bureau of Standards. In 1991, he was posthumously awarded the National Metal of Technology for his innovations of long distance refrigeration.

Frederick McKinley Jones is credited with single-handedly creating safe national and international markets, and delivering fresh meat and produce to those markets by a variety of refrigerated transport vehicles. So, the very next time we see a McDonald's food trucks, or any refrigerated food trucks, on the highway or unloading at the supermarket pod bays; or enjoy fresh food on a cruise ship; or order cold drinks aboard an airline flight; let us all remember the African American inventor whose efforts marked a new direction in the marketing of fresh foods and his success in revolutionizing fresh food transport. And let's not forget the innovations he created for the radio and movie industries also.

S cott Joplin was an African American musician and composer and one of the greatest piano players in history. He is called the father of Ragtime music. Ragtime was the music style that flourished before the turn of the 20th century. Although lacking the improvisation or the Blues feeling inherent in Jazz, Ragtime was a strong influence on the earlier forms of Jazz. Ragtime's structure and syncopations, blending together aspects of classical music, marches, and African rhythms with Creole influences, strongly hinted at Jazz. Ragtime also included early American folk tunes set to a syncopated beat. Ragtime became an African American music form that represented the past as well as the present.

Joplin was born in Texarkana, Texas. His parents were Giles and Florence Joplin. He had three brothers and two sisters. The whole family was very musically talented. Giles Joplin played the violin and Florence sang and played the banjo. So, Joplin got his first music lessons at home. He then took lessons from several white teachers who had heard him play. By the time Scott was a teenager, he was already in great demand around Texarkana. He played for churches, parties, picnics, and dances. To hone his skills, Joplin even played in less wholesome places, like bars and nightclubs.

Not much is known about Scott's early life. He had few educational opportunities. But more than anything else, he wanted to play and enjoy music. His father, however, wanted him to work with him on the railroad. Scott's father had been born into slavery, so having a "good" job was important to the elder Joplin. The two argued constantly about Scott's musical future. It is not known exactly when, but Scott left home to go on the road in his middle teens after fighting with his father for that last time about music.

By 1885, Scott Joplin had settled in St. Louis, Missouri, playing the piano at the Silver Dollar Saloon. There, Scott played "jig piano," which was what Ragtime was first called. It was an obvious reference to race. In 1895, Scott moved to Sedalia, Missouri to work at the Maple Leaf Club. By this time, he had the desire to become a more respectable musician. So, at the age of twenty-seven, he enrolled in the George R. Smith College for Negroes to study music. Shortly afterwards, Scott began to compose and publish music. His "rag" tunes made him famous and successful.

The most famous Joplin "rag" tunes includes classics such as *Maple Leaf Rag*, *Magnetic Rag*, *Wall Street Rag*, and *The Entertainer*. Joplin also wrote "rag" ballads and "rag" operas. In 1907, Joplin moved to New York City. The next year, he published *The School of Ragtime – Six Exercises for Piano*. His book of piano exercises became extremely popular. And Scott was finally able to prove to his father that he could make a "good" living from music. Scott was popular with women. In 1901, he married a woman named Belle. But by 1904, he married Freddie Alexander who died a few months later. In 1908 Scott was married Lottie Stokes, who became his greatest fan and music publishing partner.

One of Scott's operas was very dear to him, and dedicated it to the memory of his second wife, Freddie. He called it *Treenonisha*. It contained a superb variety of black music including folksongs, spirituals, ragtime, and the blues. He published the opera himself in 1911, but he could not convince anyone to produce it on stage. He became despondent, mostly because he longed for recognition as an artist of worth. He had a mental collapse and entered the hospital. He recovered from the breakdown, but never completely regained his health. Scott died in New York City on April 1, 1917.

Scott Joplin's tremendous volume of music lives on. And Jazz musicians speak of him as one of the early pioneers of their art form. In recent years many of his songs have been re-discovered. Major orchestras now play Ragtime music. The song, *The Entertainer*, was featured in the hit movie, *The Sting*, with Paul Newman and Robert Redford. And *Tremonisha* was lavishly staged, recorded, and critically acclaimed. It earned a posthumous Pulitzer Prize for Joplin in 1976. Finally, the meritorious achievement he wanted.

BARBARA JORDAN (1936-1996)

B arbara Jordan was an African American educator, statesman, and the first black and the first woman to be elected to the United States House of Representatives from the state of Texas. She was an orator of enormous talents and gave an eloquent discourse during the House impeachment hearings of President Richard M. Nixon after the Watergate Scandal.

Barbara Charlaine Jordan was born in Houston, Texas in 1936 to Benjamin and Arlyne Patton Jordan. Rev. Jordan was a full-time warehouseman and a Baptist minister. The Jordan's had three daughters and ran a very strict household. In her early life, Barbara and her sisters sang Gospel music and appeared as the Jordan Sisters. But it was her passion and talent for debate that marked Jordan's childhood and adolescence. By 1952, she had a large collection of honors, including an award presented by Zeta Phi Beta Sorority. It was at Phyllis Wheatley High School in Houston that Jordan decided on a career in law.

Jordan went on to do undergraduate work at Texas State University. Joining the debate team there, she won first place in junior oratory. Jordan graduated magna cum laude from Texas Southern University in 1956. She received her law degree came from Boston University in 1959 where she was known as a skilled public speaker. After qualifying for the bar in Texas and Massachusetts, Jordan moved back to Houston and set up her first office in her parents' home. Case by case, her law practice grew. At the same time, she began to take part in politics. Jordan worked for John F. Kennedy during the 1960 Presidential Election.

In 1962 and 1964, Jordan ran for election to the Texas House of Representatives. She lost both elections. Jordan later remarked: "I did not like losing." But the Voting Rights Act of 1965, signed by President Lyndon Johnson in response to successful protest from voting rights groups, inspired Jordan to run again. Since the era of Reconstruction, the political life of blacks in the South had been constrained by poll taxes and other discriminatory devices.

In 1966, using grassroots tactics, Jordan won the election by a two to one margin over her opponent. She became the first black woman to be elected and the first African American since 1883 to serve in the Texas Senate. Se also became the first to chair a committee, and the first freshman senator named to the Texas Legislative Council. In the 1972 national election, Jordan became, at age thirty-six, the first black woman elected to Congress from the South. In the U.S. House of Representatives, Jordan became a junior member of the Judiciary Committee.

It was in this committee that Jordan participated in confirmation hearings for two vice presidents and in the impeachment hearings for President Richard Nixon. The hearings were televised, so everyone in America had the opportunity to see how skillfully Jordan questioned some of the most powerful men in the country. Jordan spoke forcefully against Nixon, and at the same time, managed to be entirely nonpartisan about the whole Watergate affair. For Jordan the issue remained the U.S. Constitution, and as it became apparent, she was one of Congress' most learned authorities on that document.

Jordan believed in the Constitution. And the fact that she was only marginally included in its first two hundred years of implementation did not deter her love for the ideals and principles of democracy. It only strengthened her resolve to correct it. She spoke of it with her usually eloquence: "My faith in the Constitution is whole, it is complete, it is total, and I am not going to sit here and be an idle spectator to the diminution, subversion, the destruction of the Constitution." One of her most notable achievements was the broadening of the Voting Rights Act of 1965 to include Mexican, Asian, and Native Americans.

Jordan was the keynote speaker at the 1976 Democratic National Convention, but in 1978, she announced her retirement from political life and received an appointment as distinguished professor at the Lyndon B. Johnson School of Public Affairs at the University of Texas in Austin. Never completely out of the spotlight, Jordan was again the keynote speaker at the 1992 Democratic National Convention that nominated President Bill Clinton. In 1994, Clinton bestowed on her the nation's highest civilian honor, the Presidential Medal of Freedom. It was a most fitting tribute to this articulate freedom fighter, and the most knowledgeable Member of Congress in recent history.

J uke Joint, sometimes spelled as "jook joint," is the Black Vernacular English term for an informal establishment featuring blues music, dancing, food, and alcoholic drinks. Primarily, African Americans in the southeastern United States operated them. The term "juke" is believed to derive from the Gullah word "joog." In Gullah, joog means to be rowdy or disorderly. Gullah, which is a language and a culture, is a corruption of the word "Angola." And Angola is a country in West Africa from where many southeastern slaves were taken. The word "juke" may have derived from the Wolof linguistic group in West Africa.

Juke Joints emerged along with new patterns of African American labor following the emancipation of the slaves. At the turn of the 20th century, sharecroppers, turpentine workers, and migratory laborers needed a place to relax and socialize following a hard week of work, particularly since they were barred from white saloons by the codifying of Jim Crow Laws. Many white landowners did not mind Jukes being established on their property because it was a way of keeping black laborers isolated from the townspeople. And, of course, they could get their share of the profits in the form of "rent" from the Juke operator. Both contrivances were a means to further exploit black people.

Juke Joints were often set in ramshackle buildings or private houses on the outskirts of towns. They were very often conveniently located in or near work camps. Jukes offered food, drink, dancing, and gambling for weary workers. They were also a social outlet and a pressure valve to vent the stresses of the workweek. Operators made extra money selling groceries, homebrewed beer, and moonshine liquor to patrons. And during the Prohibition Era, just as many rural whites as blacks frequented Juke Joints. Just as often, and again because of Jim Crow segregation, they provided cheap room and board.

Juke Joints were not exclusively an African American experience, nor were they solely rural. The term was used for black establishments in the city as well as in the country. The name that was most commonly accepted to mean a white Juke Joint was "Honky Tonk." And in the Hispanic American culture, the "Cantina" served much the same purposes as a Juke Joint.

The Mississippi Delta Juke Joints are most famous in African American culture as the incubators for the Blues. The local black musicians forged a basis for the classic blues in the Delta Jukes. Virtually all the great early Blues singers and musicians traveled the Juke Joint Circuits, scraping out a living on tips and free meals. While musicians played, patrons enjoyed the dances of the period like the Jitterbug and the Slow Drag. Juke Joints were known for improvised, often humorous, styles of rhythmic dancing called "juking." A Juke Joint was also called "Barrelhouse," which was another name for the style of dancing associated with Blues, Jazz, and Funk.

Juke Joints also enjoyed many colorful monikers in their continuous history within the United States. Places like the "Do Drop Inn," the "Black Castle," the "Pink Pony," "Juicy's Place." "Monkey's Place," and "Ground Zero," are just a few of the remaining Jukes in the South. Jukes have been celebrated in African American folklore, the cinema, and in surviving photographs. In "Mules and Men," Zora Neale Hurston is credited as the first writer to define Jukes in literature. In "The Color Purple," Harpo turns his home into a Juke Joint after Sophia leaves him. Most recently, the Hip-Hop artists Outkast did a marvelous job of recreating a Juke Joint called "The Church" in their brilliant movie, "Idlewild."

The Juke Joint is an American phenomenon because every town had at least one. It was the place where local blacks came after work to relax, eat catfish and pig feet, to drink beer and whiskey, and above all, to listen and dance to the music. They were as abundant as churches and were as common as the neighborhood market. There is a quest now for the cultural preservation of the Juke Joint tradition. And a clarion call has gone out to remember the life and habits that took place in and around the Juke Joints.

J uneteenth is the oldest known celebration of the actual ending of slavery in the United States. Dating back to 1865, it was on June 19th that Federal soldiers led by Major General Gordon Granger, arrived with the news that the Civil War had ended on April 9, 1865, and that all slaves were now free. One of the first orders of business for General Granger was to read to the people of Texas General Order #3 stating:

> *"The people of Texas are informed that in accordance with a Proclamation from the Executive of the United States, all slaves are free. This involves an absolute equality of rights and rights of property between former masters and slaves, and the connection heretofore existing between them becomes that between employer and free laborer."*

Now, it is here that historical foundation needs to be imputed. Slavery was legally abolished with the enactment of the Thirteenth Amendment to the U. S. Constitution on January 31, 1865. Even before that, the Emancipation Proclamation of 1863 had freed all slaves in states that had seceded from the Union. The order included Texas and her ten Confederate sister states. However, being issued by the President of the United States, the Confederate States of America, having already formed its own sovereign country, with its own Constitution, and its own chief executive and bicameral congress, felt no compulsion to obey it. But with the surrender of Confederate commander Robert E. Lee to Union commander Ulysses S. Grant at Appomattox Courthouse in Virginia, the Confederacy no longer existed. And it initiated the demise of a way of life that the South had known for nearly two hundred and fifty years.

Even with all of that, the Union Army arrival in Texas seemed more than a little late. Lee surrendered to Grant in April 1865. More than two months before Granger's General Order. What happened during that time seems more shrouded in myth and folklore than revealed in historical fact. Technically the war did end in April, but the last fighting did not cease until May 26, 1865 in Mississippi. It wasn't until after that, the Union forces had the strength and manpower to enforce the abolition of slavery throughout the South. Coming as late as it did, still the reading of the proclamation ignited a chain of spontaneous freedom celebrations that rippled across the state and spread throughout the Southwest. The black reaction to this profound news ranged from pure shock to immediate jubilation.

The anniversary of freedom was not to be forgotten by people who had spent their entire lives in bondage – people for whom the lash had been a common punishment, but whose sting had been a momentary passing compared to the pain of family separations, the indignity of compelled deference, and the thought that only the grave would bring emancipation. So in the ensuing years, the joyous events of June 19, 1865, were re-enacted, becoming a tradition of Juneteenth celebrations. Their best Sunday dress, American flags, prayers of thanksgiving, baseball games and massive quantities of food, characterized these African American gatherings. In Texas, where it began, rodeos, fishing, and barbecues were the standard. Often guest speakers were brought in and recounts of the events of the past served as a catalyst for spontaneous worship services that were also a major part of these celebrations.

In true African American style, music and dance figured prominently in the impromptu celebrations that erupted across the state in 1865. It is believed that the Negro Spiritual containing the words "Free at Last, Free at Last, Thank God Almighty I am Free at Last" has its origins in Texas during the Emancipation revelry. Juneteenth remains essentially a Southern celebration for African Americans, but throughout the 1980s and 1990s, it enjoyed a growing and healthy interest from communities and organizations all over the nation. Places like the Smithsonian Institute, the Henry Ford Museum, and others have begun sponsoring Juneteenth-centered activities. In more recent years, a number of National Juneteenth Associations have arisen to take their place along side older organizations – all with the same mission to promote and cultivate knowledge and an appreciation of the history and culture of African Americans.

P ercy Julian was an African American research chemist, and pioneer in the chemical synthesis of medical drugs. As a research scientist, he always hungered for the deepest secrets of plant chemistry. His dogged determination and his grace under the pressure of prejudice helped to overcome his obstacles with personal triumphs. He was inducted into the National Academy of Sciences in 1973 in recognition of his scientific achievements. And he was inducted into the National Inventors Hall of Fame in 1990.

He was born Percy Lavon Julian in Montgomery, Alabama on April 11, 1899. His father was a railway mail clerk and his mother was a teacher. Julian attended the State Norman School for Negroes, a private high school in Montgomery. After graduation he went to Greencastle, Indiana where he enrolled in DePauw University. He was valedictorian of the graduation class and a member of two honor societies, Phi Beta Kappa and Sigma Chi. He received a B.A. in 1920. Julian taught at Fisk University before entering Harvard University, where he earned an M.S. degree in Chemistry in 1923.

After accepting a teaching position at West Virginia College for Blacks, he later transferred to Howard University in Washington, D.C., serving as associate professor of Chemistry and acting chair of the department for two years. In 1929, with financial backing from the General Education Board, Julian went abroad to Vienna, to study for his doctorate. While studying there, he became interested in the research of soybeans. In 1931, he received a Ph.D. in Organic Chemistry. Upon receiving a four-year fellowship in organic chemistry at DePauw, he and his assistant were the first to synthesize physostigmine, a drug used in the treatment of glaucoma. The Dean of the University wanted to appoint Julian as chairman of the chemistry department, but was advised against it because Julian was black.

Dr. Julian left DePauw accepting employment at the Glidden Company, a manufacturer of paints and varnishes in 1936. He was appointed Chief Chemist and Director of Research of the Soya Products Division from 1945 – 1953. His appointment was viewed as a turning point regarding the acceptance of black scientists in America. In 1954, Dr. Julian was director of research of the Vegetable Oil and Food Division where he successfully developed new processes for paints as well as perfecting a method of extracting *sterol* from soybean oil for the manufacturing of sex hormones.

Dr. Julian saved the lives of thousands of servicemen in World War II with his invention of "aero-foam" derived from soybeans, which was used to extinguish fires. In 1954, Dr. Julian founded Julian Laboratories, Inc. in Oak Park, Illinois, and Laboratories Julian de Mexico in Mexico City. In just a few years, Julian Laboratories grew to be one of the largest producers of drugs in the country. The company was devoted mainly to the production of synthetic cortisone in large quantities and at a reasonable cost. Before Dr. Julian's work, cortisone, used in the treatment of rheumatoid arthritis, was available only in limited quantities and it was extremely expensive.

In 1961, Dr. Julian sold the Oak Park Laboratories to the pharmaceutical company of Smith, Kline and French for more than two million dollars but maintained his position as President and continued as a consultant to Julian Labs until 1964. During his long and productive career, he received numerous awards, published over 200 papers in respected science journals, and had more than 125 patents to his credit. He received the NAACP Springarn Medal for outstanding contributions to research in chemistry in 1947. He served as Vice President of the Board of Directors of Roosevelt College in 1948 and Vice President of the Board of Trustees of Provident Hospital in Chicago in the same year. He also served as a Trustee of Fisk University.

Percy L. Julian achieved so much in his lifetime. His accomplishments extend well beyond the scope of this biographical essay. He led a fulfilled life and he realized his dream of seeing the emergence of black scientists entering universities where their creative talents could find uninhibited outlets.

THE KENTUCKY DERBY (EST. 1875)

The Kentucky Derby stands as the oldest consecutively held Thoroughbred Horse Race in America. It may not seem an appropriate subject for a Black History Essay Book, but there are facts present in the history of the Derby that are not generally known. The history of the Kentucky Derby and African American horsemen will be forever intertwined. For it was these men who helped shaped America's greatest horse race. The first Kentucky Derby winning jockey was black. In fact, fourteen of the fifteen jockeys in the first Derby were black. Black jockeys won fifteen of the first twenty-eight Derby races. And interestingly, black horse trainers trained six of the first seventeen Derby champion thoroughbreds.

The first Kentucky Derby was held on May 17, 1875. Popular African American jockey, Oliver Lewis rode H.P. McGrath's thoroughbred, Aristedes, to victory in the first running of the 1.5 mile contest. His winning time was two minutes and 37 seconds. Another African American, Ansel Anderson, had trained Aristedes. In 1877, black trainer, Ed Brown, trained Derby champion, Baden-Baden. Black jockeys, Alonzo Clayton and James Perkins won their respective Derby's when they were only 15 years of age. Black jockeys, Willie Simms and Isaac Murphy were not only Derby winners, but Triple Crown winners, winning the Preakness and the Belmont Stakes, as well. Murphy was the first jockey to win three Kentucky Derby races, winning in 1884, 1890, and 1891. In 1896 the racecourse was shorten to 1.25 mile when Simms won the race in two minutes and seven seconds.

The accomplishments of African American horsemen in the very early years of horse racing are often forgotten. In the Antebellum South, slaves rode for their masters. Many even obtained their freedom as payment for winning important races. In the years between the end of the Civil War and the turn of the 20th century, African American jockeys were very influential. The sport was erected on the backs of black jockeys and black trainers. In the early years of the Derby, many black jockeys owned and had trained the horses they rode. They were expert horsemen who possessed the skill and power necessary to spur a horse to glorious victories.

After the turn of the 20th century, thoroughbred horse racing started to be a higher profile sport and blacks were mostly seen only as stable help. The last black jockey to win the Kentucky Derby was Jimmy Winkfield, who won in both 1901 and 1902. He eventually left the United States to race in Europe where attitudes toward blacks were more liberal. In recent years, African Americans have started to come back to the mainstream of horseracing. Entertainer M.C. Hammer owned the successful Oaktown Stables that raced the excellent filly, Lite Light, winner of the Kentucky Oaks and other prestigious races. Barry Gordy, famed *Motown* music mogul, also had some success with his horses. There is now on the horseracing scene, a young black jockey named Marlon St. Julien. He has been very successful on the Texas and Chicago racing circuits.

Although Major League Baseball has replaced Thoroughbred Horseracing as the national pastime, the Kentucky Derby continues to serve as a unique American tradition. The spectacle that was first witnessed by only 10,000 people in 1875, today annually attracts crowds of over 130,000 people. Millions more view the event on television, and around the world via satellite. To some it is just a horserace, but to horseracing enthusiasts, it is the most exciting two minutes in sports. Traditionally the Kentucky Derby has been called the "Run for the Roses" because of the garland of roses tossed around the winning horse. Today, the main attraction to the sport has been the earnings and prestige it generates for the owners.

The Kentucky Derby is held annually on the first Saturday in May. Now that there is a slow-paced trend of blacks returning to the sport, it will be interesting to observe whether they will ever come to dominate it again. As with other sports, like Baseball, Basketball, Boxing, Football, Tennis, and now Golf, the rule has been that if blacks enter in it – they are likely to become preeminent in it.

CORETTA SCOTT KING (1927-2006)

I n the recent passing of Coretta Scott King, widow of slain Civil Rights leader, Martin Luther King, we are challenged to remember what she stood for. With March being National Women's History Month, we are also confronted by this year's theme: "Women – Builders of Communities and Dreams." Mrs. King's dream was the same as her husband's. And she lived to see how that dream was fulfilled after his death. She could have retired after the 1968 assassination. But she continued to devote herself to their shared dream of an America in which black people achieved equal rights and all people obtained social justice.

At birth she was given the name Coretta, but everyone called her Corey. She was the second of three children born to Obadiah and Bernice McMurry Scott, in Heiberger, Alabama. Her father's farm had been in his family since Reconstruction. But they were still cash poor and every member of the family worked the land. Her father was the first black man in the county to own a truck. Her life was not untouched by Jim Crow segregation. She and her brother and sister had to walk five miles a day to attend the one-room Crossroad School in Marion, Alabama while white students rode buses to a closer all-white school.

Later, Mrs. Scott decided that the only black high school was too far away for her children to walk. So she hired a bus and drove all the black students in the area to and from school daily. The only alternative to that would have been to have the students boarded for the week, coming home only on weekends. Young Corey was an excellent student, especially in music, and was valedictorian of her graduating class at Lincoln High School. She received a scholarship to Antioch College in Yellow Springs, Ohio, where her sister, Edythe had been the first black, fulltime student to live on campus. As an undergraduate, she took an active interest in the budding Civil Rights Movement. She joined the Antioch chapter of the NAACP, and the college's Race Relations and Civil Liberties Committees.

Scott graduated with a B.A. Degree in music and education and won another scholarship for postgraduate study in concert singing at the New England Conservatory of Music in Boston, Massachusetts. She supplemented her income by working in the Library. By this time she had already decided to become a concert singer, thus bypassing the racism involved with the teaching profession. In Boston, her life changed forever. She met a very young M.L. King, Jr. He was a Morehouse College graduate, enrolled at Boston College working toward a doctorate degree, and he was two years her junior. The two were married on June 8, 1953 by M.L. King, Sr. The Kings remained in Boston long enough for Corey to receive her advanced degree in voice and violin.

In September 1953 Scott-King moved with her husband to Montgomery, Alabama where he had been called to the pastorate of Dexter Avenue Baptist Church. In less than one year, the couple would become public figures when Rosa Parks refused to surrender her dignity on a segregated bus. And the next few years would see Corey sharing as a full partner in her husband's work, walking beside him in marches, traveling abroad with him, and giving speeches when he was unable to do so. On behalf of the Women's Strike for Peace, she was a delegate at the 1962 Disarmament Conference in Geneva, Switzerland. And as she was still keeping up with her music, she often gave concerts on behalf of the Civil Rights Movement.

Upon the death of her husband, Coretta Scott King became a revered public figure and an important leader in her own right. In a very savvy business move, she was issued copyrights on her husband's image, taped voice, and writings. As the "First Lady" of the Civil Rights Movement, a title she shied away from, she gave many hundreds of speeches, abroad and at home, became active in numerous organizations, published a collection of Dr. King's speeches and her own autobiography, and built the King Center for Nonviolent Social Change in Atlanta, Georgia. In her remaining years, she devoted much energy to HIV/AIDS awareness and curbing gun violence. When we esteem Dr. Martin Luther King, Jr., we must also appreciate this courageous woman who dared to build a community on a shared dream.

DR. MARTIN LUTHER KING, JR. (1929-1968)

He was born Michael Lewis King, Jr. on January 15, 1929 in Atlanta, Georgia. He was the middle child in the middleclass family of M.L., Sr. and Alberta Williams King. As a student, the young King had an insatiable thirst for knowledge. Throughout his academic career he maintained an exceptionally high scholastic standing which enabled him to skip three grades and enter Morehouse College at age 15. He received a B.A. in sociology at age 19 and afterwards entered Crozer Theological Seminary in Chester, Pennsylvania. He graduated from Crozer in 1951 with a 4.0 grade point average. He became an ordained minister, following in the footsteps of his father, maternal grandfather, and great grandfather.

In 1953, Dr. King married Corretta Scott, a music student he met at Boston University. The couple later had four children: Yolanda, Martin III, Dexter, and Bernice. Dr. King started in the ministry as the assistant pastor to his father at the Ebenezer Baptist Church in Atlanta. He became an ordained minister, following in the footsteps of his father, maternal grandfather, and great grandfather. By 1955, King had completed his dissertation in philosophy and was awarded a Ph.D. degree from Boston University.

Dr. King was later called to the Dexter Avenue Baptist Church in Montgomery, Alabama. It was there that he rose to national prominence as president of the Montgomery Improvement Association and the leader of the Montgomery Bus Boycott that lasted 385 days. After the arrest of Rosa Parks, King advised blacks not to use Montgomery public transportation. This nonviolent protest led the Bus Company into bankruptcy and forced it to negotiate with Dr. King. The cohesiveness of blacks during the crisis effected change in the company's racial policies and resulted in a 1956 U.S. Supreme Court decision declaring Alabama's bus segregation laws to be unconstitutional.

In 1957, Dr. King organized and became the president of the Southern Christian Leadership Conference (SCLC) to further advance the cause of social justice. The SCLC became the clearinghouse for numerous church-based demonstrations and rallies. Although Baptist ministers dominated, the SCLC transcended denominational lines and provided churches with a vehicle to express their solidarity with each other and with the Civil Rights Movement. The SCLC reflected Dr. King's philosophy of achieving social justice by nonviolent demonstration. It became his base of operation until his assassination. Dr. King called upon African Americans to understand that nonviolence is not a symbol of weakness or cowardice, but as Jesus Christ had demonstrated, nonviolent resistance transforms weakness into strength and breeds courage in the face of danger. In his own words, Dr. King stated: *"we had the protection of our knowledge that we were more concerned about realizing our righteous aims than about saving our own skins."*

Dr. King was the most dynamic speaker ever produced by the Black Church. He became the undisputed leader of the Civil Rights Movement and the ultimate spokesman for the whole era. He was a man of prodigious talent. His writings were superb syntheses of religious thought, social philosophy, and commentary on the black cause. The "I Have A Dream" speech, delivered to an assembly of 250,000 people during the 1963 March on Washington, is still recited to his honor. Dr. King was primarily a religious thinker. His convictions were theologically conditioned. For him, "the dream" was radically rooted in biblical prophetic vision. His dream was grounded not in the hopes of white America, but in God. For that reason, Dr. King looked not to the secular Enlightenment tradition, but to his religious faith to promote social reform.

In his all too brief life, Martin Luther King, Jr. received more than 300 honors and awards, including the coveted Nobel Peace Prize. The Nobel was a most fitting tribute to honor the peaceful warrior who exposed the contradictions of the American dream to the eyes of the world. And just like the renowned religious reformer, Martin Luther, whose moniker and mantle he assumed, Dr. King transformed the world and changed the way we would forever imagine ourselves in it.

SUSIE KING TAYLOR (1848-1912)

S usie King Taylor was the first African American nurse to serve in the Civil War. She also worked as a laundress, teacher, and domestic worker. Her story is not unique for the women of that era. What was unique was that she kept a diary. Even more unique, in 1902 King published a memoir from that journal entitled: "Reminiscences of my Life in Camp With the 33rd U.S. Colored Troops."

She was born Susie Baker, the first of nine children born to Raymond Baker and Hagar Ann Reed Baker, on the Grest Plantation, Isle of Wright, Georgia on August 5, 1848. When she was seven, Susie and one of her brothers obtained permission of the Grest family to move to Savannah to live with their maternal grandmother. The grandmother, Dolly Reed, had earned her freedom. She had a wagon business trading in fruits, eggs, molasses, live chickens, and any notion she thought she could sell or barter.

Susie's grandmother could also read and write and saw to it that her grandchildren could do the same. Susie attended "secret schools" like blacks had to so that no one would know that they were being taught to read. The children hid their books in flour sacks or wrapped them up like bundles of laundry to keep the secret. The children were taught in the kitchens and parlors of their grandmother's friends. The last person to teach Susie was a white girl who played with her and knew how to keep the secret. By the time Susie was twelve, she could read and write well enough to forge slave passes.

Susie's grandmother was fearful for the children in Savannah as Civil War fighting came closer. She was forced to send Susie and her brother back to their Georgia Sea Island enslavement for their own safety. Ironically, Union Soldiers liberated the Sea Islands first. Susie became "contraband" of war and was taken to St. Simon's Island, Georgia. She served with the First Regiment of South Carolina volunteers, comprised of slaves freed by the Union Army. She was first used as a laundress for the soldiers, but when it was realized that she was a fluent reader, she began to teach black soldiers how to read and write.

Also at age fourteen, Susie married Sergeant Edward King, one of the members of the 33rd. It was with this regiment that she began to nurse wounded men. She developed an aptitude to assist camp doctors in caring for injured soldiers. In 1863, there were several cases of vitriolic fever, a mild form of the smallpox virus. As doctors treated the disease, Susie volunteered to assume responsibility for patient care. She continued to nurse sick and wounded soldiers for four years until she and Edward were mustered out of the regiment in 1866. As Susie awaited the birth of their first child, she opened a school in Georgia for former slaves and their children. But just three months before the baby was due, on September 16,1866, Edward was killed in a dock accident as he worked as a longshoreman.

After her son was born, Susie could only find work as a maid in the South. As Black Codes were being instituted to restrict their freedom, African Americans were no longer allowed to be nurses. She moved to Boston, but found conditions limited there also. But she did marry again in 1879 to Russell Taylor, who afforded her the opportunity to stop working and become a homemaker for her family. Susie remained concerned about people and their circumstances. She put her organizational skills and her values to work in support of various causes. She organized a group of volunteers for the Women's Relief Corp. They helped aging veterans and their families; and they volunteered their services to hospitals and infirmaries.

Susie Baker King Taylor died at the age of sixty-four, and was buried without fanfare and without herald. After outliving the brutality of slavery; after bravely nursing soldiers for four years and writing about it; after being denied a pension; after starting a Georgia Island school for African Americans; and after committing herself to continuous public service and the uplifting of her race, there was not even a marker for her Boston grave. But because she had the foresight to keep a journal, history did mark her compassionate and courageous passage through it by the fresh telling and retelling of her story.

E theridge Knight was an Indianapolis resident and Pulitzer Prize nominated poet. He was an advocate of poetry as an oral art form and believed in its application as performance art. Even though he spent nearly nine years confined to the Indiana State Prison system, he became a leading figure in the militant Black Arts Movement that held a close philosophical affinity to the Black Nationalism Movement.

Etheridge Knight was born in Corinth, Tishomingo County, Mississippi on April 19, 1931. He was the third of seven children born to Etheridge Knight, Sr. and Belzora Cozart Knight. He grew up attending the local schools in Corinth and Paducah, Kentucky, dropping out by ninth grade. But his education would continue in a different venue. Knight began exploring the world of juke joints, pool halls, and the many other clandestine activities that the streets had to offer undereducated, unskilled, and ill-prepared black youth. Knight developed a joy in language usage and began to master the art of the "Toast." A Toast is a form of long, improvised, humorous poetry that dates back to the nineteenth century African American tradition of Signifyin', which has its roots in the African storytelling tradition. The Toast exploits the unexpected, using quick verbal surprises, and humor, but it is characterized by non-malicious criticism.

From age sixteen to nineteen, Knight served an enlistment period in the United States Army. He saw action in the Korean War where he received a severe shrapnel wound that was treated with morphine. With a history of adolescent drug experimentation, Knight developed an addiction to drugs and alcohol. Upon his discharge from the service, he turned to years of crime to support his drug habit. In 1960 he was arrested for armed robbery and spent more than eight years at an Indiana state correctional facility. But it was in prison that Knight began to write poetry that related directly to his experience.

In writing about that period of his life, Knight penned: "I died in Korea from a shrapnel wound / and narcotics resurrected me / I died in 1960 from a prison sentence / and poetry brought me back to life." Knight also began to submit his writings to publishing houses. Following numerous rejection letters from publishers, he received his first acceptance letter from the Negro Digest. They published a poem he wrote soon after the death of rhythm and blues singer Dinah Washington. The poem was aptly titled "To Dinah Washington." During this time he corresponded with, and received visits from such established African American literary figures as Chicago's Gwendolyn Brooks and New York City's Sonia Sanchez. Dudley Randall of Broadside Press published Knight's first book, "Poems from Prison" (1968).

Knight was briefly married to Sanchez when he was released from prison. His continued drug use may have contributed to the brevity of the marriage. Also, upon his release form prison, he found himself in the middle of the Black Arts Movement that aesthetically tied the artist to the black community by experience. He was also led to the Black Power Movement with its concepts of disenfranchisement and alienation from the broader American culture. The Black Arts Movement produced art that spoke directly to the needs and aspirations of black America, and Knight embraced those ideals into his own work. He edited a collection of poems entitled "Black Voices from Prison" (1970). He followed with: "Belly Song & Other Poems" (1973), "Born of a Woman" (1981), and "The Essential Etheridge Knight" (1986).

Knight's poetic themes included family relationships, prison, life and death, love and connection, addiction and incarceration. His legacy continues in Indianapolis with the Etheridge Knight Foundation and an annual Arts Festival that benefits at risk youth. He received many honors and awards posthumously and while he lived from the National Endowment for the Arts, Poetry Society of America, and the Indiana Governor's Literature Award. He was the artist in residence at two universities and he held a Guggenheim Fellowship. In 1990 he earned two bachelor degrees in American Poetry and Criminal Justice from Martin University in Indianapolis. Fitting credentials for a talented "jailhouse poet."

K wanzaa is an African American celebration observed in the United States since 1966. It is a seven-day holiday that begins December 26 and continues through January 1. African American scholar and social activist, Maulana Karenga, developed Kwanzaa. As the originator of Kwanzaa, Karenga wanted it to be a celebration to honor black culture around the world, and to uphold black unity, the black community, and the black family. His goal was to institute an alternative celebration to Christmas for African Americans.

Kwanzaa has its roots in the ancient first-fruits harvest celebrations from which it takes its name. Many African villagers celebrate the first reaping from the harvest in which nature is praised and the gods are thanked. *"Matunda ya Kwanza"* is Swahili for "the first fruits of harvest." Swahili is the lingua franca, or business language, of East Africa. Karenga added another *"a"* to the word so that it would have seven letters. Certainly seven letters could then more suitably reflect the seven principles of Kwanzaa. Another reasonable explanation for the change of spelling is that it distinguishes the African American word from the African word.

Kwanzaa is organized around five fundamental activities common to other African first-fruits celebrations. The first activity to celebrate is the gathering of family, friends, and community. Secondly, is the reverence for the creator and creation, including thanksgiving and the recommitment to respect the environment. The third concept to celebrate is the commemoration of the past, which included the honoring of ancestors, the learning of lessons, and the emulating of achievements in African history. Fourth, the recommitment to the highest cultural ideals of the African community is emphasized. This is represented by truth, justice, respect for people and nature, care for the vulnerable, and respect for elders. And last is the celebration of the "good of life" which includes life, struggle, achievement, family, community, and culture.

As is the case in most African celebrations, singing and dancing is a large part of the Kwanzaa celebration. And also included are rituals, dialogue, narratives, poetry, music, and feasting. A central practice of Kwanzaa is the lighting of the mishumaa saba or the seven Kwanzaa candles. A single candle is lit each day to highlight each of the Nguzo Saba or seven principles. The seven principles

327

to live by establish the overall framework and the supporting structure of Kwanzaa. Each day a different principle is referenced and tribute placed upon it.

These seven principles or Nguzo Saba, in Swahili and English, are: kujichagulia (self-determination); umoja (unity); ujima (collective work and responsibility); ujamaa (cooperative economics); nia (purpose); kuumba (creativity); and imani (faith). Kwanzaa ends with a day of assessment in which celebrants raise and answer questions of cultural and moral grounding and consider their worthiness in family, community, and culture.

Seven symbols are used in the Kwanzaa ceremony: a straw place mat (*mkeka*), symbolizing the history of African Americans; a seven-branched candleholder (*kinara*), representing Africa and the African ancestors; seven candles (*mishumaa saba*) three green, three red, and one black; fruits and vegetables (*mazao*) representing the fruits of collective work; ears of corn (*muhindi*), symbolizing black children; a communal cup (*kikombe cha umoja*), to be passed among celebrants; and gifts (*zawadi*), shared on the seventh day (January 1) as a reward for principles upheld.

Although many African Americans commemorate both traditions, Kwanzaa can never be a substitute for Christmas. Kwanzaa celebrates culture while Christmas celebrates God's miraculous gift. Kwanzaa promotes many cultural positives. But unlike Christianity, it does not promote salvation, or the God who gives it. There can be found many more cultural positives in Christianity. Within the faith is given all the morals to govern cultures, families, and individuals. It is the framework by which Christians are shown to be the "light of the world" without the use of candles.

I f the name "John Mercer Langston" strikes a familiar chord to the reader it is because of one of his most well known descendants, James Mercer "Langston Hughes." Langston Hughes was a prolific writer and one of the brightest stars of the *Harlem Renaissance.*

John Mercer Langston was born free in Louisa County, Virginia. He was the youngest of four children born to Lucy Langston, an emancipated slave of African and Indian ancestry. His father was Ralph Quarles, a wealthy white planter and slaveholder. Both of Langston's parents died in 1834 after brief, unrelated illnesses. The children were left with sizable inheritances that ensured their financial independence. A white friend of Quarles, who lived in Chillicothe, Ohio, cared for John and his brothers, Charles and Gideon until 1838 when he moved to Missouri. To protect their inheritance, the Langston brothers moved to Cincinnati rather than a slave state.

In Cincinnati, Langston lived with an African American family, in a tight-knit community of freedmen, who persevered in the face of relentless bigotry. Inspired by their experiences, Langston grew up involved in the black rights movement. In 1848, at the invitation of Frederick Douglass, Langston delivered an impromptu speech to the National Black Convention in Cleveland, condemning those who refused to help fugitive slaves.

Langston obtained both Bachelor and Master of Arts degrees from Oberlin College. However, he was denied entry to law school. Angry, but undeterred, he read law under Philemon Bliss and became the first black lawyer in Ohio, passing the Bar in 1854. With the aid of his brothers, he organized antislavery societies at both the state and local level. He also helped runaway slaves to escape along the Ohio section of the *Underground Railroad.* Langston married Caroline Wall and settled in Brownhelm, Ohio where he established a law practice. He quickly became involved in local politics and won election to the post of Town Clerk, perhaps becoming the first African American elected to public office in the United States. He became a radical proponent of armed resistance, conspiring with John Brown but declining to participate in the raid on Harper's Ferry.

Langston returned to Oberlin in 1856 where he again involved himself in town government. With the coming of the Civil War, he organized black volunteers for the Union cause. As chief western recruiter for black soldiers, he assembled the Massachusetts 54th, the nations' first black regiment, the Massachusetts 55th, and the 5th Ohio. Selected by the Black National Convention to lead the National Equal Rights League in 1864, Langston carried out extensive suffrage campaigns in Ohio, Kansas, and Missouri. From 1865 to 1867, he served as a city councilman in Oberlin and from 1867 to 1868 he served on the board of education. With an established and respected law practice, he even handled legal matters for the town. He vigorously supported Republican candidates for local and national office.

Appointed Educational Inspector for the Freedmen's Bureau, Langston traveled throughout the South advocating educational opportunity, political equality and economic justice coupled with individual responsibility. In 1868, he organized the law department at Howard University, serving as the first dean. He was also vice-president and became the acting president. In a dispute with the Trustees of Howard, Langston was forced out of his position and the entire law faculty resigned in protest.

In the eight years following his Howard University tenure, Langston entered the diplomatic corps as the Consul-General to Haiti. He assumed the presidency of Virginia Normal and Collegiate Institute in 1885. And in 1888 he sought and won a seat in the U.S. House of Representatives. Although his victory was contested afterwards, he became the first African American elected to Congress from Virginia. John Mercer Langston was a statesman of the highest caliber and was fully committed to the cause of freedom and equality for all African Americans.

NELLA LARSEN (1891-1964)

Nella Larsen was a novelist and the first African American woman to win a Guggenheim Fellowship Award for creative writing. She was most notably associated with the Harlem Renaissance. Although Larsen's career as a writer during that fabled period was short-lived, she was one of the artists who helped to establish it as an era of literary revitalization. And she was one of the women who gave a new voice to African American women. Her modernist use of irony and symbolism enabled her to introduce novels with multiple themes threaded throughout.

In her lifetime Larsen deliberately obscured her background. Her own biographical statements were very guarded and mysterious. She was born Nella Walker in Chicago in 1891. She was the only child of Mary Hanson Walker, a Danish woman, and Peter Walker, a West Indian immigrant. After the death of her father in 1893, her mother quickly remarried Peter Larsen, who was also Danish. Nella's stepfather began to resent her blackness after the birth of his daughter with Nella's mother. Both Nella and her half-sister attended public and private schools in Chicago. But because she was half black, her presence in the family began to be an embarrassment and she was treated like an outsider.

Larsen's stepfather enrolled her in the Normal School of Fisk University in 1907. It was the beginning of the permanent alienation from her family. She never returned home for weekend or holiday breaks. Instead, she became an avid reader. Larsen continued at Fisk, studying science through 1910. She claims to have spent 1910 through 1912 in Copenhagen, Denmark, auditing classes at the university there. By 1912 Larsen had resurfaced in New York City where she enrolled in the nursing program at Lincoln University. In 1915, she then moved to Alabama and became the assistant superintendent of nurses at the prestigious Tuskegee Institute.

Larsen was miserable in the Jim Crow South. She returned to New York City as a public health nurse in 1916. In Harlem, she met and married Samuel Elmer Imes, a black physicist, in 1919. In Harlem, she became acquainted with people influential in the burgeoning Harlem arts movement. It was in this environment that Larsen's interest in literature began to blossom. She left her nursing position in 1921 and became a children's librarian and attended library classes at Columbia University. She continued at the Harlem Library until

1926, honing her skills as a writer by penning several short works of fiction. With her strikingly Scandinavian physical features and her keen writing abilities, Larsen became the darling of the Harlem Renaissance and praised as one of its most important contributors.

In 1928, Larsen published *Quicksand*. It was praised by people like W.E.B. Dubois, and won a Harmon Foundation Bronze Medal for literature. In it she related some of her own personal experiences, ideas, thoughts, and beliefs. Her second novel, *Passing* appeared in 1929. It too contained bits and pieces from Larsen's life. Both novels involved semi autobiographical accounts of women whose racial and sexual confusion contribute to their unfulfilled quest for identity. As a modernist writer, Larsen addressed gender related issues such as empowerment and sexuality. At the same time she also addressed the issues of race and economics through women who could pass for white and thereby escape the cycle of poverty. Larson's other works include: *The Wrong Man* (1926), *Freedom* (1926), and *Sanctuary* (1930).

In 1934, Larsen's career took a nosedive. She became embroiled in a bitter divorce from her unfaithful husband and she was accused of plagiarism. She shed the husband and recovered nicely from the taint of plagiarism. But she never published anything else. Until 1964, she lived the life of a nurse in total obscurity, as Nella Larsen Imes. She continued her fascination with books and read incessantly. She never rekindled any of her Harlem Renaissance relationships. Neither did she publish novels or short stories. She was found dead in her New York apartment just as she lived the last thirty years – alone. The secrecy she had always sought for the beginning of her life, had now woven its way to the end of her life. And today still, Nella Larsen remains an enigma – a puzzle, cloaked in mystery.

LEWIS HOWARD LATIMER (1848-1928)

L ewis Latimer was an African American inventor and innovator. He was a pioneer in the development of the electric light bulb and the telephone. He was the only black member of the *Edison Pioneers*, a group of distinguished scientists and inventors who worked for Thomas Edison's companies over the years. He was also an educator of sorts. At the turn of the 20th century, he taught English and drafting to immigrant groups at the Henry Street Settlement House.

Latimer, whose father was a former slave was born in Chelsea Massachusetts and raised in Boston. At age sixteen, Latimer enlisted in the Navy and served as a cabin boy on the *U.S.S. Massasoit* for the remainder of the Civil War. In 1865, after receiving an honorable discharge, he returned to Boston. His skill in mechanical drawing enabled him to secure a position with Crosby & Gould, patent solicitors. The work of the patent draftsmen fascinated the young Latimer, and he taught himself draftsmanship skills. Becoming confident, he asked to be allowed to submit some drawings. The request was begrudging granted, but Latimer's impressive work earned him the position of junior draftsman and in a very short time, he was advanced to chief draftsman.

In 1876, Alexander Graham Bell was in need of a highly skilled draftsman to prepare blueprints for his new invention, the Telephone. Bell went to Crosby & Gould, and it was Latimer who was assigned to draw the plans for Bell's telephone patent. Latimer also held the patent on the transformer that Bell would use in transporting sound over great distances through telephone lines. In 1879, Latimer left Crosby & Gould to work as a draftsman for Hiram Maxim, the inventor of the machine gun and head of the U.S. Electric Lighting Company in Bridgeport, Connecticut. In Maxim's employ, he was responsible for supervising the installation of electric light in New York, Philadelphia, Montreal, and London. With his experience with patents, Latimer eventually began working for patent lawyers as an expert witness in patent dispute lawsuits.

Electricity was in its infancy, but everyone knew it was the wave of the future, and Latimer held the same perception. He proceeded to work on improving the carbon filament used in the light bulb. In 1882, he received a patent for what was probably his most important invention – an improved process for manufacturing carbon filaments. This process proved far superior to any other due to the longer lasting properties of the carbon filaments made from the cellulose of cotton thread or bamboo, and their excellent conductivity. Latimer assigned this patent and others to the U.S. Electric Lighting Company.

Latimer left Maxim and transferred to the engineering department at the Edison Company in 1884. He supervised the installation of Edison's electric light systems in New York, Philadelphia, Canada and London. In 1890, Latimer was assigned to the legal department where he performed an invaluable service as an expert witness, defending Edison's patents in court. Based on Latimer's testimony, Edison won his cases because of Latimer's vast knowledge of electrical patents. He was a man of many talents and skills, and not limited to electrical inventions. He privately published volumes of his own poetry. In addition, he authored a definitive technical textbook in 1890 entitled *Incandescent Electric Lighting.*

Lewis Latimer did more than just help to bring electric lights to the streets of New York and its office buildings, homes and subway stations. Through his many activities, he brought "light" to the lives of those around him. He worked for civil rights organizations, and taught immigrants mechanical drawing and the English language in a New York City community center. Latimer is a man that history cannot forget. A public school in Brooklyn, dedicated in 1968, bears his name. During Black History Month, all of the Bell Systems Labs pay homage to his patented transformer that allows voices to be heard through telephone lines. And in New York City, the Consolidated Edison Electric Utility stands as a "glowing" reminder of the talent and genius of this great African American inventor.

J arena Lee was the first woman preacher of the African Methodist Episcopal (AME) Church and the first African American woman to write an extended account of her own life. Although not officially ordained as a minister by church hierarchy, Lee was known for her powerful preaching and missionary work during 19th century. She became an itinerate preacher, traveling more than 2,300 miles along the east coast, and as far west as Ohio, delivering 178 sermons.

Jarena was born in Cape May, New Jersey on February 11, 1783 to free African American parents. History does not record the names of her parents, so her maiden name is not known. Not much is known of her early childhood either, or anything about her early education. It is known that she was literate enough as a young adult to read, teach and preach from the Bible with exceptional clarity. And in 1836, Lee penned her religious conversion experiences by writing: *"The Life and Religious Experience of Mrs. Jarena Lee."* By 1849, she had completed a more expanded version.

Jarena worked as a house servant in homes close to Philadelphia. At age twenty-one she became a devout Christian. Almost mystical, she had a series of ecstatic religious experiences and visions. Subsequently, at age twenty-four, she felt called to preach. The religious restrictions of the day caused even her to resist the idea of something so rare as a woman preacher. But Jarena became the first official challenge to the restrictions on women preachers in a black denomination when, in 1809, she approached Richard Allen, who had become the pastor of the newly established Bethel AME Church in Philadelphia, for a license.

Jarena never obtained that license, nor did not having it impede her from preaching. Although Allen could see women leading prayer meeting, he drew the theological line against female preaching and refused to issue the license Jarena requested. Allen could not sanction Jarena's call, claiming that the Methodist Church "did not call for women preachers." In 1811 Jarena married an AME clergyman, Rev. Joseph Lee, pastor of a congregation at Snow Hill. At her husband's urging, Jarena took control of the Christian educational needs of the Snow Hill congregation by organizing the Sunday School.

By 1816, Richard Allen had become the first Bishop of the AME denomination and they were now officially established as a connectional of the Methodist organization. Jarena again sought to legitimize her activities by seeking permission to become ordained. And again it was denied. But this time Allen did not put her off. She was permitted to hold prayer meetings in her home and to "exhort" at assemblies. Allen further encouraged Jarena by admitting her to meetings with recognized ministers. He also saw that she had speaking engagements at the churches in his bishopric. After she was widowed, he took her to Methodist conferences and served as her mentor and protector. And the most amazing thing of all, Allen kept her youngest son for two years while she traveled away from Philadelphia to preach.

Jarena never accepted the Methodist polity that denied women the right to preach the gospel. In her 1836 book, she argued that since Jesus had died to save the entire human race, women as well as men, there were no legitimate grounds for refusing women the right to preach His gospel. She served as a traveling revivalist, accepted by many pastors and preaching to mixed crowds of believers in several states. Even after the death of her friend and mentor, she continued to preach and bring men and women to Christ.

Jarena Lee displayed holy boldness, not only in preaching, but also in facing a society that allowed her to be the mother of men, but not the spiritual leader of men. She envisioned a world without sexism, racism, or any form of hatred. In 1837, while in the slave state of Maryland, she preached against slavery while invoking the memory of Nat Turner without ever calling his name. She mystically predicted the coming of a great civil strife, long before the start of the American Civil War in 1861. Lee died in the 1850s without seeing an end to slavery, but still keeping the faith that its end would come.

WILLIAM LEIDESDORFF (1810-1848)

William Leidesdorff was a merchant, trader, ship owner, land baron, and diplomat. He was the leading citizen of San Francisco when California was still a Mexican province. He was appointed Vice Council to Mexico, serving under the jurisdiction of Commodore Stockton, then Military Governor of California in 1845. It was in that capacity that he gave aid to the Americans during the Bear Flag Rebellion at Sonoma.

He was born William Alexander Leidesdorff to a Danish sugar planter by the same name and an African woman named Anna Marie Spark on St. Croix, Virgin Islands. He left the Islands as a youth. He and two of his brothers managed the family's cotton holdings in New Orleans from 1834 until 1840 when his father died. Leidesdorff later inherited money from the sale of that business. He then moved to New York, where he worked as a seafarer, serving as a ship's master on several voyages, participating in shipping and commercial trading until 1845.

Leidesdorff sold all his personal effects in New Orleans to buy the 106-ton schooner, *Julia Ann*. His move to California coincided with a critical time in American history. There was great controversy over whether California should remain in alliance with Mexico, become independent like Texas, or be annexed by the United States. And of course, there was the issue of slavery. If California were annexed, would it be slave or free? By the time Leidesdorff sailed in to the Bay area, these were still unanswered questions.

When Leidesdorff arrived in San Francisco, it was still part of Mexico. There were very few comforts in the city. There were no hotels, stores, or roads. Yet Leidesdorff was able to secure two very large tracts of land from the Mexican government. He later built a store and a home on the land. He quickly became very popular with Mexican officials who were frequent quests in his home. He became a Mexican citizen in order to obtain more land in 1844, and received from Mexico a 35,000-acre ranch. He named it *Rancho Rio de Los Americanos.*

Leidesdorff threw himself into the making of California history, finding the innumerable demands of a community experiencing birth pangs suiting his interest. He built San Francisco's first hotel on a lot he owned at the corner of Clay and Kearny. He opened California's first public school. He was the first to bring horse racing to California. Among the several business ventures claiming his attention was the launching of the first steamboat, the Sitka, to sail into the San Francisco Bay. To expand his business as a Hawaiian sugar importer and beef tallow exporter, he built a warehouse at the corner of California and Leidesdorff streets. In 1846 the Mexican mayor of San Francisco gave Leidesdorff more land within the city. By this time he was the city treasurer, a council member, and chairman of the school board.

Although Mexico still owned California, the United States and Great Britain were both trying to seize control of the territory. Liedesdorff played a key role in the struggle for California. Though a Mexican citizen, Leidesdorff aided the Americans by telling them about the city's defenses. The American Navy waited off the coast of California as the U.S. Marines landed and took over the city's government in 1846. The day before, Leidesdorff warned the citizens what was about to happen. He translated the soldiers' orders from English to Spanish for those who did not understand. Two weeks after the invasion, he gave a victory party for the Americans at his grand home as he had done so often for Mexican officials. Grateful for his help, the Americans allowed him to keep his land, property, and titles.

William Leidesdorff died at the age of thirty-eight of Typhoid Fever. He lived a short but eventful life. In a brief time he had become a man of great political power and enormous wealth. Without being an American citizen, he made American history by being a man with an adventurous spirit and incredible business acumen. Just as Jean Baptiste DuSable is forever a part of the history that belongs to Chicago, William Alexander Leidesdorff is forever a part of the history that belongs to San Francisco.

Marie Leveau is perhaps the most compelling and fascinating figure in New Orleans history. She is famous even today as the most powerful Voodoo priestess who ever lived. But history can produce very few hard facts about her life. Portraits of her show that she was a very handsome woman with golden completion, dark curly hair, and penetrating eyes. She was an expert practitioner of Voodoo, and even held the title of queen for years after her death. However, it is only legend that presents the most insight into her life as the nineteenth century "Voodoo Queen" of New Orleans.

She was born in the French Quarter in New Orleans in the 1790s. Her mother was a black woman, possibly even a slave. Her father was a wealthy white planter. She was raised as a devout Catholic and had a close relationship with Père Antoine, the priest of St. Louis Cathedral. At age twenty-five, she married a freeman name Jacques Paris. By accounts it was a happy marriage until Marie began claiming to be his widow, even before Jacques was known to have died. With his disappearance, it was presumed that he really was dead, although there was never a body produced for burial.

After Jacques Paris' mysterious disappearance, Leveau became a hairdresser who catered to wealthy white families in New Orleans. It was then that she began to collect secrets about influential people and she delved more deeply into the seamy underworld of voodoo. She also began a relationship with Christopher Duminy de Glapion, a freeman of color from Haiti. Between these two men, Leveau produced fifteen children. One daughter, also named Marie, is said to have greatly resembled her mother. This daughter is thought to be the reason Marie Leveau was said to have been seen even after her death.

Leveau's best-documented exploits of Voodoo involved a murder trial of a young Creole gentleman who promised Marie his house if she could work her magic to render a not guilty verdict. Marie placed charms throughout the courthouse and a not guilty verdict was obtained. And Marie began to live in grand style in New Orleans. She gained the attention of the city's elite. Her fame also spread abroad. Important visitors to the city like author Oscar Wilde could be seen promenading around with Marie Leveau. During the War of 1812, Marie helped the wounded during the Battle of New Orleans and was so noted for her efforts that she was invited to the state funeral of General Jean

Humbert, a hero of that battle.

Leveau was also a community-minded person. She visited the sick in prisons and was called upon by city officials to help combat the Yellow Fever epidemic of the 1850s. She was a feared and respected figure. Her voodoo beliefs were inextricably tied to her Catholic faith. Her most famous religious rituals were held on the banks of Bayou St. John every June 23. She also practiced rituals on the shore of Lake Pontchartrain near her cottage, Maison Blanche. It is said that sometimes Marie would dance with her large snake, Zombi, wrapped around her. Everyone believed that her snake possessed great powers too.

Leveau was adept with charms and potions of all kinds. But her real power came from her extensive network of spies and informants. The New Orleans upper class had a careless habit of discussing their most confidential affairs in front of their slaves and servants who then reported to Marie out of fear and respect. As a result, Leveau had an almost magical knowledge of the workings of the political and social power in New Orleans. And as her daughter became a practicing priestess, legend of Marie's powers grew to the extent that she now appeared ageless, with the ability to traverse time and space.

Marie Leveau was considered to be the quintessential Voodoo Queen. To this day, floral tributes are left at her graveside in New Orleans for favors granted in her name. She also appears in many 19th century novels and was known to have had an international following. But it is such a pity that we have only American folklore and Voodoo legend left behind to tell the intricate story of Marie Leveau. Because of this we will never know the true character of this captivating woman who teetered between light and dark.

E dmonia Lewis was a nineteenth century sculptress. She was the first African American woman to win international acclaim for her art. Her medallions and sculptures continue to inspire minority art students even into this new millennium. She overcame obstacles of gender and race to achieve artistic greatness.

Edmonia Lewis was born to a Chippewa mother and an African American father in Ohio or New York in 1843 or 1845. She is believed to be the first sculptress of African American and Indian heritage. Little is known of her early life. Lewis had an older brother, Samuel, whose Indian name was *Sunrise*. He had become a wealthy adult after going west. Lewis began her life with the Indian name *Wildfire*. She was only three when her mother died. Her mother's two sisters in the Ojibwa community in New York raised her until age twelve. The Chippewa lived a semi-nomadic lifestyle. In her own words she recalled, *"I led this wandering life, fishing and swimming. I did as my mother's people did. I made baskets and pincushions, embroidered moccasins and I went into the cities with my mother's people to sell them."*

From 1860 to 1862, with funds supplied by her brother, Lewis attended Oberlin College in Ohio. Oberlin was the first co-educational college in the United States. There she changed her name to Mary Edmonia, but generally signed her sculptures and her correspondence as "Edmonia." At Oberlin College, Lewis excelled at drawing but admitted that she had always preferred to make "the form of things." She developed a keen interest in sculpture. Lewis never graduated from Oberlin, though. Instead, her life took a terrifying turn. When an art instructor missed some paintbrushes, Lewis was accused of theft. The two white co-eds, who accused her of stealing the art supplies, fell ill after drinking mulled wine, which Lewis allegedly served them.

Lewis was put on trial for attempted murder and was defended by noted African American lawyer, John Mercer Langston. In a well-publicized trial, Lewis was acquitted of all charges. But she was beaten by townspeople who did not agree with the verdict. The attack was in part due to Lewis' perceived guilt and in part to the racist sentiment of the town. The attack left Lewis bedridden for weeks and scared for life. Since she was not permitted to graduate, she moved to Boston in 1863.

In Boston, Lewis met prominent black and white abolitionists and established her first studio. William Lloyd Garrison introduced her to portrait sculptor Edward Brackett who became her first mentor. Her earliest sculptures were medallions with portraits of white antislavery leaders and Civil War heroes such as Garrison, Charles Sumner, Wendell Phillips and others. She also produced portrait busts of abolitionist John Brown and Col. Robert Gould Shaw, leader of the all black 54th Massachusetts Regiment.

As a neo-classical artist, Lewis moved in the artistic circles of Europe. She traveled extensively to London, Paris, and Florence before opening a studio in Rome. Rome became her home because of the abundant marble and cheap labor supplies. She was readily accepted into the fold of other female sculptors like Harriet Hosmer, Louisa Lander, and Anne Whitney. From Rome Lewis produced marvelous sculptures: *The Freed Woman and her Children (1866); Forever Free (1867); Hagar (1868); Hiawatha and Minnehaha (1871); The Old Arrow Maker (1872)*. Perhaps her greatest work was *The Death of Cleopatra* produced for the Centennial Exposition in Philadelphia in 1876.

Lewis proved to be a courageous woman who did not let race and gender hinder her from achieving her artistic goals. She had talent and focused all her energy and creativity into her sculptures, infusing elements of her heritage into her works. She drew upon her dual ancestry for inspiration. Lewis was part of the neoclassical artistic movement in the late 19th century, a movement and period into which she brightly fit. She was reported as still living in Rome in as late as 1911, but just as with her birth, the date and location of her death cannot be verified. But we will always be able to celebrate the life and art of Mary Edmonia Lewis as she herself celebrated her heritage through her work.

G eorge Liele was the first black Baptist minister of the independent Black Church Movement, and the founder of the earliest black Baptist churches in America. And through great missionary zeal, he was also instrumental in spreading the Baptist faith to blacks in Jamaica.

Liele was born in Virginia around 1750, as was the case with slavery; he could never recount his birth date. But he remembered his birth father was a religious man influenced by the eighteenth century religious revivals called the Great Awakening. Sometime before the start of the American Revolution, while still in his teens, he traveled extensively with his owner, Henry Sharpe, a Baptist Deacon.

Liele was converted to Christ while residing in Burke County, Georgia, and was baptized in 1772 by Matthew Moore, pastor of Big Buckhead Baptist Church. Liele received further religious instruction from Pastor Moore, as well as being continuously taught by Sharpe. Showing a gift for public speaking, he was invited to address a church quarterly meeting. He so greatly impressed the congregation that he was given a probationary license to exhort the slaves on the Sharpe, and neighboring plantations.

Liele was ordained as a Baptist minister in 1775, on the eve of the War of Independence. Like many other slaves, Liele had embraced Christianity during the evangelistic revivals that followed the Great Awakening. Now, as a fully licensed preacher, he could perform mission work among all Christians throughout the colonies. But the mission churches he established among the slave on various plantations, as well as the trading post church at Silver Bluff in South Carolina, was short lived as a consequence of conflicts associated with the Revolutionary War.

Liele was emancipated in 1777 and began to fully engage in the independent Black Church movement. He preached mostly to blacks, slave and free, in Virginia, Georgia, and South Carolina. By the end of that year, he had established at least two other churches. One of these continues to this day as the First African Baptist Church of Savannah. Liele pastored that church while keeping in close communication with other churches he had established in Georgia. When Liele had to leave, he left the churches in the capable hands of converts like Andrew Bryan and David George, whom he had baptized and trained in the faith.

Liele was a Loyalist, like his mentors, Sharpe and Moore. His sympathies were with the British even as Great Britain was loosing the war to the American patriots. This created an untenable situation for a free black man living in the South. As the British were evacuating in defeat, it was British Colonel James Kirkland who advised Liele to leave British North America in order to remain free. And In 1783, Liele immigrated to Jamaica and became the first black foreign missionary to settle on the Island.

In Jamaica, Liele continued the missionary work he had begun in what was by this time the United States of America. His evangelism in the West Indies began before the English Baptist came. By the time the British had sent their first missionary to Jamaica, Liele had already established a church in Kingston with more than 500 members. Despite some initial opposition from officials, his movement grew, and continued to flourish. By the time of his death, Liele had converted possibly ten percent of the island's black population to the Baptist faith. By the 1830s there were twenty-one black Baptist churches in Jamaica, along with twenty-seven Baptist schools serving some 4,000 black students.

Liele's missionary efforts to spread the Baptist faith place him among the most important of the early African American religious leaders. He did not create a denomination specifically for African Americans as Richard Allen had. But he did take an existing denomination and create a place for African American worship that did not previously exist. In the United States, the Baptist faith has more people of African descent than any other single denomination, partly due to the pioneer work of the Rev. George Liele.

D r. Alain Locke was perhaps the greatest social thinker of modern times. If Langston Hughes was the poet laureate of the Harlem Renaissance, that extraordinary period of creativity among African American writers, artists, musicians, and actors; then Locke was the founding father of the "New Negro Movement" that sparked it. He played the greatest and most influential role in identifying, nurturing, and publishing the works of young black artists. It was Locke's philosophy and intellect that served as the motivating aesthetic in keeping the energy and passion of the movement in the forefront of American culture, to wit, we are all most grateful beneficiaries.

Alain Leroy Locke was born on September 13, 1886, the only child of one of Philadelphia's elite black families. His parents, Pliny Ishmael and Mary (Hawkins) Locke, afforded their son the best education. He attended Central High School and the School of Pedagogy. He entered Harvard University in 1904 and distinguished himself as a Phi Beta Kappa, and by graduating magna cum laude in 1907. Locke spent the following three years studying abroad. He became the first black Rhodes Scholar at Oxford University. And he spent another year pursing an advanced degree in philosophy at the University of Berlin.

Locke began a forty year distinguished career at Howard University in 1912 as an Assistant Professor of English and Philosophy. In 1916 he took a sabbatical to obtain a Ph.D. in philosophy at Harvard. He returned to Howard in 1918 as a full Professor of Philosophy, eventually chairing the department before his retirement in 1953. He used philosophy and other social sciences in the analysis of social problems in the United States. His personal focus hinged on three issues: values and evaluation, cultural pluralism, and race relations. His thinking on social and ethnic problems was informed by a philosophical view that he set forth as cultural pluralism. Locke felt that each culture group had its own identity and each cultural group was entitled to protect and promote it. He further philosophized that in the particular context of America, the claim to cultural identity was in no way in conflict with American citizenship.

Locke's career as a teacher and writer covered the wide range of his interests. He had a significant part in the development of the curriculum of Howard's College of Liberal Arts. He believed in academic excellence and was one of the founders of the Gamma Chapter of Phi Beta Kappa. At Howard, he

345

advanced the study of philosophy both as an independent discipline and an ally with other social sciences. He energetically supported and was a staunch advocate for the black visual arts. He founded the Drama Department at Howard. He stressed the need for blacks to draw upon their rich heritage for inspiration and resource. He knew that black visual arts would come to make its mark on American culture in the profound way that black music had.

Locke was the author and editor of many books, including the quintessential *The New Negro*, the anthology published in 1925 that ushered in a focus on black art and literature. He also wrote *When Peoples Meet: A Study in Race and Cultural Contacts"* He contributed to *The Negro in America, The Negro and his Music,"* and *The Negro in Art*. His books stressed black culture, but always showed how it fit into the whole of American life. Locke also wrote for journals such as *Crisis, Opportunity*, and *Phylon*. In addition, he was also widely known for his work in Adult Education. He was the leading black advocate in that movement throughout the 1930s and 1940s. Also included with his tenure at Howard, were fellowships and visiting professorships at the nation's most prestigious colleges and universities.

Historically, Alain Locke's life spanned the post Reconstruction era to the onset of the Civil Rights Movement. His influence on modern culture was so immense, his interests so broadly varied, his education so intense, and his acclaim so wide, that he can truly be called "a man for all seasons." He was a philosopher and an interpreter of African American cultural achievements. But more than that, he was the recognized authority on the contributions of African Americans in literature, art, and the humanities.

J oe Louis was the second African American prizefighter to become Heavyweight Champion of the World. He was affectionately called the "Brown Bomber" because he could pack a wallop. No other African American had become an idol to all Americans regardless of color. Before Mohammad Ali captured the imagination of boxing enthusiasts all over the world with his boisterous self-acclamation of "I am the greatest," it was Joe Louis who captured the hearts of Americans and became a dramatic symbol of racial harmony in the process.

He was born Joseph Louis Barrow in a sharecropper's shack in Lexington, Alabama on May 13, 1914. He was the seventh of eight children born to Monroe and Lillie Barrow. His pedigree was typical for a son of the south. He was the son of sharecroppers, the great grandson of slaves, and the great, great grandson of a slaveholder. His father was institutionalized in a mental hospital two years after Joe's birth. The family was erroneously notified of his father's death, and his mother unknowingly remarried. When Joe was ten, his mother, stepfather, and his siblings became a part of the *Great Migration* and moved to Detroit.

Because education conditions were deplorable for blacks in the South, Joe was placed in classes with children considerably younger than himself. This caused him to develop a self-conscious stammer. He found solace in taking violin lessons. When he later attended a vocational school to learn cabinetmaking, a classmate got him interested in amateur boxing. At age seventeen he left school and began training for amateur bouts. He boxed under the name "Joe Louis" so that his mother would not find out.

Louis lost his first amateur fight, but racked up an impressive record of winning 50 of 54 bouts. This included more than 40 knockouts. In 1934 he won a national amateur title in the light heavyweight division. He turned professional in that year after coming to the attention of John Boxborough, the kingpin of the numbers rackets in Detroit's black neighborhoods. This racketeer gave him surprisingly good advice on how to become a good fighter and he managed Louis all the way to the championship.

Louis' professional career was even more stellar than his amateur career. In his first year, he won 27 bouts that included 23 knockouts, a TKO of Primo

Carnea, and a KO of Max Baer. Both men were former heavyweight champions. His winning streak ended on Jun 19, 1936 when German boxer, Max Schmeling knocked him out in the fourth round. It was only a small setback, but Louis was emotionally devastated by this loss. But on June 22, 1937, after a seven-bout winning streak, he took the title from James Braddock, joining the category of Jack Johnson, the first black Heavyweight Champion of the World.

Louis again had to face Schmeling in June 1938. This time it was not just a fight of two men it was a fight of two ideologies. Adolph Hitler and the Nazi Party controlled Germany and another World War was looming in Europe. Schmeling, although not a Nazi, represented totalitarianism, and Louis, who was now the champion, represented Democracy. The press and radio media played up this sporting event the same way they had the 1936 Berlin Olympics. And again it was proven that German athletes were not superior to African Americans. Louis took down Schmeling in short order. In only 124 seconds into the first round, Louis scored a stunning knockout, making him the most popular athlete in the world. Louis and Schmeling met in the ring only twice, but they would remain friends for the duration of their lives.

During World War II Louis enlisted in the army as a Technical Sergeant. He fought over 100 exhibition bouts before two million service men. Along with his humble shyness, his patriotism was another quality that endeared him to the American public. Although it was not reported, Louis had a troubled personal life. He was married four times, twice to his first wife. And he had affairs with Hollywood stars Lena Horne, Sonja Henie, and Lana Turner. Joe Louis held the Heavyweight Title from 1937 until 1948. Even with two failed comeback attempts, his final record remains "the bomb" at 68 wins and 3 losses.

NAT LOVE A.K.A. "DEADWOOD DICK" (1854-1921)

Nat Love was born the youngest of three children in a Tennessee slave cabin in 1854. At age fifteen, he was one of so many southern blacks who found their way west to escape the oppressive aftermath of slavery. But life in the western territories was dangerous for everyone. There was gross lawlessness. Mobs calling themselves *vigilantes* improvised a homemade frontier justice and executed men they thought guilty of crimes. Even the presence of federal soldiers and marshals could not always prevent outlaws from terrorizing settlers. Even women and children occasionally fell victim to a generally violent way of life.

Frontier towns in the 1870s possessed few redeeming features. There were a great many saloons, dance halls, and gambling houses. Apparently these "dens of iniquity" drew no color line, so that black cowboys were accommodated on the same terms as white ones – as long as they had money. Upon his arrival in Dodge City, Love found work as a cowboy earning $30.00 a month. It was the beginning of what he termed in his 1907 autobiography as "an unusually adventurous life." Love immediately earned the admiration of the other cowboys for his ability to ride unbroken horses.

For nearly two decades he took part in the long cattle drives that guided Texas beef into Kansas and all points north. While his autobiography does confirm the large-scale participation of black cowboys on the long drives up the Chisholm Trail, Love provides very little insight into the intricacies of western racial relationships. Its unusual that he does not mention a single instance of discrimination or bias, yet such incidents did take place and it is difficult to believe that Love neither encountered nor witnessed them.

At the Centennial Fourth of July celebration in 1876, after a cattle drive to Deadwood, South Dakota, Nat Love earned the nickname that he would ware proudly for the rest of his life. He competed against the best cowboys in the West in a series of contests displaying riding and shooting skills. He won the contest to rope, throw, tie, bridle, saddle, and mount an untamed bronco. He accomplished this feat in a record nine minutes. He won the shooting contests with a rifle at 100 and 250 yards and with a Colt-45 at 150 yards. Winning these contests required great marksmanship. Afterwards, his admiring fans gave him the nickname "Deadwood Dick."

Later that same year, Love was captured by Indians and "adopted" into the tribe, more or less against his will. But he made a daring escape riding a bareback horse one hundred miles in twelve hours of darkness. He was shot twice during his escape. This is only one of the many harrowing experiences Love writes about in his autobiography. His stories are filled with exciting almost unbelievable escapades. With obvious relish and complete self-confidence he claims to have fought off Indians, braved the elements, battled wild animals and wilder men, and lived to tell it. Love was known for his ability to hunt and track wild animals as well as his skill with a gun. But by his own narrative account, he was larger than life. He could shoot targets from the hip at fourteen feet when the other cowboys could only manage eight feet. He entered shooting and roping contests and walked away the winner of purses valued at $200 or better.

While Love and other cowboys were yet riding the range, the great era of the West was passing into history. Progress in the form of the Railroad was making them obsolete. No longer was it necessary for men on horseback to drive cattle thousands of miles to market. Trains could carry Texas beef to eastern consumers in less time and with greater ease than the long cattle drive up the Chisholm Trail. In 1890 Nat Love left the range for a job with the Railroad as a Pullman Porter. It was the best type of position open to African American men at that time. His autography entitled: *The Life and Adventures of Nat Love: Better known in the Cattle Country as "Deadwood Dick,"* provides us with remarkable insight into that bygone western era, and the code by which the cowboys lived. But what do we really know from the Nat Love story? There were black cowboys, for sure. But Love being as wild as he claimed begs further research.

M aroon Societies were bands of freedom seeking runaway slaves who established communities of their own in remote areas, where slave catchers could not easily recapture them. Maroon Societies had varying degrees of stability. The most stable societies included men and women, who may have engaged in sustaining agrarian pursuits, and developed trade with outsiders. They instituted identities through language and culture absent from the social structure of the slave owners' homesteads and plantations. The least stable societies were gangs of escaped males who wandered in a region, living hand-to-mouth by fishing, hunting, and raiding local plantations.

In English, the word "maroon" means to be stranded or stuck in a place. But in Spanish, the word comes from "cimarrón," which is defined as "wild, savage, fugitive, and runaway." The literal Spanish meaning is "to live on mountaintops." Maroon populations were proven to have located throughout all of the Americas – North, Central, and South. They were also frequently noted in all of the West Indies. Remote areas like the Amazon River Basin, the hills of North Carolina, and the Florida Everglades hosted exceptional Maroon Societies. These communities sought in varying ways to duplicate the African cultures from which they came. The most stable of them built communal agricultural societies, raised crops, and bred animals and fowl. And above all, they maintained families with African kinship patterns.

Long before the Underground Railroad became an effective antislavery device, slaves were running away. Some were men, women, and children, singularly, in pairs, and in groups. Running away was first and foremost the most common and effective form of slave resistance. But when runaway slaves had no destination, they went so as far as to organize themselves into these settlements. In Maroon Societies, runaway slaves lived in these independent, albeit, hidden communities. Although attention and credit have been given to Maroon societies and their struggles in other parts of the Western Hemisphere, comparatively little has been written about Maroon Societies in the United States. But what is known is that their formation represented only one of a number of ways that Africans resisted slavery in the Americas.

The forests, mountains, and swamps of the Southern United States were the favorite Maroon locations. Virginia, North and South Carolina, Georgia,

Louisiana, Mississippi, Alabama, and Florida all had Maroon Societies existing within their borders. The largest and most notable communities in the United States existed in the Dismal Swamp, along the Virginia – North Carolina border, and in Florida in union with the Seminole Indians. Maroons proved to be troublesome to the planters who sought to maintain strict order on their plantations. They were sources of refuge for fugitive slaves daring enough to escape their masters and reach them. The Maroon Societies were also bases from which to launch raids on plantations for supplies or just for retaliation.

Maroon Societies represented the reality and possibility of self-determination and power to other slaves. Both their existence and their victories against search-and-destroy expeditions by slaveholders, and their successful attacks against plantations reaffirmed this reality. The Maroons raided plantations to free other enslaved Africans and to provide the leadership and the inspiration for future slave insurrections.

There is evidence of the establishment of at least fifty Maroon Societies between 1672 and 1864 with varying life spans within the United States. Mostly isolated, with limited means of subsistence, and with regular search-and-destroy measures launched against them, the Maroons' capacity to expand was somewhat limited. They were also restricted in their capability to wage effective guerilla warfare. But the contribution they did make to the overall process and legacy of resistance to slavery stands out, and it is increasingly recognized and greatly respected as just one of the ways that slaves resisted the slave system.

THURGOOD MARSHALL (1908-1993)

T hurgood Marshall was an African American jurist who achieved many "firsts" in his long and eventful life. He was the first black appointed to serve as an Associate justice on the United States Supreme Court in 1967. Before that, President Johnson had appointed him as the first black Solicitor General to the U.S. Supreme Court. He believed wholeheartedly in the Constitution. He was twice married with two sons.

He was born "Thoroughgood" Marshall to William and Norma Marshall in 1908 in Baltimore, Maryland. His grandfather had been a slave. His parents were a middleclass couple that promoted education over all else. Marshall attended the city's public schools. He changed his name to "Thurgood" during this time. Marshall graduated with honors form Lincoln University in 1930 and graduated at the top of his class from Howard University Law School in 1934.

Marshall's career began when he entered private law practice in Baltimore in 1934. Later that year he became counsel for the local National Association for the Advancement of Colored People (NAACP). In 1936 he joined the organization's national legal staff. He became its chief legal officer in 1938 and handled all cases that dealt with the constitutionality of African American rights. Marshall was appointed to the position of director-counsel of the NAACP's Legal Defense and Educational Fund in 1950. He spearheaded the elimination of practices and laws that prevented African Americans from enjoying full rights of citizenship.

Marshall's career with the NAACP was the most distinguished in its legal history. Among his greatest triumphs was the 1954 United States Supreme Court case, *Brown vs. the Board of Education of Topeka, Kansas*. He and his associates successfully challenged the legality of racial segregation in the nation's public schools. It was a landmark case that struck down the "separate but equal" doctrine that had been so much a part of the oppressive culture of the South. It also opened the door to challenge other forms of discrimination against African Americans.

President John F. Kennedy nominated Marshall for appointment to the Second Circuit Court of Appeals on September 23, 1961. The Senate confirmed him the next year. After President Lyndon B. Johnson was sworn in to fill the remainder of President Kennedy's term, he appointed Marshall as Solicitor

General (SG) of the United States in 1965. He became the first black to hold that position. The SG is the government's primary advocate before the Supreme Court. Even though it is the fourth highest-ranking person in the Justice Department, it is perhaps the most powerful position in the department next to the Attorney General.

The pinnacle of Marshall's distinguished career came in June 1967 when President Johnson nominated him as an Associate Justice of the Supreme Court. He was then confirmed by the Senate in August and took the constitutional oath in September 1967. Marshall again made history as the first person of African descent to serve on the Supreme Court. From all reports Marshall remained a larger-than-life figure even while serving on the Court. He had always had strong sentiments in support of human rights and equal justice. And he was particularly protective of the civil rights gains of African Americans. He further distinguished himself as a spokesman for racial equality and the rights of the underprivileged.

He outspokenly criticized the government for not understanding the role that African Americans played in expanding justice. But he was always reticent when it came to speaking about his achievements. Marshall observed, at his retirement in 1991, that he wanted to be remembered simply as a man who had done *"what he could with what he had."* And what he had was a brilliant legal mind, a deep and abiding respect for the Constitution, and a distinguished career in the law. In the African American struggle to end racial discrimination in the United Stated, no one played a more salient role than Thurgood Marshall.

BRIDGET "BIDDY" MASON (1818-1891)

B iddy Mason became an African American entrepreneur, philanthropist, and founder of the oldest black church in Los Angeles, California, First African Methodist Episcopal (AME) Church. She rose from slavery in the South to prominence in the West through hard work, good business sense, and a generous spirit. Her charity for the sick, homeless, and her supportive prison ministry, are still celebrated today.

She was born Bridget Mason, a slave, on August 15, 1818, on the John Smithson plantation in Hancock, Mississippi. Her parents are not known to history. In 1836, her owners gave her as a wedding gift to Robert Marion Smith and Rebecca Crosby Smith. After converting to Mormonism in 1847 the Smith family, their slaves, and a number of other families comprised a caravan of 300 wagons and made a 2,000-mile journey to the Utah Territory.

Making the trek with Mason were her three daughters, Ella, Ann, and Harriet, who in all likelihood were fathered by Smith. She acted as the cook, midwife, nurse, cattle herder, and caretaker for the whole caravan. After four years in Salt Lake City, Smith uprooted again and moved his household to San Bernardino, California, where Brigham Young was starting a new Mormon community. In 1850 California had been declared a "free state" and slavery was not legal there. It is not known whether Smith knew this before his arrival or he simply forgot. When in 1855 he decided to leave California with his slaves and move to Texas, Mason had other ideas. She convinced the local sheriff to block Smith's departure with a writ of habeas corpus. The case was eventually heard in the United States District Court of Appeals.

Under California law Mason and her children could not legally be held as slaves and on January 1, 1856 they were freed. With manumission papers in hand and children in tow, Mason moved to Los Angeles and quickly found work as a nurse and midwife. Her nursing skills soon afforded her economic independence. By 1866 she had saved enough money to purchase property in downtown Los Angles at 331 South Spring Street and built a clapboard house that she occupied until her death on January 15, 1891. Today this site is in the center of the commercial district in the heart of Los Angeles. The address became the base for her philanthropic work and a haven where the poor and homeless of all races could find safety and food. It also served as a haven for newcomers and any others needing assistance. She became the first black female property owner and philanthropist in Los Angeles.

Mason purchased a commercial building, which she leased to tenants from whom she earned a substantial income. With this money she and her son-in-law, Charles Owens, founded the first Los Angeles branch of the African Methodist Episcopal Church in 1872. It is the oldest black church in Los Angeles. It was there that Mason operated a nursery and food pantry. In addition, she aided flood victims and brought food to the malnourished men in local jails. In 1884 Mason sold a parcel of land for $1500 and built a commercial building with spaces for rental on the remaining land. As the town developed, most of her early investments became prime urban real estate and formed the basis of her considerable wealth. She continued to make wise decisions in her business and real estate transactions and her financial fortunes continued to increase until she accumulated a personal fortune of almost $300,000.

Through clever investments Bridget "Biddy" Mason acquired large tracts of land. Some of these she donated for schools, churches, nursing homes and other charities. Many knew but few ever forgot the generosity of Biddy Mason. At the time of her death she was buried in an unmarked grave. In 1988 the first African American mayor of Los Angles, Tom Bradley, erected a tombstone for her. In 1989, November 16 was declared "Biddy Mason Day," and a large timeline depicting the highlights of her life was dedicated on the wall of the Broadway Spring Center in Los Angeles. It was a fitting tribute for a woman that rose from being thought of as property, to one of the most philanthropic property owners.

JAN MATZELIGER (1852-1889)

J an Earnst Matzeliger made possible the modernization of the shoe industry by designing and patenting a "shoe lasting" machine that would automatically stitch the leather of the shoe to the sole. And it could make shoes ten times faster than by hand crafting. This invention also resulted in a lower cost to both the shoe manufacturer and the customer.

Matzeliger was born in Paramibo, Surinam (Dutch Guiana). His mother was a native black of Surinam, and his father was an educated Dutch engineer from a wealthy and aristocratic family in Holland. At age ten, Matzeliger worked as an apprentice in a government machine shop, where his remarkable talent for mechanics surfaced. At age nineteen, he signed on a merchant ship as a seaman for two years. After leaving the ship in Philadelphia, he worked at various jobs. One year later, Matzeliger arrived in Lynn, Massachusetts, where he remained for the rest of his life. Lynn was one of the leading shoe manufacturing centers, producing over half of the shoes made in the United States.

Matzeliger was able to secure a job with Harney Brothers, a shoe manufacturing company. He attended evening school and learned to speak fluent English. While working for the Harneys, Matzeliger solved a problem that had baffled the shoe industry for many years. He invented a "shoe lasting" machine that made handcrafted shoes obsolete. Before Matzeliger's automatic shoe lasting machine, a costly and tedious manual process did the task of attaching the leather uppers to the sole. Handlasters were highly skilled, and well paid for those times, but their work was slow and inefficient for the industrial age. As a result, the price of shoes was extremely expensive.

The "last" was a wooden model of the human foot. After a shoemaker had judged that the leather had been drawn over the "last" properly, the edges if the upper leather were sewn to the innersole. The excess leather at the toe was cut and drawn into plaits, which were shaved off to produce a smooth leather surface when it was attached to the outer sole. Matzeliger's invention made all these complex operations more efficient, increasing shoe production to 700 pairs per day.

Matzeliger first constructed a miniature prototype of his shoe lasting machine out of pieces of wood and bits of scrap hardware in 1880. Six months later, he produced a larger model. He was offered miniscule amounts of money for his prototype, but he refused all offers. He eventually secured financial backing for his project that enabled him to build a working model. Matzeliger's invention enabled him to produce shoes ten times faster than a shoe craftsman.

Matzeliger's invention made Lynn, Massachusetts the shoe manufacturing capitol of the world. Over the next few years, he was able to obtain four more patents on specific improvements to the shoe lasting machine. By 1889, the demand for the new "laster" had become international. The companies that emerged from the fruits of Matzeliger's labor formed the United Shoe Machinery Corporation and by 1955 had holdings of over a billion dollars.

Jan Matzeliger died of Tuberculosis at the age of 37. In his short life, he revolutionized the shoemaking industry. Even today, shoe manufacturers still use machinery similar to the Matzeliger original. He emerged from the industrial era as a giant in his field. At a time when machines were being invented to do the work of men, Matzeliger, and so many other black inventors, were taking America into a new era of industrial revolution – an era that cared less about cultural heritage and more about personal accomplishment.

L iberia is a small West African country located on the Atlantic coast, bordered by Sierra Leone, the Republic of Guinea, and the Ivory Coast. It is the oldest republic on the African continent and owes its establishment to the American Colonization Society (ACS) that was founded in 1816 to resettle freed American slaves in Africa. Thus Liberia has its roots in the controversy that raged in antebellum America over the institution of slavery and the destiny of African Americans, both slave and free. White reformers, who could not envision racial harmony in American society if or when slavery came to an end, controlled the ACS. They began the colonization movement mostly to be rid of the black presence in white America. Certainly sentiments including missionary zeal and paternalism also helped form the foundation of the movement.

Many black people, in the face of overt discrimination, also felt that repatriation of blacks to Africa was a practical idea, and worked just as hard as whites to achieve that end. By 1822 agents acting on behalf of ACS secured land from native rulers and named the first settlement Monrovia, in honor of President James Monroe. Full-scale immigration of African Americans to Liberia never materialized. Fewer than 5,000 free people of color and manumitted slaves had reached Africa by 1843. The Liberian colony grew slowly as the ACS and its state auxiliaries established other separate settlements along the coast between Sierra Leone and the Ivory Coast. Conflicts arose between the black settlers and the ACS. By the time Joseph Jenkins Roberts became the first black governor in 1841, the decision had been made to give the settlers almost full control of the government.

A constitution modeled on that in the United States was drawn up, a tripartite government was instituted, and Liberia became an independent republic in July 1847. Roberts was its first president, serving until 1856. Great Britain and France recognized the country within the first five years. But the U.S. did not recognize Liberia until 1862. Motivated by the desire to escape slavery and racial discrimination, and yet clinging tenaciously to American values and culture, the African American settlers, whether free or freed, resisted absorption by Liberia's more numerous indigenous peoples. The settlers became known as the Americo-Liberians and quickly fashioned an existence that became stratified along economic and social lines. At the outset a small elite group of leading citizens from among the free black emigrants set the tone and pace.

They brought to Africa the advantages of literacy and personal property and success in mercantile commerce. They also used their relative prosperity to dominate settler politics and establish prevailing social standards by founding churches, benevolent societies and fraternal orders, and other community institutions. Moreover, they consolidated their status position through the bonds of marriage making proper family ties an enduring feature of settler political and social dynamics. To this day, power and status can be traced to the elite African American settler families who repatriated Liberia but remains only 5% of the overall population. The indigenous Malinke, Kru, and Gola peoples hold the majorities. The African American settlers, regardless of individual background or status, were united in their determination that Christianity and Western civilization would be Liberia's cultural foundation.

Convinced that their life-style was superior, Americo-Liberians assumed the mission of imposing their values on the indigenous Africans. Inevitably, conflicts ensued that could have been avoided. Whenever negotiations of their differences failed to bring peaceful resolutions, neither group hesitated to resort to military force to advance their interests. The settlers organized militia companies for self-defense but also used them as instruments of territorial expansion and to make punitive raids on native slave traders. Relations between settlers and Africans, forged in a climate of mutual suspicion in the 19th century, evolved into today's patterns of uneasy coexistence characterized by intermittent warfare and protracted civil strife.

D r. Benjamin Mays was an author, educator, Baptist minister, civil rights activist, and the president of Atlanta's Morehouse College for twenty-seven years. He has the distinction of being a wise enough sage to have been a great influence on, and gave valuable advice to, Martin Luther King, Jr. Mays delivered the exquisite eulogy at King's funeral. He was an enlightened "man for all seasons," possessing nearly thirty honorary doctorate degrees and other honors and awards too numerous to list.

He was born Benjamin Elijah Mays on August 1, 1895 in Epworth, South Carolina. He was one of eight children born to former slaves, Hezekiah and Louvenia Carter Mays. After attending Virginia Union University, Mays transferred to Bates College in Maine and earned a bachelor's degree in 1920. He was ordained as a Baptist minister in 1921. And from 1921 to 1924, he taught math at Morehouse College. He received his first advanced degree, a master's, from the University of Chicago in 1925. But it would take another ten years to earn his Ph.D. from the same institution.

While undertaking graduate study, he taught English for several years at South Carolina State College and worked in various positions for the state government. Also, he was an activist and organizer for the National Urban League. In 1934 he became dean of the school or religion at Howard University. It was at that time he had the opportunity to travel to India and speak with Mohandas K. Gandhi. The "Mahatma" or "great soul," as Gandhi was called, taught Mays the principles of nonviolent direct action. Like most Americans, Mays was already well acquainted with American-born writer Henry David Thoreau and his theories and principles, and his essay on Civil Disobedience.

In 1940 Mays was offered the presidency of Morehouse College, the most prestigious of the historically black colleges. He directed Morehouse until his retirement in 1967, and was then named President Emeritus. Mays was an extraordinary president who vigorously attracted the philanthropic support that would ensure Morehouse to be an outstanding institution for years to come. He was a role model for all students entering the college. Perhaps his greatest legacy was that he exerted a strong personal influence on many students. Mays became to King what Socrates was to Plato. He was more than an advisor and mentor to King; he introduced him to the principles that would govern his life.

King spoke of Dr. Mays as his "intellectual father." And the Mays name continues to be a draw for freshmen classes.

As Dr. Mays' status of college president was assured and expanded, he became outspoken on several issues. He was an early advocate of the value of education for African Americans and strongly encouraged them to attend college. As a proponent of civil rights, he spoke out early and often against segregation and discrimination. He coauthored a civil rights manifesto entitled, *The Durham Statement* in 1941. He also became a central figure in the National Association for the Advancement of Colored People (NAACP), the World Council of Churches, the International Young Men's Christian Association (YMCA), and the United Nations Children's Fund. In 1977 Mays became an advisor to Georgia-born President Jimmy Carter.

Dr. Mays was also a scholar of the Black Church. His publication with coauthor, Joseph W. Nicholson, *The Negro's Church* (1933), was a survey of black churches in twelve cities. *The Negro's God as Reflected in His Literature* (1938), was both a theological study and one of the first extended works of criticism of black literature by an African American. *Disturbed About Man* (1969) was a sociological treatise on American life, and *Born To Rebel* (1971) was his autobiography.

Dr. Benjamin Mays' whole life revealed a combination of sharp intellect with religious commitment and prophetic conviction. If you enjoy circular logic, think about this: Dr. Benjamin Mays had a profound impact on Martin Luther King, Jr., who, in turn, had a profound impact on the whole world.

ELIJAH MCCOY (1843-1929)

E lijah McCoy was a black mechanical engineer and the inventor of a revolutionary device that made it possible to lubricate the moving parts of a machine while it was operating. His lubricator for locomotives changed the railroad industry forever. Folklore and legend has it that whenever railroad men wanted to be assured of getting the authentic McCoy lubricator coupler, they asked for the "Real McCoy."

He was born Elijah J. McCoy in Colchester, Ontario, Canada. He was one of twelve children. The date of his birth has been variously recorded as March or May in 1843 or 1844. His parents, George and Mildred McCoy, escaped slavery from Kentucky and fled to Canada, by way of the Underground Railroad. While living in Canada, his father had obtained 160 acres of land in return for his service to the British during a Canadian armed rebellion.

McCoy was sent to study abroad at age fifteen. He went to Edinburgh, Scotland. Upon the completion of his studies, he entered the United States as a well-trained engineer and immediately began to seek employment. He was repeatedly denied engineering positions because of his race. Finally, accepting a job as a fireman for the Michigan Central Railroad, he had the menial task of shoveling coal into the engine and oiling all of the train's moving parts. It was at this time that McCoy began experimenting with a mechanical self-lubricating device. McCoy was married twice with no children. The first time in 1868, he married Ann Elizabeth Steward. Sadly, she was killed in an accident. A year later, he married Mary Eleanor Delaney. They were married for fifty years. Of course, the major stressor in McCoy's life would have been victimization due to prejudice. He had to take menial jobs instead of engineering jobs for which he was qualified.

In 1870, McCoy gained instant fame in the field of mechanical engineering. He started the *Elijah McCoy Manufacturing Company* in Detroit, Michigan. In this shop, he invented the first automatic lubricator, called the "lubricator cup", and was granted a U.S. patent on July 2, 1872. His device allowed small amounts of oil to drip continuously onto the moving parts of a machine while it was in operation. Prior to his invention, all motorized machinery had to be periodically brought to a complete stop so that lubricants could be applied manually. McCoy's lubricator cup became an extremely important invention to industry because it reduced time and labor costs significantly, and increased business profits substantially.

In time, any manufacturer who owned a machine containing the self-lubricating mechanism bragged of having "the real McCoy", an expression that is still used today to signify genuine quality. McCoy soon improved upon his first model with more sophisticated ones. For the next twenty-five years, he made various changes and patented more than fifty different automatic lubricators. Later he specialized in lubricating devices for special kinds of machinery such as air brakes and steam engines.

Invitations poured in from large industries, here and abroad, asking McCoy to serve as a consultant or lecturer. Although major industrialist requested his services and expertise in the field, many were not aware of his race. They were often taken aback to learn that this ingenious invention was conceived by a black man. There were times when they would cancel McCoy's scheduled appearances because of racial prejudice; some even refused to use the lubricator they so badly needed.

Elijah McCoy died in Detroit at the age of 85 in 1929. He suffered physical, mental, and emotional distress in his later years. He even spent time in the Eloise Asylum in Michigan. The "real McCoy" process is still employed in modern day machinery such as automobiles, locomotives, ships, rockets, and a vast number of other machines. While his inventions earned others millions of dollars in savings, they provided him with only a modest existence. But McCoy's inventions will always be remembered as some of the most modernizing mechanisms of the industrial world.

H attie McDaniel was an African American singer and actress of minstrelsy and later theater, radio, movies, and television. She is perhaps best known as the first black to be nominated for, and to receive, the Academy Award for best-supporting actress for her portrayal of "Mammy" in the 1939 epic film classic, *Gone With the Wind (GWTW)*. She later donated her Oscar to Howard University.

Hattie McDaniel was the last of thirteen children born to Henry McDaniel, a Baptist minister and former Civil War veteran, and Susan Holbert McDaniel, a church choir singer. She was born in Wichita, Kansas, but was raised in Denver, Colorado. Her talent for singing and drama was noticed very early on. Her first stage appearance was in her father's traveling minstrel show at thirteen. She was also a regular performer in her high school programs and plays until she dropped out to perform fulltime.

When her father retired from performing, McDaniel began touring with other minstrel shows. In 1920 she appeared with George Morrison's *Melody Hounds* and received rave reviews. She appeared in vaudeville shows that included the Shrine, Elks, and Pantages circuits until the onset of the Great Depression. She then took a job as a bathroom attendant in a Milwaukee nightclub. The club owner soon discovered her vocal talents and she spent another year as the club's featured singer before leaving for Los Angeles.

In 1931, McDaniel's brother found a role for her on a radio show called *The Optimistic Do-Nuts* in Los Angeles. Almost immediately she became the show's main attraction portraying a character known as "Hi-Hat Hattie." Her film debut came in 1932 when she found herself singing a duet with Will Rogers in *Judge Priest*. She appeared in many films for the remainder of the 1930s, and throughout the 1940s. She became a feature in all Hollywood film genres. McDaniel was also featured on numerous radio shows throughout that nearly twenty-year span. She was a huge favorite on the beloved *Amos 'n Andy* Series and on the *Eddie Cantor Show*.

Beside McDaniel's Oscar winning performance in *GWTW*, other significant roles include her appearance as "Queenie" in *Show Boat* and as "Fedelia" in *Since You Went Away*. In the 1942 film, *In This Our Life*, she played "Minerva Clay," a woman who openly confronted racial issues. She played domestics in

The Little Colonel, Alice Adams, Saratoga, and *The Golden West.* In fact, most of her roles were that of subservient or cantankerous maids. She became widely recognized on film as the typical Hollywood "Mammy." It was those roles that weighed heaviest on her. But they represented the vast majority of the film work available to a woman of color in those days. A famous McDaniel quote was: *"I'd rather play a maid and make $700, than be a maid and make $7."*

From 1947 to 1952, McDaniel starred in *The Beulah Show*, first on radio, and then on the new medium of television. *Beulah* was the first radio show to have a black playing the staring role. She portrayed a maid again, but on her own terms. She refused to employ the typical dialect of the Black Vernacular English. She acted the role of a woman who worked in service, yes, but a woman with dignity. In this role of Beulah, she was never accused of perpetuating a stereotype, as had been the case in roles previous to it.

Hattie McDaniel was a prolific actress of immense talent who appeared in more than 300 films. She was one of the great American character actors of her day. She is said to have had enough clout with David O. Selznick to call for most eliminations of the word "nigger" in the *GWTW* script. Despite her talent, she was relegated to portraying the limiting roles of housemaids. She was stereotyped and typecast as the good-natured "Mammy" in all that Hollywood could offer her at that time. But she acted those roles with dignity, investing her characters with humanity, and transforming them into something that we have all come know and love – fiercely independent African American women.

OSCAR MICHEAUX (1884-1951)

O scar Micheaux was a writer, director, publicist, producer, and a pioneer in the African American film industry. He was the first black filmmaker to produce a silent movie, a feature-length sound movie, and to premiere a movie opening on Broadway. He was known as the "dean" of the black filmmakers for the positive way his films portrayed African American life.

He was born on January 2, 1884 in Metropolis, Illinois, and the fifth of thirteen children. At age seventeen he went to Chicago, where he worked first as a shoeshine boy and later as a Pullman porter on the Chicago-Portland run. In 1904 Micheaux used his savings to buy a homestead on Indian land that was newly opened to settlement. He began farming and ranching, and expanded his homestead to 500 hundred acres. His experiences as an African American settler in the rough environment of the South Dakota frontier would later provide him with material for several of his most important novels and films.

Micheaux's creative outlet began with a string of novels that he later produced as films. *The Conquest: the Story of a Negro Pioneer* (1913) followed the adventures of a black self-made settler caught between his love for a white woman and the perceived demands of his racial identity. *The Forged Note: A Romance of the Darker Races* (1915) was his second novel. *The Homesteader* (1917) was an epic with a plot similar to his first novel. In 1924, the Micheaux film, *Body and Soul,* featured African American singer and actor, Paul Robeson in his first American screen appearance. Another retelling of his pioneer memories appeared in 1944 as *The Wind From Nowhere.*

In 1919 Micheaux produced *Within Our Gates,* a movie whose sole purpose was to counter the awful racial stereotypes and bigotry promoted in the D.W. Griffin film, *Birth of a Nation.* Micheaux attacked the negative images of blacks head-on in every film he made just by never pandered to the white establishment by depicting blacks in negative stereotypical way.

Micheaux used the proceeds from his first novel to start a Sioux City business, the Western Book & Supply Company, which published several of his novels. When black filmmakers George and Noble Johnson negotiated unsuccessfully with him to film *The Homesteader* in 1919, Micheaux turned his attention to movie making. He filmed *The Homesteader* himself. It was the first African

American silent film. He subsequently renamed his business the Micheaux Book & Film Company. He went on to produce, write, and direct possibly forty films. The exact number is historically unclear, but is variously recorded as being between 30 – 44 films. The first African American feature-length talking film, *The Exile* (1931), was a Micheaux creation. Although his film, *The Betrayal* (1948), was not a commercial success, it was the first film by an African American to have a Broadway premiere.

The budget for Micheaux's many film projects came from his own entrepreneurial efforts. He personally transported prints from town to town, sometimes for single showings, and edited his films on the road. To raise money for theater owners, Micheaux used a stock of actors from the Lafayette Players Stock Company to give private performances of scenes from upcoming productions. At the height of his success, branch offices of his film company, by then renamed the Oscar Micheaux Corporation (OMC), opened in New York City and Chicago.

Too many of Micheaux's films have been lost to us. Those films that do survive are a testament to this groundbreaking genius of the filmmaking genre. His works dramatized individual characters' struggle against prejudice within the black community as well as in opposition to outer racism. He addressed African American concerns while framing them within the familiar narratives of white mainstream writing. His portrayals of the black middle class are today considered to be the undermining antidote to the racial stereotypes he had to endure in his day.

O f all the horrors of slavery, the slave trade, and the slave system, no aspect was more dehumanizing than the Middle Passage. It was the second leg of the Trans Atlantic Slave Trade. It was the Middle Passage that delineated the transportation of kidnapped Africans from the West Coast of Africa to the Americas. The Europeans created a triangular pattern of trade across the Atlantic Ocean. European ships would leave the continent laden with goods for trade along the African coast. In return for those goods, they would receive captured Africans and load them aboard the ships which then sailed away to the Americas.

Most of the slaves were unloaded on the Caribbean Islands. The Caribbean was the mid-point between North and South America. It served as a good dividing spot where the slaves could be sent either north or south, efficiently. The planters of the American South preferred to purchase slaves who had been "seasoned" in the islands for a period of time. Slaves directly from Africa were not easily "broken in."

The ships were then loaded with slaves already held in the *baracoons* or slave markets in the islands. Sugar and spices were added to the cargo list, and all was taken to the United States. From there, the ships again unloaded their cargo and reloaded with rum, molasses, and other U.S. goods bound for European markets, and sailed back across the Atlantic. Voyages lasted from six weeks to three months depending on prevailing conditions.

The Middle Passage was the part of the triangular trade that was so brutal on the Africans that many jumped overboard when the opportunity presented itself. Ships began to be outfitted with safety nets surrounding them to stop that. Slaves were stripped naked and branded like animals to identify ownership. And because they were considered to be commodities, they were stowed as cargo in ships bound for the Americas. Slavery was a lucrative business, so the higher the ratio of slaves per cubic foot of hold space, the greater the income. Mal-nourishing the slaves with skimpy rations further maximized profits.

Slaves were chained together, usually by shackles on the ankles, and arranged in cramped ships' holds, unable to move, turn, or stand, Often they had to lie against each other like spoons on shelves only eighteen inches high. Women and children were usually allowed more mobility. The ship's crew required the separation of slave women and men. They wanted easy access to the women. Assault by white sailors was common practice. Possibly for this reason, it was thought that it was the women that instigated mutinies aboard slave ships.

In the ships' holds, copious sweat and human excrement fouled the air. There was no ventilation and many died from suffocation and pestilence. Sick slaves were chained together and jettisoned overboard. Slaves were allowed on deck once or twice daily where they were forced to dance for exercise. Africans used dance as a large part of their religious practice and ritual, but "forced dance" was profane to them and it took away any consolation of faith.

It has been conservatively estimated that the number of African stolen from Africa passes the ten million mark. Fifteen percent of that number is thought to represent the loss of human life during the Middle Passage alone. In light of the terrible reality of the cruel and barbarous voyages that brought Africans to the Americas, it amazes historians that the loss was not larger. But, of course, those with Afro-centric viewpoints do estimate the numbers transported and lost to be much greater.

The Trans-Atlantic Slave Trade is recorded as the largest forced migration of people the world has ever seen. The forced migrations of the Trans-Saharan, Red Sea, and Indian Ocean Slave Trades in total did not equal it. Nobel Prize winning author, Toni Morrison speaks of the Middle Passage in this way: *"the passage was so horrible, no song, tale, legend, or conscious memory of it was retained by the survivors."*

DORIS "DORIE" MILLER (1919-1943)

D orie Miller was an African American Navy cook stationed at Pearl Harbor, Hawaii on December 7, 1941. If there was ever a story of daring and sheer audacity, it is the story of Dorie Miller. He is recognized as the first American Naval hero of World War II. When the Japanese attacked the American Naval Base on that Sunday morning, Miller, although untrained to do so, shot down enemy aircraft. For that deed he was the awarded the coveted Navy Cross.

He was born Doris Miller, was one of four sons born to sharecroppers, Connery and Henrietta Miller on October 12, 1919. Young Dorie experienced all the difficulties of that hard life growing up on a small farm in Waco, Texas. His education was like any other child of the sharecropping system – he was mostly self-taught. While in high school, he became interested in sports. Dorie was fascinated with football and became the "star" fullback of his high school team. At age nineteen, he enlisted in the United States Navy, where he was destined to serve his country with honor and distinction. At this time, the armed forces were still racially segregated and extremely discriminatory in many of its practices. Blacks were confined exclusively to cooking and meal service details. They didn't have the same opportunities to serve as whites did.

One Sunday morning, in December of 1941, while most of the U.S. naval fleet was anchored at Pearl Harbor, Japanese airplanes flew over and bombed most of the base. Some ships were sunk immediately with all hands aboard. It was sudden and completely without warning. There was no time for any effective response. But Dorie Miller, a young African American cook aboard the battleship, U.S.S. Arizona, untrained as a gunner, manned an anti-aircraft gun and downed four enemy planes during the height of the surprise air attack on America's primary naval base in the South Pacific.

Miller's actions aboard the U.S.S. Arizona have been described as *"perhaps the only American victory on that day."* His fellow seamen praised him highly for the courage he had displayed. Dorie Miller received the Navy Cross on May 27, 1942, from Admiral Chester W. Nimitz for his heroism in saving the life of the ship's captain and for gunning down four enemy planes.

In a radio address to the American people, apprising them of the attack, and in his address to the bicameral Congress, President Franklin Delano Roosevelt called December 7, 1941 *"a date that will live in infamy."* That surprise attack by the Imperial Japanese Navy marked only the second time in U.S. history that it had been attacked on its own soil. But it behooves African Americans not to dwell so much on the attack, but on the heroic deeds of all U.S. servicemen and women who have fought in every war to defend American freedom.

Dorie Miller seized the moment and defended a nation that had thought him unfit to train because of his race. And yet, he shot down enemy aircraft and rescued his captain by pulling him out of harms way. History will never have much to say about Dorie Miller because he was cut down in the flower of his youth. He was only twenty-four when he was killed in a later battle in the Pacific. It is known that he was a son, a brother, a friend, a sailor, a cook, and a hero. And according to those at Pearl Harbor on that day, those who called him friend, those who served with him, all still say that Miller was a nice guy.

History may not be able say much about a life cut so short, but it can speak volumes about the courage and valor of Dorie Miller. He may forever be associated with *a date that will live in infamy*. But his heroism overshadows that reprehensible act. In A.E. Housman's novel, *A Shropshire Lad*, is entered the poem, *To An Athlete Dying Young*. The words seem to bespeak Dorie Miller's all too brief but eventful life:

> *Smart lad to slip betimes away / From fields where glory does not stay /*
> *And early though the laurel grows / It withers quicker than the rose.*

FLORENCE MILLS (1895-1927)

Florence Mills was one of the most successful entertainers of the 1920s. She was a child prodigy who began singing and dancing at an early age. She was a vaudevillian who went on to become an important dancer, singer, and comedic actress on Broadway. Her most notable work was as an accomplished dancer, introducing new routines to the nation.

She was born Florence Winfrey, the youngest of three daughters born to John and Nellie Simon Winfrey. History does not record much about her early life. She was born in or around the Washington, D.C. area. Her parents had been slaves in Amherst County, Virginia and later worked as tobacco processors until economic depression hit the industry. They moved from Lynchburg to Washington, D.C. where her father was a day laborer and her mother took in laundry. Because of slavery, both her parents were illiterate.

Throughout her childhood, she performed under the stage name of "Baby Florence." By age four, she was already performing in revues, and by age five, she was winning Cakewalks and Buck Dancing Contests. Her first appearance in show business was with a white minstrel show as a "pickaninny," the only role available for black children. The highpoint of her childhood career was at age eight with her appearance in the road company production of the *Sons of Ham* with Bert Williams and George Walker. Afterwards, a traveling white vaudeville team hired her. After moving to New York with her mother and sisters, she organized a traveling song and dance act with her sisters. By age fourteen, she was performing with them as the "Mills Trio." Florence did not think that "Winfrey" was a good enough stage name.

Just before World War I, Mills moved from Vaudeville to Cabaret singing and was hired at the Panama Café by Ada Smith. She formed another group, the Panama Trio, with herself, Smith, Cora Green, and Tony Jackson on piano. But the Panama Café was soon closed because it was a front for so much vice. However, stardom did come for Mills in 1921 when she replaced Gertrude Sanders as the star of the Eubie Blake and Noble Sissle musical, *Shufflin' Along*. She sang and danced with tremendous ease. Her voice was cheery and bright. And there was no dance step too difficult for her to perform. She introduced the public to the "Baltimore Buzz," a dance that stunned the show's audiences.

Mills' popularity helped to end the male domination in Vaudeville. She became the queen of the black vaudevillian stage. She had been building a repertoire since the age of four. Aida Overton Walker taught he to sing *Miss Hannah from Savannah*. Dancers Bill "Bojangles" Robinson and Ulysses Thompson, her second husband and an acrobatic dancer, had introduced her to polished dance routines. In 1923, Mills toured Europe in *Dover Street to Dixie*. The show became *Dixie to Broadway* when it returned to New York in 1924. At the same time, Duke Ellington wrote a musical portrait entitled "Black Beauty" that was supposedly a special tribute to her.

In 1926 Mills starred in *Blackbirds*, an all-black revue that showcased much of the black talent of the day. After a successful run on Broadway, the show toured London and Paris and Mills was once more an international success. Her signature musical number in the show was "I'm A Little Blackbird." She sang it in a high bird-like voice done with such exquisite poignancy that it raised lumps in the throats of listeners. After a brief respite in Germany, Mills returned home for an appendectomy that had been put off much too long. She died on November 1, 1927. Her funeral was the most spectacular that Harlem had ever seen. Five thousand people packed into the church while 150,000 lined the streets. As the procession moved slowly through the streets of Harlem, a low flying airplane released a flock of blackbirds.

Florence Mills was an uncomplicated personality in a world made still more complex by race and gender issues. She was more than an activist for racial equality or a feminist pioneer. She was a crusader for human rights, wanting only to touch the humanity in everyone who witnessed her performances.

T he story of Malcolm X is by now generally well known. Alex Healy co-authored with Malcolm a best-selling autobiography. There is also a best-selling biography by Bruce Perry simply titled: *Malcolm*. And by now, everyone has seen or at least heard of the Academy Award-nominated film by Spike Lee, which adhered closely to Haley's book.

He was born Malcolm Little on May 19, 1925, in Omaha, Nebraska. His father Earl was a preacher and organizer for the Marcus Garvey's Universal Negro Improvement Association. Malcolm always believed that his father was murdered by white supremacists. His mother, Louise, was a West Indian mulatto born on the island of Grenada. She was unsuccessful in her attempt to hold the family together after the death of her husband. At one point Malcolm was placed in the foster care of a white couple and by his admission, was very well treated.

White supremacists ran the Little family out of Nebraska, and they settled in Lansing, Michigan, where Malcolm spent his early childhood. He was the fourth of eight children, and eventually lived with an older sister in Boston. It was there that Malcolm became a small-time hustler and petty criminal before the age of twenty-one. He was sent to prison, where he encountered and was converted by the Nation of Islam (NOI). Malcolm discarded his surname as the product of dehumanizing slavery, and like other Black Muslims in the sect, took the surname "X" to symbolize the lost identity stolen by American slavery.

While in prison, Malcolm used his time wisely for self-education, avid reading, and other scholarly pursuits. By the time of his release in 1952, he possessed the vocabulary of a college graduate and an ideology that gave new meaning to his life. Embracing the hate-filled doctrine of the NOI fit Malcolm's psyche that had never recovered from his father's murder and his mother's resulting mental instability. America had already taught Malcolm to hate. But it was the NOI and the Honorable Elijah Mohammad who taught him how to channel that hate.

Elijah Mohammad served as a surrogate father to Malcolm, elevating him even above his own sons. Malcolm became the Information Officer and chief spokesman for the Black Muslims. Nationally, he was second only to Elijah

Mohammad. Malcolm was completely subservient to Elijah Mohammad, whom he saw as the agent in redeeming his life, a role model, and undoubtedly as the missing father figure. In 1956, Malcolm's Harlem Temple was cited as one of the most successful temples of the NOI. By the early 1960s, Malcolm was one of the most controversial and popular black men in America, completely overshadowing Elijah Mohammad. Malcolm was suspended from the ministry for reasons that are still debated to this day. Nevertheless, Malcolm continued to idolize Mohammad.

In 1963, Malcolm X and the NOI ended their long association. He founded the Muslim Mosque, Inc. and the Organization of Afro-American Unity. He began traveling throughout the United States with a message of black manhood and independence. He was also a busy guest lecturer at universities, and a frequent guest on national radio and television talk shows. He overcame hatred and began to advocate black pride and black economic self-reliance.

In 1964, Malcolm made a pilgrimage to Mecca, Saudi Arabia and also journeyed throughout Africa. The experience changed him greatly and he renounced the NOI and Elijah Mohammad's teachings of hate. With his pilgrimage, came his name change. He became El Hajj Malik El Shabazz and became a Sunni Muslim, fully embracing the teachings of the Prophet Mohammad and the doctrine of Islam. And he rejected the hate-filled rhetoric of Elijah Mohammad. Malcolm X was assassinated in New York City on February 21, 1965. But before his death, he had overcome his hatred for whites and had begun to realize that all people could work together to build a democratic society.

W hite people wearing "blackface" makeup were the originators of Minstrelsy. Minstrel shows began to take shape the 1830s, and became the most popular form of American entertainment throughout most of the nineteenth century. Applying burnt cork to actors' faces, necks, and hands to make a caricature of a black person created the blackface. After the end to the American Civil War, African American troupes created their versions of minstrel shows. To further entertain their white audiences, blacks kept the tradition of corking their faces just as whites did.

Minstrelsy apparently began when white entertainer, Thomas Rice, saw an old crippled black stable-hand in Cincinnati performing alone for his own amusement an awkward dance, and singing this curious little ditty:

/ Weel about, and turn about and do jis so /
Ebry time I weel about I jump Jim Crow /

The song, the dance, and the shabby clothes were copied and introduced into Rice's act. It became an instant and popular sensation. This beginning established Minstrelsy as a national craze. And the term Jim Crow was introduced into the language very early on as a euphemism for Negro, but later to signify the South's elaborate system of legally and socially enforced racial segregation statutes.

In terms of content, Minstrelsy was essentially white people imitating their version of the appearance, humor, manner, vernacular, and speech patterns of black people. The imitation was a crass and vulgar caricature of African Americas. Minstrelsy helped institutionalize racism by serving as a mechanism for social characterization and definition. It portrayed blacks as too ridiculous ever to be taken seriously. Or it sentimentally showed them yearning for the happier days of slavery, a condition for which they were demonstrably better suited than they were for freedom and independence.

Minstrelsy had a set collection of characters, all of which were grotesque stereotypes of black people. There was the infantile, inherently comic, superstitious, lazy, buffoon named Sambo. The pretentious, sharply dressed, womanizing urban dude was Jim Dandy. The black preachers were always bombastically and humorously misusing words. There were only two types of women, the fat mammies and the provocative and coquettish wenches. The children were depicted as pickanninies, which is an old southern term making reference to black children. Of course the children, for whatever talents they could display, had to be poorly dressed with messy hair and dirty clothes, and wildly misbehaving. The stock scenes pictured the nostalgic, idyllic, and carefree antebellum days on the old plantation, crooning songs and shuffling dances outside the cabin door. The finalé of the Minstrel Show was always the walk-around in which all performers appeared on stage to in a competitive dance, usually to the tune of *Dixie*.

Tragically Minstrelsy distorted authentic African American folk music, dance, speech, humor and style, but it did introduce elements of black culture, however refracted, to white audiences. One reason for Minstrelsy's century-long appeal was its claim to satisfy white people's curiosity about the exotic black strangers in their midst. Minstrel Shows often billed themselves as "Ethiopian delineators" and promised to provide character studies and lifelike impersonations of blacks. Blackface for white performers was just a mask behind which they could act out their racial fears and fantasies, as well as be free from their inhibitions to distain black people. In addition they could capriciously perpetuate negative stereotypes.

Many well-known singers, actors, and dancers were at first minstrel performers. Sammy Davis, Jr., the comedy team of Williams and Walker, Ethel Waters, Hattie McDaniel, W.C. Handy, and so many others were in Minstrelsy before their breakthroughs. Al Jolson, a white singer and actor, performed in blackface in vaudeville, on Broadway, and in movies. Minstrelsy had a great influence on a number of other artistic outlets. Its structure evolved into forms later taken by vaudeville, variety shows, burlesque, and Broadway musical theater. Even today's Comedy Clubs are a type of Minstrelsy. But unfortunately for African Americans, Minstrelsy perverted, obscured, distorted, and mockingly imitated our legitimate culture.

378

W es Montgomery is widely regarded as one of the finest jazz guitarists ever. He received his first national exposure in 1948, but was not featured prominently on a recording until 1957. His unique style set a new standard in playing. Modern jazz guitarists still consistently list him as one of the major influences in their lives.

He was born John Leslie Montgomery, the second of three brothers of a musical family, in Indianapolis on March 6, 1923. He adopted the name Wes in later life. His family was not wealthy so he was not able to receive any formal training in music. In fact, throughout his life, Montgomery could not read musical notation or chord symbols. Despite this, he maintained a strong interest in music and was able to apply it when his brother bought him a tenor guitar in 1935. His early musical influence was Charlie Christian, playing "Solo Flight." In 1943 Montgomery bought his first electric guitar and amplifier and tried to duplicate other solos by Christian. The following year he was hired by the 440 Club in Indianapolis as a solo guitarist, playing mostly Christian's compositions.

Ironically, Wes was the last of the musical Montgomery brothers to become nationally known. He worked briefly with Lionel Hampton from 1948-1950, but returned Indianapolis to raise his family. While he was developing his revolutionary style working club dates by night, he was a welder by day. His brothers, electric bass innovator Monk, and vibist/pianist Buddy, had moved to San Francisco and were enjoying successful careers. While still working the club scene in Indy, Wes would join Monk and Buddy on several recording sessions in the late 1950s. Interestingly, Wes was not a skilled music reader. He could learn complex melodies just by listening.

When trumpet great, Cannonball Adderley, came to Indianapolis and heard Montgomery, it created a groundswell of interest in the guitarist among New York opinion-makers that led to his Riverside recording contract in 1959. Montgomery was an immediate success with critics who poured out praise for his musical style. He became the model for an entire new generation of guitarists, as well as for some established guitar players who recognized the future in Montgomery. The general public and jazz enthusiasts, who could hear warmth and passion in his playing, just as avidly celebrated him.

For a while, Montgomery retained a local trio with Mel Rhyne, but was soon reunited with Monk and Buddy as the "Montgomery Brothers." Despite studio partnerships with greats like Adderley and Jimmy Smith, live recordings with the Wynton Kelly Trio, and a brief stint with the John Coltrane Band in 1961, most of Montgomery's work was in bands with Rhyne or his brothers. As he moved to larger record labels and more commercial projects, his popularity kept pace and his albums began to appear in the upper reaches of the pop charts. He became the quintessential model for every aspiring guitarist in the United States and abroad. His most commercially successful recordings were: *Scarborough Fair, Eleanor Rigby*, and *I Say a Little Prayer for You.*

Montgomery's live performances left musicians and jazz audiences speechless with his virtuosity. His unique style often described as "impossible," set a new standard in guitar playing. And yet, he was modest enough to see himself only as the provider for his large family, not as the man who produced music that redefined the possibilities of the jazz guitar. Praise for his playing style has continued almost unabated for the nearly forty years since his untimely death of a heart attack. He left behind his wife of many years, five children, and fans too numerous to count.

Few musicians in jazz history were more innovative, or more unassuming than this legendary Hoosier. Wes Montgomery developed an incredible thumb-picking style, played octave and chord passages with the fluency and nuance of single lines. And he organized these astounding techniques in solos of daring detail. He revealed his musical self completely and honestly to jazz enthusiasts everywhere.

GARRETT A. MORGAN (1875-1963)

G arrett Augustus Morgan invented the gas mask widely used by firemen in American cities in the early 1900s. And later soldiers on the battlefields of Europe used the mask during World War I. But he is mostly remembered for his invention of the three-way automatic traffic signal that brought order to the nation's chaotic streets, greatly improving traffic safety, and again saving lives.

Morgan was born March 4, 1875, in Paris, Kentucky, the seventh of eleven children born to Sydney and Elizabeth Morgan, former slaves. As a youth, his time was disproportionately divided between attending school and working on the family farm. He left school at the age of fourteen, having completed the fifth grade. But in his adult life, he would hire a tutor to help him improve his grammar. He went to Cincinnati, where he secured a job as a sewing machine repairman for a textile manufacturer. Later he opened his own sewing machine repair shop. In fact, it was in Cincinnati that he developed several commercially successful enterprises.

Morgan's first invention was a belt fastener for sewing machines, which he sold in 1901 for $50.00. In 1907 he opened his own sewing machine repair shop. By 1909 Morgan had opened a tailoring shop, employing thirty-two workers, manufacturing dresses, suits, and coats. After only one year in this business he was able to buy a home for his wife, Mary Anne. They later had three sons. In 1913, he inadvertently discovered a substance that would straighten hair, which he later marketed. The business profits reaped from the *G.A. Morgan Hair Refining Company* guaranteed Morgan the financial relaxation to be able to concentrate on his other inventions.

The most important of his various inventions was a "breathing device" that served as the prototype for the modern gas mask. Morgan directed his attention to the frequent instances of firemen being overcome by fumes and thick smoke when they entered burning buildings. Many respiratory devices of that time were not dependable and frequently malfunctioned. Consequently he perfected a breathing device that he patented in 1914. On July 25, 1916, Morgan, his brother Frank, and two others, demonstrated the use of his invention by wearing the devices as they rescued twenty-four workers trapped by an explosion in a smoke-filled tunnel under Lake Erie.

Afterwards, the city of Cleveland awarded Morgan a medal for heroism and ingenuity in the rescue efforts. Newspapers across the nation carried the story about his wonderful invention. Numerous city fire departments ordered the breathing device, which Morgan later modified to carry its own air supply. He founded the *National Safety Device Company* and extensively utilized the new advertising media to promote his invention. The United States Navy awarded his company the contract to develop the breathing device for use in war. The gas mask began to be widely used by engineers, chemists and workmen who were exposed to noxious fumes or dust or for any hazardous breathing situations.

In 1922, Morgan patented yet another great invention. He invented the three-way automatic traffic signal. This signal light became the forerunner of the overhead and sidewalk traffic lights that we use each day. He sold the rights to the traffic light in 1923 to the *General Electric Company* for $40,000. Before this time, traffic signals had no yellow caution light. Morgan's signal gave drivers a warning to slow down before a red stoplight. This brought about a marked improvement in traffic safety.

In the 1920s Morgan also embarked upon civil rights endeavors. He and his colleagues started a newspaper, the *Cleveland Call*, which later became the *Cleveland Call And Post*. With his business acumen, the paper had one of the largest circulations of any black newspaper in the Midwest. Morgan died at the age of eighty-eight in Cleveland, Ohio after a long and successful life. Because of Garrett Morgan, his inventive genius and creative mind, we can all breathe a little easier and drive a little safer.

Toni Morrison is an African American educator, editor, and since being awarded a Pulitzer Prize for fiction, and the Nobel Prize for literature, one of the world's most prominent modern authors. Her novels and short stories have taken their place in the canon of American literature and are taught at colleges and universities. Her work is most notable for epic themes, vivid dialogue, and richly detailed African American characterizations.

She was born Chloe Anthony Wofford to George and Rahmah Wofford on February 18, 1931, in Lorain, Ohio. For Morrison, both parents were visible homilies of black dignity and resolve. Her father, a welder in an aircraft factory during World War II, put his signature to every plane on which he had welded a perfect seam. Morrison graduated with honors from Lorain High School. She changed her name to "Toni" while at Howard University where she obtained a B.A. degree in English. After receiving an M.A. degree from Cornell with a thesis on the theme of suicide in the works of William Faulkner and Virginia Wolf, she taught at Texas Southern University and Howard University. Her most notable student at Howard was Stokely Carmichael.

She met and married Harold Morrison and the couple had two sons before their marriage ended. It was while teaching at Howard that Morrison began to meet informally with a small group of poets and writers. It was there that she formulated what became her first novel, "The Bluest Eye" (1969). The novel was an incisive probe into the complex dynamics of black self – hatred. Morrison resigned from Howard in 1964 and took a job as a textbook editor for Random House Publishing Company where she remained until 1985. She rose to become a senior editor and was able to encourage such black writers as Toni Cade Bambara, Angela Davis, and Muhammad Ali. Her editorship of "The Black Book" (1974) was an experimental collage of African American history and literature and was a major event in the world of African-American letters.

Morrison has also taught at Yale University, State University of New York at Purchase, and held the prestigious Albert Schweitzer Chair in the Humanities at the State University of New York at Albany. She is currently the Robert F. Goheen Professor in the Humanities at Princeton. Morrison's other novels include: "Sula" (1973), nominated for the National Book Award; "Song of Solomon" (1977), winner of National Books Critic's Circle Award; "Tar Baby" (1981), where she explores the folkloric dimensions of African

American culture; "Beloved" (1987), the Pulitzer Prize winner which highlights the effects of slavery on the enslaved; "Playing in the Dark" (1992); "Jazz" 1992; and "Paradise" (1997). In recent years, she has published a series of children's books with her son, Slade Morrison.

Morrison emerged in the in the 1970s and 1980s as an authoritative, African American novelist. Her influence has grown with each novel. She has explored themes ranging from childhood madness to the supernatural and is recognized as one of the most prestigious writers of the twentieth century. Morrison has received many honors and awards, but the most important international recognition of her work came in 1993 when she was awarded the Nobel Prize in literature. She is the first African American to be honored with the world's most prestigious literary award. In her acceptance speech Morrison said: "We die. That may be the meaning of life. But we do have language. That may be the measure of our lives."

Toni Morrison is an epic storyteller who compels us to remember those unspeakable terrors that have shaped African American culture. She skillfully draws upon race, gender, and communal experience, of which she is heir, for the substance of her novels. Morrison is a deeply spiritual writer, concerned with the perennial questions of love and death, the will to be free and the forces – both internal and external – that circumscribe that freedom. Let us reflect on and esteem this deeply insightful, hugely talented, Pulitzer and Nobel award winning author.

J elly Roll Morton was a pioneer of modern jazz. He was a virtuoso pianist, bandleader, and the first true jazz composer. He was a most colorful character who could generate his own publicity by "overstating" the truth. His business cards referred to him as the "creator of jazz and swing." Of course, that was not the truth, but he was the most influential of the early jazz musicians. He was known for mixing individual improvisation within rehearsed group arrangements, a format that became the staple of modern jazz.

He was born Ferdinand Joseph Le Menthe in the Creole section of downtown New Orleans. His parents were both fair skinned Creoles. All his life he considered himself to be more white than black. He harbored much resentment to his black heritage. He passed for white whenever he could. His father, also a musician, left the family early in his life and Morton grew up under a stepfather named Mouton, which he anglicized to Morton. He received guitar lessons at age six, but soon abandoned it for the piano. By age twelve, he was an accomplished pianist. Orphaned early, he was raised by his grandmother, Eulalie Echo.

The early influence of Morton's aunt, a voodoo practitioner, left him in a confused state of Catholicism. In his adolescence he was a barrel maker for $3 a week until he got a job as the pianist in a high-class bordello in the New Orleans red light district of Storyville. That wild, wide-open, district ran on drugs, alcohol, gambling, prostitution, brawls, and murders 24/7. But it had the greatest constellation of musical genius ever concentrated in one place. Morton made $20 in tips the first night. When his grandmother realized where all his money was coming from, she threw him out of the house. It left him free, in his late teens, to travel most of the gulf coastal towns, and to mingle with the best musicians of the early jazz age.

Morton was known to write at least two versions of all his compositions, one in ragtime and one in jazz. He was greatly influenced by ragtime pianist, Tony Jackson. He received some formal training at St. Joseph's College in St. Benedict, Louisiana. Beginning with his trip to the St. Louis World's Fair in 1904, Morton embarked on a decade of itinerant music making that carried him throughout the South, to Chicago, and New York City. He played with vaudeville acts and minstrel shows, and supplemented his income by gambling, hustling pool, and hustling women. He was a known swindler, braggart, and womanizer. Even the lyrics in some of his songs reflected a great degree of immorality. He assumed the moniker "Jelly Roll" which was itself a vulgar term filled with sexual innuendo.

Morton traveled for a time with an all-girl dance revue that was a front for prostitution. He finally settled in Chicago from 1911–1915. He began producing music that set him apart from other jazz pianists of the time. He toured the West Coast before resettling in Chicago. He began solo recordings with RCA Victor in 1923 and 1924. From 1926 to 1930 he led the Red Hot Peppers Ensemble featuring legendary performer, Kid Ory. Morton's best known recordings include: *Jelly Roll Blues, Black Bottom Stomp, Wolverine Blues*, and *King Porter Blues*. In 1928 Morton moved to New York City where he had trouble finding musicians who wanted to play his style of jazz. But the onset of the Great Depression of the 1930s diminished his popularity. His musical career ended in the way that it started, in dives where fighting was so commonplace, he sustained many injuries from which he would never fully recover.

For all his musical genius, Jelly Roll Morton was so conflicted by his race, that he was a mass of contradictions. He despised his black heritage, but gravitated to the musical styling of African Americans. He had a name that would have identified him as French, but he chose an ordinary English version of another French name. He was a staunch Catholic, but practiced the black arts of voodoo. He couldn't decide whether to become a musical genius, or a panderer of women, so he became both. But for all his many quandaries, he was the best musical mind of the jazz age. But only in death did he rise to the highest tier of musical acclaim. His influence was seen in musicians from Fletcher Henderson to Benny Goodman to Duke Ellington. And just like Morton himself, his body of work crossed the color line.

ELIJAH MUHAMMAD (1897-1975)

lijah Muhammad was the leader of the black separatist quasi-religious movement known as the Nation of Islam (NOI), but most commonly called the Black Muslims. He led the group virtually unopposed from 1934 until his death in 1975. His most famous disciple, and one time challenger, was his chief minister, Malcolm X. The two became bitter adversaries when Malcolm embraced orthodox Islam and began to espouse and practice racial inclusion as found therein.

He was born Elijah Poole near Sandersville, Georgia. He was the sixth of thirteen children born to an itinerant Baptist preacher William, and his wife, Mariah Poole. Elijah had been named by his grandfather and was teasingly called "the Prophet" by the other children. His formal education ended at age nine when he and a sister began chopping wood for a living. In early adolescence, he witnessed the atrocities of racism that left him ripe for a separatist ideology. But it would be many years before the break with Christianity would be permanent.

In 1923 Poole migrated with his wife and two children into the industrial area of Detroit, Michigan. There he found economic and social conditions not much better than in Georgia. He worked at a series of odd jobs and menial tasks in order to feed his growing family. But in 1931, Poole met and became a disciple of Wallace D. Fard, founder of the Nation of Islam. Poole became fully immersed in the movement, abandoning his slave name and becoming Elijah Karriem. Within a year, he became Fard's chief minister, and had established the Nation of Islam Temple # 2 in Chicago by 1933.

When Fard mysteriously disappeared in 1934, Poole changed his name to Muhammad and seized the mantle of leadership. He moved the NOI Headquarters to Chicago. As the supreme leader, his distinctive ideological emphases emerged free of Fard's overshadowing. Muhammad not only claimed to be the messenger of Allah to the Nation of Islam, completely assuming Fard's organizational leadership, but he also reinterpreted who Fard was. He preached that Fard had been Allah (God) in disguise and that he had shared with him secrets known to no one else. Muhammad effectively presented himself as the sole custodian of Fard's revelation to the African American community. And he spent the next eight years recruiting followers throughout the country based on that revelation.

In 1942 he was imprisoned for urging blacks to resist military draft. After his release in 1946, the Nation of Islam Movement spread quickly and prospered under his leadership. In the 1950s and 1960s it peaked mostly due to the charismatic leadership of his principal lieutenant, Malcolm X. And at its peak, the NOI posed a big challenge to black Christianity. Its focus on Islam as a "black religion" drew blacks from their Christian faith, as it attempted to uncouple the history of blacks from that of whites in America.

Despite the use of Muslim references to God, the Nation of Islam does not espouse the same Islam as founded in Arabia in the eighth century A.D. But as a Black Nationalist organization, with a separatist ideology, the NOI promotes self-improvement and self-help initiatives. Muhammad ordered a strict code of behavior governing such matters as diet, dress, and interpersonal relations. He also enjoined the membership to loosely follow Islamic religious rituals, but insisted that they pray five times a day.

Muhammad's strong sense of community brought on the establishment of accredited schools in numerous cities. The organization has sent produce from their farmland by their own trucks and airplanes throughout the U.S. The Final Call, their current weekly newspaper, was founded as Muhammad Speaks, and has a wide national circulation, and now, an Internet version. Many African Americans were attracted to Elijah Muhammad's ideologies and found them consistent with their interpretation of their own life experiences. NOI membership records were always kept secret under Elijah Muhammad but it is believed that the influence of the ideology extends far beyond NOI official membership rolls.

T he Negro leagues were black baseball teams, including players, managers, and owners. The leagues were created out of necessity, since African Americans were excluded from the existing mainstream Baseball Leagues due to the existing racial prejudice in the United States.

In response, the black baseball hero Andrew "Rube" Foster created the Negro National League (NNL). Foster was himself an excellent athlete and a shrewd player. He is credited with inventing the infamous bunt-and-run play, and he insisted that team players play the game using their minds as well as their physical skills. His sharp business sense led him to bring together the other owners of successful black ball clubs in Kansas City in 1920. Together, these men wrote their own constitution and established the Negro National League (NNL).

There were eight clubs in the league, with teams based in Chicago, Dayton, Detroit, Indianapolis, and St. Louis. Blacks, except for the Kansas City Monarchs, which was owned by a white man, owned all the Negro League teams. Foster himself owned the Chicago American Giants. The NNL was fairly successful in the beginning, with a consistent attendance record and a yearly income of $200,000 in 1923. Because of the success of the NNL, an Eastern Colored League (ECL) was organized in 1924. African American fans, too, loyally supported it. The ECL was predominately white-owned and frequently raided the NNL of its best players by enticing them with higher wages.

The most frustrating problem of the leagues was the inconsistency and unpredictability of game schedules. Few black teams owned their own ballparks, so club owners were forced to cooperate with white businessmen in order to have a "home" ballpark. Black clubs in this predicament had to make sure their games were played when the white team was on the road. Also, if weather canceled a game or the other team was a no-show, it was virtually impossible to reschedule. Another league problem was that of acquiring umpires. Many black players and their coaches resented the presences of white umpires. At that time blacks were not allowed to umpire any games.

Gus Greenlee, a black numbers czar and league organizer, developed the idea of the East-West All-Star Game in 1933. It became black baseball's biggest feature. By 1940, the Negro Leagues were better attended than their white counterparts. The leagues produced superstars like James "Cool Papa" Bell, Satchel Paige, Ted "Double-Duty Radcliffe, Moses "Fleet" Walker, Josh Gibson, and of course, the pioneering Jackie Robinson. The Negro Leagues also boasted of something the Major Leagues have still yet to explore, women players. Toni Stone, Connie Martin, and the diminutive Mamie "Peanut" Johnson were female players on various Negro League Teams.

The Negro League teams became known for their talent and adroit skill on baseball diamonds in every city in which they played. The players were unmatched in their abilities and expertise, and in many instances, they were overall better players than those on the white teams. The black players combined creativity and athletic ability to develop what became known as "tricky baseball." It essentially included imaginative ways of scoring base runs through base-stealing, the bunt-and-run, the run-and-hit, special do-or-die sacrifice plays, and many other breathtaking stratagems.

Integration exhausted the Negro Leagues of many of their star athletes and the interest in them seriously declined. Willie Mayes, Hank Aaron, Ernie Banks, and Roy Campanella were all Negro League players before they followed Robinson into Major League Baseball. Interestingly in 1946, Eddie Klep became the first white player for a Negro League team. The final Negro League East-West All-Star Game was held in Kansas City in 1963. But by the 1970s the Negro Leagues had all but disappeared, becoming more comedic than competitive. And instead of continuing as a part of the summer fabric of the American landscape, they became a stellar page in American history.

In the New England Colonies, Election Day was a special time for white citizens. But it was just as special for blacks also. Depending on the location within the Northeast, slaves were permitted to elect their own governors, and in some cases, kings, to serve as official representatives of the black community. Blacks were given the opportunity to play important social roles in several northeastern colonies, even after they became states. The role of these kings and governors was to serve as the buffer between slaves and slave owners, and white government leaders. In some cases, black governors and kings could mete out minor punishment or reward for slaves.

The title of governor or king did not entitle the slave to full power over other slaves. But it did give them considerable regional authority in dealing with day to day mundane issues and provided them with added stature within the slave community. In an oddly inverted way, black governors and kings brought a great deal of status and prestige to their owners. Their owners provided slaves with any support they could afford to insure the winner would be a slave from their household. Most slaves borrowed clothing from their masters and mistresses. The most popular attire was a uniform because they were considered to be the most dignified. Slave owners were keenly aware of the importance of his slave's attire. Slaves held the same status as their owners, so a poorly dressed slave was a reflection on his owner.

The first elections of black kings and governors began in the early 18th century in northeastern capital cities and charter colonies. Elections were held in Newport, Rhode Island in 1756; Hartford, Connecticut in 1766; and by the 1770s, in Norwich, Connecticut; and Salem, Massachusetts. By the end of the 18th century, similar elections took place in Portsmouth, New Hampshire, and North Bridgewater, Danvers, and Lynn in Massachusetts. These cities welcomed the idea of blacks being able to handle much of their own social and disciplinary issues. It was beneficial to whites to have the kings or governors as the enforcers of social propriety. In some areas whites even allowed blacks to elect their own sheriff who held the title for life. Slave owners endorsed the idea of black elections, considering it more of an amusement than any threat to their authority.

Black elections took place over the course of a week and occurred at the same time as white elections. As was the case with white elections, only men were allowed to vote. But black women could lobby for their favorite candidates. In many instances, blacks were given time off from work to take part in the elections and the attendant celebrations. Black Election Day did prove to be a festive event, much like Pinkster Celebrations in New York and New Jersey. There was food, wine, music, and dancing. There were also events such as wrestling, running, jumping, and stick fighting to highlight the week.

Following the elections, the candidates were honored in an inaugural parade with the winning governor or king sporting a powered wig during the 1700s, and a tall silk hat during the 1800s. The winner would lead the parade, and in many cases would ride a fine horse. The slave owner whose slave was elected always hosted a post-election party at his home, complete with more food, wine, music, and dancing. To top the evening's festivities, there would be fireworks or good-natured celebratory gunfire.

Once dismissed as childish parodies of white elections, "Negro 'Lection Day" has come to be seen as an important political and social phenomenon that blended African and European traditions. While whites were busy casting ballots in colonial and early state elections, marginalized blacks gathered for a mixture of fun, athleticism, and socializing, culminating in voting and a flashy inaugural parade. Elected blacks wielded authority within their community and mediated disputes among blacks, which had no legal standing in the greater community. It can only be surmised, but the celebration of Election Day must have livened up bland, uninspiring, white colonial celebrations. And it most assuredly helped to construct the later phenomenon of the American parade.

HUEY NEWTON (1942-1989)

uey Newton will be long remembered as one of the founding members of the Black Panther Party (BPP) in the United States. The BPP was Huey's brainchild and probably the most defining organization of the Black Nationalist Movement. The rise of the BPP was purely a 1960s phenomenon with an unmistakable impact on 1960s and 1970s pop culture. When Newton and the Panthers appeared in public, wearing black polo shirts, black leather jackets, dark glasses, and black berets, they created an aura of revolution.

He was born Huey Percy Newton in Monroe, Louisiana on February 17, 1942, the youngest of seven children. His father, who was an active NAACP leader, named him after the radical Louisiana politician, Huey P. Long. Huey grew up in Oakland, California, a place that would become the West Coast center of the American Black Nationalist Movement. He was a troubled teen, involved in gangs and beset by other police problems. But he took his studies seriously before graduation and taught himself to read.

While attending Merritt College, Huey met Bobby Seale, and they began work on a project to diversify the school's curriculum. It was then that Huey fell under the sway of leftist revolutionaries like Fidel Castro and Mao Tse-tung. He became critical of the racist oppression of blacks in the U.S. and the capitalist system that reinforced their exploitation. In response to incidences of police brutality and institutional racism, and as an illustration of the need for black self-defense, Newton and Seale formed the *Black Panther Party for Self-Defense* in 1966. At the height of its popularity during the late 1960s, the party had 2,000 members in chapters in urban areas across the country.

Huey co-authored the party's ten-point program that called for: full employment, improved education and housing, an end to police brutality and the exemption of blacks from military service. As the Black Panther Defense Minister, he set up the group to monitor the police. He organized shotgun-armed patrols in black neighborhoods, which were deemed legal as long as they were visible. These "justice patrols" sought to inform blacks of their rights and counter the history of police brutality against them. Huey understood and created a culture of revolution. Not surprisingly, the BPP developed a hostile relationship with police departments across the nation. But Huey became the main target of police harassment.

In 1967 Huey was convicted of voluntary manslaughter in the death of a police office, but his conviction was overturned 22 months later, and he was released from prison. The trial provoked a "Free Huey" campaign, drawing thousands to Panther rallies and greatly increasing its prestige and membership. By 1970 though he saw the party weakened by regional and internal strife because of disputes about militant programs. In 1971 he advised the party to adopt a nonviolent manifesto and to dedicate itself to providing social services to the black community. He advocated political education and programs that he believed would link the Panthers to the broader black community.

In 1974 Huey was accused of another murder and fled to Cuba for three years before returning to face charges. He endured two trials that resulted in hung juries before the state dropped the case. He received a Ph.D. in social philosophy from the University of Santa Cruz in 1980. His dissertation was entitled the "War Against the Panthers: A Study of Repression in America." The Black Panther Party disbanded in 1982 after succumbing to factionalism and extreme pressure from FBI and other policing agencies.

Huey Newton's personal life took a downward spiral as the prominence of the Panthers declined. He was plagued by rumors of drug use, and conflict with the law persistently troubled him. In March 1989 he was sentenced to a six-month jail term for misappropriating public funds intended for a Panther-founded Oakland school. Tragically, Huey died like a true revolutionary. He was shot to death while walking along a street in Oakland in 1989. Although he had renounced violence in 1971, he was never able to break the cycle of violence that surrounded him, nor escape the personal demons that besieged him.

T his term may or may not be familiar to the younger readers, but it refers to the strategy employed by the late Dr. Martin Luther King, Jr. during the civil rights era. Direct actions were primarily defined by their confrontational, public, disruptive and possibly illegal nature. When large masses of black people became directly involved in economic boycotts, street marches, mass meetings, going to jail by the thousands, and a whole range of disruptive tactics, the term that best described this strategy was nonviolent direct action.

During the American Civil Rights Movement, direct action protests came largely from the philosophy of Dr. King, who was the acknowledged leader of the movement and the ultimate spokesman of an era. Dr. King had been greatly influenced by the Indian statesman, Mohandas K. Gandhi. It was Gandhi who led his people to throw off the yoke of colonization by challenging the authority of Great Britain. He inspired the Indian people to use nonviolent, but disruptive, tactics to decrease the efficiency of British Colonial administration. Gandhi's technique was so successful that the British were forced to grant independence to India in 1947. Dr. King combined the rhetoric of righteousness and American democracy with Baptist eloquence and a Ghandian philosophy of nonviolent passive resistance to oppose discriminatory laws and customs. He employed general noncompliance to achieve social justice in America.

Another great influence on the politics of the late Dr. King was the 19th century American writer and poet, Henry David Thoreau. Thoreau was a staunch proponent of non-cooperation with injustice, whether it was law or custom. In his well-known essay, *Civil Disobedience*, Thoreau expressed his willingness to be imprisoned in defiance of injustice. But since Dr. King was primarily a religious thinker, he was more consumed by theology and the example of Jesus as set forth in the Bible. As the leader of the movement, King knew that the demonstrators would be met with violence. Police, dogs, and torrents of water from fire hoses assaulted them. And true to his faith, Dr. King taught his followers to love the enemy and not retaliate during any protest demonstration. King's philosophy was so "God driven" that even those who did not believe in nonviolence as a way of life, were inspired to employ it as a strategy to achieve the goals of the movement.

Nonviolent direct action protest fits into a rich tradition of black resistance to white control. The significance of black resistance lies in the fact that it has been forever present in some form. The persistent struggle of African Americans has given rise to a resistance tradition that includes hundreds slave revolts, the Underground Railroad, and numerous protest organizations. It also gave rise to a once popular coded form of English called Pig Latin. Whether it is called passive resistance, civil disobedience, or direct action protest, it was the strategy that was used to challenge the established systems of segregation and long held patterns of racial injustice in America. It was this same strategy of nonviolent direct action that finally bought a huge measure of Reconstruction to the American South.

While the Civil Rights Movement did much to improve the lives of African Americans, there is still a long way to go before racial equality is fully achieved. And the struggle to overcome this country's legacy of racism is an ongoing process. What has become apparent as we ease into the new millennium is that while hate cannot be legislated from a person's heart, the legislation passed in that era has done a tremendous job in closing the citizenship gap that previously existed. The 1964 Civil Rights Act and the 1965 Voting Rights Act produced the most sweeping reforms ever. Without a doubt, they have had the most influence on the political expansion and social fabric of the country.

Since nonviolent direct action can be utilized as a political and moral philosophy to achieve social or political change, it has been described as the technique utilized by the masses. It is the politics of ordinary people, reflecting its historically mass-based use by populations throughout the world. Nonviolent direction action did not end with the Civil Rights Movement, it is ongoing, it is effective, and it is universal.

BARACK OBAMA (1961-)

B arack Obama has got to be the most fascinating man of this new millennium. One must marvel at his skyrocketing propulsion on to the national scene and his history making assent to the highest office in the nation. President-elect Barack Obama will become the 44th President of the United States on January 20, 2009. He was the second African American to be elected to the Senate from the State of Illinois, with Carol Moseley Braun being the first. Obama is the first African American to win the nomination from a major political party. And he is the first African American to win a national election for the presidency. This has been more than historic. It has been phenomenal. America has had any number of seminal moments in its history, but Obama's landslide victory this past November must rank with the greatest. In the 232 years since the first declaration of independence from a sovereign in Europe, it seems that the United States of America has finally lived up to the creed it has held out to the world. It has at last become *one nation under God.*

From the moment that Barack Obama began his run for the presidency, he started a groundswell of enthusiasm that had been unequalled since the John F. Kennedy campaign of 1960. For those old enough to remember, it may have seemed like *Camelot* all over again. He is eerily similar to Kennedy. He is young and vital, with bright ideas and polished idealism. He is smart and dynamic, which is pretty much to be expected from a Harvard graduate. But as we watch Obama with his youthful good looks and lanky build; as we listen to his sublime eloquence; this is not *Camelot* we were seeing and hearing. It is *Kismet.* He was fated to be the next president. It was destiny that put him here at this time in history to fulfill a purpose. Whatever that purpose, possibly yet to be realized, will certainly keep us engaged for at least the next four years.

Obama campaigned with a slogan of "Change." And change is exactly what we got. He has changed the way campaigns will be conducted from this time forward. His was the most high-tech campaign that this country or any other country had ever seen. The use of television and radio were pretty standard. But his use of email, text-messaging, You-Tube, and Face Book reached a whole new demographic. His grassroots efforts were unstoppable. There was a campaign office in every major city, staffed by young people and powered by older volunteers. He flew to the most populace cities and engaged people, groups, clubs, and unions. He told their stories in his campaign speeches. He visited every state, whether it was red or blue, several times over. And every time, he won voters with his calm demeanor and eloquent oratory. Obama's capacity to raise campaign funds overwhelmed his Democratic opponents in the Primaries, and simply killed his Republican counterpart in the National Election.

What is most intriguing about Obama is that even though he is an African American, he brings none of the attendant history of slavery with him. His mother was a Caucasian American but his father was not African American, but East African. That is pretty far removed from the West African coast that engaged so ruthlessly in the Trans-Atlantic slave trade that brought Africans into the Americas. The Obama history is very different from the history of other African Americans in that respect only. For I am sure his experience has been very much the same when facing the racism that is so slowly dying in America. One cannot be black in America and not come to know the weight of all that it means to be black in America, even if you were raised by white grandparents.

He was born Barack Hussein Obama II on August 4, 1961 at a maternity hospital in Honolulu, Hawaii. His mother was Stanley Ann Dunham, but everyone called her Ann. She was a nineteen year old college student. And his father was Barack Hussein Obama, Sr., a foreign exchange student from Kenya. The couple met while attending the University of Hawaii at Manoa. His father left his mother to continue his studies at Harvard in 1963. Eventually, Obama Sr. returned to Kenya, his Kenyan family and numerous Kenyan children.

By the time Barack II was six years old, his mother was married to Lolo Soetoro and was living in Jakarta, Indonesia with Barack and his baby sister, Maya. When that marriage ended, Ann remained in Indonesia, but sent Barack to live in Hawaii with her parents. From that time forward, Obama was raised by his grandfather Stanley Dunham and his wife, Madelyn. He saw his mother on her frequent visits to Hawaii. But he would see his father only once again when he was ten years old.

There are many black children in America being raised by grandparents. But few are raised with so much diversity in their backgrounds. Obama was raised by his white maternal grandparents in the remotest state from the mainland. His only sibling from his mother is half Indonesian. But from his father, there are many Kenyan half brothers and sisters. Obama attended public and parochial schools in Jakarta until age ten. From fifth grade through twelfth grade, Obama attended the Punahou Preparatory School, an independent private school on Oahu, until his graduation in 1979.

Upon finishing high school, Obama moved to Los Angeles and enrolled in Occidental College. He led a protest against South Africa's apartheid system, calling for America to divest, all the while struggling with his black, white, Hawaiian identity. He remained there for two years and transferred to Columbia University in New York City. There he majored in political science, specializing in international relations. After obtaining a B.A. from Colombia in 1983, Obama worked for one year for Business International Corporation (BIC). It was then a publishing and advisory company dedicated to assisting American companies operating abroad. From there Obama joined the New York Public Interest Research Group (NYPIRG), a nonpartisan political organization. Obama was their Project Coordinator for "Mayday," a community-wide effort to draw attention to the poor conditions of the New York City subway stations. It was a very pointed protest against the Mass Transit Authority and it was his first community organizer job after graduating from Columbia.

It was in Chicago though that Obama's organizational skills and business acumen readily emerged. From 1985 to 1988, he was the Director of the Developing Communities Project (DCP), a faith-based community organization on the far Southside. His achievements at the DCP included instituting a college preparatory tutoring program, setting up a job training program, and organizing a tenants' rights association in a housing project. Obama increased his staff from one (himself) to thirteen. He also astoundingly grew the budget from $70,000 to $400,000 annually. He also found the time to consult with and teach at the Gamaliel Foundation, a community organizing institute.

Before he entered Harvard Law School in 1988, Obama took the summer to tour Europe and travel to Africa. After attending schools away from the mainland, and in Indonesia, international mingling was nothing new to him. He visited Kenya and met for the first time his father's extensive family, including his Kenyan siblings, aunts, uncles, and surrogate grandmothers. After such an eventful summer, he was settled and ready to tackle Harvard. By the end of his first year, Obama was selected to be the editor of the *Harvard Law Review*. He was elected the first black president of the journal in his second year. This caused the national spotlight to shine on him for the first time. During the summers he journeyed back to Chicago to work as an associate at two law firms there. Obama graduated magna cum laude from Harvard Law School in 1991, receiving a Doctor of Jurisprudence.

In 1989, Obama met Michelle Robinson, his summer advisor at the law firm in which he was working. At first, she declined his offers for dates, but the couple became engaged in 1991 and married in 1992. They have two children Malia

Ann and Natasha, known as Sasha. In 1995, Obama became a published author with the best-selling *"Dreams from My Father: A Story of Race and Inheritance."* His second book, *"The Audacity of Hope: Reclaiming the American Dream,"* became a great sensation when it was released in 2006 and endorsed by Oprah Winfrey for her Book Club. Much of Obama's campaign strategy and rhetoric is found in his second book.

From 1997 to 2004, Obama served as an Illinois State Senator in Springfield. His focus was on government reform and health care initiatives. In January 2003, he announced his candidacy for the U.S. Senate and handily defeated the Republican perennial candidate, Allan Keyes. He became the only Senator in the Congressional Black Caucus. In the U.S. Senate, Obama carried with him the same spirit of bipartisanship he had always held. He sought ways to engage his idealism on every committee on which he worked. He voted against the war in Iraq, but he worked tirelessly on behalf of veterans. He directed his concern for people to the areas of healthcare, education, and environmental affairs. He worked diligently on the powerful Senate Foreign Relations Committee with Senators Dick Lugar and Joe Biden.

Having achieved the greatest "first" of his political career, one would think that Obama would wear it as a badge of honor. If there is anything he has down-played the most, it is that he was the first African American to achieve so much in such a short time. And he has never once welcomed the spotlight to be focused on race. This may stem from his youthful inner conflict about race. But more than likely, it stems from the man he has grown to be. Obama was widely quoted as saying: *"There is no white America and no black America; there is only the United States of America."* He has vowed to be the President of that America, not an America divided by racial issues. He seems humbled by the overwhelming number of popular and electoral votes that made him President-elect of the United States in the first place. He is even more humbled by the manner in which America has seized on his dream of what America can be. And with that America firmly galvanized behind him, Barack Obama is calmly poised on the precipice of being the most powerful leader of the most powerful country in the world.

P ete O'Neal is an African American living in self-imposed exile in Africa since 1970. He is one of the last American exiles from and era when activists considered themselves at war with the United States government. In 1968 when he founded the Kansas City chapter of the Black Panther Party, he was a streetwise urban revolutionary, touting the rhetoric that was so much a part of Black Nationalism.

He was born Felix Peter O'Neal in 1940 in Kansas City, Missouri. It is a city so sprawling that it geographically enjoins two states, Kansas and Missouri. He was raised on the city's historic 12th Street, home to such musical legends as Charlie "Bird" Parker and Count Basie. Growing up in that impoverished environment in the 1950s and 1960s, O'Neal quickly became involved in drug selling and any other hustle the streets had to offer. He developed a misguided sense of values that centered on having expensive clothes, jewelry, and fancy cars.

Upon hearing his first Black Panther Party speech by Huey Newton and Bobby Seale in Oakland, California, O'Neal's life was completely changed. His values became more communitarian. When he returned home, he set up a Black Panther Party and became a dynamic leader in his own right. All Panthers looked and dressed the same. They were conspicuous by their shotguns, black berets, leather jackets and political posturing as evidenced by their clenched fists. Their rhetoric was pointed and articulate, and merciless to U.S. political or government figures.

From 1968 to 1970, O'Neal was the leader of the Kansas City BPP. Most panther activities were based on a strong desire for black self-determination and community control. Panthers became a symbol of black solidarity. And Kansas City was no different. A blanket Panther program furnished breakfast for inner city children in every city that had a chapter of the BPP. O'Neal had organized the Kansas City chapter to feed in excess of 700 children a day through donations of food from businesses in the city.

The Panthers, nationwide, took a strong stance against law enforcement agencies. They were organized to monitor police and community relations. During O'Neal's leadership in Kansas City, he gained notoriety in the black community for publicly accusing the Kansas City police chief of funneling guns to right-wing organizations. He even disrupted the hearings of the U.S. Senate, which was considering the matter. Shortly after that hearing, in October 1969, he was arrested for carrying an illegal firearm across state lines, from Kansas City, Missouri to Kansas City, Kansas.

While out on bail awaiting trial in 1970, O'Neal weighed his options and decided to skip out on what he considered to be trumped up charges. He and his young wife, Charlotte, fled to Sweden, and then to Algeria, using fake passports. In Algeria they worked for two years with the International Black Panther Party, founded by Eldridge and Kathleen Cleaver. They migrated to Tanzania and built a homestead in a rural village between Mt. Meru and Mt. Kilimanjaro. Still considered a fugitive, O'Neal cannot return to the United States unless pardoned by authorities. But his wife, an artist, has returned on several visits. Still O'Neal continues to be in a state of revolt against the inequities that exists in the United States. And he feels that it makes him an American patriot of the highest order.

In Africa O'Neal still has the Panther spirit but uses that spirit in innovative ways. He founded the United African American Community Center (UAACC), a nonprofit organization created for the enrichment of the local people. The UAACC offers computer classes and English instruction. He also operates a Bed and Breakfast for tourists. He is the coordinator of the Study Abroad Program for a number of universities in Tanzania. He also provides an international exchange program where he sends Tanzanian youth to the U.S. to further their education. And he brings urban American youth to Tanzania for cultural enrichment programs. Ironically, it is in Africa that Pete O'Neal is the most revolutionary, sponsoring programs that live up to the Black Panther rallying cry, giving "All Power to the People."

By the eighteenth century, African slavery was already deeply entrenched in the Americas. The institution of slavery was only slightly different in the British North American Colonies. Climate and soil restricted the development of commercial agriculture in the northern colonies. And slavery never became as economically important in the North as it did in the South. The number of slaves in the North was typically low and most of them were domestic servants. But even so, the vast population of whites in the North did not question the institution of slavery until after the American Revolution.

Slaves brought an understanding of medicinal minerals, plants, and herbs from Africa to the Americas that often surpassed European medical science of that time. Traditional African medicine is a holistic art that incorporates spiritualism and a considerable use of indigenous herbal medicines. But scientific use of herbal medicines has proven to be efficient, and also provides the basis of Western medicine. For instance, Kaolin, the active ingredient in Kaopectate, has always been used to treat diarrhea in Mali. To cure skeletal-muscular diseases, Bantu healers have prescribed the bark of trees that yield salicylic acid, an active ingredient in aspirin. African medical knowledge proved invaluable in the spring of 1721, when a smallpox epidemic erupted in Boston carried in on a ship returning from the island of Tortuga in the Barbados. Before the epidemic finished its course, it had killed nearly 1,000 people.

At that time Cotton Mather was one of the leading and most influential Puritan ministers of colonial New England and a part of the famed Mather family. He watched three of his own children nearly die from smallpox and urged doctors to begin performing inoculations against the disease. Mather had learned of the ancient practice of inoculation from his slave, Onesimus, who had been inoculated as a child in Africa. Onesimus was thought to have come from the Sudan. But at the time that term was generic, and applied to any part of sub-Saharan Africa. Mather first heard of inoculation when he asked Onesimus whether he had ever had smallpox. His response was: "Yes and no." It was then that Onesimus described the procedure, common to Africa where pus from smallpox sores was placed into a cut in the arm of a non-infected person. When this was done successfully, it allowed the non-infected person to develop a resistance to smallpox. It was the precursor to today's common

403

practice of vaccination.

As a slave, Onesimus had no voice in American society and could not speak on behalf of his own experience, not even to relieve the suffering of smallpox victims. But emboldened by Onesimus' story, Mather urged all Bostonians to undergo inoculation. The cause of inoculation was very unpopular in Puritanical New England where medicine relied more on the all-wise providence of God and less on the artifice of men. The process of inoculation was politically, medically, and religiously opposed in the British colonies and in Europe. Mather's home was even attacked by an angry mob that tossed a makeshift firebomb through his window. Fortunately, the bomb was not set off.

One physician heeded Mather's secondhand account of Onesimus' firsthand experience. Dr. Zabdiel Boylston experimented with the concept by first inoculating his own son, and then his two household slaves. The experiment was enormously successful. Eventually two other doctors joined Boylston in inoculating nearly 300 Bostonians. Following this innovative treatment inspired by Onesimus, the death rate in Boston was drastically reduced from one-in-twelve to one-in-forty.

There is a bittersweet conclusion to Onesimus' story. There was no Gospel fulfilling end to the oppressive relationship between slave and master. But Mather eventually did free Onesimus. He was not freed because his knowledge was instrumental in saving countless lives. He was freed because his owner considered him to be a disobedient servant. Through Mather's first-hand written account, and medical accounts of the day, history has made note of Onesimus' recall of a traditional African medical practice that sparked the introduction of smallpox inoculation in what was to become the United States.

S atchel Paige was perhaps the most talented American baseball player ever. He was the first African American pitcher in the American League, and the first representative of the *Negro Leagues* to be inducted into the *Baseball Hall of Fame*. Paige was the most widely known African American baseball player until Jackie Robinson integrated the major leagues in 1947.

He was born Leroy Robert Paige to John and Lulu Paige in Mobile, Alabama. His father was a gardener and his mother was a laundress. Paige acquired his nickname in his youth while working as a baggage handler in the Mobile train station. He was sent to the Mount Meigs, Alabama reform school at an early age for stealing. It was there that he learned to fling a ball and play the game he came to love and would become famous for.

Paige began his career with the Birmingham Black Barons in the 1920s. For more than two decades he pitched for many teams of the Negro Leagues in the United States. As a free agent he played in Canada. And during the North American winter season, he played with Caribbean, Central American, and South American teams. He even barnstormed throughout the U.S. to play in exhibition games. In one year he traveled 30,000 miles. By some accounts, Paige pitched over 2,500 career games. By his own account, he won 2,000 of those games and threw 55 no-hitters. Paige is most remembered for the speed and variety of his pitches, including the *hesitation ball*, which involved stopping his pitching motion momentarily during a pitch.

Satchel Paige was a colorful and engaging man and the consummate showman. Once he had the audacity to send the infield to the dugout while he faced the best hitters in the opposition lineup. His success in head-on contests against white stars became legendary and filled the coffers of exhibition game promoters through the 1930s and 1940s. More importantly for the Negro Leagues as a whole, as Paige's fame grew, white patrons by the thousands filled ballparks across America, even in the South, to see him perform, regardless of the competition. More often than not the competition came from other Negro Leagues teams. So the benefits of Paige's popularity were bestowed not only on him but also upon all Negro Leagues players.

Paige, by virtue of his tremendous pitching talent and his often-tested ability to defeat the best that white major leaguers had to offer, was a rebel who challenged the claimed superiority of major league baseball. His boasting taunted the white fans to buy tickets. His successful claims always impressed the crowds in the stadiums. Paige's showmanship made palatable the inability of the most talented white players to gain any consistent advantage over him.

In 1948, one year after Jackie Robinson integrated major league baseball, Paige became the first black pitcher for the Cleveland Indians. With Paige on the pitcher's mound, the Indians won the World Series during his first year on the team. From 1951 to 1953, he was a relief pitcher for the St. Louis Browns. By 1952, he was pitching on the American League All-Star squad. Paige pitched his last major league game in 1965. He pitched his last baseball game for the Indianapolis Clowns, a Negro League team, in 1967. And in 1971, he was inducted into the Baseball Hall of Fame, the first member of the Negro League ever to be so honored. Paige later spent many years as a pitching coach for the Atlanta Braves of the National League.

Satchel Paige had a distinctive baseball career that spanned nearly five decades. He never disclosed his true birth date thereby keeping secret his true age. He was thought to be well into his forties when he entered the newly integrated major leagues. He was quoted as saying:

"Age is a question of mind over matter: if you don't mind, it doesn't matter."

CHARLIE "BIRD" PARKER (1920-1955)

C harlie "Bird" Parker was a jazz saxophonist, composer, and one of the most important and influential improvisation soloists in the history of jazz. Parker did more to create the "bebop" style than any other single artist, and is the most celebrated for it. The celebrity surrounding Parker stems from his spiced improvised melodies with unexpected accents and perfectly played flurries of notes. Some of his finest recordings were with small groups on the Dial and Savoy record labels.

He was born Charles Christopher Parker, Jr., the only child of Charles and Addie Parker in Kansas City, Kansas. In his youth, he acquired the nickname "Yardbird" because he loved fried chicken. As a young man his musician friends shortened it to "Bird." In 1927 his parents separated and he moved with his mother to Kansas City, Missouri, an important center for African American music during the 1920s and 1930s. When he was eleven, his mother brought him his first saxophone and he received his first music lesson in public school. He was largely self-taught, but had the ability to listen and a willingness to practice that enabled him to make rapid progress. In a short time, he could play with local jazz musicians.

Parker was an unmotivated high school student and dropped out early. But by age fifteen, he was a fulltime musician, had a wife, and was beginning to acquire a lifelong addiction to drugs. He worked chiefly in the Kansas City area from 1935 to 1939, playing with a variety of blues and jazz bands. Being self-taught, his ideas frequently exceeded his technical abilities. After being embarrassed in a jam session with the classically trained Count Basie, Parker spent the summer with the George Lee Band at a resort, memorizing solo recordings. Upon his return, his future promise could be heard in a style that had phenomenally developed.

In 1940 Parker went to live in New York City, the hub of jazz musical and business activity. He worked intermittently at Clark Monroe's Uptown House and was invited to join the Jay McShann Band. He participated in many jam sessions with well-known musicians and never again embarrassed himself. In fact, he became bored with the stereotyped chord changes then in use. Parker began to complain that his mind could hear something different but he could not yet play it. His individual style emerged when he discovered that he could develop a melody line utilizing the higher intervals of a chord while backing

407

these intervals with appropriately related chords. Finally, he could play the music that was in his head.

Parker's style crystallized further as he often sat in with groups conducted by Noble Sissle and Earl "Fatha" Hines. Newcomers like Miles Davis flocked to him. But modern jazz bebop style matured into a movement as the result of the musical relationship Parker formed with Dizzy Gillespie; and along with the work of Thelonious Monk, Kenny Clarke, and others. Though musicians valued and respected Parker's work, he had to contend with many jazz critics and more traditional musicians who disliked any new development in jazz. And at that time, Parker had yet to make an impact on the general public.

But the years from 1947 to 1951 proved to be Parker's most inspired period, one in which he produced more than half of his recorded work. In recording, playing nightclubs and concerts, and radio broadcasts, he utilized his own small combo, a string group, and Afro-Cuban bands. When traveling without his band, he frequently appeared as a guest soloist with various musical groups. Parker's bebop was disseminated to jazz aficionados around the world, and his melody patterns, his methods of playing those patterns, and even entire solos of his were being enjoyed. In 1949, *Birdland*, a jazz nightclub, was named to honor him.

Charlie Parker's mastery of the saxophone and his distinctive tone raised the art of jazz improvisation to a new peak of maturity. He experienced many personal difficulties throughout his short life. Often in debt and addicted to drugs and alcohol, he endured broken marriages, several suicide attempts, and even imprisonment. Although he had a short life, containing less than praiseworthy elements, he was long on talent and ability, and he left a stamp on jazz that will never be erased.

ROSA PARKS (1913-2005)

T he name, Rosa Parks, is inextricably connected to the Civil Rights Movement. She gave no resounding speeches, led no massive demonstrations against the citadels of segregation, wrote no petitions, and argued no particular points of law. But what she did was simple and electrifying. She took a public bus in Montgomery, Alabama, that would land her in history as one of the most inspirational people of all time. Later, Mrs. Parks would be christened "the Mother of the Civil Rights Movement."

On December 1, 1955, Mrs. Parks, a forty-two-year old black seamstress, took action that shook the racist South and signaled to African Americans that the time had come at last to unequivocally answer "No" to racial segregation and discrimination. While riding the public bus from her job at the Montgomery Fair Department Store, this tired black worker was approached by a white man who boarded the bus and who remained standing rather than sit down next to a black woman. The bus driver demanded that she surrender her seat, as the Jim Crow Laws of Alabama required. He had probably done so many times without incident.

Mrs. Parks refused to move to the "colored" section of the bus and allow the white man to take her seat. Her feet were tired she was later to remark. More than likely, her soul was tired. She said "No," and remained in her seat. The bus driver became irate and stopped the bus to call the police. Rosa Parks was arrested. This incident caused the entire African American community to rise up, as it had never done before in any city. During the Montgomery Bus Boycott, no black person rode the buses for 381 days.

The fight to vindicate Mrs. Parks ignited the Civil Rights Movement and thrust to the foreground the young Martin Luther King, Jr. Her "No" became the indignant rallying cry for black people throughout America. Montgomery marked the first flash of organized and sustained mass action and nonviolent revolt against the Southern way of life. In Montgomery, there emerged a courageous and collective challenge in protest against the American order, which promised so much for everyone else, while it perpetuated indignities and brutalities against oppressed African Americans.

In addition to being a seamstress, Rosa Parks had been the recording secretary for the NAACP and was then running the office its president. In the summer prior to her courageous act, she had gone for a summer workshop at the Highlander Folk School in Monteagle, Tennessee. Highlander had a long history of training labor organizers. In the 1950s, it turned to providing instruction and support for the new civil rights activists from all over the South. Before her Highlander experience, Parks had a history of passive resistance to bus drivers and had actually been thrown off the same bus by the same driver who would have her arrested. Although Montgomery whites had not expected this extent to her civil disobedience, her "stand" was no surprise to those who knew her. To her credit, and to no one else, is laid the praise for the courage it takes to be the first to take a stand against injustice.

Dr. Martin Luther King, Jr., when hearing the accusation that a local civil rights group instigated Mrs. Parks' arrest, subsequently and eloquently described Parks' action this way: "She was not "planted" there by the NAACP, or any other organization; she was planted there by her own personal sense of dignity and self-respect. She was anchored to that seat by the accumulated indignities of days gone by and the boundless aspirations of generations yet unborn. She was a victim of both the forces of history and the forces of destiny. She had been tracked down by the Zeitgeist – the spirit of the time."

For the last fifty years of her life, amid countless accolades and honors too numerous to mention, by every local, state, and national dignitary, from every glamorous movie star and on-air personality, from every rap and rock artist, and from every athlete, Rosa Parks was called the mother of the Civil Rights Movement. But she was called "home" at the age of ninety-two to receive an even greater reward. Her courage and moral uprightness bespoke the well-ordered steps of a life well-spent.

P assing refers to the ability of a person to be regarded as a member of a particular group other than his or her own, such as a different race, ethnicity, class, or gender, generally with the purpose of gaining social acceptance. For the purposes of this discourse, racial identification will be the key factor. The very term of "passing" is simply a clipped form of the phrase "pass for." As it pertains to race, it has the meaning of an impostor "passing as" another person. In an ethnic sense for African Americans, it has always meant that there are those of us whose complexions are so fair, features so keen, and hair so silken, that they can literally "pass for white."

Culturally, passing has usually meant black and biracial people who have been successfully accepted as a member of the ethnic majority. While it is extremely uncommon for dark Europeans to aspire to pass as black, at some stages in American history, some whites living in the U.S. who may have been excluded from white American society and categorized as "non whites," allied themselves with African Americans during the Civil Rights Movement. The term "passing" is used derisively and it is not considered to be politically correct to aspire or attempt to pass, or to accuse another person of aspiring or attempting to pass as white. Passing is associated with deceit and pretense. Where black-to-white passing is in question, the phenomenon of passing is considered to be immoral, blameworthy, and untrue to self.

The term "passing" has rarely been used in recent years. With the easing of racial discrimination and the social injustice associated with being black, there has been no great necessity to pass in order to increase economic and social opportunities. It was common in the 19th and early 20th centuries for some African Americans to claim Hispanic or Native American ancestry, seeking greater acceptance in white society. Today, most people who have redefined themselves from black to white or Hispanic, make no secret of their African ancestry. They just do not feel that this trifling fact should stop them from adopting a racial self-identity that matches their appearance. The misadventure of enforcing strict racial identities on people who may not fit neatly into the American caste system has been the fuel for many novels, plays, movies, and lately, music. Rock band, Big Black, released a song regarding this subject called "Passing Complexion" on their 1986 album, "Atomizer."

The novel *Passing* by Nella Lawsen; the novel *Showboat* by Edna Ferber that developed into a Broadway musical; the novel *Pinky* by Cid Ricketts Sumner that grew into an Academy Award nominated film; the novel *Imitation of Life* that became a blockbuster movie melodrama; and most recently, *The Human Stain,* a novel by Philip Roth, and a film starring Sir Anthony Hopkins, all display tragic figures who have shifted identities. A common theme in these novels is the fear of discovery and the assumed rejection that follows. And it is that fear that consumes the central characters. It is after all, that abnormal fear that compels the protagonists to pass as white in the first place.

Passing is a real life oddity that exists not just in the United States, but on every continent that has ever hosted African slavery. The peculiarity in the U.S. is that of class and ethnic mobility as fundamental components of the "American Dream." And it has been a dream held, on average, by one African American in one thousand, in every year of this nation's history. When examined in this light, "passing" has not yet become passé.

There are paradoxes associated with passing as a person of another ethnicity. The absurdities of these contradictions undermine the very essence of racial classification. The first being, in principle, there is only one race, and that one race is human. If passing is race-based, and race, as progressive thinkers know, does not really exist, then how can anyone pass as anything else? Passing from one race to another assumes that there are distinct races to pass in and out of. Secondly, when someone who looks white, isn't white, who then, is white? And lastly, if black is the absence of all color and white is the reflection of all color, why then aren't white people categorized as "colored." As circular as my logic may be, it does so readily speak to the hypocrisy of race. And the mere question of race poses these conundrums.

laves were always regarded with suspicion and some crimes attributed to them, such as planning an insurrection and harming a white person, were viewed as threats to the social order of the slavocracy. One of the devices set up as a mechanism of control and to enforce Slave Codes, the rules and regulations that controlled the conduct of slaves, was the "patrol system." The patrollers were white men were who were called upon to serve for a stated period of time, usually one to six months. They were to apprehend slaves out of place and return them to their masters or commit them to jail; visit slave quarters and search for various kinds of weapons than might be used in an uprising; and visit assemblies of slaves where disorder might develop or where conspiracy might be planned. The slaves considered the patrollers, or "patterollers" as they called them, to be an insidious group comprised mostly of "poor white trash."

The legislatures of the slave states required patrol service from men and women slaveholders alike on the grounds that all should contribute to the service and security of that district where their interests lied. In those states, persons unwilling to serve might hire substitutes or else pay a penalty for not doing so. The slaves' description of the "patterollers" as poor whites is then accurate. They were men whose economic status did not allow the luxury of hiring substitutes, or men who welcomed such paid employment. In most slave states, the patrol system was intricately linked to state militias. Patrols were organized in the military style of the militia, with captains, sergeants, and patrollers (privates). The patrollers were always the property-less, non-slaveholding class while the officers were wealthy planters. The patrol system gave poor whites a degree of authority over blacks that they would not otherwise have experienced, and it enlisted them in support of an institution whose economic rewards largely excluded them.

The prominent position occupied by patrols in African American folklore suggests that they performed their duties more systematically and with an added degree of cruelty than is often supposed. Every slave at some point encountered the "patterollers." Black oral tradition celebrated the triumphs of wily slaves who could outwit the "patterollers." They were also used as a form of "bogeymen" to frighten errant black children. Slave parents threatened their misbehaving children with visits by the "patterollers." But frequent too were substantiated court records of abuses the slaves suffered at their hands. Mostly

413

the "patterollers" divided counties into sectors and frequently patrolled across the countryside to flush out runaway slaves. Or they would respond to the apprehension of planters and store owners who complained about slaves roaming at night committing robberies. A more corrupted form of the patrol system came into existence during the emergencies created by slave uprisings or just the rumors of them. At such times, it was not unusual for "patterollers" to disregard all caution and prudence and kill any black, slave or free, that they encountered in their search. The patrols frequently became lynch mobs.

Slaveholders welcomed the patrol service in keeping public roads free from wandering slaves. But some of them hotly resented the patrollers' occasional trespass on their premises in search of weapons or to break up slave gatherings, and the enthusiastic punishment they sometimes inflicted on the slaves. Laws in every slave state empowered patrols to apprehend violators, determine their guilt, pronounce sentence, and inflict punishment on the spot – without concurrence or review by any other authority. In most states and at most times patrols might administer ten lashes to those judged guilty.

Slave patrols began as a special institutional device to maintain worker discipline and servile status in the New World colonial empires where the growth of commercial agriculture led to a concentration of slave labor. But the tradition of the "patterollers," their summary justice, and the resentment thereby established, outlived the institution of slavery and did not easily die away. The Ku Klux Klan (KKK) and other white vigilante terror groups, that in later years sought to maintain or reestablish white dominance, had no legal basis. Yet their roots lay deep in the dark past of the institution of slavery in America. And they continue to brutalize and attempt to maintain control over the lives of African Americans and others.

JAMES W.C. PENNINGTON (1807-1870)

J ames Willard Charles Pennington is perhaps the most self-inventive personality in African American history. He was born a slave, but constantly reinvented himself until he had become a stonemason, blacksmith, teacher, abolitionist and moral reformer, author and historian, and finally, a minister. But his restlessness did not stop there. He was first a Presbyterian minister, and then an African Methodist Episcopal (AME) minister, before becoming Presbyterian again. Yet through these changes, he remained steadfast and unwavering in his integrity.

He was given the name James when he was born on a plantation on Maryland's eastern shore. He was the second of twelve children born into the slave family of Brazil and Nelly Pembroke. He grew up in the precarious fashion of a slave, with his very life and well being dependent on the whim of various slave masters. The family was split up on a couple of occasions when their owners' finances needed bolstering. As a slave, James did not receive a formal education but he obtained skills as a stonemason and a blacksmith after he escaped. While free, his intensive studies led him to become a teacher and preacher.

When James was twenty years old an altercation between his father and their master, punctuated by his own savage beating, caused him to plot an escape. Without telling his parents, but trusting no one else, James escaped on a Saturday night. He retreated to a secret place and changed into clothes he had hidden away. Following the North Star, he struck out on his harrowing journey to freedom. Slave catchers apprehended and held him for a time though he managed a second escape. Eventually he made his way to Pennsylvania, where a Quaker harbored him and began his formal education. Of course, as a runaway slave, he had to change his name to evade future slave catchers. In 1828 Pennington relocated to New York City, working as a blacksmith by day and attending school at night.

Under the spiritual guidance of a Presbyterian minister, Dr. S.H. Cox, Pennington cultivated a devout belief in Christ. His faith was closely tied to the reform movements of the time. He began to involve himself in abolitionist activities as well as participating in several conventions of free blacks in Philadelphia in the early 1830s. He met and worked with the usual abolition leaders like, William Lloyd Garrison and Lewis Tappan. He created temperance societies for African Americans. In 1834, Pennington relocated to New Haven, Connecticut where he audited classed at Yale University and became an ordained minister. He would also become a key player in the infamous Amistad Affair of the late 1830s. In 1838, Pennington conducted the wedding of a 21-year old runaway slave named Frederick Douglass.

In 1839, Pennington became the pastor of a newly formed Congregational church in Brooklyn. In 1840, he left for Hartford, Connecticut, to become the pastor of Talcott Street Colored Congregational Church. He was twice elected president of the Hartford Central Association of Congregational ministers, a group composed of whites. In 1841, Pennington published the *"Text Book of the Origin and History of the Colored People."* In it he asserted the African origin of western European civilization. He also argued against European claims to superiority over Africans. He became the founder and president of Union Missionary Society (UMS), a black-led group created to evangelize Africa and Jamaica, and other places of the African Diaspora. His work as head of UMS launched him into national and international prominence, becoming the Connecticut delegate to the World Anti-Slavery Convention in London

The man who became James Willard Charles Pennington was an exceptional human being. He did not like WHAT he was, so he changed it. He did not like where he was, so he left it. He created a whole new persona for himself. He spent his life in service to the disaffected and the down trodden in nineteenth century America. Supported by his faith, Pennington became a free man in every sense of the word. And in the process, Pennington became a source of inspiration to people of his generation and a source of pride to people of this generation.

P erhaps the greatest cowboy who ever lived was Bill Pickett. He said he invented the cowboy sport of "bulldogging" (steer-wrestling) and no one disputed his claim. Bulldogging involves riding after a steer and then leaping out of the saddle to grab it by the horns. Then with boot heels digging in the ground, the cowboy wrestles the steer to the ground by twisting its head back and its nose up. Pickett not only did this with relative ease, but also added the touch of sinking his teeth into the steer's upper lip and raising his hands in the air to show that his teeth were the only grip on the animal.

Pickett was born in 1870, the second of thirteen children to Black Cherokees in Oklahoma. The Cherokee were slaveholding planters in Georgia until the 1830s when the United States government, under President Andrew Jackson, forcibly removed them from their lands and settled them in the West. The Cherokee were peaceful slaveholding cotton farmers until gold was discovered on their land. And from that moment, the white power structure purposed to take their land and move them to what was called "Indian Territory."

After completing the fifth grade, Pickett left the dull confines of a frontier classroom for the wild life of the range. He landed a job as a ranch hand and developed his roping and riding skills. Legend has it that he was only ten years old when he began to practice his technique for steer wrestling. Whenever he started, whether a child or an adult, Pickett was the inventor and the master practitioner of steer wrestling.

As an adult, Pickett was only five foot six inches tall and never weighed more than 145 pounds. Nevertheless, his small frame swept through his bulldogging feat with the strength of a much larger man and the agility of a ballet dancer.

Pickett married and eventually fathered nine children. To provide for his family, he landed a job with the huge 101 Ranch in Oklahoma run by the Miller brothers. The Millers hired the best cowboys they could find for their ranch and rodeo. The Miller Rodeo won so many local prizes that they were soon barred from local cowboy competition. It was then that the Millers took the rodeo on the road and Pickett and two assistants, Tom Mix and Will Rogers, were the greatest box office draws. Pickett's brand of bulldogging was one of seven major rodeo events, and the only one invented by an individual.

Until he became famous, Pickett had to dress as a Mexican toreador since many rodeos did not admit black contestants. Pickett entertained in Mexico City, London, New York, and in Argentina and Canada. And in every city, he was the featured act. He was billed as the "Dusky Demon" or the "Wonderful Colored Cowboy". Always added to those terms was the one he was most famous for: "The Bulldogger."

In his later years Pickett made two silent films. One was a full-length, black cowboy mystery movie starring Pickett and Anita Bush, an internationally known stage actress. It was entitled *The Crimson Skull,* and set in the all black town of Boley, Oklahoma. As was the case with the stars of all western movies, Pickett outwitted the bad guys and got the girl. His other film performance, appropriately called *The Bulldogger*, a Richard E. Norman film made by Norman Studios, demonstrated Pickett's steer-wrestling artistry for the camera. There are many surviving photographs of Picket and his favorite horse, Spradley, and grouped with other cowboys like Mix and Rogers. There are also surviving film posters of Pickett from those silent films.

Pickett died in 1932, eleven days after the horse he had tried to rope while on foot, kicked and fell on him. With his masterful skills, Pickett won fame and a decent living. He has been described as *"the greatest sweat and dirt cowhand that ever lived – bar none."* But he was far more than that. Bill Picket was an inventor and master of a perilous technique for handling steers on ranches who turned the concept into a superb rodeo performance. He started life in the 19th century as a talented cowboy with a large family to feed, and ended life in the 20th century as a cherished performer with a large audience to entertain.

THE PINEY WOODS SCHOOL (EST. 1909)

The Piney Woods Country Life School is the largest of four historically Black Boarding Schools. At one time there were 83 such schools, but in the late 1950s and early 1960s most of these were closed once access to public schools became officially open to African American students in the South.

Laurence Clifford Jones, a 1907 University of Iowa graduate, envisioned a school where the concept of "head, heart, and hands" education would be available for rural black youth. In the spring of 1909, he arrived in a poor section of Mississippi, just twenty miles southeast of Jackson, in an area known simply as "the piney woods." It was there, on forty acres of land and a dilapidated log cabin donated by a former slave, that his vision began to take shape. Dr. Jones started teaching in a small clearing near a fallen cedar log that served as a school bench.

News spread quickly about the determined teacher and his school in rural Mississippi. Students of varying ages desiring an education and a brighter future flocked to the school. The townspeople saw the earnestness and honesty of the young teacher and contributed lumber, nails and small amounts of food and money to the effort. From the beginning, the Piney Woods School consisted of vocational subjects along with the educational basics. Dr. Jones felt that many of his students would never go on for higher education and must be prepared to earn a living at a useful trade.

In a segregated America, Jones' educational vision of "head, heart, and hands" of poor, rural black students in a residential campus setting was unique but not entirely unheard of. The same vision had been conceptualized on a college level at the Tuskegee Institute under Booker T. Washington in neighboring Alabama. At a time when Jim Crow laws prevented black children from attending the same public schools as whites, the idea of the residential campus for black students stemmed from necessity. The school grew out of the traditions of self-help and mutual assistance cultivated by African Americans long before the post-Reconstruction era.

By 1913, the school had received a charter from the state of Mississippi. Many teachers, black and white, joined the staff and worked for little or no salary as the school endeavored to train teachers for the State Department of Education and to teach handicapped and blind children. In 1938 the International Sweethearts of Rhythm, an all-female swing band, was organized to perform throughout the United States to raise money for the school. In 1954 the television program, *This Is Your Life*, featured Dr. Jones. The program host, Ralph Edwards, asked each viewer to send $1 to the school, resulting in an avalanche of small donations totaling $750,000. The dividends from that money serve as the basis for the school's endowment fund. However, the school continues to solicit and accept private donations.

The school shortened its name to the Piney Woods School in 1998 to accurately reflect America's change to an urban society. It is still located in the same area, though, but it now rests on over 2,000 acres. The school campus has expanded to 60 acres; the remainder includes a 500-acre working farm; and 1500 acres of numerous lakes and extensive woodlands. Students do not pay the full tuition cost, but all are expected to devote ten hours a week to work on campus. The school has a focused academic climate, strict dress code, consistent discipline, and strong ethical and spiritual values reinforced by non-denominational Christian worship services.

All the school's former students are deeply indebted to it for its high academic achievement and the spiritual and moral values it imparted to the students. All of the graduates of the Piney Woods School deeply esteem the school with their *head, heart, and hands*. It is a pleasure to present this historic school in Mississippi to highlight the concept of the Black Boarding School. Its inclusion in this text merely serves to underscore the sad history of the educational policies in the Jim Crow South. And as in every case, it emphasizes African Americans survival skills in a hostile environment.

Pinkster is a holiday that was celebrated over several days by African slaves and the Dutch in the colony of New Amsterdam (later New York). Pinkster is derived from the word "Pinksteren," the Dutch name for Pentecost. It is an important festival on the Christian calendar. Pentecost is celebrated seven weeks after Easter, in May or early June. The religious implications of the festival related to renewal of life. Its practical application related to the planting of crops. After planting, Pinkster festival marked a break from the tedious work associated with farming. Apparently it possessed all of the fun associated with carnivals.

The Dutch observed Pinkster by attending church services. Important church functions like baptisms and confirmations were often held during the festival. Neighbors visited one another and children dyed eggs and ate gingerbread. Blacks and whites alike enjoyed drinking, game playing, dancing, and music at these festivals. Vendors adorned market stalls and carts with greenery and flowers like the Azalea that was so closely associated with the Pinkster festival. Whites hired skillful black dancers to draw crowds to their vendors' booths. Dances such as the jig, breakdown, or double shuffle, synthesized African and European elements with newly invented dance steps. They were the forerunners of today's tap and break dancing.

During the late 1700s and early 1800s, the Pinkster Festival was presided over by a "King" who was himself a slave. This was an inversion of the usual social order. The "crowning" of the Pinkster King was like the "election" of governors and generals during other holidays celebrated by black people elsewhere in the northeast. Pinkster celebrations endowed respected members of the black and slave communities with distinction, and it conferred a symbolic power over the white community. Celebrations featuring this sort of inversion of rank can be traced both to West African and European antecedents. Pinkster is most related in this way to better known New World festivals such as "Mardi Gras" in New Orleans, the "Goombay" and "Junkanoo" festivals in the Bahamas, and "Carnivale" in Brazil.

The Dutch first introduced Pinkster to the Hudson Valley in the early 1700s. It has been suggested that perhaps at first the slaves simply stood on the sidelines and watched as the Dutch engaged in all the activities of celebration. But by the middle of the 1700s it had already became an African festival. It was not that the whites withdrew so much as the blacks merely took it over. For them it was a way of preserving their tradition into their new way of life. African slaves must have seen something in the extant Pinkster celebration that they could use as a vehicle to give expression to their past African experience.

Despite the Dutch origins of Pinkster, blacks in New York and New Jersey were so successful in incorporating their own heritage into the celebration that by the early 1800s Pinkster was widely considered to be a black holiday. Slave owning families granted time off to their slaves. Pinkster gave many of them the opportunity to reunite with loved ones and family members who often lived many miles away. Most slaves journeyed from the rural areas into New York City with its significantly larger population of both free and enslaved black people. Market places in New York City and Brooklyn attracted large gatherings at Pinkster celebrations. Black men and women sold such items as berries, herbs, sassafras bark, beverages, and oysters at these markets. And in turn, they used the money they earned to participate more fully in the Pinkster festival.

Pinkster, as an African American creative expression, reached its peak from 1780 to 1820. In the weeks prior to the festival, temporary shelters woven from brush, and clearly based on African design were set up. Of course, Pinkster meant different things to different people. To the Dutch, it was a religious holiday and a respite from work, and a time to enjoy family and friends. For enslaved Africans, Pinkster meant all of that and much more. Slaves enjoyed temporary independence, made money and purchased goods. More importantly for them, though, it meant the opportunity to preserve, reconstruct, and express African traditions despite the restrictions fostered on them by slavery in the Americas.

T he terms "Numbers Racket," "Numbers Game," and "Policy Making" all refer to a once highly popular illegal betting game, played on a daily basis in African American communities across the nation. Betting was referred to as "Playing the Numbers." With the advent of state lotteries, the black community's Numbers Game has declined considerably. Although it still exists, it has only a fraction of the scope that it once enjoyed. Policy Shops were in the United States prior to 1860. As to when it actually took a firm hold in the black community is unclear. As early as 1875 a report of a select committee of the New York State Assembly reported Policy Making to be "the lowest, meanest, worst form of gambling."

The Numbers Game or Policy Making as it started in the black community has a long history. It caught on quickly because a bettor could bet as little as one penny. In a community where most of the people are either on relief or in the lowest income brackets, the rewards seemed great. Also associated with this long history is the full autonomy enjoyed by the black organizers of the game. A hierarchy developed and great status was achieved based on how big a Numbers Bank a Numbers Chief could run.

An entire culture, employment industry, and lexicon developed around the Numbers Game. There were "Numbers Chiefs" who backed the game and guaranteed the pay off of the bets. There were the "Numbers Runners" that carried the bets and betting slips from the betting parlors to the "clearing house" called the "Numbers Bank" or "Policy Bank." The word "policy" is used interchangeably with "numbers" and it stems from a similarly cheap insurance that was common. In the black community, both were seen as a gamble on the future. Blacks began buying Dream Books to understand the numerology associated with their dreams and then play the number that corresponded to that dream.

In "Policy Parlors," the bettors' attempts to pick three or four digit numbers to match those that will be randomly drawn the following day. The gambler could place his or her bet using just the spare change found on a kitchen table. The penny and dime games opened up Numbers Playing to even the poorest of people. The game's main attraction to low income and working class bettors was the ability to bet small amounts of money. This explains why it was so popular among African Americans. Also, unlike today's state lotteries, policy men would extend credit to the bettor.

A player would win if his or her numbers matched a preset series of three numbers, which were found in daily newspapers as the last three digits of either the New York Stock Exchange total, U.S. Treasury balance, or total bets at a selected racetrack. The Numbers Game seldom favored the players because the results were often fixed. The Numbers Game made its Policy Bankers very wealthy. It was not unusual for them to extend loans and financing to inner city residents that could not be obtained from white operated financial institutions. The Policy Bankers would also contribute funds for various community services and causes, as well as the financing for educational institutions for black children.

Different Numbers and Policy Banks would offer different rates to bettors, though a payoff of 600 to 1 was typical. But since the odds of winning were well over 1 to 1,000, the profits for Numbers Game and those who controlled it were enormous. However, for the bettor, who only had little more than a few cents with which to bet, the returns were small by comparison. If a person in the Depression Era 1930s bet one penny, and his number "hit," he would win $6. By today's monetary values, that is not a lot of money. But in the 1930s, a loaf of bread was 10 cents, and $6 would have easily fended off starvation.

The overt exclusion of blacks from the nation's, economic, social and political processes only served to foment alterative means of survival. Blacks were frequently denied access to all that made America great. Some blacks turned to illegal resources to offset economic deprivation. It is no surprise that a nonviolent crime like "Playing the Numbers" became such a cultural phenomenon within the black community.

MARY ELLEN "MAMMY" PLEASANT (1814-1904)

M ary Ellen Peasant's great claim to fame is that she was the largest single financer of John Brown's ill-fated raid on Harper's Ferry, contributing $30,000 of her own money. And her most infamous notoriety came at the hands of the San Francisco newspapers that gave her the epithet of "Mammy" in a trial of scandal and deception in the 1880s. But the truth of her life, and the most powerful from a historical standpoint, is that she was an American original. She was an entrepreneur during the California Gold Rush. And she was a fierce warrior for civil and human rights, before and after the American Civil War.

By her own account, Mary Ellen was born on a plantation near Augusta, Georgia. Her father was said to have been the youngest son of a Virginia governor. Her mother was an enslaved voodoo priestess, originally from Haiti. She witnessed her mother's death at the hands of a plantation overseer when she was quite young. She learned to make her way all alone from that point. In one of her many biographies, Mary Ellen is said to have been rescued out of slavery by a sympathetic white man and sent for education in an Ursaline Convent in Louisiana. From there she became an unpaid servant in the home of John and Ellen Williams in Cincinnati. She began using the name "Mary Ellen Williams." A Quaker family in Nantucket held her as an indentured servant for nine years. It was their suggestion that she pass as white.

In early adulthood, after leaving the service of a Quaker family named Hussey, Mary Ellen became a tailor's assistant in Boston. She also became a paid church soloist. It was in Boston that she met and soon married James W. Smith, a wealthy contractor and merchant who could also pass for white. He was an abolitionist and a regular contributor for William Lloyd Garrison's newspaper, the *Liberator*. In addition, he rescued slaves for the Underground Railroad. Mary Ellen also became a conductor on that trackless series of homes and volunteers who helped escaped slaves. She sometimes dressed as a jockey to steal onto plantations to help escapees. Sometimes she was disguised as a delivery man driving a wagon.

When Smith died between 1844 and 1848, he left Mary Ellen with lucrative land investments in San Francisco, California and a plantation in Harper's Ferry, Virginia staffed by freed slaves they had rescued via the Underground Railroad. Smith requested that Mary Ellen devote a portion of the money he would leave to the cause of emancipating the slaves. She did that, and so much more. Continuing to support the Abolitionists activities of Wendell Phillips, she also subscribed to and supported the Liberator newspaper. In addition, she continued her activities with the Underground Railroad. She even got new husband John Pleasant (no relation to her white father) to help with slave rescues. But after her part in John Brown's raid, by means of money and activities, she and her new husband decided to move west for her safety.

Once in San Francisco, Pleasant continued to help runaway slaves. She was able to get them jobs with the best families in the city, or she hired them herself. She operated several boarding houses and restaurants. Still passing as a white woman, she used her business acumen and made social inroads with San Francisco's wealthiest citizens. She had a particularly fruitful 30-year business affiliation with Thomas Bell, director of the Bank of California. A full understanding of their relationship is yet to be revealed. Black citizens knew her as a philanthropist who used her financial resources to help them obtain a footing in the city. She also paid lawyer fees for them to defend their civil rights through lawsuits against the city.

At the close of the Civil War, much to the chagrin of prominent whites, Mary Ellen let it be known to all that she was indeed black. She may have been born a slave with no name. But today she has been given the title "Mother of Civil Rights in California" for work begun in the 1860s. Her achievements went unsurpassed until the Civil Rights Movement in the 1960s. Her dramatic life was part of the story of slavery, abolition, the gold rush, and civil war. She helped to shape early San Francisco and amassed a joint $30 million fortune in the process. African American history has no other story that is at once as scandalous and venerated. No other figure with as much mystery and intrigue as Mary Ellen Pleasant.

426

S alem Poor was a Minuteman, and one of the over 5,000 blacks who fought in the American Revolution to gain liberty for the Thirteen North American Colonies belonging to Great Britain. The independence that the United States has enjoyed for 230 years is owed to those freedom-loving patriots, both black and white, that fought in a protracted struggle for American liberty.

The first record of Salem, boy servant to John and Rebecca Poor, is found in 1747, when he was baptized in the North Parish Congregational Church in Andover, Massachusetts. His youth and early adulthood were spent in slavery on the Andover farm of John Poor and his son, John, Jr. In 1769, when Salem was only twenty-two he had accumulated 27 pounds to purchase his freedom from Poor. But his manumission did not become official record until 1772.

In 1771, Salem married Nancy Parker, the mixed African and Native American servant of Captain James Parker. There is a baptismal record, again from North Parish Church, of their one son, Jonas, who was born in September 1776. No records of other children for the couple have ever been uncovered. Neither are there any records of Salem's occupation in Andover after the completion of his military service. Nor is there any record of his death and burial site. In fact, there are only limited accounts of Salem's life before and after his Revolutionary War experience.

In March 1774, after the Continental Congress designated certain units of the Massachusetts militia to serve as Minutemen, the Massachusetts Committee of Safety permitted black volunteers to join town and village companies. In 1775, Salem Poor enlisted in the First Andover Company as a private. Like other militia Minutemen, he was trained to respond to British aggression at a minute's notice. It was in Massachusetts, at the battle of Lexington and Concord in April 1775 that the Minutemen first fired, what history has recorded as, "the shot heard 'round the world."

Shortly after the British retreat from Lexington, Salem enlisted under Capt. Samuel Johnson in the Fifth Massachusetts Regiment. During the American retreat from Bunker Hill (Breed's Hill), Salem saw British Lieut. Col. James Abercrombie leading the elite grenadiers, raise his arms in victory. Salem took aim and fired, and then watched the British officer fall, mortally wounded by his shot. Salem was an excellent marksman and a trained musketeer. During the American Revolution he was used extensively as a sharpshooter who could pickoff the British in all the battles in which he was engaged.

Salem's military career seems to come right out of U.S. history books. Besides being one of the thirty-six blacks at Bunker Hill, he was in other famous battles as well. He fought with the patriots at Saratoga. He was in the last major battle of the New England Colonies at Monmouth in New Jersey. He spent that legendary frozen winter of 1777-78 with General George Washington at Valley Forge. He also served in the crucial battles of White Plains, New York and Providence, Rhode Island. Attitudes about the use of black soldiers varied during the course of the struggle for American independence. Washington would waiver and be swayed by public opinion and his own need for committed soldiers. But records show that from 1775 until 1780, Salem was never away from active duty for more than a few months at a time.

Salem Poor was an American hero at a seminal moment in United States history. The loosely joined colonies were forging a nation with the revolutionary idealism of the Age of Enlightenment. Those same ideals would define what America would become and how it would respond to stimuli from that moment, and through the rest of its history. And African Americans held those same enlightened sentiments. While the war did lead to the abolition of slavery in northern states, slavery entrenched itself even more deeply in the southern states. African Americas continued to face discrimination in every aspect of American life, especially education, employment, and housing, for 200 of its 232-year history.

THE NATIONAL ASSOCIATION FOR THE ADVANCEMENT
OF COLORED PEOPLE

The National Association for the Advancement of Colored People (NAACP) is perhaps the preeminent civil rights organization in the United States. With its brilliant staff of constitutional attorneys, it has led the fight for the establishment of African American rights and elimination of all discriminatory practices.

The origins of the NAACP are certainly found in the movement launched by W.E.B. Dubois. In 1905 Dubois formed the Niagara Movement because in his words: *"today, we have no organization devoted to the general interests of the African race in America."* Twenty-nine educated blacks from fourteen states answered Dubois' call. A manifesto was issued attacking fifteen areas of discrimination against blacks. Vowing to protest tirelessly, the group's members pledged to "assail the ears of America with the story of its shameful deeds toward us." For a time, the Niagara Movement was a success. But its membership did not grow quickly, and it lacked funds. And the movement gradually ebbed away.

The NAACP began where the Niagara Movement left off. Blacks led a precarious existence, filled with threats, attacks against their rights, and little economic progress. One editor of an African American newspaper wrote: *"We are going nowhere, and the world we live in is a mean one, turned against us."* This indictment prompted Oswald Garrison Villard, a grandson of Boston abolitionist William Lloyd Garrison, to call for a national meeting for the renewal of the struggle for civil and political liberties for African Americans.

Answering Villard's call in 1909 were fifty-three prominent black and white Americans, representing a crow-section of concerned citizens. Among them were political advocate and anti-lynching crusader Ida Wells Barnett; social worker and writer Mary White Ovington; Rabbi Stephen S. Wise; Bishop Alexander Walters of the African Methodist Episcopal Zion Church; and of course, W.E.B. Dubois. The early organization was ambitious. National in scope, it opened state and local branches, controlled by an interracial board of directors. Most far-reaching was the group's pledge to make the 11,000,000 African Americans socially free from insult and politically free from disfranchisement.

One of the NAACP's early targets was the federal government. Federal agencies like the post office and the treasury department were segregating their restrooms and cafeterias and demoting black employees. The NAACP then took on tougher problems: judge and jury prejudice, worker protection, attacks on voters, and black-white labor tensions. NAACP workers traveled to any scene of heightened racial tension to collect information, which they transmitted to the press. Without the NAACP, a strategy for dealing with these racial and reform issues would not have matured.

In 1915, NAACP lawyers won their first legal victory before the United States Supreme Court. The Court declared unconstitutional the *grandfather clause* that kept blacks off the voting rolls in the South. The clause stipulated that only citizens voting on or before January 1, 1857 were eligible to vote. Obviously, this excluded blacks because it was a date that preceded the adoption of the Fifteenth Amendment. Its greatest triumph was the 1954 U.S. Supreme Court case *Brown vs. the Board of Education*. It was the landmark decision that struck down the awful "separate but equal" doctrine that had been so much a part of the culture of the South.

The NAACP served as the foremost civil rights advocate for African Americans in the twentieth century. It stood for black rights when the country was awash in racial violence and prejudice. The NAACP was founded for the purpose of improving the conditions under which African Americans lived at that time. Although these conditions have improved enormously, many differences still exist in the rights of United States citizens solely because of race or ethnic origin. The NAACP continues to seek a single class of citizenship for every American.

C olin Luther Powell was born in Harlem, New York City on April 5, 1937. His parents, Luther and Maude, were Jamaican immigrants. Powell has a complex West Indian bloodline that includes: African. English, Irish, Scottish, and possibly, Arawak or Caribbean Indian ancestry. When the history of slavery in the Caribbean and its corollary, miscegenation, is considered, such ancestry is not out of the ordinary.

Powell never distinguished himself in high school. But in college he found the structure and discipline he needed. In 1954 he entered the City College of New York City and its R.O.T.C. program and rose to the rank of cadet colonel. He was made a second lieutenant in the army upon graduating in 1958. His first post was in Germany, where he served for two years before returning to the U.S. It was then that he met Alma Johnson, whom he married in 1962, and with whom he had three children. A few months after the wedding, Powell was sent to Vietnam.

During his first tour of duty in Vietnam, Powell performed with distinction as an advisor to South Vietnamese troops. He was awarded the Purple Heart for an injury in the line of duty. In 1963 he returned to the U.S. It was an America racked with turmoil. It was the proverbial "best of times and worst of times." The war was becoming increasingly unpopular. Social unrest filled the news. A backlash against the Civil Rights Movement caused four young girls in Birmingham to be killed in a church bombing. Also Powell's returned coincided with the assassination of President John F. Kennedy in November.

Powell's next years would be occupied with climbing the rungs necessary to a military career. He performed so well at the Fort Benning Infantry School that he was asked to become an instructor. In 1966, he was promoted to the rank of Major. He then graduated second in his class from the United States Army Command and General Staff College before getting another tour in Vietnam in 1968. On his second tour, he worked at staff headquarters in the rear, though he once again received a Purple Heart and a Soldier's Medal when he rescued men from a helicopter crash.

With two tours in Vietnam behind him, Powell obtained an MBA from George Washington University in 1971. The following year he was honored with a White House Fellowship. At this point the "soldier" was thrown more and more into the realm of politics. Powell served the Carter Administration as an executive assistant in both the Energy and Defense Departments. During the Reagan Administration, Powell was chosen as senior military assistant to Defense Secretary Weinberger. Powell later held his first Cabinet position when President Reagan appointed him National Security Advisor in 1987.

In 1989 Powell was appointed Chairman of the Joint Chiefs of Staff by President George Herbert Bush. He became the first African American to hold that post. In that position, General Powell was the top military leader in the nation. The world witnessed his expert military strategy during Desert Shield and Desert Storm. He emerged as the architect of operations designed to execute the most high tech military campaign in history. During military briefings and press conferences concerning air strikes against Iraq, President Bush deferred to him.

Colin Powel was honored at his retirement as Chairman of the Joint Chiefs of Staff, where he commented: *"All I ever wanted to be was a soldier."* But his talent and ability had taken him much further. Each time his country had called him to higher posts, he answered those calls. He possesses a standard of right conduct, integrity, and morality that has been visibly lacking in many on today's political scene. It is the class of conduct into which America seeks to put its trust. In January of 2001, Powell was appointed to a Cabinet post by then President-elect, George Walker Bush, and became the first African American to be named Secretary of State. Any of the positions that Powell has held could have been the pinnacle of great military and political careers. But it is felt that all that Colin Powell can be... is yet to be.

L eontyne Price was the first African American soprano to achieve international diva status, an accomplishment that opened doors for other aspiring black women in the field of opera. Over the years she has received twenty Grammy Awards for her contributions to opera and classical music. At an early age she was greatly inspired by the work of Marian Anderson, the famed African American concert contralto.

She was born Mary Violet Leontine Price in Laurel, Mississippi, on February 10, 1927, the elder of two children of James Anthony and Katherine Baker Price. Her father worked at a lumber company, and her mother served as a midwife. Both parents were musically inclined. At the age of three, Leontyne began to take piano lessons, and soon added singing to her musical studies. By age eleven she was playing piano at church services, as well as playing and singing at weddings, funeral, and private gatherings.

In high school, Price sang first soprano in the choral group and played piano at school concerts. In 1943 she played and sang at her first formal public recital. After graduation in 1944, she attended Wilberforce College in Ohio where she studied voice with Catherine Van Buren. Price graduated with a B.A. degree in 1948 and accepted a scholarship to the prestigious Juilliard School of Music in New York City, where she received advanced vocal training from Florence Page Kimball, a former concert singer.

While at Juilliard, Price saw live opera performances for the first time in her life, attending productions at the Metropolitan Opera. Excited by what she saw and heard, Price decided to become an opera singer. She joined Juilliard's Opera Workshop under the direction of Frederic Cohen. When composer-critic Virgil Thompson heard her perform the role of Mistress Ford in Verdi's "Falstaff," he invited her to sing in a revival of his opera, "Four Saints in Three Acts." Her portrayal of Saint Cecilia in that work at the Broadway Theater marked her professional debut as an opera singer in 1952. Leaving Juilliard, she traveled to Paris, France to repeat the performance.

Later in 1952, Price began an extended American and European tour as Bess in a revival of George Gershwin's "Porgy and Bess." But the performance that truly revealed the enormous range of her operatic ability was her sensational singing of the title role of Giacomo Puccini's tragic melodrama "Tosca" in

1955. It was at that point she entered the popular imagination with NBC's dramatic and unprecedented broadcast of a black person as the principal character singing opera on national television. That performance counts as a historic moment in television.

After her stunning television debut, Price appeared in major works in the United States, Europe, and Australia. She single-handedly caused African American opera companies to appear, creating opportunities for blacks working in the operatic arena. Throughout the 1960s she remained exceptionally active as a performer of various roles with many opera companies in San Francisco, Chicago, Berlin, Paris, Salzburg, and other cities. On January 27, 1961, Price made her debut at the New York Metropolitan Opera performing Leonora in Verdi's "Il trovatore." She received an unprecedented forty-two minute ovation. Price went on to be a resident member of the Met for the next twenty-four years.

Leontyne Price defied race, class, and region to pursue a life in the world of opera. Everyone who heard her fine soprano voice likened it to the finest of instruments, the Stradivarius violin. Whether we are celebrating February as National Black History Month, March as National Women's History Month, or just the sheer majesty of music, we should esteem to honor this artistically gifted performer.

P earl Primus was a modern dancer, choreographer, teacher, and anthropologist whose work helped to establish the importance of African American dance in American culture. She was nationally and internationally recognized for her contributions to the performing arts. Primus was known for primitive, high-energy routines, always physically taxing, and sometimes causing her to leap five feet in the air. Her dancing also examined social issues in the United States and cultural issues in Africa and the Caribbean.

She was born in Port of Spain, Trinidad in 1919 to Edward Primus and Emily Jackson Primus. Her family moved to New York when she was only two. She was a product of the city public school system. A gifted athlete who excelled in track and field, she attended Hunter High School and earned a biology degree from Hunter College. While attending evening school at New York University, Primus took courses in psychology and health education and was preparing for a career in medicine.

Primus became an understudy for the National Youth Administration's dance group. After rapid progress, she won a scholarship with the New Dance Group in 1941. She was one of the first African Americans to receive such a scholarship. Primus pursued other forms of employment while she was involved in her dance training. At various times she was employed as a clerk, factory worker, welder, photographer, switchboard operator, and health education teacher. By 1942, however, she knew she would embark on a career in dance. And she knew she would draw inspiration from various subjects of black culture.

In 1943 Primus performed at the New York Men's Hebrew Association. She later secured feature engagements at Café Society Uptown and Downtown, two of the most prestigious nightclubs in Manhattan. Also during the 1940s, Primus launched her own dance troupe, which included folksinger, Josh White. The troupe also included four male dancers, two drummers, two other singers, and a jazz band. Between 1944 and 1945, Primus performed in a series of solo concerts in NYC, Chicago, Trenton, and Newark. Her choreography continuously showed a creative interest in the African Diasporas.

Primus' first major choreographic work, "African Ceremonial" attested to her early interest in black heritage. "Slave Market," employed spirituals to express the way these songs were used in the Underground Railroad. "Rock Daniel," showed the influence of jazz on American culture. Primus lectured and taught dance and anthropology throughout the United States and West Africa. She continued to develop dance concepts, creating a series of six dance groupings. The first group drew on African and Afro-Caribbean cultures that she saw as having essential dignity despite the world's misrepresentations of all things black. Her other groupings were based on African American cultural concepts such as the Langston Hughes poem, "The Negro Speaks of Rivers." Social commentary entered her work as she interpreted the Lewis Allen poem, "Strange Fruit." In it she explored the inane practice of lynching.

In 1959, Primus received her M.A. in education from NYU and traveled to Liberia to be the Artistic Director of their National Dance Company. She created "Fanga," an interpretation of a traditional Liberian invocation to the earth and sky. In 1978, she received her Ph.D. from NYU and created "Michael, Row Your Boat Ashore." It was a sociopolitical comment about the 1963 Birmingham church bombing. Her original dance troupe grew into the Pearl Primus Dance Language Institute. And her method of blending African, African-American, and Afro-Caribbean dance styling is still taught.

In her lifetime, Pearl Primus received applause, accolades, and awards too numerous to list here. In 1991, she was awarded the coveted National Medal of Arts, the highest award of the National Endowment of the Arts presented to her by President George Bush. She combined modern dance with classical ballet, moving powerfully and rhythmically with measured steps to metered sound. When Primus danced, she did not just entertain – she taught. Her every performance was a lesson of cultural significance.

AFRICAN AMERICAN QUILTING TRADITION

I n the African American tradition, quilting is a form of needlework, created by slaves and greatly influenced by the African aesthetic of religious and cultural traditions. Many intricately designed quilts or bed coverlets, hand stitched, mostly from wool and cotton, recorded family histories, legends, and songs. Quilts were also a great place to record political, religious, and personal philosophies. Many such ideas were related despite the illiteracy of many black quilters.

The textile traditions of African peoples are less thoroughly documented than other aspects of their folk art such as music and dance. What is known can be traced back to the prominent influences of four ethnic groups of Central and West Africa. The Mende-speaking peoples of Guinea, Mali, Senegal, and Burkino Faso; the Yoruba and Fon peoples in Benin and Nigeria, the Ejagham peoples of the Cameroons; and the Kongo peoples in Zaire and Angola are the West African progenitors of most African Americans.

African slaves and African textiles were traded heavily throughout the Caribbean, Central and South America, and of course, the Southern United States. Distinct weaving of each of the before mentioned regions became intermixed. By the time early African American quilting became a tradition in and of itself, it was already a hybrid of many African textile traditions, not to mention European and Native American traditions. Quilts that preserved West African origins were passed down through generations, thereby making them preserves of family histories. They were also used in baptismal ceremonies and to adorn gravesites.

The patchwork-quilt, those with geometric designs cut from old or worn clothing, began as squares and rectangles that were then pieced into both patterned and free-formed quilts. They were used to make diamond patterns. The diamond is symbolic of life itself: birth, life, death, and rebirth. They could also be used to display cultural information about the quilter's family or plantation life. Folklore has it that runaway slaves could read quilts hung on clotheslines and fences to find their way to freedom. If nothing else, we know that quilts were used to denote a safe house for escaped slaves. And certain free-form quilts were used as roadmaps to mark the guiding stars or to find the way North. There is a cache of freedom quilts at the Smithsonian.

In Africa, men wove most of the textiles. Yet when brought to the U.S. their work was divided according to Western patriarchal standards, and women took over the textile tradition. Slave girls sometimes quilted beside their mistresses, learning to spin cotton and wool and to cut patterns from discarded clothing. Because quilts and clothing were both in great demand in an age before the sewing machine, slave women who became skilled quilters and seamstresses often enjoyed more liberties for themselves and their families. Devoting many hours a day to the craft, quilters, beginning at about the age of twelve, created both practical and decorative quilts. They generally stitched African motifs. They created mythological figures or reptilian symbols for black quilt buyers, while sewing the traditional Anglo-American designs for white families.

Although the idea of quilts with secret slave encryptions woven into them is now in dispute, it still engages our imagination. On occasion a theory is advanced that offers an intriguing view of the past. The theory may not have substance and may not be substantiated in any scholarly way, but it provides a vehicle through which we believe we can better understand our past. Appliquéd quilts frequently preserved African American oral and folk traditions through the quilters' utilization and blending of African mythological figures and Christian symbolism. There is no doubt that African Americans did create message quilts. And to this day, those quilts are speaking volumes to a whole generation that still remains clueless about the daily degradation in the life of a slave.

A. PHILLIP RANDOLPH (1889-1979)

A Phillip Randolph was a powerful union organizer and tireless civil rights advocate. He was a force to be reckoned with from the 1920s through the 1960s. He spent nearly fifty years of his life fighting for higher wages and better working conditions. He single-handedly put pressure on four different United States presidents concerning the rights of laborers and blacks in this country.

He was born Asa Phillip Randolph on April 15, 1889 in Crescent City, Florida. He was one of two sons of the Reverend James William and Elizabeth Robinson Randolph, both descendants of slaves. The Randolph family moved to Jacksonville in 1891, where both Asa and his older brother, James, excelled in their studies at Cookman Institute, the first high school for African Americans in Florida. In 1911, Randolph became part of the Great Migration when he left the south and traveled to Harlem, New York.

Randolph enrolled in City College, and bowing to his parents' objections to an acting career, switched his aspirations from drama to politics and economics, and joined the Socialist party. It was during this time that he met his future wife, Lucille Green, a young widow. He also formed an acquaintance with Chandler Owen, a Columbia University student. The two shared the same political ideas, became "soapbox orators," and established *The Messenger*, a radical Harlem magazine in 1917. The magazine was never a financial success. However, it served as a vehicle for Randolph's viewpoints against war and capitalism.

His view as a socialist was that decent, well paying jobs was the first step towards social and political freedom. Randolph saw the degraded condition of African Americans and other minorities as the symptom of a larger social illness of an unfair distribution of power, wealth, and resources with racism at the root of it all. By 1925, the Pullman Company, builders and operators of sleeping cars and parlor cars for the nation's railroads, was the largest single employer of blacks in the United States. It paid its 12,000 porters $60.00 per month for 400 hours or 11,000 miles (whichever came first). Porters were required to pay for their meals and to purchase their own uniforms and equipment. They were not compensated for the five hours of preparation time before trips or any overtime. Additionally, they worked straight through without layover time.

The porters secretly sought out Randolph because they considered him a good orator, a tireless fighter for the rights of African Americans and most importantly, because he was not a porter and immune to Pullman vengeance. After several meetings, the Brotherhood of Sleeping Car Porters (BSCP) was formed on August 25, 1925. The Pullman Company did everything in its power, legally and illegally, to stop the BSCP. They subsidized efforts by the African American press to wage an all-out offensive against the union. Ministers and politicians joined the attack, decrying the union as "Communists" who dared attack the Pullman Company, the "benefactor of the Negro race."

On August 25, 1937, Pullman's president announced to the Brotherhood negotiators that the company was ready to sign an agreement. Randolph and the BSCP made history. It was the first time a contract had been signed between a black union and a U.S. corporation. The contract awarded a settlement of $1.25 million to the porters and their work month was reduced to 240 hours. In the courageous twelve-year battle with Pullman, Randolph and the BSCP earned the admiration and respect of many labor and liberal leaders, including the American Federation of Labor (AFL), with whom the BSCP would later affiliate. Black churches and newspapers eventually joined the National Association for the Advancement of Colored People (NAACP) and National Urban League (NUL) in support of the BSCP.

A. Phillip Randolph emerged as a national spokesman for African American rights and a staunch defender of the labor movement. In his lifetime, he challenged four presidents in the cause of civil rights and was the first to propose a "March on Washington" in the 1940s. This restless warrior went on to become the highest-ranking African American in the labor movement when he became Vice-President of the AFL – CIO Executive Council.

C ongressman Charles Rangel is serving his seventeenth term in the U.S. House of Representatives. He represents the 15th congressional district of East / Central Harlem, the Upper Westside, and Washington Heights. He is a longtime supporter of African American causes and a staunch civil rights proponent. He is also a founding member and past chairman of the very well respected Congressional Black Caucus.

He was born Charles Bernard Rangel in New York City on June 11, 1930. His mother and grandfather raised him in Harlem after his parents' separation. He was educated in the local schools but dropped out in his junior year of high school. He worked odd jobs until his enlistment in the United States army in 1948. Rangel distinguished himself in the Korean Conflict. He received a Bronze Star and Purple Heart for leading forty men from behind Chinese lines. He was honorably discharged with the rank of sergeant.

Rangel's military experience convinced him that he would never be satisfied with the kinds of jobs that he had held before the war. Consequently, he resumed his education upon his return to New York. He earned his high school diploma in 1953 and entered college. He graduated with a B.S. degree from New York University School of Commerce in 1957. After being awarded a three-year scholarship to law school, he obtained a J.D. degree as a dean's list student in 1960. While in law school, Rangel served as a law assistant to the New York County district attorney from 1953-1957 as a special investigator for the local elections fraud bureau.

Rangel was admitted to the bar in 1960. He started out as a tireless crusader for civil rights before being appointed assistant United States attorney in the Southern District of New York by Attorney General, Robert F. Kennedy. He resigned after only one year. He then founded the John F. Kennedy Democratic Club in Harlem. His political career began in 1966 when he was elected the first of two terms in the New York state assembly. Of course, his voting record reflected his liberal views. He supported the liberalization of abortion laws and legalization of the lottery while opposing stiffer penalties for prostitution as ineffective.

Rangel came to national prominence in 1970. A growing interest in national affairs led him to run for a seat in Congress. He successfully challenged the powerful Adam Clayton Powel, Jr. Citing Powell's poor congressional attendance record he defeated the incumbent by fewer than 200 votes. But in the general election, Rangel drew 88 percent of the vote to win easily. Early on he championed liberal causes. He has authored legislation to benefit minorities and women. He voted to reduce military spending. He was a very vocal critic of the bombing of Cambodia. He held to his liberal standards on domestic issues as well. He voted for busing and against the deregulation of natural gas. He supported the creation of a consumer protection agency and the implementation of automobile pollution controls.

Rangel's political mastery resulted in his appointment to several high-profile committees during the 1970s. He was chairman of the House Judiciary Committee during the impeachment hearings of President Richard M. Nixon. He was appointed to the powerful House Ways and Means Committee, making him the first African American to receive this honor. Eventually he became chairman of its Health subcommittee. In the 1980s Rangel began to assert a great influence within his own party and became a member of the Democratic Steering and Policy committee. Rangel is perhaps best known for authoring driving anti-drug legislation. He has crossed party lines, pushing for tougher and more stringent drug importation laws. Rangel has emerged as one of the leading strategists in America's war on drugs.

Even though Charles Rangel is the epitome of liberal politics, he is seldom hampered by conservative backlash. And he is, without a doubt, one of the most powerful, politically adroit, and charismatic African American statesmen of the late twentieth century and the new millennium.

Although emerging in the 1970s, it was in the 1980s that Rap Music became a widespread definitive statement of a new African American musical art form. It is important to note that there are various schools of Rap Music defined by itself and by lyrical stress. There are three major forms of Rap: *Teacher Rap,* which stresses social consciousness, social commitment, and social struggle; *Gangsta Rap,* which glorifies violence; and *Player/Lover Rap,* which demeans women. There are other forms that can be categorized differently, and even these are not always clear-cut. More often than not, the various forms of Rap Music overlap and greatly resemble each other.

Rap artists, while denying their debt to predecessors in Rhythm and Blues and Jazz, nevertheless add depth and color to their Rap by using R&B music as background. Rap pretends "self genesis," thereby wrongly dismissing the rich cultural history of the African American music tradition. Rap Music has a distinctiveness all its own, but like all African American music forms, it follows the African oral tradition. The cadence, rhythms, and body movements, even when performed by white rap artists, clearly display the African character of Rap Music.

As with the advent of any music form, history will most assuredly contain many detractors, and some will be quite vocal. Not everyone appreciated Ragtime, or the Blues, or Jazz, or even Rhythm and Blues. Certainly, most of the dominant culture had its share of problems with Rock n' Roll. But unlike any music before it, Rap initiates a passionate discourse of supporters and critics. This is essentially because of its dual character and mixed messages, and its relevance to both youth culture and the black music tradition. Too often the lyrics demean black women, reducing them to objectified, anatomical parts. Closely related to this is the theme of violent domination of women.

There is a widespread tendency of some Rap Music to reject the boundaries of propriety and good taste with the interjection of vulgarities. Also, some Rap Music fosters an anti-Christian belief that existence is senseless and useless. Rap is very often extremely nihilistic; promoting the idea that there can be no social or economic progress until all existing institutions have been destroyed. And above it all, Rap heralds the belief that societal conditions warrant destruction "by any means necessary." In this respect, Rap is heavily used to

443

criticize the United States and all its flaws. But Rap does not propose any creative or life affirming solutions to U.S. societal problems.

The most negative forms of Rap Music offer an easy vocabulary with three and four-letter words abounding. Rap offers a depreciative image that stereotype African Americans and gives license to use degrading vocabularies. With the word "nigger," in all its various and sundry disguises (nigga, niggas, nigggaz), defaming an entire ethnic group, it is any wonder that the largest consumers of Rap Music are white males, ages 18 – 35. It must be comforting to them to hear the word their fathers taught them set to music by the very ones for which it was coined. That disgusting word can neither be made chic nor fashionable by setting it to rhyme and music.

Finally, Rap Music, for all its controversy, has spoken to African American youth in a special, albeit, foul way. From urban street corners to suburban malls, the look and sound of American adolescence has been forever transformed by this popular culture phenomenon that Rap artists have created. They have produced a raw street language, hip-hop clothing, and the rhythm-driven music that uses the rhymed spoken word, and the free sampling of the hits of earlier popular artists. It remains to be seen whether Rap Music will someday offer any positive social practice or even loose this unacceptable sway that it holds over our young people. But one thing is certain Rap Music is an African American musical art form. And like all previous African American music varieties, it is unique, it is popular, and it is global – embraced by every culture in every nation.

The "Red Ball Express" was the United States Army codename for a massive logistical operation during World War II. It was a fleet of over 6,000 trucks and trailers that delivered 500,000 tons of ammunition, food, and fuel to the Allied Armies in the European Theater of Operations between August 25 and November 16, 1944. The Red Ball was operated primarily by African American soldiers, who drove two and a half ton trucks, delivering gasoline for General George Patton's Third Armored Division, and other vital supplies to the frontlines as American troops pushed the Germans out of France and back toward Berlin. The Battle of the Bulge, the definitive encounter of the war, was successfully executed because of the unbroken supply lines supported by the brave black soldiers of the Red Ball Express.

World War II was the first truly mechanized war. It placed unprecedented demands on the Army Quartermaster Corps for petroleum. General Patton's bold armored advance across France in 1944 is credited historically as a significant contribution to the Allied victory in Europe. American tanks burned up and average of 400,000 gallons of gasoline a day. That placed a huge demand on Quartermasters to provide an almost insatiable need for gasoline and other petroleum supplies. General Omar Bradley, senior commander of the First Army, crossed the Seine River, but being critically low on food and ammunition, he then had to wait until supply lines could catch up with his forward advance.

By early August, gasoline reserves and even food were nearly depleted. Nevertheless, the armies managed to continue this highly mobile type of warfare, driving eastward for another three weeks before being halted by the exhaustion of supplies of all types. Believing victory to be firmly within their grasp, the armies outran their supply lines and were forced to live hand-to-mouth for several days. In a desperate effort to bridge the gap between the lack of supplies at the front and the mounting stockpiles of petroleum, ammo, and food back at the beachhead in Normandy, a long distance, one-way, highway system, dubbed the Red Ball Express was conceived. "Red Ball" is and old railroad term meaning priority freight. The trucks of the Red Ball Express displayed a red ball insignia that gave them the right-of-way over all other traffic on the supply route. The supply route was marked with red balls all along the way.

The Red Ball Express truck convoy system stretched from St. Lo in Normandy to Paris, and eventually to the frontlines along France's northeastern border. On an average day, 900 fully loaded vehicles were on the Red Ball route 24 hours a day, with drivers officially ordered to observe 60-yard intervals and a top speed of 25 miles per hour. At night, the speed was reduced because the truck headlights were shielded so that the Germans could not bomb the whole convoy. Some of the trucks were mounted with .50-caliber machine guns for self-defense should the enemy be encountered.

Communications and transportation officials were responsible for overseeing Red Ball activities, but it required the support and coordination of many branches to succeed. While the engineers were busy maintaining roads and bridges, MPs were on hand at each major check point to direct traffic and record pertinent data. Quartermasters, truck drivers, material handlers, and petroleum specialists were ever present along the route and at forward areas. Any trucks that broke down were pushed to the side of the road, repaired in place by roving mechanical repair teams. Repaired trucks re-joined the convoy as soon as possible, or they were evacuated to rear area depots.

The Red Ball Express was finally halted in November 1944. It had reached a point of diminishing returns. As the route got increasingly longer, the Red Ball vehicles began using almost as much gasoline, over 300,000 gallons a day, as it delivered to the frontlines. Tire replacement rose to over 55,000 just in that September alone. And accidents, because of driver fatigue, increased significantly. Truck and trailer maintenance also factored in to the equation. Finally, the logistics of maintaining so great a supply route did what the German army never could – it stopped the African Americans on the Red Ball Express.

Bass Reeves was the first commissioned African American United States Deputy Marshal West of the Mississippi River. He was easily recognizable by his six feet two inch, 190-pound frame, large black straight-brimmed hat, and two Colt revolvers. Judge Isaac Parker, also known as the "hanging judge," appointed him a Deputy for the Fort Smith, Arkansas area and the Oklahoma "Badlands" Territory. Reeves was a legendary lawman of the Western Frontier, capturing over 3,500 outlaws, male and female, and only killing fourteen men in the performance of his duties.

He was born to a slave woman named Pearlalee, on the farm of Arkansas Legislator, William Steel Reeves. His given name was perhaps "Sebastian," which was shortened to "Bass" as he grew up. The year of his birth has been variously recorded between 1824 and 1840. In 1846, William Reeves moved his family and slaves to the Red River bottomland near Sherman, Texas. In 1861, William's son, George, founded a cavalry company that later served the Confederacy. Bass became George's body servant and aide-de-camp. But he escaped to Indian Territory and lived with the "Five Civilized Tribes," mostly the Creek Indians, as a fugitive slave until 1863. He bought land near Van Buren, Arkansas, and became a successful stockman and farmer. He married Texas native, Nellie Jinney, in 1864 and they raised ten children together. After Nellie's death, Reeves married Winnie Sumter of Muskogee, Oklahoma and started a second family.

On May 10, 1875 Parker was appointed judge of the Federal Western District Court at Fort Smith. His appointment was to bring law and order to the Indian Territory. His first official act was to swear in a U.S. Marshall and appoint 200 Deputies to curb lawlessness in the 75,000 square mile area. White outlaws had so terrorized the Seminole and Creek Indians, that white people, with or without badges, were not welcome there. Reeves was recruited because he was well acquainted with tribal languages and customs, and he knew the territory so well. Because he was black, he did not suffer from the reputation for abuse that stigmatized whites among the Indians.

Reeves had a well-deserved reputation for law enforcement during his thirty-two year career. He could bring in outlaws, dead or alive. While assigned to the federal district courts at Paris and Sherman, Texas he killed Bob Dozier, a master criminal whose activities included, murder, land swindles, and cattle and horse theft. Dozier, who had eluded Reeves for many years, was shot after refusing to surrender. Tom Story, murderer and horse thief from 1884-1889, died in a gunfight with Reeves. Jim Webb, a horse thief with many notches on his gun belt, was killed after a running gun battle with Reeves.

Dependability and devotion to duty were the benchmarks of Reeves' service to the government. Many district courts requested him for his reliability in serving warrants. Never having learned to read or write, Reeves would have someone read the subpoenas or warrants to him until he memorized which name belonged to each warrant. If the outlaw could not read, then Reeves had to locate someone who could make sure that he had the right person. He never refused to serve any warrant. Reeves arrested his son after a two-week manhunt. The younger Reeves was tried, convicted, and sentenced to life in prison for killing his wife, but was later given a full pardon.

After 1907 the role and the duties of the U.S. Deputy Marshals as the primary law-enforcement officers were assumed by other state agencies. And Oklahoma Statehood brought "Jim Crow" laws that relegated the aging Reeves to patrolman status with the Muskogee city police department. But from 1907 to 1909 there were reportedly no crimes committed on his watch. In 1909 his health failed and he died on January 12, 1910 of Bright's disease. It was a very sad ending to a life more exciting than any dime-novel hero of the wild, Wild West.

NORBERT RILLIEUX (1806-1894)

Norbert Rillieux was the engineer who invented the Multiple Evaporation process that transformed the sugar industry. Before his invention, sugar had been so expensive that only rich people used it on special occasions. He is credited with turning that previously upper-class luxury into an ordinary household item.

He was born in New Orleans in 1806 to Constance Viviant, a freed slave living on the plantation of his father, Vincent Rillieux, who was an engineer and the inventor of the steam-operated cotton bailing press. Young Rillieux displayed his father's intelligence and mechanical aptitude at an early age. He received his early education in the New Orleans Catholic school system, but he was sent to Paris to study at L'Ecole Centrale. Rillieux excelled at his studies and showed a particular talent for engineering. At the age of twenty-four, he became their youngest instructor of applied mechanics and published a series of papers on the steam engine and steam economy.

For the next ten years Rillieux experimented with steam engines and steam evaporation concepts that would form the basis for his important invention. His strong interest in his father's plantation, coupled with his theory on multiple-effect evaporation prompted his return to New Orleans in the 1830s. He used this opportunity to put his experiments with evaporation to practical use. The sugar refining process at that time was called the "Jamaica Train." It was a slow, expensive, labor-intensive production process. Sugar refinement was so hazardous that many slaves lost their lives during the refining process. Rillieux's invention not only refined sugar safely, quickly, and efficiently, but also produced a finer grade of sugar.

Rillieux developed a special evaporating pan, which was essentially a vacuum pan with condensing coils that could boil liquid at a controlled temperature. Heat control was critical since sugar caramelized at high temperatures. His refining method was a series of vacuum pans combined to make the heated vapor evaporate cane liquid, pan-by-pan, into crystallized granules. The Rillieux innovation has been hailed as one in the greatest in the history of chemical engineering. For the consumer, the innovation reduced the cost of sugar. It also resulted in saved lives, fuel, manpower and time, giving the United States sugar industry worldwide supremacy.

Rillieux's invention became a process in and of itself. He attempted to devise his evaporation process in 1834 and failed. He failed again in 1841. It was not until 1843 that he succeeded in obtaining a patent. In 1846, he received yet another patent for an improvement on his original evaporation design. The years between 1845 and 1855 were successful for Rillieux. His system was employed everywhere in Louisiana and stood in sharp contrast to the older methods in which slaves transferred the boiling liquid from one steaming open kettle to the next by means of long ladles. Just one laborer manipulating a few valves could operate the completely enclosed Rillieux apparatus.

Today, the process of multiple-effect evaporation is virtually unchanged from the basic principle that Rillieux applied. Even though there is now new technology supporting Rillieux's innovation, it is still universally used for the manufacturing of sugar, soap, gelatin, condensed milk, and glue. The Rillieux method is also employed in the recovery of waste liquids in distilleries and factories.

History is unclear as to the date of Rillieux's return to Paris, possibly in the 1850s. But it does record that he served as Headmaster of his alma mater, L'Ecole Centrale. Although he earned plenty of money from the patent of his invention, the lack of recognition for the sugar revolution that he began troubled him through the end of his life. In his later years he developed a passion for Egyptology and began deciphering hieroglyphics. It was thirty years after his death that the movement to honor Norbert Rillieux began in Holland. And it quickly spread to every sugar producing country in the world. It would have been a bittersweet victory for the man who sweetened everyone's life.

PAUL ROBESON (1898-1976)

Paul Robeson was a multitalented African American scholar, athlete, actor, singer, and human rights advocate. He was one of the most broadly talented people of the 20th century. He had to suffer greatly for his beliefs and it cost him dearly, but nevertheless, he took a stance against injustice and fought it when and wherever he found it.

Paul Robeson was born in Princeton, New Jersey, on April 29, to Drew and Anna Robeson. His father had been born a slave, but worked his way through college and became a minister. Paul was one of those people who seemed to have been born with every imaginable talent. He was an outstanding athlete, a brilliant student, a great actor, and gifted singer. Paul won a scholarship to attend Rutgers College. He excelled in sports and became an All-American. He sang in the college choir and won many oratory contests. He was elected Phi Beta Kappa. After graduating with the highest grade point average in his class, Paul enrolled in Columbia University to study law. He worked his way through law school by playing professional football.

In 1921, Paul married Eslanda Cardozo Goode. The couple's only child, Paul, Jr., was born in 1927. It was Eslanda who urged Paul to become an actor. In 1925, he got the lead in Eugene O'Neill's play, *The Emperor Jones*. For the next twenty years, Paul had a very successful career in concert halls and on stage and screen. He appeared in Shakespeare's *Othello* playing the part of the Moor and receiving critical acclaim for it. He gave music concerts, singing spiritual, folk songs, and operatic arias. He starred in the early movie productions of *The Emperor Jones, Jericho, King Solomon's Mines,* and *Saunders of the River.* He is probably most remembered for the song, *Ole Man River,* which he sang in *Showboat,* the play and movie.

As long as African Americans were openly discriminated against and lacked equality, Paul was not content with fame and fortune. He saw the injustice and spoke out against the United States for its mistreatment of black people. Living mostly in Europe from 1928 to 1939 and traveling extensively in Asia and Africa, the Robesons were increasingly drawn into leftist politics and international issues. They eventually came to fully embrace Communism. After that, Robeson fought for trade unionism and developed very particular ideas against colonialism in Africa.

The Robesons were brought before the United States Congress by the House Un-American Activities Committee and asked whether they were Communists. They refused to answer because they believed that government had no right to question their beliefs. Increasingly, Robeson found it difficult to earn a living in the U.S. and was forced to sell his home. The State Department revoked his passport, thus cutting off his lucrative overseas income in 1950. It was not until 1958 that the Supreme Court restored it to him. He was b*lacklisted* in the United States and was barred from Broadway, Hollywood, recording companies, concert halls, radio and television.

Roberson and Eslanda left the U.S. for England in 1958. They lived off-and-on in the Soviet Union until 1963. Traveling widely, Paul gave many concerts and spoke for the cause of freedom for people everywhere. He learned to speak Russian, Chinese, and six other languages, including two African languages. He became known as a citizen of the world. He was as comfortable in Russia and Kenya as he was in Harlem. Counted among his friends were listed to be Indian Prime Minister Nehru, African statesman Jomo Kenyatta, and authors James Joyce and Ernest Hemmingway.

In 1963, Paul Robeson came back to the United States to work for the Civil Rights Movement. He participated in the Selma March in that same year. He eventually campaigned against the Vietnam War. But none of his later protest activities damaged him financially as his earlier protests did.

BILL "BOJANGLES" ROBINSON (1878-1949)

B ill Robinson was an African American tap artist, comedic entertainer, vaudevillian, and actor of the late nineteenth, into the early twentieth century. He was known for his skill and originality in creating a unique dance style characterized by highly rhythmic, syncopated and complex footwork. He is also credited with originating the phrase; "Everything is copasetic," which to him meant: *life is good.*

He was born Luther Robinson on May 25, 1878, the son of Maxwell and Marla Robinson. His father was a machinist and his mother was a singer. Robinson and his brother, Bill, whose name he would later appropriate, were orphaned when their parents died in 1885. Following that the boys lived with their paternal grandmother. Robinson worked as a shoeshine boy and danced on the street corners for money. During this time he began to use the nickname "Bojangles," which possibly derived from the word "jangle," a slang term for fighting.

At age twelve, Robinson ran away to Washington, D.C., where he continued street performances as well as working as a stable boy at a racetrack. His first professional job came in 1892 as a member of the "Pickaninny Chorus," a group of African American children who sang backup for the main performer, in the revue, *The South Before the War.* After a two-year enlistment in the United States Army, Robinson moved to New York City in 1900.

Robinson emerged as one of the first black stars of vaudeville. At the time, whites in "blackface" normally performed black roles, but from 1902 to 1914 Robinson toured the vaudeville circuit as the partner of black comedian, George Cooper. Cooper played straight man to Robinson's clown. While theirs was not a dance team, when the two broke up, Robinson got his manager to book him as a solo dance performer. His vaudevillian career culminated in a European tour in 1926.

In 1917 Robinson performed for the American armed forces that were ordered to Europe during World War I. In 1918 he premiered at New York's legendary Palace Theater where he performed his trademark "stair dance," a rapid tap dance up and down a five-step staircase, to a standing ovation. Because of the complexity of his dance steps, which he made look so easy, Robinson became one of the first black stars of Broadway. He debuted as the lead in the all-black revue, *Blackbirds of 1928*. Newspaper reviews hailed him as the best tap dancer ever. Robinson's other notable staring performances on Broadway include: *Brown Buddies* (1930); *Blackbirds of 1933*; *The Hot Mikado* (1939), *All In Fun* (1940); and *Memphis Bound* (1945).

Robinson began to make Hollywood Movies in the 1930s, at a time when the film industry offered few opportunities to blacks. His films include: *Dixiana* (1930); *Harlem is Heaven* (1933); *Hooray for Love* (1935); and *Stormy Weather* (1945). His most popular films, however, were the four he made with then child star, Shirley Temple: *The Littlest Colonel* (1935); *The Littlest Rebel* (1935); *Just Around the Corner* (1938); and *Rebecca of Sunnybrook Farm* (1938). When research was completed, Robinson's personal life seemed contradictory. He was married three times but had no children. He carelessly threw money away at the racetracks but he loving donated to so many more worthwhile causes. In his lifetime he earned a fortune but he died with little money.

But in this one thing, there is no contradiction. Bill Robinson was a consummate performer. His show business career spanned fifty years. He amazed his audiences with his dancing wherever he went. Even in his sixties, his footwork was complex, graceful, and often improvised. Usually bedecked in tails and a top hat that was tilted to one side, he charmed his audiences with an irresistible smile. When contemporary tap performers speak of him, they call him the greatest tap dance artist of all time. That alone makes everything about the life of Bill "Bojangles" Robinson truly "copasetic."

He was born John Roosevelt Robinson on January 31, 1919 in Cairo, Georgia to a family of poor sharecroppers. But he will be forever remembered as "Jackie." He had always exhibited athletic ability. And he became a star athlete at Pasadena's John Muir High School. He attended Pasadena Junior College in California and the University of California at Los Angles. At UCLA he demonstrated exceptional athletic ability and became the first student-athlete in the school's history to become "All American." He earned varsity letters in four sports – football, basketball, baseball, and track and field.

By 1941, Robinson was the assistant athletic director of the National Youth Camp (NYC) in Atascadero, California, playing semiprofessional football with the Los Angles Bulldogs throughout the year. Later, in the same year, Robinson joined the United States Army. After graduating Officers Candidate School (OCS) at Fort Riley, Kansas, he became a second lieutenant in what was then a segregated army. Troubled by the mistreatment of black soldiers, Robinson protested the army's discriminatory practices. Military police at Fort Hood, Texas arrested him when he refused the driver's order to move to the back of a bus. He was acquitted at court-martial. Robinson was honorably discharged in 1944 with the rank of first lieutenant.

Robinson began his professional baseball career in 1945 with the Kansas City Monarchs, one of the leading teams of the Negro Leagues. Later that same year, he signed with Branch Rickey, the general manager of the Brooklyn Dodgers. Rickey had been longing to tap into the rich resources of the Negro Leagues. Robinson spent the 1946 season playing for the Montreal Royals of the International League. The Royals were a minor league affiliate of the Dodgers. After one season in the minor league, he was called up to the Brooklyn team. Robinson became the first African American to play major league baseball in the 20th century. Starting as a first baseman, he made his debut in a Brooklyn Dodger's uniform on April 15, 1947.

Breaking baseball's color barrier was a serious challenge, and Robinson met fierce resistance from many players and fans who believed in the separation of people on the basis of race. He endured malicious catcalls and racial slurs shouted from the stands, but never acknowledged the taunts. Some rival players went beyond verbal abuse in an effort to intimidate him. They threw pitches at his head, spat on him when he slid into a base, and attempted to injure him with the spikes on their shoes, but Robinson never retaliated. With the support of Dodger management and the encouragement of teammates, the determined Robinson survived these attacks and helped the Dodgers win the National League (NL) pennant in 1947. He led the NL with a .297 batting average, a league-leading 29 stolen bases, and earned the Rookie of the Year award. Graceful fielding, timely hitting, and aggressive base running typified Robinson's style.

The rest of Robinson's career was even more spectacular. In 1949 he won the Most Valuable Player (MVP) award. During his ten seasons with the Dodgers, batted an average of .311, led the team to six pennants and a World Series Championship. With stellar talent, athletic grace, and personal and racial dignity, he helped bring down racial barriers in other team sports as well. For his outstanding performance and lasting example, Robinson was inducted into the National Baseball Hall of Fame in 1962.

Although Jackie Robinson did many memorable things in his life – as an athlete, a soldier, civil rights activist and business executive – he will always be remembered for the storm of controversy that arose around him as he broke the color barrier in major league baseball. The 1947 season opened up a whole new world for black ballplayers in America as well as for African Americans in their long march toward full civil rights. On Sunday, April 15, 2007, the entire Los Angeles Dodgers staff, managers and players, wore Robinson's famed number "42" to honor the sixtieth year of his 1947 debut into Major League Baseball, into U.S. History, and into the hearts of all Americans.

R oot doctors are a part of the African American body of Folk Medicine, with approaches to health and healing that dominated life during slavery and has continued to influence some people's understanding of medical practice. They were herbalists who used various plant and animal parts to cure or create ailments. Rarely administered in their raw forms, the herbs were ground into powders or rendered liquid, and then combined with other plants to form the concoctions. Like a drug store pharmacist, the root doctor provided specific directions for its use.

During slavery many African Americans maintained the same spiritual view of health that had characterized their African ancestors. The nature of an illness determined the way it was treated by the root doctor. All illnesses without natural explanations were believed to have been the result of supernatural forces. Poor health, they believed, arose from discord. Sickness could stem from the curses of others, deviance from religious integrity, or conflict with the natural environment. They believed that good health arose from harmony with nature and other people. Outside United States, especially in the Caribbean Island nations and Latin America, these beliefs combined with Roman Catholicism to produce syncretic religions like Voodoo.

Since the beginning of the 20th century, root doctors have been more visible in practicing their craft than voodoo priests. In the early days of slavery, Voodoo encompassed elements of divination, manipulation, and roots that gave it the appearance of a magical rather than a religious system. But Voodoo as a religion was suppressed because of its ties to slave uprisings. For that reason, and for various others, Voodoo began to operate covertly, while the medicinal aspect of roots was viewed as a more benign pursuit and operated overtly. Slave owners, who usually scorned continuations of African culture, permitted slaves to practice their traditional medicine. These root cures absolved them of the responsibility to pay white physicians for their slaves.

From the Antebellum period to the present, root cures have been primarily, but not exclusively, the domain of older women. The knowledge was often passed from one generation to the next. Slave culture regarded root doctors (root women and witch doctors) with high esteem and valued herbal cures, such as Mullen leaves, camphor, sulfur, and multifarious roots. One tetanus or lockjaw remedy involved squeezing out the excess blood from the puncture wound, and then wrapping it with bacon, tobacco leaves, and a penny. Given the quality of medical care in the antebellum South, root cures were often just as effective as anything else.

Throughout the 20th century, a retaining of the old ways paralleled the growth of scientific practice, and root cures were often viewed as acceptable supplements to modern medicine. Eating beets built the blood. Asafetida bags worn around the neck promoted wellness. A teaspoon of coal oil and sugar would not cure the cold, but it would stop the cough. The same concoction hardened into candy could be used as cough drops. Goose grease rubbed on the chest, prevented colds. Sulfur taken internally rid the body of "bad humors." Sulfur and Vaseline applied to the skin made it smooth. Sulfur compounds applied to the scalp made hair grow. And every would-be mother knew that there was "a baby in every bottle" of *Lydia E. Pinkham Vegetable Compound.*

Still in drug stores today are remnants of the root cures used by African Americans of a by-gone era. In addition to conventional drugs and those mentioned above, these stores sell camphor, spirits of turpentine, and oil of clove, as well as some patent medicines such as *Carter's Liver Pills*, *Humphries 11*, and *Black Draught*. Today's root doctors have gone high tech and are advertising *High John the Conqueror Root Oil* for sale at reasonable prices over the Internet. It seems that the old adage of *"that what doesn't kill us only makes us stronger"* is true after all.

JOSEPHINE ST. PIERRE RUFFIN (1842-1924)

Josephine St. Pierre Ruffin had a long career of humanitarian work beginning with the Civil War when she and husband, George L. Ruffin, recruited soldiers for the Fifty-Fourth and Fifty-Fifth Colored Regiments of Massachusetts. She gained national prominence as a civic leader and an organizer of black women's clubs before the turn of the 20th century. She was also the founder of the famed New Era Club of Boston and instrumental in publishing the first black women's newspaper in the United States.

She was born in Boston on August 31, 1842, the sixth child of John and Eliza St. Pierre. Both parents were of mixed English, French, Indian, and African ancestry. Her mother had been born in Cornwall, England and her father was a clothing merchant and the founder of Zion Baptist Church in Boston. According to family records, her paternal grandfather was an African who escaped from a slave ship near an Indian settlement. Josephine's early education involved boarding schools in Salem, Massachusetts because Boston public schools were segregated. She continued her education until she was married at age sixteen to Ruffin.

Hoping to escape racial discrimination, the Ruffin family lived in Liverpool, England until the start of the Civil War. Upon returning to the U.S. they became fighters in the struggle for black equality. George worked as a barber while attending Harvard University and later became a state legislator, city council member, and Boston's first black municipal judge. Josephine, while successfully raising their five children, directed her efforts in promoting black causes and busying herself with public welfare concerns and the women's suffrage movement.

In 1879 Ruffin help organize the Boston Kansas Relief Association that provided food, clothing, and money to the masses of African Americans relocating to Kansas. She was a charter member of the Association Charities of Boston, and an executive board member of the Massachusetts Moral Education Association. In 1894 she started the Women's New Era Club and edited its monthly newspaper, "Women's Era." Within one year, she called in other clubs that led to the organization of the National Federation of Afro-Women's (NFAW) Clubs. Its aim was to demonstrate the existence of a large and growing class of intelligent, cultured black women, and to refute public charges of ignorance and immorality alleged against them.

In 1896, the NFAW merged with a rival organization headed by the illustrious Mary Church Terrell to become the National Association of Colored Women (NACW). Also in the same year, Ruffin was instrumental in the formation of the Northeastern Federation of Women's Clubs. She became a member of the New England Women's Press Association and an executive board member of both the Massachusetts State Federation of Women's Clubs and the General Federation of Women's Clubs. In 1900, as a delegate of one black and two white clubs, Ruffin attended the National Convention of Women's Clubs in Wisconsin.

Resistance to integration by the convention led to what history calls the "Ruffin Incident." She was highly insulted when opposed by southern white women, the convention refused to ratify the acceptance of the all-black New Era Club. Ruffin emphatically refused to represent the white clubs because of the denial of membership to the black club. Although Northern and Midwestern delegates backed Ruffin, the Southern contingent successfully blocked her participation. But Ruffin remained active for the betterment of blacks and women. She founded two training centers for black youths and was active in the establishment of National Association for the Advancement of Colored People (NAACP) in Boston. Ruffin died at age eighty-one after giving tirelessly to her family and community, having proven that African American women get it done!

B ayard Rustin was a brilliant and controversial civil rights theoretician, organizer, and strategist. He was active in the struggle for human rights, and economic and social justice for over fifty years. Being openly gay, he became a strong advocate for gay and lesbian rights. Through his long association with A. Phillip Randolph, Rustin planned a March on Washington as early as 1941. But it was called off when President Franklin D. Roosevelt made important political concessions to Randolph.

Rustin was born on March 17, 1910 in West Chester, Pennsylvania. His grandmother raised him in a Quaker community. The pacifism he learned from the Society of Friends remained with him throughout his life. He had a comfortable childhood, excelling in academics, music, and sports in high school. His first exposure to racism came at an out of town football game when he was refused service in a restaurant. After high school he studied at West Chester State College, Cheyney State College, and Wilberforce University. Rustin moved to New York City during the Harlem Renaissance and studied at City College. He sang in local clubs with African American folk artists Josh White and Huddie Ledbetter to earn extra money.

Rustin found himself attracted to the Young Communist League's stance on race issues and joined the group in 1936. He was an organizer and worker until he quit the party in 1941. His involvement with communism would be used against him many times, but he never waived in his beliefs. In 1941 he began a long association with the Fellowship Of Reconciliation (FOR). Serving as its Race Relations Secretary, he toured the country conducting race relations' institutes designed to facilitate communication and understanding between racial groups. But Rustin's strategies were sometimes international in scope. He visited Africa and India and consulted with state leaders to bring an end to British colonial rule. He worked to end Apartied in South Africa. He supported the plight of the Vietnamese boat people and the Haitian refugees. He worked for the freedom of Soviet Jews and was an early advocate for the Ethiopian Jews in their struggle to immigrate to Israel.

Rustin's domestic strategies were used in a number of causes. He organized the New York branch of CORE in 1941 and became field secretary in 1947. He led the first "Freedom Ride" in North Carolina, which resulted in a 30-day sentence on a chain gang in 1947. This protest ride was the model for the

Freedom Rides of the 1960s. His account of the chain gang experience was serialized in the New York Post and spurred an investigation that resulted in the abolition of chain gangs in North Carolina. He became executive secretary of the War Resisters League (1953).

Rustin was the special aide to Martin Luther King (1955-1962) helping to guide the Montgomery Bus Boycott, and drafting the original plan for the Southern Christian Leadership Conference. He organized civil rights demonstrations at the Democratic and Republican National Conventions (1960). He organized the New York Public Schools boycott (1964). Also in 1964 he became executive director of the A. Phillip Randolph Institute in New York City, which served as a bridge between the African American community and organized labor. He continued to serve in leadership roles at the institute until the end of his life.

Though he was largely behind the scenes, Rustin will always be remembered as the organizing genius and master planner of the historic March on Washington in August 1963. He brought together dignitaries, labor leaders, entertainers, and the leading civil rights figures of the day. Throughout his life, he pursued causes about which he felt strongly. Whether at home or abroad, Rustin was always prepared and completely unafraid to take a stand. Extensive background in the theory, strategies, and tactics of nonviolent direct action proved invaluable to the causes for which he was passionate. His detractors and supporters have spoken in agreement that there has been no one since who has accomplished the enormous logistical tasks of mass political movements along with the delicate diplomacy of coalition building like Bayard Rustin.

Although Peter Salem was the best-known black hero of the American Revolutionary War, very little of his life was ever recorded. He played a decisive role in the Battle of Bunker Hill (Breed's Hill). History can accurately state that Salem was born into slavery in Framingham, Massachusetts, but as was the case with slavery, it cannot accurately state the year. He was a cane weaver by trade. His original owner was Jeremiah Belknap who later sold him to Lawson Buckminister of Framingham. Salem was allowed to enlist in the Continental Army. And in exchange for his enlistment, Salem was granted his freedom.

Salem was one of about 5,000 blacks that fought with the Americans during the Revolution. He fought in the early pivotal battles of Lexington and Concord in April 1775, and Bunker Hill in June 1775. He was a member of the Massachusetts Militia, or Minutemen, as they were called. Eyewitnesses credited Salem with firing the decisive shot that killed British Major John Pitcairn at Bunker Hill. According to one story, the colonial troops were near defeat, and Pitcairn ordered them to surrender. Salem stepped forward and shot Pitcairn causing the British to be so stunned that the Americans were able to retreat. Presumably, the musket he used is preserved in the Bunker Hill Museum. Also, in 1882 at the centennial celebration marking the end of the American Revolution, a statue of Salem was unveiled in Framingham.

Although the American colonists were ultimately victorious in the war, choosing sides and deciding whether to fight in the war was far from an easy choice to make. The great majority of them were loyal to King George III. For black people, what mattered most was freedom. As the Revolutionary War spread through every region, those in slavery sided with whichever army promised them personal liberty. The British actively recruited slaves belonging to Patriots while leaving the Loyalists' slaves unmolested.

After the Battle of Bunker Hill, Salem served until the end of the war. African Americans were instrumental in the American Revolution in spite of George Washington's attempt to ban them from the Continental Army. Even Washington eventually had to face the fact that African Americans were able and willing fighters. After all, the first martyr of the Revolution was Crispus Attucks, a black man. However, it wasn't until the bitter winter at Valley Forge and the overall large-scale desertion rate in the Continental Army that

Washington was forced by circumstances to re-think his views and accept African Americans into his army.

The British, on the other hand, recruited slaves hoping to disrupt American production. They promised emancipation for all slaves who fought for the Crown. This produced a flood of black volunteers in the British Army. The escaped slaves were not only good soldiers but they were passionate about their freedom and saw the British cause as a way to rebel against their American masters. Whereas the Americans could only count 5,000 blacks that fought with them, the British could count many more. It is estimated that between 50,000 and 100,000 slaves escaped, fought, and many died fighting for the British cause during the American Revolution.

Blacks, slave and free, saw the American Revolutionary War as a mixed blessing. The principles of the Revolution unambiguously implied the end to slavery. But there was an inherent contradiction in whites wanting to gain independence from England while enslaving blacks at the same time. This contradiction had its roots in the white concept of liberty as opposed to that of blacks. To whites, the war meant freedom and liberty in a politico-economic sense. To blacks, the war meant a release from the personal bondage under which they suffered.

Peter Salem was a daring American hero who fought in the American Revolutionary War on the side of the American Patriots. For his efforts he gained his own personal freedom, but he died in obscure poverty, never having the patriotic ideals and principles for which he so bravely fought fully applied to his life.

The Dred Scott Case was just one of the many debates of the contentious 1850s that eventually led to the American Civil War that began in 1861. The case intensified ongoing debates over slavery, and further polarized the North and South on the question surrounding slavery in United States Territories and in the American West. The case also prompted a Constitutional debate about the inviolate right of property. The Fifth Amendment disqualified any law that would deprive a slaveholder of his property.

Dred Scott was born into slavery in Virginia possibly in 1800. His owner, Peter Blow, moved to St. Louis in 1830, where he sold Scott to John Emerson, a U.S. Army surgeon. In 1836 Emerson and Scott moved to Fort Snelling, an army post in what is now Minnesota, and what was then in U.S. territory that banned slavery under the Missouri Compromise. At Fort Snelling Scott married Harriet Robinson, who was also a slave. In 1837 Emerson left Fort Snelling for Jefferson Barracks near St. Louis. Scott and his wife stayed behind in Fort Snelling, but later joined Emerson in 1838. The Scott family eventually returned to St. Louis with Emerson in 1840.

In 1846, after Emerson died, Scott sued to prove that he, his wife Harriet, and their two daughters, were legally entitled to their freedom. Scott argued that living in free states, where slavery was banned, essentially made him and his family free. And once free, they remained free, even after returning to Missouri. In 1850, the St. Louis Circuit Court concluded that Scott's two years of residence in a free state and a free territory made him free. However, in 1852 the Missouri Supreme Court reversed the decision, claiming that due to Northern hostility toward slavery, Missouri would no longer recognize federal or state laws that might have emancipated Scott.

In 1854 Scott turned to the federal courts and renewed his request for freedom in the U.S. Circuit Court in Missouri. Scott's owner at this time was Emerson's brother-in-law, John Sanford, who argued that blacks could never be citizens of the United States and therefore could never sue in federal court. Federal Judge Robert Wells ruled that if Scott was free he was entitled to sue in federal court as a citizen. However, after trial, Wells decided Scott was still a slave. After being tried in Missouri state courts and in a federal circuit court, the case went before the United States Supreme Court.

The Supreme Court heard the case, formally known as *Scott vs. Sanford*, in the spring of 1856, but did not decide on it that year. Instead, the court ordered new arguments, to be conducted in December 1856, after the upcoming presidential election. Scott received free legal counsel from George Blair, later a Cabinet member under President Abraham Lincoln, and George Curtis, brother of Supreme Court Justice Benjamin Curtis. Representing Sanford for free was U.S. Senator Henry Geyer of Missouri, and Reverdy Johnson, a Maryland politician and close personal friend of Chief Justice Roger B. Taney. In March 1857 the Supreme Court ruled in a 7 to 2 decision that Scott was still a slave and therefore not entitled to sue in court. Taney wrote the majority decision for the Court. The Justices issuing the dissenting opinions, John McLean and Benjamin Curtis, were both non-slaveholders.

The Supreme Court essentially ruled that Scott was not a citizen of Missouri, or any state, and that as a slave he was only property and his owner could take him to any place within the jurisdiction of the United States. In further shocking words, Taney declared that blacks were *"so far inferior, that they had no rights which the white man was bound to respect."* Curtis further argued that since it was ruled that the Court lacked jurisdiction to hear the case, its only recourse was to dismiss the case without prejudice and not pass judgment on the merits of the case. Slavery was the cause and reason for the American Civil War. The Dred Scott Case was one of the issues surrounding slavery that hastened the country into civil war. The decision itself is universally viewed as the worse Supreme Court decision in the history of U.S. jurisprudence. Even now, it is an affront to the doctrine of liberty upon which this country was founded.

H azel Scott was an exceptional pianist, singer, recording artist, and radio and television performer. She was best known for her jazz improvisations on familiar classical pieces. She was also the first black woman to host her own television show, "The Hazel Scott Show," until 1951.

She was born Hazel Dorothy Scott to Thomas and Alma Scott in Port of Spain, Trinidad. Under the tutelage of her mother, Hazel began playing the piano at the age of two and debuted in her native Trinidad by the age of three. She did not begin formal music training until after the family moved to the United States in 1924. Scott was raised in New York City where she eventually attended the public schools there. She made her formal American debut at New York's Town Hall by age six. And by age nine, had acquired six scholarships to the Julliard School of Music in New York City.

Scott attempted to enter Julliard at age fourteen but was under age. The school had a minimum age requirement of sixteen. But she began touring with her mother's group, an all-girl band after her father died. By the time Scott was sixteen, she was a radio star on the Mutual Broadcasting System and playing at the Roseland Dance Hall with the Count Basie Orchestra. In the late 1930s she appeared in the Broadway musical "Sing Out the News." After that, she appeared in "Priorities of 1942."

Scott's film credits include "Something to Shout About," "I Dood It," "Tropicana," "The Heat is On," "Broadway Melody," and "Rhapsody in Blue." It was in 1945 that Scott married the popular preacher and politician, Adam Clayton Powell, Jr. It was the social event of the season, but the marriage was rocky from the beginning. The couple managed to have one son even though they separated several time before finally divorcing in 1956.

In the late 1940s Scott became the first black woman to host her own television show. But due to McCarthy era politics and the accusation of being a communist sympathizer, her show was canceled in 1951. She defended her position at fundraising events and by fighting for equal rights. Scott refused to perform in segregated theaters and became a very outspoken critic of both McCarthyism and the social and political climate oppressing African Americans. She was widely recognized for her efforts in the struggle for racial justice. Scott made an outstanding contribution to music because of her combination of two approaches to piano in classical and jazz. She was called a musical "chameleon" for her flawless ability to shirt from jazz to classical to blues. Scott also released a few dozen albums in her career. Her most famous hit was "Tico Tico." Her album "Relaxed Piano Moods," with Charles Mingus and Max Roach, is the album most highly regarded by critics today. Scott's musical style was stride boogie-woogie, a genre made popular throughout the 1940s.

Scott lived in Paris, France for five years during the 1960s. In 1967 she returned to the U.S. and to her television and nightclub career. She had a recurring role on "The Julia Show" starring Diahann Carroll and appeared on "The Bold Ones." Scott also returned to motherhood because Powell had left the country to live on the Caribbean island of Bimini to escape his legal problems, thus leaving their son. In 1978 Scott was inducted into the Black Filmmakers Hall of Fame. She continued to perform until her death.

Hazel Scott was a talented child prodigy and an important artist until the end of her life. She can be celebrated in February for National Black History Month and March for National Women's History Month. Whenever we chose to honor this gifted musician and courageous warrior for freedom and social justice, we are esteeming all Americans with a pioneering spirit.

S *cottsboro Boys* was the collective name given to Olen Montgomery, Clarence Norris, Haywood Patterson, Ozzie Powell, Willie Roberson, Charles Weems, Roy White, Eugene Williams, and Andy White. They were called "boys" partly because of they were all teenagers, but mostly because the American South always referred to black males of any age as "boy." It was then, and still now, a term of disrespect, always used to demean and insult. The Scottsboro incident was just one of the more infamous cases of extreme prejudice and miscarriage of justice imposed against African Americans in the South.

In 1929, hard times came to the United States with the Great Depression. No group of Americans was hit harder than rural blacks. The price of cotton spiraled downward from eighteen to six cents a pound. Two-thirds of over two million black farmers either made no money or went into debt. Those who could find work might do so for fifteen cents a day worth of credit by a landlord or from a company store. African Americans by the thousands abandoned their fields and traditional homes for northern cities, but fared little better there. By 1931 the United States was well into its most serious economic depression and thousands of homeless and out-of-work men, or hobos as they came to be called, would secretly ride in railroad freight cars to go looking for work or just to stay on the move.

In the Scottsboro Case of March 25, 1931, a white hobo stepped on the hand of a black hobo and the incident escaladed into a fight. The blacks won, and threw the whites off the train. The whites, incensed at having been defeated by blacks, ran to local law enforcement and complained of an assault by black men. The sheriff telegraphed ahead to the next town of Paint Rock, Alabama to stop the train and arrest all blacks on it. An angry mob of gun toting, rope-carrying whites greeted the train an hour later. They seized nine black youths; some of them not even involved in the incident, and snatched them from the train. The blacks ranged in age from twelve to nineteen.

As the sheriff continued to search the train, he discovered what seemed to be two young white men. But in fact, it turned out to be two white women. Ruby Bates, age seventeen, and Victoria Price, age twenty-one, were dressed in men's clothing and also riding the rails that night. Suddenly the assault charge levied against the blacks for fighting with whites was elevated to rape charges

469

against all nine black youths. Apparently, the white women had been encouraged by the sheriff to make the accusation. The women had previous arrest records on solicitation charges and were threatened with, and afraid of, incurring new charges. All nine youths were arrested and taken on the back of a flatbed truck to the Jackson Count Seat in Scottsboro, Alabama. Word of the incident spread, a lynch mob immediately gathered, and the young men were saved from certain death by the protective presence of 120 Alabama National Guardsmen.

On April 6, 1931 the first of many trials of the Scottsboro Case was begun. In less than two weeks, and with a presumption of guilt, the blacks had been tried and sentenced to death for rape. The trial was so patently unfair that two organizations came to the aid of the young black men. The National Association for the Advancement of Colored People (NAACP), and a communist group, the International Labor Defense (ILD), treated the case as a *cause celebre*. Both groups had radically different ideas on how to broach racism. In 1933, in a retrial, a judge dismissed the death sentences because of weak evidence. But another retrial in 1934 reinstated it. The Scottsboro Case was even reviewed by the U.S. Supreme Court.

In short, none of the nine were ever executed for any of the charges. But they spent a collective total of 100 years in Alabama jails and penitentiaries. Court trials, retrials, and appellate decisions were handed down until the 1940s. Even though the women had long recanted their false allegations, the last Scottsboro "boy" was paroled from prison in 1950. After nineteen years of trials, retrials, and imprisonment, he finally obtained his freedom. But like the other eight in the case, some of whom died in prison, he never obtained justice.

In the eighteenth century, before Florida was part of the United States, it proved unique to the history of the nation as a location where large communities of runaway slaves could live in relative freedom. Escaped slaves, living as maroons, became Florida's first settlers. They came from Georgia and Alabama to escape the harsh reality of being someone else's property. About the same time, a group of Creek Indians left Georgia and established their own community in Florida. They were known as Seminoles after the Creek word for "runaway." Like some other Indian groups, the Seminoles kept African slaves. Contemporary accounts have shown that unlike white slave owners, Seminoles allowed their slaves to live freely with their families in exchange for a percentage of their harvests.

By the early nineteenth century, Spain, which owned Florida, was half-heartedly abiding by the international treaty banning the Trans-Atlantic Slave Trade. As increasing numbers of black slaves escaped to Florida, the Spanish Crown freed them and gave them land to cultivate. Before long, intermarriage between escaped African Americans and the Seminoles and their black slaves became quite common, and the groups formed strong kinship bonds.

Africans proved far more adaptable to Florida's tropical terrain than the Spanish or the Seminoles. They transplanted a rice cultivation method practiced in the West African countries of Senegambia and Sierra Leone. Use to a more temperate climate, the Seminoles began to learn how to survive in Florida from these ex-slaves. From the beginning of the merging of their cultures, the Indians depended upon the Africans for their survival.

The Seminole nation offered something valuable to Africans in return. Blacks and other ethnic groups within the nation enjoyed an independent village status. Their only obligation was to pay a small agricultural tax to be used for the common defense. If blacks needed something besides freedom, it was a strong defense against the slave hunters from the north, so their tax was well spent. Georgia slaveholders were soon invading Florida, seeking their runaways, and soon meeting a united resistance by armed red and black Seminoles.

Whites in neighboring states were enraged at the loss of their slave property in Spanish Florida, and pressed the United States government for action. In 1816, following a series of failed negotiations Congress authorized the use of a combined armed force of soldiers and sailors to invade Florida. This marked the opening of the first Seminole War that lasted two years with no winner. The first war was followed by an uneasy peace, interrupted often by white slave hunters and Creek Indians raiding to capture escaped slaves.

When Spain ceded Florida to the U.S. in 1819, the institution of slavery was threatened by the mere presence of free blacks holding valuable land. Again the government intervened, adopting a policy that relocated the Seminoles, black and red, west of the Mississippi River, to the Indian Territory in present-day Okalahoma. From 1835 – 1842 the U.S. and Seminoles engaged each other in continuous battles of an undeclared war. The Seminoles always refused to negotiate a treaty that did not provide for the protection of their black allies and kin.

Clearly, the Seminoles lost the second war by attrition. It is unknown how many blacks and Indians lost their lives in their fight to remain free. It is estimated that 500 blacks were returned to slavery, 2000 Seminoles were forced to go west, and the government simply stopped hunting for those few who remained in the Florida swamps. The story of the Seminole is yet another tragic tale in the long list of tragedies the United States of America created in the fight to keep its property rights inviolate.

THE SECRET MEANINGS OF THE NEGRO SPIRITUALS

"One of these morning / it won't be very long / you'll look for me / and I'll be gone"

WE.B. Dubois called the Negro Spirituals, also known as the slave songs and plantation songs, "the slaves' one articulate message to the world." In the years following the American Civil War, the spirituals were almost lost to us because the freed slaves refused to sing them after slavery was abolished. The newly freed slaves identified the songs with slavery and thus a part of their collective experience that they wanted to forget. But the efforts of the Fisk University Jubilee Singers, who gathered and recorded on paper the songs of the slaves, have preserved them for all posterity.

The spirituals were primarily religious in nature, often recounting and retelling the Bible stories that the slaves had been taught or perhaps read on their own. There were over six thousand of those songs and when strung together, they complete the biblical narrative. They range in title from *"Adam and Eve in the Garden"* to *"John the Revelator."* While it is true that many of the songs contained deep theological concepts, it is also true that many of them held secret meanings. The spirituals were used in worship, and also to communicate secretly with one another. Often this was done in the presence of their white masters.

What made the spirituals do double duty as religious hymns and coded messages were their common themes of slavery, flight, deliverance, and heaven. One of the best known, and one of the clearest symbolically, *is "Go Down, Moses."* Enslaved Africans closely identified with the children of Israel who were eventually delivered out of their bondage in Egypt by God:

"When Israel was in Egypt land / Let my people go /
Oppressed so hard they could not stand / Let my people go /
Go down, Moses, way down in Egypt land / Tell ole Pharaoh /
Let my people go."

While this was a recycling of scriptural narrative, it was also a personal expression of faith, and a most profound statement of social protest against the institution of slavery. In quoting another spiritual, *"If I had my way / I would*

473

tear this house down." And this too was a clear indictment against slavery. Many other spirituals articulated important religious truths while also conveying radical, egalitarian, social, and political principles:

> *"Didn't my Lord deliver Daniel / deliver Daniel / deliver Daniel*
> *Didn't my Lord deliver Daniel / and why not every man?"*

The conductors of the Underground Railroad often used coded spirituals to instruct slaves plotting their escape. Spirituals containing references to the "Jordan River" were interpreted to mean the Ohio River, which bordered the slave state of Kentucky and the free states of Ohio and Indiana. The Promised Land in the Bible usually represented Canada, the North in general, or any free state. As the slaves sang of their spiritual freedom though faith, they also hoped for physical freedom through emancipation or escape. The line of one spiritual, *"you'll look for me / and I'll be gone"* did not refer to death, but to a plan to escape slavery.

The Negro Spirituals were a unique body of work and a tremendous art form. It was just one way African slaves expressed themselves to the world. In that light, truly those songs and the singers of those songs achieved much. They spelled out the slaves' deep religious faith, and at the same time, interwove both protest against oppression and demonstration on behalf of freedom. The actual singing of the spirituals was perhaps the very first nonviolent protest in African American history. This fact was not lost on the Civil Rights Movement of the 1960s. The movement resurrected the Negro Spirituals and continued the protest in the same spirit and the same words of the slaves in the American South. And even today, in this new millennium, those haunting melodies and powerful lyrics can still touch us:

> *"We shall overcome / we shall overcome / we shall overcome some-d-a-y.*
> *O Deep in my heart / I do believe / we shall overcome some-day."*

TUPAC AMARU SHAKUR (1971-1996)

T upac Shakur was an African American Hip-Hop Artist who produced socially relevant, Afrocentric, and thought provoking Rap Music. He was listed in record books as the best-selling Rap artist of all time. His lyrics were renowned for the interjection of descriptive terms relating to harshness of life on the streets, violence, racism, and other societal problems. But the starkness of his lyrics did not diminish its poetry.

Tupac Amaru, which means, "shining serpent," was the name of the last Inca Chief. Shakur means, "thankful to god." But he was born Lesane Parish Crooks in the Bronx, New York City, on June 16, 1971. As the son of former Black Panther, Afeni Shakur, he was initiated into the world of Black Nationalism from his earliest days. Continually struggling, often destitute, Tupac Shakur and his mother moved throughout his youth, finally settling in Marin City, California, in 1988. He had acted on stage while attending the Baltimore School for the Arts, but it wasn't until moving to California that Tupac began to concentrate exclusively on music.

Tupac left home to join the Rap group, Strictly Dope. After three years with them, he had little more than a book of rhymes, but he rapped his way onto Digital Underground's 1991 hit *"Same Song."* Later that year, Shakur released his first solo album *2Pacalypse Now,* it went gold almost immediately. One of the feature songs on that album was *"Brenda's Got a Baby."* It was a keen but mournful observation about the all to common fate of teenage motherhood. But most of his topics touched on social issues and held some incisive social importance.

His second album, *Strictly 4 My N.I.G.G.A.Z.,* launched him into the pop charts with singles such as *"I Get Around"* and *"Keep Ya Head Up."* His subsequent album releases, *Me Against the World* and *All Eyez on Me*, established Tupac Shakur as a multi-platinum recording artist in the ever-expanding world of Hip Hop. He employed a resonant baritone voice with a distinctive rhyme cadence that young people could recognize easily as his style. His lyrics engaged language that is typical of Hip Hop music–angry, with four letter words abounding, and by and large, unprintable. A little known fact about Tupac was that he was an avid reader who was oddly taken by the timeless poetry of William Shakespeare, the political views of Niccolò Machiavelli, and the social relevance of J.D. Salinger.

Two of the songs from his *Me Against the World* album, *"If I Die 2Nite"* and *"Death Around the Corner,"* were chillingly prophetic of his own violent end. Tupac Shakur was shot outside of the Las Vegas MGM Grand Casino following a Mike Tyson title bout on September 7, 1996. He never recovered from those injuries and died six days later. He was just twenty-five years old. Before his death, Tupac starred in two movies, *Juice* and *Poetic Justice* for which he received good reviews. After his death, three other films in which he appeared were released: *Bullet, Gridlock'd,* and *Gang Related.*

With all his fame and wide acclaim, he was constantly embroiled in legal battles. In October 1993, he was arrested for allegedly shooting two off-duty police officers in Atlanta. Over the next two years he returned to courtrooms on numerous occasions, including an assault on a film director and an alleged assault on a young woman. Just days before his conviction on that assault charge, Tupac was robbed of $40,000 in jewelry and shot twice as he entered a New York City recording studio.

Tupac's life spun out of control. He fell victim to an art form he helped define – gangsta rap. And that art form has continuously fed on itself. Tupac has not been the only rapper to loose his life to the violence driven by this particular music industry. The question on many minds is did Tupac's life imitate the art or did the art imitate his life? In any case, rap music possesses a rage that holds an unacceptable sway over African American youth. Tupac's music reached millions and his life epitomized the vitality and sadly the violence of an entire generation of urban youth.

BENJAMIN "PAP" SINGLETON (c. 1809-1892)

Pap Singleton was known as the "Father of the Exodus" that brought hundreds of thousands of southern African Americans for western settlement into Kansas, Oklahoma, Nebraska, Indiana, and other areas from the post-Reconstruction South. In keeping with the biblical theme of the old Negro Spirituals, the freed slaves were called the "Exodusters." And nearly 100,000 blacks migrated to Kansas alone during the late 1870s and early 1880s. Building politically powerful, landowning, all black townships, Singleton helped blacks to exit the oppressive, Jim Crow South.

He was born Benjamin Singleton, a slave in Davidson County, Tennessee, possibly around 1809. As he grew up he was trained as a cabinet-maker. He was sold several times but always managed to escape. After being sold and sent to New Orleans, he escaped back to Nashville, then to Detroit, and finally Canada. Eventually he resettled in Detroit where he ran a boardinghouse that frequently sheltered runaway slaves. During the Civil War years, Singleton left Detroit and returned to Nashville, which was under Union Army occupation. He made a living building cabinets and coffins. While peddling his wares, he preached to idle, destitute, former slaves about going west to farm and own federal homestead lands.

By 1869, Singleton was convinced that his mission was to help his people improve their lives. He set his sights on Kansas, where he and a partner, Columbus Johnson, scouted out black settlements in Cherokee County and later Morris County. He spread the word about his settlements through posters that circulated widely throughout the South. He and Johnson formed a company, "The Real Estate and Homestead Association," that helped blacks from Tennessee and many other southern states move to Kansas between 1877 and 1879.

In 1880, Singleton was called to testify at Congressional hearings about the alarming rate at which blacks were migrating from the South. He testified that his company was responsible for 8,000 of the 100,000 blacks that migrated into Kansas. Southern planters and farmers were the most alarmed by the loss of the black labor force. And yet, they were the ones most responsible for it. Blacks were discontented with inadequate labor prices and the delays in paying their wages. Whites had used violent intimidation tactics and work techniques similar to enslavement to keep freedmen tied to the land. In a word, they had

477

attempted to re-enslave black people.

By 1881, Singleton had begun a new phase in his campaign to aid African Americans by organizing a political party called the United Colored Links. Affiliated with the Greenback Party, a white workers' party that called for fundamental social change in the United States, the Links Party was intended to help African Americans acquire their own factories and start their own industrial enterprises. Unfortunately, it was soon discovered that there was not enough capital within the black community to achieve this goal.

In 1883, when the black westward migration was effectively ended, Singleton felt compelled to organize a back-to-Africa movement and formed a company that encouraged African Americans to immigrate to Africa. His Trans-Atlantic Society was designed to help black people move back to their ancestral homelands in Africa. But by 1887 this too had proven to be unsuccessful and for the same reason – not enough black capital to complete the enterprise.

Near the end of his life, suffering poor health, Benjamin "Pap" Singleton was forced to give up his self-appointed mission. He died in St. Louis in 1892. But his nineteenth century vision would live on in a twentieth century hero named Marcus Garvey. Singleton's vision of a society in which African Americans owned the land, directed the industries, and held power found a charismatic champion in Garvey whose Universal Negro Improvement Association (UNIA) of the early 1920s briefly realized many of Pap Singleton's dreams to empower African Americans.

N oble Sissle was a successful bandleader, musician, composer, actor, and producer. He co-wrote "Shuffle Along" with the great Eubie Blake, the most successful musical comedy created by African Americans for the Broadway stage. Sissle also led a number of fine orchestras that featured some of the best musicians available, among them Sidney Bechet, Otto "Toby" Hardwicke, Tommy Ladnier and Buster Bailey.

Sissle was born on July 10, 1889 in Indianapolis, Indiana. His first singing engagement was at his father's Methodist church. He was also the featured soloist in his Cleveland high school glee club. He attended DePauw University, and Butler University in Indianapolis. His early career was spent largely in vaudeville as a singer. He toured on the Chautauqua circuit, with the Thomas Hahn Jubilee Singers from 1911–1913 and with the Joe Porter Serenaders from 1913–1915. He spent 1915 touring as the Dixie Duo with Eubie Blake. Sissle became the protégé of James Reese Europe, serving as the drum major in the all-black 369th Regiment from 1916–1919.

After World War I, Sissle's talents as a songwriter drew him to Broadway where he renewed the collaboration with Blake. Sissle achieved a major breakthrough with Blake when they co-wrote "Shuffle Along," an all-black musical revue that opened on May 21, 1921. Observers like James Weldon Johnson call it "epoch-making." Arna Bontemps said it was the "overture to an era of hope." It was rare for black entertainers to gain acceptance along the "great white way," but the success of this musical is credited with sparking the Harlem Renaissance. Langston Hughes claimed that "Shuffle Along" "gave a scintillating send-off to that Negro vogue in Manhattan... that spread to books, African sculpture, music and dance." It changed Broadway musical theater by introducing a Jazz dancing chorus line and the vitality and style of African American music to a more refined mainstream theater.

"Shuffle Along" presented a succession of songs, dances, and sketches that were attuned to the new musical sounds of the day. Sissle and Blake utilized Ragtime and the newly emerging, Jazz. There was a faint continuing element of minstrelsy as a concession to the white audience in the comedy sketches, but hardly any in the music. For the first time since the 1890s, people of color presented real African American song, dance, humor, and style to a broad American audience. Black artist were changed as a result of the musical. They now were able to earn money and recognition by performing elements of their own cultural tradition. Whites were also changed and enriched by having experienced unique black culture performed on Broadway.

The most memorable songs from Shuffle Along were: *I'm Just Wild About Harry*, *Love Will Find A Way*, *Honeysuckle*, and *Boogie-Woogie Beguine*. The musical featured the performances of then lesser-known black talents like Josephine Baker and Paul Robeson. Sissle's association with Blake also produced other Broadway Musicals: *Elsie* (1923), *Chocolate Dandies* (1924), *Runnin' Wild* (1924), and *Keep Shufflin'* (1928). In the late 1920s, Sissle led bands in Paris and London, and during the 1930s, led successful bands in New York and elsewhere in the United States. He founded the Negro Actors Guild in 1937, becoming its first president. He wrote columns for the *New York Age* and the *Amsterdam News*. He toured with a United Service Organization (USO) Camp Show that staged *Shuffle Along* in 1945–1946.

Noble Sissle continued touring during the 1940s and 1950s, but gradually directed his attention toward music publishing. In 1952 he became a disc jockey at New York City's W-MGM Radio Station. At one point, he was named the unofficial mayor of Harlem. It was a fitting tribute for the man who set the standard for Broadway musicals, and legitimized black musicals as a genre.

One of the most daring and dramatic stories to emerge from the Civil War era comes from the life of a slave named Robert Smalls. With his experience as a boat pilot, he was able to escape to freedom with his wife, two small children and fourteen other slaves. He commandeered a steamboat and sailed it out of Charleston Harbor past five fortified Confederate forts, and relinquished it to the Union Navy that had formed a blockade around the port of Charleston. This only began the journey that would take him all the way to the United States Congress as the first African American elected to the House of Representatives from the state of South Carolina.

Smalls was born into slavery April 5, 1839 on a plantation in Beaufort, South Carolina to slaves, Robert and Lydia Smalls. He never accustomed himself to being a slave and secretly learned to read and write. In 1851, at the age of 12, he was sent to Charleston and began work as an outfitter for ships. This job allowed Smalls to become very familiar with ships, sailing, and other seafaring arts. But most importantly he became familiar with Charleston Port. By 1861, Smalls had developed a working knowledge of the steamer that was later to make him famous. Smalls was called a *wheelman* because the title of *pilot* was always reserved for whites.

On May 13, 1862, the Confederate steamboat *Planter* was taken out of the port of Charleston by Smalls and delivered to one of the vessels of the Federal fleet then blockading the port. The day before, the ship had retuned to Charleston from an engagement which including moving guns from Cole's Island to James Island. The previous week, the *Planter* had supplied guns to various fortifications and then strategically planted bombs under the waters of the bay.

The officers had gone ashore and slept overnight in the city, leaving on board a crew of eight slaves. Among them was Robert Smalls who had earlier been ordered by Confederates to serve on the ship. At some point, Smalls decided that he could steer the ship out of Charleston Harbor and surrender it to the Union blockade. Consulting with the other slaves, Smalls discovered that two of them wanted to remain.

Every precaution was taken by Smalls to avoid detection of his plan. Being resolved to do this deed, he planned the action to the smallest detail. Under his command, wood was taken on the ship, steam was put on, and with her valuable cargo of guns and ammunition, intended for a new fortification at Fort Ripley, the *Planter* moved out of the harbor at 2:00 a.m. Smalls steered the ship beyond the North Atlantic wharf, where his wife, two children, and eight other people were waiting to embark. These passengers were taken aboard at 3:25 a.m.

With nine men, five women, and three children on board, the perilous journey had begun. Smalls passed Fort Johnson, blew the usual salute on the steam-whistle, and proceeded down the bay. When he had reached the area of Fort Sumter, he stood in the pilothouse leaning out of the window as the captain had usually done. Smalls even folded his arms in the same manner and wore the same kind of straw hat as the captain. The required signal given as a ship passed out into the sea was blown, as coolly as any other captain would have done.

Fort Sumter answered by signal, "all right," and the ship headed toward Morris Island, which was occupied by a light artillery unit, and then passed beyond the guns of Fort Sumter. When Fort Sumter soldiers discovered that the ship was headed for the Federal fleet they signaled to the Morris Island contingent to stop her. But it was too late. The ship had passed beyond the range of the Morris Island guns and was making her way toward a Union vessel. As the ship approached the Union forces, Smalls displayed a white flag, but because it was not seen at first, Union forces stood ready to defend the fleet. Just as they were about to fire, they noticed the flag of truce.

Noted black historian and scholar, Albert Raboteau, has called the religion of the slaves the *invisible institution*. It flourished in brush arbors, near waterfalls, and secret praise houses, apart from white eyes and ears, and where worshipers prayed and sang, and shouted into buckets to muffle the sound. The invisible institution allowed the slaves to continue their African traditions and inject them into the new American worship. And to them, it was quite visible.

In black worship service, the slaves could preserve their African characteristics. Even more amazingly, those characteristics could be applied to their Christianity. Today, we call those African characteristics, "African survivals." They are traits that can still be found in African American worship today. For example, the "call-and-response" between preacher and congregation is a communal feature that is purely African in origin. It was implemented so that every member of the village could participate in religious ceremonies. And the call-and-response can still be heard in black churches to this day...Amen?

Another African survival is shouting. In Africa worshipers had a ritual called the "ring shout." Worshipers moved in a counter-clockwise circle, and shuffled one foot behind them, until an emotional outburst was released. Having worship services inside buildings with pew and chairs to impede movement, black churches had to resort to jumping and shouting in a vertical movement. White churches also employ this type of ecstatic behavior. But in the case of African Americans, scholars have concluded that it is most assuredly an African survival.

The Christian use of hymns was interspersed throughout white Protestant worship services. But in the African concept of worship, music and dance were an inseparable part of their religious ritual. They could not conceive of the one without the other. Again, building constraints do not permit the type of space needed for dance in American churches. The simple definition of the word "dance" is "to move rhythmically to music." So, every handclap, every foot-tap, every head-nod, and every shoulder-rock, performed to the beat of music is a dance. Only African American church choirs sway rhythmically as they sing, and this too is an African adaptation of dance.

It is not surprising that the old black preachers, or "exhorters" as they were called in the slave community, were the ones who spoke for their people. Whatever their ethnic origin, the authority of major religious leaders on the plantation owed much to the African tradition of divine-kingship found throughout West Africa. And for that reason exhorters were least likely to have their authority questioned by the slaves that they were spiritually guiding. Whereas the "warrior-king" was typical in Europe, much of black Africa was characterized by the "priest-king," which gave all black religious leaders a high status in slave communities. This helps to explain the power and influence that black preachers have even to this day. The most notable leaders of the Civil Rights Movement were the black clergy.

White control of the semi-independent black churches was never completely relaxed. Therefore there was always some tension because the slaves preferred their own preachers. And they wanted to conduct their religious services according to their own mode of worship. This tension was heightened when free blacks attended slave worship services. Whites did not trust this slave / free mixture created when their worship was combined. They felt that conspiracies were being formed and slave insurrections were being fomented. This tension did not resolve itself until the slaves were emancipated in 1865.

Of all of the institutions created by African Americans, the Black Church is the least changed of them all. The worship services are still technically the same. The music is still an important part of the service. And the worship experience is still passionate, expressive, and personal. One noteworthy exception to the *invisible institution* is that the previously unlearned exhorter has become the college-educated, seminary-trained pastor.

B essie Smith was undoubtedly the most talented and influential female blues singer during her lifetime. She deservedly earned the title of "Empress of the Blues." The Blues was an African American art form that grew into distinctive shape at the turn of the twentieth century. Smith took the rural folk blues songs of black southern common people, added a vaudeville tinge, and elevated this music to a unique and unparalleled level of artistry.

She was born in Chattanooga, Tennessee to William and Laura Smith. Her father was a laborer and part-time Baptist preacher who died soon after her birth. Her mother died not many years later. An older sister, Viola, took in laundry to support the surviving siblings in a one-room shanty on Charles Street. By the age of nine, Bessie was already earning money by singing for coins on the streets of Chattanooga. But by age fourteen, she found a way out of poverty.

Smith began working in the black vaudeville circuit and appeared in a wide variety of other entertainment venues, including cabarets, dance halls, traveling carnivals and minstrel shows. She was in one troupe that included Gertrude "Ma" Rainey, the first great female blues singer. It was Rainey who taught her the art of country blues singing. Although taught by the best, Smith was unsurpassed in her ability to apply emotional intensity to the blues and deliver a song with majesty. By 1920 Smith was producing her own shows on the road in which she danced and sang, and acted in comic and dramatic sketches.

After touring all over the South, where she had a strong following, Smith met pianist-composer, Clarence Williams, who was also a representative of the Columbia Phonograph Company. He took her to New York City to make recordings. In February 1923 she made her first record for Columbia, *Downhearted Blues*, a duet with Williams, with *Gulf Coast Blues* on the flip side. It established her as the most successful black performing artist of her time. The three minutes and twenty-five second record sold an unbelievable 750,000 copies in the first six months.

What made Smith so immensely popular and soon propelled her to become a $2,000 a week entertainer was innate talent and her special feeling for the blues. Of course it didn't hurt that thousands of African Americans transposed from the rural South into the urban North during the Great Migration were hungry for her down-home style. Her contralto voice was so rich and powerful that she disdained to use a microphone during live performances. She was one of the principal developers of the "growl," a rough tone achieved by subtly manipulating the throat and mouth.

Smith made a total of 159 three-minute recorded sides for Columbia Records. She alone is credited with bringing the company back from the brink of bankruptcy. Over the years she recorded with a number of the most important names in jazz and blues, including a young Louis Armstrong. She left a treasury of great blues songs: *Back Water Blues, Nobody Knows You When You're Down and Out, Ticket Agent Ease Your Window Down*, and *Gimme a Pigfoot*, to name a few. In 1929 she starred in an unforgettable short film, *St. Louis Blues*, in which the Fletcher Henderson Band and the Hall Johnson Choir backed her.

Sadly, Bessie Smith's personal life was far less spectacular than her entertainment life. Her problems were many and varied. Some of the problems stemmed from early and unsuccessful marriages. Other problems resulted from poor judgment in choosing lovers and companions. She shared her affections equally with men and women. Hers was a frequently bawdy and troubled lifestyle, filled with excessive drinking, and tempestuous and destructive relationships. Even her life's end fit the "blues scenario." She was killed in an auto accident, traveling on a narrow road to a show date in Mississippi. Only those who appreciate the blues can see that, in so many ways, her life imitated her art.

The Student Nonviolent Coordinating Committee (SNCC), pronounced, "Snick," was a civil rights and political organization formed in 1960 by African American college students dedicated to overturning segregation in the South and giving young blacks a stronger voice in the Civil Rights Movement. It was organized to advance the "sit-in" movement, a protest technique that became prominent when four black college students refused to leave their seats after being denied service at a segregated lunch counter. Afterwards, SNICK broadened its agenda to include all forms of protests. From the very beginning, SNICK wanted to establish itself as an independent entity that would harness its youthful energy and frustration; and to challenge white racism, as well as the larger more conventional black civil rights groups.

Martin Luther King argued that a united movement would be stronger than a divided one and invited the students to create a wing within the Southern Christian Leadership Conference (SCLC). Other civil rights groups, National Urban League (NUL) and National Association for the Advancement of Colored People (NAACP) made similar invitations. But the students rejected all offers to become the student arm of any existing civil rights group. However, they did adopt King's strategy of nonviolent protest. In April 1960, the students announced the formation of SNICK and, although integrated, it would be led and staffed primarily by blacks. In its first months SNICK served mostly as a conduit for student groups to communicate and coordinate the sit-in campaign. National television images of neatly groomed, peaceful students being refused a cup of coffee and, in some instances, being forcefully removed and carried off to jail, generated sympathy from blacks and whites across the country. Several SNICK protesters capitalized on the publicity with a "jail-no-bail" campaign. Refusing to post bonds or pay fines, the students served jail sentences, filling Southern jails and increasing media coverage.

SNICK did join with the Congress of Racial Equality (CORE) to test the 1961 Supreme Court decision that declared segregation in interstate bus and train stations to be unconstitutional. "Freedom Riders" challenged segregated restrooms, restaurants, and waiting rooms at interstate bus facilities along an extended route from Washington D.C. through the Carolinas, Georgia, Alabama, and Mississippi. Along the way, riders were beaten, arrested, and a bus was set afire by white a mob. By the end of the summer, the protests had spread to train stations and airports throughout the South.

In November the Interstate Commerce Commission (ICC) issued strict rules prohibiting segregated transportation facilities. SNICK then shifted its focus to voting rights and joined CORE, NUL, SCLC, and the NAACP in a voter education project that sought to increase the number of Southern blacks registered to vote. Sadly in Mississippi the Ku Klux Klan (KKK) killed three SNICK voter registration activists. Afterwards, SNICK helped to create the Mississippi Freedom Democratic Party (MFDP) to provide an alternative to the official white-controlled state Democratic Party.

In 1967, after growing tension with Dr. King and SCLC, SNICK began cooperating on various levels with the Black Panther Party. A faction of SNICK, controlled by Stokely Carmichael, took over the organization and began to eject its white members. Carmichael called for "Black Power," a term used to describe a series of new tactics and goals, including the use of violence as a legitimate means of self-defense.

In 1969, Carmichael's successor, H. "Rap" Brown, also a symbol of black radicalism, changed the name of the organization to Student National Coordinating Committee, indicating that the group would retaliate violently if forced to. The irony of SNICK is that it started as a nonviolent protest organization, born of the Civil Rights Movement whose thrust was integrationist. But SNICK was seduced by the violence-laden ideology of Black Nationalism whose thrust was separatist. And it was that ideology that effectively killed off the Civil Rights Movement.

S oul food, such as red beans and rice, chitterlings, crackling bread, black-eyed peas, etc., is the cuisine characteristic of African Americans. It is closely related to the cuisines of both Africa and the Caribbean Island nations. African slaves brought to the Americas many of their native fruits and vegetables, including yams, watermelons, okra, and several varieties of beans, all of which were soon adopted into the diets of their owners. Slaves were taken into plantation kitchens as cooks and learned to combine their food with the food of the owners. Today, soul food is looked upon as the savory blend of the three cultures – European, Native American, and African.

African American cuisine also grew out of the slaves' resourcefulness in utilizing the cast-off ingredients of the masters' meals. They developed methods to cook parts of the pig not eaten by slave owners and feasted on the snout (nose), ears, feet, tails, ribs, thighs (hocks), stomach (maw), and small intestines (which when boiled or fried are known as chitterlings, or just "chitlins"). The West African tradition of cooking all edible parts of plants helped the slaves to survive in the United States. Slaves often prepared collard greens by simmering them in oil, peppers, and spices. They also creatively processed and cooked corn, the food most often made available to them by their owners. Slaves made corn bread, grits, hoecakes (cornmeal cooked on the blade of a garden tool over fire), and hush puppies (deep-fried cornmeal with onions and spices)

The West African diet featured starchy foods such as rice and yams, both of which became important staples in the African American diet. Although African slaves did not introduce rice into the Americas, their experience with rice cultivation in Africa helped to make possible the large-scale rice production in the Carolinas and the Gulf Coast states. Using both African and American cooking methods, slaves roasted, boiled, fried, and baked native yams and sweet potatoes. Sweet potato pie continues to be a popular African American dessert.

Beans were a major component of the African diet and were brought to the Americas by slaves. As in Africa, these bean varieties, including black-eyed peas and kidney beans, were typically simmered and flavored with a piece of meat. Another popular import, the okra plant, was usually fried or boiled and is the principal ingredient in gumbo, a spicy stew associated with the Creole culture of Louisiana, which has its roots in seventeenth century Afro-European culture.

Chicken, fish, and goat constituted important sources of protein for West Africans. While they usually cooked these meats in stews or over flames, many slaves in America adopted the European practice of frying meat, which best preserved it from spoiling on road trips. Fried chicken was developed in the South during the nineteenth century and quickly became popular throughout the United States. In addition to chicken and pork, deer, rabbit, opossum and raccoon were widely hunted and consumed by slaves.

In the southeastern part of the United States the mingling of Native, European, and African cultures produced a hybrid cuisine that included, among other things, barbecue. Many of the Africans who came to colonial South Carolina arrived from the Spanish controlled West Indies, where, as linguistic evidence suggests, barbecue originated from the Spanish word, "barbacoa." Thus enslaved Africans may have learned some culinary techniques, including barbecue, from the Caribbean.

As they began cooking over an open fire, the American slaves began to baste their meats with sauce instead of serving it on the side, as had been practiced in Africa. Because of regional differences in livestock, barbecue has come to mean pork in the eastern U.S. and beef in the western U.S. In whatever region, African Americans can usually recognize what food has "soul" just by the taste. It is more than greens being simmered in those pots; it is the history of a people.

Mary Fields was born a slave, possibly in 1832, in Hickman County, Tennessee. She was owned by Judge Dunn and grew up on his family farm as a servant-companion to his daughter, Dolly. There is no record of the names of her parents or her siblings; she seems to have been a slave "orphan." She never married, had no children, and possessed no formal education.

Sometime after the Civil War, Fields left Tennessee. She moved to Mississippi where she worked as a chambermaid on the steamship, Robert E. Lee. Historical accounts place her aboard the Lee during its great race against another steamship, the Natchez, in June 1870. When she recounted the exciting experience of the race, she said that crewmen tossed anything they could get their hand on – even barrels of resin and sides of ham and bacon into the boiler while men sat on the relief valves to boost the steam pressure. It was so hot in the cabins that the passengers were forced to take to the decks and it was expected that the boilers would explode.

By 1884, Dolly Dunn had become Mother Amadeus, the Mother Superior of the Ursuline Nuns in Toledo, Ohio. Fields joined them as the cook and handywoman of the Order. Being a tall powerfully built woman, 6 feet tall and weighing 200 pounds, Fields did all the hauling, lifting, and heavy work for the sisters of the convent. Mother Amadeus left Toledo when she was called to take a position in Cascade, Montana to open a school for Blackfoot Indian girls. But when she fell ill in Montana, Fields came to her aid. After nursing Mother Amadeus back to health, Fields decided to stay and help build the St. Peter's Mission School and became the protector of the nuns. For ten years Fields washed clothes and sacristy linen; cared for as many as 400 chickens; and tended large gardens for the sisters. As a crack shot with revolver and rifle, she also killed all predators of the convent's livestock.

It was in Montana that Fields began to dress in the comfortable clothes of a man, including wool cap and boots. She wore a revolver strapped around her waist under her apron. She had a standing bet that she could knock a man out with one punch, and she never lost a dime to anyone foolish enough to take her up on that bet. She broke more that a few noses in her day. By order of the mayor, she was the only woman of reputable character in Cascade allowed to drink in the local saloon. And while she enjoyed that privilege, she never drank to excess. She smoked cigars in public, something else that women did not do.

The convent nuns tried to smooth Fields' rough edges by inviting her to participate in services and practice her Catholic faith. They urged her to stop fighting, smoking, drinking and to become more "ladylike." But she preferred the rougher company of the men who worked around the convent and never gave up the privilege of frequenting saloons. Bonding with men and being in their rough company eventually cost her the job at the convent. After hearing complaints of her fistfights with men, and after she shot a man, the Bishop of Montana ordered the convent to remove her. Fields appealed the firing, but it did no good. In 1895, with the help of Mother Amadeus, she secured a wagon and team of horses for a U.S. mail route, becoming only the second woman in the country to so.

Fields carried mail, freight, and passengers between Cascade and Helena, earning the nickname, "Stagecoach Mary." Many of her passengers never realized that she was a woman in her seventies. On several occasions, her horses could not cross the snowdrifts so she walked a mule named Moses to deliver the mail. In 1903, Fields gave up her mail route and settled into town life. She started a laundry business and in the process began to baby-sit most of the children in the area. She became a big fan of the game of baseball and attended every game held in Cascade. She died in 1914 and was buried in a small cemetery between Cascade and St. Peter's Mission. In 1959, Mary Fields was memorialized in a story written about her in *Ebony Magazine* by Montana native and famed film star, Gary Cooper, who had only fond memories of a strong and caring character who earned the moniker of "Stagecoach Mary."

MARIA W. STEWART (1803-1879)

M aria Stewart is generally acknowledged as the first American woman, black or white, to lecture in public. She is best known for speeches that addressed issues of black economic empowerment, the abolition of slavery, and black pride. Although she touched on worldly matters in her speeches, the tone for her commentary was generally religious.

She was born Maria Miller to free parents in Hartford, Connecticut in 1803. Her parents died when she was only five years old. And from the time of their death until she was fifteen, Maria was indentured to a local clergyman and his family. Afterwards, she supported herself as a domestic worker. While working as a domestic servant, Maria attended Sunday School where she took literacy classes along with religious instruction.

On August 10, 1826, Maria married James W. Stewart in Boston. The ceremony was officiated by Rev. Thomas Paul, founding pastor of Boston's African Baptist Church. James Stewart had served in the American Navy, aboard three different ships in the War of 1812. He was much older than Maria and had become wealthy as an independent shipping agent for whaling and fishing vessels. After the wedding, the couple settled in Boston among the black middle class. Maria incorporated her husband's last name and his middle initial into her name.

Maria's marriage to James was short-lived. He died on December 17, 1829. Despite his success as a businessman, after a legal battle over his estate, Maria was fraudulently stripped of her inheritance by a group of unscrupulous white lawyers, leaving her virtually penniless. A year after the death of her husband, Maria suffered further loss when David Walker, the author of *The Appeal*, was found dead under suspicious circumstances. Maria had been strongly influenced by Walker's ideas. His influence would be most evident in her subsequent lectures and writings.

After all these trials, Stewart made a public confession of her faith in Christ and underwent a conversion that led her to become a religious and political witness. She began speaking out against tyranny, victimization, and injustice. She gave speeches and wrote essays against slavery and political and economic exploitation. When Stewart began to lecture publicly, such activity was unheard of for nineteenth century American women. Abolitionist, William

Lloyd Garrison, published her essays in pamphlet form and in his abolitionist newspaper, *The Liberator*. In her essays, she acknowledged that her life could be in danger, but asserted that she was ready to be a martyr for the cause of freedom. Like David Walker, Steward directed her essays to blacks instead of whites, urging them to exercise virtue and character equal to the white standard and their equality would be recognized.

In 1833 Stewart left Boston under severe criticism for her "unladylike" behavior of public speaking. She moved to New York where she participated in literary and anti-slavery activities. She later became a teacher and taught school in Manhattan, Brooklyn, even opening a school in Washington, D.C. In 1878 she became eligible to receive a pension as a widow of a veteran of the War of 1812. She used the money to publish a new edition of her collected works, *Meditations from the Pen of Mrs. Maria W. Stewart*, accompanied by letters from friends and colleagues.

Maria Miller Stewart was a woman ahead of her time. Her speeches and writings emphasized women's ability and activism. She criticized racism and sexism in an era in which it was thought of as inappropriate for women to participate publicly in political debates. Yet she defied gender and race to speak to issues that concerned her. It is deemed an honor when history showcases forward thinking, thought provoking, black feminists. And Mrs. Stewart is worthy of double honor for overcoming racial prejudice and gender bias.

WILLIAM STILL (1821-1902)

William Lloyd Still was an African American abolitionist and author who documented the experiences of fugitive slaves in his book, *The Underground Railroad*, and hired agents to insure the book's wide distribution. He is called the father of the Underground Railroad for aiding 649 runaway slaves, mostly through his Philadelphia home, and for establishing a network of safe houses and contacts stretching from the upper South into Canada.

He was the youngest of eighteen children born to Levin and Charity Still in the Pine Barrens forest of Burlington County, New Jersey. His parents were former slaves who changed their name from "Steel" to "Still" to disguise their identity. William's father had purchased his freedom from a Maryland farmer and moved to New Jersey. But his mother had twice escaped from the same farmer to join her husband. She avoided capture and re-enslavement by changing her name.

Still spent his early years working on his father's New Jersey farm. There was no time for him to learn to read and write. He languished in illiteracy until early adulthood. In 1844, Still settled in Philadelphia. For three years he worked at various jobs in a private home, as a waiter, and in a brickyard. In those years he taught himself to read and write. In 1847 he took a job as a clerk for the Pennsylvania Anti-Slavery Society and immediately became involved in the broader activities of the abolition movement. He married Letitia George and had four children. He also established a profitable coal business that supported his varied philanthropic activities.

The Fugitive Slave Act of 1850 gave great powers to southern slaveholders seeking to recapture their escaped slaves. But the oppressive legislation only served to further sectionalize the country. It increased northern sympathy for the plight of slaves and boosted traffic on the Underground Railroad. The Fugitive Slave Act also caused Philadelphia's Abolitionist community to organize a Vigilance Committee. The committee's purpose was to assist the increasingly large number of fugitive slaves passing through the city. Still was named chairman of the committee. He managed the finances, which were used to assist Harriet Tubman and her rescue efforts. He helped fugitive slaves find shelter on their way to safe places in the North and Canada.

Perhaps Still's most dramatic experience as an Underground Railroad agent came in August of 1850. A runaway slave named Peter told Still he was looking for his parents. As the man detailed his story, Still stood mesmerized. Peter was looking for Levin and Charity Steel. Peter was an older brother that William had never met. Still later reported that the incident inspired him to keep more accurate records of runaway slaves in the hope that it might enable them to find family members and loved ones. He assisted as many as 60 runaways a month, kept careful records of his secret activities, and often hid fugitives in his home. After John Brown's unsuccessful raid on Harper's Ferry, Still sheltered some of Brown's men and helped them to escape.

After the Civil War, Still devoted his time to combating racism and discrimination. These efforts were begun as early as 1859 when he started a campaign to stop racial discrimination on the railroad cars of Philadelphia. He exposed the practice to the press. Also in 1861 he helped to organize a social, civil, and statistical association to collect and preserve information about black Americans. Still established an orphanage for the children of African-American soldiers and sailors. He founded a Mission Sabbath School. He served on the freedmen's Aid Commission to help former slaves.

In 1873 Still published the account of the freedom network in which he championed hundreds of fugitive slaves who bravely made their way to the North. In 1880 he was one of the first organizers of the YMCA for black youths and served on Philadelphia's Board of Trade. Without question, William Still is one of the great heroes of African American history.

The Stono Rebellion occurred on Sunday, September 9, 1739, near the Stono River just 20 miles west of Charleston, South Carolina. It was the first and largest slave uprising in the British North American Colonies, prior to the American Revolutionary War. Historians have longed searched for an incident that may have triggered the rebellion as if freedom itself was not a just enough cause. Historically, with the odds so heavily stacked against resistance, the vast majority of slaves resigned themselves to the overwhelming authority of the white power structure.

By the summer of 1739 the South Carolina black majority had begun to organize a massive rebellion. A slave named Jemmy emerged as the leader of the uprising. Little is known about him. His slave occupation remains a mystery. Historians believe that he was captured in his early teens and forced into slavery. Most of the slaves of South Carolina came from the rice growing regions of West Africa, particularly, Angola. Their kinship and linguistic ties made secrecy and communicating plans about the insurrection easy. Information about how the uprising was planned is not known, but first-hand narratives provide vivid details about its execution.

Early on the morning of September 9, about 20 slaves assembled in St. Paul's Parish, located at the western edge of the Stono River. At daybreak the group marched to the bridge and broke into the firearms store and seized boxes of guns and ammunition. The storeowners stumbled upon the intruders and were killed in the struggle. The slaves left their severed heads on the store's front porch. A slave army developed as they marched along the river, freeing fellow slaves, killing their masters, and burning plantations. Twenty-five whites were killed, including women and children, as the slaves marauded through the plantations lining the river. Many of Charleston's most valuable estates were burned and stores destroyed. Amid the familiar beat of African drums and shouts of "Liberty," many more slaves were drawn into the struggle.

Late in the evening an army of white militia surrounded the celebrating slaves and a battle ensued. The slaves were badly out numbered and outgunned. Many slaves who attempted to fight were shot and killed. Some tried to return to their plantations, hoping they could avoid being implicated in the uprising. But most of them were captured, convicted at trial, and executed. The heads of those executed were placed on mile markers and fence posts throughout the

Charleston area. A small group of slaves actually managed to escape and hide for several weeks. But armed militia eventually caught and killed them after a brief gun battle.

In response to the Stono Rebellion, South Carolina officials tried to reduce the provocation for future insurrections. Penalties were imposed on slaveholders who overworked their slaves or beat them excessively. Colonial officials established a "Negro School" in Charleston, largely to teach slaves selected Christian values like obedience and submissiveness. But this benevolence of the colonial officials was overshadowed by the legal attacks on the mobility and limited personal liberties of South Carolina slaves. Some of the definitive measures taken after the uprising led to the abolition of the "talking drums" during any slave gathering. Freedom of assembly, even for religious worship, and freedom to earn money and to raise food were severely curtailed. The freedom to learn to read English, which had always been restrictive, was abolished altogether. All South Carolinians began to rigorously enforce rules regarding the black-to-white ratio, and closely monitored them.

The Stono Rebellion was not successful. But it did succeed in persuading many whites to leave South Carolina for colonies with white majorities. Neither did crushing the rebellion succeed in crushing the will of the slaves to continuously seek their freedom and liberty in the British North American Colonies, nor in the superseding United States of America.

BILLY STRAYHORN (1915-1967)

B illy Strayhorn was an African American prodigy, and later a classically trained pianist. He was the world's most versatile orchestra arranger, and one of America's greatest and most prolific composers. At a very early age, he made major contributions to the world of jazz music. Even though Strayhorn produced an album in his own name, the 1950 "Billy Strayhorn Trio," and recorded with other artists, his main body of work remains as the collaborations with the great Duke Ellington.

He was born William Thomas Strayhorn to James Nathaniel and Lillian Young Strayhorn in 1915, in Dayton, Ohio. His family relocated after his birth to Hillsborough, North Carolina, and finally to Pittsburgh, Pennsylvania. In 1923, Billy began the first grade in a Hillsborough one-room wooden schoolhouse. But he had shown an aptitude for the piano at a much earlier age. In fact, he played from the time he could reach the keys. His mother took him to Pittsburgh to join his father who had found work there. His father immediately hired Charlotte Catlin to give his son private piano lessons.

By the time Strayhorn entered high school, he was practicing everyday and becoming so engrossed in playing that he would forget all else. He played piano for his high school orchestra. While still in high school, he wrote a musical revue that toured featuring a yet unknown Billy Eckstine. While still in his teens, Strayhorn composed "Lush Life." It was a sophisticated work with mature, worldly lyrics. He played it for friends, but did not publish it until 1949. Strayhorn's father enrolled him in a Pittsburgh musical institution where he studied classical music. This gave him more classical training than most jazz musicians of his time. It was the only privilege he enjoyed in an otherwise disadvantaged youth.

In 1937 Strayhorn met Duke Ellington who hired him immediately as an arranger and second piano. But it was his lyrical compositions that attracted the most attention. The Ellington – Strayhorn artistic collaboration would last for thirty years. Ellington affectionately called him "Sweet Pea." And Strayhorn thrived undeniably in Ellington's shadow. For it was in shadow that he found the security to vent his musical gifts, cultivate his artistic interests, but live a lifestyle that could not otherwise bear scrutiny.

Some of Strayhorn's musical gems include: "Chelsea Bridge," "Rain Check," and "Lotus Blossom." In 1941, following the Duke's written subway instructions to his house, Strayhorn composed the music for and wrote the lyrics to "Take the A Train." It became a major hit and Ellington's theme song. The product of the first year of the Ellington – Strayhorn collaboration was the renowned "Something to Live For" with Strayhorn at the piano. Among his other collaborations with Ellington were: "Day Dream," "Love You Madly," "Johnny Come Lately," "Star Crossed Lovers," and "Satin Doll." The almost telepathic connection between Strayhorn and Ellington made it difficult to decipher where one began and the other ended. They were so in sync, and their talents so entwined, they could finish each other's sentences.

Strayhorn lived a tremendously productive life. He wrote at least one song every week until his death in 1967. Even as he lay dying of cancer, he penned "Blood Count." Ellington was devastated by the loss of his good friend and long-time collaborator. Strayhorn influenced so many people, and yet he remained very modest and unassuming all the while. For a time he coached Lena Horne in classical music to broaden her knowledge and improve her style. He toured the world with Ellington's orchestra and for a brief time lived in Paris. Strayhorn's music is known internationally and honored on its own merits. He and Ellington co-wrote the "Queen's Suite" for Elizabeth II and gave her the only recorded copy.

Billy Strayhorn lived his life under girded by four basic freedoms – freedom from hate, freedom from self-pity, freedom from fear, and freedom from pride. Governed by these principles, his musical genius flowed freely from his soul and onto the pages of jazz music history. Even though he played and composed for all those that we may call gifted, Billy Strayhorn seems to have been the most gifted of all.

HENRY O. TANNER (1859-1937)

Henry Ossawa Tanner was an artist who was not only famous for painting religious art but for genre scenes of African American life, including his best known works, *The Banjo Lesson* (1893) *The Music Lesson* and *The Thankful Poor* (1894). His paintings hang in museums in Paris, London, New York, and Chicago. In 1996, the White House purchased his *Sand Dunes at Sunset* for its permanent collection. Tanner was the first African American artist to be inducted into the National Academy and one of the first American artists to achieve international fame.

Tanner was born in Pittsburgh, Pennsylvania on June 21, 1859. He was the oldest of seven children born to Benjamin Tucker Tanner and Sarah Miller Tanner. His father was a leader in the black community, a writer and minister who later became a bishop in the African Methodist Episcopal (AME) Church. His parents gave Henry the unusual middle name of "Ossawa" in honor of John Brown's antislavery raid at the Osawatomie site in Kansas.

Tanner's talent for art was recognized very early. He began painting at age thirteen but did not become an art student at the Philadelphia Academy of Art until 1880. There he studied under Thomas Eakins, one of the premier painters of America. After two years with Eakins, he entered the Pennsylvania Academy of Design. While there, and through 1890, Tanner painted traditional European subjects such as landscapes and animals. He sold drawings to magazines to make extra money for his dream of going to Paris. Starting in the 1890s and throughout the rest of his life, he painted mostly African American subjects.

Tanner's parents did not think he could earn a living as an artist due to pervasive racial prejudice in the United States. He left art school and took a teaching position at Atlanta's Clark College from 1889 through 1891. His Atlanta friends held an art show for him, but only they bought the paintings. After that Tanner relocated to France where he continued to live and paint until his death in 1937. He made only occasional trips to American for exhibitions. Paris was the art capital of the world. In Paris he took courses at the Academie Julien and won critical acclaim. The city became more than just a place to study and exhibit his art it also became his home.

From 1894 to 1914 Tanner regularly exhibited his work at the Salon de la

Societe Artistes Francais in Paris. After 1900 he also widely exhibited in the United States. He became known for his paintings of biblical subjects, a theme he began exploring in the mid-1890s. *Daniel in the Lion's Den* (1896) was the first of his biblical genre, winning an honorable mention in an art show. The next year he won a prize for *The Raising of Lazarus*. He painted many more biblical scenes and made many trips to Palestine and other places mentioned in the Bible.

In 1899 Tanner married Jessie Olssen and they had one son, Jesse Ossawa Tanner. From all reports it was a happy marriage. The family made many trips to the U.S. but Paris remained their home. They stayed in France even during World War I, when most Americans were fleeing Europe altogether. In 1923 the French government named Tanner a chevalier of the French Legion of Honor, the highest civilian award. But sadly his wife died in 1925. Over the next year his son was stricken with an illness that lasted for many years. But through it all Tanner continued to immerse himself in his art.

At the time of his death he had attained the stature of being the most respected African American artist of his day. His artistic style was Realism, meaning he saw the world as it was. The best descriptor of his work has to be Formalism, meaning his work was truly beautiful. He knew that his art would never have the impact he wanted to make in the intolerable racial climate of the United States. So he exiled himself from his country and his countrymen in order to achieve the level of success and respect his art deserved. And he became the first African American artist to win international commendation.

MARSHALL "MAJOR" TAYLOR (1878-1932)

Marshall Walter Taylor was born into poverty in rural Marion County, Indiana on January 26, 1878. He was a world champion bicycle racer and became one of his generation's wealthiest and most famous athletes. Taylor's father, Gilbert, was a Civil War veteran who worked as a coachman for the Southard family of Indianapolis. His mother, Saphronia, was a devoutly religious woman and instilled her beliefs into her son. As a companion for young Daniel Southard, Marshall received many benefits not normally accorded an African American child of that era. Two of those benefits included a semiformal education and his very own bicycle.

In 1892, Taylor's skills on his bike earned him a dollar-a-day job as a trick rider for the local Hay and Willits bicycle shop. He performed the stunts to advertise the company. The military style uniform provided for the position gained him the nickname "Major." Around that same time, when he was only fourteen, he defeated a top amateur field in a 10-mile road race. When he was just fifteen he won a professional 75-mile road race between Indianapolis and Matthews, Indiana. In August of 1896 he set several unofficial records at Indianapolis' Capital City bicycle track. Such feats resulted in numerous death threats, and Indianapolis tracks were subsequently restricted to whites only.

Seeking greater racing opportunities, Taylor and his mentor, Louis "Birdie" Munger, owner of the Munger Bicycle Company, moved to Worcester, Massachusetts in 1896. Over the next decade, Taylor, still dressed in military style uniforms, established world bicycle racing records for seven different distances. His 1898 race at Indianapolis' Newby Oval drew over 18,000 fans. He reigned as the American Champion in 1898 and as the World One-Mile Sprint Champion in 1899. A 1901 barnstorming tour of Europe produced forty-two victories in fifty-seven races against the European champions.

Racing before admiring throngs throughout Europe and Australia between 1902 and 1909, Taylor earned as much as $35,000 annually. He and his wife, Daisy, and daughter, Sydney, traveled first class on great French and German steamships, stayed in elegant continental hotels, and dined at the world's finest restaurants. Taylor dominated the sports world in an era when baseball, prizefighting, and bicycle racing vied for America's sports attention.

Here in the United States Taylor faced constant racial bigotry and harassment.

He was often prohibited from racing on American tracks. In cities where he was allowed to race, he had difficulty finding lodgings and accommodations. Though widely admired for the religious devotion inspired by his mother, Taylor endured racist cycling organizations, physical assaults from other competitors, and promoters who lacked integrity. Extreme mental and physical exhaustion led to his retirement in 1910.

Little is known of Taylor's later years. He lost $15,000 in the failed manufacture of a patented automobile wheel prior to World War I. Other bad investments, the financial failure of his 1928 autobiography, *The Fastest Bicycle Rider in the World;* his 1930 divorce from Daisy, and costly treatment for chronic heart disease left him penniless. He moved from Worcester to Chicago after his divorce and took residence in the South Wabash Avenue YMCA. He died in 1932 in the charity ward of Cook County Hospital and was buried in a pauper's grave. In 1948 he was re-interred in a private cemetery with a monument paid for by Frank Schwinn of the Schwinn Bicycle Company.

Marshall Taylor was a sports legend in his own time and is still considered to be so, even by current standards. His connection to Indianapolis has been commemorated with the naming of the *Major Taylor Velodrome* in his honor. The Velodrome was built in 1982 and is a cycling track that has been host to many national and international competitions. It is a fitting tribute to a national and international bicycling champion who had to endure unrivaled hardships.

MARY CHURCH TERRELL (1863-1954)

The life of Mary Church Terrell spanned an entire history of struggle. Born in 1863, the year of the Emancipation Proclamation, Terrell died in 1954, the year of the *Brown v. the Board of Education* decision. During her life, Mrs. Terrell worked as a writer, lecturer, and educator. She is remembered best for her contribution to the struggle for the rights of African American women.

She was born Mary Eliza Church on September 23, 1863, in Memphis, Tennessee to parents who had been born into slavery. But her family came to be one of the wealthiest in Memphis. She was the eldest daughter of Robert Church Sr. Her father was a pioneer businessman after the Civil War. Through his hard work, he became the South's first black millionaire. Her family's wealth, however, could not protect her from segregation and the humiliation of Jim Crow laws. While traveling on the train, she and her family were sent to the Jim Crow car. This experience, along with others, led her to realize that racial injustice was evil and that it and all other forms of injustice must be fought.

As a graduate of Oberlin College in 1884, Mary Church was among the first black women in the country to obtain a college education. She majored in the classics and spent two years in Europe studying French, German, and Italian to broaden her education. Mary's father urged her to lead the genteel life of a lady of refinement, but she rejected that course and embarked on a teaching career. After graduation, she taught in Wilberforce, Ohio and then at the Preparatory School for Colored Youth in Washington, D.C.

Not only was did Mary become a teacher, but a principal as well. She was also appointed to the District of Columbia Board of Education, the first black woman in the United States to hold such a position. After marrying Robert Terrell, Mary was forced to resign her teaching post in Washington, D.C. in 1891. She embarked to spend the rest of her life as a lecturer, women's rights activist, and leader of the Black Clubwomen's Movement. Many 19th century women commented on Terrell's dignity and diligence as a factor in the social elevation of women.

Terrell became one of the first Presidents of the Bethel Literary and Historical Association. The association discussed major issues and questions of the day.

There was negative reaction to her leadership, but it was concluded, "She could preside with ease and grace, plan with foresight and execute with vigor." During the late nineteenth century, numerous local black women's service clubs were formed. The black club members found that they could not affiliate themselves with the National Federation of Women's Clubs nor could they be represented at the 1893 World's Fair. Black women came together to form the National Association of Colored Women (NACW) in 1896.

Terrell was the first President of the NACW. The club addressed issues ranging from lynching, Jim Crow, suffrage and the plight of rural women. She and Ida Wells Barnett were the only two founding women members of the National Association for the Advancement of Colored People (NAACP). In 1914 she organized Delta Sigma Theta Sorority and wrote the *Delta Creed* that outlined a code of conduct. In 1940 she wrote her autobiography, *A Colored Woman in a White World*. At the age of eighty-nine she led a picket line while on a cane to desegregate Kressge's Dime Stores. In 1953, at the age of ninety, she led a successful drive to end the segregation of public facilities in Washington, D.C.

The story of Mary Church Terrell is an inspiring one. And there is tribute in its retelling. It was deeply immersed in a host of efforts to improve the plight of blacks and women. Terrell died at the age of ninety-one. We esteem to honor a life spent in service to her people. We esteem to honor a life spent in struggle for human rights. We esteem to honor a life so boldly courageous that the speaking of it never dies. We esteem to honor Mary Church Terrell and all those of the Black Clubwoman's Movement.

At the Constitutional Convention of 1787 held in Philadelphia, delegates from all thirteen states met to develop a Constitution for the fledging new nation of the United States of America. The unity the thirteen colonies had employed to defeat their mother country was beginning to crack as the thirteen states tried to forge together a political system. The adoption of the federal Constitution ushered in an era of compromise as sectionalism began to order the steps of government. It was easy to see that the schism dividing the nation would be between the North and the South. And the issues that would separate them the most would be the ones surrounding the institution of slavery. But the United States was willing to work any compromise to set in place its "experiment in liberty."

All of the delegates at the Convention felt "government should rest upon the dominion of property." Since only white males who owned property were entitled to vote, property rights became inviolate within the framing of the Constitution. In the North property included commerce and industry. In the South property included slaves since all its capital and resources were tied to the institution. In the protection of this right of property, the Constitution gave recognition to human slavery without ever naming it as such. The document indirectly endorsed the continued bondage of people of African descent. The words, slave and slavery, were never written into the Constitution until the ratification of the Thirteenth Amendment that abolished slavery in 1865.

It was James Madison who offered delegates the "three-fifths compromise" to determine a state's representation in the U.S. House of Representatives. The compromise was a way to settle the question of how to count slaves as part of a state's population. But the issue of how to count slaves split the convention delegates into two orders. Northerners regarded slaves as property that should receive no representation. And since slaves were property, slaveholders should pay a $10 tax for each slave they owned. Southerners demanded that slaves be counted equally with free people, but only for the purpose of apportionment. The South wanted a strong central government to protect its rights, but not one that would interfere with the right to own slaves.

The notorious three-fifths clause in the Constitution allowed states to count three-fifths of their total slave population in apportioning political representation in the House. The framers of the Constitution believed that a concession on slavery was the price for southern support for a strong central government. Of the fifty-five convention delegates, twenty-five owned slaves. But none of the delegates believed in racial equality. The northern delegates were convinced, and rightly so, that some southern states would refuse to ratify the Constitution and possibly not join the Union at all. However, by compromising the slavery issue, the framers set in motion a system of political inferiority for blacks, and they planted the seeds for the future conflict regarding slavery.

The three-fifths compromise seemed to guarantee that the South would be strongly represented in the House and would have a disproportionate power in electing Presidents. But over the long term, the compromise did not work as the South had anticipated. Since the North's white population grew more rapidly than the South's, by 1820, southern representation in the House had fallen to 42 %. But the compromise did influence the election of slaveholding Presidents from 1800 until the 1850s.

The three-fifths compromise was strictly a matter of determining political representation in the House of Representatives. At the Constitutional Convention, the framers willingly accepted the challenge and responsibility of their new political freedom by establishing the machinery and safeguards that ensured the continued enslavement of African Americans. The right of property was the central core value in the Constitution. But there existed a strange irony in establishing the protection of liberty for white America, while effectively killing the hope of freedom for black America.

Emmett Till was an African American teenager who was unaccustomed to the intensity of racial loathing in the South, and fell victim to a hate crime of the most despicable nature. His death at the hands of two white men caused a national outcry from blacks and whites, and it gained national attention as the fledgling Civil Rights Movement began a nationwide thrust for social justice. Even though Till was just one of the more than 3,000 blacks summarily killed in the Jim Crow South since the end of the Civil War, he did not die in obscurity. His death prompted unprecedented cooperation between local law enforcement agencies and the NAACP legal staff and field investigators.

He was born Emmett Louis Till on July 25, 1941 in Chicago, Illinois to Louis and Mamie Till. His mother, a clerk for the Air Force procurement office and later a teacher, essentially raised Emmett alone since she and her husband soon separated in 1942. By the time of Emmett's death, his mother had remarried and divorced again. His father was a soldier in the Army during World War II who was executed in 1945 in Italy for rape and murder. In his short life, Emmett attended the Chicago Public School System and had just finished the seventh grade at the all-black McCosh Elementary School on Chicago's Southside.

Emmett was nicknamed "Bobo" by friends and family. His height was listed between 5'4" and 5'5". He possessed a muscular frame to carry his stocky 160 pounds of weight. Emmett had a speech impediment resulting from a bout of non-paralytic polio when he was only three. He had a stammer that prevented him from pronouncing certain words distinctly. However, that did not prevent him from growing into a self-assured and assertive young man who was always well dressed. He even had a reputation as a fun-loving prankster and a risk taker. By all subsequent reports, "Bobo" was well liked by everyone.

In late August 1955, Emmett's mother decided to send her son to visit relatives in the Mississippi Delta town called Money. She had been born in Mississippi and understood the South and the hatred of all things black. She warned her son to mind his manners with white people. What was exposed at trial was that Emmett whistled at a white woman and her husband and his half-brother killed him for it. And of course, those men were acquitted by the all-white LeFlore County jury. Whether his mother's admonition went unheeded, or whether

Emmett was filled with youthful exuberance cannot be identified by this late date. But what is crystal clear is that Emmett should not have died for either.

With so many violent acts committed against African Americans in Mississippi in the forms of shootings, firebombing, beatings, lynching, and general mayhem, it is difficult to name one act more heinous than another. But Emmett Till, a Chicago boy just turning fourteen, was kidnapped and murdered for allegedly flirting with a white woman. When his body was found, days later, it was determined that he had been shot in the head, one eye gouged out, and his head smashed in on one side All this was done before his neck was bound with barbwire, tied to a heavy cotton bale fan and dumped off the Tallahatchie Bridge into the River in Money, LeFlore County, Mississippi. The two men had taken his clothes and shoes and burned them. Emmett's nude body was found by fishermen. He was only identifiable by the ring that he wore that had belonged to his father.

Even though Till's body was severely damaged and badly decomposing and missing his left ear, his mother still courageously ordered an open casket funeral so the that whole world could see the brutality done to her son. The surviving pictures of Emmett Till in his casket bear no resemblance to Emmett Till as he really was. And it is sickening to think that, to this day, there is yet that same spirit of hate laden in the souls of some people. The U.S. criminal justice system now finds hate crimes to be federal offenses, and punishable by the death penalty, when proven. But that comes too late for too many like Emmett Till.

Jean Toomer was one of the most talented of the African American Harlem Renaissance writers. Critics agree that the best book to come out of that period was Toomer's "Cane." He studied in France, where he developed, and inserted into his writings, the art of introspective contemplation. He moved freely among European and American literary circles and fully immersed himself in a variety of experiences while coming to the idealistic conclusion that he could transcend race in America.

He was born Nathan Pinchback Toomer in Washington, D.C. on March 30, 1894. He was the son of Nathan Toomer and Nina Pinchback Toomer. Because of their racial backgrounds, Toomer and his parents could and often did pass for white. Until the age of eighteen, Toomer lived alternately as black and white. His father was a bi-racial, well-to-do planter. And his mother, also of mixed heritage, was the daughter of P.B.S. Pinchback, the first black governor of Reconstruction era Louisiana.

In 1895, Nathan abandoned his family, leaving Nina and her son to live with her somewhat tyrannical father. Pinchback agreed to support them only if Nina would change her son's name from Nathan to Eugene. Though his name was not legally altered, his grandparents began calling him Eugene Pinchback, but in school he was known as Eugene Pinchback Toomer. Even as a fatherless youth, Toomer grew up amid the wealth and luxury afforded by Washington's "blue veined" black aristocracy. They lived in a white neighborhood, but he attended the all black Garnet Elementary School.

When his mother remarried in 1896, the family moved to New Rochelle, New York where they lived in a white neighborhood and Toomer attended an all white school. In 1909, his mother died and Toomer returned to Washington and attended the all black Paul Lawrence Dunbar High School. After graduation in 1914, he renounced all racial classifications and sought to live only as an American, and not as a member of any racial group. During the next three years, he studied agriculture, literature, physical education and psychology at several different colleges and universities. But he never earned any degree.

As Toomer began to write, he changed and shortened his name, and gave to it a French pronunciation. Between 1918 and 1923, he wrote many short stories.

His writings were critically acclaimed and lauded in the literary circles of some of the best American writers. As with much of his work, his 1923 book, "Cane" delved deep into the despair and exploitation of African American life. And yet in 1930, he declined to be included in James Weldon Johnson's "Book of Negro Poetry" on the defense that he was not a "Negro." In two Toomer poems, the lyrical "First American," and the epic "Blue Meridian," much of his philosophy on race is explained and his democratic idealism is crystalline.

Toomer was married twice to white women, and had only one daughter who did not know that her father possessed any black blood. His intense good looks produced numerous illicit affairs with many women, including the wives of his closest friends. He was vilified in the press as a notorious womanizer for his amorous adventures with high society white women. In his quest for self-discovery, Toomer embraced the teachings of Russian mystic Georges Ivanovitch Gurdjieff. It was through the Gurdjieff teachings that Toomer was able to express and define his holistic identity. And he was able finally to reconcile his red, black, and white American racial heritage.

Jean Toomer was a prolific short story writer who lived in relative obscurity during the last thirty years of his life. He was a philosopher who defied any and all racial classifications, simply calling himself the "First American." He denied that he was a black man who appeared white. And his bloodline refused to be labeled anything other than "American." Toomer was never convinced that he was purely black or purely white. But he was convinced that he was the primogenitor of a "new American race." Even though he was largely misunderstood, he was a gentle man with courage of conviction and strength of character.

T he best-known African American woman of the 19th century was Sojourner Truth. She was born into slavery, but she reinvented herself, choosing a name which means "itinerant preacher" to match the new identity she fashioned. Sojourner Truth was a gospel preacher, a member of a strange religious commune, a reformer, an abolitionist, and a pioneering feminist. Truth was one of the great communicators of the age even though she never learned to read or write.

She was born Isabella Baumfree to slave parents, James and Elizabeth, in Ulster County, New York. She was one of their thirteen children and grew up speaking Dutch in this area near Kingston. Six different masters owned her before the age of thirty. From 1810 to 1827 she was owned by John Dumont, whom she forged a strong lifelong tie despite beatings and other abuses from Dumont and his wife. In 1827, New York granted legal emancipation to enslaved Africans, but Isabella's master refused to release her. She escaped but was caught and would have been returned had not a friend agreed to pay for her services for the remainder of the year.

Isabella later adopted his name, Van Wagenen, until, as she stated; *"And the Lord gave me Sojourner because I was to travel up and down the land showing the people their sins and being a sign unto them. Afterwards I told the Lord I wanted another name, cause everybody else had two names, and the Lord gave me Truth because I was to declare the truth to the people."*

During her very first year of freedom, Truth joined the Methodist Church in Kingston. In her newfound independence, she also discovered the courage to sue for the return of her son Peter, who had been sold into the South to avoid New York's emancipation law. In 1828 she went to New York City where she worked as a housekeeper to earn a living, and became involved in evangelical religious circles and activities, including frequent preaching at religious revivals.

In her religious zeal, Sojourner Truth came under the influence of a radical religious group, the New York Perfectionists, and of Robert Matthews, their charismatic leader and messianic figure. He called himself the "Prophet Matthias" and established a religious commune in Sing Sing, New York. Truth also spent time in the utopian colony in Northampton, Massachusetts in the

513

1840s and participated in various abolitionist and feminist causes. In 1850 she dictated her autobiography, *The Narrative of Sojourner Truth: A Northern Slave,* to abolitionist Olive Gilbert. Before long she was sharing antislavery speaking platforms with the likes of Frederick Douglass, Wendell Phillips, and William Lloyd Garrison.

In 1852, she gave her best-known speech at the Second National Women's Suffrage Convention in Akron, Ohio, using the rhythmic refrain *"Ain't I a Woman?"* Today, this speech ranks as one of the 19th century's most remarkable public addresses. Truth was six feet tall, with a dark complexion, very slender, and possessed a deep voice. She usually dressed in Quaker garb and a turban. In all her public speaking engagements she presented herself as a person of stature, always bearing herself like a queen, even though she was born a slave. During the Civil War, Truth fearlessly visited many Union army camps. By 1864, she had sufficient stature to get a White House audience with President Abraham Lincoln.

At the war's end, she worked with the freedmen in Washington, D.C. With the abolitionist cause no longer necessary, Truth embraced others. Besides women's suffrage, she was also involved in the Temperance League's campaigns against alcohol and tobacco, and a movement to obtain land grants in the West for the freed former slaves. Sojourner Truth died in 1883, in Battle Creek Michigan, where she settled sometime after the Civil War. She had led one of the most colorful and eventful lives of any American citizen. She lived through one of the most seminal moments in the nation's history. And she will always be remembered as one of the ones who gave definition to the era.

P erhaps the most recognizable name in African American history is that of Harriet Tubman. She fled slavery, adopted her mother's name, and guided other runaway slaves to freedom in the North and into Canada for more than ten years before the start of the American Civil War. During the war she served as a scout, spy, and nurse for the United States Army. In her later years she continued to work for the rights of blacks and women.

Tubman was born Araminta Ross circa 1820 to slaves Benjamin Ross and Harriet Greene. She was one of 11 Ross children on a plantation in Dorchester County Maryland. She was put to work at age 5, serving as a maid and a children's nurse before becoming a field hand when she was 12 years old. Early abuse from her master or possibly an overseer left her with permanent neurological damage. At age 13, one or the other struck her on the head with a heavy object that caused her to experience lethargy, stupors, and sudden blackouts throughout the rest of her life.

In 1844 Araminta Ross received permission from her owner to marry John Tubman, a free black. For the next five years she lived in a state of semi-slavery: legally she remained a slave, but her owner allowed her to live with her husband. She never had children. The death of Tubman's master in 1847, followed by the death of his son and heir two years later, made her status uncertain. Fearing that the family's slaves would be sold to settle the estate, she fled North to freedom.

In Pennsylvania, Harriet Tubman joined the Abolitionist cause, working to end slavery. She became a "conductor" on the Underground Railroad, a network of antislavery activists who helped slaves escape from the South. During the decade preceding the war, she made an estimated 19 expeditions to the South and personally escorted between 300-400 slaves to freedom in the North. Tubman faced great personal danger guiding slaves to freedom. The Fugitive Slave Law of 1850 made aiding and abetting runaway slaves a Federal crime punishable by death.

Southerners offered large cash rewards for Tubman's capture. She had a $40,000 bounty on her head. It was the largest bounty ever for any black person. This did not stop her from making treks into the South to free her family and hundreds of others. It did cause her to move to Ontario, Canada, a city that was the destination of many escaped slaves. But by the late 1850s, a number of Northern states passed personal liberty laws that protected the rights of fugitive slaves. It was only then that Tubman was able to purchase land and move to Auburn, New York, a center of antislavery sentiment.

Tubman never lost any of her charges and seemed to have an uncanny ability to find food and shelter during her hazardous missions. She carried a sleeping powder to stop babies from crying and always carried a gun to prevent her charges from backing out once the journey to freedom had begun. She constantly changed her route and her method of operation, though she almost always began her escapes on Saturday night. Owners did not make their slaves work on Sundays and might not miss them until Monday, after which time the runaways had already traveled a full day and a half. Also, newspapers reporting the escape would not be published until the beginning of the week, so by the time copies reached readers, Tubman and the fugitive slaves were likely to be close to their northern destination.

Abolitionist John Brown referred to Tubman as "the General" because her strategies were so workable and she was dedicated to the struggle for freedom. Among African Americans she came to be known as "Moses", after the Biblical hero who led the Hebrews out of slavery in Egypt. The Civil War was the only thing that stopped Tubman's freedom trail. By the end of the war she realized her mission was accomplished. Harriet Tubman was a 19th century reformer that saw the dawn of the 20th century. She lived long enough to see that her people were free but not long enough to see them equal.

The Nat Turner Rebellion was the most famous slave revolt in United States History. Only the Turner insurrection of 1831, in rural Virginia, got beyond the planning stage. Slave uprisings ranged in size from one or two isolated slaves in the countryside to literally thousands in urban areas. While some were undoubtedly reacting to cruel personal treatment, most had a grand and international vision of black liberation. Some slave revolts were quick and spontaneous, but most were the result of careful thought, intelligent planning, and inspired leadership. Behind them, and in the case of the Nat Turner Rebellion as well, was full knowledge of the American Revolution, its creed and its ideals.

What is known primarily about United States slave revolts is that there were many more of them, and they were much more important, than conventional history generally admits. Slaveholders played down slave rebellions for two reasons. First, rebellion contradicted their myth of contented and docile slaves. Secondly, the planter class, usually severely outnumbered by the slaves, was deeply fearful that news of any one insurrection might inspire others.

Nat Turner was born into slavery on October 2, 1800, on a plantation in Southampton County, Virginia. It was reported that Nat's mother, unable to bear the thought of surrendering her son to the slave system, had to be restrained from killing him at birth. Nat's parents and his grandmother instilled in him the need to resist slavery. While still a young child, Nat was overheard describing events that had happened before he was born. This, along with his keen intellect, and other signs marked him in the eyes of the other slaves as a "prophet" intended for some great purpose.

Turner grew up to be a deeply religious person; he studiously avoided mixing in the company of others, and wrapped himself in mystery. He devoted his free time to prayer and fasting, he recited long passages of scripture from the Bible, and he began to preach. Although he was largely self-taught, the son of his master did help him learn to read and write. He was seemingly a "model" slave. He worked in cotton and tobacco fields and was mechanically gifted. He had learned enough about science and mechanics to take charge of farm equipment. In 1821, Turner ran away from the overseer, returning after thirty days because of a vision in which the Holy Spirit told him to return to his "earthly" master. Following that, his popularity as a religious leader increased, convincing many others that he was a leader chosen by God.

Spirits that spoke only to him constantly beleaguered Turner. He saw and believed in "signs." Visions also regularly filled his head. And those visions were always associated with blood. He came to believe that he was God's executioner on earth, an insistent deathblow against the sins of white men and the evils of the slave system. In his visions, spirits told him that it was his God-given duty to struggle against the enslavement of his people. Turner believed God sanctioned him. He became known as a forceful preacher and exhorter who believed that God wanted him to free the slaves. And this conviction led him to plan the most famous slave insurrection in Antebellum America.

In 1825, after seeing strange lights in the sky, Turner prayed to understand the meaning of it. A second vision followed. While laboring in the fields, he saw great drops of blood cover the corn and hieroglyphic characters written in blood. In 1828, Turner had his third vision in which the Holy Spirit again appeared to him and said: *"The time is fast approaching when the first should be last and the last should be first."* He was told to wait for a sign in the heavens.

Then, in February 1831, there was an eclipse of the sun. Turner took this to be the sign that he had been promised. He confided his plan to the four slaves he trusted the most, Henry, Hark, Nelson, and Sam. They decided to stage an insurrection on July 4, and began planning a strategy. But they had to postpone action because Turner became ill. On August 13, there was an atmospheric anomaly in which the sun appeared bluish-green. This was Nat's final sign, and a week later, on August 21, he and his men met in the woods to eat dinner and make final plans.

The Turner insurrection began at midnight on August 21, 1831, when a small group of seven slaves began roaming the woods in rural Virginia. Turner started the uprising by killing his own master first. His small group then killed the rest of the household and set off down the road repeating the process at other farmhouses. They were joined by other slaves and began marauding the countryside. Slaves from neighboring plantations, swelling their number to seventy, joined in the rebellion.

For thirty-six hours, Turner's insurrection continued unabated and was responsible for the deaths of sixty white people. In his confession, Turner admitted that he had no clear plan to guide him. He mapped out no route for eluding pursuers. An advance guard of the most trusted fifteen or twenty of his men rode in front, hurtling toward their victims to elicit horror and prevent escape. Sometimes Turner didn't reach a plantation until the killing had already commenced. Even without a clear plan though, Turner had wanted to kill every slave owner and then storm the county courthouse.

Just three days into the insurrection, white militiamen brought the rebellion under control by killing or scattering Turner's men. By August 23, federal forces from Fort Monroe as well as detachments from the warships USS Warren and USS Natchez had been mobilized to join the Virginia militia. All slave rebellions caused fear in the South. But this fear took the form of a devastating retaliatory strike. Approximately three thousand white men fought to squash the insurrection, and hundreds of innocent blacks died in their answer to Nat Turner's rebellion.

In total, the state executed fifty-five people, banished many more, and acquitted only a few. The state reimbursed the slaveholders for the loss of their slave property. But in the hysterical climate that followed the Turner Rebellion, close to two hundred black people, many of whom had nothing to do with the rebellion, were murdered by white mobs. In addition, slaves as far away as North Carolina were accused of having a connection to the insurrection, and were subsequently tried and executed. Although most of the insurrectionists were rounded up and executed almost immediately, Nat Turner evaded capture for another six weeks. He was finally taken into custody on October 30. And on November 5, he was hastily tried in the Southampton County Court and sentenced to death by hanging.

During the last week of his life, as he awaited execution, Turner granted an interview that was later published as *"The Confession of Nat Turner."* In the interview, he expressed no feelings of guilt or remorse. Neither was there a plea for mercy. When the time came for him to die, Turner walked calmly to his execution. His intellect was still in tact, but the effects of slavery upon his life perverted his understanding of biblical prophecy. On November 11, 1831, Nat Turner was hanged. And with his death, he not only passed into history, but into folklore as well. It was said that Old Nat's body was further mutilated. It was skinned and drawn and quartered by four horses. Other legends say his body was buried in four different parts of Virginia. History, of course, cannot corroborate any of this.

But history has verified that in the aftermath of the Nat Turner Rebellion, southern states supported a decidedly repressive policy against black people, slave and free. Cruelties were meted out for the slightest infractions. The Black Church was especially eyed with suspicion, as it was viewed to be the principle agency in which slaves fomented and plotted insurrection. And free black people were even less tolerated in the South as they were seen as the slaves' chief allies in the abolition of slavery altogether. As the 177th anniversary of the death of Nat Turner approaches, his story remains one of the most riveting in the chronicles of United States history. And, perhaps, because of our modern-day enlightenment, the Nat Turner story is the most poignant and lamentable in the history of humanity.

T he Tuskegee Airmen were the African American fighter pilots during World War II who flew escort missions with other American bombers during the Italian campaign. The white bomber crews called them "Red Tailed Black Angels" because of the markings on their planes and because they never lost a single American bomber to German fighter planes while they were on escort duty. They trained under what has been called the "Tuskegee Experiment" by which the Army Air Corp program trained blacks to fly and maintain aircraft. All pilots, and air and ground support were a part of the program.

As airplanes and flying developed following World War I, African Americans began pressuring for the formation of training units for black airplane pilots. But it was not until 1939, as Europe prepared for World War II, did Congress pass Public Law 18, which called for a major expansion of American air forces. The bill provided for the establishment of training programs for blacks, but only in support services. But one program was authorized to train black pilots. The 66th Air Force Flying School was established at Motion Airfield in Tuskegee, Alabama. The site was chosen because the weather in Alabama permitted year round training and because the South was already heavily segregated.

Nearly 500 black men entered the Tuskegee program, which was run by white officers. Since those in charge, both expected and wanted the program to fail, blacks were expelled for the slightest reasons, resulting in a high dropout rate. The first class preparing to be pilots began training on August 25, 1941. The class consisted of 13 men, 5 of whom graduated in June 1942. That class included Benjamin O. Davis, Jr. who later rose to become the country's first three-star general of African descent.

Because the white officers at Tuskegee held negative stereotypes considering black pilots unfit for combat, and thus insisting on prolonging their practice time, the Tuskegee pilots emerged from the program especially well trained. The men who survived the rigorous training programs were an elite group, largely college educated and highly motivated. Eventually, nearly 1,000 black men won their wings as trained pilots and received commissions as Lieutenants in the United States Air Force. Another 1,000 graduated from the program with various support skills. When finally allowed to, 450 Tuskegee Airmen flew

521

combat missions during World War II.

Black pilots wanted to be integrated into the regular air force but most whites, civilian and military, did not want them to serve at all. A segregated unit was the only compromise. The War Department authorized the creation of an all-black flying unit, the 99th Pursuit Squadron, later renamed the 99th Fighter Squadron. It was specifically formed to accommodate the Tuskegee Airmen. Later the segregated black 332nd Fighter Group was formed, comprising four fighter squadrons, the 99th, 100th, 301st, and 302nd. Assigned largely to Italy, the Tuskegee Airmen compiled an impressive record. Their fighter planes escorted bombers on their way to Europe. In 1,578 missions escorting 15,552 sorties, the Tuskegee Airmen never lost a bomber.

The Tuskegee Airmen destroyed or damaged 409 enemy planes. They even sank a German destroyer, marking the first time a ship of that size and offensive capability had ever been sunk simply by aircraft machine-gun fire. By the war's end the Fighter Group had lost 66 men and been awarded 100 Distinguished Flying Crosses. On September 15, 1946, the government disbanded the fighter units and closed the Tuskegee Air Base. Partly because of the record of the Tuskegee Airmen, the War Department had reassessed its policies of segregation in the armed forces by 1948.

Today there are over forty chapters of Tuskegee Airmen, Incorporated nationwide. Staffed by retired Air Force personnel and others, they are now black and white, male and female. And they celebrate the legacy of the African American escort fighter pilots whose name and insignia they proudly bear.

C olonel Tye was the most feared and respected guerrilla commander of the American Revolution. He was one of the many enslaved Africans who escaped and fought for the British. There are many reasons why Colonel Tye is unfamiliar to most African Americans. Americans will never glorify anyone who fought for the British during the American Revolution, so he is not in any United States history books. And the British are still embarrassed by their loss of the American colonies, so they never speak of the American Revolution. For those two reasons alone, Colonel Tye was destined become an unsung hero.

He was born into slavery in the British Colony of New Jersey, and given the name Titus at birth. Tye grew to be one of four young men owned by John Corlies of Shrewsbury, in the eastern part of Monmouth County, New Jersey. Shrewsbury Quakers, under increasing pressure from their Philadelphia-influenced counterparts, slowly began to end slavery among themselves in the 1760s. Corlies did not follow the local practice of educating his slaves nor of freeing them on their twenty-first birthdays. And by 1775, he was one of the few remaining Quaker slaveholders in Monmouth County, New Jersey.

In November 1775, John Murray, Earl of Dunmore and the Royal Governor of the Virginia Colony, issued a proclamation offering freedom to all male slaves who would join the British forces. The idea was to disrupt production in the colonies. And the offer was good in all thirteen. The news of it spread quickly up and down the Atlantic coast, and blacks, tasting freedom, grew bold. One day after hearing of the offer, Titus fled his master and joined the flood of Monmouth County blacks seeking refuge with the British as soldiers, sailors, and general workers. He changed his name and gained tremendous notoriety three years later as "Captain Tye," the pride of Lord Dunmore's "Ethiopian Regiment."

While not formally commissioning black officers, the British army often bestowed titles out of respect, and Tye quickly earned their respect. In his first known military incursion, the June 1778 Battle of Monmouth, Tye captured a captain in the Monmouth militia. In July 1779, Tye's band launched a raid on Shrewsbury, and carried away clothing, furniture, horses, cattle, and two of the town's inhabitants. With his "motley crew" of black and white refugees known as "cowboys," Tye continued to attack and plunder patriot homes, using his knowledge of Monmouth County's swamps, rivers and inlets to strike suddenly and disappear quickly. These raids, often aimed at former masters and their friends, were a combination of banditry, reprisal, and commission. Tye and his men were well paid by the British, sometimes earning payments in gold.

During the harsh winter of 1779, Tye was among an elite group of twenty-four black Loyalists, known as the Black Brigade, who joined with the Queen's Rangers, a British guerrilla unit, to protect New York City and conduct raids for food and fuel. By 1780, Colonel Tye had become an important military force. Within one week in June, he led three actions in Monmouth County. On June 12 while the British attacked Washington's dwindling troops, Tye and his unit launched a daring attack on the home of Barnes Smock, capturing the militia leader and twelve of his men, destroying their cannons, depriving George Washington of needed reinforcements, and striking fear in the hearts of local patriots.

In a series of raids throughout the summer, Tye continued to debilitate and demoralize the patriot forces. In a single day, he and his men captured eight militiamen, plundered their homes and took them prisoner to New York. In September 1780, Tye led his final raid on the home of an American Patriot that the British had tried for years to capture. Tye held him down with musket fire until Loyalists forces flushed him out by setting a fire. During the battle, Tye was shot in the wrist. It was considered to be a minor injury until he was stricken with tetanus and died weeks later at the age of twenty-seven. Tye was a fierce fighter, not for any revolutionary cause, but in defense of his own personal liberty. He died a free son of Africa in North America, which would hold his kindred in subjection for another eighty-five years.

The Underground Railroad was an Antebellum, or pre-Civil War, network of abolitionists that illegally helped fugitive slaves reach safety in one of the Free states or Canada. Black and white abolitionists worked together to provide secret safe houses and clandestine escape routes during the slaves' perilous journeys to freedom. The network was begun in the 1780s under Quaker auspices, who at that time were the only religious sect that did not condone slavery.

As a metaphor, the term *underground railroad* first appeared in print in the early 1840s. After that, other railroad related terminology was added to the mix. The escaping slaves were called *passengers*. Those who guided the slaves were called *conductors*. Any home, church, or facility that provided shelter for the escapees was called a *station*. This jargon gives the impression that the Underground Railroad was a very organized and highly secretive organization but that is not altogether true. Slave escapes were more spontaneous than planned. The Underground Railroad was probably the worse kept secret of all secrets. The North used it as propaganda against the South to highlight the evils of slavery. And the South used it against the North to underscore their betrayal of fugitive slave laws.

The Underground Railroad acquired legendary fame after the 1830s because of people like conductor Harriet Tubman, a former slave. Tubman was called the "Moses" of her people because she made so many trips South to lead slaves to freedom. Levi Coffin, a Cincinnati Quaker, also ran a safe house out of southern Indiana, was another famous abolitionist. But there were countless unknown plantation slaves who must have aided other slaves who ventured along an escape route. Since history cannot record their deeds, their portion continues to be underestimated.

There is no way of knowing, and history may never reveal, just how many slaves traveled via the Underground Railroad. It has been estimated that between 60,000 and 100,000 slaves gained their freedom in this way. There were stations all along the Mason-Dixon Line leading to the free states. There were even terminals for quick escape to Canada. In addition, a great many slaves from Texas, Arkansas, Louisiana, and adjoining areas slipped across the border into Mexico. But there is little documentation at all about this route, and very few people are aware of it having existed.

There are interesting historical accounts of how blacks made there way North using ingenious methods. One of the most unusual was Henry Brown of Richmond, Virginia who had himself nailed into a crate and shipped via the Adams Express Company to Philadelphia. Carried by train, ferry, and wagon for twenty-six hours, the large box arrived at the antislavery office at 107 North Fifth Street. The package was opened, and to and to everyone's surprise, Brown emerged, reached out his hand and greeted the surprised recipients. He was forever after known as "Box" Brown.

Perhaps the most dramatic of all slave narratives concerning an escape is that of Ellen and William Craft, a slave couple from Georgia. She was fair-skinned enough to pass for white, and disguised herself as a young Southern gentleman. William Craft pretended to be her faithful black body servant. Claiming to have an abscessed tooth, she wore a scarf to hide her feminine face, and pretending to have a broken wrist, she wore her arm in a sling, since she couldn't write. They traveled by train and stayed in hotels in Charleston, Richmond, and Baltimore. After several dangerously close calls and almost being detected, they safely crossed out of a slave state and onto Philadelphia.

For every one reported brave and daring story of African Americans, history has lost a hundredfold others. Fugitive slave laws became more stringent until the outbreak of the Civil War. With the passing of fugitive slave laws, it became a Federal offence to aid or abet a runaway slave. The penalties were severe enough to include death by hanging for anyone caught participating in such a crime. This is the reason that slave escapes had to be more spontaneous than planned. The element of surprise was more helpful than a design when lives were being risked for the cause of abolition.

The Underground Railroad continued its activities in defiance of the law until the outbreak of the Civil War. Southerners were increasingly provoked by Abolitionists who systematically absconded with their slave-property. Antagonism over fugitives and the publicity accorded them were just one of the issues fueling the flames of sectional strife that eventually led to the American Civil War.

D enmark Vesey was a respected black businessman of Charleston, South Carolina, who planned a slave insurrection of immense proportions. He had planned this war of liberation for July 14, 1822, but his plans were revealed before the uprising could take place. What is so remarkable about Vesey is that at the time of the planned uprising, he had already gained his freedom and was making a good living as the owner of a carpentry shop. But his intense detestation of slavery made it impossible for him to stand still and do nothing while other blacks suffered enslavement.

Vesey is credited with organizing a massive conspiracy of a slave insurrection that involved thousands of enslaved and free blacks, possibly as many as 9,000 that lived in and around Charleston, South Carolina. With co-conspirators, "Gullah Jack" Prichard and Monday Gell, and with connections to as far away as Haiti, Vesey formulated a sophisticated plan to seize Charleston, liberate those men and women who were held in slavery, and leave the United States by ship.

Vesey planned and organized an uprising of city and plantation black slaves and freemen. The rebels would strike at midnight, blocking bridges and seizing all key points. The plan reportedly called for the rebels to attack guardhouses and arsenals, seize guns and ammunition, kill all whites, burn or otherwise destroy the city, and free all slaves. Vesey felt confident of their chances of taking the city. Every detail had been carefully worked out. Although the figures are in dispute, it is believed between 6,000 and 9,000 black people may have been involved.

He was born Telemanque either a free person in West Africa, or a slave on St. Thomas in the Virgin Islands. History cannot verify the date of his birth, but it is believed to be around 1767. In fact, not much is known about him before 1781 when he was purchased by the Danish captain of a slave ship. Captain Joseph Vesey brought him and 390 other slaves from St. Thomas to Saint-Dominque (Haiti). Telemanque was sold and put to work on a sugar plantation. On day when Telemanque fell to the ground in an epileptic seizure, his new owner returned him to Captain Vesey as "unsound goods" when the ship returned to port.

The captain renamed him Denmark and gave him his last name. Since

Denmark was not suited to heavy labor, he became the captain's personal slave for the next twenty years. As a personal slave he lived a comfortable life when compared to slaves who worked on plantations, but as a slave he was still subject to the whims of his master. For the first two years, Denmark had to witness the horrors of the slave trade as he sailed with the captain on his voyages between Africa and the West Indies. In 1783 the captain gave up the slave trade and settled in Charleston. Denmark had become educated through his travels and remarkable well versed in abolitionism. Having spent time in Saint-Domingue, he followed the events there with interest in 1791 when a successful slave insurrection created the new nation of Haiti whose president was black.

In 1800 Denmark won a street lottery prize of $1,500. He purchased his freedom with $600 and used the rest to open a carpentry shop in Charleston. Vesey proved to be a highly skilled artisan, and his business did so well that he grew wealthy and became a respected member of the black community. In 1816, he and other free blacks established an African Methodist Episcopal (AME) Church in Charleston. By 1820, the church had 3,000 members and Vesey was an elder with a growing family. He used the pulpit to sow the seeds of rebellion. He urged his congregation to break free from slavery and quoted verses from the Bible to validate his argument.

Vesey was not content with his relatively successful life. He possessed a profound hatred for slavery and slaveholders. He became well versed in all the antislavery arguments and spoke out against the abuse and exploitation of his people. He believed in equality for everyone and vowed not to rest until his people were free. He became a political provocateur, agitating and moving slaves to resist their enslavement. He gained the respect from slaves who looked to him for guidance.

Twice the white power structure closed the church particularly because of Vesey's inflammatory rhetoric. The entire congregation responded with anger. Closing the church intensified their desire to fight slavery. Vesey became an itinerate preacher, traveling from plantation to plantation spreading his message. Blacks began to see him as their liberator, and he had no difficulty gathering recruits for his intended rebellion.

As the conspiracy unfolded on May 30, 1822, a slave named George Wilson, informed his master of a planned insurrection that involved thousands of free and enslaved blacks who lived in and around the Charleston area. Charleston authorities subsequently uncovered evidence of the most extensive slave insurrection in American history. The city's closing of the African Methodist Church, which boasted of a membership of over 3,000, provided the catalyst for the revolt. Among Vesey's co-conspirators was "Gullah Jack" Pritchard, an African priest from Mozambique; Monday Gell, who had written two letters to the black president of Haiti enlisting support for the insurrection; Ned and Rolla Bennett, slaves of the governor of South Carolina; and Peter Poyas, the carpenter of a slave ship.

When it was known to Vesey that city officials were put on alert, he responded by pushing the date of the uprising forward to June 16. But no sooner had he informed his followers, the new date was also betrayed. Charleston filled with soldiers, with patrols in the streets and guards at every bridge. When Vesey realized that nothing could be done, he burned all lists of names and all correspondences, and sent his followers away. But names had been leaked and many people knew who the leaders were. Charleston officials moved stealthily to arrest and question the leaders. During the next few weeks, hundreds were rounded up, including Vesey, who had evaded authorities but was captured after a two-day search.

During the lengthy trial after the insurrection had been thwarted, the intricate plans of the massive uprising emerged in court testimony. If Vesey's plan were to be carried out as it had been in Haiti every white person would have to be killed. What was really shocking to whites was that blacks, slave or not, who were approached about the uprising gave it their blessing and cooperation, even though it meant killing the families for which they had been working. Following trial, Vesey and thirty-six others were hanged. On the day of Vesey's execution, state militia and federal troops had to be called out to contain a demonstration by black supporters. Despite arrests and beatings, many blacks defied authorities by wearing mourning black as they witnessed the execution of their leader.

As a result of the Vesey Conspiracy, slave codes were stiffened and free blacks were discouraged from living in South Carolina, altogether. When the mayor of Charleston published the report of the Vesey conspiracy he arrogantly editorialized: *"there is nothing they [blacks] are bad enough to do, that we [whites] are not powerful enough to punish."* But there was vindication for this when one of the first black regiments formed, the Fifty-Fourth Massachusetts Infantry, invoked the name of "Vesey" as their battle cry when they courageously stormed the fortified walls of Fort Wagner, South Carolina during one of the bloodiest battles of the Civil War.

What was so remarkable about Denmark Vesey's story was the fact that he was a free man who could not peacefully co-exist with slavery. He was also dissatisfied with his second-class status as a freedman and determined to help relieve the far more oppressive condition of involuntary servitude for his family and friends. It is believed that he had several children by slave women and that his own children were also enslaved. Denmark Vesey became a symbol in the fight to end slavery in America. Like so many others who lost their lives in the antislavery battle, his memory grew to be an inspiration for the abolitionist movement that came later.

Voodoo is a religion with roots in West Africa. It became an admixture of Christianity and some of the ancient deities of Africa. The belief system is polytheistic and includes the use of demons and zombies, the "living dead." Its practices include the use of rituals, charms, herbs, and potions to control reality and events. Spirit possession is central to Voodoo. The spirits have two names, a Catholic saint's name and an African name. Under the control of the spirits, the devotee becomes the "horse" as he allows the spirits to use his body and voice. Although Voodoo relies on a system of magic, it is not its fundamental aspect.

In Africa it was used to unite groups to fight against a common enemy, and during enslavement in North America it became a force to organize, rally, and strengthen those rebelling against enslavement. Its support for rebellion was the compelling reason for slave owners to suppress the meetings and services associated with Voodoo. With the outlawing of the religious aspect, the magic aspect, with its use of charms and herbal rituals and the creation of Voodoo objects, became more pronounced.

The word Voodoo, which is Dahomean in origin and means spirit or deity, is derived from the word Vodou in the Fon and Ewe languages. The word and the religious system arrived in North American when the first twenty Africans arrived in Jamestown, Virginia in 1619 aboard a Dutch man-of-war. The number of Voodoo worshipers increased as more Africans arrived first as indentured servants, and later as slaves directly from Africa or via the West Indies, where African slavery was introduced as early as 1504.

With the influx of more slaves into the Americas, Voodoo became deeply entrenched in the Caribbean, and to a certain extent, in the British North American colonies and later in the United States. Although there is no record of the introduction of Voodoo worship in Louisiana, it is a reasonable certainty that New Orleans was the birthplace of Voodoo in North America. The Louisiana colony received fresh cargoes of slaves directly from Africa as well as seasoned slaves from the French colonies of Martinique, Guadeloupe, and Santo Domingo (Haiti). All three colonies were known to be home to major cults of Voodooism.

The Haitian Revolution of 1791 reinforced Voodoo in and around New

Orleans as hundreds of Haitian refugees, many of which were Voodoo cult leaders and adherents, settled in the area. The most renowned and earliest Voodoo leaders in New Orleans came either directly from Africa or by way of the West Indies. The priests and priestesses are commonly called "voodoos," and throughout the southern United States the term is also used as a verb. To "voodoo" someone means to punish by magical means. Even today, Voodoo (a.k.a. "hoodoo"), as well as "conjure," "root work," and "witchcraft," are terms used to refer to a diverse collection of traditional practices among descendants of African slaves in the Americas.

With the intense Christianization of the slaves throughout the eighteenth and nineteenth centuries, Voodoo came to be viewed with ambivalence by blacks. Polytheism has always presented concerns to the one-God belief system of Christianity. Although Voodoo is not widely practiced in the United States in the African American community today, its footprint can be seen in the sizable Haitian-American communities of New York City, Miami, and New Orleans. It is still very prevalent among blacks in Haiti, Jamaica and other parts of the Caribbean, and in Brazil.

It is estimated that the Trans-Atlantic Slave Trade displaced countless millions of Africans. It was the largest forced migration of people in the history of the world, uprooting societies, traditional religious practices, and belief and value systems. We may never fully understand how Voodoo benefited traditional African culture. But History does understand that Voodoo became a perversion as it was forced to blend with other worldviews and value systems, and then adapt itself to the horrors of slavery in the Americas.

T he Voting Rights Act, adopted initially in 1965 and extended in 1970, 1975, 1982, and 2007, is generally considered to be the most successful piece of civil rights legislation ever adopted by the United States Congress. The Act codifies and effectuates the 1870 Fifteenth Amendment's permanent guarantee that, *in this country, no person shall be denied the right to vote because of race or color.* In addition, the Voting Rights Act of 1965 contains several special provisions that impose even more stringent requirements in certain jurisdictions throughout the nation.

Adopted at a time when African Americans were substantially disenfranchised in many Southern states, the Voting Rights Act employed measures to restore the right to vote and intruded in matters previously reserved to the individual states. *Section Four* of the Act ended the use of literacy requirements for voting in the Southern states of Alabama, Georgia, Louisiana, Mississippi, South Carolina, Virginia, and several counties in North Carolina. In these states, voter registration and voter turnout in the 1964 presidential election was less that 50% of the voting-age population.

Under *Section Five* of the Act, no voting changes were legally enforceable in the above jurisdictions until approved either by a three-judge court in the District of Columbia or by the Attorney General of the United States. Other sections of the Act authorized the Attorney General to appoint the federal voting examiners who could be sent into the covered jurisdictions to ensure that legally qualified persons were free to register for federal, state, and local elections, or to assign federal observers to oversee the conduct of the elections. It is *Section Five* that comes up for review, renewal, and possible expansion at certain intervals of time. It is this periodic review of *Section Five* that has caused urban legends to arise that African Americans will not be allowed to vote after a specified time.

Those rumors stating that the Voting Rights Act of 1965 will expire are patently untrue. The basic provision of the Voting Rights Act which prevents discrimination in voting is a permanent right which will never expire. The special provisions of the Act which allow the United States Attorney General to intervene in areas in which there is a disparity between the numbers and qualifications of voters did, however, come up for review in the year 2007. Originally intended to be of limited duration, these provisions were extended in 1970, 1975, and 1982. These special provisions were again reviewed in 2007, and again extended. The other provisions which require certain states to obtain pre-clearance or approval of the U. S. Attorney General before making any changes to their voting laws were also reviewed and extended in 2007.

Surely the recent historic 2008 Primary Elections have put all such rumors to rest. With Barack Obama being the first African American to win the Democratic Party's nomination for President, unfounded rumors and urban legends should vanish away for awhile, at least. But just in case they do not, every citizen should know the facts. The most easily verifiable fact comes from the United States Justice Department: Both the Fifteenth Amendment to the United States Constitution and the Voting Rights Act of 1965 guarantee that no person can be prohibited from voting because of race or color. And that guarantee is without expiration.

In passing the Voting Rights Act, Congress determined that such a far-reaching statute was necessary in response to compelling evidence of continued interference with attempts by African American citizens to exercise their right to vote all over the South. As the United States Supreme Court stated in its 1966 decision upholding the constitutionality of the Act, *"the previous case-by-case litigation has been inadequate to combat the widespread, persistent discrimination in voting."* After enduring ninety-five years of systematic resistance to the Fifteenth Amendment, Congress acted wisely in shifting the advantage from the discriminatory practices of the states to the aid of African Americans who were victimized by illegal "Jim Crow" Laws.

At the time that the Voting Rights Act was adopted, only one-third of all African Americans of voting age were on the registration rolls in the specially covered states, while twice that many whites were registered. To date, black voter registration rates are approaching parity with that of whites in many areas. Not very far behind African Americans are Hispanic voters in the previously mentioned jurisdictions that were added to the list of those specifically covered by the Act in 1975. An added incentive to the enforcement of the Act has been the increased opportunity of Black and Hispanic voters to elect representatives of their choice, thereby providing a vehicle for challenging discriminatory election methods such as at-large elections, racially gerrymandering districting plans, and run-off requirements that may dilute minority voting strength.

The 1965 Voting Rights Act was passed to ensure the principle of universal adult suffrage for the first time in American history. The Act dealt a final blow to such discriminatory practices as the use of literacy tests, property taxes, or poll taxes, as conditions for voter qualification. The Act also provided for affirmative intervention by the federal government to increase voter registration in areas of low voter turnout. Blacks were virtually excluded from all public offices in the South in 1965. But now they are substantially represented in the state legislatures and local governing bodies throughout the region. It behooves all African Americans to vote, not because it is our right, but because it is our duty to demonstrate to the next generation that we affirm the struggle of all previous generations.

A   lice Walker is one of the best known of the contemporary African American writers. She is a poet, short story writer, essayist, biographer, and political and civil rights activist. Her focus is mostly on women of color as they relate to their respective cultures. Her critically acclaimed novel, *The Color Purple* (1982), was the first by an African American woman to win a Pulitzer Prize. And the movie was nominated for several Academy Awards.

Alice Malsenoir Walker was born in Eatonton, Georgia, February 9, 1944. She was the youngest of eight children born to sharecroppers Willie Lee Walker and Minnie Grant Walker. After high school graduation, Walker studied at Spelman College in Atlanta from 1961 to 1963, but finished her undergraduate studies at Sarah Lawrence College in Bronxville, New York in 1965. After graduating from Sarah Lawrence, she returned to the South, helping with voter registration drives in Georgia and participating in campaigns for welfare rights and children's programs in Mississippi.

In 1967 Walker married Melvyn Leventhal, a Jewish civil rights attorney, and although interracial marriage was illegal in Mississippi at that time, she and Leventhal lived there and had a daughter, Rebecca. She and Leventhal worked together to desegregate Mississippi schools. Walker served as a writer in residence and teacher of Black Studies at two Mississippi colleges: Jackson State College (1968-69) and Tougaloo College (1970-71). In the North, she lectured on literature at Wellesley College in Wellesley, Massachusetts, and at the University of Massachusetts in Boston (1972-73). After her divorce in 1976, she moved to New York City and then, in 1979, to San Francisco, where she still lives and writes.

Walker has received many grants and fellowships, including a Guggenheim Fellowship, the Lillian Smith Award, American Book Award, and the Richard and Hinda Rosenthal Foundation Award. Her fiction, nonfiction, and poetry works include: *In Love and Trouble: Stories of Black Women* (1973); *In Search of Our Mothers' Gardens: Womanist Prose* (1983); *Horses Make a Landscape Look More Beautiful* (1984); *The Temple of My Familiar* (1989); *Her Blue Body Everything We Know: Earthling Poems, 1965-1990 Complete* (1991); and *The Same River Twice: Honoring the Difficult:...*(1996).

Walker is an original thinker as well as a prolific writer. She alone is a "womanist" while the rest are merely "feminists." Her definition of a womanist is of one "committed to the survival and wholeness of an entire people, male and female." This different slant on feminism has given her great impact on contemporary literature and the lives of her readers. Her coin of the term womanist also differentiates black feminists from white ones. By her writings, she has committed to exploring the lives of black women in the United States and abroad.

One of Walker's most important achievements in her quest to reconnect black women with their heritage was to rescue the neglected writings of another southern literary figure, Zora Neale Hurston. In her writings, Walker repeatedly makes the point that black women can survive and flourish in spite of racism and sexism "by armoring themselves with the knowledge of the heroic lives of their foremothers." Walker still possesses the spirit of the "60s" and has enlarged her activism for civil rights and women's rights in the United States to those same issues in other countries.

In 1995 Walker participated in an effort to pressure Nigeria's military government to restore democracy. She vehemently denounces and continues to write against the barbaric custom of female circumcision practiced against women in certain African, Asian, and central European cultures. Alice Walker has played a major role in giving a long-overdue voice to women of color everywhere. When celebrating February as National African American History Month, or March as National Women's History Month, it is always fitting to showcase this powerful and highly motivated "Womanist."

MADAME C.J. WALKER (1867-1919)

Madam Walker was born Sarah Breedlove to former slaves on a plantation in the poverty ridden Louisiana Delta. She was orphaned at age seven when both parents died. She and her older sister survived by working in the cotton fields around Vicksburg, Mississippi. At age fourteen she married Moses McWilliams to escape the abuse and cruelty from her brother-in-law. Her only daughter, Lelia was born in 1885. When her husband died two years later, she joined relatives in St. Louis, saving enough money from her work as a washerwoman to educate her daughter.

At the turn of the century, Sarah began to suffer from a stress, diet, and hygiene related scalp ailment known as alopecia, which caused her to lose her hair. She tried many products, including those of Poro founder, Annie Malone, another black woman entrepreneur. In 1905 Sarah moved to Denver as a Poro sales agent and then married an old friend and newspaperman, Charles Joseph Walker.

Once married, Sarah and her husband went into business together. She took the title of "Madam," like French beauty experts as she spread her hair-care gospel. Using her husband's initials, Sarah became "Madam C.J. Walker." Her new name gave her enterprise a sense of flair, but her business planning made her a success. Although lacking any formal training, she was arguably the most astute marketing expert of her day. The Walkers first promoted and sold with great success, *Madam C.J. Walker's Wonderful Hair Grower*, a scalp conditioning formula she claimed came to her in a dream.

Madam Walker traveled for a year and a half throughout the heavily black South and Southeast, selling her products door to door, demonstrating her scalp treatments in churches and lodges, and devising sales and marketing strategies. She even traveled to Central America and the Caribbean to expand her business. In 1908, she moved her base to Pittsburgh where she opened Lelia College to train Walker "hair culturists." By early 1910, Madam Walker had settled in Indianapolis, then the nation's largest inland manufacturing center, where she built a factory, hair and manicure salon and another training school.

Madam Walker's friendships with churchwomen and clubwomen exposed her to a new way of viewing the world. She came to have a great philanthropic spirit. Less than a year after her arrival in Indianapolis, she gained national attention by donating $1,000 to the building fund of the "colored" YMCA. She was also a strong supporter of the Bethel A.M.E. Church that she attended while in Indianapolis. She donated handsomely to the NAACP's anti-lynching movement. And she also encouraged political and social activism among her sales and staff workers.

Madam Walker maintained Townhouses in Indianapolis and New York City before moving to a mansion in Irvington-on-Hudson, New York in 1916. She left the daily operations of *The Madam C.J. Walker Manufacturing Company* in Indianapolis to F.B. Ransom, her attorney and general manager. By the time of her death at her estate, *Villa Lewaro*, she had helped to define the role of the 20th century, self-made American businesswoman; established herself as a pioneer of the modern black hair-care and cosmetics industry; and set standards in the African American community for corporate and community giving. More than anything else, Madam Walker was a shinning example of what African Americans can accomplish when the African communitarian principles of self-help and mutual assistance are applied throughout their communities.

Madam C.J. Walker's own words to the National Negro Business League Convention in 1912 convey her life's accomplishments quite succinctly: *"I am a woman who came from the cotton fields of the South. From there I was promoted to the washtub. From there I was promoted to the cook kitchen. And from there I promoted myself into the business of manufacturing hair goods and preparations...I have built my own factory on my own ground."* Madam also built her own version of the American Dream on her own terms.

D avid Walker was born in Wilmington, North Carolina on September 28, 1785. He was the son of a slave father and a freeborn black woman. In adulthood, one of his contemporaries described Walker's personal appearance as "pre-possessing, being six feet in height, slender, and well proportioned; his hair – loose, his complexion – dark." His imposing looks and his articulate, intolerance of slavery characterized David Walker as one the most dynamic of the Abolitionists.

Since his mother was free, David was also free. Although details of his life in the South are vague, it is known that in the 1820s he devoted much time to travel, witnessing firsthand the sorrow wrought by slavery. From various plantations he saw a son forced to whip his naked mother until she died, a man forced to whip his pregnant wife until the child was lost. Such atrocities forced Walker to conclude: *"If I remain in this bloody land, I will not live long."* In 1825, Walker settled in Boston. He opened a clothing store on Brattle Street where he sold new and second-hand clothes. White clothing dealers tried to force him out of business, he and two other clothing dealers were subjected to police harassment. They were indicted and tried for receiving stolen goods. Walker and one of the others were acquitted, and charges against the third were dropped.

Walker became deeply involved in the concerns of the black community in Boston, working to improve education for black children, establish black churches, and increase employment opportunities for blacks. He became a leader in the Massachusetts General Colored Association, an organization founded in 1826 to abolish slavery and improve racial conditions for blacks. He spoke before that assembly, stressing that a cohesive, singularly focused community was the first step in the quest for freedom. *"Ought we not to form ourselves into a general body to protect, aid, and assist each other to the utmost of our power?"* He was also Boston's agent and occasional contributor to the newspaper, *Freedom's Journal*.

By 1828, Walker had defined his purpose. He was destined to break through the surface of the abolitionist movement toward a more energized radicalism. In 1829 Walker published a fiery, seventy-six page pamphlet entitled *Appeal to the Colored Citizens of the World*. At that time, few dared oppose the institution of slavery with the force David Walker exhibited in his *Appeal*. It was the most powerful piece of anti-slavery literature of its time. The most amazing thing about the *Appeal* was its Pan-African scope. It was addressed to Africans of the Diaspora. That had not been done before Walker's time. *The Appeal* was divided into four articles. The first dealt with slavery and its evil consequences; the second dealt with black's lack of education; the third addressed the upholding of the slave system by the Christian ministry; and the fourth concerned a plan to colonize African Americans back to Africa.

Response to Walker's *Appeal* was immediate, volatile, and intense. The South posted rewards of $1,000 dead or $10,000 alive for Walker. In response to the *Appeal* Georgia and South Carolina passed laws against incendiary publications. Georgia made the circulation of such documents a capital offense. Walker's writings caused Northern Abolitionists to fear retaliation against their cause from the powerful slaveholding South. Southern reaction was so strong against Walker that his friends urged him to go to Canada but he insisted on remaining in Boston.

The *Appeal* was in its third printing in 1830 when David Walker was found dead outside his shop. In prophetic rhetoric expressing the same sentiment as Dr. Martin Luther King in his "Mountaintop" speech, Walker emphatically stated: *"I count my life not dear to me, but I am ready to be offered at any moment. For what is the use of living, when in fact I am dead."* If you have ever wondered or even considered the words of orators like Martin Luther King and Malcolm X, and asked: "How did they think of that?" I must direct you to 19th century America and the profound words in *David Walker's Appeal*. The astute minds of King and Malcolm, who understood history, would have read with avarice the words of David Walker.

B efore Jackie Robinson entered Major League Baseball in 1947, there was Fleet Walker, an African American who played professional baseball in nineteenth century America. Walker excelled as a college player at Oberlin College in Ohio before playing professionally from 1883 until 1889.

He was born Moses Fleetwood Walker on October 7, 1857 in Mt. Pleasant, Ohio, an important stop on the Underground Railroad. He was the fifth child of Moses W. Walker, a cooper and blacksmith, and Caroline Walker, a midwife. During Fleet's childhood, the family moved to Steubenville, where his father began to study medicine. The family grew in wealth and prominence as his father practiced medicine and later became a minister. Dr. Walker was one of the most highly regarded black professionals in the state.

The Walker children were educated in black schools until the Steubenville school system integrated. Fleet attended Steubenville High School, taking college preparatory classes. He enrolled in Oberlin College in 1878. His brother, Weldy Wilberforce Walker, followed him in 1881. Oberlin was nationally recognized for its liberal admission policies regarding blacks and women. Fleet and Weldy both excelled academically and in sports. Like Fleet, Weldy also gained the reputation as a great baseball player.

In order to earn money to pay for Law School at the University of Michigan, Fleet began playing professionally with the Toledo Blue Stockings in 1883. In 1884, the Blue Stockings joined the Major League sanctioned American Association, making Fleet the first African American in the Major Leagues. Several other blacks, including Fleet's brother, Weldy, played League baseball during this time. But there was a mounting sentiment, soon to become fact, that Major League baseball should be open only to white players. By 1889, Fleet was the only remaining black player in the Major Leagues. And there began the tacit agreement among owners and player that no blacks would enter Major League Baseball again. This form of institutional racism would last until 1947.

After playing for the Blue Stockings, Fleet played for other league teams in Cleveland, Newark, and Syracuse. Of course there were many hardships to face because of his race. When the team traveled, accommodations would be denied to Fleet because of Jim Crow Laws. There were racial slurs from other players, racist chants from some spectators, and ill treatment from team managers. As the team catcher, his teammates often refused to accept his signals. Crowds of spectators would jeer at the "nigger." Often managers would not protest or even insist on game forfeiture when the other teams refused to play with Fleet in the lineup. But mostly, people appreciated his superb skills as a catcher and his hitting style at bat. It was assured that when Fleet was in the lineup, his team would win the game.

Following his career in the Major Leagues, Fleet played in exhibition games with other black players against white teams. When he stopped playing the game, he worked as a postal clerk, hotel operator, and he owned an opera house. He and Weldy also published *The Equator*, a newspaper dedicated to African American causes and issues. In 1908, embittered but not broken, he published a book, *Our Home Colony*, which called for black emigration back to Africa as the only alternative to racial prejudice.

Toward the end of his life, and after the death of his first wife, Fleet battled unsuccessfully with alcohol addiction. He was acquitted of second-degree murder following an intrusion into his home by a burglar. He participated in his own defense although he never obtained his law degree. Of all the black Major League baseball players, Fleet Walker suffered the most, was damaged the worse, and paid the highest price for his celebrity. And yet, he is practically unspoken of by today's black baseball players or baseball enthusiasts anywhere. Perhaps the poet who composed the lines: *What happens to a dream deferred? / Does it dry up / Like a raisin in the sun? / Or does it fester like a sore – / And then run?* was indeed singing the praises of this unsung baseball hero, Moses Fleetwood Walker.

MAGGIE LENA WALKER (1867-1934)

Maggie Lena Walker was an African American who became the nation's first woman bank president. She was the organizer and founder of the St. Luke Bank and Trust Company of Richmond, Virginia. She came from an impoverished background, but her personal wealth grew tremendously over the course of her life. Maggie was born to William Mitchell and Elizabeth Draper, servants of the Van Lew family. Elizabeth Van Lew had been a Union spy and harbored Union soldiers after they escaped from Confederate prisons in Richmond. The Van Lew estate, with its mansion, various out buildings, extensive grounds, and garden had also been a station on the Underground Railroad.

Walker was a gifted student who finished high school at the head of her class and began a teaching career at age sixteen. Later she took a position as the executive secretary of the Independent Order of St. Luke Society. It was a black self-help organization. The purpose of the Order was to assist sick and aged members, and to provide funeral and burial services. In the late 1800s, insurance policies for African Americans were unheard of. Without any previous training, Walker achieved immediate success for the Order, maintaining complete and accurate membership records. Within ten year she was promoted to grand secretary-treasurer, a position she held for thirty-five years.

In 1890 Maggie married Arstead Walker, a wealthy businessman of her church. The couple had two sons, Russell (1895) and Melvin (1897). But Walker remained a career-minded woman, increasing her household staff to include a nurse and tutor for her children. She devoted the majority of her time to the Order of St. Luke. She continued to move up in rank, establishing new services as she advanced. In 1895 she formed the Juvenile Branch of the Order, drafting its governing by-laws. In 1903 Walker instigated an important move, changing the name of the St. Luke Penny Savings Bank to the St. Luke Bank and Trust Company. During the Great Depression St. Luke absorbed other black banks to become the Consolidated Bank and Trust Company with Walker as chairman of the board.

Walker conceived the notion of teaching members how to save and invest their money. From this idea grew her plan for founding the St. Luke Penny Savings Bank, of which she became president. When she assumed the position of secretary-treasurer in 1899, St. Luke had about 3,400 members, with no reserved funds or property, and an inadequate staff. By 1924, Walker had increased the membership to 100,000, acquired a $100,000 office building, maintained a cash reserve of $70,000, and had hired 55 full-time staff employees with 145 field workers. Also, the membership could follow the course of her progress by reading the *St. Luke Herald* newspaper another venture she launched.

Walker organized and stood at the helm of many civic organizations like the St. Luke Educational Fund to help black children get an education. She was the organizer and president of the Council of Colored Women. She was a trustee of the National Training School in Washington, D.C. and a national director of the NAACP. She was a board member of the National Urban League and an appointee of various governors of Virginia. She was also the instigator for the establishment of a home for delinquent girls in Richmond. She organized 1,400 women into a council that made the down payment of $5,000 to purchase land for the institution. In 1934 black-owned businesses and black clubwomen paid her a great tribute by declaring the month of October to be "Maggie L. Walker Month."

Walker made giant strides in her lifetime. She was a solid citizen respected by blacks and whites alike. Her sense of community and her forward thinking was unsurpassed in her lifetime. She was an astute businesswoman, a shrewd financier, an esteemed clubwoman, a perceptive newspaper founder, a humble community servant, and one of the first modern feminist thinkers. Maggie Lena Walker was a nineteenth century woman with a twenty-first century vision.

W yatt T. Walker is an African American minister, author, and social activist. He came to national prominence as the lead strategist for the Southern Christian Leadership Conference 1960-1964. In many photographs from the 1960s, he was the quiet young man in the black horn rim glasses, standing close to Dr. Martin Luther King, Jr.

He was born Wyatt Tee Walker on August 16, 1929, in Brockton, Massachusetts. As a New Jersey high school student in the 1940s, he joined the Young Communist League. One of his high school papers was a treatise on the feasibility of a Soviet-style economy in the United States. His college advisors, however, steered him away from politics into the ministry. Walker obtained a B.S. from Virginia Union University, graduating magna cum laude in 1950 and received his M. Div. summa cum laude in 1953.

Walker's first pastorate was at the Gillfield Baptist Church in Petersburg, Virginia. Organized in 1797, it was the regional center for the black aristocracy, much like Dexter Avenue Baptist Church in Montgomery, Alabama. Until shortly before Walker's arrival in 1952, the Gillfield congregation had segregated itself by skin color, with the lighter blacks sitting on one side and the darker ones on the other. Under the tutelage of renowned pastor, Vernon Johns, Walker preached against such class division.

Walker began his fifty-year career in civil rights activism in Virginia where he developed a record as a force in the local civil rights movement. He simultaneously served as President of the Petersburg Branch of the NAACP, state director of CORE, and President of the Petersburg Improvement Association (PIA). Since PIA was an early affiliate of SCLC, and King being drawn to the kind of energy that Walker possessed, it did not take long for Walker to be noticed. King appointed him the first full-time Executive Director of the fledgling SCLC. But King would have to wait for Walker to finish his jail sentence in Petersburg for attempting to integrate the Petersburg Library. And complications of salary and pulpit arrangements further delayed Walker's entrance into SCLC.

When Walker did arrive at SCLC, he proved to be an excellent tactician, authoring many protest strategies, including the Birmingham campaign of 1963. He had a passion for nonviolent direct action. His style was flamboyant, and the ways he thought of to violate segregation laws was inspiring. Walker introduced monthly budget control sheets, a stable secretarial service, 501(c)(4) tax status, established personnel procedures, systematic press releases and press relations, and organization discipline on the staff level. He also increased philanthropic donations by courting northern liberal organization and the black middle class. The SCLC income more than doubled in the first year of his administration. In addition to supervising the SCLC staff, Walker usually traveled with King and Ralph Abernathy. He also organized King's speaking engagements to maximize effective fund-raising.

After building SCLC into a national civil rights powerhouse, Walker relocated to New York City in 1964 to develop the Negro Heritage Library, the first series of books on black life and history. His seminal work "Somebody's Calling My Name: Black Sacred Music and Social Change" (1979) is considered a classic, and his three-volume "Spirits That Dwell in Deep Woods," a pioneer work in the field of ethnomusicology. He is considered to be the foremost authority on black spirituals. He has studied abroad in Nigeria and Ghana, as well as in the U.S., obtaining many advanced and honorary degrees.

Walker returned to the pastorate in 1967 as Senior Pastor of Canaan Baptist Church of Christ in Harlem where he continues to lead the congregation. He is a key figure in the physical renaissance of Harlem and one of the two largest developers of affordable housing in NYC. He is the current Chairman of the Board of the National Action Network, headed by the Rev. Al Sharpton. Walker is also Dean of the Doctoral Studies Program of United Theological Seminary in Dayton, Ohio. Wyatt Tee Walker is looked upon as the last of a dying breed that could, and often did, harness the power of African American protest.

He was born Booker Taliaferro, a slave on a plantation in rural Franklin County, Virginia. In his autobiography, *Up From Slavery*, tongue in cheek Washington says: *"I am not quite sure of the exact place or exact date of my birth, but at any rate I suspect I must have been born somewhere and at some time."* His mother, Jane, was the cook; his father was a white man whose identity he never knew. Booker worked as a house servant until he and his family were liberated by Union troops near the end of the Civil War. Following the war, the family moved to Malden, West Virginia, where they joined Washington Ferguson, also a former slave, whom Jane had married during the war.

To help support the family Booker worked first in a salt furnace, then in coal mines, and later as a houseboy in the home of Gen. Lewis Ruffner, who owned the mines. He came under the influence of Viola Ruffner, the general's wife, who taught him respect for cleanliness, efficiency, and order. During this time, and despite opposition from his stepfather, Booker started to attend a school for blacks while continuing to work. At school, for reasons still debated by historians, he gave himself the last name "Washington." In his autobiography he was reminiscent about the incident. He admired those blacks that were freeborn and had first, middle, and last names, when all his life he was only ever called "Booker."

In 1872 Washington walked to Virginia to attend a newly founded school for blacks, Hampton Institute. After graduation he taught for two years in Malden and then studied at Wayland Seminary in Washington, D.C. In 1879 he became an instructor at Hampton Institute where he helped to organize a night school and was in charge of the industrial training of seventy-five Native Americans. The school was so successful that in 1881, Hampton founder, educator Samuel Chapman Armstrong, appointed Washington as organizer and principal of a black school in Tuskegee, Alabama, the Tuskegee Institute. Washington made the institution into a major center for industrial and agricultural training. It became widely known as the "Tuskegee Machine" for the way it cranked out educated, self-sufficient black students.

A good deal of Washington's work took place beyond the school's walls. He placated the hostile whites of Tuskegee with assurances that he was counseling his students to set aside political activism in favor of economic gains. He also assured skeptical legislators that his students would not flee the south after their education but instead would be productive contributors to rural economies. These messages resonated with whites not just in the South but also in the North among Tuskegee's benefactors. Tuskegee was the first black institution of higher learning to have an all black faculty. The enrollment reached 2,000 and its endowment rose to over $2 million.

Steel magnet, Andrew Carnegie, who became the most generous donor to Tuskegee during Washington's lifetime, praised him as "one of the most wonderful men who ever lived." Most blacks also praised the man who built a school from the dirt of the Deep South that had succeeded, by 1890, in training 500 African Americans a year on 500 hundred acres of land. Presidents Taft, (Teddy) Roosevelt, and McKinley sought Washington's advice on racial and Southern issues. Blacks soon learned that Washington's endorsement was essential for any political appointment or backing by white philanthropic groups who readily deferred to his opinion.

In 1895 Washington made a speech that historians have labeled the "Atlanta Compromise." In this address he urged blacks to accept their inferior social status for the present and to strive to raise themselves through vocational training and economic self-reliance. Many whites, pleased by his views, and many blacks, awed by his prestige, accepted Washington as the chief spokesman of African Americans. More militant blacks, like W.E.B. Dubois objected to Washington's accommodationist policies and strongly opposed him. But oppose him or not, everyone respected Booker T. Washington, the "Wizard" of Tuskegee, and his Tuskegee "Machine."

W atch Night Services are a 146-year tradition of the Black Church in the United States. On New Year's Eve, African Americans across the nation gather to "watch" the old year go out and welcome in the New Year. As we do this we give thanks to God for his guidance through another year. The first Watch Night Service, from whence the tradition began, occurred on December 31, 1862. It was the eve of the Emancipation Proclamation that would become law on January 1, 1863. That first Watch Night Service was called *Freedom Watch Night* in honor of the impending historic event.

Under pressure from abolitionists and in an attempt to undermine the Confederacy by weakening its labor supply, President Abraham Lincoln made known his intent to free the slaves in the states that were in rebellion against the Union of the United States. The document was read first to his Cabinet Staff in the summer of 1862. The Cabinet Secretaries advised him to wait until Union Army forces were in a more advantaged position. The advantage came in September after the Union Army narrowly defeated Confederate forces at the Battle of Antietam. It was one of the Civil War's bloodiest battles. But it was enough of a victory for President Lincoln to use it as the backdrop to introduce the Emancipation Proclamation.

In September 1862 news of the impending document was made public. To summarize the proclamation it simply said that slaves in the Confederate States would be "thenceforward, and forever free." The law would take effect at the stroke of midnight on January 1, 1863 if the rebel states continued in their rebellion. Lincoln gave the South one hundred days to decide whether to continue and have all their slaves freed or end the rebellion and thus keep their slaves. Meanwhile, many slaves were self-emancipating by escaping to Union lines, or being set free by Union officers as they advanced southward and captured Southern cities.

The Abolitionists were less than thrilled with the Emancipation Proclamation for a few good reasons. The issue of slavery was made a war aim nearly too late in the war. And slavery was only being abolished in the states in rebellion against the Union. There were still nearly a million slaves in the border-states whose status would remain completely unchanged by the terms of the document. And, of course, there was Delaware, a Northern slaveholding state, also exempt from the document. The Abolitionists' greatest fear was that the South would accept the terms of the document, end the war, and still keep the system of slavery in tact.

Waiting for New Year's Day must have seemed like an eternity for everyone involved. Expectations were exceedingly high. Word of possible freedom reached blacks on Southern plantations very quickly. African Americans have always passed information or news through informal verbal networks that we have come to call the "grapevine." News of the expectant freedom announcement reinforced what everyone already knew, that the nation could not exist "half slave and half free." On New Year's Eve 1862, Northern churches filled with people waiting for the Emancipation Proclamation to become law. Blacks and whites talked, sang, prayed, and preached throughout the night.

These church assemblies had in attendance such well-known people as Harriett Tubman, Frederick Douglass, William Wells Brown, William Lloyd Garrison, Harriet Beecher Stowe, Charles B. Ray, and other freedom fighters. The underlying fear for them was that Lincoln would not keep his word. He had vacillated before about the issue of slavery. But in any event, the South ignored or refused the offer. And this time Lincoln did not waver nor go back on his word. And the reaction was explosive. Telegraph wires hummed with the news. There were marches through the cold streets of Philadelphia, Boston, and New York. And in Washington, D.C., groups of former slaves who had escaped during the war gathered together to pray and sing.

The Watch Night tradition continues for African Americans. It is no longer *Freedom Watch Night* nor do we think to commemorate that episode of our history. Watch Night Services are now purely for praise and worship. In our 389-year history of being black in America, we have survived assaults on our person and insults to our citizenship. All of which results in trauma to our psyche. But we know that we have survived these ordeals by the Grace of God. And for every Watch Night Service that African Americans attend from now on, let us borrow from the wording of the Emancipation Proclamation and be *henceforward and forever* <u>thankful</u>.

PHYLLIS WHEATLEY (c. 1753-1784)

For years United States History textbooks contained fewer that five African American names. One of those named was Phyllis Wheatley. She was a young slave girl living in Boston with her owners. Phyllis never tried to run away, lead an insurrection, or incite anyone to riot. Her claim to fame was her calm demeanor and a keen intellect that was not thought to be present in Africans. He was a poet and writer of letters and elegies. She was eventually freed, married, and had children. But history only regards her as the little slave girl who could write poetry.

Phyllis Wheatley was born in Senegal along the Gambia River in West Africa. She was brought to the United States on the slave ship, *The Phyllis,* for which she was named. John and Susanna Wheatley purchased her in Boston in July 1761. They named her for the ship on which she was held captive and gave her their surname. Soon after beginning to work for the Wheatleys, as a personal maid, Phyllis started to show signs of being intellectually gifted. The wealthy family raised Phyllis more like a daughter than a slave. The Wheatley's daughter, Mary, instructed her in the Bible. After just sixteen months in the new world, Phyllis could read English, and later mastered Latin. After only four years, Phyllis Wheatley began to write poetry.

Wheatley's first published poem appeared in the Newport Mercury, a Rhode Island newspaper, on December 21, 1767. In the fall of 1770 she established a widespread readership with the publication of an elegy on the death of the Reverend George Whitehead, an internationally popular Methodist evangelist. Over the next few years she published several other well-received elegies in broadsides and newspapers in North America and England. In 1772, Wheatley attempted to find subscribers in Boston for a proposed volume of her poems, but her efforts failed.

With her owners' permission, Wheatley sailed to England in the spring of 1773 to supervise the publication of her work. The volume, published in September 1773, was entitled: *Poems on Various Subjects, Religious and Moral by Phyllis Wheatley, Negro Servant to Mr. John Wheatley of Boston in New England.* Wheatley was almost immediately celebrated as an American phenomenon. Under pressure from Phyllis' friends and admirers, John Wheatley set her free shortly after her return to Boston. Although free, Wheatley did not quit her former master's household. She nursed them until their deaths.

There was no militancy in Wheatley's poetry. She concentrated mostly on religious themes, praising, for example, the circumstances that brought her in contact with the Christian creed. In addition to faith subjects, she wrote about American patriotism and the equality of souls. When Washington was commissioned as Commander-in-Chief of the Continental forces in 1776, Wheatley wrote a poem expressing her genuine delight over the occasion in a tribute to him. In return, Washington invited her to visit him at his headquarters, which she accepted.

In April 1778, Wheatley married John Peters, a free black man who ultimately failed at various business ventures, but who displayed immense personal dignity and was a strong advocate on behalf of blacks before the Massachusetts tribunals. Wheatley died shortly after giving birth to her third child. The baby, like her previous two children, did not survive.

Phyllis Wheatley had no literary models to guide her except those of Europe and America. Mastering those, and drawing on her childhood memories of Africa and her experiences as a slave, she created a new, African American Literature. Wheatley cannot be called an activist or a radical; she did not use her talents to attack the system of slavery. However, what she did was significant because her worked proved to all that Africans could think. At a very early time in American history, she dispelled the stereotype that Africans had no mental or intellectual gifts. The fact that she was effective in the literary world, thought at the time to be outside the capability of Africans, makes her a figure of historic proportions.

WALTER FRANCIS WHITE (1893-1955)

W alter White was a civil rights leader who built the foundations of the Civil Rights Movement as an official of the National Association for the Advancement of Colored People (NAACP). He was also an influential author of the Harlem Renaissance. He fought for equality in voting rights, challenged segregation and discrimination in education and travel, and drew national attention to the evil of lynching.

White was born on July 1, 1893, in Atlanta, Georgia, to George and Madeline White. His father was a postal worker who raised his son in a racially mixed, middle-class neighborhood. Possessing mixed heritage, he and his father had fair complexions, silken hair, and blue eyes. They could have "passed" for white but chose not to do so. White credited a 1906 race riot in Atlanta, during which he and his father defended the family's home from fire, as the incident that ignited his race consciousness as a black man.

After graduating from Atlanta University in 1916, White became active in the black community. When the Atlanta board of education sought to end public education for blacks after the sixth grade, he organized a campaign and fought the board's decision. The school board was forced to change its policy. This incident led to the formation of a local branch of the NAACP with White as secretary. By 1918 White gained the attention of James Weldon Johnson who was at that time the NAACP field secretary.

When Johnson became the first African American Executive Secretary of the NAACP in 1920, he appointed White as his assistant. Together they firmly established black leadership in the NAACP and expanded the branch system of the organization. White was also an invaluable researcher for the NAACP's aggressive anti-lynching campaign. Passing for white, he investigated some of the most shocking lynchings and other racially motivated crimes of mob violence without hindrance. He was able to infiltrate secret meetings of hate groups and secure valuable information. On one such occasion in Arkansas, he barely escaped being lynched himself.

In 1929, while Johnson was on leave, White served as acting executive of the NAACP. During this time he directed the efforts to block the confirmation of John J. Parker, a segregationist judge from South Carolina, to the U.S. Supreme Court. By 1931, White's appointment to succeed Johnson as

Executive Secretary of the NAACP was made official. White's administration remained committed to the fight for the enforcement of black constitutional rights. By strengthening the legal arm of the NAACP, he was able to direct campaigns for federal civil rights legislation in the form of anti-lynching laws, voting rights, laws banning poll taxes and discrimination in the U.S. armed forces, and laws in favor of desegregation and the equalization of schools.

Together with union activist, A. Phillip Randolph, White persuaded President Franklin D. Roosevelt to issue an executive order prohibiting discrimination in the defense industry in 1941. He also lobbied for the establishment of the Fair Employment Commission. White was also a writer. In addition to numerous articles and two syndicated newspaper columns, White authored several books, including two novels and his autobiography. His exposé on bigotry in the military, *A Rising Wind*, was one of the influences on President Harry S. Truman executive order to end segregation in the armed forces. With all his pressing duties, he still found time to be a delegate to the Second Pan-African Congress in 1921 and a consultant to the U.S. delegation at the San Francisco Conference that organized the United Nations in 1945.

Walter White was the preeminent strategist of the NAACP. He led the organization from 1931 until his death in 1955. Under his leadership it became a major force for political change and social justice in the United States. The crowning achievement of White's NAACP career was the fight to desegregate public schools. It culminated in the historic 1954 United States Supreme Court landmark decision, *Brown vs. Board of Education of Topeka, Kansas*.

C harlie Wiggins is one of the forgotten heroes of auto racing. He was an extraordinary mechanic and racecar driver during the ugly days of segregation. When the governing body of auto racing, the American Auto Association (AAA), and the Indianapolis Motor Speedway turned away black drivers and mechanics, Wiggins involved himself in the racing league for African Americans, the "Gold and Glory."

He was born Charles Edwin Wiggins on July 15, 1897 in the segregated section of Evansville, Indiana called "Baptisttown." City officials too often ignored petitions and other organized efforts by African Americans to improved conditions in the neighborhood. Charlie was the oldest of four sons born to Sport Wiggins, a dockworker and later a miner; and Jennie Wiggins, a laundress for elite white families in Evansville. Ramshackle houses lined the dusty, unpaved streets where Charlie and his brothers, Lawrence, Walter, and Hershel, grew up. Amid those rough conditions though, Sport supported his family modestly enough, but the boys hardly ever saw their father.

At an early age Wiggins enjoyed organizing neighborhood races, games and wrestling matches. He was small for his age but had a reputation as a tough kid with an unwavering resolve, a quality that would characterize him throughout his life. That special kind of "daredevil" courage he displayed in his youth would also be life-long. He showed tremendous maturity by helping his mother with the three younger boys while his father was always working. Sadly, his mother died of fever when he was only nine. He earned money by shining shoes in the afternoons. It proved to be so profitable that by age eleven, he was routinely skipping school and earning a dollar a day.

Wiggins had two customers who would change his life. Henry Benninghof and Eugene Nolan were auto parts manufacturers and mechanical repair shop owners. They also owned automobile plants in Terre Haute and Indianapolis. The two men allowed Wiggins to watch and listen to the auto mechanics in their shop; and later broke all the social rules of the day by letting him become an apprentice. By the time Wiggins married and was able to move to Indianapolis, he was a highly skilled mechanic who could diagnose an engine's problems just by listening to it.

Wiggins and his wife, Roberta, settled in a house on West Street, two blocks south of Indiana Avenue, in the heart of the city's African American district in the fall of 1922. "Avenue" life was very different from the bleakness they had endured in Evansville. Roberta reveled in the city's gay social scene of jazz and dance clubs. Indianapolis increased Wiggins' opportunity to work on automobiles. After a unique interview, he earned the position of chief mechanic at Sagalowsky's Garage just south of Monument Circle. Once, to circumvent the rules of segregation, the 1934 Indy 500 winner, "Wild Bill" Cummings, hired Wiggins as his mechanic but told officials of the Motor Speedway that Wiggins was his janitor.

For the 1924 inaugural Gold and Glory Sweepstakes for black racers, Wiggins was denied entry because he was small in stature. But by 1925, he had built his first racecar by scavenging parts from various abandoned vehicles and crafting ones that could not be found. He entered the Gold and Glory in the "Wiggins Special." It was his first professional race and he finished fifth. It would be the lowest finish of his career. Afterwards, he came to be a dominant force on the colored racing circuit, which included winning the "Gold and Glory" in Indianapolis in 1926, 1931, 1932, and 1933.

Charlie Wiggins had earned for himself the title of "Negro Speed King" until his career ended in the 1936 racing accident that took his right leg. But he continued to work as an extremely talented mechanic and racecar builder after fashioning prosthesis for himself. And he always remained an enthusiast of the auto racing sport and a nurturing mentor for African American auto racers.

BERT WILLIAMS (1874-1922)

ert Williams was the preeminent black entertainer of his day and one of the most admired comedians of the era. He became a hugely popular Vaudeville performer, and partnered with George Walker to form the comedic song and dance team of "Walker and Williams."

He was born Egbert Austin Williams was born on the island of Antigua in the West Indies in 1874. His parents brought him to the United States at age two. The family eventually settled in Riverside, California, where Williams grew up. After high school, he briefly studied civil engineering in San Francisco, but he soon abandoned that for the field of entertainment.

Williams became a singing, dancing, banjo-playing comedian. He performed in vaudeville acts in San Francisco, New York City, and London. In the Broadway musical, *The Gold Bug* (1896), Williams reintroduced the old slave dance, the Cakewalk. The Cakewalk was an exaggerated, strutting style dance that lent itself very well to the syncopated beat of a new African American musical art form, Ragtime.

Williams began his career by joining a small minstrel troupe that played the mining and lumber camps of California and Oregon. In 1895 he met another African American performer, George Walker, and the two became partners. They formed a comedy team and followed the vaudeville circuit. The Williams and Walker Production Company produced *Senegambian Carnival* (1897). Their repertory company later included Jessie Shipp, Alex Rogers, Will Marion Cook, Lottie Williams and Ada Walker.

Williams and Walker opened in *The Song of Ham* in 1902. It was a musical farce that played in New York City for two years. In 1904, they produced an all-black musical comedy, *Williams & Walker In Dahomey*, The musical farce captivated Broadway and even played in London for eight months, including a command performance before King Edward VII. The team followed up with similar musical successes, *Williams & Walker in Abyssinia* and *Williams & Walker in Bandanna Land*. They became the first internationally famous team of African American stars in the history of American entertainment.

Walker died in 1909 and Williams gave up producing to become a featured performer in otherwise all white Broadway productions. In 1910 he signed a long-term contract that earned him many thousands of dollars in the *Ziegfield Follies*. But he continued to write his own songs and skits. Williams recorded songs that included: *I'm in the Right Church, but the Wrong Pew, Jonah*, and *Nobody*. He also appeared in two films: *Darktown Jubilee* (1914) and *A Natural Born Gambler* (1916). In addition, he starred in two Broadway shows developed exclusively for him, *Broadway Brevities* (1920) and *Under the Bamboo Tree* (1922).

While appearing in *Under the Bamboo Tree*, Williams collapsed on stage in Detroit, Michigan. Afterwards, he was taken to his New York City home where he died a month later. At the turn of the century, Williams was one of America's top comedians. He was a contemporary of, and greatly admired by such performers as Eddie Cantor and W.C. Fields. Those two comedians regarded him as the funniest man on the vaudevillian stage. His comedic timing and delivery were flawless.

Bert Williams was the first African American to succeed on the American stage. He was also the first African American to be asked to join the ever-popular *Ziegfield Follies* and the *Midnight Frolics* on Broadway. Williams was more than a comedic genius. His range of talents made him a pioneer in the entertainment industry. His success opened the door for scores of other African American comedians, musicians, composers, lyricists, musical directors and producers, stage managers, and all others associated with the American stage.

P erhaps the most peculiar story from the annals of African American history is that of Cathay Williams or "William Cathay" as she came to be known. She successfully masqueraded as a man during her brief enlistment as a Buffalo Soldier in a newly formed all-black regiment stationed in the western territory.

By her own account of her birth, Cathay was born to a freeman and a slave woman owned by a wealthy farmer, William Johnson, near Independence, Missouri. She and her mother were moved to Jefferson City while she was still a young girl. Her master died there. When the Union soldiers swept through Missouri, Cathay and other blacks became what history has labeled "Contraband." The *Contrabands* were those self-liberated slaves who followed the Union troops as southern cities and towns fell before them. Until the war's end, Cathay traveled through the South as a cook with the Thirteenth Army.

On November 15, 1866 Cathay enlisted in the 38th Infantry as a freedman named William Cathay and was sent to New Mexico for duty. An army record listed her age as twenty-two, but even that is uncertain. It was not uncommon for young men to state that they were older just so they could get into the army. She may have done the same thing. Cathay is described as having black eyes and hair, standing 5 foot 9 inches tall. She must have been very slender because there was no visible sign of her femininity on the cursory, pre-enlistment medical examination provided. In those days the brief physical probably served only to point out any obvious defects that would make a recruit "unfit" for duty. Since United States Army regulations forbade the regular enlistment or commissioning of women, it is certainly felt that neither the recruiting officer nor the doctor ascertained the truth of her gender.

Only a male cousin and a particular male friend, who also joined the regiment with her, knew that Cathay was in fact a woman. Her reasons for becoming a soldier are pure conjecture. But by her own admission, she wanted to make an independent living for herself "without depending on relations or friends." Post Civil War America was difficult in the South. For single women, it must have been even more so. In the army Cathay found steady work and higher pay; and more importantly, food, shelter, and clothing. Along with a decent livelihood, historians presume that the army offered a greater semblance of respect for African American men than civilian life offered African American women.

Very little is known about the details of Cathay's service. But it seems she was an average soldier. She stood guard and performed other duties. She carried a musket and marched like other soldiers. When the company was not on the march, they did garrison duty, drilled and trained, and went scouting for signs of hostile Indians. Cathay participated in her share of the obligations facing Company-A. Her career was not illustrious or even exciting. She neither distinguished herself nor disgraced the uniform. It was only when she faked an illness that the post surgeon discovered she was a woman. Her deception demanded her immediate discharge. All the men in the company wanted to get rid of her when the truth was revealed. *"Some of them acted real bad to me,"* she later recounted.

Cathay was discharged on October 14, 1868. Afterwards, she resumed the garb and identity of a woman, even marrying and divorcing. She worked as a cook for an officer in the New Mexico Territory. From there, she went to Pueblo, Colorado and remained for two years, working in the Dunbar Laundry. From Pueblo, Cathay moved to Las Animas and again worked as a laundress. As late as 1891 she was reported to be living in Trinidad, Colorado while protesting the denial of her army pension.

Just like the date of her birth, the date of her death cannot be verified. But Cathay Williams is assured a place in United States history as the only documented female Buffalo Soldier. Further, she was the only recognized African American woman to serve in the United States Army prior to the 1948 law that officially allowed the enlistment of all women.

PAUL R. WILLIAMS (1894-1980)

aul Williams was an extremely talented African American who became one of the preeminent architects of Southern California, producing and incredible number of buildings over a career that spanned nearly sixty years. During his exceedingly productive career, Williams designed nearly 3,000 residential and commercial structures, and became known as Southern California's "architect to the stars."

He was born Paul Revere Williams in 1894 in downtown Los Angeles soon after his family arrived from Memphis, Tennessee. His father was a hotel waiter. He was orphaned before he was five, and a foster family raised him. He was the only black in his elementary school and showed an early aptitude for drawing buildings. A friend of his foster family, and a builder, suggested that he become an architect. Upon learning what architects did, he became completely consumed by the idea.

Williams received no encouragement toward his chosen profession from anyone outside of his family. By the time he reached Polytechnic High School, his guidance counselor tried hard to dissuade him from such an occupation. The counselor pointed to the fact that at the time blacks did not build fine homes or expensive offices buildings. He directed Williams toward the career choices of medicine and the law. He was not discouraged though he could only think of one black architect, William S. Pittman, the son-in-law of Booker T. Washington. He was quoted as saying: "If I allow the fact that I am a Negro to checkmate my will to do, now, I will inevitably form the habit of being defeated." Upon graduation from high school, Williams enrolled in a Los Angles extension of New York's Beaux Arts Institute of Design. He excelled at the Institute, eventually winning the school's medal of excellence.

At age twenty, Williams won first place in a city planning competition in Pasadena, California. And he did well in two other design competitions before enrolling as an architectural engineering student at the University Of Southern California (USC). After graduation from USC, Williams attended three arts schools before joining the offices of residential architect Reginald D. Johnson, where he was given the assignment to design a $150,000 home. Williams later joined the commercially oriented firm of John C. Austin, where he helped prepare construction drawings of the Shrine Auditorium and the First Methodist Church. Williams became a licensed architect in 1921, and one year later started his own architecture firm, Paul R. Williams and Associates. To give back to the community, he became a member of Los Angles' first City Planning Commission, one of many local, state, and federal boards and commissions on which he would serve.

In 1923, Williams joined the Southern California chapter of the American Institute of Architects (AIA), becoming the first African America member of the national organization. He would later become the first elected to the AIA College of Fellows. He designed the home of dancer William "Bojangles" Robinson. But most of his business came from well-to-do white clients, building homes in Los angles, Beverly Hills, Bell Air, Pacific Palisades, and San Marino. His clientele included Lon Chaney, Gary Grant, Lucille Ball and Dezi Arnaz, Zsa Zsa Gabor, and Frank Sinatra. He designed the home of automobile magnate E.L. Cord that included an eighteen-car garage. His architectural signature included sliding pocket doors that disappeared into the walls and the cascading spiral staircase. He even perfected the skill of drawing upside-down so that his clients would not have to look over his shoulder.

On occasion Williams received commissions from L.A.'s black community including, Second Baptist Church, Connor-Johnson Mortuary, and the city's first black YMCA. On that project, he included the likenesses of Frederick Douglass and Booker T. Washington in the building's façade. Paul Williams established an impeccable reputation, designing homes with smart, contemporary looks and elegant informality in the most exclusive neighborhoods. But the bizarre irony was he would not be allowed to live in those exclusive neighborhoods because he was African American.

V anessa Williams has had many "firsts" in her young, accomplished life. She rose to prominence by becoming the first African American to win the Miss America title in the history of the pageant. Unfortunately, she was also the first to be asked to abdicate the title because of scandal.

She was born Vanessa Lynn to Milton and Helen Williams on March 18, 1963 in New York City. She has one younger brother, Christopher, and both children were raised to appreciate music by their parents who possessed advanced musical degrees. The family moved to the small town of Millwood just thirty miles north of the city when Vanessa was just a year old.

From the time Vanessa could reach the piano bench, she was subjected to a grueling schedule of music lessons that also included the French horn. By the time she reached high school, she was already an accomplished singer and musician. At Horace Greeley High School in Chappaqua, New York, she began acting, dancing, and modeling. She became a star performer in plays and musicals. She sang in the school chorale and played French horn in the school orchestra and the band. She was also named to the All-State Women's Choir and the All-County Orchestra.

In 1981 Williams enrolled at Syracuse University, where she majored in musical theater. In 1983 the executive director of the Miss America Greater Syracuse Pageant was impressed by her performance in a college musical and asked her to enter the contest. Williams entered because much of the contest centered on talent competition and she thought the exposure would benefit her theatrical ambitions and musical aspirations. And if she won the top Miss America prize, she would earn large personal appearance fees.

Williams won the Miss America Greater Syracuse Pageant and soon thereafter took the Miss New York State pageant. But it was in September 1983 that she won a place in history as the first African American to be crowned Miss America. She so impressed the judges enough with a combination of beauty, intelligence, and singing talent to handily win the title. Williams was the odds on favorite very early in the contest. It seems to have been a banner year for the establishment of a black standard of beauty because the first runner up in the Miss America pageant was Suzette Charles, the first black Miss New

Jersey. Sadly, Williams held the crown for only ten months. In July 1984 it was discovered that in the summer of 1982, she had posed for a series of explicit and nude photographs. At age nineteen, she made an unwise decision in posing for the pictures and it returned to haunt her. Williams relinquished her title to avoid the embarrassment of seeing them published while she was the reigning Miss America. She was also under tremendous pressure from pageant officials to avoid scandalizing the Miss America pageant.

After relinquishing her title Williams also abandoned her plans to continue studies at Syracuse. Instead she immediately plunged into her career as a professional entertainer. She began making appearances on various television programs and music specials. In 1987 she married Ramon Hervey II, a public relations specialist who became her manager. Before their divorce ten years later, he had succeeded in helping Williams put her career on track. He guided her into a recording career by signing her to a division of Polygram Records. Her debut album was the "Right Stuff" and contained several tracts that became hits.

While achieving singing stardom, Williams also built an equally illustrious reputation as an actress. For television, she portrayed Suzanne De Pass in "The Jacksons: An American Dream" (1991). Also in the 1990s she appeared in an impressive list of films including "New Jack City," "Eraser," "Soul Food," and "Dance With Me." And she was a huge success in the title role of the Broadway musical "Kiss of the Spider Woman." Versatile singing and acting achievements have made Vanessa Williams one of the most popular entertainers of her time. And Williams has one of the most spectacular "comeback" stories of modern time.

August Wilson was a Pulitzer Prizewinning African American playwright. His singular achievement and literary legacy is a cycle of ten plays, each set in a different decade, depicting the comedy and tragedy of the African American experience in the twentieth century. His early childhood experiences in low-income communities informed his dramatic writings.

He was born Frederick August Kittel on April 27, 1945 in a Pittsburgh slum called the "Hill." It was a very poor section of town where blacks, Italians, and Jews all lived in relative peace together. He was the fourth of six children born to Frederick Kittel, a German immigrant baker, and Daisy Wilson Kittel, a black cleaning woman from North Carolina. Because his father never spent time with the family, Wilson's mother had to raise her six children alone in a two-room, cold-water apartment, with no telephone, behind a grocery store.

Wilson learned to read when he was only four and developed a voracious appetite for books. By age twelve, he spent regular hours at the local library. Despite this, he was a very unexceptional student. He had a reputation for talking out of turn in class. His reaction to the harsh and constant racism he faced in an all-white parochial school left him wounded and uninspired. Students would leave notes on his desk saying: "Nigger go home." And the abusive teachers would accuse him of plagiarizing his well-written term papers and book reports. He finally dropped out high school at age fifteen. But he continued to self-educate at the public library. He also developed a fascination for language and word usage. He became an avid listener as he soaked up the conversations he overheard in coffee shops and on street corners. In his head he could construct stories just from listening.

In 1965, Fredrick Kittel died leaving Wilson free to sever the last tie to his father and to honor his mother by using her maiden name. The symbolic starting point of Wilson's serious writing career came in the same year when he bought a used typewriter, paying for it with the $20 that his sister gave him for writing her term paper. By his twenties, Wilson was already writing poetry and short stories. He was fully dedicated himself to the task of becoming a writer. Although his poems were published in some small literary magazines over the next few years, he failed to achieve recognition as a poet. He entered the United States Army, but was discharged a year later. He returned to

Pittsburgh to work odd jobs as a dishwasher, cook, porter, and gardener.

In the late 1960s Wilson discovered the militant writings of Malcolm X and began to espouse "cultural nationalism." Cultural nationalism meant to Wilson that black people could work toward self-definition and self-determination though the higher pursuits of theater and the arts. In 1968 he founded the "Black Horizon Theater in the Hill District of Pittsburgh and served as the resident playwright and director for the next ten years. In 1978 Wilson moved to St. Paul, Minnesota and found his writers voice. He drafted "Jitney," a play set in a gypsy cab station. He submitted the play to the Minneapolis Playwright's Center and won a $200 per month fellowship and acceptance at the 1982 National Playwright's Conference. His next work was "Fullerton Street" which was produced at the Allegheny Repertory Theater.

Wilson's breakthrough work was "Ma Rainey's Black Bottom." Opening on Broadway in 1984, it was a popular and critical success. In 1985 Wilson won a Tony Award and Pulitzer Prize for "Fences." He also won the Pulitzer for "The Piano Lesson" in 1986. Following in 1988, "Joe Turner's Come and Gone" was critically acclaimed, receiving the New York Drama Critic's Circle Award as best new play of the year. Wilson stayed culturally true to his art form and refused to give in to the allure of Hollywood. Although the lives of many of his characters were bleak, and no one else could bespeak the Blues like August Wilson, he always maintained a degree of optimism about the situations faced by Africans in American. On October 2, 2005, he died knowing that the human spirit was indomitable, and black culture yet lives.

O prah Winfrey is an actress, producer, magazine publisher, and most importantly, a talk show host. She is the most famous and successful African American woman in history. She is currently ranked as America's first black woman billionaire. *The Oprah Winfrey Show*, a ratings powerhouse, has become the stage on which Oprah preaches self-improvement, empowerment, and compassion. She is known for her easy intimacy and powerful connection with her audiences, who hug her, cry on her shoulder, and share with her their struggles and triumphs. It is this skill that Oprah has parlayed into media superstardom. Her innate abilities are evident in her television show, Production Company, and philanthropic foundation. Just with her popular and influential book club, Oprah has revolutionized the publishing industry

She was born Oprah Gail Winfrey to Vernon Winfrey, a twenty year-old soldier, and Vernita Lee, an eighteen year-old farm girl. Her parents were ill-prepared to raise a child and sent Oprah to live with her paternal grandmother. Oprah's life was often harsh and lonely, with her only social outlet being the church. Vernita Lee retrieved her daughter after six years and took Oprah to live in Milwaukee. Oprah alleges to have been repeatedly victimized as a young girl by an adult relative and family friend while in her mother's care. Although she continued to excel in school, she began to exhibit behavioral problems.

Finally, at age fourteen, Oprah was sent to live with her father and stepmother in Nashville. The change, according to Oprah, saved her from becoming a juvenile delinquent. Flowering under her father's strict but loving discipline; Oprah focused on her studies and gained enough popularity to become senior class president of her predominately white high school. A local Nashville radio station hired Oprah to read the news on the air several times a day. She earned a full scholarship to attend Tennessee State University in 1970. In the evenings, she anchored a local television news program.

In 1976 Oprah left Nashville to anchor Baltimore's ABC affiliate. When that proved to be disastrous, the station offered her a different role co-hosting a morning talk show. It was called *People Are Talking*, and it revealed all of Oprah's people skills and showed her effortless, unscripted, on-air style. After eight years of ever-increasing popularity, in 1984 she left Baltimore to host

A.M. Chicago, a morning talk program consistently ranked second after that of the city's talk-television king, Phil Donahue. Within months Oprah had doubled her ratings over Donahue. *A.M. Chicago* was renamed *The Oprah Winfrey Show* and went into national syndication in 1986. The deal netted her an estimated $30 million. But more than that, the program introduced a new kind of television that emphasized women's voices, the appeal of personal stories, and the power of sharing them.

Oprah's acting credits include, *The Color Purple*, a 1986 Steven Spielberg film, and *The Women of Brewster Place* (1988). Oprah stared in and produced the 1999 movie *Beloved*, starring Danny Glover. Oprah became the first African American woman to form her own television and film production company, *Harpo Productions*. Since then she has expanded into radio and launched her own print media periodicals with *O The Oprah Magazine* and *O At Home*. They are journals that are as smart, chic, and sophisticated as any on the market. She remade and produced *The Color Purple* as a Broadway Musical. And it is getting rave reviews in New York, and it now successfully touring throughout the United States.

Even Oprah's philanthropic activities are staggering. Whether she is building villages for Hurricane Katrina relief in New Orleans, or building individual homes for *Habitat For Humanity* elsewhere. More than a mover and shaker, she is a giver, and is good at harnessing the giving of others. Recently she built a school for young girls in South Africa because of a promise she made to Nelson Mandella. Oprah Winfrey is a multitalented, multifaceted, multimedia superstar whose impact on American popular culture has been phenomenal. Over 40 million people view her daily worldwide. Her outreach has been immeasurable. And she seems to have acquired the "Midas Touch" and gold is produced wherever she puts her hands.

CARTER G. WOODSON (1875-1950)

C arter G. Woodson was an African American educator, author, and historian. He was an early proponent of the theories of African cultural retention in African Americans. Woodson was one of the first to recognize the rich heritage of African Americans, and to insist that African culture survived the Atlantic crossing and could still be seen in many aspects of contemporary African American life. He was the primary initiator of "Negro History Week" in the 1920s that grew to become "Black History Month" in the 1970s. Woodson was a pioneer in the scholarly research and dissemination of African American history and culture.

Carter Godwin Woodson was one of nine children born to former slaves, James Woodson and Eliza Riddle Woodson, on December 19, 1875, at New Canton in Buckingham County, Virginia. Woodson's father had helped the Union soldiers during the Civil War. His mother had secretly learned to read and write as a young slave girl. When they heard they were building a high school for blacks in Huntington, West Virginia, the whole family moved there. The Woodson family was large and, of course, very poor. Carter could never regularly attend such schools as were being provided during the Reconstruction era.

Woodson was largely self-taught to master the fundamentals of basic school subjects by the time he was seventeen. In addition, relatives attending Freedmen's Bureau Schools helped to further tutor him and cultivate his interest in education. While still in his teens, Woodson had to earn his living as a miner in the Fayette County coalfields. It was not until 1895 that he was able to enter the Frederick Douglass High School in Huntington. He received his high school certificate in just two years, despite working long hours in the mines. By 1903, Woodson earned a degree from Berea College, in Kentucky after only two years of study.

Ever the seeker of more knowledge, Woodson had earned his B.A. and M.A. degrees from the University of Chicago by 1908. To top off his educational achievements, Woodson earned a PhD. in History in 1912. He became only the second African American to receive a doctoral degree from Harvard University. In his travels, Woodson enjoyed a year of study in Asia and Europe, and a semester at the Sorbonne in Paris. His teaching and travels abroad gave him a mastery of several languages. He also received a research grant from Laura Spelman Rockefeller for the study of the 1830 Census that listed the blacks that had owned slaves.

In Dr. Woodson's career as an educator, he served as a teacher and the principal of Douglass High School. He was Supervisor of schools in the Philippines, teaching English to Spanish speaking students. He was a Language teacher for ten years at Paul Lawrence Dunbar High School in Washington, D.C. He became the Dean of the School of Liberal Arts at Howard University and West Virginia State College. Dr. Woodson became convinced that among scholars, the role of his own people in American history was being either ignored or misrepresented. He realized the need for special research into the neglected past of the American Negro. With that realization, he founded The Association for the Study of Negro Life and History (ASNLH) in 1915. The following year, Dr. Woodson began the publication of the *Journal of Negro History* that has never missed an issue. To this day, the *Journal* publishes works of black and white scholars who research and write about people of color.

Carter G. Woodson was a prolific writer and author of many scholarly works, such as: *The Education of the Negro Prior to 1861* (1915), *A Century of Negro Migration* (1918), *The History of the Negro Church* (1927), and *The Mis-Education of the Negro* (1933). The chronicle of Dr. Woodson's far-reaching achievements must include the organizing of Associated Publishers in 1920. It is the oldest black publishing company in the nation. The founding of the publishing company made possible the publication of books about blacks when the subject was not then acceptable to most publishers.

RICHARD WRIGHT (1908-1960)

Richard Wright came to prominence in the modernist literary period surrounding World War II. It became clear that he was the master of the short story as he joined the ranks of contemporary American writers. He is best known for the way he described the stark, tragic realism and frustration of a young black man living in the blighted slums of an American city in his introductory novel, *Native Son* (1940). His critically acclaimed autobiography, *Black Boy* (1945), was also a searing portrait of American racism.

He was born Richard Nathan Wright, the grandson of slaves in Natchez, Mississippi in 1908. His parents, Nathan Wright, an illiterate sharecropper, and Ella Wilson Wright, a schoolteacher, had another son, Leon, two years later. In 1911 Ella took the children to Memphis and Nathan later followed to work in the mills. But within a year, Nathan deserted the family for another woman. In the absence of her husband, Ella found work as a cook and other menial jobs to support her two sons. But in the wake of such emotional trauma, her health failed rapidly. Wright and his brother were forced to live with various relatives from Arkansas to Mississippi when his mother suffered a debilitating stroke. Many of these relatives were steeped in the Southern religious tradition that Wright found difficult to embrace.

Upon the completion of the ninth grade Wright headed to Memphis again and then to Chicago. In the North Wright discovered leftist philosophy and became a member of the Communist Party. He became acquainted with the works of notable authors like H.L. Mencken, Fyodor Dostoyevsky, Theodore Dreiser, and Sinclair Lewis. He took a job with the U.S. Post Office and his employment remained stable until the Stock Market Crash in 1929. Wright was the first black writer to have a novel selected as the "Book of the Month." He also published articles in Marxist journals like the Anvil, Left Front, and New Masses. *Uncle Tom's Children* (1938) was a collection of short stories based on his childhood in the South.

Wright was a Communist from 1935 until his brake from it in 1942. In 1944 he published, "I Tried To Be A Communist." In it he expressed his disillusionment with the dogma of Communism and its tacit refusal to speak to civil rights issues specific to the black experience. In 1935 Wright joined the Federal Writers Project and followed it to New York City in 1937. In 1938 he won a Guggenheim Fellowship and resigned from the project. He was a prolific writer and won many critical awards for short stories and novels. He also wrote *Twelve Million Black Voices* and *The Man Who Lived Underground* (1941); *The Outsider* (1953); *Black Power* (1954); *The Color Curtain* (1956); *White Man, Listen* and *Pagan Spain* (1957). Some of his writings made him the target of FBI investigations for sedition.

Wright remained in NYC until Gertrude Stein, another modernist writer, invited him to Paris to exchange ideas with other expatriates in the 1940s. The freedom must have been intoxicating because he moved his family there. He was warmly received and his work was intellectually embraced. He met Jean-Paul Satre, France's foremost Existentialist, and became a devotee. As an African American living in a hostile environment, it was easy for him to identify with Existentialism and its emphasis on isolation in a hostile universe. Wright wrote three other novels while living in France. But for numerous reasons, they were not well received in the United States. And it reinforced his conviction to never return to America.

The underling theme of the modernist writers was the "American Dream," which was different for every writer. But Richard Wright was a modernist writer who could not express the "American Dream" as long as he faced the nightmare of racism. His novels lent themselves to the destructive effects of white racism on both blacks and whites. He was faced with the challenge of living as an alien in his own country or as an alien in another country. He chose the latter as being the most sensible choice for any African American. He tried to assuage his consciousness with the social godlessness of Communism and the intellectual godlessness of Existentialism, and sadly never once returned to the God of his youth.

One of the most fascinating, yet at the same time, puzzling figures in American history is York, the slave of William Clark. York was the only African American on the Lewis and Clark Expedition that explored the North American Continent from 1804–1806. Little information survives about York to present his life in any great detail. But it is known that he was the only documented African American to explore the newly purchased Louisiana Territory, to traverse the continent, and to reach the Pacific Ocean.

York was born into slavery in Virginia near the York River. His parents, Old York and Rose were slaves owned by the Clark family. When John Clark died in 1799, his son, William, inherited several slaves, including York and his parents. York became William Clark's personal body servant and attended him until 1809 when he was freed. In all journal entries concerning the expedition, and all other documents and writings by Clark, York is never referenced as "my slave," but always as "my servant." However, it was not uncommon for southerners in those times, especially those aristocratic Virginians, not to make any distinction between the two terms.

York is described as a tall, powerfully built man, with agility and good athletic abilities; a very good swimmer and good marksman; skillful caregiver and lifesaver, all of which made him an important part of the expedition. He was even a good cook. It is recorded that York swam to a river island to pick greens for dinner. He was one of the hunters who obtained meat for the group. And often went hunting alone. It has also been recorded that York was the primary caregiver on several occasions when Sacajawea or other members of the party fell ill. York enjoyed more freedom on the expedition than at anytime before. He had an equal vote in all matters that concerned the group and more than pulled his own weight.

Possibly because of his size and stature, York was a great curiosity for the Native peoples the expedition encountered. Historians have hypothesized that this was due to his color. But the records of the expedition clearly note the color of the Indians as ranging from tan to red to black. So York's color could not have been an object of curiosity. But clearly he was different looking from all the other members of the expedition. He was often selected to be part of scouting parties with Indians or with other members of the expedition. Once, at great risk to his own life, York went out in search of Sacajawea and her baby,

Jean-Baptiste Charbonneau, and Clark when they were caught in a flash flood during a storm.

When the expedition ended, however, York did not receive fame or a land grant, nor was he granted the one thing that a slave desired most, his freedom. And it would be at least another five years before he would obtain that. Clark had York jailed for a time for misbehavior. It seems that he had become sullen and insolent because he had not been freed, and he had not been granted a long enough visit to Louisville to see his wife. Details of York's life are sketchy and vague after the discovery expedition ended.

York did finally obtain his freedom, but it is unknown if he was ever reunited with his wife. He started a hauling business in Tennessee, but his business failed when his animals died. And supposedly he died of cholera while living in Tennessee. But did he, really? In 1832 a black man who claimed to have been on the Lewis and Clark Expedition was discovered living among the Crow Indians. He was a war chief and had four wives. All those who revere justice must surely hope this to be the true ending of York's story.

York was the only member of the Lewis and Clark Expedition who had no choice about whether or not he would go. As a slave, he was bound to his master and went where he was told. Yet as a member of the discovery expedition, he had almost total freedom and fully participated in one of the seminal events in American history. In the bicentennial celebratory year of the Lewis and Clark Discovery Expedition, York remained an enigma – a puzzle cloaked in a mystery. Nevertheless, York stands as a reminder in American history that the United States of 1804 was a profoundly different place than it was in 2004.

A ndy Young is a civil rights advocate and was a close associate of civil rights leader, Dr. Martin Luther King, Jr. during the Civil Rights Movement. He went on to become the first African American ambassador to the United Nations (UN), appointed by President Jimmy Carter. He was elected for two terms as Mayor of Atlanta starting in 1981.

He was born Andrew Jackson Young into and affluent family in New Orleans, Louisiana. He was afforded educational opportunities available to few blacks in the American South. He attended Howard University in Washington, D.C. and Hartford Theological Seminary in Connecticut. He was ordained a Congregational Minister of the United Church of Christ in 1955. Upon completion of seminary training, Young accepted positions in dioceses in rural Georgia and in Alabama. Those experiences made him keenly aware of the poverty and discrimination experienced by blacks in rural southern states and inspired his work in civil rights.

In 1959 Young moved to New York City to be the assistant director of the National Council of Churches and to raise financial support for civil rights activities in the South. He returned to Georgia two years later and joined the Southern Christian Leadership Conference (SCLC). His energetic work as funding coordinator and administrator of SCLC's Citizenship Education Program gained him the admiration of Dr. King. The two men became friends and Young began to help coordinate marches, sit-ins, and other forms of non-violent direct action protests.

When Wyatt T. Walker left the executive directorship of SCLC in 1964, Dr. King picked Young to succeed him. By 1967, Young had risen to executive vice-president within the organization. After King's assassination in 1968, Young helped to guide SCLC toward activities promoting social and economic improvements for African Americans. He retired from the daily routine of SCLC in 1970 but remained on the board of directors until 1972. Also in that year, Young became the first African American to be elected to the United States House of Representatives from the state of Georgia since Reconstruction. While in Congress he played an instrumental role in winning for the presidential candidate, Jimmy Carter, the vital backing of those members of the black community who questioned Carter's commitment to black civil rights.

Young resigned from Congress in 1977 when President Jimmy Carter appointed him the U.S. ambassador to the U.N. As ambassador, Young promoted understanding between the U.S. and African nations. He was instrumental in focusing American foreign policy on sub-Saharan Africa and bringing American attention to the appalling conditions of the practice of Apartheid in South Africa. Young resigned from the position after he was criticized for his contacts with the Palestine Liberation Organization (PLO). At that time the U.S. had not formally recognized the PLO as the legitimate representative of the Palestinian people.

In 1982 Young was elected mayor of Atlanta, an office he held until 1989. He made an unsuccessful attempt for governor in the Georgia gubernatorial race in 1990 and then retired from politics. He returned to public life in 1996 as the co-chairman of the Atlanta Committee for the 1996 Summer Olympic Games.

His autobiography, *A Way Out Of No Way*, was published in 1994. It highlights his time in the Civil Rights Movement and his time at the United Nations, and is very reflective of his religious views. The title is taken from an African American folk expression: *My God can make a way out of no way*. Those words are also expressed in Gospel Music as well. For all his undertakings and accomplishments as a man of the movement, a man of politics, and a man of diplomacy, his memoir documents that through it all, the Reverend Andrew J. Young has remained a man of God.

W hitney Young was Executive Director of the National Urban League (NUL) during the Civil Rights Movement of the 1960s. He shaped the organization's policy and lobbied industry to provide employment opportunities for African Americans. While the Civil Rights Movement many have opened the doors of opportunity for blacks, it was Young and the NUL that equipped them to walk through those doors.

He was born Whitney Moore Young, Jr. to middle-class parents on July 31, 1921, in Lincoln Ridge, Kentucky. The family also had two daughters, Arnita and Eleanor. At age fourteen Whitney graduated from Lincoln Institute, a vocational high school for blacks as which his father was principal. He graduated from Kentucky State College in 1941 and enlisted in the army during World War II. In 1947, he received a master's degree in social work from the University of Minnesota. In 1954 he was appointed Dean of Atlanta University's School of social work. While living in Atlanta, Young was vice-president of the National Association for the Advancement of Colored People (NAACP).

In August 1961 the National Urban League sought a new Executive Director and approached Young. Some felt that he was too inexperienced for that post, even though he had been industrial relations secretary of the St. Paul, Minnesota branch of Urban League from 1947 to 1949. And he had also been Executive Secretary of the Omaha, Nebraska branch from 1949 to 1954. That experience notwithstanding, the NUL was still a very old and historic organization with a pedigree extending into the early 20th century. The NUL was formed in 1911 when three previously existing New York City organizations merged to improve conditions for African Americans.

When Young took control of the organization in October, it was likened to a fresh breeze. He restructured the national headquarters, expanded the scope of programs, and developed new projects to improve employment opportunities. He developed a national skills bank, which sought to place the unemployed and underemployed in marketable positions that utilized their talents. The on-the-job training programs placed unskilled workers in training positions in private industry.

During the first seven years of Young's leadership, the training programs produced 50,000 workers, and the NUL reported up to 50,000 placements annually in new or upgraded jobs. Not only did Young expand services but the organization itself grew from 63 affiliates to 98. The professional staff increased from 300 to over 1,200 and its income grew from $340,000 in 1961 to $14,749,000 by 1970. Because of Young's efforts, the NUL received over $6,000,000 for its general support during a three-year period from the Ford Foundation. For his fair housing project, Henry Ford II gave Young a yearly check for $100,000.

The Urban League was much less militant than many other organizations involved in the Civil Rights Movement. In the 1960s, the NUL did not embrace the direct action of other civil rights groups. It did not sponsor sit-ins, protest marches, bus boycotts, or voter registration drives. Instead, it took a proactive position that better aligned it with the black political and social thought of the day. It lent moral support, conducted fact-finding surveys, mediated and negotiated grievances between the demonstrators and the power structure. As the Civil Rights Movement advanced, Young led the NUL from the usual stance of sideline observance and sought to bridge the gap between the movement and the organization.

Whitney Young guided the National Urban League through one of the most socially and politically turbulent decades in United States history. In 1963 he established a dialogue with prominent civil rights leaders. As a result, the Council for United Civil Rights Leadership was formed. And at the 1963 March on Washington, his work became public knowledge. Clearly each organization and each leader had their own unique role to fulfill within the movement. As others led protests and walked picket lines, Young marched African Americans into job training centers, better housing, and institutions of higher education.

Allison, Robert J., ed. The Interesting Narrative of the Life of Olaudah Equiano. New York: Bedford Books, 1995

Appiah, Kwame Anthony and Henry Louis Gates, Jr., ed. Africana: Encyclopedia of the African and African American Experience. New York: Civitas Books, 1999

Asante, Molefi K. and Mark T. Mattson. Historical and Cultural Atlas of African Americans. New York: Macmillian Publishing company, 1992

Baldwin, Lewis V. To Make the Wounded Whole: The Cultural Legacy of Martin Luther King, Jr. Minneapolis: Fortress Press, 1992

Bentley, George R. A History of the Freedmen's Bureau. New York: Octagon Books, 1970

Berlin, Ira. Many Thousands Gone: The First Two Centuries of Slavery in North America. Cambridge, Massachusetts: Belknap Press, 1998

Blumrosen, Alfred W. and Ruth G. Blumrosen. Slave Nation: How Slavery United the Colonies & Sparked the American Revolution. Illinois, Naperville: Sourcebooks, Inc., 2005

Bowen, Catherine Drinker. Miracle at Philadelphia: The Story of the Constitutional Convention May to September 1787. New York: Back Bay Books, 1986

Bradford, Sarah. Harriet Tubman: The Moses of Her People. Massachusetts: Applewood Books, 1993

Branch, Taylor. Parting The Waters: America in the King Years 1954-63. New York: Simon & Schuster, 1988

Bundles, A'Lelia. On Her Own Ground: The Life and Times of Madam C.J. Walker. New York: Scribner, 2001

Clarke, Duncan. History of American Slavery. London: PRC Publishing Ltd., 1998

Dabney, Virginius. The Jefferson Scandals: A Rebuttal. New York: Dood, Mead & Company, 1981

Dodson, Howard, Christopher Moore and Roberta Yancy. The Black New Yorkers: The Schomburg Illustrated Chronology. New York: John Wiley & Sons, Inc., 2000

Dubois, W.E.B. Black Reconstruction in America 1860-1880. New York: The Free Press, 1998

Dubois, W.E.B. The Souls of Black Folk. Chicago: Lushena Books, Inc., 2000

Fitts, Leroy. A History of Black Baptists. Nashville, Tennessee: Broadman Press, 1985

Foner, Eric. Reconstruction: America's Unfinished Revolution 1863-1877. New York: Harper & Row, 1998

Franklin, John Hope and Genna Rae McNeil. African Americans and the Living Constitution. Washington: Smithsonian Institution, 1995

Franklin, John Hope, Alfred A. Moss. From Slavery to Freedom: A History of African Americans, 7th ed., New York: Alfred A. Knopf, 1988

Franklin, John Hope and Loren Schweninger. Runaway Slaves: Rebels on the Plantation. New York: Oxford University Press, 1999

Frazier, E. Franklin. The Negro Church in America. New York: Schocken Books, Inc., 1974

Gates, Jr., Henry Louis and Cornel West. The African American Century: How Black American Have Shaped Our Country. New York: The Free Press, 2000

Goodman, James. The Stories of Scottsboro. New York: Pantheon Books, 1994

Gordon-Reed, Annette. Thomas Jefferson and Sally Hemings: An American Controversy. USA: University Press of Virginia, 1997

586

Grant, Callie Smith. Free Indeed. Ohio: Barbour Publishing, Inc., 2003

Gould, Todd. For Gold & Glory: Charlie Wiggins and the African-American Racing Car Circuit. USA: Indiana University Press, 2002

Haber, Louis. Black Pioneers of Science and Invention. USA: Harcourt, Brace & World, Inc., 1970

Hamilton, Virginia. The People Could Fly: American Black Folktales. New York: Alfred A. Knopf, 1993

Holloway, Joseph E., ed., Africanisms in American Culture. Indiana University Press, 1991

Honey, Michael Keith. Black Workers Remember: An Oral History of Segregation, Unionism, and the Freedom Struggle. Berkeley, Los Angeles: University of California Press, 1999

Jenkins, Edward S., et. al. ed. American Black Scientists and Inventors. Washington: National Science Teachers Association, 1975

Karenga, Maulana. Introduction to Black Studies. Los Angeles, CA: University of Sankore Press, 1993

Katz, William Loren. The Black West. New York: Touchstone, 1996

Kroger, Larry. Black Slaveowners: Free Black Slave Master in South Carolina 1790-1860. USA: University of South Carolina Press, 1995

Lincoln, C. Eric. The Black Church Since Frazier. New York: Schocken Books, Inc., 1974

Lincoln, C. Eric, Lawrence H. Mamiya. The Black Church in the African American Experience. Durham: Duke University Press, 1990

Morris, Aldon D. The Origins of the Civil Rights Movement: Black communities Organizing for Change. New York: The Free Press, 1984

Nash, Gary B. Red, White & Black: The Peoples of Early North America, 4th ed., New Jersey: Prentice Hall, Upper Saddle River, 2000

Newman, Richard. Go Down, Moses: A Celebration of the African-American Spiritual. New York: Roundtable Press, 1998

Obama, Barack. The Audacity of Hope: Thoughts on Reclaiming the American Dream. U.S.A: Crown/Three Rivers Press, 2006

Obama, Barack. Dreams from My Father: A Story of Race and Inheritance. U.S.A. Three Rivers Press, 1995

Oliver, Roland, and Caroline Oliver. ed., Africa in the Days of Exploration. New Jersey: Prentice-Hall, 1965

Oshinsky, David. Worse than Slavery. New York: The Free Press, 1996

Patterson, Charles. The Civil Rights Movement. New York: Facts On File, Inc., 1995

Perry, Bruce. Malcolm: The Life of a Man who Changed Black America. New York: The Talman Company, 1991

Pierce, Paul S. The Freedmen's Bureau: A Chapter in the History of Reconstruction. USA: Iowa, 1970

Pinn, Anne H. and Anthony B. Pinn. Introduction to Black Church History. Minneapolis: Fortress Press, 2002

Raboteau, Albert J. Canaan Land: A Religious History of African Americans. New York: Oxford University Press, Inc., 1999

Raboteau, Albert J. Slave Religion: The "Invisible Institution" in the Antebellum South. New York: Oxford University Press, Inc., 1978

Rogers, J.A. Sex And Race: *Volume II*. 6th ed., New York: Helga M. Rogers, 1972

Ransom, Roger L. Conflict and Compromise: the Political Economy of Slavery, Emancipation, and the American Civil War. New York: Cambridge University Press, 1989

Smith, Carter, ed., One Nation Again: A Sourcebook on the Civil War. Connecticut: The Millbrook Press, 1993

Redding, Saunders. They Came In Chains. USA: J.B. Lippincott Company, 1950

Smitherman, Geneva. Black Talk: Words and Phrases from the Hood to the Amen Corner. New York: Houghton Mifflin Company, 1994

Stuckey, Sterling. Slave Culture: Nationalist Theory and the Foundations of Black America. New York: Oxford University Press, 1988

Tindall, George Brown, David E. Shi. America: A Narrative History. Vol. I, 4th ed. New York: W.W. Norton & Company, 1996

Thomas, Hugh. The Slave Trade: The Story of the Atlantic Slave Trade: 1440-1870. New York: Simon & Schuster, 1997

Trudeau, Noah André. Like Men of War: Black Troops in the Civil War 1862-1865. Canada: Little, Brown and Company, 1998

Tunnell, Ted. Crucible of Reconstruction: War, Radicalism, and Race in Louisiana 1862-1877. USA: Louisiana State University Press, 1984
U.S. Statutes at Large, Treaties, and Proclamations of the United States of America. Boston, 1866

Walker, David. David Walker's Appeal. Baltimore: Black Classic Press, 1993

Ward, Andrew. Dark Midnight When I Rise. New York: Farrar, Straus & Giroux, 2000

Washington, Booker T. Up From Slavery: An Autobiography. New York: Carol Publishing Group, 1993

Warren, James C. The Tuskegee Airmen: Mutiny at Freeman Field. CA: The Conyers Publishing Company, 2001

Washington, James Melvin, ed. A Testament of Hope: The Essential Writings of Martin Luther King, Jr. San Francisco: Harper & Row, Publishers, 1986

Watkins, T.H. The Great Depression: America in the 1930s. Toronto: Little, Brown & Company, 1993

Weinstein, Allen and Frank Otto Gatell, ed. American Negro Slavery. New York: Oxford University Press, 1968

Wormser, Richard. The Rise and Fall of Jim Crow. New York: St. Martin's Press, 2004

CPSIA information can be obtained
at www.ICGtesting.com
Printed in the USA
BVHW041457100920
588465BV00003B/23